BOND MARKETS, ANALYSIS AND STRATEGIES

Second Edition

Frank J. Fabozzi, CFA

Sloan School of Management
Massachusetts Institute of Technology

Prentice-Hall International, Inc.

© 1993, 1989 by Prentice-Hall, Inc.
A Simon & Schuster Company
Englewood Cliffs, New Jersey 07632

Printed in the United States of America

10 9 8 7 6 5 4 3

ISBN 0-13-032210-5

Prentice-Hall International (UK) Limited, *London*
Prentice-Hall of Australia Pty. Limited, *Sydney*
Prentice-Hall Canada Inc., *Toronto*
Prentice-Hall Hispanoamericana, S.A., *Mexico*
Prentice-Hall of India Private Limited, *New Delhi*
Prentice-Hall of Japan, Inc., *Tokyo*
Simon & Schuster Asia Pte. Ltd., *Singapore*
Editora Prentice-Hall do Brasil, Ltda., *Rio de Janeiro*
Prentice-Hall, Inc., *Englewood Cliffs, New Jersey*

To my parents
Alfonso and Josephine Fabozzi

CONTENTS

PREFACE

Prior to the early 1980s, the bond market was comprised mainly of "plain vanilla" bonds with simple cash flow structures. Thus, valuation was relatively straightforward. The market has since progressed and cash flow structures of bonds have become increasingly complex. As investment banking firms have altered the cash flows of fixed income assets to attract a wider range of investors, they have enabled borrowers to reduce their cost of raising funds.

Many securities in the bond market have options embedded in them. The idea of decomposing securities such as callable bonds into their basic components (a noncallable bond and a call option in the case of a callable bond) was considered innovative. Now this is commonplace and investment managers focus on alternative models to value the particular option components.

The bond market has received increased attention from many types of investors. Within this market, an array of securities are now available which may be combined with derivative products to facilitate portfolio strategies to control interest rate risk and/or enhance returns.

Because of the increased importance of this market, and the complex structure of the securities, participants must be well informed on forces that drive the bond market and also on the increasingly complex techniques for valuing securities. Once this is mastered, portfolio strategies mentioned in this book, as well as those which develop subsequently, can be effectively employed.

The objective of *Bond Markets, Analysis and Strategies, Second Edition* is to provide detailed coverage of the bond market. This includes coverage of the securities available in the market (Treasury securities, agency securities, corporate bonds, municipal bonds, international bonds, mortgages, and mortgage-backed securities), their investment characteristics, the state-of-the technology for valuing them, and portfolio strategies using them.

The second edition is a substantial revision of the first edition. There were 14 chapters in the first edition. There are 22 chapters in the second edition. The second edition includes more detailed coverage of the various market sectors, particularly mortgage-backed securities, such as collateralized mortgage obligations, Eurobonds and non-U.S. bond markets. Unlike the first edition, there is coverage of the option-adjusted spread technology for valuing bonds with embedded options and also expanded coverage of the valuation of mortgage-backed securities. While the first edition covered the use of options and futures in portfolio strategies, the second edition includes a chapter on customized interest rate risk control tools (interest rate swaps, caps, and floors). A new chapter on active portfolio strategies is included.

A new feature in the book is end of chapter questions. Some questions have been adapted from previous Chartered Financial Analyst examinations and I have included excerpts from *BondWeek*, a publication of Institutional Investor, Inc.

I am indebted to certain individuals who provided helpful comments on this edition and the previous one or who provided insightful discussions on some of the topics. These individuals include: Scott Amero (BlackRock Financial Management), David Askin (New Amsterdam Partners), Joseph Bencivenga (Salomon Brothers), Anand Bhattacharya (Prudential Securities), John Carlson (Daiwa Securities America), Andrew Carron (The First Boston Corporation), Peter Christensen (PaineWebber), Ravi Dattatreya (Sumitomo Bank Capital Markets), Mark Dunetz (The Guardian), Sylvan Feldstein (Merrill Lynch Capital Markets), Michael Ferri (George Mason University), John Finnerty (Fordham University), Gifford Fong (Gifford Fong Associates), Jack Francis (Baruch College, CUNY), Sean Gallop (J.P. Morgan Securities, London), Laurie Goodman (Merrill Lynch Capital Markets), Lakbir Hayre (Prudential Securities), David Jacob (J.P. Morgan Securities), Frank Jones (The Guardian), Andrew Kalotay (Fordham University), Thomas Klaffky (Salomon Brothers), Dragomir Krgin (EJV Partners), Peter Lambert (Dodge and Cox), Linda Lowell (Smith Barney), K.C. Ma (Texas Tech), Matt Mancuso (Bear Stearns), Jan Mayl (TIPS), Franco Modigliani (MIT), Ed Murphy (Merchants Mutual Insurance), Barry Nix (Bear Stearns International), Mark Pitts (Lehman Brothers), Sharmin Mossavar-Rahmani (Fidelity Management Trust), Frank Ramirez (MMAR Group), Chuck Ramsey (MMAR Group), Scott Richard (Miller, Anderson & Sherrerd), Dexter Senft (EJV Partners), Michael Smirlock (Goldman Sachs Asset Management), Roy Standfest (Salomon Brothers), Michael Waldman (Salomon Brothers), Richard Wilson (Fitch Investors Service),

Ben Wolkowitz (Morgan Stanley), David Yuen (Franklin Resources), and Yu Zhu (Merrill Lynch Capital Markets).

Portions of this manuscript were used in the Investment Banking and Markets course and the Fixed Income Seminar that I taught at MIT over the past five years. I am grateful to Stewart Myers, Chairman of the Department of Applied Economics, Finance and Accounting, for giving me the opportunity to teach the seminar.

While there have been several additions to the book, there has been one important deletion. I coauthored the first edition with my wife, Dessa Fabozzi. At the time, she was on the faculty of Rutgers University. Prior to the completion of the first edition, she joined the Financial Strategies Group of Merrill Lynch Capital Markets. Because of her commitments at Merrill Lynch, she was not able to work with me on the second edition. Nevertheless, I gained considerable insight into market developments through our daily conversations. It was invaluable to have an "in-house" expert I could turn to when I encountered difficulties. It is my hope that her work schedule will permit her to coauthor future editions of this book.

Frank J. Fabozzi

Chapter 1

INTRODUCTION

A bond is a debt instrument requiring the issuer (also called the debtor or borrower) to repay to the lender/investor the amount borrowed plus interest over some specified period of time. A typical ("plain vanilla") bond issued in the United States specifies (1) a fixed date when the amount borrowed (the principal) is due, and (2) the contractual amount of interest, which typically is paid every six months. The date on which the principal is required to be repaid is called the maturity date. Assuming that the issuer does not default or redeem the issue prior to the maturity date, an investor holding this bond until the maturity date is assured of a known cash flow pattern.

For a variety of reasons to be discussed later in this chapter, the 1980s saw development of a wide range of bond structures. In the residential mortgage market particularly, new types of mortgage designs were introduced. The practice of pooling of individual mortgages to form mortgage "pass-through" securities grew dramatically. Using the basic instruments in the mortgage market (mortgages and mortgage pass-through securities), issuers created derivative instruments such as collateralized mortgage obligations and stripped mortgage-backed securities that met specific investment needs of a broadening range of institutional investors.

SECTORS OF THE U.S. BOND MARKET

The U.S. bond market is the largest bond market in the world. (Non-U.S. bond markets include the Eurobond market and other national bond markets discussed in Chapter 8.) The size of the U.S. bond market and its composition as of December 31, 1990, are summarized in Exhibit 1-1. Of the $8.7 trillion long-term debt market, the largest component by far is the mortgage market, which we discuss in Chapter 10. The mortgage-backed securities sector (securities whose underlying collateral is a pool of

1

mortgage loans), the subject of Chapters 11 and 12, is the fastest growing sector of the long-term debt market. The second largest sector is the market for U.S. Treasury securities, while the smallest sector shown in Exhibit 1-1 is the U.S. government agency securities market.[1]

The corporate bond sector includes bonds issued by U.S. corporations as well as bonds issued in the United States by non-U.S. entities. The latter market sector is called the *Yankee bond market*. The municipal sector is where state and local governments raise funds. Bonds issued in this sector typically are exempt from federal income taxes, and it is consequently referred to as the tax-exempt sector.

**EXHIBIT 1-1   Composition of the U.S. Bond Market
as of December 31, 1990
(dollars in billions; based on par value)**

U.S. Treasury Securities		$2,210	(25.4%)
U.S. Agency Securities1		309	(3.6%)
(excluding agency pass-through securities)			
Corporate Bonds		1,506	(17.3%)
Domestic	1,387		
Yankee	119		
Municipal Securities		852	(9.8%)
Mortgages—Nonsecuritized		2,783	(32.0%)
(1-4 multifamily, farm commercial)			
Mortgage-backed Securities		1,029	(11.9%)
Total U.S. Bond Market*		$8,689	

*Excludes asset-backed securities.

Source: Prepared from data supplied by Salomon Brothers Inc.

OVERVIEW OF BOND FEATURES

In this section, we provide an overview of some important features of bonds. A more detailed treatment of these features is presented in later chapters. The bond *indenture* is the contract between the issuer and the bondholder, which sets forth all the obligations of the issuer.

Type of Issuer

A key feature of a bond is the nature of the issuer. There are three issuers of bonds: the federal government and its agencies, municipal governments, and corporations (domestic and foreign). Within the municipal and corporate bond markets, there are a wide range of issuers, each with different abilities to satisfy their contractual obligation to lenders.

---

[1]As Chapter 11 explains, a majority of the securities backed by a pool of mortgages are guaranteed by a federally sponsored agency of the U.S. government. These securities are classified as part of the mortgage-backed securities market rather than as U.S. government agency securities.

Term to Maturity

The *term to maturity* of a bond is the number of years over which the issuer has promised to meet the conditions of the obligation. The *maturity* of a bond refers to the date that the debt will cease to exist, at which time the issuer will redeem the bond by paying the principal. The practice in the bond market, however, is to refer to the "term to maturity" of a bond as simply its "maturity" or "term." As we explain below, there may be provisions in the indenture that allow either the issuer or bondholder to alter a bond's term to maturity.

Generally, bonds with a maturity of between 1 to 5 years are considered "short-term." Bonds with a maturity between 5 and 12 years are viewed as "intermediate-term," and "long-term" bonds are those with a maturity of more than 12 years.

There are three reasons why the term to maturity of a bond is important. The most obvious is that it indicates the time period over which the holder of the bond can expect to receive the coupon payments and the number of years before the principal will be paid in full. The second reason that term to maturity is important is that the yield on a bond depends on it. As will be explained in Chapter 9, the "shape" of the yield curve determines how term to maturity affects the yield. Finally, the price of a bond will fluctuate over its life as yields in the market change. As demonstrated in Chapter 4, the volatility of a bond's price is dependent on its maturity. More specifically, with all other factors constant, the longer the maturity of a bond, the greater the price volatility resulting from a change in market yields.

Principal and Coupon Rate

The *principal value* (or simply "principal") of a bond is the amount that the issuer agrees to repay the bondholder at the maturity date. This amount is also referred to as the *redemption value*, *maturity value*, *par value*, or *face value*.

The *coupon rate*, also called the *nominal rate*, is the interest rate that the issuer agrees to pay each year. The annual amount of the interest payment made to owners during the term of the bond is called the *coupon*. The coupon rate multiplied by the principal of the bond provides the dollar amount of the coupon. For example, a bond with an 8% coupon rate and a principal of $1,000 will pay annual interest of $80. In the United States and Japan, the usual practice is for the issuer to pay the coupon in two semiannual installments. For bonds issued in European bond markets or the Eurobond market, coupon payments are made only once per year.

Note that all bonds make periodic coupon payments, except for one type that makes none. These bonds, called *zero-coupon bonds*, made their debut in the U.S. bond market in the early 1980s. The holder of a zero-coupon bond realizes interest by buying the bond substantially below its principal value. Interest then is paid at the maturity date, with the exact amount being the difference between the principal value and the price paid for the bond. The reason behind the issuance of zero-coupon bonds is explained in Chapters 3 and 5.

Floating-rate bonds also exist. For these bonds coupon rates are reset periodically according to some predetermined benchmark. Although the coupon rate on most floating-rate bonds is reset on the basis of some financial index, there are some issues where the benchmark for the coupon rate is a nonfinancial index, such as the price of a commodity. Second, while the coupon on floating-rate bonds benchmarked off an interest rate benchmark typically rises as the benchmark rises, and falls as the benchmark falls, there are issues whose coupon interest rate moves in the opposite direction from the change in interest rates. Such issues are called *inverse floaters*; institutional investors use them as hedging vehicles.

In the 1980s, new structures in the high-yield (junk bond) sector of the corporate bond market have provided variations in the way coupon payments are made. One reason is that a leveraged buyout or a recapitalization financed with high-yield bonds, with consequent heavy interest payment burdens, places severe cash flow constraints on the corporation. To reduce this burden, firms involved in LBOs and recapitalizations have issued *deferred-coupon bonds* that let the issuer avoid using cash to make interest payments for a specified number of years. There are three types of deferred-coupon structures: (1) deferred-interest bonds, (2) step-up bonds, and (3) payment-in-kind bonds. Another high-yield bond structure requires that the issuer reset the coupon rate so that the bond will trade at a predetermined price. High-yield bond structures are discussed in Chapter 6.

In addition to indicating the coupon payments that the investor should expect to receive over the term of the bond, the coupon rate also indicates the degree to which the bond's price will be affected by changes in interest rates. As illustrated in Chapter 4, all other factors constant, the higher the coupon rate, the less the price will change in response to a change in interest rates. Consequently, the coupon rate and the term to maturity have opposite effects on a bond's price volatility.

Embedded Options

It is common for a bond issue to include a provision in the indenture that gives either the bondholder and/or the issuer an option to take some action against the other party. The most common type of option embedded in a bond is a *call feature*. This provision grants the issuer the right to retire the debt, fully or partially, before the scheduled maturity date. Inclusion of a call feature benefits bond issuers by allowing them to replace an old bond issue with a lower-interest cost issue if interest rates in the market decline. A call provision effectively allows the issuer to alter the maturity of a bond. For reasons explained in the next section, a call provision is detrimental to the bondholder's interests.

The right to call an obligation is also included in all mortgage loans and therefore in all securities created from these loans. This is because the borrower (i.e., the homeowner) has the right to pay off a mortgage loan at any time, in whole or in part, prior to the stated maturity date of the loan.

An issue may also include a provision that allows the bondholder to change the maturity of a bond. An issue with a *put provision* included in the indenture grants the bondholder the right to sell the issue back to the issuer at par value on designated dates. Here the advantage to the investor is that if interest rates rise after the issue date, thereby reducing a bond's price, the investor can force the issuer to redeem the bond at par value.

A *convertible bond* is an issue giving the bondholder the right to exchange the bond for a specified number of shares of common stock. Such a feature allows the bondholder to take advantage of favorable movements in the price of the issuer's common stock. An *exchangeable bond* allows the bondholder to exchange the issue for a specified number of common stock shares of a corporation different from the issuer of the bond. These bonds are described in Chapter 6.

Some issues allow either the issuer or the bondholder the right to select the currency in which a cash flow will be paid. This option effectively gives the party with the right to choose the currency the opportunity to benefit from a favorable exchange rate movement. Such issues are described in Chapter 8.

The presence of embedded options makes the valuation of bonds complex. It requires investors to have an understanding of the basic principles of options, a topic covered in Chapters 13 and 18. The valuation of bonds with embedded options frequently is complicated further by the presence of several options within a given issue. For example, an issue may include a call provision, a put provision, and a conversion provision, all of which have varying significance in different situations.

RISKS ASSOCIATED WITH INVESTING IN BONDS

Bonds may expose an investor to one or more of the following risks: (1) interest-rate risk; (2) reinvestment risk; (3) call risk; (4) default risk; (5) inflation risk; (6) exchange-rate risk; (7) liquidity risk; and (8) volatility risk. While each of these risks is discussed further in later chapters, we describe them briefly below.[2]

Interest-Rate Risk

The price of a typical bond will change in the opposite direction from a change in interest rates: As interest rates rise, the price of a bond will fall. As interest rates fall, the price of a bond will rise. This property is illustrated in Chapter 4. If an investor has to sell a bond prior to the maturity date, an increase in interest rates will mean the realization of a capital loss (i.e., selling the bond below the purchase price). This risk is referred to as *interest-rate risk* or *market risk*. This risk is by far the major risk faced by an investor in the bond market.

As noted earlier, the actual degree of sensitivity of a bond's price to changes in market interest rates depends on various characteristics of the issue, such as coupon and maturity. It will also depend on any options embedded in the issue (e.g., call and put provisions), because, as we explain in later chapters, these options are also affected by interest rate movements.

Reinvestment Risk

As explained in Chapter 3, calculation of the "yield" of a bond assumes that the cash flows received are reinvested. The additional income from such reinvestment, sometimes called "interest-on-interest," depends upon the prevailing interest rate levels at the time of reinvestment, as well as on the reinvestment strategy. Variability in the reinvestment rate of a given strategy because of changes in market interest rates is called *reinvestment risk*. This risk is that the interest rate at which interim cash flows can be reinvested will fall. Reinvestment risk is greater for longer holding periods, as well as for bonds with large, early, cash flows, such as high-coupon bonds. This risk is analyzed in more detail in Chapter 3.

It should be noted that interest-rate risk and reinvestment risk have offsetting effects. That is, interest-rate risk is the risk that interest rates will rise, thereby reducing a bond's price. In contrast, reinvestment risk is

---

[2] In later chapters, other risks such as yield curve risk, event risk, and tax risk are also introduced.

the risk that interest rates will fall. A strategy based on these offsetting effects is called immunization, a topic covered in Chapter 22.

Call Risk

As explained earlier, many bonds include a provision that allows the issuer to retire or "call" all or part of the issue before the maturity date. The issuer usually retains this right in order to have flexibility to refinance the bond in the future if the market interest rate drops below the coupon rate.

From the investor's perspective, there are three disadvantages to call provisions. First, the cash flow pattern of a callable bond is not known with certainty. Second, because the issuer will call the bonds when interest rates have dropped, the investor is exposed to reinvestment risk, i.e., the investor will have to reinvest the proceeds when the bond is called at relatively lower interest rates. Finally, the capital appreciation potential of a bond will be reduced, because the price of a callable bond may not rise much above the price at which the issuer will call the bond.[3]

Even though the investor is usually compensated for taking call risk by means of a lower price or a higher yield, it is not easy to determine if this compensation is sufficient. In any case, the returns from a bond with call risk can be dramatically different from those obtainable from an otherwise comparable noncallable bond. The magnitude of this risk depends upon various parameters of the call provision, as well as on market conditions. Call risk is so pervasive in bond portfolio management that many market participants consider it second only to interest-rate risk in importance. Techniques for analyzing callable bonds are presented in Chapters 13 and 14.

Default Risk

Default risk, also referred to as *credit risk*, refers to the risk that the issuer of a bond may default, i.e., will be unable to make timely principal and interest payments on the issue. Default risk is gauged by quality ratings assigned by commercial rating companies such as Moody's Investors Service; Standard & Poor's Corporation; Duff & Phelps; McCarthy, Crisanti & Maffei; and Fitch Investors Service, as well as the credit research staffs of securities firms.

Because of this risk, bonds with default risk trade in the market at a price that is lower than comparable U. S. Treasury securities, which are considered free of default risk. In other words, a non-U.S. Treasury bond

---

[3] The reason for this is explained in Chapter 13.

will trade in the market at a higher yield than a Treasury bond that is comparable otherwise.

Except in the case of the lowest-rated securities, known as "high-yield" or "junk bonds," the investor is normally more concerned with the changes in the perceived default risk and/or the cost associated with a given level of default risk than with the actual event of default. Even though the actual default of an issuing corporation may be highly unlikely, they reason, the impact of a change in perceived default risk, or the spread demanded by the market for any given level of default risk, can have an immediate impact on the value of a bond.

Inflation Risk

Inflation risk or *purchasing-power risk* arises because of the variation in the value of cash flows from a security due to inflation, as measured in terms of purchasing power. For example, if investors purchase a bond on which they can realize a coupon rate of 7%, but the rate of inflation is 8%, the purchasing power of the cash flow actually has declined. For all but floating-rate bonds, an investor is exposed to inflation risk because the interest rate the issuer promises to make is fixed for the life of the issue. To the extent that interest rates reflect the expected inflation rate, floating-rate bonds have a lower level of inflation risk.

Exchange-Rate Risk

A nondollar-denominated bond (i.e., a bond whose payments occur in a foreign currency) has unknown U.S. dollar cash flows. The dollar cash flows are dependent on the exchange rate at the time the payments are received. For example, suppose an investor purchases a bond whose payments are in Japanese yen. If the yen depreciates relative to the U.S. dollar, then fewer dollars will be received. The risk of this occurring is referred to as *exchange-rate* or *currency risk*. Of course, should the yen appreciate relative to the U.S. dollar, the investor will benefit by receiving more dollars.

Liquidity Risk

Liquidity or *marketability* risk depends on the ease with which an issue can be sold at or near its value. The primary measure of liquidity is the size of the spread between the bid price and the ask price quoted by a dealer. The wider the dealer spread, the more the liquidity risk. For an investor who plans to hold the bond until the maturity date, liquidity risk is less important.

Volatility Risk

As explained in Chapter 13, the price of a bond with certain types of embedded options depends on the level of interest rates and factors that influence the value of the embedded option. One of these factors is the expected volatility of interest rates. Specifically, the value of an option rises when expected interest rate volatility increases. In the case of a bond that is callable, or a mortgage-backed security, where the investor has granted the borrower an option, the price of the security falls, because the investor has given away a more valuable option. The risk that a change in volatility will affect the price of a bond adversely is called *volatility risk.*

FINANCIAL INNOVATION AND THE BOND MARKET

Since the 1960s, there have been a surge of significant financial innovations, many of them in the bond market. Observers of financial markets have categorized these innovations in different ways. For example, the Economic Council of Canada classifies financial innovations into three broad categories:[4]

- *market-broadening instruments*, which augment the liquidity of markets and the availability of funds by attracting new investors and offering new opportunities for borrowers;
- *risk-management instruments*, which reallocate financial risks to those who are less averse to them, or who have offsetting exposure, and who are presumably better able to shoulder them; and
- *arbitraging instruments and processes*, which enable investors and borrowers to take advantage of differences in costs and returns between markets, and which reflect differences in the perception of risks, as well as in information, taxation, and regulation.

Another classification system of financial innovations based on more specific functions has been suggested by the Bank for International Settlements: *price-risk-transferring innovations, credit-risk-transferring instruments, liquidity-generating innovations, credit-generating instruments,* and *equity-generating instruments.*[5] Price-risk-transferring innovations are those that provide market participants with more efficient means for dealing with price or exchange rate risk. Credit-risk-transferring instruments reallocate the risk of default. Liquidity-generating innovations do three things: (1) they increase the liquidity of the market, (2) they allow

---

[4] *Globalization and Canada's Financial Markets* (Ottawa, Canada: Supply and Services Canada, 1989), p. 32.

[5] Bank for International Settlements, *Recent Innovations in International Banking* (Basle: BIS, April 1986).

borrowers to draw upon new sources of funds, and (3) they allow market participants to circumvent capital constraints imposed by regulations. Credit-generating and equity-generating innovations increase the amount of debt funds available to borrowers, and increase the capital base of financial and nonfinancial institutions, respectively.

Professor Stephen Ross suggests two classes of financial innovation: (1) new financial products (financial assets and derivative instruments) better suited to the circumstances of the time (e.g., to inflation and volatile interest rates) and to the markets in which they trade, and (2) strategies that primarily use these financial products.[6]

One of the objectives of this book is to explain the financial innovations that are taking place in the bond market. As you read the chapters on various bond sectors and various bond portfolio strategies, be sure you understand the factors behind the innovations in that market.

OVERVIEW OF THE BOOK

The next three chapters of this book set forth the basic analytical framework necessary to understand the pricing of bonds and their investment characteristics. Chapter 2 explains how the price of a bond is determined. The various measures of a bond's return are illustrated and critically evaluated in Chapter 3, which is followed by an explanation of the price volatility characteristics of bonds in Chapter 4.

Chapters 5 through 12 describe the various sectors of the debt market. As Treasury securities provide the benchmark against which all bonds are valued, it is imperative to have a thorough understanding of the Treasury market. Chapter 5 discusses Treasury securities, Treasury derivative securities (zero-coupon Treasury securities or "stripped" Treasury securities), and federally sponsored credit agency securities. In Chapters 6, 7, and 8 the investment characteristics and special features of U.S. corporate debt, municipal securities, and non-U.S. bonds, respectively, are explained. The term structure of interest rates, that is, the relationship between maturity and yield, is the subject of Chapter 9.

Chapter 10 focuses on the various mortgage instruments. Mortgage-backed securities are discussed in Chapters 11 and 12, with the former covering mortgage pass-through securities and the latter covering derivative mortgage-backed securities (collateralized mortgage obligations and stripped mortgage-backed securities).

---

[6]Stephen A. Ross, "Institutional Markets, Financial Marketing, and Financial Innovation," *Journal of Finance* (July 1989), p. 541.

The various methodologies for valuing bonds and mortgage-backed securities with embedded options are presented in Chapters 13 through 15. The analysis of convertible bonds is covered in Chapter 16.

Chapters 17, 18, and 19 explain the different instruments that can be used to control portfolio risk. Chapter 17 covers interest rate futures contracts; Chapter 18 covers interest rate options; and Chapter 19 explains interest rate swaps and interest rate agreements (caps, floors, collars, compound options). Coverage includes the pricing of these contracts and their role in bond portfolio management.

Portfolio strategies are covered in the last three chapters of the book. Chapter 20 explains the objectives of bond portfolio management and the various types of portfolio strategies, active and structured, the latter of which are designed to achieve the performance of some predetermined benchmark. These strategies include indexing, the subject of Chapter 21, and liability funding strategies (immunization and cash flow matching), the subject of Chapter 22.

QUESTIONS FOR CHAPTER 1

1. a. Which sector of the U.S. bond market is referred to as the tax-exempt sector?

   b. What is meant by the Yankee bond sector of the U.S. bond market?

2. Who are the major types of issuers of bonds in the United States?

3. a. What is the cash flow of a ten-year bond that pays coupon interest semiannually, has a coupon rate of 7%, and has a par value of $100,000?

   b. What is the cash flow of a seven-year bond that pays no coupon interest and has a par value of $10,000?

4. a. Give three reasons why the maturity of a bond is important.

   b. Generally, in terms of years how does one classify bonds as short-term, intermediate-term, and long-term?

5. a. What is a floating-rate bond?

   b. What is an inverse floating-rate bond?

   c. Can you determine today what the cash flow of either a floating-rate bond or an inverse floating-rate bond will be?

6. a. What does the call feature in a bond entitle the issuer to do?

   b. What is the advantage of a call feature for an issuer?

   c. What are the disadvantages of a call feature for the bondholder?

7. What does the put feature in a bond entitle the bondholder to do?

8. What is a convertible bond? An exchangeable bond?

9. Does an investor who purchases a zero-coupon bond face reinvestment risk?

10. What risks does an investor face in purchasing a French corporation's bond whose cash flows are denominated in French francs?

11. Why may liquidity risk and interest-rate risk be unimportant to an individual who invests in a three-year bond and plans to hold that bond to the maturity date?

Chapter 2

PRICING OF BONDS

In this chapter we explain how the price of a bond is determined, and in the next we discuss how the yield on a bond is measured. Basic to understanding pricing models and yield measures is an understanding of the time value of money. Therefore we begin this chapter with a review of the time value of money.

REVIEW OF TIME VALUE OF MONEY

The notion that money has a time value is one of the basic concepts in the analysis of any financial instrument. Money has time value because of the opportunity to invest it at some interest rate.

Future Value

To determine the future value of any sum of money invested today, equation (2.1) can be used:

$$(2.1) \quad P_n = P_0 (1 + r)^n$$

where n = number of periods

P_n = future value n periods from now (in $)

P_0 = original principal (in $)

r = interest rate per period (in decimal form)

The expression $(1 + r)^n$ represents the future value of $1 invested today for n periods at a compounding rate of r.

For example, suppose a pension fund manager invests $10 million in a financial instrument that promises to pay 9.2% per year for 6 years. The future value of the $10 million investment is $16,956,600; that is:

$$P_6 = \$10,000,000\ (1.092)^6$$
$$= \$10,000,000\ (1.69565)$$
$$= \$16,956,500$$

This example demonstrates how to compute the future value when interest is paid once per year (that is, the period is equal to the number of years). When interest is paid more than one time per year, both the interest rate and the number of periods used to compute the future value must be adjusted as follows:

$$r = \frac{\text{Annual interest rate}}{\text{Number of times interest is paid per year}}$$

$n =$ Number of times interest is paid per year x Number of years

For example, suppose that the portfolio manager in the first example invests $10 million in a financial instrument that promises to pay an annual interest rate of 9.2% for 6 years, but the interest is paid semiannually (that is, twice per year). Then:

$$r = \frac{.092}{2} = .046$$
$$n = 2 \times 6 = 12$$

and

$$P_{12} = \$10,000,000\ (1.046)^{12}$$
$$= \$10,000,000\ (1.71546)$$
$$= \$17,154,600$$

Notice that the future value of $10 million when interest is paid semiannually ($17,154,600) is greater than when interest is paid annually ($16,956,500), even though the same annual rate is applied to both investments. The higher future value when interest is paid semiannually reflects the greater opportunity for reinvesting the interest paid.

Future Value of an Ordinary Annuity

When the same amount of money is invested periodically, it is referred to as an *annuity*. When the first investment occurs one period from now, it is referred to as an *ordinary annuity*. The future value of an ordinary annuity can be found by finding the future value of each investment at the end of the investment horizon and then adding these future values. However, it is easier to compute the future value of an ordinary annuity using equation (2.2).

$$(2.2) \quad P_n = A \left[\frac{(1+r)^n - 1}{r} \right]$$

where A = amount of the annuity (in $)

The term in the brackets is the *future value of an ordinary annuity of $1* at the end of n periods.

To see how this formula can be applied, suppose that a portfolio manager purchases $20 million par value of a 15-year bond that promises to pay 10% interest per year. The issuer makes a payment once a year, with the first annual interest payment occurring one year from now. How much will the portfolio manager have if (1) the bond is held until it matures 15 years from now, and (2) annual payments are invested at an annual interest rate of 8%?

The amount that the portfolio manager will have at the end of 15 years will be equal to:

1. The $20 million when the bond matures
2. 15 annual interest payments of $2,000,000 (.10 x $20 million)
3. The interest earned by investing the annual interest payments at 8% per year.

We can determine the sum of the second and third items by applying equation (2.2). In this illustration the annuity is $2,000,000 per year. Therefore:

$$A = \$2,000,000$$
$$r = .08$$
$$n = 15$$

and

$$P_{15} = \$2,000,000 \left[\frac{(1.08)^{15} - 1}{.08} \right]$$

$$= \$2,000,000 \left[\frac{3.17217 - 1}{.08} \right]$$

$$= \$2,000,000 \left[27.152125 \right]$$

$$= \$54,304,250$$

The future value of the ordinary annuity of $2,000,000 per year for 15 years invested at 8% is $54,304,250. Because $30,000,000 (15 × $2,000,000) of this future value represents the total dollar amount of annual interest payments made by the issuer and invested by the portfolio manager, the balance of $24,304,250 ($54,304,250 − $30,000,000) is the interest earned by reinvesting these annual interest payments. Thus the total dollars that the portfolio manager will have at the end of 15 years by making the investment will be:

Par (maturity) value	$20,000,000
Interest payments	30,000,000
Interest on reinvestment of interest payments	24,304,250
Total future dollars	$74,304,250

As you shall see in the next chapter, it is necessary to calculate these total future dollars at the end of a portfolio manager's investment horizon in order to assess the relative value of a bond.

Let's rework the analysis for this bond assuming that the interest is paid every six months (based on an annual rate), with the first six-month payment to be received and immediately invested six months from now. We shall assume that the semiannual interest payments can be reinvested at an annual interest rate of 8%.

Interest payments received every 6 months are $1,000,000. The future value of the 30 semiannual interest payments of $1,000,000 to be received plus the interest earned by investing the interest payments is found as follows:

$$A = \$1,000,000$$

$$r = \frac{.08}{2} = .04$$

$$n = 15 \times 2 = 30$$

$$P_{30} = \$1,000,000 \left[\frac{(1.04)^{30} - 1}{.04} \right]$$

$$= \$1,000,000 \left[\frac{3.2434 - 1}{.04} \right]$$

$$= \$1,000,000 \left[56.085 \right]$$

$$= \$56,085,000$$

Because the interest payments are now equal to $30,000,000, the interest earned on the interest payments reinvested is $26,085,000. The opportunity for more frequent reinvestment of interest payments received makes the interest earned of $26,085,000 from reinvesting the interest payments greater than the $24,304,240 interest earned when interest is paid only one time per year.

The total future dollars that the portfolio manager will have at the end of 15 years by making the investment are as follows:

Par (maturity) value	$20,000,000
Interest payments	30,000,000
Interest on reinvestment of interest payments	26,085,000
Total future dollars	$76,085,000

Present Value

We have explained how to compute the future value of an investment. Now we illustrate how to work the process in reverse; that is, we show how to determine the amount of money that must be invested today in order to realize a specific future value. This amount is called the *present value*. Because, as we explain later in this chapter, the price of *any* financial instrument is the present value of its expected cash flows, it is necessary to understand present value in order to be able to price fixed-income instruments.

What we are interested in is how to determine the amount of money that must be invested today at an interest rate of r per period for n periods to produce a specific future value. This can be done by solving the formula for the future value given by equation (2.1) for the original principal (P_0):

$$P_0 = P_n \left[\frac{1}{(1+r)^n} \right]$$

Instead of using P_0, however, we denote the present value by PV. Therefore the present value formula can be rewritten as:

$$(2.3) \quad PV = P_n \left[\frac{1}{(1+r)^n} \right]$$

The term in the brackets is the present value of $1; that is, it indicates how much must be set aside today, earning an interest rate of r per period, in order to have $1 n periods from now.

The process of computing the present value is also referred to as *discounting*. Therefore the present value is sometimes referred to as the *discounted value*, and the interest rate is referred to as the *discount rate*.

To illustrate how to apply equation (2.3), suppose a portfolio manager has the opportunity to purchase a financial instrument that promises to pay $5 million seven years from now with no interim cash flows (i.e., the interest payments are automatically reinvested). Assuming that the portfolio manager wants to earn an annual interest rate of 10% on this investment, the present value of this investment is computed as follows:

$$r = .10$$

$$n = 7$$

$$P_7 = \$5,000,000$$

$$PV = \$5,000,000\left[\frac{1}{(1.10)^7}\right]$$

$$= \$5,000,000\left[\frac{1}{1.948717}\right]$$

$$= \$5,000,000(.513158)$$

$$= \$2,565,791$$

The equation shows that if $2,565,791 is invested today at 10% annual interest, the investment will grow to $5 million at the end of seven years. Suppose that this financial instrument is actually selling for more than $2,565,791. Then the portfolio manager would be earning less than 10% by investing in this financial instrument at a purchase price greater than $2,565,791. The reverse is true if the financial instrument is selling for less than $2,565,791. Then the portfolio manager would be earning more than 10%.

There are two properties of present value that you should recognize. First, for a given future value at a specified time in the future, the higher the interest rate (or discount rate), the lower the present value. The reason the present value decreases as the interest rate increases should be easy to understand: the higher the interest rate that can be earned on any sum invested today, the less has to be invested today to realize a specified future value.

The second property of present value is that, for a given interest rate (discount rate), the farther into the future the future value will be received, the lower its present value. The reason is that the farther into the future a given future value is to be received, the more opportunity there is for interest to accumulate. Thus fewer dollars have to be invested.

Present Value of a Series of Future Values

In most applications in portfolio management a financial instrument will offer a series of future values. To determine the present value of a series of future values, the present value of each future value must first be computed. Then these present values are added together to obtain the present value of the entire series of future values.

Mathematically, this can be expressed as follows:

$$(2.4) \quad PV = \sum_{t=1}^{n} \frac{P_t}{(1+r)^t}$$

For example, suppose a portfolio manager is considering the purchase of a financial instrument that promises to make these payments:

Years from Now	Promised Payment by Issuer
1	$ 100
2	100
3	100
4	100
5	1,100

Assume that the portfolio manager wants a 6.25% annual interest rate on this investment. The present value of such an investment can be computed as follows:

Years from Now	Future Value of Payment	Present Value of $1 at 6.25%	Present Value of Payment
1	$ 100	.9412	$ 94.12
2	100	.8858	88.58
3	100	.8337	83.37
4	100	.7847	78.47
5	1,100	.7385	812.35
		Present value =	$ 1,156.89

Present Value of an Ordinary Annuity

When the same dollar amount of money is received each period or paid each year, the series is referred to as an *annuity*. When the first payment is received one period from now, the annuity is called an *ordinary annuity*. When the first payment is immediate, the annuity is called an *annuity due*. In all the applications discussed in this book, we shall deal with ordinary annuities.

To compute the present value of an ordinary annuity, the present value of each future value can be computed, then summed. Alternatively, a formula for the present value of an ordinary annuity can be used:

$$(2.5) \quad PV = A \left[\frac{1 - \dfrac{1}{(1+r)^n}}{r} \right]$$

where A = amount of the annuity (in $)

The term in the brackets is the *present value of an ordinary annuity of $1 for n periods.*

Suppose that an investor expects to receive $100 at the end of each year for the next eight years from an investment, and that the appropriate discount rate to be used for discounting is 9%. The present value of this ordinary annuity is:

$A = \$100$

$r = .09$

$n = 8$

$$PV = 100 \left[\frac{1 - \dfrac{1}{(1.09)^8}}{.09} \right]$$

$$= \$100 \left[\frac{1 - \dfrac{1}{1.99256}}{.09} \right]$$

$$= \$100 \left[\frac{1 - .501867}{.09} \right]$$

$$= \$100 (5.5348)$$

$$= \$553.48$$

Present Value When Payments Occur More than Once per Year

In our computations of the present value we have assumed that the future val to be received or paid occurs each year. In practice, the future value to be receiv may occur more than once per year. When that is the case, the formulas we have developed for determining the present value must be modified in two ways. First, the annual interest rate is divided by the frequency per year.[1] For example, if the future values are received semiannually, the annual interest rate is divided by 2; if they are paid or received quarterly, the annual interest rate is divided by 4. Second, the number of periods when the future value will be received must be adjusted by multiplying the number of years by the frequency per year.

PRICING A BOND

The price of any financial instrument is equal to the present value of the *expected* cash flows from the financial instrument. Therefore to determine the price requires:

1. Estimate of the expected cash flows
2. Estimate of the appropriate required yield

The expected cash flows for some financial instruments are simple to compute; for others, the task is more difficult. The required yield reflects the yield for financial instruments with *comparable* risk, or so-called alternative (or substitute) investments.

The first step in determining the price of a bond is to determine its cash flows. The cash flows for a bond that the issuer cannot retire prior to its stated maturity date (that is, a noncallable bond[2]) consist of:

1. Periodic coupon interest payments to the maturity date
2. The par (or maturity) value at maturity

Our illustrations of bond pricing use three assumptions to simplify the analysis:

1. The coupon payments are made every six months. (For most domestic bond issues coupon interest is in fact paid semiannually.)
2. The next coupon payment for the bond is received exactly six months from now.
3. The coupon interest is fixed for the term of the bond.

Consequently, the cash flow for a noncallable bond consists of an annuity of a fixed coupon interest payment paid semiannually and the par or

---

[1] Technically, this is not the proper way for adjusting the annual interest rate. The technically proper method of adjustment is discussed in the next chapter.

[2] In Chapter 13 we discuss the pricing of callable bonds.

maturity value. For example, a 20-year bond with a 10% coupon rate and a par or maturity value of $1,000 has the following cash flows from coupon interest:

$$
\begin{aligned}
\text{Annual coupon interest} &= \$1,000 \times .10 \\
&= \$100 \\
\text{Semiannual coupon interest} &= \$100\,/\,2 \\
&= \$50
\end{aligned}
$$

Therefore there are 40 semiannual cash flows of $50, and a $1,000 cash flow 40 6-month periods from now.

Notice the treatment of the par value. It is *not* treated as if it is received 20 years from now. Instead, it is treated on a basis consistent with the coupon payments, which are semiannual.

The required yield is determined by investigating the yields offered on comparable bonds in the market. By comparable, we mean noncallable bonds of the same credit quality and the same maturity.[3] The required yield typically is expressed as an annual interest rate. When the cash flows occur semiannually, the market convention is to use one-half the annual interest rate as the periodic interest rate with which to discount the cash flows.

Given the cash flows of a bond and the required yield, we have all the analytical tools to price a bond. As the price of a bond is the present value of the cash flows, it is determined by adding these two present values:

1. The present value of the semiannual coupon payments
2. The present value of the par or maturity value at the maturity date

In general, the price of a bond can be computed using the following formula:

$$
P = \frac{C}{(1+r)^1} + \frac{C}{(1+r)^2} + \frac{C}{(1+r)^3} + \cdots + \frac{C}{(1+r)^n} + \frac{M}{(1+r)^n}
$$

or

$$
(2.6) \quad P = \sum_{t=1}^{n} \frac{C}{(1+r)^t} + \frac{M}{(1+r)^n}
$$

---

[3] In Chapter 4 we introduce a measure of interest-rate risk known as duration. There, instead of talking in terms of bonds with the same maturity as being comparable, we recast the analysis in terms of duration.

where P = price (in $)
    n = number of periods (number of years times 2)
    C = *semiannual* coupon payment (in $)
    r = periodic interest rate (required annual yield divided by 2)
    M = maturity value
    t = time period when the payment is to be received

Because the semiannual coupon payments are equivalent to an ordinary annuity, applying equation (2.5) for the present value of an annuity gives the present value of the coupon payments:

$$(2.7) \quad C \left[\frac{1 - \dfrac{1}{(1+r)^n}}{r} \right]$$

To illustrate how to compute the price of a bond, consider a 20-year 10% coupon bond with a par value of $1,000. Let's suppose that the required yield on this bond is 11%. The cash flows for this bond are as follows:

1. 40 semiannual coupon payments of $50
2. $1,000 to be received 40 six-month periods from now

The semiannual or periodic interest rate (or periodic required yield) is 5.5% (11% divided by 2).

The present value of the 40 semiannual coupon payments of $50 discounted at 5.5% is $802.31, calculated as:

$C = \$50$

$n = 40$

$r = .055$

$$= \$50 \left[\frac{1 - \dfrac{1}{(1.055)^{40}}}{.055} \right]$$

$$= \$50 \left[\frac{1 - \dfrac{1}{8.51332}}{.055} \right]$$

$$= \$50 \left[\frac{1 - .117463}{.055} \right]$$

$$= \$50(16.04613)$$

$$= \$802.31$$

The present value of the par or maturity value of $1,000 received *40 6-month periods from now*, discounted at 5.5%, is $117.46, as follows:

$$\frac{\$1,000}{(1.055)^{40}}$$

$$= \frac{\$1,000}{8.51332}$$

$$= \$117.46$$

The price of the bond is then equal to the sum of the two present values:

	Present value of coupon payments	= $ 802.31
+	Present value of par (maturity value)	= 117.46
	Price	= $ 919.77

Suppose that, instead of an 11% required yield, the required yield is 6.8%. The price of the bond would then be $1,347.04, demonstrated as follows:

The present value of the coupon payments using a periodic interest rate of 3.4% (6.8%/2) is:

$$\$50 \left[\frac{1 - \dfrac{1}{(1.034)^{40}}}{.034} \right]$$

$$= \$50 \, (21.69029)$$

$$= \$1,084.51$$

The present value of the par or maturity value of $1,000 received *40 six-month periods from now* discounted at 3.4% is:

$$\frac{\$1,000}{(1.034)^{40}} = \$262.53$$

The price of the bond is then:

	Present value of coupon payments	= $ 1,084.51
+	Present value of par (maturity) value	= 262.53
	Price	= $ 1,347.04

If the required yield is equal to the coupon rate of 10%, the price of the bond would be its par value, $1,000, as the following calculations demonstrate.

Using a periodic interest rate of 5.0% (10%/2), the present value of the coupon payments is:

$$\$50 \left[\frac{1 - \dfrac{1}{(1.050)^{40}}}{.050} \right]$$

$$= \$50(17.15909)$$

$$= \$857.95$$

The present value of the par or maturity value of $1,000 received *40 six-month periods from now* discounted at 5% is:

$$\frac{\$1,000}{(1.050)^{40}} = \$142.05$$

The price of the bond is then:

	Present value of coupon payments	= $ 857.95
+	Present value of par (maturity) value	= 142.05
	Price	= $1,000.00

Pricing Zero-Coupon Bonds

Some bonds do not make any periodic coupon payments. Instead, the investor realizes interest as the difference between the maturity value and the purchase price. These bonds are called *zero-coupon bonds*. The price of a zero-coupon bond is calculated by substituting zero for C in equation (2.6):

$$(2.8) \quad P = \frac{M}{(1+r)^n}$$

Equation (2.8) states that the price of a zero-coupon bond is simply the present value of the maturity value. In the present value computation, however, the number of periods used for discounting is not the number of years to maturity of the bond, but rather *double* the number of years. The discount rate is one-half the required annual yield.

For example, the price of a zero-coupon bond that matures 15 years from now, if the maturity value is $1,000 and the required yield is 9.4%, is $252.12, as shown:

$$M = \$1,000$$
$$r = .047(.094/2)$$
$$n = 30(2 \times 15)$$

$$P = \frac{\$1,000}{(1.047)^{30}}$$
$$= \frac{\$1,000}{3.96644}$$
$$= \$252.12$$

Price/Yield Relationship

A fundamental property of a bond is that its price changes in the opposite direction from the change in the required yield. The reason is that the price of the bond is the present value of the cash flows. As the required yield increases, the present value of the cash flow decreases; hence the price decreases. The opposite is true when the required yield decreases: the present value of the cash flows increases, and therefore the price of the bond increases. This can be seen by examining the price for the 20-year, 10% bond when the required yield is 11%, 10%, and 6.8%. Exhibit 2-1 shows the price of the 20-year, 10% coupon bond for various required yields.

If we graph the price/yield relationship for any noncallable bond, we will find that it has the "bowed" shape shown in Exhibit 2-2. This shape is referred to as *convex*. The convexity of the price/yield relationship has important implications for the investment properties of a bond, as we explain in Chapter 4.

The Relationship Between Coupon Rate, Required Yield, and Price

As yields in the marketplace change, the only variable that can change to compensate an investor for the new required yield in the market is the price of the bond. When the coupon rate is equal to the required yield, the price of the bond will be equal to its par value, as we demonstrated for the 20-year, 10% coupon bond.

EXHIBIT 2–1   Price/Yield Relationship for a 20-Year, 10% Coupon Bond

Yield	Price
0.045	$1,720.32
0.050	1,627.57
0.055	1,541.76
0.060	1,462.30
0.065	1,388.65
0.070	1,320.33
0.075	1,256.89
0.080	1,197.93
0.085	1,143.08
0.090	1,092.01
0.095	1,044.41
0.100	1,000.00
0.105	958.53
0.110	919.77
0.115	883.50
0.120	849.54
0.125	817.70
0.130	787.82
0.135	759.75
0.140	733.37
0.145	708.53
0.150	685.14
0.155	663.08
0.160	642.26
0.165	622.59

When yields in the marketplace rise above the coupon rate at *a given point in time*, the price of the bond adjusts so that the investor can realize some additional interest. If it did not, investors would sell the bond for an alternative, higher-yielding issue; the resulting lack of demand would cause the price to fall and thus the yield on the bond to increase. This is how a bond's price falls below its par value.

The capital appreciation realized by holding the bond to maturity represents a form of interest to the investor to compensate for a coupon rate that is lower than the required yield. When a bond sells below its par value, it is said to be selling at a *discount*. In our earlier calculation of bond price we saw that when the required yield is greater than the coupon rate, the price of the bond is always lower than the par value ($1,000).

EXHIBIT 2-2   Shape of Price/Yield Relationship

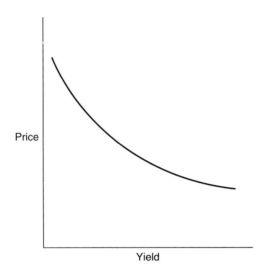

When the required yield in the market is below the coupon rate, the bond must sell above its par value. This is because investors would have the opportunity to purchase the bond at par would be getting a coupon rate in excess of what the market requires. As a result, investors would bid up the price of the bond because its yield is so attractive. The price would eventually be bid up to a level where the bond offers the required yield in the market. A bond whose price is above its par value is said to be selling at a *premium*. The relationship between coupon rate, required yield, and price can be summarized as follows:

Coupon rate < required yield <————> price < par (discount bond)
Coupon rate = required yield <————> price = par
Coupon rate > required yield <————> price > par (premium bond)

Relationship Between Bond Price and Time if Interest Rates are Unchanged

If the required yield does not change between the time the bond is purchased and the maturity date, what will happen to the price of the bond? For a bond selling at par value, the coupon rate is equal to the required yield. As the bond moves closer to maturity, the bond will continue to sell at par value. Its price will remain constant as the bond moves toward the maturity date.

The price of a bond will *not* remain constant for a bond selling at a premium or a discount. Exhibit 2-3 shows the time path of a 20-year, 10% coupon bond selling at a discount and the same bond selling at a premium as it approaches maturity. Notice that the discount bond increases in price as it approaches maturity, assuming the required yield does not change. For a premium bond, the opposite occurs. For both bonds, the price will equal par value at the maturity date.

Reasons for the Change in the Price of a Bond

The price of a bond will change for one or more of the following three reasons:

1. There is a change in the required yield owing to changes in the credit quality of the issuer.
2. There is a change in the price of the bond selling at a premium or a discount, without any change in the required yield, simply because the bond is moving toward maturity.
3. There is a change in the required yield owing to a change in the yield on comparable bonds (that is, a change in the yield required by the market).

Reasons 2 and 3 for a change in price are discussed in this chapter. Predicting a change in an issue's credit quality (reason 1) before that change is recognized by the market is one of the challenges of investment management.

COMPLICATIONS

The framework for pricing a bond discussed in this chapter assumes that:

1. The next coupon payment is exactly six months away.
2. The cash flows are known.
3. The appropriate required yield can be determined.
4. One rate is used to discount all cash flows.

Let's look at the implications of each assumption for the pricing of a bond.

Next Coupon Payment Due in Less Than Six Months

When an investor purchases a bond whose next coupon payment is due in less than six months, the accepted method for computing the price of the bond is as follows:

EXHIBIT 2-3   Time Path for the Price of a 20-Year, 10% Bond Selling at a Discount and Premium as it Approaches Maturity

Year	Discount Bond Selling to Yield 12% Price	Premium Bond Selling to Yield 7.8% Price
20.0	$849.54	$1,221.00
19.5	850.51	1,218.62
19.0	851.54	1,216.14
18.5	852.63	1,213.57
18.0	853.79	1,210.90
17.5	855.02	1,208.13
17.0	856.32	1,205.24
16.5	857.70	1,202.25
16.0	859.16	1,199.14
15.5	860.71	1,195.90
15.0	862.35	1,192.54
14.5	864.09	1,189.05
14.0	865.94	1,185.43
13.5	867.89	1,181.66
13.0	869.97	1,177.74
12.5	872.17	1,173.67
12.0	874.50	1,169.45
11.5	876.97	1,165.06
11.0	879.58	1,160.49
10.5	882.36	1,155.75
10.0	885.30	1,150.83
9.5	888.42	1,145.71
9.0	891.72	1,140.39
8.5	895.23	1,134.87
8.0	898.94	1,129.13
7.5	902.88	1,123.16
7.0	907.05	1,116.97
6.5	911.47	1,110.53
6.0	916.16	1,103.84
5.5	921.13	1,096.89
5.0	926.40	1,089.67
4.5	931.98	1,082.16
4.0	937.90	1,074.37
3.5	944.18	1,066.27
3.0	950.83	1,057.85
2.5	957.88	1,049.11
2.0	965.35	1,040.02
1.5	973.27	1,030.58
1.0	981.67	1,020.78
0.5	990.57	1,010.59
0.0	1,000.00	1,000.00

$$(2.9) \quad P = \sum_{t=1}^{n} \frac{C}{(1+r)^{v}(1+r)^{t-1}} + \frac{M}{(1+r)^{v}(1+r)^{n-1}}$$

where

$$v = \frac{\text{Days between settlement and next coupon}}{\text{Days in six - month period}}$$

Note that when v is 1 (that is, when the next coupon payment is six months away), equation (2.9) reduces to equation (2.6).

The Cash Flows May Not Be Known

For noncallable bonds, assuming that the issuer does not default, the cash flows are known. For most bonds, however, the cash flows are not known with certainty. This is because an issuer may call a bond before the stated maturity date. With callable bonds, the cash flow will, in fact, depend on the level of current interest rates relative to the coupon rate. For example, the issuer will typically call a bond when interest rates drop far enough below the coupon rate so that it is economic to retire the bond issue prior to maturity and issue new bonds at a lower coupon rate.[4] Consequently, the cash flows of bonds that may be called prior to maturity are dependent on current interest rates in the marketplace.

Determining the Appropriate Required Yield

All required yields are benchmarked off yields offered by Treasury securities, the subject of Chapter 5. The analytical framework that we develop in this book is one of decomposing the required yield for a bond into its component parts, as we discuss in later chapters.

One Discount Rate Applicable to All Cash Flows

Our pricing analysis has assumed that it is appropriate to discount each cash flow using the same discount rate. As explained in Chapter 12, a bond can be viewed as a package of zero-coupon bonds, in which case a unique discount rate should be used to determine the present value of each cash flow.

---

[4] Mortgage-backed securities discussed in Chapter 15 are another example; the borrower has the right to prepay all or part of the obligation prior to maturity.

PRICE QUOTES, ACCRUED INTEREST, AND INVOICE PRICE

Price Quotes

Throughout this chapter we have assumed that the maturity or par value of a bond is $1,000. A bond may have a maturity or par value greater or less than $1,000. Consequently, when quoting bond prices, traders quote the price as a percentage of par value.

A bond selling at par is quoted as 100, meaning 100% of its par value. A bond selling at a discount will be selling for less than 100; a bond selling at a premium will be selling for more than 100. The following examples illustrate how a price quote is converted into a dollar price.

Price Quote (1)	Converted to a Decimal (2) [=(1)/100]	Par Value (3)	Dollar Price (4) = [(2) × (3)]
97	.9700000	$ 10,000	9,700.00
85 1/2	.8550000	100,000	85,500.00
90 1/4	.9025000	5,000	4,512.50
80 1/8	.8012500	10,000	8,012.50
76 5/32	.7615625	1,000,000	761,562.50
86 11/64	.8617188	100,000	86,171.88
100	1.0000000	50,000	50,000.00
109	1.0900000	1,000	1,090.00
103 3/4	1.0375000	100,000	103,750.00
105 3/8	1.0537500	25,000	26,343.75
103 19/32	1.0359375	1,000,000	1,035,937.50

Accrued Interest

When an investor purchases a bond between coupon payments, the investor must compensate the seller of the bond for the coupon interest earned from the time of the last coupon payment to the settlement date of the bond.[5] This amount is called *accrued interest*. The computation of accrued interest depends on the type of bond. For a Treasury coupon security, discussed in Chapter 5, accrued interest is based on the actual number of days the bond is held by the seller. For corporate and municipal bonds, accrued interest is based on a 360-day year, with each month having 30 days.

---

[5] The exceptions are bonds that are in default. Such bonds are said to be quoted *flat*, that is, without accrued interest.

Invoice Price

The invoice price is the total amount that the buyer of the bond pays the seller. The invoice price is equal to the price agreed upon by the buyer and the seller plus accrued interest. This is often referred to as the *full price* of a bond or the *dirty price*. The price of a bond without accrued interest is called the *clean price*.

SUMMARY

This chapter has shown how to determine the price of a noncallable bond. The price is simply the present value of the bond's expected cash flows, the discount rate being equal to the yield offered on comparable bonds. For a noncallable bond, the cash flows are the coupon payments and the par value or maturity value. For a zero-coupon bond, there are no coupon payments. The price is equal to the present value of the maturity value, where the number of periods used to compute the present value is double the number of years, and the discount rate is a semiannual yield.

The higher (lower) the required yield, the lower (higher) the price of a bond. Therefore a bond's price changes in the opposite direction from the change in the required yield. When the coupon rate is equal to the required yield, the bond will sell at its par value. When the coupon rate is less (greater) than the required yield, the bond will sell for less (more) than its par value and is said to be selling at a discount (premium).

Over time, the price of a premium or discount bond will change even if the required yield does not change. Assuming the credit quality of the issuer is unchanged, the price change on any bond can be decomposed into a portion attributable to a change in the required yield and a portion attributable to the time path of the bond.

QUESTIONS FOR CHAPTER 2

1. A pension fund manager invests $10 million in a debt obligation that promises to pay 7.3% per year for four years. What is the future value of the $10 million?

2. Suppose that a life insurance company has guaranteed a payment of $14 million to a pension fund 4.5 years from now. If the life insurance company receives a premium of $10.4 million from the pension fund and can invest the entire premium for 4.5 years at an annual interest rate of 6.25%, will it have sufficient funds from this investment to meet the $14 million obligation?

3. a. The portfolio manager of a tax-exempt fund is considering investing $500,000 in a debt instrument that pays an annual interest rate of 5.7% for four years. At the end of four years, the portfolio manager plans to reinvest the proceeds for three more years and expects that, for the three-year period, an annual interest rate of 7.2% can be earned. What is the future value of this investment?

   b. Suppose that the portfolio manager in 3(a) has the opportunity to invest the $500,000 for seven years in a debt obligation that promises to pay an annual interest rate of 6.1% compounded semiannually. Is this investment alternative more attractive than the one in 3(a)?

4. Suppose that a portfolio manager purchases $10 million of par value of an eight-year bond that has a coupon rate of 7% and pays interest once per year. The first annual coupon payment will be made one year from now. How much will the portfolio manager have if she (1) holds the bond until it matures eight years from now, and (2) can reinvest all the annual interest payments at an annual interest rate of 6.2%?

5. a. If the discount rate that is used to calculate the present value of a debt obligation's cash flow is increased, what happens to the price of that debt obligation?

   b. Suppose that the discount rate used to calculate the present value of a debt obligation's cash flow is x%. Suppose also that the only cash flow for this debt obligation is $200,000 four years from now and $200,000 five years from now. For which one of these cash flows will the present value be greater?

6. The pension fund obligation of a corporation is calculated as the present value of the actuarially projected benefits that will have to be paid to beneficiaries. Why is the interest rate used to discount the projected benefits important?

7. A pension fund manager knows that the following liabilities must be satisfied:

Years from now	Liability
1	$ 2.0 million
2	3.0
3	5.4
4	5.8

Suppose that the pension fund manager wants to invest a sum of money that will satisfy this liability stream. Assuming that any amount that can be invested today can earn an annual interest rate of 7.6%, how much must be invested today to satisfy this liability stream?

8. Calculate for each of the bonds below the price per $1,000 of par value assuming semiannual coupon payments.

Bond	Coupon Rate	Years to Maturity	Required Yield
A	8%	9	7%
B	9	20	9
C	6	15	10
D	0	14	8

9. Consider a bond selling at par ($100) with a coupon rate of 6% and ten years to maturity.
   a. What is the price of this bond if the required yield is 15%?
   b. What is the price of this bond if the required yield increases from 15% to 16%, and by what percentage did the price of this bond change?
   c. What is the price of this bond if the required yield is 5%?
   d. What is the price of this bond if the required yield increases from 5% to 6%, and by what percentage did the price of this bond change?
   e. From your answers to 9(b) and 9(d), what can you say about the relative price volatility of a bond in high compared to low interest rate environments?

10. Suppose you purchased a debt obligation three years ago at its par value of $100,000. The market price of this debt obligation today is $90,000. What are some of the reasons why the price of this debt obligation could have declined since you purchased it three years ago?

11. Suppose you are reviewing a price sheet for bonds and see the following prices (per $100 par value) reported. You observe what seem to be several errors. Without calculating the price of each bond, indicate which bonds seem to be reported incorrectly, and explain why.

Bond	Price	Coupon Rate	Required Yield
U	90	6%	9%
V	96	9	8
W	110	8	6
X	105	0	5
Y	107	7	9
Z	100	6	6

12. What is the maximum price of a bond?
13. What does the invoice price of a bond include?

Chapter 3

MEASURING YIELD

In the previous chapter we showed how to determine the price of a bond, and we described the relationship between price and yield. In this chapter we discuss various yield measures and their meaning for evaluating the relative attractiveness of a bond. We begin with an explanation of how to compute the yield on any investment.

COMPUTING THE YIELD OR INTERNAL RATE OF RETURN ON ANY INVESTMENT

The yield on any investment is the interest rate that will make the present value of the cash flows from the investment equal to the price (or cost) of the investment. Mathematically, the yield on any investment, y, is the interest rate that satisfies the equation:

$$P = \frac{CF_1}{(1+y)^1} + \frac{CF_2}{(1+y)^2} + \frac{CF_3}{(1+y)^3} + \dots + \frac{CF_N}{(1+y)^N}$$

This expression can be rewritten in shorthand notation as:

$$(3.1) \quad P = \sum_{t=1}^{N} \frac{CF_t}{(1+y)^t}$$

where CF_t = cash flow in year t

P = price of the investment

N = number of years

The yield calculated from this relationship is also called the *internal rate of return.*

Solving for the yield (y) requires a trial-and-error (iterative) procedure. The objective is to find the interest rate that will make the present value of the cash flows equal to the price. An example demonstrates how this is done.

Suppose a financial instrument selling for $903.10 promises to make the following annual payments:

Years from Now	Promised Annual Payments (cash flow to investor)
1	$ 100
2	100
3	100
4	1,000

To compute yield, different interest rates must be tried until the present value of the cash flows is equal to $903.10 (the price of the financial instrument). Trying an annual interest rate of 10% gives the following present value:

Years from Now	Promised Annual Payments (cash flow to investor)	Present Value of Cash Flow at 10%
1	$ 100	$90.91
2	100	82.64
3	100	75.13
4	1,000	683.01
	Present value = $	931.69

Because the present value computed using a 10% interest rate exceeds the price of $903.10, a higher interest rate must be used in order to reduce the present value. If a 12% interest rate is used, the present value is $875.71, computed as follows:

Years from Now	Promised Annual Payments (cash flow to investor)	Present Value of Cash Flow at 12%
1	$ 100	$ 89.29
2	100	79.72
3	100	71.18
4	1,000	635.52
	Present value = $	875.71

Using 12%, the present value of the cash flow is less than the price of the financial instrument. Therefore a lower interest rate must be tried in order to increase the present value. Using an 11% interest rate:

Years from Now	Promised Annual Payments (cash flow to investor)	Present Value of Cash Flow at 11%
1	$ 100	$90.09
2	100	81.16
3	100	73.12
4	1,000	658.73
	Present value =	$903.10

Using 11%, the present value of the cash flow is equal to the price of the financial instrument. Therefore the yield is 11%.

Although the formula for the yield is based on annual cash flows, it can be generalized to any number of periodic payments in a year. The generalized formula for determining the yield is:

$$(3.2) \quad P = \sum_{t=1}^{n} \frac{CF_t}{(1+y)^t}$$

where CF_t = cash flow in period t

n = number of periods

Keep in mind that the yield computed is now the yield for the period. That is, if the cash flows are semiannual, the yield is a semiannual yield. If the cash flows are monthly, the yield is a monthly yield. To compute the *simple* annual interest rate, the yield for the period is multiplied by the number of periods in the year.

Special Case: Investment with Only One Future Cash Flow

In one special case it is not necessary to go through the time-consuming trial-and-error procedure to determine the yield. This is where there is only one future cash flow from the investment. When an investment has only one future cash flow at period n (CF_n), equation (3.2) reduces to:

$$P = \frac{CF_n}{(1+y)^n}$$

Solving for yield, y:

$$(3.3) \quad y = \left(\frac{CF_n}{P}\right)^{1/n} - 1$$

To illustrate how to use equation (3.3), suppose that a financial instrument currently selling for $62,321.30 promises to pay $100,000 six years from now. The yield for this investment is 8.20%, as follows:

$$y = \left(\frac{100,000.00}{62,321.30}\right)^{1/6} - 1$$

$$= (1.60459)^{1/6} - 1$$

$$= 1.082 - 1$$

$$= .082 \text{ or } 8.2\%$$

Note in equation (3.3) that the ratio of the future cash flow in period n to the price of the financial instrument (i.e., CF_n / P) is equal to the future value per $1 invested.

Annualizing Yields

In the previous chapter we annualized interest rates by multiplying by the number of periods in a year, and we called the resulting value the *simple annual interest rate*. For example, a semiannual yield is annualized by multiplying by 2. Alternatively, an annual interest rate is converted to a semiannual interest rate by dividing by 2.

This simplified procedure for computing the annual interest rate given a periodic (weekly, monthly, quarterly, semiannually, etc.) interest rate is not accurate. To obtain an effective annual yield associated with a periodic interest rate, the following formula is used:

Effective annual yield = (1 + periodic interest rate)^m – 1
where m = frequency of payments per year

For example, suppose the periodic interest rate is 4% and the frequency of payments is twice per year. Then:

Effective annual yield $= (1.04)^2 - 1$
$= 1.0816 - 1$
$= .0816 \text{ or } 8.16\%$

If interest is paid quarterly, then the periodic interest rate is 2% (8%/4), and the effective annual yield is 8.24%, as follows:

$$\text{Effective annual yield} = (1.02)^4 - 1$$
$$= 1.0824 - 1$$
$$= .0824 \text{ or } 8.24\%$$

We can also determine the periodic interest rate that will produce a given annual interest by solving the effective annual yield equation for the periodic interest rate. Solving, we find:

$$\text{Periodic interest rate} = (1 + \text{effective annual yield})^{1/m} - 1$$

For example, the periodic quarterly interest rate that would produce an effective annual yield of 12% is:

$$\text{Periodic interest rate} = (1.12)^{1/4} - 1$$
$$= 1.0287 - 1$$
$$= .0287 \text{ or } 2.87\%$$

CONVENTIONAL YIELD MEASURES

There are three bond yield measures commonly quoted by dealers and used by portfolio managers: (1) current yield; (2) yield to maturity; and (3) yield to call. In this section we discuss each yield measure and show how it is computed. In the next section we critically evaluate each measure in terms of its usefulness in identifying the relative value of a bond.

Current Yield

Current yield relates the annual coupon interest to the market price. The formula for the current yield is:

$$\text{Current yield} = \frac{\text{Annual dollar coupon interest}}{\text{Price}}$$

For example, the current yield for a 15-year, 7% coupon bond with a par value of $1,000 selling for $769.40 is 9.10%, as shown:

$$\text{Current yield} = \frac{\$70}{\$769.40} = .0910 \text{ or } 9.10\%$$

The current yield calculation takes into account only the coupon interest and no other source of return that will affect an investor's yield. No consideration is given to the capital gain that the investor will realize when a bond is purchased at a discount and held to maturity; nor is there any recognition of the capital loss that the investor will realize if a bond purchased at a premium is held to maturity. The time value of money is also ignored.

Yield to Maturity

In the first section of this chapter we explained how to compute the yield or internal rate of return on any investment. The yield is the interest rate that will make the present value of the cash flows equal to the price (or initial investment). The yield to maturity is computed in the same way as the yield (internal rate of return); the cash flows are those that the investor would realize by holding the bond to maturity. For a semiannual pay bond, the yield to maturity is found by first computing the periodic interest rate, y, that satisfies the relationship:

$$P = \frac{C}{(1+y)^1} + \frac{C}{(1+y)^2} + \frac{C}{(1+y)^3} + \cdots + \frac{C}{(1+y)^n} + \frac{M}{(1+y)^n}$$

$$(3.4) \quad P = \sum_{t=1}^{n} \frac{C}{(1+y)^t} + \frac{M}{(1+y)^n}$$

where P = price of the bond

C = *semiannual* coupon interest (in $)

M = maturity value (in $)

n = number of periods (number of years $\times$ 2)

For a semiannual pay bond, doubling the periodic interest rate or discount rate (y) gives the yield to maturity. However, recall from our discussion of annualizing yields that doubling the periodic interest rate understates the effective annual yield. Despite this, the market convention is to compute the yield to maturity by doubling the periodic interest rate, y, that satisfies equation (3.4). The yield to maturity computed on the basis of this market convention is called the *bond-equivalent yield*.

The computation of the yield to maturity requires a trial-and-error procedure. To illustrate the computation, consider the bond that we used to compute the current yield. The cash flow for this bond is (1) 30 coupon payments of $35 every six months and (2) $1,000 to be paid 30 six-month periods from now.

To get y in equation (3.4), different interest rates must be tried until the present value of the cash flows is equal to the price of $769.42. The present value of the cash flows of the bond for several periodic interest rates is as follows:

Annual Interest Rate	Semiannual Rate (y)	Present Value of 30 Payments of $35 [1]	Present Value of $1,000 30 Periods from Now [2]	Present Value of Cash Flows
9.00	4.50	570.11	267.00	837.11
9.50	4.75	553.71	248.53	802.24
10.00	5.00	538.04	231.38	769.42
10.50	5.25	532.04	215.45	738.49
11.00	5.50	508.68	200.64	709.32

When a 5% semiannual interest rate is used, the present value of the cash flows is $769.42. Therefore y is 5%, and the yield to maturity on a bond-equivalent basis is 10%.

It is much easier to compute the yield to maturity for a zero-coupon bond because equation (3.3) can be used. As the cash flow in period n is the maturity value M, equation (3.3) can be rewritten as:[3]

$$(3.5) \quad y = \left(\frac{M}{P}\right)^{1/n} - 1$$

For example, for a ten-year zero-coupon bond with a maturity value of $1,000, selling for $439.18, y is 4.2%, as shown:

$$y = \left(\frac{\$1,000}{\$439.18}\right)^{1/20} - 1$$

$$y = (2.27697)^{.05} - 1$$

$$y = 1.042 - 1 = .042$$

---

[1] The present value of the coupon payments is found using this formula:

$$\$35 \left[\frac{1 - \dfrac{1}{(1+y)^{30}}}{y} \right]$$

[2] The present value of the maturity value is found using this formula:

$$\$1,000 \left[\frac{1}{(1+y)^{30}} \right]$$

[3] That is, M is substituted for CF_n.

Note that the number of periods is equal to 20 semiannual periods, which is double the number of years. The number of years is not used because we want a yield value that may be compared with alternative coupon bonds. To get the bond-equivalent annual yield, we must double y, which gives us 8.4%.

The yield to maturity calculation takes into account not only the current coupon income but also any capital gain or loss that the investor will realize by *holding the bond to maturity*. In addition, the yield to maturity considers the timing of the cash flows.

The relationship among the coupon rate, current yield, and yield to maturity looks like this:

Bond Selling at	Relationship
Par	Coupon rate = current yield = yield to maturity
Discount	Coupon rate < current yield < yield to maturity
Premium	Coupon rate > current yield > yield to maturity

Yield to Call

For a bond that may be called prior to the stated maturity date, another yield measure is commonly quoted—the *yield to call*. The cash flows for computing the yield to call are those that will result if the issue is called on its first call date.[4] The yield to call is the interest rate that will make the present value of the cash flows equal to the price of the bond if the bond is held to the first call date.

Mathematically, the yield to call can be expressed as follows:

$$P = \frac{C}{(1+y)^1} + \frac{C}{(1+y)^2} + \frac{C}{(1+y)^3} + \dots + \frac{C}{(1+y)^{n^*}} + \frac{M^*}{(1+y)^{n^*}}$$

$$(3.6) \quad P = \sum_{t=1}^{n^*} \frac{C}{(1+y)^t} + \frac{M^*}{(1+y)^{n^*}}$$

where M^* = call price (in $)

n^* = number of periods until first call date (number of years $\times$ 2)

---

[4] Practitioners can compute a yield to call for every possible call date. The procedure for computing the yield to any call date is the same as that described for computing the yield to the first call date.

For a semiannual pay bond, doubling the periodic interest rate (y) gives the yield to call on a bond-equivalent basis.

To illustrate the computation, consider an 18-year, 11% coupon bond with a maturity value of $1,000 selling for $1,168.97. Suppose that the first call date is 13 years from now and that the call price is $1,055. The cash flows for this bond if it is called in 13 years are (1) 26 coupon payments of $55 every six months and (2) $1,055 due in 26 six-month periods from now.

The value for y in equation (3.6) is the one that will make the present value of the cash flows to the call date equal to the bond's price of $1,168.97. The process of finding the yield to call is the same as that for finding the yield to maturity. The present value at several periodic interest rates is:

Annual Interest Rate	Semiannual Rate (y)	Present Value of 26 payments of $55 [5]	Present Value of $1,055 26 Periods from Now [6]	Present Value of Cash Flows
8.0	4.00	879.05	380.53	1,259.58
8.5	4.25	855.59	357.50	1,213.09
9.0	4.50	833.06	335.91	1,168.97
9.5	4.75	811.43	315.68	1,127.11
10.0	5.50	790.64	296.71	1,087.35

Because a periodic interest rate of 4.5% makes the present value of the cash flows equal to the price, 4.5% is y, the yield to call. Therefore the yield to call on a bond-equivalent basis is 9%.

Investors typically compute both the yield to call and the yield to maturity for a callable bond selling at a premium. They then select the lower of the two as a measure of return. [7]

---

[5] The present value of the coupon payments is found using this formula:

$$\$55 \left[\frac{1 - \dfrac{1}{(1+y)^{26}}}{y} \right]$$

[6] The present value of the call price is found using this formula:

$$\$1,055 \left[\frac{1}{(1+y)^{26}} \right]$$

[7] The lowest yield based on every possible call date and the yield to maturity is referred to as the *yield to worst*.

Yield (Internal Rate of Return) for a Portfolio

The yield for a portfolio of bonds is not simply the average or weighted average of the yield to maturity of the individual bond issues in the portfolio. It is computed by determining the cash flows for the portfolio and determining the interest rate that will make the present value of the cash flows equal to the market value of the portfolio.[8]

Consider a three-bond portfolio as follows:

Bond	Coupon Rate	Maturity	Par Value	Price	Yield to Maturity
A	7.0%	5 years	$10,000,000	$ 9,209,000	9.0%
B	10.5%	7 years	$20,000,000	$20,000,000	10.5%
C	6.0%	3 years	$30,000,000	$28,050,000	8.5%

To simplify the illustration, it is assumed that the coupon payment date is the same for each bond. The portfolio's total market value is $57,259,000. The cash flow for each bond in the portfolio and the whole portfolio follows:

Period Cash Flow Received	Bond A	Bond B	Bond C	Portfolio
1	$350,000	$1,050,000	$900,000	$2,300,000
2	350,000	1,050,000	900,000	2,300,000
3	350,000	1,050,000	900,000	2,300,000
4	350,000	1,050,000	900,000	2,300,000
5	350,000	1,050,000	900,000	2,300,000
6	350,000	1,050,000	30,900,000	32,300,000
7	350,000	1,050,000	—	1,400,000
8	350,000	1,050,000	—	1,400,000
9	350,000	1,050,000	—	1,400,000
10	10,350,000	1,050,000	—	11,400,000
11	—	1,050,000	—	1,050,000
12	—	1,050,000	—	1,050,000
13	—	1,050,000	—	1,050,000
14	—	21,050,000	—	21,050,000

---

[8] In Chapter 4 we discuss the concept of duration. A good approximation to the yield for a portfolio can be obtained by using duration to weight the yield to maturity of the individual bonds in the portfolio.

To determine the yield (internal rate of return) for this three-bond portfolio, the interest rate must be found that makes the present value of the cash flows shown in the last column of the table above equal to $57,259,000 (the total market value of the portfolio). If an interest rate of 4.77% is used, the present value of the cash flows will equal $57,259,000. Doubling 4.77% gives 9.54%, which is the yield on the portfolio on a bond-equivalent basis.

Yield Measure for Floating-Rate Securities

The coupon rate for a floating-rate security changes periodically according to some predetermined index. Because the value for such a benchmark in the future is not known, it is not possible to determine the cash flows. This means that a yield to maturity cannot be calculated for a floating-rate bond.

A conventional measure used to estimate the potential return for a floating-rate security is the security's *effective margin*. This measure estimates the average spread or margin over the underlying index that the investor can expect to earn over the life of the security. The procedure for calculating the effective margin is as follows:

1. Determine the cash flows assuming that the index rate does not change over the life of the security.
2. Select a margin (spread).
3. Discount the cash flows found in (1) by the current index rate plus the margin selected in (2).
4. Compare the present value of the cash flows as calculated in (3) to the price. If the present value is equal to the security's price, the effective margin is the margin assumed in (2). If the present value is not equal to the security's price, go back to (2) and try a different margin.

For a security selling at par, the effective margin is simply the spread over the index.

To illustrate the calculation, suppose that a six-year floating-rate security selling for 99.3098 pays a rate based on some interest rate index plus 80 basis points.[9] The coupon rate is reset every six months. Assume that the current interest rate for the index is 10%. Exhibit 3-1 shows the calculation of the effective margin for this security. The first column shows the current interest rate for the index. The second column sets forth the cash flows for the security. The cash flow for the first 11 periods is

---

[9] A basis point is equal to .01% or .0001. One hundred basis points are equal to 1%.

equal to one-half the current interest rate index (5%) plus the semiannual spread of 40 basis points multiplied by 100. In the twelfth six-month period, the cash flow is 5.4 plus the maturity value of 100. The top row of the last five columns shows the assumed margin. The rows below the assumed margin show the present value of each cash flow. The last row gives the total present value of the cash flows.

For the five assumed yield spreads, the present value is equal to the price of the floating-rate security (99.3098) when the assumed margin is 96 basis points. Therefore, the effective margin on a semiannual basis is 48 basis points and 96 basis points on an annual basis. (Notice that the effective margin is 80 basis points, the same as the spread over the index, when the security is selling at par.)

A drawback of the effective margin as a measure of the potential return from investing in a floating-rate security is that the effective margin approach assumes that the index will not change over the life of the security. Second, if the floating-rate security has a cap or floor, this is not taken into consideration. Techniques described in Chapter 14 can allow interest rate volatility to be considered and can handle caps or floors.

EXHIBIT 3-1   Calculation of the Effective Margin
for a Floating -Rate Security

Floating-rate security: Maturity = 6 years
Coupon rate = index + 80 basis points
Reset every six months

Present Value of Cash Flow:

Assumed Annual Yield Spread (in b.p.)

Period	Index	Cash Flow*	80	84	88	96	100
1	10%	5.4	5.1233	5.1224	5.1214	5.1195	5.1185
2	10	5.4	4.8609	4.8590	4.8572	4.8535	4.8516
3	10	5.4	4.6118	4.6092	4.6066	4.6013	4.5987
4	10	5.4	4.3755	4.3722	4.3689	4.3623	4.3590
5	10	5.4	4.1514	4.1474	4.1435	4.1356	4.1317
6	10	5.4	3.9387	3.9342	3.9297	3.9208	3.9163
7	10	5.4	3.7369	3.7319	3.7270	3.7171	3.7122
8	10	5.4	3.5454	3.5401	3.5347	3.5240	3.5186
9	10	5.4	3.3638	3.3580	3.3523	3.3409	3.3352
10	10	5.4	3.1914	3.1854	3.1794	3.1673	3.1613
11	10	5.4	3.0279	3.0216	3.0153	3.0028	2.9965
12	10	105.4	56.0729	55.9454	55.8182	55.5647	55.4385
	Present Value		100.0000	99.8269	99.6541	99.3098	99.1381

*For periods 1-11: Cash flow = 100 (Index + Assumed Margin) (0.5)
 For period 12: Cash flow = 100 (Index + Assumed Margin) (0.5) + 100

POTENTIAL SOURCES OF A BOND'S DOLLAR RETURN

An investor who purchases a bond can expect to receive a dollar return from one or more of these sources:

1. The periodic coupon interest payments made by the issuer
2. Any capital gain (or capital loss—negative dollar return) when the bond matures, is called, or is sold
3. Income from reinvestment of the periodic interest payments (the interest-on-interest component)

Any measure of a bond's potential yield should take into consideration each of these three potential sources of return. The current yield considers only the coupon interest payments. No consideration is given to any capital gain (or loss) or interest-on-interest. The yield to maturity takes into account coupon interest and any capital gain (or loss). It also considers the interest-on-interest component; implicit in the yield-to-maturity computation, however, is the assumption that the coupon payments can be reinvested at the computed yield to maturity. The yield to maturity, therefore, is a *promised* yield— that is, it will be realized only if (1) the bond is held to maturity, and (2) the coupon interest payments are reinvested at the yield to maturity. If neither (1) nor (2) occurs, the actual yield realized by an investor can be greater than or less than the yield to maturity.

The yield to call also takes into account all three potential sources of return. In this case, the assumption is that the coupon payments can be reinvested at the yield to call. Therefore the yield-to-call measure suffers from the same drawback inherent in the implicit assumption of the reinvestment rate for the coupon interest payments. Also, it assumes that the bond will be held only to the call date.

Determining the Interest-on-Interest Dollar Return

The interest-on-interest component can represent a substantial portion of a bond's potential return. The potential total dollar return from coupon interest and interest-on-interest can be computed by applying the future value of an annuity formula given in the previous chapter. Letting r denote the semiannual reinvestment rate, the interest-on-interest plus the total coupon payments can be found from equation (3.7):

Coupon interest

$$(3.7) \qquad + \qquad = C\left[\frac{(1+r)^n - 1}{r}\right]$$

Interest - on - interest

The total dollar amount of coupon interest is found by multiplying the semiannual coupon interest by the number of periods:

Total coupon interest $= nC$

The interest-on-interest component is then the difference between the coupon interest plus interest-on-interest and the total dollar coupon interest, as expressed in equation (3.8).

$$(3.8) \quad \text{Interest - on - interest} \quad = C\left[\frac{(1+r)^n - 1}{r}\right] - nC$$

The yield-to-maturity measure assumes that the reinvestment rate is the yield to maturity.

For example, let's consider the 15-year, 7% bond that we have used to illustrate how to compute current yield and yield to maturity. The yield to maturity for this bond is 10%. Assuming an annual reinvestment rate of 10% or a semiannual reinvestment rate of 5%, the interest-on-interest plus total coupon payments using equation (3.7) is:

$$\begin{array}{c} \text{Coupon interest} \\ + \\ \text{Interest-on-interest} \end{array} = \$35\left[\frac{(1.05)^{30} - 1}{.05}\right]$$

$$= \$2,325.36$$

Using equation (3.8), the interest-on-interest component is:

$$\begin{aligned} \text{Interest-on-interest} \quad &= \$2,325.36 - 30\,(\$35) \\ &= \$1,275.36 \end{aligned}$$

Yield to Maturity and Reinvestment Risk

Let's look at the potential total dollar return from holding this bond to maturity. As mentioned earlier, the total dollar return comes from three sources:

1. Total coupon interest of $1,050 (coupon interest of $35 every six months for 15 years)
2. Interest-on-interest of $1,275.36 earned from reinvesting the semiannual coupon interest payments at 5% every six months
3. A capital gain of $230.60 ($1,000 minus $769.40)

The potential total dollar return if the coupons can be reinvested at the yield to maturity of 10% is then $2,555.96.

Notice that if an investor places the money that would have been used to purchase this bond, $769.40, in a savings account earning 5%

semiannually for 15 years, the future value of the savings account would be:

$769.40 $(1.05)^{30}$ = $3,325.30

For the initial investment of $769.40, the total dollar return is $2,555.90.

So, an investor who invests $769.40 for 15 years at 10% per year (5% semiannually) expects to receive at the end of 15 years the initial investment of $769.40 plus $2,555.96. This is precisely what we found by breaking down the dollar return on the bond assuming a reinvestment rate equal to the yield to maturity of 10%. Thus it can be seen that for the bond to yield 10%, the investor must generate $1,275.36 by reinvesting the coupon payments. This means that to generate a yield to maturity of 10%, approximately half ($1,275.36/$2,555.96) of this bond's total dollar return must come from the reinvestment of the coupon payments.

The investor will realize the yield to maturity at the time of purchase only if the bond is held to maturity and the coupon payments can be reinvested at the yield to maturity. The risk that the investor faces is that future reinvestment rates will be less than the yield to maturity at the time the bond is purchased. This risk is referred to as *reinvestment risk.*

There are two characteristics of a bond that determine the importance of the interest-on-interest component and therefore the degree of reinvestment risk: maturity and coupon. For a given yield to maturity and a given coupon rate, the longer the maturity, the more dependent the bond's total dollar return is on the interest-on-interest component in order to realize the yield to maturity at the time of purchase. In other words, the longer the maturity, the greater the reinvestment risk. The implication is that the yield-to-maturity measure for long-term coupon bonds tells little about the potential yield that an investor may realize if the bond is held to maturity. For long-term bonds, the interest-on-interest component may be as high as 80% of the bond's potential total dollar return.

Turning to the coupon rate, for a given maturity and a given yield to maturity, the higher the coupon rate, the more dependent the bond's total dollar return will be on the reinvestment of the coupon payments in order to produce the yield to maturity anticipated at the time of purchase. This means that when maturity and yield to maturity are held constant, premium bonds are more dependent on the interest-on-interest component than bonds selling at par. Discount bonds are less dependent on the interest-on-interest component than bonds selling at par. For zero-coupon bonds, none of the bond's total dollar return is dependent on the interest-on-interest component. So a zero-coupon bond has zero reinvestment risk if held to maturity. Thus the yield earned on a zero-coupon bond held to maturity is equal to the promised yield to maturity.

TOTAL RETURN

In the previous section we explain that the yield to maturity is a *promised* yield. At the time of purchase an investor is promised a yield, as measured by the yield to maturity, if both of the following conditions are satisfied:

1. The bond is held to maturity.
2. All coupon interest payments are reinvested at the yield to maturity.

We focused on the second assumption, and we showed that the interest-on-interest component for a bond may constitute a substantial portion of the bond's total dollar return. Therefore reinvesting the coupon interest payments at a rate of interest less than the yield to maturity will produce a lower yield than the yield to maturity.

Rather than assume that the coupon interest payments are reinvested at the yield to maturity, an investor can make an explicit assumption about the reinvestment rate based on personal expectations. The *total return* is a measure of yield that incorporates an explicit assumption about the reinvestment rate.

Let's take a careful look at the first assumption—that a bond will be held to maturity. Suppose, for example, that an investor who has a five-year investment horizon is considering the following four bonds:

Bond	Coupon	Maturity	Yield to Maturity
A	5%	3 years	9.0%
B	6%	20 years	8.6%
C	11%	15 years	9.2%
D	8%	5 years	8.0%

Assuming that all four bonds are of the same credit quality, which one is the most attractive to this investor? An investor who selects Bond C because it offers the highest yield to maturity is failing to recognize that the investment horizon calls for selling the bond after five years, at a price that depends on the yield required in the market for ten-year, 11% coupon bonds at the time. Hence there could be a capital gain or capital loss that will make the return higher or lower than the yield to maturity promised now. Moreover, the higher coupon on Bond C relative to the other three bonds means that more of this bond's return will be dependent on the reinvestment of coupon interest payments.

Bond A offers the second highest yield to maturity. On the surface, it seems to be particularly attractive because it eliminates the problem of realizing a possible capital loss when the bond must be sold prior to the maturity date. Moreover, the reinvestment risk seems to be less than for the other three bonds because the coupon rate is the lowest. However, the investor would not be eliminating the reinvestment risk because after three years the proceeds received at maturity must be reinvested for two more years. The yield that the investor will realize depends on interest rates three years from now on two-year bonds when the proceeds must be rolled over.

The yield to maturity doesn't seem to be helping us to identify the best bond. How, then, do we find out which is the best bond? The answer depends on the investor's expectations. Specifically, it depends on the interest rate at which the coupon interest payments can be reinvested until the end of the investor's planned investment horizon. Also, for bonds with a maturity longer than the investment horizon, it depends on the investor's expectations about required yields in the market at the end of the planned investment horizon. Consequently, any of these bonds can be the best alternative, depending on some reinvestment rate and some future required yield at the end of the planned investment horizon. The total return measure takes these expectations into account and will determine the best investment for the investor depending on personal expectations.

The yield-to-call measure is subject to the same problems as the yield to maturity. First, it assumes that the bond will be held until the first call date. Second, it assumes that the coupon interest payments will be reinvested at the yield to call. If an investor's planned investment horizon is shorter than the time to the first call date, the bond may have to be sold for less than its acquisition cost. If, on the other hand, the investment horizon is longer than the time to the first call date, there is the problem of reinvesting the proceeds from the time the bond is called until the end of the planned investment horizon. Consequently, the yield to call doesn't tell us very much. The total return, however, can accommodate the analysis of callable bonds.

Computing the Total Return for a Bond

The idea underlying total return is simple. The objective is first to compute the total future dollars that will result from investing in a bond assuming a particular reinvestment rate. The total return is then computed as the interest rate that will make the initial investment in the bond grow to the computed total future dollars.

The procedure for computing the total return for a bond held over some investment horizon can be summarized as follows. For an assumed reinvestment rate, the dollar return that will be available at the end of the investment horizon can be computed for both the coupon interest payments and the interest-on-interest component. In addition, at the end of the planned investment horizon the investor will receive either the par value or some other value (based on the market yield on the bond when it is sold). The total return is then the interest rate that will make the amount invested in the bond (that is, the current market price plus accrued interest) grow to the future dollars available at the end of the planned investment horizon.

More formally, the steps for computing the total return for a bond held over some investment horizon are as follows:

Step 1: Compute the total coupon payments plus the interest-on-interest based on the assumed reinvestment rate. The coupon payments plus the interest-on-interest can be computed using equation (3.7). The reinvestment rate in this case is one-half the annual interest rate that the investor assumes can be earned on the reinvestment of coupon interest payments.

Step 2: Determine the projected sale price at the end of the planned investment horizon. The projected sale price will depend on the projected required yield at the end of the planned investment horizon. The projected sale price will be equal to the present value of the remaining cash flows of the bond discounted at the projected required yield.

Step 3: Sum the values computed in Steps 1 and 2. The sum is the total future dollars that will be received from the investment, given the assumed reinvestment rate and the projected required yield at the end of the investment horizon.[10]

Step 4: To obtain the semiannual total return, use the formula:

$$(3.9) \quad \left(\frac{\text{Total future dollars}}{\text{Purchase price of bond}} \right)^{1/h} - 1$$

where h is the number of six-month periods in the investment horizon.

Notice that this formula is simply an application of equation (3.3), the yield for an investment with just one future cash flow.

Step 5: As interest is assumed to be paid semiannually, double the interest rate found in Step 4. The resulting interest rate is the total return.

---

[10] The total future dollars computed here differ from the total dollar return that we used in showing the importance of the interest-on-interest component in the previous section. The total dollar return there includes only the capital gain (or capital loss if there was one), not the purchase price, which is included in calculating the total future dollars. That is:

Total dollar return = Total future dollars − Purchase price of bond

To illustrate computation of the total return, suppose that an investor with a 3-year investment horizon is considering purchasing a 20-year, 8% coupon bond for $828.40. The yield to maturity for this bond is 10%. The investor expects to be able to reinvest the coupon interest payments at an annual interest rate of 6% and that at the end of the planned investment horizon the then-17-year bond will be selling to offer a yield to maturity of 7%. The total return for this bond is found as follows.

Step 1: Compute the total coupon payments plus the interest-on-interest, assuming an annual reinvestment rate of 6%, or 3% every six months. The coupon payments are $40 every six months for three years or six periods (the planned investment horizon). Applying equation (3.7), the total coupon interest plus interest-on-interest is:

Coupon interest
+
Interest-on-interest

$$= \$40 \left[\frac{(1.03)^6 - 1}{.03} \right]$$

$$= \$40 \left[\frac{1.1941 - 1}{.03} \right]$$

$$= \$40(6.4684)$$

$$= \$258.74$$

Step 2: Determining the projected sale price at the end of three years, assuming that the required yield to maturity for 17-year bonds is 7%, is accomplished by calculating the present value of 34 coupon payments of $40 plus the present value of the maturity value of $1,000, discounted at 3.5%. The projected sale price is $1,098.51.[11]

Step 3: Adding the amounts in Steps 1 and 2 gives total future dollars of $1,357.25.

---

[11] The present value of the 34 coupon payments discounted at 3.5% is:

$$= \$40 \left[\frac{1 - \frac{1}{(1.035)^{34}}}{.035} \right] = \$788.03$$

The present value of the maturity value discounted at 3.5% is:

$$\frac{\$1,000}{(1.035)^{34}} = \$310.48$$

The projected sale price is $788.03 plus $310.48, or $1,098.51.

Step 4: To obtain the semiannual total return, compute the following:

$$\left(\frac{\$1,375.25}{\$828.40} \right)^{1/6} - 1$$

$$= (1.63840)^{.16667} - 1$$

$$= 1.0858 - 1$$

$$= .0858 \text{ or } 8.58\%$$

Step 5: Double 8.58% for a total return of 17.16%.

There is no need in this case to assume that the reinvestment rate will be constant for the entire investment horizon. An example will show how the total return measure can accommodate multiple reinvestment rates.

Suppose that an investor has a six-year investment horizon. The investor is considering a 13-year, 9% coupon bond selling at par. The investor's expectations are as follows:

1. The first four semiannual coupon payments can be reinvested from the time of receipt to the end of the investment horizon at a simple annual interest rate of 8%.

2. The last eight semiannual coupon payments can be reinvested from the time of receipt to the end of the investment horizon at a 10% simple annual interest rate.

3. The required yield to maturity on seven-year bonds at the end of the investment horizon will be 10.6%.

Using these three assumptions, the total return is computed as follows:

Step 1: Coupon payments of $45 every six months for six years (the investment horizon) will be received. The coupon interest plus interest-on-interest for the first four coupon payments, assuming a semiannual reinvestment rate of 4%, is:

$$\begin{matrix} \text{Coupon interest} \\ + \\ \text{Interest-on-interest} \end{matrix} = \$45 \left[\frac{(1.04)^4 - 1}{.04} \right]$$

$$= \$191.09$$

This gives the coupon plus interest-on-interest as of the end of the second year (four periods). Reinvested at 4% until the end of the planned investment horizon, four years or eight periods later, $191.09 will grow to:

$$\$191.09\,(1.04)^8 = \$261.52$$

The coupon interest plus interest-on-interest for the last eight coupon payments, assuming a semiannual reinvestment rate of 5%, is:

$$\begin{array}{c} \text{Coupon interest} \\ + \\ \text{Interest-on-interest} \end{array} = \$45\left[\frac{(1.05)^8 - 1}{.05}\right]$$

$$= \$429.71$$

The coupon interest plus interest-on-interest from all 12 coupon interest payments is $691.23 ($261.52 + $429.71).

Step 2: The projected sale price of the bond, assuming that the required yield is 10.6%, is $922.31.[12]

Step 3: The total future dollars are $1,613.54 ($691.23 + $922.31).

Step 4: Compute the following:

$$= \left(\frac{\$1,613.54}{\$1,000.00}\right)^{1/12} - 1$$

$$= (1.61354)^{.08333} - 1$$

$$= 1.0407 - 1$$

$$= .0407 \text{ or } 4.07\%$$

Step 5: Doubling 4.07% gives a total return of 8.14%.

---

[12] The present value of the coupon payments discounted at 5.3% is:

$$= \$45\left[\frac{1 - \dfrac{1}{(1.053)^{14}}}{.053}\right] = \$437.02$$

The present value of the maturity value discounted at 5.3% is:

$$\frac{\$1,000}{(1.053)^{14}} = \$485.29$$

The projected sale price is $437.02 plus $485.29, or $922.31.

Applications of the Total Return (Horizon Analysis)

The total return measure allows a portfolio manager to project the performance of a bond on the basis of the planned investment horizon and expectations concerning reinvestment rates and future market yields. This permits the portfolio manager to evaluate which of several potential bonds considered for acquisition will perform the best over the planned investment horizon. As we have emphasized, this cannot be done using the yield to maturity as a measure of relative value.

Using total return to assess performance over some investment horizon is called *horizon analysis*. When a total return is calculated over an investment horizon, it is referred to as a *horizon return*. In this book we use the terms horizon return and total return interchangeably.

Horizon analysis is also used to evaluate bond swaps. In a bond swap the portfolio manager considers exchanging a bond held in the portfolio for another bond. When the objective of the bond swap is to enhance the return of the portfolio over the planned investment horizon, the total return for the bond being considered for purchase can be computed and compared with the total return for the bond held in the portfolio to determine if the bond being held should be replaced. We shall discuss several bond swap strategies in Chapter 20.

An often-cited objection to the total return measure is that it requires the portfolio manager to formulate assumptions about reinvestment rates and future yields, as well as to think in terms of an investment horizon. Unfortunately, some portfolio managers find comfort in measures such as the yield to maturity and yield to call simply because they do not require incorporating any particular expectations. The horizon analysis framework, however, enables the portfolio manager to analyze the performance of a bond under different interest rate scenarios for reinvestment rates and future market yields. Only by investigating multiple scenarios can the portfolio manager see how sensitive the bond's performance will be to each scenario. Chapter 12 explains a framework for incorporating the market's expectation of future interest rates.

SUMMARY

In this chapter we have explained the conventional yield measures commonly used by bond market participants: current yield, yield to maturity, and yield to call. We then reviewed the three potential sources of dollar return from investing in a bond—coupon interest, interest-on-interest, and capital gain (or loss)—and showed that none of the three conventional yield measures deals satisfactorily with all of these sources.

The current yield measure fails to consider both interest-on-interest and capital gain (or loss). The yield to maturity considers all three sources, but is deficient in assuming that all coupon interest can be reinvested at the yield to maturity. The risk that the coupon payments will be reinvested at a rate less than the yield to maturity is called reinvestment risk. The yield to call has the same shortcoming; it assumes that the coupon interest can be reinvested at the yield to call. We then presented a yield measure, the total return, that is more meaningful than either yield to maturity or yield to call for assessing the relative attractiveness of a bond given the investor's or the portfolio manager's expectations and planned investment horizon.

QUESTIONS FOR CHAPTER 3

1. A debt instrument offers the following payments:

Years from now	Cash flow to investor
1	$2,000
2	2,000
3	2,500
4	4,000

   Suppose that the price of this debt instrument is $7,704. What is the yield or internal rate of return offered by this debt instrument?

2. What is the effective annual yield if the semiannual periodic interest rate is 4.3%?

3. a. What is meant by the "yield to maturity" of a bond?

   b. What is meant by the yield to maturity calculated on a bond-equivalent basis?

4. a. Show the cash flows for the four bonds below, each of which has a par value of $1,000 and pays interest semiannually:

Bond	Coupon Rate	No. of Years to Maturity	Price
W	7%	5	$884.20
X	8	7	948.90
Y	9	4	967.70
Z	0	10	456.39

   b. Calculate the yield to maturity for the four bonds.

5. A portfolio manager is considering buying two bonds. Bond A matures in three years and has a coupon rate of 10% payable semiannually. Bond B, of the same credit quality, matures in ten years and has a coupon rate of 12% payable semiannually. Both bonds are priced at par.

   a. Suppose the portfolio manager plans to hold the bond that is purchased for three years. Which would be the best bond for the portfolio manager to purchase?

   b. Suppose the portfolio manager plans to hold the bond that is purchased for six years instead of three years. In this case, which would be the best bond for the portfolio manager to purchase?

   c. Suppose that the portfolio manager is managing the assets of a life insurance company that has issued a five-year guaranteed investment contract (GIC). The interest rate that the life insurance company has agreed to pay is 9% on a semiannual basis. Which of the two bonds should the portfolio manager purchase to assure that the GIC payments will be satisfied, and that a profit will be generated for the life insurance company?

6. Demonstrate that the yield to call for an 11% coupon bond, callable in six years at a call price of $1,055, and selling for $1,233.64 is 7.1%.

7. Explain how to calculate the yield on a portfolio.

8. An investor is considering the purchase of a 20-year, 7% coupon bond selling for $816 and a par value of $1,000. The yield to maturity for this bond is 9%.

   a. What would be the total future dollars if this investor invested $816 for 20 years earning 9% compounded semiannually?

   b. What are the total coupon payments over the life of this bond?

   c. What would be the total future dollars from the coupon payments and the repayment of principal at the end of 20 years?

   d. In order for the bond to produce the same total future dollars as in 8(a), how much must the interest-on-interest be?

   e. Calculate the interest-on-interest from the bond assuming that the semiannual coupon payments can be reinvested at 4.5% every six months, and demonstrate that the resulting amount is the same as in 8(d).

9. What is the total return for a 20-year zero-coupon bond selling to offer a yield to maturity of 8%?

10. a. Explain why the total return from holding a bond to maturity will fall between the yield to maturity and reinvestment rates.

   b. For a long-term, high-coupon bond, do you think that the total return from holding a bond to maturity will be closer to the yield to maturity or to the reinvestment rate?

11. Suppose that an investor with a five-year investment horizon is considering purchasing a seven-year, 9% coupon bond selling at par. The investor expects that the coupon payments can be reinvested at an annual interest rate of 9.4% and that at the end of the investment horizon two-year bonds will be selling to offer a yield to maturity of 11.2%. What is the total return for this bond?

Chapter 4

BOND PRICE VOLATILITY

To employ effective bond portfolio strategies, it is necessary to understand the price volatility of bonds resulting from changes in interest rates. The purpose of this chapter is to explain the price volatility characteristics of a bond and to present several measures to quantify price volatility.

A REVIEW OF THE PRICE/YIELD RELATIONSHIP FOR OPTION-FREE BONDS

As we explain in Chapter 2, a fundamental principle of an option-free bond (that is, a bond that does not have an embedded option) is that the price of the bond changes in the opposite direction from a change in the required yield for the bond. This principle follows from the fact that the price of a bond is equal to the present value of its expected cash flows. An increase (decrease) in the required yield decreases (increases) the present value of its expected cash flows, and therefore decreases (increases) the bond's price. Exhibit 4-1 illustrates this property for the following six hypothetical bonds, where the bond prices are shown assuming a par value of $100 and pay interest semiannually:

1. A 9% coupon bond with 5 years to maturity
2. A 9% coupon bond with 25 years to maturity
3. A 6% coupon bond with 5 years to maturity
4. A 6% coupon bond with 25 years to maturity
5. A zero-coupon bond with 5 years to maturity
6. A zero-coupon bond with 25 years to maturity

When the price/yield relationship for any option-free bond is graphed, it exhibits the shape shown in Exhibit 4-2. Notice that as the required yield rises, the price of the option-free bond declines. This relationship is not linear however (that is, it is not a straight line). The shape of the price/yield relationship for any option-free bond is referred to as *convex*.

The price/yield relationship that we have discussed refers to an instantaneous change in the required yield. As we explain in Chapter 2, the price of a bond will change over time as a result of (1) a change in the perceived credit risk of the issuer, (2) move toward par as a discount or premium bond approaches the maturity date, and (3) a change in market interest rates.

EXHIBIT 4-1   Price/Yield Relationship for Six Hypothetical Bonds

——————————— Price at Required Yield ———————————

Required Yield	9%/5	9%/25	6%/5	6%/25	0%/5	0%/25
6.00%	112.7953	138.5946	100.0000	100.0000	74.4094	22.8107
7.00	108.3166	123.4556	95.8417	88.2722	70.8919	17.9053
8.00	104.0554	110.7410	91.8891	78.5178	67.5564	14.0713
8.50	102.0027	105.1482	89.9864	74.2587	65.9537	12.4795
8.90	100.3966	100.9961	88.4983	71.1105	64.7017	11.3391
8.99	100.0395	100.0988	88.1676	70.4318	64.4236	11.0975
9.00	100.0000	100.0000	88.1309	70.3570	64.3928	11.0710
9.01	99.9604	99.9013	88.0943	70.2824	64.3620	11.0445
9.10	99.6053	99.0199	87.7654	69.6164	64.0855	10.8093
9.50	98.0459	95.2539	86.3214	66.7773	62.8723	9.8242
10.00	96.1391	90.8720	84.5565	63.4881	61.3913	8.7204
11.00	92.4624	83.0685	81.1559	57.6712	58.5431	6.8767
12.00	88.9599	76.3572	77.9197	52.7144	55.8395	5.4288

**EXHIBIT 4-2
Shape of Price/Yield
Relationship for an
Option-Free Bond**

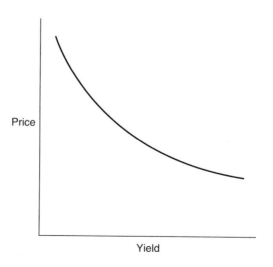

THE PRICE VOLATILITY CHARACTERISTICS OF OPTION-FREE BONDS

Exhibit 4-3 shows for the six hypothetical bonds in Exhibit 4-1 the percentage change in the bond's price for various changes in the required yield, assuming that the initial yield for all six bonds is 9%. An examination of Exhibit 4-3 reveals several properties concerning the price volatility of an option-free bond.

Property 1: Although the prices of all option-free bonds move in the opposite direction from the change in required yield, the percentage price change is not the same for all bonds.

Property 2: For very small changes in the required yield, the percentage price change for a given bond is roughly the same, whether the required yield increases or decreases.

EXHIBIT 4-3   Instantaneous Percentage Price Change for Six Hypothetical Bonds

Six Hypothetical bonds, priced initially to yield 9%:

9% coupon, 5 years to maturity, price	=	100.0000
9% coupon, 25 years to maturity, price	=	100.0000
6% coupon, 5 years to maturity, price	=	88.1309
6% coupon, 25 years to maturity, price	=	70.3570
0% coupon, 5 years to maturity, price	=	64.3928
0% coupon, 25 years to maturity, price	=	11.0710

Yield Changes to	Change in Basis Points	9%/5	9%/25	6%/5	6%/25	0%/5	0%/25
6.00%	−300	12.80%	38.59%	13.47%	42.13%	15.56%	106.04%
7.00	−200	8.32	23.46	8.75	25.46	10.09	61.73
8.00	−100	4.06	10.74	4.26	11.60	4.91	27.10
8.50	−50	2.00	5.15	2.11	5.55	2.42	12.72
8.90	−10	0.40	1.00	0.42	1.07	0.48	2.42
8.99	−1	0.04	0.10	0.04	0.11	0.05	0.24
9.01	1	−0.04	−0.10	−0.04	−0.11	−0.05	−0.24
9.10	10	−0.39	−0.98	−0.41	−1.05	−0.48	−2.36
9.50	50	−1.95	−4.75	−2.05	−5.09	−2.36	−11.26
10.00	100	−3.86	−9.13	−4.06	−9.76	−4.66	−21.23
11.00	200	−7.54	−16.93	−7.91	−18.03	−9.08	−37.89
12.00	300	−11.04	−23.64	−11.59	−25.08	−13.28	−50.96

Property 3: For large changes in the required yield, the percentage price change is not the same for an increase in the required yield as it is for a decrease in the required yield.

Property 4: For a given change in basis points, the percentage price increase is greater than the percentage price decrease. The implication of this property is that if an investor owns a bond (that is, is "long" a bond), the price appreciation that will be realized if the required yield decreases is greater than the capital loss that will be realized if the required yield rises by the same number of basis points. For an investor who is "short" a bond, the reverse is true: the potential capital loss is greater than the potential capital gain if the required yield changes by a given number of basis points.

An explanation for these four properties of bond price volatility lies in the convex shape of the price/yield relationship. We will investigate this in more detail later in the chapter.

Characteristics of a Bond that Affect its Price Volatility

There are two characteristics of an option-free bond that determine its price volatility: coupon and term to maturity.

Characteristic 1: For a given term to maturity and initial yield, the price volatility of a bond is greater, the lower coupon rate. This characteristic can be seen by comparing the 9%, 6%, and zero-coupon bonds with the same maturity.

Characteristic 2: For a given coupon rate and initial yield, the longer the term to maturity, the greater the price volatility. This can be seen in Exhibit 4-3 by comparing the 5-year bonds to the 25-year bonds with the same coupon.

An implication of this characteristic is that investors who want to increase a portfolio's price volatility because they expect interest rates to fall, all other factors being constant, should hold bonds with long maturities in the portfolio. To reduce a portfolio's price volatility in anticipation of a rise in interest rates, bonds with shorter-term maturities should be held in the portfolio.

The Effects of Yield to Maturity

We cannot ignore the fact that credit considerations cause different bonds to trade at different yields, even if they have the same coupon and maturity. How, then, holding other factors constant, does the yield to maturity affect a bond's price volatility? As it turns out, the higher the yield to maturity that a bond trades at, the lower the price volatility.

To see this, compare the 9%, 25-year bond trading at various yield levels in Exhibit 4-4. The first column shows the yield level the bond is trading at, and the second column gives the initial price. The third column indicates the bond's price if yields change by 100 basis points. The fourth and fifth columns show the dollar price change and the percentage price change. Note in these last two columns that the higher the initial yield, the lower the price volatility.

An implication of this is that, for a given change in yields, price volatility is greater when yield levels in the market are low, and price volatility is lower when yield levels are high.

EXHIBIT 4-4   Price Change for a 100-Basis Point Change in Yield for a 9%, 25-Year Bond Trading at Different Yield Levels

Yield Level	Initial Price	New Price (∗)	Price Decline	Percent Decline
7%	123.46	110.74	12.72	10.30%
8%	110.74	100.00	10.74	9.70%
9%	100.00	90.87	9.13	9.13%
10%	90.87	83.07	7.80	8.58%
11%	83.07	76.36	6.71	8.08%
12%	76.36	70.55	5.81	7.61%
13%	70.55	65.50	5.05	7.16%
14%	65.50	61.08	4.42	6.75%

*as a result of a 100 basis point increase in yield.

MEASURES OF BOND PRICE VOLATILITY

Money managers, arbitrageurs, and traders need to have a way to measure a bond's price volatility to implement hedging and trading strategies. Three measures that are commonly employed are (1) price value of a basis point, (2) yield value of a price change, and (3) duration.

Price Value of a Basis Point

The *price value of a basis point,* also referred to as the *dollar value of a basis point,* is the change in the price of the bond if the required yield changes by one basis point. Note that this measure of price volatility indicates *dollar price volatility* as opposed to percentage price volatility (price change as a percent of the initial price). Typically, the price value of a basis point is expressed as the absolute value of the change in price.

Owing to property 2 of the price/yield relationship, price volatility is the same for an increase or a decrease of one basis point in required yield.

We can illustrate how to calculate the price value of a basis point by using the six bonds in Exhibit 4-1. For each bond, the initial price, the price after increasing the required yield by one basis point (from 9% to 9.01%), and the price value of a basis point (the difference between the two prices) are as follows:

Bond	Initial Price (9% yield)	Price at 9.01%	Price Value of a Basis Point*
5-year, 9% coupon	100.0000	99.9604	.0396
25-year, 9% coupon	100.0000	99.9013	.0987
5-year, 6% coupon	88.1309	88.0945	.0364
25-year, 6% coupon	70.3570	70.2824	.0746
5-year, zero-coupon	64.3928	64.3620	.0308
25-year, zero-coupon	11.0710	11.0445	.0265

*Absolute value per $100 of par value

Because this measure of price volatility is in terms of dollar price change, dividing the price value of a basis point by the initial price gives the percentage price change for a one-basis-point change in yield.

Yield Value of a Price Change

Another measure of the price volatility of a bond used by investors is the change in the yield for a specified price change. This is estimated by first calculating the bond's yield to maturity if the bond's price is decreased by, say, X dollars. Then the difference between the initial yield and the new yield is the yield value of an X dollar price change. The smaller this value, the greater the dollar price volatility, because it would take a smaller change in yield to produce a price change of X dollars.

As we explain in Chapter 5, Treasury notes and bonds are quoted in 32nds of a percentage point of par. Consequently, in the Treasury market investors compute the yield value of 1/32. The yield value of 1/32 for our two hypothetical 9% coupon bonds is computed as follows, assuming that the price is decreased by 1/32.

Bond	Initial Price Minus 32nd*	Yield at New Price	Initial Yield	Yield Value of a 32nd
5-year, 9% coupon	99.96875	9.008	9.000	.008
25-year, 9% coupon	99.96875	9.003	9.000	.003

*Initial price of 100 minus 1/32 of 1%

Corporate bonds and municipal bonds, the subject of Chapters 6 and 7, are traded in 8ths of a point. Consequently, investors in these markets compute the yield value of an 8th. The calculation of the yield value of 1/8 for our two hypothetical 9% coupon bonds is as follows, assuming that price is decreased by 1/8:

Bond	Initial Price Minus 8th*	Yield at New Price	Initial Yield	Yield Value of an 8th
5-year, 9% coupon	99.8750	9.032	9.000	.032
25-year, 9% coupon	99.8750	9.013	9.000	.013

*Initial Price of 100 minus 1/8 of 1%

Duration

In Chapter 2 we explained that the price of an option-free bond can be expressed mathematically as follows:[1]

$$(4.1) \quad P = \frac{C}{(1+y)^1} + \frac{C}{(1+y)^2} + ... + \frac{C}{(1+y)^n} + \frac{M}{(1+y)^n}$$

where P = price of the bond
C = semiannual coupon interest (in $)
y = one-half the yield to maturity or required yield
n = number of semiannual periods (number of years x 2)
M = maturity value (in $)

To determine the approximate change in price for a small change in yield, the first derivative of equation (4.1) with respect to the required yield can be computed:

$$(4.2) \quad \frac{dP}{dy} = \frac{(-1)C}{(1+y)^2} + \frac{(-2)C}{(1+y)^3} + ... + \frac{(-n)C}{(1+y)^{n+1}} + \frac{(-n)M}{(1+y)^{n+1}}$$

Rearranging equation (4.2) we obtain:

$$(4.3) \quad \frac{dP}{dy} = - \frac{1}{(1+y)} \left[\frac{1\,C}{(1+y)^1} + \frac{2\,C}{(1+y)^2} + ... + \frac{n\,C}{(1+y)^n} + \frac{n\,M}{(1+y)^n} \right]$$

---

[1] Equation (4.1) assumes that the next coupon payment is exactly six months from now and that there is no accrued interest. As we explain at the end of Chapter 2, it is not difficult to extend the model to account for the first coupon payment occurring less than six months from the valuation date and to adjust the price to include accrued interest.

The term in brackets is the weighted average term to maturity of the cash flows from the bond, where the weights are the present value of the cash flow.

Equation (4.3) indicates the approximate dollar price change for a small change in the required yield. Dividing both sides of equation (4.3) by P gives the approximate percentage price change:

$$(4.4) \quad \frac{dP}{dy}\frac{1}{P} = -\frac{1}{(1+y)}\left[\frac{1\,C}{(1+y)^1} + \frac{2\,C}{(1+y)^2} + ... + \frac{n\,C}{(1+y)^n} + \frac{n\,M}{(1+y)^n}\right]\frac{1}{P}$$

The expression in the brackets divided by the price (or here multiplied by the reciprocal of the price) is commonly referred to as *Macaulay duration*.[2] That is:

$$\text{Macaulay duration} = \frac{\dfrac{1\,C}{(1+y)^1} + \dfrac{2\,C}{(1+y)^2} + ... + \dfrac{n\,C}{(1+y)^n} + \dfrac{n\,M}{(1+y)^n}}{P}$$

which can be rewritten as:

$$(4.5) \quad \text{Macaulay duration} = \frac{\displaystyle\sum_{t=1}^{n}\frac{t\,C}{(1+y)^t} + \frac{n\,M}{(1+y)^n}}{P}$$

Substituting Macaulay duration into equation (4.4) for the approximate percentage price change gives:

$$(4.6) \quad \frac{dP}{dy}\frac{1}{P} = -\frac{1}{(1+y)}\ \text{Macaulay duration}$$

Investors commonly refer to the ratio of Macaulay duration to $(1 + y)$ as modified duration; that is:

---

[2] In a 1938 National Bureau of Economic Research study on bond yields, Frederick Macaulay coined this term and used this measure rather than maturity as a proxy for the average length of time that a bond investment is outstanding. (See Frederick Macaulay, *Some Theoretical Problems Suggested by the Movement of Interest Rates, Bond Yields, and Stock Prices in the U.S. Since 1856* [New York: National Bureau of Economic Research, 1938].) In examining the interest rate sensitivity of financial institutions, Redington and Samuelson independently developed the duration concept. (See F. M. Redington, "Review of the Principle of Life Office Valuation," *Journal of the Institute of Actuaries*, 1952, pp. 286-340; and Paul A. Samuelson, "The Effect of Interest Rate Increases on the Banking System," *American Economic Review*, March 1945, pp. 16-27.)

(4.7) Modified duration $= \dfrac{\text{Macaulay duration}}{(1+y)}$

Substituting equation (4.7) into equation (4.6) gives:

(4.8) $\dfrac{dP}{dy}\dfrac{1}{P} = -\text{Modified duration}$

Equation (4.8) states that modified duration is related to the approximate percentage change in price for a given change in yield. Because for all option-free bonds modified duration is positive, equation (4.8) states that there is an inverse relationship between modified duration and the approximate percentage change in price for a given yield change. This is to be expected from the fundamental principle that bond prices move in the opposite direction of interest rates.

Exhibits 4-5 and 4-6 show the computation of the Macaulay duration and modified duration of two five-year coupon bonds. The durations computed in these exhibits are in terms of duration per period. Consequently, the durations are in half-years because the cash flows of the bonds occur every six months. To adjust the durations to an annual figure, the durations must be divided by 2, as shown at the bottom of Exhibits 4-5 and 4-6. In general, if the cash flows occur m times per year, the durations are adjusted by dividing by m. That is:

Duration in years $= \dfrac{\text{Duration in } m \text{ periods per year}}{m}$

Macaulay duration and modified duration in years for the six hypothetical bonds are as follows:

Bond	Macaulay Duration (in years)	Modified Duration (in years)
9%/5-year	4.13	3.96
9%/25-year	10.33	9.88
6%/5-year	4.35	4.16
6%/25-year	11.10	10.62
0%/5-year	5.00	4.78
0%/25-year	25.00	23.92

EXHIBIT 4-5   Calculation of Macaulay Duration and Modified Duration for 9%, 5-Year Bond Selling to Yield 9%

Coupon rate   =   9.00%
Term (years)   =   5
Initial yield   =   9.00%

Period (t)	Cash Flow*	PV of $1 at 0.045	PV of CF	t x PVCF
1	$ 4.50	.956937	4.306220	4.30622
2	4.50	.915729	4.120785	8.24156
3	4.50	.876296	3.943335	11.83000
4	4.50	.838561	3.773526	15.09410
5	4.50	.802451	3.611030	18.05514
6	4.50	.767895	3.455531	20.73318
7	4.50	.734828	3.306728	23.14709
8	4.50	.703185	3.164333	25.31466
9	4.50	.672904	3.028070	27.25262
10	104.50	.643927	67.290443	672.90442
Total			100.000000	826.87899

*Cash flow per $100 of par value

$$\text{Macaulay duration (in half years)} = \frac{826.87899}{100.000000} = 8.27$$

$$\text{Macaulay duration (in years)} = \frac{8.27}{2} = 4.13$$

$$\text{Modified duration (in years)} = \frac{4.13}{1.0450} = 3.96$$

Rather than use equation (4.5) to calculate Macaulay duration and then equation (4.7) to obtain modified duration, we can derive an alternative formula that does not require the extensive calculations required by equation (4.5). This is done by rewriting the price of a bond in terms of its two components: (1) the present value of an annuity, where the annuity is the sum of the coupon payments, and (2) the present value of the par value. That is, the price of a bond per $100 of par value can be written as follows:[3]

---

[3] The first term in equation (4.9) is the present value of the coupon payments from equation (2.7) in Chapter 2 discounting at y.

EXHIBIT 4-6   Calculation of Macaulay Duration and Modified Duration for 6%, 5-Year Bond Selling to Yield 9%

Coupon rate   =   6.00%
Term (years)   =   5
Initial yield   =   9.00%

Period (t)	Cash Flow*	PV of $1 at 0.045	PV of CF	t x PVCF
1	$ 3.00	.956937	2.870813	2.87081
2	3.00	.915729	2.747190	5.49437
3	3.00	.876296	2.628890	7.88666
4	3.00	.838561	2.515684	10.06273
5	3.00	.802451	2.407353	12.03676
6	3.00	.767895	2.303687	13.82212
7	3.00	.734828	2.204485	15.43139
8	3.00	.703185	2.109555	16.87644
9	3.00	.672904	2.018713	18.16841
10	103.00	.643927	66.324551	663.24551
Total			88.130923	765.89520

*Cash flow per $100 of par value

Macaulay duration (in half years) $= \dfrac{765.89520}{88.130923} = 8.69$

Macaulay duration (in years) $= \dfrac{8.69}{2} = 4.35$

Modified duration (in years) $= \dfrac{4.35}{1.0450} = 4.16$

$$(4.9) \quad P = C\left[\dfrac{1 - \dfrac{1}{(1+y)^n}}{y}\right] + \dfrac{100}{(1+y)^n}$$

By taking the first derivative of equation (4.9) and dividing by P, we obtain another formula for modified duration:

$$(4.10) \quad \text{Modified duration} = \dfrac{\dfrac{C}{y^2}\left[1 - \dfrac{1}{(1+y)^n}\right] + \dfrac{n(100 - c/y)}{(1+y)^{n+1}}}{P}$$

where the price is expressed as a percentage of par value.

Macaulay duration can be expressed by multiplying equation (4.10) by $(1 + y)$.

To illustrate how to apply equation (4.10), consider the 25-year, 6% bond selling at 70.357 to yield 9%. Then:

$C = 3$ (.06 x 100 $\times$ 1/2)
$y = .045$ (.09 $\times$ 1/2)
$n = 50$
$P = 70.357$

Substituting into equation (4.10):

$$\text{Modified duration} = \frac{\dfrac{3}{(.045)^2}\left[1 - \dfrac{1}{(1.045)^{50}}\right] + \dfrac{50\,(100 - 3/0.045)}{(1.045)^{51}}}{70.357}$$

$$= \frac{1,481.481(0.88929) + 176.5704}{70.357}$$

$$= 21.23508$$

Converting to an annual number by dividing by 2 gives a modified duration of 10.62. Multiplying by 1.045 gives 11.10, which is Macaulay duration.

Properties of Duration: As can be seen from the various durations computed for the six hypothetical bonds, the modified duration and Macaulay duration of a coupon bond are less than the maturity. It should be obvious from the formula that the Macaulay duration of a zero-coupon bond is equal to its maturity; a zero-coupon bond's modified duration, however, is less than its maturity. Also, the lower the coupon, generally the greater the modified and Macaulay duration of the bond.[4]

There is a consistency between the properties of bond price volatility we discussed earlier and the properties of modified duration. We showed earlier that when all other factors are constant, the longer the maturity, the greater the price volatility. A property of modified duration is that when all other factors are constant, the longer the maturity, the greater the modified duration. We also showed that the lower the coupon rate, all other factors being constant, the greater the bond price volatility.

---

[4] This property does not hold for long-maturity deep-discount bonds.

As we have just seen, generally the lower the coupon rate, the greater the modified duration. Thus, the greater the modified duration, the greater the price volatility.

Finally, as we noted earlier, another factor that will influence the price volatility is the yield to maturity. All other factors constant, the higher the yield level, the lower the price volatility. The same property holds for modified duration, as can be seen below which shows the modified duration of a 25-year, 9% coupon bond at various yield levels:

Yield	Modified duration
7%	11.21
8%	10.53
9%	9.88
10%	9.27
11%	8.70
12%	8.16
13%	7.66
14%	7.21

Approximating the Percentage Price Change: If we multiply both sides of equation (4.8) by the change in the required yield (dy), we have the following relationship:

$$(4.11) \quad \frac{dP}{P} = - \text{Modified duration} \times dy$$

Equation (4-11) can be used to approximate the percentage price change for a given change in required yield.

To illustrate the relationship, consider the 6%, 25-year bond selling at 70.3570 to yield 9%. The modified duration for this bond is 10.62. If yields increase instantaneously from 9% to 9.10%, a yield change of +0.0010 (10 basis points), the *approximate* percentage change in price using equation (4-11) is:

$$-10.62 (+.0010) = -.0106 \text{ or } 1.06\%$$

Notice from Exhibit 4-3 that the actual percentage change in price is −1.05%. Similarly, if yields decrease instantaneously from 9% to 8.90% (a 10-basis point decrease), the approximate percentage change in price using equation (4.11) would be +1.06%. According to Exhibit 4-3, the actual percentage price change would be +1.07%. This example illustrates that, for small changes in the required yield, modified duration gives a good approximation of the percentage change in price.

Instead of a small change in required yield, let's assume that yields increase by 200 basis points, from 9% to 11% (a yield change of +0.02). The approximate percentage change in price using equation (4-11) is:

$$-10.62\,(+.02) = -.2124 = -21.24\%$$

How good is this approximation? As can be seen from Exhibit 4-3, the actual percentage change in price is only −18.03%. Moreover, if the required yield decreased by 200 basis points, from 9% to 7%, the approximate percentage change in price based on duration would be +21.24, compared to an actual percentage change in price of +25.46%. Modified duration provides not only a flawed approximation but also a symmetric percentage price change, which, as we point out earlier in this chapter, is not a property of the price/yield relationship for bonds when there are large changes in yield.

We can use equation (4.11) to provide an interpretation of modified duration. Suppose that the yield on any bond changes by 100 basis points. Then, substituting 100 basis points (.01) into equation (4.11), the following is obtained:

$$\frac{dP}{P} = -\text{ Modified duration }(.01) = -\text{ Modified duration}\,\%$$

Thus, modified duration can be interpreted as the approximate percentage change in price for a 100-basis point change in yield.

Approximating the Dollar Price Change: Modified duration is a proxy for the percentage change in price. Investors also like to know the dollar price volatility of a bond. Of course, equation (4-2) can be used to compute the dollar price volatility. Alternatively, multiplying both sides of equation (4-8) by P gives:

$$(4.12) \quad \frac{dP}{dy} = (-\text{ Modified duration})\,P$$

The expression on the right-hand side is called *dollar duration*. That is:

$$(4.13) \quad \text{Dollar duration} = -(\text{ Modified duration })\,P$$

Once we know the percentage price change, and the initial price, the estimated dollar price change using modified duration can be determined. Alternatively, the estimated dollar price change can be obtained by multiplying both sides of equation (4.11) by P, giving

$$dP = -(\text{Modified duration })\,P(dy)$$

From equation (4.13) we can substitute dollar duration for the product of modified duration and P. Thus:

(4.14) $dP = -(\text{Dollar duration})(dy)$

For small changes in the required yield, equation (4-14) does a good job in estimating the change in price. For example, consider the 6%, 25-year bond selling at 70.3570 to yield 9%. The dollar duration is 747.2009. For a 1-basis point (.0001) increase in the required yield, the estimated price change per \$100 of face value is:

$dP = -(\$747.2009)(.0001)$

$= -\$.0747$

From Exhibit 4-1, we see that the actual price is 70.2824. The actual price change would therefore be .0746 (70.2824 − 70.3570). Notice that the dollar duration for a one-basis point change is the same as the price value of a basis point.

Now let's see what happens when there is a large change in the required yield for the same bond. If the required yield increases from 9% to 11% (or 200 basis points), the approximate dollar price change per \$100 par value is:

$dP = -(\$747.2009)(.02)$

$= -\$14.94$

From Exhibit 4-1, we see that the actual price for this bond if the required yield is 11% is 57.6712. Thus the actual price decline is 12.6858 (57.6712 − 70.3570). The estimated dollar price change is more than the actual price change. The reverse is true for a decrease in the required yield. This result is consistent with what we illustrated earlier. When there are large movements in the required yield, dollar duration or modified duration are not adequate to approximate the price reaction. Duration will overestimate the price change when the required yield rises, thereby underestimating the new price. When the required yield falls, duration will underestimate the price change and thereby underestimate the new price.

CONVEXITY

The three measures for price volatility that we describe in the previous section are good measures for small changes in yield or price. We have explained how these measures are related. Exhibit 4-7 does this more formally.

EXHIBIT 4-7   Measures of Bond Price Volatility and Their Relationships to One Another

Notation:

D	=	Macaulay duration
D^*	=	modified duration
$PVBP$	=	price value of a basis point
$YV32$	=	yield value of a 32nd
y	=	yield to maturity in decimal form
Y	=	yield to maturity in percentage terms ($Y = 100 \times y$)
P	=	price of bond
m	=	number of coupons per year

Relationships:

$$D^* = \frac{D}{(1 + y / m)} \qquad \text{by definition}$$

$$\frac{\Delta P / P}{\Delta y} \approx D^* \qquad \text{to a close approximation for a small } \Delta y$$

$\Delta P / \Delta Y \approx$ slope of price / yield curve — to a close approximation for a small ΔY

$$PVBP \approx \frac{D^* \times P}{10000} \qquad \text{to a close approximation}$$

$$YV32 \approx \frac{1}{3200 \times PVBP} \qquad \text{to a close approximation (when the yield is in percentage terms)}$$

$$PVBP \approx \frac{1}{3200 \times YV32} \qquad \text{to a close approximation (when the yield is in percentage terms)}$$

For bonds at or near par:

$PVBP \approx D^* / 100$ — to a close approximation

$D^* \approx \Delta P / \Delta Y$ — to a close approximation for small ΔY

Because all the duration measures are only approximations for small changes in yield, they do not capture the effect of the convexity of a bond on its price performance when yields change by more than a small

EXHIBIT 4-8 Line Tangent to the Price/Yield Relationship

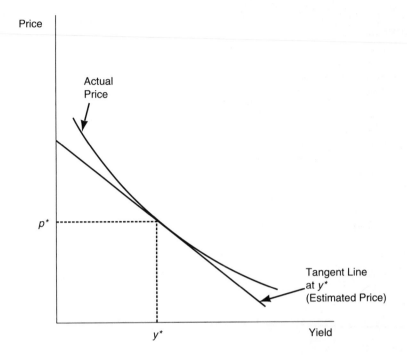

amount. The duration measure can be supplemented with an additional measure to capture the curvature or convexity of a bond. In this section, we tie together the convex price/yield relationship for a bond and several of the properties of bond price volatility discussed earlier.

In Exhibit 4-8, a tangent line is drawn to the price/yield relationship at yield y^*. The tangent shows the rate of change of price with respect to a change in interest rates at that point (yield level). The slope of the tangent line is closely related to the price value of a basis point. Consequently, for a given starting price, the tangent (which tells the rate of absolute price changes) is closely related to the duration of the bond (which tells about the rate of percentage of price changes). The steeper the tangent line, the greater the duration; the flatter the tangent line, the lower the duration. Thus, for a given starting price, the tangent line and the duration can be used interchangeably and can be thought of as one and the same method of estimating the rate of price changes.

Notice what happens to duration (steepness of the tangent line) as yield changes: as yield increases (decreases), duration decreases (increases). This property holds for all option-free bonds as we noted earlier.

EXHIBIT 4-9   Price Approximation Using Duration

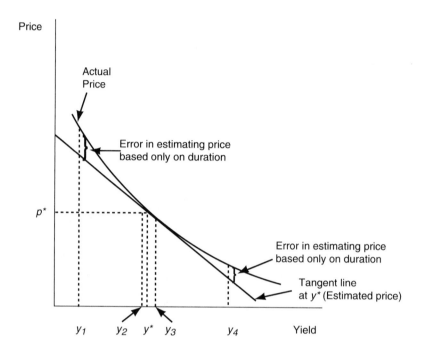

If we draw a vertical line from any yield (on the horizontal axis), as in Exhibit 4-9, the distance between the horizontal axis and the tangent line represents the price approximated by using duration starting with the initial yield y^*. The approximation will always understate the actual price. This agrees with what we demonstrated earlier about the relationship between duration (and the tangent line) and the approximate price change. When yields decrease, the estimated price change will be less than the actual price change, thereby underestimating the actual price. On the other hand, when yields increase, the estimated price change will be greater than the actual price change, resulting in an underestimate of the actual price.

For small changes in yield, the tangent line and duration do a good job in estimating the actual price. However, the farther away from the initial yield y^*, the worse the approximation. It should be apparent that the accuracy of the approximation depends on the convexity of the price/yield relationship for the bond.

Measuring Convexity

Duration (modified or dollar), attempts to estimate a convex relationship with a straight line (the tangent line). Is it possible to specify a mathematical relationship that provides a better approximation to the price of the bond if the required yield changes?

We can use the first two terms of a Taylor series to approximate the price change as follows:[5]

$$(4.15) \quad dP = \frac{dP}{dy}dy + \frac{1}{2}\frac{d^2P}{dy^2}(dy)^2 + \text{Error}$$

Dividing both sides of equation (4.15) by P to get the percentage price change gives us:

$$(4.16) \quad \frac{dP}{P} = \frac{dP}{dy}\frac{1}{P}dy + \frac{1}{2}\frac{d^2P}{dy^2}\frac{1}{P}(dy)^2 + \frac{\text{Error}}{P}$$

The first term on the right-hand side of equation (4.15) is equation (4.11); that is, it is the dollar price change based on dollar duration. Thus the first term in equation (4.15) is our approximation of the price change based on duration. In equation (4.16), the first term on the right-hand side is the approximate percentage change in price based on modified duration.

The second term in equations (4.15) and (4.16) includes the second derivative of the price function (equation (4.1)). It is the second derivative that is used as a proxy measure for the convexity of the price/yield relationship. Market participants refer to the second derivative of price (equation (4.1)) as the *dollar convexity* of the bond. That is:

$$(4.17) \quad \text{Dollar convexity} = \frac{d^2P}{dy^2}$$

The product of the dollar convexity and the square of the change in the required yield indicates the estimated price change due to convexity. That is, the approximate change in price due to convexity is:

$$(4.18) \quad dP = (\text{Dollar convexity})(dy)^2$$

The second derivative divided by price is a measure of the percentage change in the price of the bond due to convexity, and is referred to simply as *convexity*. That is:

$$(4.19) \quad \text{Convexity} = \frac{d^2P}{dy^2}\frac{1}{P}$$

---

[5] A Taylor series, discussed in calculus textbooks, can be used to approximate a mathematical function. Here, the mathematical function to be approximated is the price function.

and the percentage price change due to convexity is:

$$(4.20) \quad \frac{dP}{P} = \frac{1}{2}(\text{Convexity})(dy)^2$$

The second derivative of the price equation (4-1) is:

$$(4.21) \quad \frac{d^2P}{dy^2} = \sum_{t=1}^{n} \frac{t(t+1)C}{(1+y)^{t+2}} + \frac{n(n+1)M}{(1+y)^{n+2}}$$

Exhibits 4-10 and 4-11 demonstrate how to calculate the second derivative (equation (4.21)), annualized dollar convexity, and annualized convexity for the two five-year coupon bonds. The convexity measure is in terms of periods squared. To convert the convexity measures to an annual figure, equations (4.17) and (4.19) must be divided by 4 (which is 2 squared). In general, if the cash flows occur m times per year, convexity is adjusted to an annual figure as follows:

$$\text{Convexity in years} = \frac{\text{Convexity in } m \text{ periods per year}}{m^2}$$

Annualized convexity and annualized dollar convexity for our six hypothetical bonds can be summarized as follows:

Bond (per $100 par)	Second Derivative	Annualized Convexity (per $100 par)	Annualized Dollar Convexity
9%/5-year	7,781.02	19.45	1,945.26
9%/25-year	64,288.42	160.72	16,072.00
6%/5-year	7,349.45	20.85	1,837.36
6%/25-year	51,476.26	182.92	12,869.70
0%/5-year	6,486.30	25.18	1,621.42
0%/25-year	25,851.93	583.78	6,463.02

Alternatively, the second derivative can be determined by taking the second derivative of equation (4.9). By doing so, we can simplify equation (4.21) as follows:

$$(4.22) \quad \frac{d^2P}{dy^2} = \frac{2C}{y^3}\left[1 - \frac{1}{(1+y)^n}\right] - \frac{2Cn}{y^2(1+y)^{n+1}} + \frac{n(n+1)(100 - C/y)}{(1+y)^{n+2}}$$

To illustrate how to use equation (4.22), consider the 6%, 25-year bond selling at 70.357 to yield 9%. The second derivative is:

$$\frac{2(3)}{(0.045)^3}\left[1-\frac{1}{(1.045)^{50}}\right]-\frac{2(3)(50)}{(0.045)^2(1.045)^{51}}+\frac{50(51)(100-3/0.045)}{(1.045)^{52}}$$

$$= 65,843.62\ (.88929)-15,695.14+8,617.31$$

$$= 51,476.26$$

This agrees with the value reported earlier.

Approximating Percentage Price Change Using Duration and Convexity

Equation (4.16) tells us that the percentage price change of a bond can be estimated using both duration and convexity. To illustrate how this is done, consider the 6%, 25-year bond selling to yield 9%. The modified duration for this bond is 10.62, and the convexity is 182.92. If the required yield increases by 200 basis points, from 9% to 11%, the approximate percentage change in the price of the bond is:

Percentage change in price due to duration from equation (4.11)
$= -$ (Modified duration) (dy)
$= -$ (10.62) (.02) $= -.2124 = -21.24\%$

  plus

Percentage change in price due to convexity from equation (4.20)

$$= \frac{1}{2}\ (\text{Convexity})\ (dy)^2$$

$$= \frac{1}{2}\ (182.92)\ (.02)^2\ =\ .0366\ =\ 3.66\%$$

The estimated percentage price change due to duration and convexity is:

$$- 21.24\% + 3.66\% = -17.58\%$$

From Exhibit 4-3 we see that the actual change is -18.03%. Using duration and convexity measures together gives a better approximation of the actual price change for a large movement in the required yield. Suppose, instead, that the required yield *decreases* by 200 basis points.

EXHIBIT 4-10   **Calculation of Convexity and Dollar Convexity for 9%, 5-Year Bond Selling to Yield 9%**

Coupon rate   =   9.00%
Term (years)   =   5
Initial yield   =   9.00%
Price   =   100

Period (t)	Cash Flow*	$\dfrac{1}{(1.045)^{t+2}}$	$t(t+1)$ CF	$\dfrac{t(t+1)\,\text{CF}}{(1.045)^{t+2}}$
1	$ 4.50	.876296	9	7.886
2	4.50	.838561	27	22.641
3	4.50	.802451	54	43.332
4	4.50	.767895	90	69.110
5	4.50	.734828	135	99.201
6	4.50	.703185	189	132.901
7	4.50	.672904	252	169.571
8	4.50	.643927	324	208.632
9	4.50	.616198	405	249.560
10	104.50	.589663	11,495	6,778.186
Total			12,980	7,781.020

*Cash flow per $100 of par value.

Second derivative   = $7,781.02$

Convexity (half years)   = $\dfrac{7,781.020}{100.0000}$ = 77.8102

Convexity (years)   = $\dfrac{77.8102}{4}$ = 19.4526

Dollar Convexity   = 100×19.4526 = $1,945.26$

EXHIBIT 4-11   Calculation of Convexity and Dollar Convexity for 6%, 5-Year Bond Selling to Yield 9%

Coupon rate   =   6.00%
Term (years)   =   5
Initial yield   =   9.00%
Price   = 88.1309

Period (t)	Cash Flow*	$\dfrac{1}{(1.045)^{t+2}}$	t (t+1) CF	$\dfrac{t(t+1)\,CF}{(1.045)^{t+2}}$
1	$ 3.00	.876296	6	5.257
2	3.00	.838561	18	15.094
3	3.00	.802451	36	28.888
4	3.00	.767895	60	46.073
5	3.00	.734828	90	66.134
6	3.00	.703185	126	88.601
7	3.00	.672904	168	113.047
8	3.00	.643927	216	139.088
9	3.00	.616198	270	166.373
10	103.00	.589663	11,330	6,680.891
Total			12,320	7,349.446

*Cash flow per $100 of par value.

Second derivative   =   7,349.45

Convexity (half years)   = $\dfrac{7,349.45}{88.1309}$ =   83.3924

Convexity (years)   = $\dfrac{83.3924}{4}$ =   20.8481

Dollar convexity   =   88.1309 × 20.8481   =   1,837.36

Then the approximate percentage change in the price of the bond using modified duration and convexity is:

Percentage change in price due to duration from equation (4.11)

$$= -\text{(Modified duration)} \, (dy)$$

$$= -(10.62 \, (-.02) = +.2124 = +21.24\%$$

plus

Percentage change in price due to convexity from equation (4.20)

$$= \frac{1}{2} \, (\text{Convexity}) \, (dy)^2$$

$$= \frac{1}{2} \, (182.92) \, (-.02)^2 \; = \; .0366 \; = \; 3.66\%$$

The estimated percentage price change due to duration and convexity is:

+21.24% + 3.66% = 24.90%

From Exhibit 4-3 we see that the actual change is +25.46%. Once again, using both duration and convexity provides a good approximation of the actual price change for a large movement in the required yield.

The Value of Convexity

Up to this point, we have focused on how taking convexity into account can improve the approximation of a bond's price change for a given yield change. The convexity of a bond, however, has another important investment implication, which is illustrated in Exhibit 4-12. The exhibit shows two bonds, A and B. The two bonds have the same duration and are offering the same yield; they have different convexities, however. Bond B is more convex (bowed) than Bond A.

What is the implication of the greater convexity for B? Whether the market yield rises or falls, B will have a higher price. That is, if the required yield rises, the capital loss on Bond B will be less than it will be on Bond A. A fall in the required yield will generate greater price appreciation for B than for A.

Generally, the market will take the greater convexity of B compared to A into account in pricing the two bonds. That is, the market will price convexity. Consequently, while there may be times when a situation such as that depicted in Exhibit 4-12 will exist, generally the market will require investors to "pay up" (accept a lower yield) for the greater convexity offered by Bond B.

The question is: How much should the market want investors to pay up for convexity? Look again at Exhibit 4-12. Notice that if investors expect that market yields will change by very little—that is, they expect low interest rate volatility—the advantage of owning Bond B over Bond A

**EXHIBIT 4-12   Comparison of Convexity
                        of Two Bonds**

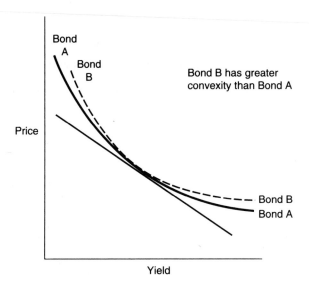

is insignificant because both bonds will offer approximately the same price for small changes in yields. In this case, investors should not be willing to pay much for convexity. In fact, if the market is pricing convexity high, which means that A will be offering a higher yield than B, investors with expectations of low interest rate volatility would probably be willing to "sell convexity"—that is, to sell B if they own it and buy A. In contrast, if investors expect substantial interest rate volatility, Bond B would probably sell at a much lower yield than A.

Properties of Convexity

All option-free bonds have the following convexity properties.

Property 1: As the required yield increases (decreases), the convexity of a bond decreases (increases). This property is referred to as *positive convexity*. An implication of positive convexity is that the duration of an option-free bond moves in the right direction as market yields change. That is, if market yields rise, the price of a bond will fall. The price decline is slowed down by a decline in the duration of the bond as market yields rise. In contrast, should market yields fall, duration increases so that percentage price change accelerates. With an option-free bond, both these changes in duration occur.

This is portrayed graphically in Exhibit 4-13. The slope of the tangent line in the exhibit gets flatter as the required yield increases. A flatter tangent line means a smaller duration as the required yield rises. In contrast, the tangent line gets steeper as the required yield decreases, implying that the duration gets larger. This property will hold for all option-free bonds. Also, from this graphical presentation we can see that the convexity is actually measuring the rate of change of the dollar duration as market yields change.

Property 2: For a given yield and maturity, the lower the coupon, the greater the convexity of a bond. This can be seen from the computed convexity of our hypothetical bonds. Of the three 5-year bonds, the zero-coupon bond has the highest convexity, and the 9% coupon bond has the lowest convexity. The same is true of the 25-year bonds.

Property 3: For a given yield and modified duration, the lower the coupon, the smaller the convexity. The investment implication of this property is that zero-coupon bonds have the lowest convexity for a given modified duration.

EXHIBIT 4-13   Change in Duration as the Required Yield Changes

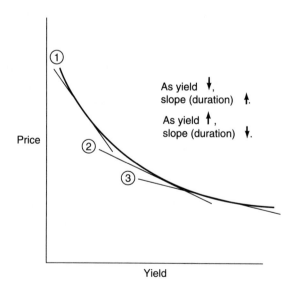

ADDITIONAL CONCERNS WHEN USING DURATION

Our illustrations have demonstrated that relying on duration as the sole measure of the price volatility of a bond may mislead investors. There are two other concerns about using duration that we should point out.

First, in the derivation of the relationship between modified duration and bond price volatility, we started with the price equation (4.1). This price equation assumes that all cash flows for the bond are discounted at the same discount rate. The appropriateness of this assumption is examined in Chapter 9, where we analyze the yield curve. Essentially, the derivation of equation (4.3) assumes that the yield curve is flat and all shifts are parallel. In Chapter 20, we show the limitations of applying duration when this assumption does not hold, and the yield curve does not shift in a parallel fashion.

Our second concern is misapplication of duration to bonds with embedded options. The principles we have illustrated apply only to option-free bonds. When changes in yields result in a change in the expected cash flow for a bond, which is the case for bonds with embedded options, the duration and convexity measures are appropriate only in certain circumstances. We discuss the price volatility of bonds with embedded options in Chapters 13 and 14.

SUMMARY

In this chapter we have discussed the price volatility characteristics of option-free bonds and reviewed three measures of bond price volatility: price value of a basis point, yield value of a price change, and duration. We then focused on the various duration measures—Macaulay duration, modified duration, and dollar duration—showing the relationship between bond price volatility and each of these measures. Finally, we looked at the convexity of a bond, showing how convexity can be used to illuminate the price volatility of a security and the investment implications of convexity.

QUESTIONS FOR CHAPTER 4

1. The price value of a basis point will be the same whether the yield is increased or decreased by one basis point. The yield value of 100 basis points, however (i.e., the change in price for a 100 basis point change in interest rates) will not be the same if the yield is increased or decreased by 100 basis points. Why?

2. Calculate the requested measures below for bonds A and B (assume each bond pays interest semiannually):

	A	B
Coupon	8%	9%
Yield to maturity	8%	8%
Maturity (in years)	2	5
Par	100.00	100.00
Price	100.000	104.055

a. Price value of a basis point
b. Macaulay duration
c. modified duration
d. convexity

3. For bonds A and B in question 3:

a. Calculate the actual price of the bonds for a 100-basis point increase in interest rates.

b. Using duration, estimate the price of the bonds for a 100-basis point increase in interest rates.

c. Using both duration and convexity, estimate the price of the bonds for a 100-basis point increase in interest rates.

d. Comment on the accuracy of your results in (b) and (c), and state why one approximation is closer to the actual price than the other.

e. Without working through calculations, indicate whether the duration of the two bonds would be higher or lower if the yield to maturity is 10% rather than 8%.

4. Can you tell from the information below which of the following three bonds will have the greatest price volatility, assuming each is trading to offer the same yield to maturity?

Bond	Coupon Rate	Maturity
X	8%	9 years
Y	10	11 years
Z	11	12 years

5. State why you would agree or disagree with the following statements:

a. As the duration of a zero-coupon bond is equal to its maturity, the responsiveness of a zero-coupon bond to interest rate changes is the same regardless of the level of interest rates.

b. When interest rates are low, there will be little difference between the Macaulay duration and modified duration measures.

c. If two bonds have the same dollar duration, yield, and price, their dollar price sensitivity will be the same for a given change in interest rates.

d. For a one-basis point change in yield, the price value of a basis point is equal to the dollar duration.

6. The November 26, 1990, issue of *BondWeek* includes an article, "Van Kampen Merritt Shortens." The article begins as follows:

Peter Hegel, first v.p. at Van Kampen Merritt Investment Advisory, is shortening his $3 billion portfolio from 110% of his normal duration of 6 1/2 years to 103-105% because he thinks that in the short run the bond rally is near an end.

Explain Hegel's strategy and his use of the duration measure in this context.

7. Consider two Treasury securities:

Bond	Price	Modified duration
A	100	6
B	80	7

Which bond will have the greater dollar price volatility for a 25-basis point change in interest rates?

8. What are the limitations of using duration as a measure of a bond's price sensitivity to interest rate changes?

9. The excerpt following is taken from an article entitled "Denver Investment to Make $800 Million Treasury Move," that appeared in the December 9, 1991, issue of *BondWeek*, p. 1:

Denver Investment Advisors will swap $800 million of long zero-coupon Treasuries for intermediate Treasuries.... The move would shorten the duration of its $2.5 billion fixed-income portfolio... .

Why would the swap described above shorten the duration of the portfolio?

Chapter 5

TREASURY AND AGENCY SECURITIES

The second largest sector of the bond market (after the mortgage market) is the market for U.S. Treasury securities; the smallest sector is the U.S. government agency securities market. We discuss them together in this chapter.[1] The appendix to this chapter discusses repurchase agreements and their use in the Treasury market.

TREASURY SECURITIES

U.S. Treasury securities are backed by the full faith and credit of the United States government. Consequently, market participants view them as having no credit risk. Interest rates on Treasury securities are the benchmark interest rates throughout the U.S. economy as well as in international capital markets. Market participants talk of interest rates on non-Treasury securities as trading above (or below) a particular Treasury security.

Two factors account for the prominent role of U.S. Treasury securities: volume (in terms of dollars outstanding) and liquidity. The Department of the Treasury is the largest single issuer of debt in the world, with Treasury securities accounting for $1.9 trillion (represented by over 180 different Treasury note and bond issues and 30 Treasury bill issues). The entire U.S. corporate bond market accounts by contrast for about $1.4 trillion and over 10,000 issues; the U.S. municipal bond market similarly accounts for about $802 billion, with more than 70,000 separate issuers and millions of individual issues.

The large volume of total debt and the large size of any single issue have contributed to making the Treasury market the most active and hence the most liquid market in the world. The spread between bid and ask

---

[1]As explained in Chapter 11, a majority of the securities backed by a pool of mortgages are guaranteed by federally sponsored agencies of the U.S. government. These securities are classified as part of the mortgage-backed securities market rather than as U.S. government agency securities.

prices is considerably narrower than in other sectors of the bond market, and most issues can be purchased easily. Many issues in the corporate and municipal markets are illiquid by contrast, and cannot be traded readily.

There are two categories of government securities—discount and coupon securities. The fundamental difference between the two types lies in the form of the stream of payments that the holder receives, which is reflected in turn in the prices at which the securities are issued. Coupon securities pay interest every six months, plus principal at maturity. Discount securities pay only a contractually fixed amount at maturity, called maturity value or face value. Discount instruments are issued below maturity value, and return to the investor the difference between issue and maturity price.

Current Treasury practice is to issue all securities with maturities of one year or less as discount securities. These securities are called Treasury bills. All securities with maturities of two years or longer are issued as coupon securities. Treasury coupon securities issued with original maturities between two and ten years are called notes; those with original maturities greater than ten years are called bonds. While there is therefore a distinction between Treasury notes and bonds, in this chapter we refer to both as simply bonds. Although Treasury notes are not callable, many outstanding Treasury bond issues are callable within five years of maturity. Treasury bonds issued since February 1985 are not callable.

Treasury securities are available in book-entry form at the Federal Reserve Bank. This means that the investor receives only a receipt as evidence of ownership instead of an engraved certificate. An advantage of book-entry is ease in transferring ownership of the security. Treasury bills come only in book-entry form, and Treasury coupon securities issued after January 1, 1983, are required to be in book-entry form.
Interest income from Treasury securities is subject to federal income taxes but is exempt from state and local income taxes.

The Primary Market

Treasury securities typically are issued on an auction basis according to regular cycles for securities of specific maturities. Three-month and six-month Treasury bills are auctioned every Monday. The amounts to be auctioned are ordinarily announced the previous Tuesday afternoon. The one-year (52-week bill) Treasury bills are auctioned in the third week of every month, with announcement on the preceding Friday. When the Treasury is temporarily short of cash, it issues *cash management bills*. The maturities of cash management bills coincide with the length of time for which the Treasury anticipates the shortfall of funds.

The Treasury regularly issues coupon securities with maturities of 2, 3, 5, 7, 10, and 30 years.[2] Exhibit 5-1 summarizes the issue schedule for Treasury coupon securities. Two- and 5-year notes are auctioned each month. At the beginning of the second month of each calendar quarter (February, May, August, and November), the Treasury conducts its regular refunding operations. At this time, it auctions 3-year, 10-year, and 30-year Treasury securities. The Treasury announces on the Wednesday of the month preceding: (1) the amount that will be auctioned, (2) what portion of that amount is to replace maturing Treasury debt, (3) what portion of that amount is to raise new funds, and (4) its estimated cash needs for the balance of the quarter and how it plans to obtain the funds. During the second half of each calendar quarter, the Treasury conducts its "mini-refunding" operations and issues 7-year Treasury notes.

EXHIBIT 5-1   Treasury Coupon Securities Auctioned by Month

Number of Years to Maturity

Month	2	3	5	7	10	30
January	x		x			
February	x	x	x		x	x
March	x		x	x		
April	x		x			
May	x	x	x	x	x	x
June	x		x			
July	x		x			
August	x	x	x		x	x
September	x		x	x		
October	x		x			
November	x	x	x		x	x
December	x		x	x		

x = auctioned in month indicated.

---

[2] Prior to April 1986, the Treasury issued 20-year bonds. The most recent change in the Treasury auction cycle occurred in December 1990, when the Treasury discontinued the quarterly auction of the 4-year Treasury note and began a monthly auction of the 5-year Treasury note, which had previously been auctioned quarterly.

The auction for Treasury bills and Treasury coupon securities is conducted on a yield basis. Competitive bids must be submitted on a yield basis.[3] Noncompetitive tenders may also be submitted for up to a $1 million face amount. Such tenders are based only on quantity, not yield. The price paid by noncompetitive bidders is the average price determined by the competitive bidders.

The auction results are determined by first deducting the total noncompetitive tenders and nonpublic purchases (such as purchases by the Federal Reserve itself) from the total securities to be auctioned. The remainder is the amount to be awarded to the competitive bidders. The lowest-yield (i.e., highest price) bidders are awarded securities at their bid price. Successively higher-bidding bidders are awarded securities at their bid price until the total amount offered (less noncompetitive tenders) is awarded. The highest yield accepted by the Treasury is referred to as the "stop yield," and bidders at that price are awarded a percentage of their total tender offer. The difference between the average yield of all the bids accepted by the Treasury and the stop is called the "tail."

Exhibit 5-2 shows the results of an auction for seven-year Treasury notes auctioned on April 17, 1989. The amount auctioned was $7.02 billion. Competitive bidders were awarded $6.37 billion and noncompetitive bidders $0.65 billion. The average yield was 9.39%, and the high yield (that is, the stop yield) was 9.40%. Thus, the tail is 0.01 (9.40 minus 9.39). Each bidder at the stop yield was awarded 38% of the amount they bid. For example, if a financial institution had bid for $100 million at 9.40%, it would have been awarded $38 million. Bidders higher in yield than 9.40% "missed" or were "shut out."

Primary Dealers: Any firm can deal in government securities, but in implementing its open market operations, the Federal Reserve will deal directly only with dealers that it designates as primary or recognized dealers. Basically, the Federal Reserve wants to be sure that firms requesting status as primary dealers have adequate capital relative to the positions they assume in Treasury securities, and that they do a reasonable amount of volume in Treasury securities (at least 1% of Treasury market activity). Exhibit 5-3 lists the primary government dealers as of January 1992.

Until 1992, primary dealers and large commercial banks that were not primary dealers would submit bids for their own account and for their customers. Others who wished to participate in the auction process could only submit competitive bids for their own account, not their customers.

---

[3]Bids on Treasury bills are submitted in terms of yield on a bank discount basis, which we discuss more fully later in the chapter.

EXHIBIT 5-2   Results of Auction of 7-Year Notes

FOR IMMEDIATE RELEASE   CONTACT: Office of Financing
April 12, 1989   202/376-4350

RESULTS OF AUCTION OF 7-YEAR NOTES

The Department of the Treasury has accepted $7.020 million of $18,630 million of tenders received from the public for the 7-year notes, Series F-1996, auctioned today. The notes will be issued April 17, 1989, and mature April 15, 1996.

The interest rate on the notes will be 9-3/8%. The range of accepted competitive bids, and the corresponding prices at the 9-3/8% interest rate are as follows:

	Yield	Price
Low	9.38%*	99.975
High	9.40%	99.874
Average	9.39%	99.924

*Excepting 1 tender of $4,000.
Tenders at the high yield were allotted 38%.

TENDERS RECEIVED AND ACCEPTED (In Thousands)

Location	Received	Accepted
Boston	$ 32,782	$ 32,782
New York	16,515,361	6,334,941
Philadelphia	15,657	15,657
Cleveland	27,446	27,446
Richmond	23,021	17,996
Atlanta	36,871	36,871
Chicago	1,196,315	312,769
St. Louis	41,985	22,745
Minneapolis	16,665	16,658
Kansas City	29,579	29,579
Dallas	13,481	11,480
San Francisco	677,414	157,009
Treasury	3,855	3,840
Totals	$18,630,432	$7,019,773

The $7,020 million of accepted tenders includes $650 million of noncompetitive tenders and $6,370 million of competitive tenders from the public.

In addition to the $7,020 million of tenders accepted in the auction process, $600 million of tenders was awarded at the average price to Federal Reserve Banks as agents for foreign and international monetary authorities. An additional $110 million of tenders was also accepted at the average price from Federal Reserve Banks for their own account in exchange for maturing securities.

8.50 - 104.543

Consequently, a broker-dealer in government securities that was not a primary dealer could not submit a competitive bid on behalf of its customers. Moreover, unlike primary dealers, nonprimary dealers had to make large cash deposits or provide guarantees to assure that they could fulfill their obligation to purchase the securities for which they bid.

Well publicized violations of the auction process by Salomon Brothers in the summer of 1991 forced Treasury officials to more closely scrutinize the activities of primary dealers and also reconsider the procedure by which Treasury securities are auctioned.[4] Specifically, the Treasury announced that it would allow qualified broker-dealers to bid for their customers at Treasury auctions. If a qualified broker-dealer establishes a payment link with the Federal Reserve system, no deposit or guaranty would be required. Moreover, the auction would no longer be handled by the submission of hand-delivered sealed bids to the Federal Reserve. The new auction process will be a computerized auction system which can be electronically accessed by qualified broker-dealers.

The Secondary Market

The secondary market for Treasury securities is an over-the-counter market where a group of U.S. government securities dealers provide continuous bids and offers on specific outstanding Treasuries.[5] The secondary market is the most liquid financial market in the world. Daily average trading volume for all Treasury securities by primary dealers for the week of January 22, 1992, was about $164.869 billion, with the distribution among Treasury securities as follows:[6]

Treasury bills	$ 33.157 billion
Coupon securities maturing in	
under 3.5 years	50.068
3.5 years to under 7.5 years	44.285
7.5 years to under 15 years	18.857
15 years and over	18.502

---

[4] Salomon Brothers admitted that it repeatedly violated a restriction that limited the amount that any one firm could purchase at the Treasury auction. The firm also admitted that it submitted unauthorized bids for some of its customers.

[5] Some trading of Treasury coupon securities does occur on the New York Stock Exchange, but the volume of these exchange-traded transactions is very small when compared to over-the-counter transactions.

[6] This figure represents immediate transactions of purchases and sales in the market as reported to the Federal Reserve Bank of New York on January 22, 1992. Immediate transactions are those scheduled for delivery in five days or less. The figure excludes all transactions under purchase and reverse repurchase agreements. (These transactions are described in the appendix to the chapter.)

EXHIBIT 5-3   Primary Government Securities Dealers

Bank of America NT & SA
Barclays de Zoete Wedd Securities Inc.
Bear, Stearns & Co., Inc.
BT Securities Corporation
Carroll McEntee & McGinley Incorporated
Chase Securities, Inc.
Chemical Securities, Inc.
Citicorp Securities Markets, Inc.
CRT Government Securities, Ltd.
Daiwa Securities America Inc.
Dean Witter Reynolds Inc.
Deutsche Bank Government Securities, Inc.
Dillon, Read & Co. Inc.
Discount Corporation of New York
Donaldson, Lufkin & Jenrette Securities Corporation
The First Boston Corporation
First Chicago Capital Markets, Inc.
Fuji Securities Inc.
Goldman, Sachs & Co.
Greenwich Capital Markets, Inc.
Harris Government Securities Inc.
Kidder, Peabody & Co., Incorporated
Aubrey G. Lanston & Co., Inc.
Lehman Government Securities, Inc.
Merrill Lynch Government Securities Inc.
J.P. Morgan Securities, Inc.
Morgan Stanley & Co. Incorporated
The Nikko Securities Co. International, Inc.
Nomura Securities International, Inc.
PaineWebber Incorporated
Prudential Securities, Inc.
Salomon Brothers Inc.
Sanwa-BGK Securities Co., L.P.
Smith Barney, Harris Upham & Co., Inc.
SBC Government Securities Inc.
UBS Securities Inc.
S.G. Warburg & Co., Inc.
Yamaichi International (America), Inc.

Source: Market Reports Division, Federal Reserve Bank of New York, January 3, 1992.

In the secondary market, the most recently auctioned Treasury issues for each maturity are referred to as "on-the-run" or "current coupon" issues. Issues auctioned prior to the current coupon issues typically are referred to as "off-the-run" issues; they are not as liquid as on-the-run issues. That is, the bid-ask spread is larger for off-the-run issues than for on-the-run issues.

Dealer profits are generated from one or more of three sources: (1) the bid-ask spread, (2) appreciation in the securities held in inventory, or depreciation in the securities sold short, and (3) the difference between the interest earned on the securities held in inventory and the cost of financing that inventory. The last source of profits is referred to as *carry*, and depends on the shape of the yield curve. Dealers obtain funds to finance inventory position using the repo market, which we describe in the appendix.

Another component of the Treasury secondary market is the "when-issued market," or "wi market," where Treasury securities are traded prior to the time they are issued by the Treasury. When-issued trading for both Treasury bills and Treasury coupon issues extends from the day the auction is announced until the issue day. All deliveries on when-issued trades occur on the issue day of the Treasury security traded.

Government Brokers: Treasury dealers trade with the investing public and with other dealer firms. When they trade with each other, it is through intermediaries known as government brokers. Dealers leave firm bids and offers with brokers who display the highest bid and lowest offer in a computer network tied to each trading desk and displayed on a monitor. The dealer responding to a bid or offer by "hitting" or "taking" pays a commission to the broker. The size and the prices of these transactions are visible to all dealers at once.

Treasury dealers use brokers because of the speed and efficiency with which trades can be accomplished. Brokers never trade for their own account, and they keep the names of the dealers involved in trades confidential. Five major brokers handle about 50% of the daily trading volume. They include Fundamental Brokers, Inc.; RMJ Securities Corp.; Garban Ltd.; Cantor, Fitzgerald Securities Corp.; and Chapdelaine & Company Government Securities, Inc. These five firms service the primary government dealers and a dozen or so other large government dealers aspiring to be primary dealers.

The quotes provided on the government dealer screens represent prices in the "inside" or "interdealer" market, and the primary dealers have resisted attempts to allow the general public to have access to them. Only one government broker, Cantor, Fitzgerald Securities Corp., disseminates prices to nonprimary dealers. In 1989, when RMJ Securities offered to disseminate quotes to some large institutional investors, pressure from the primary dealers persuaded the broker to withdraw its offer.

Bid and Offer Quotes on Treasury Bills: The convention for quoting bids and offers is different for Treasury bills and Treasury coupon securities. Bids and offers on Treasury bills are quoted in a special way. Unlike bonds that pay coupon interest, Treasury bill values are quoted on a *bank discount basis*, not on a price basis. The yield on a bank discount basis is computed as follows:

$$Y_d = \frac{D}{F} \times \frac{360}{t}$$

where Y_d = annualized yield on a bank discount basis (expressed as a decimal)
     D = dollar discount, which is equal to the difference between the face
          value and the price
     F = face value
     t = number of days remaining to maturity

As an example, a Treasury bill with 100 days to maturity, a face value of $100,000, and selling for $97,569 would be quoted at 8.75% on a bank discount basis:

D   = $100,000 − $97,569
    = $2,431

Therefore:

$$Y_d = \frac{\$2,431}{\$100,000} \times \frac{360}{100}$$
$$= 8.75\%$$

Given the yield on a bank discount basis, the price of a Treasury bill is found by first solving the formula for Y_d for the dollar discount (D), as follows:

$$D = Y_d \times F \times t/360$$

The price is then:

Price = F − D

For the 100-day Treasury bill with a face value of $100,000, if the yield on a bank discount basis is quoted as 8.75%, D is equal to:

D   = 0.0875 × $100,000 × 100/360
    = $2,431

Therefore:

Price $= \$100,000 - \$2,431$

$\qquad = \$97,569$

The quoted yield on a bank discount basis is not a meaningful measure of the return from holding a Treasury bill for two reasons. First, the measure is based on a face value investment rather than on the actual dollar amount invested. Second, the yield is annualized according to a 360-day rather than 365-day year, making it difficult to compare Treasury bill yields with Treasury notes and bonds, which pay interest on a 365-day basis. The use of 360 days for a year is a money market convention for some money market instruments, however. Despite its shortcomings as a measure of return, this is the method dealers have adopted to quote Treasury bills. Many dealer quote sheets and some reporting services provide two other yield measures that attempt to make the quoted yield comparable to that for a coupon bond and other money market instruments.

The measure that seeks to make the Treasury bill quote comparable to Treasury notes and bonds is called the bond-equivalent yield, which we explained in Chapter 3. The CD-equivalent yield (also called the money market-equivalent yield) makes the quoted yield on a Treasury bill more comparable to yield quotations on other money market instruments that pay interest on a 360-day basis. It does this by taking into consideration the price of the Treasury bill rather than its face value. The formula for the CD-equivalent yield is:

$$\text{CD - equivalent yield} \ = \ \frac{360\,Y_d}{360 - t\left(Y_d\right)}$$

As an illustration, consider once again the hypothetical 100-day Treasury bill with a face value of $100,000, selling for $97,569, and offering a yield on a bank discount basis of 8.75%. The CD-equivalent yield is:

$$= \frac{360\,(.0875)}{360 - 100\,(.0875)}$$

$$= 8.97\%$$

Bids and Offer Quotes on Treasury Coupon Securities: Treasury coupon securities are quoted in a different manner from Treasury bills. They trade on a dollar price basis in price units of 1/32 of 1% of par (par is taken to be $100). For example, a quote of 92-14 refers to a price of 92 and 14/32. On the basis of $100,000 par value, a change in price of 1% equates to $1,000, and 1/32 equates to $31.25. A plus sign following the number of 32nds means that a 64th is added to the price. For example, 92-14+ refers to a price of 92 and 29/64 or 92.453125% of par value.

On quote sheets and screens, the price quote is followed by some "yield to maturity" measure. Yield quotes can be based on the Street or the Treasury method. The difference between the two yield measures is the procedure used to discount the first coupon payment when it is not exactly six months away.[7] This occurs for two reasons. First, for certain securities, the first coupon payment may be more or less than six months away. This situation is referred to as an "odd" or "irregular" first coupon payment. When the first coupon payment is more than six months away, it is said to have a long first coupon.[8] When the first coupon payment is less than six months from the date of issuance, the Treasury security is said to have a short first coupon.[9] The second circumstance when the first coupon payment may come in less than six months is when a security is purchased between coupon dates. From a practical point of view, once a security is issued and traded in the secondary market, investors and traders use the Street method.

Accrued Interest and Invoice Price: When an investor purchases a bond between coupon payments, if the issuer is not in default, the investor must compensate the seller of the bond for the coupon interest earned from the

---

[7] The difference between the Street and Treasury practices for computing yield is the procedure for discounting over a long first coupon period and over a fractional six-month period. The Treasury method (also called the "Fed" method) assumes simple interest over the period from the valuation date to the next coupon payment. The Street method (also called the Securities Industry Association or "SIA" method) assumes compound interest over the period from the valuation date to the next coupon payment. For example, suppose that the next coupon payment is X days from the valuation date (or previous coupon date), and W is the number of days between the issuance date (or previous coupon date) and the first coupon date (or next coupon date). Letting K denote the ratio of X to W, the discounting of a coupon payment, C/2, for both methods for a semiannual yield to maturity, y, is

Simple interest over period (Treasury method):

$$\frac{C/2}{(1+Ky)}$$

Compound interest over period (Street method)

$$\frac{C/2}{(1+y)^K}$$

[8] The five-year Treasury note issued prior to January 1991 is an example of a Treasury security usually issued as a long first coupon security. The first coupon payment for the five-year Treasury note was made approximately eight months after the issuance date.

[9] The Treasury issues a security with a short first coupon when the auction date is the fifteenth or the end of the month, but that day falls on a weekend or holiday. In such cases, the Treasury issues the security on the next business day, but pays the first coupon on the fifteenth or at the end of the month six months later. Thus, the first coupon payment is less than six months away.

time of the last coupon payment to the settlement date of the bond. This amount is called accrued interest and is computed as follows:

$$\frac{C}{2} \times \frac{\text{Number of days from last coupon payment to settlement date}}{\text{Number of days in coupon period}}$$

Market conventions determine the number of days in a coupon period and the number of days from the last coupon payment to the settlement date. For a Treasury coupon security, both are equal to the actual number of days. (This is referred to as "actual over actual" basis.)[10] The accrued interest for a Treasury coupon security is therefore determined as follows:

$$\frac{C}{2} \times \frac{\text{Actual number of days from last coupon payment to settlement date}}{\text{Actual number of days in coupon period}}$$

The *invoice price* is the total proceeds that the buyer of the bond pays the seller. The invoice price is equal to the price agreed upon by the buyer and the seller plus accrued interest.

Completed Transactions and Public Quotation System: In the stock market there has been a movement toward a consolidated tape for reporting trades on exchanges and the over-the-counter market and a composite quotation system for the collection and display of bid and ask quotations. In the Treasury market, however, despite the fact that trading activity is concentrated in the over-the-counter market, and that daily trading volume exceeds $100 billion, reporting of trades does not exist. Nor is there any record of bid and ask quotations that provides reliable price quotes at which the general public can transact. Such quotations do exist, as we explained earlier, in the interdealer market on government broker screens.

An example will show how the price of a specific government security can vary among dealers at a given time. Portfolio managers of a large institutional investor telephoned five major government dealers to obtain a price quote for the 10.75% coupon Treasury maturing on August 15, 2005.[11] The five quotes were:

---

[10] For corporate and municipal bonds, the day count convention is "30/360" which means a year is treated as having 360 days and a month as having 30 days. Therefore, the number of days in a coupon period is 180.

[11] Sharmin Mossavar-Rahmani, "Understanding and Evaluating Index Fund Management," in Frank J. Fabozzi and T. Dessa Garlicki (eds.), *Advances in Bond Analysis and Portfolio Strategies* (Chicago: Probus Publishing, 1987), p. 438.

Dealer	Bid Price	Ask Price
A	128-2	128-6
B	128-3	128-5
C	128-4	128-8
D	128-5	128-9
E	128-6	128-8

Recall that the number after the hyphen indicates the number of 32nds of 1%. Consequently, the difference between the highest and lowest price that this Treasury issue could be sold for is 4/32, or 1/8 of 1% (the difference between the bid prices of dealer A and dealer E). The difference between the lowest and highest ask price if this issue were to be purchased is also 4/32 (dealer D's ask price minus dealer B's ask price). In dollar terms, for a transaction involving $10 million, the difference between the best and the worst transaction price would be $12,500, a significant price difference in what is the most active and liquid bond market in the world. Also notice how the bid-ask spread differs from dealer to dealer, from 2/32 for two of the dealers to 4/32 for the other three.

This example highlights shortcomings of not only the U.S. Treasury market, but all the bond markets that we discuss: lack of both a reporting system for completed transactions and a quotation system. Two passages from a recent General Accounting Office study of the securities market seem to indicate that the bond market will come under increasing Congressional scrutiny:

The bond market is increasingly important to both corporate and government financing, but the operation of these markets is not well known to policy makers. A policy-oriented assessment of the changes underway in bond markets may be far overdue.

And,

A near monopoly on provision of bond market quotations by one vendor has persisted for years, largely because of the absence of regulation in this field. Since the size and importance of this market is increasing, there may be important but hidden policy questions here that should be explored. No substantial policy studies of bond markets have been conducted for use by Congress, and one may be much needed.[12]

---

[12] GAO, *Securities Markets in the Electronics Age*, Chapter 1, in manuscript, pp. 8 and 32.

Stripped Treasury Securities

The Treasury does not issue zero-coupon notes or bonds. In August 1982, however, both Merrill Lynch and Salomon Brothers created synthetic zero-coupon Treasury receipts. Merrill Lynch marketed its Treasury receipts as "Treasury Income Growth Receipts" (TIGRs); Salomon Brothers marketed its as "Certificates of Accrual on Treasury Securities" (CATS). The procedure they followed was to purchase Treasury bonds and deposit them in a bank custody account. The firms then issued receipts representing an ownership interest in each coupon payment on the underlying Treasury bond in the account and a receipt on the underlying Treasury bond's maturity value. This process of separating each coupon payment, as well as the principal (called the corpus), to sell securities against them is referred to as "coupon stripping." Although the receipts created from the coupon stripping process are not issued by the U.S. Treasury, the underlying bond deposited in the bank custody account is a debt obligation of the U.S. Treasury, so the cash flow from the underlying security is certain.

To illustrate the process, suppose $100 million of a Treasury bond with a 20-year maturity and a coupon rate of 10% is purchased to create zero-coupon Treasury securities. The cash flow from this Treasury bond is 40 semiannual payments of $5 million each ($100 million times 0.10 divided by 2) and the repayment of principal (corpus) of $100 million 20 years from now. This Treasury bond is deposited in a bank custody account. Receipts are then issued, each with a different single payment claim on the bank custody account. As there are 41 different payments to be made by the Treasury, a receipt representing a single payment claim on each payment is issued, which is effectively a zero-coupon bond. The amount of the maturity value for a receipt on a particular payment, whether coupon or corpus, depends on the amount of the payment to be made by the Treasury on the underlying Treasury bond. In our example, 40 coupon receipts each have a maturity value of $5 million, and one receipt, the corpus, has a maturity value of $100 million. The maturity dates for the receipts coincide with the corresponding payment dates by the Treasury.

Other investment banking firms followed suit by creating their own receipts.[13] They all are referred to as trademark zero-coupon Treasury securities because they are associated with a particular firm.[14] Receipts of

---

[13] Lehman Brothers offered "Lehman Investment Opportunities Notes" (LIONs); E.F. Hutton offered "Treasury Bond Receipts" (TBRs); and Dean Witter Reynolds offered "Easy Growth Treasury Receipts" (ETRs.). There were also GATORs, COUGARs, and—you'll like this one—DOGS (Dibs on Government Securities).

[14] They are also called "animal products" for obvious reasons.

one firm were rarely traded by competing dealers, so the secondary market was not liquid for any one trademark. Moreover, the investor was exposed to the risk—as small as it may be—that the custodian bank may go bankrupt.

To broaden the market and improve liquidity of these receipts, a group of primary dealers in the government market agreed to issue generic receipts that would not be directly associated with any of the participating dealers. These generic receipts are referred to as "Treasury Receipts" (TRs). Rather than representing a share of the trust as the trademarks do, TRs represent ownership of a Treasury security. A common problem with both trademark and generic receipts was that settlement required physical delivery, which is often cumbersome and inefficient.

Prior to June 1982, the Treasury was not a supporter of coupon stripping. In fact, a strongly worded letter from the Federal Reserve Bank of New York to primary government dealers stated, "in our view trading in Treasury securities stripped of coupons, or trading in the detached coupons themselves, is not a desirable market practice and should be discouraged."[15] The Treasury's objection was that taxpayers were able to undertake transactions involving stripped Treasuries that could reduce their tax liability. In June 1982, the Treasury withdrew its objections to coupon stripping when provisions of the Tax Equity and Fiscal Responsibility Act of 1982 eliminated such tax abuses.

Although the Treasury benefited indirectly from coupon stripping through a heightened demand for its securities, in February 1985 it announced its Separate Trading of Registered Interest and Principal of Securities (STRIPS) program to facilitate the stripping of designated Treasury securities. Specifically, all new Treasury bonds and all new Treasury notes with maturities of ten years and longer are eligible. The zero-coupon Treasury securities created under the STRIPS program are direct obligations of the U.S. government. Moreover, the securities clear through the Federal Reserve's book entry system.[16] Creation of the STRIPS program ended the origination of trademarks and generic receipts. By December 1988, 65% of the zero-coupon Treasury market consisted of those created under the STRIPS program. About 14% were TRs, and the balance were trademarks (with CATS and TIGRs having the "lion's" share of 8% and 13%, respectively).[17]

---

[15] See Thomas J. Kluber and Thomas Stauffacher, "Zero Coupon Treasury Securities," Chapter 11 in Frank J. Fabozzi (ed.), *The Handbook of Treasury Securities* (Chicago: Probus Publishing, 1986).

[16] In 1987, the Treasury permitted the conversion of stripped coupons into book-entry form under its Coupons Under Book-Entry Safekeeping (CUBES) program.

[17] Monte Shapiro and Carol E. Johnson, "Overview of Government Zero Market and Investment Strategies," Chapter 5 in Frank J. Fabozzi (ed.), *The Handbook of Treasury and Agency Securities* (Chicago: Probus Publishing, 1990).

The profit potential for a government dealer who strips a Treasury security lies in arbitrage resulting from the mispricing of the security. This will be explained in Chapter 9.

FEDERAL AGENCY SECURITIES

The federal agency securities market can be divided into two sectors—the *federally sponsored agency securities market* and the *federally related institution securities market*. Federally sponsored agencies, also called *government sponsored entities*, are privately owned, publicly chartered entities. They were created by Congress to reduce the cost of capital for certain borrowing sectors of the economy deemed to be important enough to warrant assistance. The entities in these privileged sectors include farmers, homeowners, and students. Federally sponsored agencies issue securities directly in the marketplace. The market for these securities, while smaller than that of Treasury securities, has in recent years come to represent an active and important sector of the bond market.

Federally related institutions are entities that are arms of the federal government that generally do not issue securities directly in the marketplace (although they did prior to 1973). Instead, they obtain all or part of their financing by borrowing from the Federal Financing Bank, an entity created in 1973. The relatively small size of these issues made the borrowing cost for individual issues significantly higher than that for Treasury securities. Creation of the Federal Financing Bank was intended to consolidate and reduce the borrowing cost of federally related institutions.

Federally related institutions include: the Commodity Credit Corporation, the Export-Import Bank of the United States, the Farmers Home Administration, the General Services Administration, the Government National Mortgage Association, the Maritime Administration, the Private Export Funding Corporation, the Rural Electrification Administration, the Rural Telephone Bank, the Small Business Administration, the Tennessee Valley Authority, and the Washington Metropolitan Area Transit Authority. All federally related institution securities are exempt from SEC registration. With the exception of securities of the Private Export Funding Corporation and the Tennessee Valley Authority, the securities are backed by the full faith and credit of the United States government. As of November 1989, the amount of federally related institution debt outstanding was $36.9 billion.[18]

---

[18] *Federal Reserve Bulletin*, March 1990

Federally Sponsored Agency Securities

There are eight federally sponsored agencies. The Federal Farm Credit Bank System is responsible for the credit market in the agricultural sector of the economy. The Farm Credit Financial Assistance Corporation was created in 1987 to address problems in the existing Farm Credit Bank System. Three federally sponsored agencies—Federal Home Loan Bank, Federal Home Loan Mortgage Corporation, and Federal National Mortgage Association—are responsible for providing credit to the mortgage and housing sectors. The Financing Corporation was created in 1987 to recapitalize the Federal Savings and Loan Insurance Corporation. Because of continuing difficulties in the savings and loan industry, the Resolution Trust Corporation was created in 1989 to liquidate or bail out insolvent institutions. The Student Loan Marketing Association provides funds to support higher education.

The federally sponsored agencies issue two types of securities: discount notes and bonds. Discount notes are short-term obligations, with maturities ranging from overnight to 360 days. Bonds are sold with maturities greater than 2 years. The issues may be callable. The same features of corporate bonds to be described in Chapter 6 are seen in securities issued by federally sponsored agencies. These include floating-rate notes and zero-coupon bonds.

With the exception of the securities issued by the Farm Credit Financial Assistance Corporation, federal agency securities are not backed by the full faith and credit of the U.S. government, as is the case with Treasury securities. Consequently, investors purchasing a federally sponsored agency security are exposed to some credit risk. The yield spread between these securities and Treasury securities of comparable maturity reflects differences in perceived credit risk and liquidity. The spread attributable to credit risk reflects financial problems faced by the issuing federally sponsored agency and any likelihood that the federal government will allow the credit agency to default on its outstanding obligations.

Two examples will illustrate this point. In late 1981 and early 1982, the net income of the Federal National Mortgage Association weakened, causing analysts to report that the securities of this credit agency carried greater risk than previously perceived. As a result, the yield spread over Treasuries on its debt rose from 91 basis points (on average) in 1981 to as high as 150 basis points.[19] In subsequent years, the Federal National

---

[19] Michael J. Moran, "The Federally Sponsored Credit Agencies: An Overview," *Federal Reserve Bulletin* (June 1986), p. 380.

Mortgage Association's net income improved, and its yield spread to Treasuries narrowed. As another example, in 1985 the yield spread on securities of the Farm Credit Bank System rose substantially above those on comparable maturity Treasuries because of the agency's financial difficulties. The spread between 1985 and 1986 varied with the prospects for Congressional approval of a bailout measure for the system.

The price quotation convention for federally sponsored agency securities is the same as that for Treasury securities. That is, the bid and ask price quotations are expressed as a percentage of par plus fractional 32nds of a point. There are some issues of federally sponsored agencies that trade with almost the same liquidity as Treasury securities. Other issues that are supported by only a few dealers trade much like off-the-run corporate bonds.

Below we provide a brief description of six of the eight federally sponsored agencies. The two agencies not discussed here—Federal Home Loan Mortgage Corporation and Federal National Mortgage Association—are covered in Chapter 11.

Federal Farm Credit Bank System: The purpose of the Federal Farm Credit Bank System (FFCBS) is to facilitate adequate, dependable credit and related services to the agricultural sector of the economy. The Farm Credit System consists of three entities: the Federal Land Banks, Federal Intermediate Credit Banks, and Banks for Cooperatives. Before 1979, each entity issued securities in its own name. Starting in 1979, they began to issue debt on a consolidated basis as "joint and several obligations" of the FFCBS. All financing for the FFCBS is arranged through the Federal Farm Credit Banks Funding Corporation, which issues consolidated obligations through a selling group consisting of approximately 150 members. For discount notes, the selling group consists of only four dealers.

Farm Credit Financial Assistance Corporation: In the 1980s, the FFCBS faced financial difficulties because of defaults on loans made to farmers occasioned largely by high interest rates in the late 1970s and early 1980s and depressed prices on agricultural products. To recapitalize the Federal Farm Credit Bank System, in 1987 Congress created the Farm Credit Financial Assistance Corporation (FACO). This federally sponsored agency is authorized to issue debt to assist the FFCBS. FACO bonds, unlike the debt of other federally sponsored government agencies, are backed by the Treasury.

Federal Home Loan Bank System: The Federal Home Loan Bank System (FHLBS) consists of the 12 district Federal Home Loan Banks (which are instrumentalities of the U.S. government) and their member banks. An independent federal agency, the Federal Home Loan Bank Board, was originally responsible for regulating all federally chartered savings and loan associations and savings banks, as well as state-chartered institutions insured by the Federal Savings and Loan Insurance Corporation. These responsibilities have been curtailed since 1989. The major source of debt funding for the Federal Home Loan Banks is the issuance of consolidated debt obligations. These obligations are joint and several obligations of the 12 Federal Home Loan Banks.

Financing Corporation: The deposits of savings and loans were once insured by the Federal Savings and Loan Insurance Corporation (FSLIC), overseen by the Federal Home Loan Bank Board. When difficulties encountered in the savings and loan industry raised concerns about FSLIC's ability to meet its responsibility to insure deposits, Congress passed the Competitive Equality and Banking Act in 1987. This legislation included provisions to recapitalize FSLIC and establish a new federally government sponsored agency, the Financing Corporation (FICO), to issue debt in order to provide funding for FICO.

FICO is capitalized by the nonvoting stock purchased by the 12 regional Federal Home Loan Banks. FICO issued its first bonds in September 30, 1987—a 30-year noncallable $500 million issue. The issue was priced 90 basis points over the 30-year Treasury security at the time. The principal of these bonds is backed by zero-coupon Treasury securities. The legislation permits FICO to issue up to $10.825 billion but not more than $3.75 billion in any one year. FICO is legislated to be dismantled in 2026, or after all securities have matured, whichever comes sooner.

Resolution Trust Corporation: The 1987 legislation that created FICO did not go far enough to resolve the problems facing the beleaguered savings and loan industry. In 1989, Congress passed more comprehensive legislation, the Financial Institutions Reform, Recovery and Enforcement Act (FIRREA). This legislation has three key elements. First, it transfers supervision of savings and loans to a newly created Office of Thrift Supervision. Second, it shifts the FSLIC insurance function to a Savings Association Insurance Fund, placed under the supervision of the Federal Deposit Insurance Corporation. Third, it establishes the Resolution Trust Corporation (RTC) as a federally sponsored agency charged with the responsibility of liquidating or bailing out insolvent savings and loan institutions. RTC is to obtain its funding from the Resolution Funding Corporation (REFCORP), which is authorized to issue up to $40 billion of long-term bonds. The principal of this debt is backed by zero-coupon

Treasury bonds. REFCORP has issued both 30-year and 40-year bonds.[20]

Student Loan Marketing Association: Popularly known as "Sallie Mae," the Student Loan Marketing Association provides liquidity for private lenders participating in the Federal Guaranteed Student Loan Program, the Health Education Assistance Loan Program, and the PLUS loan program (a program that provides loans to the parents of undergraduate students). Sallie Mae is permitted to purchase and offer investors participation in student loans. Sallie Mae issues unsecured debt obligations in the form of discount notes. In January 1982, Sallie Mae first issued floating-rate securities based on the bond-equivalent yield on 91-day Treasury bills. Sallie Mae also has long-term fixed-rate securities and zero-coupon bonds outstanding.

Future Regulation of Federally Sponsored Agencies

The U.S. bailout of the savings and loan industry raised increasing concerns in Congress over the potential cost of bailing out federally sponsored agencies. The Financial Institutions Reform, Recovery and Enforcement Act of 1989 mandated the General Accounting Office (GAO) and the Secretary of the Treasury to study the issues and prepare reports for Congress. Specifically, both the GAO and the Treasury were to investigate whether each federally sponsored agency maintained appropriate capital levels, given the risks associated with their activities. The Treasury was also charged with assessment of the impact of the activities of federally sponsored agencies on federal borrowing.

The Treasury interim report recommends that a federally sponsored agency be required to maintain a triple-A credited rating from two nationally recognized rating companies. (We discuss rating companies in the next chapter.) The rating must be achieved in the absence of government sponsorship (i.e., as a stand-alone private entity). Failure to obtain such a credit rating would result in the loss of sponsorship by the federal government. The GAO interim report puts forth two possible forms of regulation. One is the same as that recommended by the Treasury. The alternative is to require federally sponsored agencies to maintain a specified level of risk-weighted capital similar to the risk-weighted capital requirements for commercial banks. At the time of this writing, Congress has not settled upon the form of regulation, if any, to implement.

---

[20] The 40-year bonds represent the first offering of such a government or government agency bond since the Treasury issued 40-year bonds in the 1950s. The auction for the $5 billion, 40-year bond offering in January 1990 was not a successful undertaking.

SUMMARY

The U.S. Treasury market is closely watched by all participants in the financial markets because interest rates on Treasury securities are the benchmark interest rates throughout the world. The Treasury issues three types of securities: bills, notes, and bonds. Treasury bills have a maturity of one year or less, are sold at a discount from par, and do not make periodic interest payments. Treasury notes and bonds are coupon securities. Treasury securities are issued on a competitive bid auction basis, according to a regular auction cycle. The auction process relies on the participation of the primary government securities dealers, with which the Federal Reserve deals directly. The secondary market for Treasury securities is an over-the-counter market, where dealers trade with the general investing public and with other dealers. In the secondary market, Treasury bills are quoted on a bank discount basis; Treasury coupon securities are quoted on a price basis. Treasury dealers finance their positions in the repo market.

While the Treasury does not issue zero-coupon Treasury securities, government dealers have created these instruments synthetically by a process called coupon stripping. Zero-coupon Treasury securities include trademarks, Treasury receipts, and STRIPS. Creation of the first two types of zero-coupon Treasury securities has ceased; STRIPS now dominate the market. The advantage of zero-coupon Treasury securities is that they eliminate reinvestment risk. The motivation for government dealers to create these securities is the arbitrage opportunities available.

Federally sponsored agency securities and federally related institution securities make up the federal agency securities market. The former are privately owned, publicly chartered entities created to reduce the cost of borrowing for certain sectors of the economy. Federally related institutions are arms of the federal government whose debt is guaranteed by the U.S. government. While federally sponsored agencies issue their own securities, federally related institutions obtain all or part of their financing by borrowing from the Federal Financing Bank. The yield spread between securities issued by federally sponsored agencies and Treasury securities of comparable maturity depends on the agency's perceived credit risk and liquidity. Congress is considering future regulation of federally sponsored agencies.

As explained in the appendix, a repurchase agreement is a lending transaction in which the borrower uses a security as collateral for the borrowing. The transaction is referred to as a repurchase agreement because it specifies the sale of a security and its subsequent repurchase at a future date. The difference between the purchase (repurchase) price and the sale price is the dollar interest cost of the loan. An overnight repo is for one day; a loan for more than one day is called a term repo. The collateral in a repo may be a Treasury security, money market instrument, federal agency security, or mortgage-backed security. The parties to a repo are exposed to credit risk, limited by margin and mark-to-market practices included in a repo agreement. Dealers use the repo market to finance positions and cover short positions, and to run a matched book so that they can earn spread income. The Fed uses the repo market to implement monetary policy. Factors that determine the repo rate are the federal funds rate, the quality of the collateral, the term of the repo, the delivery requirement, and the availability of the collateral.

APPENDIX

REPURCHASE AGREEMENTS

A repurchase agreement is the sale of a security with a commitment by the seller to buy the security back from the purchaser at a specified price at a designated future date. Basically, a repurchase agreement is a collateralized loan, where the collateral is a security. The agreement is best explained with an illustration.

Suppose a government securities dealer has purchased $10 million of a particular Treasury security. Where does the dealer obtain the funds to finance that position? Of course, the dealer can finance the position with its own funds or by borrowing from a bank. Typically, however, the dealer uses the repurchase agreement or "repo" market to obtain financing. In the repo market the dealer can use the $10 million of the Treasury security as collateral for a loan. The term of the loan and the interest rate that the dealer agrees to pay (called the "repo rate") are specified. When the term of the loan is one day, it is called an overnight repo; a loan for more than one day is called a term repo.

The transaction is referred to as a repurchase agreement because it calls for the sale of the security and its repurchase at a future date. Both the sale price and the purchase price are specified in the agreement. The difference between the purchase (repurchase) price and the sale price is the dollar interest cost of the loan.[21]

Back to the dealer who needs to finance $10 million of a Treasury security that it purchased and plans to hold overnight. Suppose that a customer of the dealer has excess funds of $10 million. (The customer might be a municipality with tax receipts that it has just collected, and no immediate need to disburse the funds.) The dealer would agree to deliver ("sell") $10 million of the Treasury security to the customer for an amount determined by the repo rate and buy ("repurchase") the same Treasury security from the customer for $10 million the next day. Suppose that the overnight repo rate is 6.5%. Then, as will be explained below, the dealer would agree to deliver the Treasury securities for $9,998,194 and repurchase the same securities for $10 million the next day. The $1,806 difference between the "sale" price of $9,998,194 and the repurchase price

---

[21] For a more detailed description of the mechanics of repurchase agreements, see Oskar H. Rogg, "Repurchase Agreements," Chapter 8 in Frank J. Fabozzi (ed.), *The Handbook of Treasury and Agency Securities* (Chicago: Probus Publishing, 1990).

of $10 million is the dollar interest on the financing. From the customer's perspective, the agreement is called a *reverse repo*.

The formula following is used to calculate the dollar interest on a repo transaction:

Dollar interest = (Dollar principal) × (Repo rate) × Repo term/360

Notice that the interest is computed on a 360-day basis. In our example, at a repo rate of 6.5% and a repo term of one day (overnight), the dollar interest is $1,806 as we show below:

$$= \$10,000,000 \times 0.065 \times 1/360$$
$$= \$1,806$$

The advantage to the dealer of using the repo market for borrowing on a short-term basis is that the rate is lower than the cost of bank financing. (The reason for this is explained below.) From the customer's perspective, the repo market offers an attractive yield on a short-term secured transaction that is highly liquid.

While the example illustrates financing a dealer's long position in the repo market, dealers can also use the market to cover a short position. For example, suppose a government dealer sold $10 million of Treasury securities two weeks ago and must now cover the position—that is, deliver the securities. The dealer can do a reverse repo (agree to buy the securities and sell them back). Of course, the dealer eventually would have to buy the Treasury security in the market in order to cover its short position.

There is a good deal of Wall Street jargon describing repo transactions. To understand it, remember that one party is lending money and accepting a security as collateral for the loan; the other party is borrowing money and providing collateral to borrow the money. When someone lends securities in order to receive cash (i.e., borrow money), that party is said to be "reversing out" securities. A party that lends money with the security as collateral is said to be "reversing in" securities. The expressions "to repo securities" and "to do repo" are also used. The former means that someone is going to finance securities using the security as collateral; the latter means that the party is going to invest in a repo. Finally, the expressions "selling collateral" and "buying collateral" are used to describe a party financing a security with a repo on the one hand, and lending on the basis of collateral, on the other.

The collateral in a repo is not limited to government securities. Money market instruments, federal agency securities, and mortgage-backed securities are also used.

Credit Risks

Despite the fact that there may be high-quality collateral underlying a repo transaction, both parties to the transaction are exposed to credit risk. The failure of a few small government securities dealer firms involved in repo transactions in the 1980s has made market participants more cautious about the creditworthiness of the counterparty to a repo.[22]

Why does credit risk occur in a repo transaction? Consider our initial example where the dealer uses $10 million of government securities as collateral to borrow. If the dealer cannot repurchase the government securities, the customer may keep the collateral; if interest rates on government securities increase subsequent to the repo transaction, however, the market value of the government securities will decline, and the customer will own securities with a market value less than the amount it lent to the dealer. If the market value of the security rises instead, the dealer firm will be concerned with the return of the collateral, which then has a market value higher than the loan.

Repos are now more carefully structured to reduce credit risk exposure. The amount lent is less than the market value of the security used as collateral, which provides the lender with some cushion should the market value of the security decline. The amount by which the market value of the security used as collateral exceeds the value of the loan is called "margin."[23] The amount of margin is generally between 1% and 3%. For borrowers of lower creditworthiness and/or when less liquid securities are used as collateral, the margin can be 10% or more.

Another practice to limit credit risk is to mark the collateral to market on a regular basis. (Marking a position to market means recording the value of a position at its market value.) When market value changes by a certain percentage, the repo position is adjusted accordingly. Suppose that a dealer firm has borrowed $20 million using collateral with a market value of $20.4 million. The margin is 2%. Suppose further that the market value of the collateral drops to $20.1 million. A repo agreement can specify either (1) a margin call, or (2) repricing of the repo. In the case of a margin call, the dealer firm is required to put up additional collateral with a market value of $300,000 in order to bring the margin up to $400,000. If repricing is agreed upon, the principal amount of the repo will be changed from $20 million to $19.7 million (the market value of $20.1 million divided by 1.02). The dealer would then send the customer $300,000.

---

[22] Failed firms include Drysdale Government Securities, Lion Capital, RTD Securities, Inc., Belvill Bressler & Schulman, Inc., and ESM Government Securities, Inc.

[23] Margin is also referred to as the "haircut."

One concern in structuring a repo is delivery of the collateral to the lender. The most obvious procedure is for the borrower to deliver the collateral to the lender. At the end of the repo term, the lender returns the collateral to the borrower in exchange for the principal and interest payment. This procedure may be too expensive though, particularly for short-term repos, because of costs associated with delivering the collateral. The cost of delivery would be factored into the transaction by a lower repo rate offered by the borrower. The risk of the lender not taking possession of the collateral is that the borrower may sell the security or use the same security as collateral for a repo with another party.

As an alternative to delivering the collateral, the lender may agree to allow the borrower to hold the security in a segregated customer account. Of course, the lender still faces the risk that the borrower may use the collateral fraudulently by offering it as collateral for another repo transaction.

Another method is for the borrower to deliver the collateral to the lender's custodial account at the borrower's clearing bank. The custodian then has possession of the collateral that it holds on behalf of the lender. This practice reduces the cost of delivery because it is merely a transfer within the borrower's clearing bank. If, for example, a dealer enters into an overnight repo with Customer A, the next day the collateral is transferred back to the dealer. The dealer can then enter into a repo with Customer B for, say, five days without having to redeliver the collateral. The clearing bank simply establishes a custodian account for Customer B and holds the collateral in that account.

Participants in the Market

Because it is used by dealer firms (investment banking firms and money center banks acting as dealers) to finance positions and cover short positions, the repo market has evolved into one of the largest sectors of the money market. Financial and nonfinancial firms participate in the market as both sellers and buyers, depending on the circumstances they face. Thrifts and commercial banks are typically net sellers of collateral (i.e., net borrowers of funds); money market funds, bank trust departments, municipalities, and corporations are typically net buyers of collateral (i.e., providers of funds).

While a dealer firm uses the repo market as the primary means for financing its inventory and covering short positions, it will also use the repo market to run a matched book where it takes on repos and reverse repos with the same maturity. The firm does so to capture the spread at which it enters into the repo and reverse repo agreement. For example, suppose that a dealer firm enters into a term repo of ten days with a money market fund and a reverse repo rate with a thrift for ten days, for which the collateral is identical. This means that the dealer firm is borrowing funds from the money market fund and lending money to the thrift. If the rate on the repo is 7.5% and the rate on the reverse repo is 7.55%, the dealer firm is borrowing at 7.5% and lending at 7.55%, locking in a spread of 0.05% (five basis points).

Another participant is the repo broker. To understand the role of the repo broker, suppose that a dealer firm has shorted $50 million of a security. It will then survey its regular customers to determine if it can borrow, via a reverse repo, the security it shorted. Suppose that it cannot find a customer willing to do a repo transaction (repo from the customer's point of view, reverse repo from the dealer's). At that point, the dealer firm will use the services of a repo broker. When the collateral is difficult to acquire, it is said to be a "hot" or "special" issue.

The Fed and the Repo Market: The Federal Reserve influences short-term interest rates through its open market operations—that is, by the outright purchase or sale of government securities. This is not the common practice followed by the Fed, however. It uses the repo market instead to implement monetary policy by purchasing or selling collateral. By buying collateral (i.e., lending funds), the Fed injects money into the financial markets, thereby exerting downward pressure on short-term interest rates. When the Fed buys collateral for its own account, this is called a *system repo*. The Fed also buys collateral on behalf of foreign central banks in repo transactions that are referred to as *customer repos*. It is primarily through system repos that the Fed attempts to influence short-term rates. By selling securities for its own account, the Fed drains money from the financial markets, thereby exerting upward pressure on short-term interest rates. This transaction is called a *matched sale*.

Note the language that is used to describe the transactions of the Fed in the repo market. When the Fed lends funds based on collateral, we call it a system or customer repo, not a reverse repo. Borrowing funds using collateral is called a matched sale, not a repo. The terminology can be confusing, which is why we use the expressions "buying collateral" and "selling collateral" to describe what parties in the market are doing.

Determinants of the Repo Rate

There is no one repo rate; rates vary from transaction to transaction depending on a variety of factors: quality of collateral, term of the repo, delivery requirement, availability of collateral, and the prevailing federal funds rate.

The higher the credit quality and liquidity of the collateral, the lower the repo rate. The effect of the term of the repo on the rate depends on the shape of the yield curve (discussed in Chapter 9). As noted earlier, if delivery of the collateral to the lender is required, the repo rate will be lower. If the collateral can be deposited with the bank of the borrower, a higher repo rate is paid. The more difficult it is to obtain the collateral, the lower the repo rate. To understand why this is so, remember that the borrower (or equivalently the seller of the collateral) has a security that is a *hot* or *special issue*. The party that needs the collateral will be willing to lend funds at a lower repo rate in order to obtain the collateral.

While these factors determine the repo rate on a particular transaction, the federal funds rate determines the general level of repo rates. The repo rate will be a rate lower than the federal funds rate, because a repo involves collateralized borrowing, while a federal funds transaction is unsecured borrowing.

QUESTIONS FOR CHAPTER 5

1. Define the following:
   a. An on-the-run issue
   b. An off-the-run issue
   c. The when-issued market
   d. A primary dealer
2. Why do government dealers use government brokers?
3. Suppose that the price of a Treasury bill with 90 days to maturity and a $1 million face value is $980,000.
   a. What is the yield on a bank discount basis?
   b. Why is the yield on a bank discount basis not a meaningful measure of the return from holding a Treasury bill?
4. The bid and ask yields for a Treasury bill maturing on January 16, 1992, were quoted by a dealer as 5.91% and 5.89%, respectively. Shouldn't the bid yield be less than the ask yield, because the bid yield indicates how much the dealer is willing to pay, and the ask yield is what the dealer is willing to sell the Treasury bill for?
5. a. Calculate the dollar price for these five Treasury coupon securities:

	Price Quoted	Par
i.	95-4	$ 100,000
ii.	87-16	1,000,000
iii.	102-10	10,000,000
iv.	116-30	10,000
v.	102-4+	100,000

   b. Calculate the accrued interest for a Treasury coupon security trading as follows:
   Coupon rate = 8%
   Number of days from last coupon payment to settlement date = 50
   Number of days in coupon period = 181
   Par value = $1 million

6. The following is from the March 1991 monthly report published by Blackstone Financial Management:

   The Treasury also brought $34.5 billion in new securities to the market in February as part of the normal quarterly refunding.... The auctions went slightly better than expected given the significant size and the uncertainties surrounding the duration of the war. The 3-year was issued at a 6.98% average yield, the 10-year at a 7.85% average yield, and the 30-year at a 7.98% average yield. All bids were accepted at the average yield or better (i.e., with no tail), indicating ample demand for the securities.

   What is meant by the average yield and the tail? Why does the absence of a tail indicate ample demand for the Treasuries auctioned?

7. a. What is the difference among a STRIP, a trademark Treasury zero-coupon security, and a Treasury receipt?

   b. What is the most common type of Treasury zero-coupon security?

8. When stripped Treasury securities were first created, callable 30-year Treasury bonds were being issued by the Treasury. Such issues could be called by the Treasury five years before the maturity date. Why would the presence of a call feature make it difficult to strip a Treasury security?

9. a. What is the difference between a federally sponsored agency security and that of a federally related institution?

   b. Are federally sponsored agency securities backed by the full faith and credit of the U.S. government?

10. In the February 1991 monthly report of Blackstone Financial Management is the quotation:

    The Resolution Funding Corporation (REFCORP) issued $4.95 billion 30-year bonds and $2 billion 40-year bonds in January.... Since the auction, the 30-year REFCORP issue has tightened 4 basis points to a 25 basis point spread while other agency issues of similar maturities widened 3 to 4 basis points.

    In the March 1991 monthly issue, the following appeared:

    Within the agency sector, most issues tightened 2 to 5 basis points to their respective Treasury maturities, with the exception of 30-year REFCORP. These issues widened by 2 basis points. ...

    a. What is the Resolution Funding Corporation?

    b. What happened to investors' perceptions of the credit risk of REFCORP between January and February?

11. a. How can a dealer firm use a repurchase agreement to finance a long position in a Treasury security?

    b. One party in a repo transaction is said to "buy collateral," the other party to "sell collateral." Why?

    c. Why would the lender of funds in a repo transaction be exposed to credit risk?

    d. When there is a shortage of a specific security for a repo transaction, will the repo rate increase or decrease?

12. a. What is a system repo?

    b. What is a customer repo?

13. Which rate should be higher: the overnight repo rate, or the overnight federal funds rate?

Chapter 6

CORPORATE DEBT

INSTRUMENTS

As the name indicates, corporate debt instruments are obligations issued by corporations. They include bonds, medium-term notes, and commercial paper. The corporate debt instruments that we discuss in this chapter are issued by U.S. firms in the U.S. bond market and are those denominated in U.S. dollars. In Chapter 8 we examine bonds issued by foreign corporations, as well as other foreign entities, in the U.S. bond market.

CORPORATE BONDS

Corporate bonds are classified by the type of issuer. The four general classifications used by bond information services are: (1) utilities; (2) transportations; (3) industrials; and (4) banks and finance companies. Finer breakdowns are often made to create more homogeneous groupings. For example, utilities are subdivided into electric power companies, gas distribution companies, water companies, and communications companies. Transportations are further divided into airlines, railroads, and trucking companies. Industrials are the catchall class, and the most heterogeneous of the groupings with respect to investment characteristics. Industrials include all kinds of manufacturing, merchandising, and service companies.

Terms of a Corporate Bond Issue

The essential features of a corporate bond are relatively simple. The corporate issuer promises to pay a specified percentage of par value on designated dates (known as the coupon payments) and to repay par or principal value of the bond at maturity. Failure to pay either the principal or interest when due constitutes legal default, and court proceedings can be instituted to enforce the contract. Bondholders, as creditors, have a prior legal claim over common and preferred stockholders as to both income and assets of the corporation for the principal and interest due them.

The promises of corporate bond issuers and the rights of investors who buy them are set forth in great detail in contracts called *bond indentures*. If bondholders were handed the complete indenture they would have trouble understanding the wording, and even greater difficulty in determining from time to time whether the corporate issuer were keeping all the promises made. These problems are solved for the most part by bringing in a corporate trustee as a third party to the contract. The indenture is made out to the corporate trustee as a representative of the interests of bondholders; that is, the trustee acts in a fiduciary capacity for investors who own the bond issue. A corporate trustee is a bond or trust company with a corporate trust department and officers who are experts in performing the functions of a trustee.

Most corporate bonds are *term bonds*; that is, they run for a term of years, then become due and payable. Term bonds are often referred to as "bullet-maturity" bonds. Any amount of the liability that has not been paid off prior to maturity must be paid off at that time. The term may be long or short. Generally, obligations due less than 10 years from the date of issue are called *notes*. Most corporate borrowings take the form of *bonds* due in 20 to 30 years. Term bonds may be retired by payment at final maturity or retired prior to maturity if provided for in the indenture. Some corporate bond issues are so arranged that specified principal amounts become due on specified dates. Such issues are called *serial bonds*. Equipment trust certificates (discussed later) are structured as serial bonds.

Security for Bonds: As security, the issuer pledges either real property (using a mortgage) or personal property to offer security beyond that of the general credit standing of the issuer. A *mortgage bond* gives the bondholders a lien against the pledged assets. A lien is a legal right to sell mortgaged property to satisfy unpaid obligations to bondholders. In practice, foreclosure and sale of mortgaged property is unusual. If a default occurs, there is usually a financial reorganization of the issuer in which provision is made for settlement of the debt to bondholders. The mortgage lien is important, though, because it gives the mortgage bondholders a very strong bargaining position relative to other creditors in determining the terms of a reorganization.

Some companies do not own fixed assets or other real property and so have nothing on which they can give a mortgage lien as security to bondholders. Instead, they own securities of other companies; they are holding companies, and the other companies are subsidiaries. To satisfy the desire of bondholders for security, such companies will pledge stocks, notes, bonds or whatever other kind of financial asset they own. These assets are termed *collateral* (or personal property), and bonds secured by such assets are called *collateral trust bonds*.

Many years ago the railroad companies developed a way of financing purchase of cars and locomotives (called *rolling stock*) in a way that enabled them to borrow at just about the lowest rates in the corporate bond market. Railway rolling stock has for a long time been regarded by investors as excellent security for debt. The equipment is sufficiently standardized that it can be used by one railway as well as another. And it can be readily moved from the tracks of one railroad to those of another. There is generally a good market for lease or sale of cars and locomotives. The railroads have taken advantage of these characteristics of rolling stock by developing a legal arrangement for giving investors a legal claim on it that is different from, and generally superior to, a mortgage lien. The legal arrangement is one that vests legal title to railway equipment in a trustee. A railway company orders some cars and locomotives from a manufacturer. The manufacturer then transfers legal title to the equipment to a trustee who, in turn, leases it to the railroad and at the same time sells *equipment trust certificates* to obtain the funds to pay the manufacturer. The trustee collects lease payments from the railroad and uses it to pay interest and principal on the certificates. The principal is therefore paid off on specified dates unlike a term bond. Although the railway companies developed the equipment trust arrangement, it has also been used by companies engaged in providing other kinds of transportation. For example, trucking companies finance the purchase of huge fleets of trucks in the same manner; airlines use this kind of financing to purchase transport planes; and international oil companies use it to buy huge tankers.

Debenture bonds are not secured by a specific pledge of property, but that does not mean that they have no claim on property of issuers or on their earnings. Debenture bondholders have the claim of general creditors on all assets of the issuer not pledged specifically to secure other debt. And they even have a claim on pledged assets to the extent that these assets have value greater than necessary to satisfy secured creditors. Subordinated debenture bonds are issues that rank after secured debt, after debenture bonds, and often after some general creditors in their claim on assets and earnings.

The type of security issued is a factor in its cost to the issuer. For a given corporation, mortgage bonds will cost less than debenture bonds; debenture bonds will cost less than subordinated debenture bonds.

Guaranteed bonds are obligations guaranteed by another entity. The safety of a guaranteed bond depends upon the financial capability of the guarantor to satisfy the terms of the guarantee, as well as the financial capability of the issuer. The terms of the guarantee may call for the guarantor to guarantee the payment of interest and/or repayment of the principal.

It is important to recognize that a superior legal status will not prevent bondholders from suffering financial loss when the issuer's ability to generate cash flow adequate to pay its obligations is seriously eroded.

Provisions for Paying off Bonds: Most corporate issues have a call provision giving the issuer an option to buy back all or part of the issue prior to maturity. Some issues specify that the issuer must retire a predetermined amount of the issue periodically. Various types of corporate call provisions are discussed below.[1]

(1) *Call and Refund Provisions*: An important question in negotiating the terms of a new bond issue is whether the issuer shall have the right to redeem the *entire amount* of bonds outstanding on a date before maturity. Issuers generally want this right because they recognize that at some time in the future the general level of interest rates may fall sufficiently below the issue's coupon rate, so redeeming the issue and replacing it with another issue with a lower coupon rate would be attractive to them. For reasons discussed later in this chapter, this right is a disadvantage to the bondholder.

The usual practice is a provision that denies the issuer the right to redeem bonds during the first five to ten years following the date of issue with proceeds received from issuing lower-cost debt obligations ranking equal to or superior to the debt to be redeemed. This type of redemption is called *refunding*. While most long-term issues include such refunding restrictions, they still may be immediately callable, in whole or in part, if the source of funds is not lower interest cost money. Cash flow from operations, proceeds from a common stock sale, or funds from the sale of property are examples of such sources.

Investors often confuse refunding protection with call protection. Call protection is much more absolute in that bonds cannot be redeemed *for any reason*. Refunding restrictions only provide protection against the one type of redemption mentioned above. Failure to recognize this difference has resulted in unnecessary losses for some investors.

Long-term industrial issues generally have ten years of refunding protection but are then immediately callable. Electric utilities most often have five years of refunding protection, although, during times of high

---

[1] For a more detailed explanation of corporate call provisions, see: Richard S. Wilson and Frank J. Fabozzi, *The New Corporate Bond Market* (Chicago, IL: Probus Publishing, 1990).

interest rates, issues with ten years of refunding protection have been sold.

Many short-to-intermediate-term bonds and notes are not callable for the first three to seven years (in some cases, not callable for the life of the issue). Thereafter, the issue may be called for any reason.

As a rule, corporate bonds are callable at a premium above par. Generally, the amount of the premium declines as the bond approaches maturity and often reaches par after a number of years have passed since issuance. The initial amount of the premium may be as much as one year's coupon interest or as little as coupon interest for half a year. When less than the entire issue is called, the specific bonds to be called are selected randomly or on a pro rata basis. When bonds are selected randomly, the serial number of the certificates is published in *The Wall Street Journal* and major metropolitan dailies.

(2) *Sinking Fund Provision:* Corporate bond indentures may require the issuer to retire a specified portion of an issue each year. This is referred to as a sinking fund requirement. This kind of provision for repayment of corporate debt may be designed to liquidate all of a bond issue by the maturity date, or it may be arranged to pay only a part of the total by the end of the term. If only a part is paid, the remainder is called a balloon maturity. The purpose of the sinking fund provision is to reduce credit risk.

Generally, the issuer may satisfy the sinking fund requirement by either (1) making a cash payment of the face amount of the bonds to be retired to the corporate trustee, who then calls the bonds for redemption using a lottery, or (2) delivering to the trustee bonds with a total face value equal to the amount that must be retired from bonds purchased in the open market. If the bonds are retired using the first method, interest payments stop at the redemption date.

Usually, the periodic payments required for sinking fund purposes will be the same for each period. A few indentures might permit variable periodic payments, where the periodic payments vary based upon prescribed conditions set forth in the indenture. Many corporate bond indentures include a provision that grants the issuer the option to retire double the amount stipulated for sinking fund retirement. This is referred to as the *doubling option.*

Usually, the sinking fund call price is the par value if the bonds were originally sold at par. When issued at a price in excess of par, the call price generally starts at the issuance price and scales down to par as the issue approaches maturity.

Industrial issues almost always include sinking fund provisions. Finance companies almost always do not. The inclusion or absence of a sinking fund provision in public utility bonds depends on the type of public utility.

Quality Ratings

Professional money managers use various techniques to analyze information on companies and bond issues in order to estimate the ability of the issuer to live up to its future contractual obligations.[2] This activity is known as credit analysis.

Some large institutional investors and most investment banking firms have their own credit analysis department. Most individual investors and institutional bond investors make no such analytical studies. Instead, they rely primarily on commercial rating companies, which perform credit analysis and express their opinions by a system of ratings. The five commercial rating companies are (1) Moody's Investors Service, (2) Standard & Poor's Corporation, (3) Duff and Phelps, (4) McCarthy, Crisanti & Maffei, and (5) Fitch Investors Service.

The two most widely used systems of bond ratings are those of Moody's and Standard & Poor's. In both systems the term *high-grade* means low credit risk, or conversely, high probability of future payments. The highest-grade bonds are designated by Moody's by the letters *Aaa*, and by Standard & Poor's by *AAA*. The next highest grade is *Aa* or *AA*; then for the third grade both agencies use *A*. The next three grades are designated *Baa* or *BBB*, *Ba* or *BB*, and *B*, respectively. There are also *C* grades. In addition, Standard & Poor's uses a plus or minus sign to provide a narrower credit quality breakdown within each class, and Moody's uses 1, 2, or 3 to provide this breakdown. Bonds rated triple A (AAA or Aaa) are said to be *prime*, double A (AA or Aa) are of *high quality*, single A issues are *upper medium-grade* and triple B are of *medium-grade*. These four categories are referred to as *investment-grade*. Lower-rated bonds are said to have speculative elements or to be *distinctly speculative*. They are also known as *high-yield* or *junk bonds*.

There has been a dramatic decline in the credit quality of new issues in the past 15 years. According to Moody's ratings, the percentage of new issues rated Aaa has declined from a high of 42.6% in 1977 to only 11.89% in 1988. By 1988, only about 25% were rated Aaa or Aa at the time of issuance. In contrast, the proportion of issues rated Ba and lower has increased dramatically.

---

[2] For an in-depth discussion of credit analysis, see Jane Tripp Howe, "Credit Analysis for Corporate Bonds," Chapter 17 in Frank J. Fabozzi (ed.), *The Handbook of Fixed Income Securities* (Homewood, IL: Business One-Irwin, 1991).

Risks Associated with Investing in Corporate Bonds

As we explain in Chapter 1, the risks associated with investing in corporate bonds are (1) interest-rate risk, (2) reinvestment risk, (3) default risk, (4) call risk, (5) inflation risk, (6) exchange-rate risk, (7) liquidity risk, and (8) volatility risk. Below we elaborate further on default risk, call risk, and liquidity risk as they pertain to corporate bonds. We also talk about event risk.

Default Risk: Unlike Treasury securities, corporate bonds expose the investor to default or credit risk. This is the risk that the issuer will default on its obligations. At any one time, the yield offered in the market for a corporate bond varies depending on how market participants estimate the uncertainty of future payment of dollar amounts of interest and principal: It then depends on their perceived quality or credit rating. To compensate for greater credit risk, lower-quality rated issues must offer higher yields than issues with a higher rating. The yield spread between two issues that are identical in all respects except for quality is referred to as a *quality spread* or *credit spread.*

Both Moody's and Standard & Poor's periodically publish average yields at market prices on a number of long-term corporate bond issues grouped by ratings. These average yields by category always show the lowest yields on triple-A rated bonds, somewhat higher yields on double-A rated bonds, then still higher yields on single-A rated bonds. There is a relatively large differential between the average yield on single-A and triple-B bonds. Exhibit 6-1 presents Moody's average promised yields from 1976 through 1991 for its top four quality ratings.

The quality spreads between corporate bond issues of different quality and between corporate bonds and Treasury securities vary over the business cycle. Specifically, quality spreads between lower- and higher-quality bonds tend to widen when the economy is in a recession or an economic downturn but narrow during periods of economic prosperity. The narrowing of the spread between high-grade and lower-grade credit issues during periods of economic prosperity occurs because the likelihood of default is reduced even for lower-rated issues. Investors then attempt to increase yield by selling their higher-rated issues and putting the proceeds into lower-rated issues. When investors anticipate a poorer economic climate, there is often a "flight to quality," as they pursue more conservative credit-risk exposure by selling lower-quality and purchasing higher-quality issues. This widens the spread between high-grade and lower-grade credit issues.

EXHIBIT 6-1   Average Promised Yields on Corporate Bonds
by Quality Rating: 1976-1991*

Year	Aaa	Aa	A	Baa
1976	8.43%	8.75%	9.09%	9.75%
1977	8.02	8.24	8.49	8.97
1978	8.73	8.92	9.20	9.49
1979	9.63	9.94	10.20	10.69
1980	11.94	12.50	12.89	13.67
1981	14.17	14.75	15.29	16.04
1982	13.79	14.41	15.43	16.11
1983	12.04	12.42	13.10	13.55
1984	12.71	13.26	13.74	14.19
1985	11.37	11.82	12.28	12.72
1986	9.02	9.47	9.95	10.39
1987	9.38	9.68	9.99	10.58
1988	9.71	9.94	10.23	10.83
1989	9.26	9.46	9.74	10.18
1990	9.32	9.56	9.82	10.36
1991	8.77	9.05	9.30	9.80

*The annual yields are the average of the monthly averages as reported in *Moody's Bond Record*.

Call Risk: We explained earlier that corporate bonds are typically callable or redeemable. Whether the issuer has the choice to retire all or part of an issue prior to maturity, or is required to do so, the bondholder is exposed to the risk that the issue will be called away at a disadvantageous time. This risk is referred to as *call risk* or *timing risk*.

Call provisions are a disadvantage because if and when interest rates decline relative to the coupon rate to the point where call becomes an immediate or prospective danger, the market value of the bond will not rise as much as that of similar issues of the same quality. The price will be "compressed" toward the call price and will eventually coincide with it when the call is announced. This creates an asymmetric risk for the lender, who suffers the full burden of any rise in interest through a fall in price but will not reap the benefit of a higher price through lower interest rates. We discuss this risk in more detail in Chapter 13.

Recall that some indentures have a sinking fund provision with a doubling option. The doubling option effectively reduces the bondholder's call protection because, when interest rates decline, the issuer may find it advantageous to exercise this option at the special sinking fund call price in order to retire a substantial portion of the high-cost outstanding issue. Thus, while the purpose of the sinking fund provision is to reduce credit risk by paying off the majority of the issue prior to the stated maturity date, this mandatory call provision also increases call risk.

Liquidity Risk: Any bond that is quoted continually by a dealer is a marketable bond; there is a market for it. But investors who seek to implement trading and portfolio strategies want to know much more than that; they want to know how good the market is. It is useful to recognize differences in the quality of markets for different corporate bond issues.

The principal means for estimating the marketability of securities is the size of the spread between dealers' bid and ask prices. A narrow spread — say, one-quarter to one-half of 1% —indicates a very marketable issue. A wide spread—such as 2% or 3% —means low marketability. The principal determinant of the size of the spread is usually the volume of trading in an issue. This can be attributed to the fact that a high frequency of new orders means the market maker incurs both less cost of holding inventories and less risk of unfavorable price movements while inventories are being held. In addition, the number of dealers is more or less proportionate to the volume of trading. If there is a lot of business in a bond issue, there are a lot of dealers seeking the business. A large volume of trading and a large number of dealers make a highly competitive market where bid-ask spreads are pressed downward.

Event Risk: Occasionally the ability of an issuer to make interest and principal payments is seriously and unexpectedly changed by (1) a natural or industrial accident or some regulatory change, or (2) a takeover or corporate restructuring. These risks are referred to generically as *event risk.* Examples of the first type of event risk could be a change in the accounting treatment of loan losses for commercial banks or the cancellation of nuclear plants by public utilities.

An example of the second type of event risk is the 1988 takeover of RJR Nabisco for $25 billion through a financing technique known as a *leveraged buyout* (LBO). In such a transaction, the new company has a substantial amount of debt incurred to finance the acquisition of the firm.[3] In the case of RJR Nabisco, debt following the leveraged buyout amounted to $29.9 billion, compared to equity of $1.2 billion. Because the corporation had to service a larger amount of debt, its quality rating was reduced. RJR Nabisco's quality rating decreased from A1 to B3. To see

[3] For a discussion of event risk associated with takeovers, see N.R. Vijayarghavan and Randy Snook, "Takeover Event Risk and Corporate Bond Portfolio Management," in Frank J. Fabozzi (ed.) *Advances and Innovations in the Bond and Mortgage Markets* (Chicago: Probus Publishing, 1989).

how much more investors demanded because of this new capital structure with its greater proportion of debt, look at Exhibit 6-2. The exhibit shows the impact of the initial LBO bid announcement on yield spreads for RJR Nabisco's debt. The yield spread to a benchmark Treasury increased from about 100 basis points to 350 basis points.

Event risk can have spillover effects on other firms. A nuclear accident, for example, will affect all utilities producing nuclear power. And, in the case of takeovers, consider once again the RJR Nabisco LBO. An LBO of $25 billion had been considered impractical before then, but once the RJR transaction showed that size was not an obstacle, other large firms previously thought to be unlikely candidates for an LBO became fair game. To see the spillover effect, look at Exhibit 6-3, which shows how event risk fears caused yield spreads to widen for three large firms.

Bonds with Special Features

Prior to the 1970s, securities issued in the U.S. bond market had a simple structure. They had a fixed coupon rate and a fixed maturity date.

EXHIBIT 6-2   RJR Nabisco—The Impact of the Initial LBO Bid Announcement on Yield Spreads

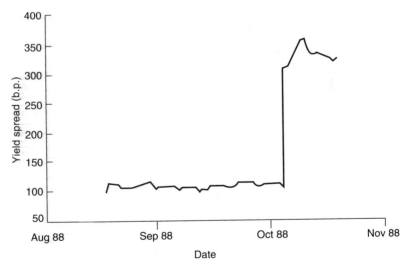

* RJR Nabisco 9 3/8 due April 2016–U.S. Treasury 8 7/8 due August 2017.

Source: N.R. Vijayarghavan and Randy Snook, "Takeover Event Risk and Corporate Bond Portfolio Management," in Frank J. Fabozzi (ed.), *Advances and Innovations in the Bond and Mortgage Markets* (Chicago: Probus Publishing, 1989), p. 55.

EXHIBIT 6-3   Anheuser Busch, Sara Lee and Union Pacific—Event Risk Fears and Widening Yield Spreads

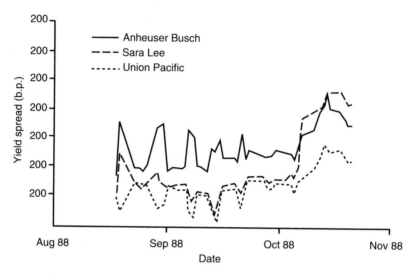

*Corporates are spread to the U.S. Treasury 8 7/8 due August 2017.

Source: Vijayarghavan and Randy Snook, "Takeover Event Risk and Corporate Bond Portfolio Management," in Frank J. Fabozzi (ed.), *Advances and Innovations in the Bond and Mortgage Markets* (Chicago: Probus Publishing, 1989), p. 56.

The only option that was available to the issuer was the right to call all or part of the issue prior to the stated maturity date. Bondholders were sometimes given the right to convert the bond for shares of common stock. The historically high interest rates that prevailed in the United States in the late 1970s and early 1980s and the volatile interest rates since the 1970s however, provided a fertile environment for both introduction of new structures and increased use of existing structures with special features that made issues more attractive to both borrowers and investors. These bond structures are reviewed below.

Convertible and Exchangeable Bonds: The conversion provision in a corporate bond issue grants the bondholder the right to convert the bond to a predetermined number of shares of common stock of the bond issuer. Exchangeable bonds grant the bondholder the right to exchange the bonds for the common stock of a firm *other* than the issuer of the bond. We discuss convertible and exchangeable bonds in more detail in Chapter 16.

Issues of Debt with Warrants: Some bonds are issued with warrants attached as part of the offer. A warrant grants the holder the right to purchase a designated security at a specified price. A warrant, therefore, is simply a call option. The warrant may permit the holder to purchase the common stock of the issuer of the debt or the common stock of a firm other than the issuer's. Or, the warrant may grant the holder the right to purchase a debt obligation of the issuer. Warrants typically can be detached from the bond and sold separately. The warrant can generally be exercised with cash or by exchanging at par the debt that is part of the unit offering. The embedded call option in the convertible bond cannot be sold separately from the bond, unlike a warrant. In the case of convertible and exchangeable bonds, only the bond may be used to exercise the option.

The holder of a bond and a warrant is in a long position in the corporate bond of the issuer and a long position in a call option on the common stock of the issuer. The same is true of a unit of debt with warrants to buy common stock of a firm other than the issuer. The holder of a bond and a warrant in this case is in a long position in the corporate bond of the issuer and a long position in a call option on the common stock of some other firm.

Putable Bonds: A putable bond grants the bondholder the right to sell the issue back to the issuer at par value on designated dates. The advantage to the bondholder is that, if interest rates rise after the issue date, thereby reducing the value of the bond, the bondholder can put the bond to the issuer for par. Thus, a putable corporate bond is a package composed of a nonputable corporate bond plus a long put option on the corporate bond. This will insure that the bond will stay close to par somewhat like instruments earning a short-term floating rate (see below), except that the former, but not the latter, also provide protection against deterioration in credit rating.

Zero-Coupon Bonds: The first public offering of zero-coupon corporate bonds was by J.C. Penney Company, Inc., in April 1982. Recall from Chapter 3 that the yield to maturity of a corporate bond when it is purchased indicates the accumulated terminal return the investor will realize if all coupon payments are reinvested at a rate equal to the yield to maturity. But the investor's actual return if a coupon corporate bond is held to maturity depends on the rate at which the coupon payments can be reinvested. That is, the investor faces reinvestment risk.

With a zero-coupon corporate bond, there are no coupon payments to reinvest or all coupons are automatically reinvested by the issuer at the yield to maturity. So the investor faces no reinvestment risk — holding a zero-coupon bond to maturity results in a return equal to the yield to maturity at the time of purchase.

Floating-Rate Securities: The coupon interest on floating-rate securities is reset periodically according to some predetermined benchmark. For example, the coupon rate may be reset every six months at a rate equal to a spread of 100 basis points over the six-month Treasury bill rate.

Floating-rate securities are attractive to some institutional investors because they allow purchase of an asset with an income stream that more closely matches the floating nature of some of their liabilities. In theory, a floating-rate security with frequent resets should trade at par if market participants consider that the appropriate spread off the benchmark since the time of issuance has not changed. For example, suppose that a single-A rated floating-rate security is issued with a coupon that resets every three months to 100 basis points over the three-month Treasury bill rate. If the perceived credit quality of this issuer, and hence the spread required by the market, has remained constant, the issue should sell at par, as the interest it pays coincides with that demanded. If, on the other hand, it deteriorates, so that the market at the reset date wants 110 basis points over the three-month Treasury bill for this bond, the price of the issue will drop below par. The opposite could occur if credit quality improves and the market is willing to accept a lower spread.

Certain floating-rate instruments are viewed by some investors as a passive substitute for short-term holdings, particularly that part of a short-term portfolio that is more or less consistently maintained at certain minimum levels. Thus, floating-rate securities save on the costs of constantly rolling over short-term securities as they reach maturity.

There may be other features in a floating-rate issue. For example, many floating-rate issues include a put option. Some issues are exchangeable, either automatically at a certain date (often five years after issuance) or at the option of the issuer, into a fixed-rate security. A few issues are convertible into the common stock of the issuer. Some floating-rate issues have a ceiling or maximum interest rate on the coupon rate; some have a floor or minimum interest rate on the coupon rate.

High-Yield Corporate Bond Sector

As explained earlier in this chapter, *high-yield bonds*, commonly called *junk bonds*, are issues with quality ratings below triple B. Bond issues in this sector of the market either were rated investment-grade at the time of issuance but have been downgraded subsequently to noninvestment-grade, or at the time of issuance were rated as noninvestment grade. Bonds that fall into the former category are termed "fallen angels." Three examples of fallen angels are ITT World Communications, Interco, and RJR Nabisco. The downgrading of the last two issues came about because of leveraged buyouts that took the companies private and substantially increased their debt/equity ratios.

There are complex bond structures in the junk bond area, particularly for bonds issued for LBO financing and recapitalizations producing higher debt. In an LBO or recapitalization, for example, the heavy interest payment burden the corporation must make places severe cash flow constraints on the firm. To reduce this burden, firms involved in LBOs and recapitalizations have issued deferred-coupon structures that permit the issuer to avoid using cash to make interest payments for a period of three to seven years. There are three types of deferred coupon structures: (1) deferred-interest bonds, (2) step-up bonds, and (3) payment-in-kind bonds.

Deferred-interest bonds are the most common type of deferred coupon structure. These bonds sell at a deep discount and do not pay interest for an initial period, typically from three to seven years.[4] *Step-up bonds* do pay coupon interest, but the coupon rate is low for an initial period before it increases ("steps up") to a higher coupon rate. Finally, *payment-in-kind (PIK) bonds* give the issuer an option to pay cash at a coupon payment date or to give the bondholder a similar bond (i.e., a bond with the same coupon rate and a par value equal to the amount of the coupon payment that would have been paid). The period during which the issuer can make this choice varies from five to ten years.[5]

In October 1987, a junk bond structure came to market that provided for the issuer to reset the coupon rate so that the bond will trade at a predetermined price.[6] The coupon rate may reset annually, and even more frequently, or reset only one time over the life of the bond. Generally, the coupon rate at the reset date will be the average of rates suggested by two investment banking firms. The new rate will then reflect: (1) the level of interest rates at the reset date, and (2) the credit spread the market wants on the issue at the reset date. This structure is called an *extendable reset bond*. Notice the difference between this bond structure and a floating-rate issue as described earlier in this chapter. With a floating-rate issue, the coupon rate resets according to a fixed spread to some benchmark. The spread is specified in the indenture. The amount of the spread reflects market conditions at the time the issue is offered. In contrast, the coupon rate on an extendable reset bond is reset according to market conditions suggested by several investment banking firms at the time of the reset

---

[4] Because no interest is paid for the initial period, these bonds are sometimes referred to as zero–coupon bonds.

[5] For a further discussion of PIK bonds, see Laurie S. Goodman and Alan H. Cohen, "Payment–in–Kind Debentures: An Innovation," *Journal of Portfolio Management* (Winter 1989), pp. 9-19.

[6] Most of the bonds have a coupon reset formula that requires the issuer to reset the coupon so that the bond will trade at a price of $101.

date. Moreover, the new coupon rate reflects the new level of interest rates and the new spread that investors seek.

The advantage to issuers of extendable reset bonds is again that they can be assured of a long-term source of funds based on short-term rates. For investors, the advantage of these bonds is that the coupon rate will reset to the market rate—both the level of interest rates and the credit spread, keeping them in principle at par. Recent experience with reset bonds, however, has not been favorable during the recent period of difficulties in the high-yield bond market. The sudden substantial increase in risk spread meant that the rise in the rate needed to keep the issue at par was so large that it would have insured the bankruptcy of the firm. As a result, the reset was sometimes insufficient to keep the issue at the stipulated price.

Secondary Market

There are two secondary corporate bond markets: the exchange market (New York Stock Exchange and American Stock Exchange) and the over-the-counter (OTC) market. Almost all trading volume takes place in the OTC market, which is the market used by institutional investors and professional money managers.

The problems we noted in Chapter 5 on Treasury securities with respect to the public reporting of completed transactions and information on reliable bid and ask prices at which an investor can transact apply as well to the corporate bond market.

Accrued Interest: In Chapter 5 we explained the market convention for determining the number of days in a coupon period and the number of days from the last coupon payment to settlement date for a Treasury coupon security. This information is needed to calculate the accrued interest. For Treasury coupon securities, it is based on the actual number of days.

While a calendar year has 365 days (or 366 days in the case of a leap year), for purposes of computing corporate bond interest the day count convention is to treat the year as having 360 days. Each month in a corporate bond year is 30 days whether it is February, April, or August. A 12% coupon corporate bond will pay $120 per year per $1,000 par value, accruing interest at $10 per month or $0.33333 per day. The accrued interest on a 12% corporate bond for 3 months is $30; for 3 months and 25 days, $38.33, and so forth. The corporate calendar is referred to as "30/360."

MEDIUM-TERM NOTES

A medium-term note is another corporate debt instrument. The unique characteristic of medium-term notes is that they are offered to investors continually over a period of time by an agent of the issuer. Investors can select from the following maturity bands: 9 months to 1 year, more than 1 year to 18 months, more than 18 months to 2 years and so on, up to 30 years. Medium-term notes are registered with the Securities and Exchange Commission under Rule 415 (the shelf registration rule). Registering under Rule 415 gives the issuer the maximum flexibility for issuing securities on a continual basis.

The yield offered on a medium-term note depends on (1) the particular maturity selected by the investor, (2) the Treasury yield curve at the time of offering, and (3) the credit risk premium demanded by the market, which depends on maturity. In other words, the medium-term note will be priced at a spread to the Treasury yield curve at the time of the offering. Medium-term notes are typically issued at par.

The medium-term note was pioneered by Merrill Lynch in 1981 to close the funding gap between commercial paper and long-term bonds.[7] The first medium-term note issuer was Ford Motor Credit Company. By 1983, GMAC and Chrysler Financial used Merrill Lynch as an agent to issue medium-term notes. The subsequent growth of the domestic medium-term note market and its importance as a funding source can be seen by comparing it to the amount of domestic public debt issued.[8] In 1982, the first full year that medium-term notes were offered, $3.8 billion was offered. This was slightly more than 10% of the $36.8 billion of domestic public debt issued. By 1989 the amount of domestic medium-term notes issued exceeded the issuance of domestic public debt: $118.4 billion versus $108.7 billion. In that year, 24.1% or $28.5 billion of the medium-term notes issued had maturities from nine months to two years; 50.1% or $59.3 billion had maturities between two years and five years. Thus, in 1989 alone $87.8 billion (74.2%) of the medium-term notes issued had maturities between nine months and five years.[9]

---

[7] Actually, in 1972 GMAC first used medium–term notes to fund automobile loans with maturities of five years and less. The medium–term notes were issued directly to investors, without the use of an agent.

[8] This includes nonconvertible, dollar-denominated debt, excluding junk bonds, mortgage-backed securities, and asset-backed securities. This information comes from IDD Information Services.

[9] As reported in "Maturity Distribution of Primary MTN Sales by Merrill Lynch," *Money Market Instruments*. (NY: Merrill Lynch Money Markets, Inc., 1989).

As of December 31,1989, the amount of medium-term notes outstanding was $339 billion. Of this amount, $261 billion was underwritten by Merrill Lynch.[10] Issuers in the market include finance companies, bank or bank holding companies, industrial companies, thrifts, utilities, and sovereign or government agencies. As of December 1989, finance companies offered the largest number of programs, followed by bank or bank holding companies and then industrials.[11]

The typical issuer of a medium-term note is one with a high quality rating. The system used by commercial rating companies to rate medium-term notes issued by corporations is the same as that used for corporate bonds described earlier in this chapter. Usually the rating matches the bond rating of the corporate issuer for instruments of the same seniority level. Consequently, unsecured medium-term notes will usually carry the same rating as the corporate issuer's unsecured bonds; secured medium-term notes will typically carry the same rating as the corporate issuer's secured bonds. While at one time restricted to high-rated issuers, the medium-term note market has been opened up to lower-rated issuers by use of credit enhancements such as letters of credit or guarantees, or by collateralizing the issue with high-quality assets.

Types of Medium-Term Note Programs Offered

Merrill Lynch medium-term notes are a good example of the types of programs offered. As of February 1990, Merrill Lynch had six programs: (1) fixed-rate MTNs; (2) floating-rate MTNs; (3) credit-supported MTNs; (4) collateralized MTNs; (5) amortizing MTNs; and (6) multicurrency MTNs.[12]

Fixed-rate MTNs pay interest semiannually, on a 30/360 day basis, just as other corporate bonds. As noted above, the yield offered is a spread to a comparable maturity Treasury security.

Floating-rate MTNs can be selected with monthly, quarterly, or semiannual reset periods. There are a wide variety of indexes for the investor to select from: LIBOR, commercial paper composite rate, Treasury bills, or prime rate. The spread that is added or subtracted from the index selected will depend on the credit rating of the issuer.

Credit-supported MTNs are backed either by an irrevocable letter of credit or by some other guarantee. The rating of a credit-supported MTN

---

[10] From "A History of Leadership," in *Money Market Instruments*.

[11] The source of this information is "Medium–Term Note Issuer Profile: 1982-1989," in *Money Market Instruments*.

[12] The information about these programs is given in *Medium–Term Notes: An Investment Opportunity* (NY: Merrill Lynch Money Markets Inc.) and *Money Market Instruments*.

will depend on the rating of the entity furnishing the credit support. Issuers such as thrifts have issued collateralized MTNs, where the collateral supporting the issue is mortgage-backed securities.[13] Despite the lower credit rating of thrifts, overcollateralization has resulted in these issues receiving the highest credit rating.

Amortized MTNs offer an investor equal periodic dollar payments over the life of the issue. The payments include both principal and interest, and are structured so that the note is fully repaid when the final payment is made. Thus, an amortized note has a structure similar to a mortgage loan.[14] Amortized MTNs are typically unsecured corporate obligations. An advantage of this form of medium-term note is that the investor's credit-risk exposure declines as each payment is made by the issuer.

Multicurrency MTNs are nondollar denominated securities. The investor can choose from more than ten foreign currencies. The investor will be paid in U.S. dollars, however, based on the exchange rate prevailing at the time of payment. A designated exchange rate agent converts the interest and principal payments from the foreign currency into U.S. dollars.

COMMERCIAL PAPER

Commercial paper is a short-term unsecured promissory note issued in the open market that represents the obligation of the issuing entity. While commercial paper has been issued by municipal entities, the primary issuers of commercial paper are corporations. The issuance of commercial paper is an alternative to bank borrowing for large corporations (nonfinancial and financial) and municipalities with strong credit ratings.

While the commercial paper market was once limited to entities with strong credit ratings, in recent years some lower-credit rated corporations have issued commercial paper by obtaining credit enhancements or other collateral to allow them to enter the market as issuers.[15] Foreign corporations and sovereign issuers also issue commercial paper.

The commercial paper market has grown from $124 billion in December 1980 to $508 billion in October 1989. Since 1988, the size of the commercial paper market has exceeded that of the Treasury bill market.

---

[13] Mortgage–backed securities are discussed in Chapters 11 and 12.

[14] See Chapter 10.

[15] Some lower–rated companies have issued commercial paper without credit enhancements or collateral. Such issues are popularly referred to as *high–yield commercial paper*.

The maturity of commercial paper is typically less than 270 days, and the most common maturity range is 30 to 50 days or less.[16] There are reasons for this. First, the Securities Act of 1933 requires that securities be registered with the SEC. Special provisions exempt commercial paper from registration so long as the maturity does not exceed 270 days. Hence to avoid the costs associated with registering issues with the SEC, issuers rarely issue commercial paper with maturities exceeding 270 days. To pay off holders of maturing paper, issuers generally obtain the proceeds by issuing new commercial paper. The risk that the investor faces is that the issuer will be unable to issue new paper at maturity. As a safeguard against this, commercial paper is typically backed by unused bank credit lines. The rating agencies also rate commercial paper.

Issuers of Commercial Paper

Corporate issuers of commercial paper can be divided into financial companies and nonfinancial companies. There are three types of financial companies: captive finance companies, bank-related finance companies, and independent finance companies. Captive finance companies are subsidiaries of equipment manufacturing companies. Their primary purpose is to secure financing for the customers of the parent company. For example, the three major U.S. automobile manufacturers have captive finance companies: General Motors Acceptance Corporation (GMAC), Ford Credit, and Chrysler Financial. GMAC is by far the largest issuer of commercial paper in the U.S. Bank holding companies may have finance company subsidiaries that provide loans to individuals and businesses to acquire a wide range of products. Independent finance companies are those that are not subsidiaries of equipment manufacturing firms or bank holding companies.

While the issuers of commercial paper are typically companies with high credit ratings, smaller and less well-known companies with lower credit ratings have been able to issue paper in recent years. They have been able to do so by means of credit support from a firm with a high credit rating (such paper is called *credit-supported commercial paper*) or by collateralizing the issue with high-quality assets (such paper is called *asset-backed commercial paper*). An example of credit-supported commercial paper is one supported by a letter of credit. The terms of a letter of credit specify that the bank issuing it guarantees that if the issuer fails to pay off the paper when it comes due, the bank will do so. The bank will charge a fee for the letter of credit. From the issuer's perspective, the

---

[16] *Money Market Instruments,* p. 16.

fee enables it to enter the commercial paper market and obtain funding at a lower cost than bank borrowing would entail. Paper issued with such a credit enhancement is referred to as *LOC paper*. The credit enhancement may also take the form of a surety bond from an insurance company.[17]

Directly-Placed versus Dealer-Placed Paper

Commercial paper is classified as either direct paper or dealer paper. Direct paper is sold by the issuing firm directly to investors without using a securities dealer as an intermediary. A large majority of the issuers of direct paper are financial companies. These entities require continuous funds in order to provide loans to customers. As a result, they find it cost-effective to establish a sales force to sell their commercial paper directly to investors.

In the case of dealer-placed commercial paper, the issuer uses the services of a securities firm to sell its paper. Commercial paper sold in this way is referred to as "dealer paper."

The Secondary Market

There is little secondary trading activity in the commercial paper market. Typically, an investor in commercial paper is an entity that plans to hold the investment until maturity. This is understandable because an investor can purchase commercial paper with the specific maturity desired. Should an investor's economic circumstances change so that there is a need to sell the paper, it can be sold back to the dealer or, in the case of directly-placed paper, the issuer may repurchase it.

Yields on Commercial Paper

Commercial paper is typically a discount instrument. That is, it is sold at a price less than its maturity value. The difference between the maturity value and the price paid is the interest earned by the investor. For commercial paper, a year is treated as having 360 days. Commercial paper is quoted on a discount basis, just as Treasury bills are. There is some commercial paper that is issued as an interest-bearing instrument.

The yield offered on commercial paper tracks that of other money market instruments. The commercial paper rate is higher than that on Treasury bills for three reasons. First, the investor in commercial paper is exposed to credit risk. Second, interest earned from investing in Treasury bills is exempt from state and local income taxes. As a result, commercial

---

[17] A surety bond is a policy written by an insurance company to protect another party against loss or violation of a contract.

paper has to offer a higher yield to offset this tax advantage of Treasury bills. Finally, the liquidity of commercial paper is less than that of Treasury bills. The liquidity premium demanded is probably small, however, because investors typically follow a buy-and-hold strategy with commercial paper and so are less concerned with liquidity.

SUMMARY

Corporate bonds are debt instruments obligating a corporation to pay periodic interest with full repayment of principal at maturity. The promises of the corporate bond issuer and the rights of the investors are set forth in the bond indenture. Provisions to be specified include call and sinking fund provisions, as well as limitations on incurring further debt and on management powers.

Security for bonds may be real or personal property. A mortgage bond grants the bondholders a lien against the pledged assets. Collateral trust bonds are secured by securities owned by the issuer. Debenture bonds are not secured by a specific pledge of property; bondholders have the claim of general creditors on all assets of the issuer not pledged specifically to secure other debt. Subordinated debenture bonds are issues that rank after secured debt, after debenture bonds, and often after some general creditors in their claim on assets and earnings.

The risks associated with investing in corporate bonds are interest-rate risk, reinvestment risk, purchasing power risk, credit risk, call risk, liquidity risk, and event risk. Credit risk can be gauged by the quality rating assigned by the commercial rating agencies. Call risk is a disadvantage to bondholders because it exposes the holder to (1) uncertainty about the timing of cash flows, (2) reinvestment risk, and (3) price compression. Event risk refers to the possibility of an event that leads investors to doubt the ability of an issuer to make interest and principal payments. Event risk can occur because of a natural or industrial accident, or a takeover or corporate restructuring.

Special corporate bond features include convertible and exchangeable bonds, units of debt with warrants, putable bonds, zero-coupon bonds, and floating-rate securities.

Junk bonds or high-yield bonds are issues with quality ratings below triple-B. Recent years have seen the introduction of several complex bond structures in the junk bond area, particularly bonds issued for leveraged buyout financing and recapitalizations producing higher levels of debt-to-equity. These include deferred-coupon bonds (deferred-interest bonds, step-up bonds, and payment-in-kind bonds) and extendable reset bonds. The high-yield bond market has permitted the shifting of corporate borrowing from commercial banks to the public bond market.

Medium-term notes are corporate debt obligations offered on an ongoing basis. Medium-term notes offer maturities ranging from 9 months to 30 years to provide a financing alternative covering the gap between terms of commercial paper and long-term bonds.

Commercial paper is a short-term unsecured promissory note issued in the open market that represents the obligation of the issuing entity. It is sold on a discount basis. The maturity of commercial paper is typically less than 270 days, and the most common maturity range is 30 to 50 days or less. Financial and nonfinancial corporations issue commercial paper, with the majority issued by the former. Direct paper is sold by the issuing firm directly to investors without using a securities dealer as an intermediary; in the case of dealer-placed commercial paper, the issuer uses the services of a securities firm to sell its paper. There is little liquidity in the commercial paper market.

QUESTIONS FOR CHAPTER 6

1. a. What are the disadvantages of investing in a callable bond?

   b. What is the advantage to the issuer of issuing a callable bond?

2. What is the difference between a noncallable bond and a nonrefundable bond?

3. Indicate whether you agree or disagree with the two statements following:

   a. "A sinking fund provision in a bond issue benefits the investor."

   b. "A guaranteed bond is safer than a debenture bond."

4. What is the difference between a convertible bond and an exchangeable bond?

5. a. "A floating-rate note will always trade in the market at par value." Do you agree with this statement?

   b. "A floating-rate note and an extendable reset bond both have coupon rates readjusted periodically. Therefore, they are basically the same instrument." Do you agree with this statement?

6. a. What is a payment-in-kind bond?

   b. An investor who purchases a payment-in-kind bond will find that increased interest rate volatility will have an adverse economic impact. If interest rates rise substantially, there will be an adverse consequence. So too will a substantial decline in interest rates have adverse consequences. Why?

7. What is event risk?

8. What is a warrant?

9. What is a putable bond?

10. What are the three types of deferred-coupon structures?

11. Explain how accrued interest is calculated in the corporate bond market.

12. a. What is a medium-term note?

    b. What determines the yield that will be offered on a medium-term note?

    c. Give several examples of the types of medium-term notes.

13. a. Why is commercial paper an alternative to short-term bank borrowing for a corporation?

    b. What is the difference between directly-placed paper and dealer-placed paper?

    c. What does the yield spread between commercial paper and Treasury bills of the same maturity reflect?

Chapter 7

MUNICIPAL SECURITIES

Municipal securities are issued by state and local governments and by governmental entities such as "authorities" or special districts. There are both tax-exempt and taxable municipal bonds. "Tax-exempt" means that interest on municipal bonds is exempt from federal income taxation, and it may or may not be taxable at the state and local levels. Most municipal bonds outstanding are tax-exempt. Municipal securities come in a variety of types, with different redemption features, credit risks, and liquidity.

Municipal securities are issued for various purposes. Short-term notes typically are sold in anticipation of the receipt of funds from taxes or receipt of proceeds from the sale of a bond issue, for example. Proceeds from the sale of short-term notes permit the issuing municipality to cover seasonal and temporary imbalances between outlays for expenditures and inflows from taxes. Municipalities issue long-term bonds as the principal means for financing both (1) long-term capital projects such as schools, bridges, roads, and airports, and (2) long-term budget deficits that arise from current operations.

INVESTORS IN MUNICIPAL SECURITIES

The single most important advantage of municipal securities to investors is the exemption of interest income from federal taxation, and the investor groups that have purchased these securities not surprisingly are those that benefit the most from this exemption. Investors dominating the municipal securities market are households (retail investors), commercial banks, and property and casualty insurance companies. Although these three groups have dominated the market since the mid-1950s, their relative participation has shifted as the tax code has changed the relative demand for municipal securities. The most recent legislation that has influenced the demand for municipal securities includes the Tax Reform Act of 1986 and the Tax Act of 1990.

143

Retail investor participation in the municipal securities market has fluctuated considerably since 1972. Retail investor market share had been trending downward, with some interruptions, but in 1981 the trend was reversed, and individual investors are now the largest holders of municipal securities. Individual investors may purchase municipal securities directly or through mutual funds and unit trusts.

Two particular provisions of the Tax Reform Act of 1986 tend to offset one another, but on balance, make municipal securities more attractive to individual investors. First, the maximum marginal tax rate for individuals was reduced from 50% before tax revision to 28%. Some previously tax-exempt municipal interest income is now subject to an alternative minimum tax. Both the reduction in maximum marginal tax rates and the potential for taxation of municipal interest income under the alternative minimum tax reduce the value of the tax exemption feature. At the same time, however, the Tax Reform Act of 1986 eliminates or reduces the attractiveness of alternative investment vehicles that individual investors had been using to shelter investment income from taxation.

Then in 1990 the Tax Act served to increase the attractiveness of municipal securities by raising the maximum marginal tax rate to 33%. In fact, the effective tax rate is higher than 33% because of various limitations on deductions that households may take.

While individual investors are not entitled to deduct any interest cost that they incur to purchase municipal securities, commercial banks (before the Tax Reform Act of 1986) had been entitled to deduct 80% of the interest cost of funds used to purchase municipal bonds.[1] The 1986 act repealed this special exemption for banks for securities purchased after August 7, 1986. As a result, bank demand for municipal securities has declined dramatically.

Commercial banks hold the obligations of state and local governments for a variety of reasons besides shielding income from federal taxation. Most state and local governments mandate that public deposits at a bank be collateralized. Although Treasury or federal agency securities can serve as collateral, in fact the use of municipal securities is favored. Obligations of state and local governments may also be used as collateral when commercial banks borrow at the discount window of the Federal Reserve. Furthermore, banks frequently serve as underwriters or market makers for

---

[1] Specifically, the Internal Revenue Code specifies that interest paid or accrued on "indebtedness incurred or continued to purchase or carry obligations, the interest on which is wholly exempt from taxes," is not tax–deductible.

municipal securities, and these functions require maintaining inventories of these securities.

Purchases of municipal securities by property and casualty companies are primarily a function of their underwriting profit and investment income. Company profitability depends primarily upon the difference between the cost of claims filed and revenues generated from insurance premiums and investment income, and claims on property and casualty companies are difficult to anticipate. Varying court awards for liability suits, the effect of inflation upon replacement and repair costs, and the unpredictability of weather are the chief factors that affect the level of claims experienced. Premiums for various types of insurance also are subject to competitive pressures and to approval from state insurance commissioners.

As can be expected then, the profitability of property and casualty companies is cyclical. Normally, intense price competition follows highly profitable years. During these high-income periods, property and casualty companies typically step up their purchases of municipal securities in order to shield income from taxation. Lower rate increases for premiums are usually granted by state insurance commissioners during this time. Underwriting losses traditionally begin to exact a toll, as premium and investment income fail to keep pace with claims settlement costs. As underwriting losses mount, property and casualty insurance companies curtail their investment in municipal securities. The profitability cycle is completed when a company wins rate increases from state commissioners after sustaining continued underwriting losses.

The 1986 act includes several provisions that reduce, but do not eliminate, the demand for municipal securities by property and casualty insurance companies.[2]

TYPES AND FEATURES OF MUNICIPAL SECURITIES

There are basically two different types of municipal bond security structures: general obligation bonds and revenue bonds. There are also securities that share characteristics of both general obligation and revenue bonds.

General Obligation Bonds

General obligation bonds are debt instruments issued by states, counties, special districts, cities, towns, and school districts. Usually, a

---

[2] For an explanation of these provisions, see Sylvan G. Feldstein and Frank J. Fabozzi, *Dow Jones–Irwin Guide to Municipal Bonds* (Homewood, IL: Dow Jones–Irwin, 1987), p. 220.

general obligation bond is secured by the issuer's unlimited taxing power. Not all general obligation bonds are secured by unlimited taxing powers. Some are backed by taxes that are limited as to revenue sources and maximum property tax millage amounts.[3] Such bonds are known as *limited-tax general obligation bonds*. For smaller governmental entities such as school districts and towns, the only available unlimited taxing power is on property. For larger general obligation bond issuers such as states and big cities, tax revenue sources are more diverse, and may include corporate and individual income taxes, sales taxes, and property taxes. The diversity of security pledges for these larger issuers, such as states, causes sometimes their bonds to be referred to as *full faith and credit obligations*.

Certain general obligation bonds are secured not only by the issuer's general taxing powers to create revenues accumulated in a general fund, but also by certain identified fees, grants, and special charges, which provide additional revenues from outside the general fund. Such bonds are known as double-barreled in security because of the dual nature of the revenue sources.

Revenue Bonds

The second basic type of security structure is found in a revenue bond. Such bonds are issued for either project or enterprise financings where the bond issuers pledge to the bondholders the revenues generated by the operating projects financed. A feasibility study is performed before the endeavor is undertaken to determine whether it can be self supporting.

In 1970, only 33.5%, or $5.96 billion of the total amount of municipal bonds issued in that year, were revenue bonds; in 1989, 65.6%, or $68.58 billion, of all municipals issued were revenue bonds.[4]

Flow of Funds Structure: For a revenue bond, the revenue of the enterprise is pledged to service the debt of the issue. The details of how revenue received by the enterprise will be disbursed are set forth in the trust indenture. Typically, the flow of funds for a revenue bond is as follows. First, all revenues from the enterprise are put into a *revenue fund*. It is from the revenue fund that disbursements for expenses are made to the following funds: *operation and maintenance fund, sinking fund, debt*

---

[3] Generally, tax rates are assessed according to millage, where one mill is equal to 0.001. So, if a municipality has a millage rate of 5 mills, and a property has an assessed value of $80,000, the tax would be 0.005 times $80,000, or $400.

[4] These data are derived from the *Merrill Lynch Fixed Income Strategy Report*, First Quarter 1990, p. 22.

service reserve fund, renewal and replacement fund, reserve maintenance fund, and *surplus fund.* [5]

Operations of the enterprise have priority over the servicing of the issue's debt, and cash needed to operate the enterprise is deposited from the revenue fund into the operation and maintenance fund. The pledge of revenue to the bondholders is a *net* revenue pledge, net meaning after operation expenses, so cash required to service the debt is deposited next in the sinking fund. Disbursements are then made to bondholders as specified in the trust indenture. Any remaining cash is then distributed to the reserve funds. The purpose of the debt service reserve fund is to accumulate cash to cover any shortfall of future revenue to service the issue's debt. The specific amount that must be deposited is stated in the trust indenture. The function of the renewal and replacement fund is to accumulate cash for regularly scheduled major repairs and equipment replacement. The function of the reserve maintenance fund is to accumulate cash for extraordinary maintenance or replacement costs that might arise. Finally, if any cash remains after disbursement for operations, debt servicing, and reserves, it is deposited in the surplus fund. The issuer can use the cash in this fund in any way it deems appropriate.

There are various restrictive covenants included in the trust indenture for a revenue bond to protect the bondholders. A rate, or user charge, covenant dictates how charges will be set on the product or service sold by the enterprise. The covenant could specify that the minimum charges be set so as to satisfy both expenses and debt servicing, or to yield a higher rate to provide for a certain amount of reserves. An additional bonds covenant indicates whether additional bonds with the same lien may be issued. If additional bonds with the same lien may be issued, conditions that must first be satisfied are specified. Other covenants specify that the facility may not be sold, the amount of insurance to be maintained, requirements for recordkeeping and for the auditing of the enterprise's financial statements by an independent accounting firm, and requirements for maintaining the facilities in good order.

Following are examples of revenue bonds:[6]

Airport Revenue Bonds: The revenues securing these bonds usually come from either traffic-generated sources—such as landing fees, concession

---

[5] There are structures allowing an entity to tap revenues of the enterprise prior to the disbursement set forth in the flow of funds structure. For example, the revenue bond could be structured so that the revenue is first applied to the general obligation of the municipality that has issued the bond.

[6] The descriptions are taken from Sylvan G. Feldstein and Frank J. Fabozzi, "Municipal Bonds," Chapter 12 in Frank J. Fabozzi and Irving M. Pollack (eds.) *The Handbook of Fixed Income Securities* (Homewood, IL: Dow Jones-Irwin, 1987), pp. 292–294

fees, and airline fueling fees—or lease revenues from one or more airlines for the use of a specific facility such as a terminal or hangar.

College and University Revenue Bonds: The revenues securing these bonds usually include dormitory room rental fees, tuition payments, and sometimes the general assets of the college or university as well.

Hospital Revenue Bonds: The security for hospital revenue bonds usually depends on federal and state reimbursement programs (such as Medicaid and Medicare), third-party commercial payers (such as Blue Cross, HMOs, and private insurance), and individual patient payments.

Single-Family Mortgage Revenue Bonds: These bonds are usually secured by the mortgages and loan repayments on single-family homes. Security features vary but can include Federal Housing Administration (FHA), Veterans Administration (VA), or private mortgage insurance.

Multifamily Revenue Bonds: These revenue bonds are usually issued for multifamily housing projects for senior citizens and low-income families. Some housing revenue bonds are secured by mortgages that are federally insured; others receive federal government operating subsidies or interest-cost subsidies; still others receive only local property tax reductions as subsidies.

Industrial Revenue Bonds: Generally, industrial revenue bonds are issued by state and local governments on behalf of individual corporations and businesses. The security for these bonds usually depends on the economic soundness of the particular corporation or business involved.

Public Power Revenue Bonds: These bonds are secured by revenues to be produced from electrical operating plants. Some bonds are for a single issuer, who constructs and operates power plants and then sells the electricity. Other public power revenue bonds are issued by groups of public and private investor-owned utilities for the joint financing of the construction of one or more power plants.

Resource Recovery Revenue Bonds: A resource recovery facility converts refuse (solid waste) into commercially salable energy, recoverable products, and a residue to be landfilled. The major revenues securing these bonds usually are (1) fees paid by those who deliver the waste to the facility for disposal, (2) revenues from steam, electricity, or refuse-derived fuel sold to either an electric power company or another energy user, and (3) revenues from the sale of recoverable materials such as aluminum and steel scrap.

Seaport Revenue Bonds: The security for these bonds can include specific lease agreements with the benefiting companies, or pledged marine terminal and cargo tonnage fees.

Sports Complex and Convention Center Revenue Bonds: These bonds usually receive revenues from sporting or convention events held at the facilities and, in some instances, from earmarked outside revenues such as local motel and hotel room taxes.

Student Loan Revenue Bonds: Student loan repayments under student loan revenue bond programs are sometimes 100% guaranteed either directly by the federal government or by a state guaranty agency.

Toll Road and Gas Tax Revenue Bonds: There are generally two types of highway revenue bonds. Bond proceeds of the first type are used to build such specific revenue-producing facilities as toll roads, bridges, and tunnels. For these pure enterprise-type revenue bonds, the pledged revenues usually are the monies collected through tolls. The second type of highway revenue bond is one where bondholders are paid by earmarked revenues outside of toll collections, such as gasoline taxes, automobile registration payments, and driver's license fees.

Water Revenue Bonds: Water revenue bonds are issued to finance the construction of water treatment plants, pumping stations, collection facilities, and distribution systems. Revenues usually come from connection fees and charges paid by the users of the water systems.

Hybrid and Special Bond Securities

Though having certain characteristics of general obligation bonds and revenue bonds, there are some municipal bonds that have more unique security structures as well. Five examples are insured bonds, letter of credit-backed bonds, moral obligation bonds, refunded bonds, and "troubled city" bailout bonds.

Insured bonds are backed by insurance policies written by commercial insurance companies, as well as by the credit of the municipal issuer. Municipal bond insurance is a contractual commitment by an insurance company to pay the bondholder any bond principal and/or coupon interest that is due on a stated maturity date but that has not been paid by the bond issuer. Once issued, this municipal bond insurance usually extends for the term of the bond issue, and it cannot be canceled by the insurance company.

Municipal bond insurance has been available since 1971. By 1990, approximately 25% of all new municipal issues were insured. Some of the largest and financially strongest insurance companies in the U.S. have been participants in this industry, as well as smaller monoline (single–line) insurance companies. The monoline companies following are major municipal bond insurers as of 1990: AMBAC Indemnity Corporation,

Capital Guaranty Insurance Company, Financial Guaranty Insurance Corporation, and Municipal Bond Investors Assurance. In general, although insured municipal bonds sell at yields lower than they would without the insurance, they tend to have yields substantially higher than triple-A-rated noninsured municipal bonds.

Some municipal bonds are backed by a commercial bank letter of credit besides being secured by the issuer's cash flow revenues. A moral obligation bond is a security structure for state-issued bonds legally authorizing but not requiring the state legislature to make an appropriation out of general state tax revenues.

Refunded bonds (also called prerefunded bonds) are bonds that originally may have been issued as general obligation or revenue bonds but that are now secured by an "escrow fund" consisting entirely of direct U.S. government obligations that are sufficient for paying the bondholders. There are three reasons why a municipal issuer may refund an issue by creating an escrow fund. First, many refunded issues were originally issued as revenue bonds. Included in revenue issues are restrictive bond covenants that the municipality may wish to eliminate. Creation of an escrow fund to pay the bondholders legally eliminates any restrictive bond covenants. Second, some issues are refunded in order to alter the maturity schedule of the obligation. Finally, when interest rates have declined after a municipal security has been issued, there is a tax arbitrage opportunity available to the issuer who can pay existing bondholders a lower interest rate and use the proceeds to create a portfolio of U.S. government securities paying a higher interest rate.[7] Most refunded bonds are structured to be called at the first call date. When the objective is to eliminate restrictive bond covenants, refunded bonds are structured to meet the maturity schedule of the original bond issue. Because refunded bonds are collateralized by U.S. government obligations, they are among the safest of all municipal obligations if the escrow is properly structured.[8]

"Troubled city" bailout bonds are structured to appear as pure revenue bonds, but in essence they are not. Revenues come from general purpose taxes and revenues that otherwise would have gone to the state or city general fund. These bond structures were created to bail out underlying general obligation bond issuers from severe budget deficits.

---

[7] Because the interest rate that a municipality pays on borrowed funds is lower than the interest rate paid by the U.S. government, in the absence of any restrictions in the tax code, a municipal issuer can realize a tax arbitrage. This can be done by issuing a bond and immediately investing the proceeds in a U.S. government security. There are tax rules that prevent such arbitrage. Should a municipal issuer violate the tax-arbitrage rules, the issue will be ruled to be taxable. However, if subsequent to the issuance of a bond, interest rates decline so that the issuer finds it advantageous to call the bond, establishment of the escrow fund does not violate the tax-arbitrage rules.

[8] For a further discussion of refunded bonds, see Chapter 5 in Feldstein and Fabozzi, *Dow Jones–Irwin Guide to Municipal Bonds*.

Examples are the New York State Municipal Assistance Corporation of the City of New York Bonds (MAC) and the State of Illinois Chicago School Finance Authority Bonds.

Municipal Notes

Municipal securities issued for periods ranging not beyond three years are considered to be short-term in nature. These include tax anticipation notes (TANs), revenue anticipation notes (RANs), grant anticipation notes (GANs), bond anticipation notes (BANs), and tax-exempt commercial paper.

TANs, RANs, GANs, and BANs are temporary borrowings by states, local governments, and special jurisdictions. Usually, notes are issued for a period of 12 months, although it is not uncommon for notes to be issued for periods as short as 3 months and for as long as 3 years. TANs and RANs (also known as TRANs) are issued in anticipation of the collection of taxes or other expected revenues. These are borrowings to even out irregular flows into the treasuries of the issuing entity. BANs are issued in anticipation of the sale of long-term bonds.

Tax-exempt commercial paper is issued for periods ranging from 30 to 270 days. Generally tax-exempt commercial paper has backstop commercial bank agreements, which can include an irrevocable letter of credit, a revolving credit agreement, or a line of credit.

Redemption Features

Municipal bonds are issued with one of two debt retirement structures or a combination of both. Either a bond has a serial maturity structure or a term maturity structure. A serial maturity structure requires a portion of the debt obligation to be retired each year. A term maturity structure provides for the debt obligation to be repaid on a final date. Usually term bonds have maturities ranging from 20 to 40 years and retirement schedules (sinking fund provisions) that begin 5 to 10 years before the final term maturity.

Municipal bonds may be called prior to the stated maturity date, either according to a mandatory sinking fund or at the option of the issuer. In revenue bonds, there is a *catastrophe call* provision that requires the issuer to call the entire issue if the facility is destroyed.

Special Investment Features

In the previous chapter, we described zero-coupon bonds, floating-rate bonds, and putable bonds in the corporate bond market. The municipal market also has securities with these features.

In the municipal bond market there are two types of zero-coupon bonds. One type is issued at a very deep discount and matures at par. The difference between the par value and the purchase price represents a predetermined compound yield. These zero-coupon bonds are similar to those issued in the taxable bond market for Treasuries and corporates. The second type is called a "municipal multiplier," or "compound interest bond." This is a bond issued at par that has interest payments. The interest payments are not distributed to the holder of the bond until maturity, but the issuer agrees to reinvest the undistributed interest payments at the bond's yield to maturity when it was issued. For example, suppose that a 10%, ten-year coupon bond with a par value of $5,000 is sold at par to yield 10%. Every six months, the maturity value of this bond is increased by 5% of the maturity value of the previous six months. At the end of ten years, the maturity value of the bond will be equal to $13,266.[9] In the case of a ten-year zero bond priced to yield 10%, the bond would have a maturity value of $5,000 but sell for $1,884 when issued.[10]

CREDIT RATINGS

While municipal bonds have long been considered second in safety only to U.S. Treasury securities, today there are concerns about the credit risks of municipal securities.[11]

The first concern came out of the New York City billion dollar financial crisis in 1975. On February 25, 1975, the state of New York's Urban Development Corporation defaulted on a $100 million note issue that was the obligation of New York City; many market participants had been convinced that the state of New York would not allow the issue to default. Although New York City was able later to obtain a $140 million revolving credit from banks to cure the default, lenders became concerned that the city would face difficulties in repaying its accumulated debt, which stood at $14 billion on March 31, 1975.[12] This financial crisis sent

---

[9] This is found by computing the future value of $5,000 20 periods from now using a 5% interest rate. That is,

$$\$5,000 \times (1.05)^{20} = \$13,266$$

[10] This is found by computing the present value of $5,000 20 periods from now using a 5% interest rate. That is,

$$\$5,000 \times \frac{1}{(1.05)^{20}} = \$1,884$$

[11] For a history of defaults of municipal bonds, see Chapter 2 in Feldstein and Fabozzi, *The Dow Jones–Irwin Guide to Municipal Bonds*.

a loud and clear warning to market participants in general—regardless of supposedly ironclad protection for the bondholder, when issuers such as large cities have severe financial difficulties, the financial stakes of public employee unions, vendors, and community groups may be dominant forces in balancing budgets. This reality was reinforced by the federal bankruptcy law taking effect in October 1979, which makes it easier for the issuer of a municipal security to go into bankruptcy.

The second reason for concern about municipal securities credit risk is proliferation in this market of innovative financing techniques to secure new bond issues. In addition to the established general obligation bonds and revenue bonds, there are now more nonvoter–approved, innovative, and legally untested security mechanisms. These innovative financing mechanisms include "moral obligation" bonds and commercial bank-backed letters of credit bonds, to name a few. What distinguishes these newer bonds from the more traditional general obligation and revenue bonds is that there is no history of court decisions or other case law that firmly establishes the rights of the bondholders and the obligations of the issuers. It is not possible to determine in advance the probable legal outcome if the newer financing mechanisms were to be challenged in court. This is illustrated most dramatically by default on bonds of the Washington Public Power Supply System (WPPSS), where bondholder rights to certain revenues were not upheld by the highest court in the state of Washington.

As with corporate bonds, some institutional investors in the municipal bond market rely on their own in-house municipal credit analysts for determining the creditworthiness of a municipal issue; other investors rely on commercial credit ratings. The two leading commercial rating companies for municipals are Moody's and Standard & Poor's, and the assigned rating system is essentially the same as that used for corporate bonds.

In evaluating general obligation bonds, the commercial rating companies assess information in four basic categories.[13] The first category includes information on the issuer's debt structure to determine the overall debt burden. The second category relates to the issuer's ability and political discipline to maintain sound budgetary policy. The focus of attention here usually is on the issuer's general operating funds and

---

[12] *Securities and Exchange Commission Staff Report on Transactions in Securities of the City of New York* (Washington, D.C.: U.S. Government Printing Office, 1977) , p. 2. The reasons for the New York City financial crisis are documented in Donna E. Shalala and Carol Bellamy, "A State Saves a City: The New York Case," *Duke Law Journal* (January 1976), pp. 1119-1126.

[13] Although there are many similarities in the ways Moody's and Standard & Poor's approach the credit rating of general obligation bonds, there are differences in their approaches as well. For a discussion of these differences, see Feldstein and Fabozzi, "Municipal Bonds," Chapter 12 in *The Handbook of Fixed Income Securities*, pp. 304-309

whether it has maintained at least balanced budgets over three to five years. The third category involves determining the specific local taxes and intergovernmental revenues available to the issuer, as well as obtaining historical information both on tax collection rates, which are important when looking at property tax levies, and on the dependence of local budgets on specific revenue sources. The fourth and last category of information necessary to the credit analysis is an assessment of the issuer's overall socioeconomic environment. The determinations that have to be made here include trends of local employment distribution and composition, population growth, real estate property valuation, and personal income, among other economic factors.

While there are numerous security structures for revenue bonds, the underlying principle in rating is whether the project being financed will generate sufficient cash flow to satisfy the obligations due bondholders.[14] A natural question to ask is: How good are the ratings? Of the municipal securities that were rated by a commercial rating company in 1929 and plunged into default in 1932, 78% had been rated double-A or better, and 48% had been rated triple-A. Since then the ability of rating agencies to assess the creditworthiness of municipal securities has evolved to a level of general industry acceptance and respectability. In most instances, ratings adequately describe the financial condition of the issuers and identify the credit risk factors. A small but significant number of recent instances still have caused market participants to reexamine their reliance solely on the opinions of the rating agencies. One example is the bonds of the Washington Public Power Supply System mentioned above. The two major commercial rating companies gave their highest ratings to these bonds in the early 1980s. While these high quality ratings were in effect, WPPSS sold over $8 billion in long-term bonds. By 1986 over $2 billion of these bonds were in default.

RISKS ASSOCIATED WITH INVESTING IN MUNICIPAL SECURITIES

The investor in municipal securities is exposed to the same risks affecting corporate bonds plus an additional one that may be labeled *tax risk*. There are two types of tax risk to which tax-exempt municipal securities buyers are exposed. The first is the risk that the federal income tax rate will be reduced. The higher the marginal tax rate, the greater the value of the tax exemption feature. As the marginal tax rate declines, the price of a tax-

---

[14] A comprehensive discussion of the analysis of various revenue bond structures is found in: Sylvan G. Feldstein, Frank J. Fabozzi, and Irving M. Pollack (eds), *The Municipal Bond Handbook: Volume II* (Homewood, IL: Dow Jones–Irwin, 1983); and Feldstein and Fabozzi, *Dow Jones–Irwin Guide to Municipal Bonds*.

exempt municipal security will decline. When in 1986 there were tax proposals to reduce marginal tax rates, tax-exempt municipal bonds began trading at lower prices.

The second type of tax risk is that a municipal bond issued as a tax-exempt issue may be eventually declared by the Internal Revenue Service to be taxable. This may occur because many municipal revenue bonds have elaborate security structures that could be subject to future adverse congressional action and IRS interpretation. A loss of the tax exemption feature will cause the municipal bond to decline in value in order to provide a yield comparable to similar taxable bonds. As an example, in June of 1980, the Battery Park City Authority sold $97.315 million in notes, which at the time of issuance legal counsel advised were exempt from federal income taxation. In November of 1980, however, the IRS held that interest on these notes was not exempt. The issue was not settled until September 1981, when the Authority and the IRS signed a formal agreement resolving the matter so as to make the interest on the notes tax-exempt.

THE PRIMARY MARKET

A substantial number of municipal obligations are brought to market each week. A state or local government can market its new issue by offering bonds publicly to the investing community or by placing them privately with a small group of investors. When a public offering is selected, the issue usually is underwritten by investment bankers and/or municipal bond departments of commercial banks. Public offerings may be marketed by either competitive bidding or direct negotiations with underwriters. When an issue is marketed via competitive bidding, the issue is awarded to the bidder submitting the best bid.

Most states mandate that general obligation issues be marketed through competitive bidding, but generally this is not required for revenue bonds. Usually state and local governments require a competitive sale to be announced in a recognized financial publication, such as *The Bond Buyer*, which is a trade publication for the municipal bond industry. *The Bond Buyer* also provides information on upcoming competitive sales and most negotiated sales, as well as the results of previous weeks' sales.

An official statement describing the issue and the issuer is prepared for new offerings.

THE SECONDARY MARKET

Municipal bonds are traded in the over-the-counter market, which is supported by hundreds of municipal bond dealers across the country.

Markets are maintained on smaller issuers (referred to as "local credits") by regional brokerage firms, local banks, and by some of the larger Wall Street firms. Larger issuers (referred to as "general names") are supported by the larger brokerage firms and banks, many of whom have investment banking relationships with these issuers. There are brokers who serve as intermediaries in the sale of large blocks of municipal bonds among dealers and large institutional investors. *The Bond Buyer's* "munifacts" teletype system, sends out a list of daily offerings and many dealers advertise their municipal bond offerings for the retail market in what is known as *The Blue List*. This is a 100-plus-page booklet published every weekday by the Standard & Poor's Corporation that gives municipal securities offerings and prices.

In the municipal bond markets, an odd lot of bonds is $25,000 or less in par value for retail investors. For institutions, anything below $100,000 in par value is considered an odd lot. Dealer spreads depend on several factors. For the retail investor, the spread can range from as low as one-quarter of one point ($12.50 per $5,000 par value) on large blocks of actively traded bonds to four points ($200 per $5,000 of par value) for odd lot sales of an inactive issue. For institutional investors, the dealer spread rarely exceeds one-half of one point ($25 per $5,000 of par value).

The convention for both corporate and Treasury bonds is to quote prices as a percentage of par value with 100 equal to par. Municipal bonds, however, generally are traded and quoted in terms of yield (yield to maturity or yield to call). The price of the bond in this case is called a basis price. The exception is certain long-maturity revenue bonds. A bond traded and quoted in dollar prices (actually, as a percentage of par value) is called a dollar bond.

YIELDS ON MUNICIPAL BONDS

Because of the tax-exempt feature of municipal bonds, the yield on municipal bonds is less than that on Treasuries with the same maturity. The ratio of municipal yields to Treasury yields varies over time. The ratio has increased recently because of the decrease in the marginal tax rate since the 1986 Tax Act, making the tax-exemption feature less attractive to investors.

A common yield measure used to compare the yield on a tax-exempt municipal bond with a comparable taxable bond is the equivalent taxable yield. The equivalent taxable yield is computed as follows:

Equivalent taxable yield = Tax-exempt yield/(1 − Marginal tax rate)

For example, suppose an investor in the 33% marginal tax bracket is considering the acquisition of a tax-exempt municipal bond that offers a yield of 8%. The equivalent taxable yield is 11.94%, as shown below:

Equivalent taxable yield = .08/(1 − .33) = .1194, or 11.94%

When computing the equivalent taxable yield, the traditionally computed yield to maturity is not the tax-exempt yield if the issue is selling at a discount because only the coupon interest is exempt from federal income taxes. Instead, the yield to maturity after an assumed tax rate on the capital gain is computed and used in the numerator of the formula above. The yield to maturity after an assumed tax on the capital gain is calculated in the same manner as the traditional yield to maturity as explained in Chapter 3. Instead of using the maturity value in computing the yield, the net proceeds after an assumed tax rate on the capital gain are used.

Yield spreads within the municipal bond market are attributable to several reasons: (1) differences between credit ratings, (2) differences between in-state and general market, and (3) differences between maturities.

Our observations about quality spreads between credit ratings for corporate bonds over the interest rate cycle are true for municipal bonds as well: quality spreads widen during recessionary periods, but narrow during periods of economic prosperity. Another factor that can cause changes in the quality spread is a temporary oversupply of issues within a market sector. For example, a substantial new-issue volume of high-grade state general obligation bonds may tend to decrease the spread between high-grade and lower-grade revenue bonds. In a weak market environment, it is easier for high-grade municipal bonds to come to market than weaker ones. Therefore, it is not uncommon for high grades to flood weak markets, while at the same time there is a relative scarcity of medium-and lower-grade municipal bond issues.

Bonds of municipal issuers located in certain states yield considerably less than issues of identical credit quality that come from other states that trade in the "general market." One reason for this is that states often exempt interest from in-state issues from state and local personal income taxes, while interest from out-of-state issues is generally not exempt. Consequently, in states with high income taxes such as New York and California, strong investor demand for in-state issues will reduce their yields relative to bonds of issuers located in states where state and local income taxes are not important considerations (for example, Florida).

In the Treasury and corporate bond markets, it is not unusual to find at different times all four shapes for the yield curve described in Chapter 9. In the municipal bond market, long-term bonds typically offer higher yields than short-and intermediate-term bonds; that is, the municipal yield curve is typically normal or upward-sloping.

REGULATION OF THE MUNICIPAL SECURITIES MARKET[15]

Congress has specifically exempted municipal securities from both the registration requirements of the Securities Act of 1933 and the periodic reporting requirements of the Securities Exchange Act of 1934. Antifraud provisions apply nevertheless to offerings of or dealings in municipal securities.

The reasons for the exemption afforded municipal securities appear to relate to (1) a desire for governmental comity, (2) the absence of recurrent abuses in transactions involving municipal securities, (3) the greater level of sophistication of investors in this segment of the securities markets (that is, institutional investors once dominated the market), and (4) the fact that there historically have been few defaults by municipal issuers. Consequently, in the period between enactment of federal securities acts in the early 1930s and the early 1970s, the municipal securities market was relatively free from federal regulation.

In the early 1970s, however, circumstances changed. As incomes rose, individuals participated in the municipal securities market to a much greater extent, and public concern over selling practices occurred with greater frequency. Moreover, the financial problems of some municipal issuers, notably New York City, made market participants aware that municipal issuers have the potential to experience severe financial difficulties approaching bankruptcy levels.

Congress passed the Securities Act Amendment of 1975 to broaden federal regulation in the municipals market. This legislation brought brokers and dealers in the municipal securities market, including banks that underwrite and trade municipal securities, under the regulatory umbrella of the Securities Exchange Act of 1934. The legislation mandates also that the SEC establish a 15-member Municipal Securities Rulemaking Board (MSRB) as an independent, self-regulatory agency, whose primary responsibility is to develop rules governing the activities of banks, brokers, and dealers in municipal securities. Rules adopted by the MSRB must be approved by the SEC. The MSRB has no enforcement

---

[15] The discussion in this section is drawn from Thomas F. Mitchell, "Disclosure and the Municipal Bond Industry," Chapter 40, and Nancy H. Wojtas, "The SEC and Investor Safeguards," Chapter 42 in Frank J. Fabozzi, Sylvan G. Feldstein, Irving M. Pollack, and Frank Zarb (eds.), *The Municipal Bond Handbook: Volume I* (Homewood, IL: Dow Jones–Irwin, 1983.)

or inspection authority. That authority is vested with the SEC, the National Association of Securities Dealers, and certain regulatory banking agencies such as the Federal Reserve Bank.

The Securities Act Amendment of 1975 does not require municipal issuers to comply with the registration requirement of the 1933 act or the periodic reporting requirement of the 1934 act, despite several legislative proposals to mandate financial disclosure. Even in the absence of federal legislation dealing with the regulation of financial disclosure, however, underwriters began insisting upon greater disclosure as it became apparent that the SEC was exercising stricter application of the antifraud provisions. Moreover, underwriters recognized the need for improved disclosure to sell municipal securities to an investing public that has become much more concerned about the credit risk of municipal issuers.

In June 1989, the SEC formally approved the first bond disclosure rule, effective January 1, 1990. While the disclosure rule has several exemptions, in general it applies to new-issue municipal securities offerings of $1 million or more.

SUMMARY

Municipal securities are issued by state and local governments and their authorities, with the coupon interest on most issues being exempt from federal income taxes. The primary investors in these securities are households (which includes mutual funds), commercial banks, and property and casualty insurance companies. Changes in the tax law have had an effect on the relative attractiveness of municipal securities for these three groups of investors.

The two basic security structures are general obligation bonds and revenue bonds. The former are secured by the issuer's general taxing power. Revenue bonds are used to finance specific projects and are dependent on revenues from those projects to satisfy the obligations. There are also hybrid securities that have certain characteristics of both general obligation and revenue bonds, and some securities that have unique structures.

Municipal notes are issued for shorter periods (one to three years) than municipal bonds. Municipal bonds may be retired with a serial maturity structure, a term maturity structure, or a combination of both. As in the case of corporate bonds, there are zero-coupon bonds and floating-rate bonds. Investing in municipal securities exposes investors to the same qualitative risks as investing in corporate bonds, with the additional risk that a change in the tax law may affect the price of municipal securities adversely. Because of the tax-exempt feature, yields on municipal securities are lower than those on comparably rated taxable securities. Within the municipal bond market, there are quality spreads and maturity spreads. Moreover, there are yield spreads related to differences between in-state issues and general market issues.

QUESTIONS FOR CHAPTER 7

1. Name the three major investors in municipal securities.

2. If it is expected that Congress will change the tax law so as to increase marginal tax rates, what do you think will happen to the price of municipal bonds?

3. Why would a property and casualty insurance company shift its allocation of funds from taxable fixed-income securities to tax-exempt fixed-income securities?

4. a. What is the difference between a general obligation bond and a revenue bond?

    b. Which type of bond would an investor analyze using an approach similar to that for analyzing a corporate bond?

5 a. In a revenue bond, which fund has priority when funds are disbursed from the reserve fund: the operation and maintenance fund, or the debt service reserve fund?

    b. In a revenue bond, what is a catastrophe call provision?

6. Define TAN, RAN, GAN, and BAN.

7. What is the tax risk associated with investing in a municipal bond?

8. "An insured municipal bond is safer than an uninsured municipal bond." Do you agree with this statement?

9. a. What is a refunded (or prerefunded) bond?

    b. Why might a municipality refund an issue by creating an escrow fund?

10. a. What is the equivalent taxable yield for an investor facing a 28% marginal tax rate who can purchase a tax-exempt municipal bond with a yield of 7.2% ?

    b. What are the limitations of using the equivalent taxable yield as a measure of relative value of a tax-exempt bond versus a taxable bond?

Chapter 8

NON-U.S. BONDS

Prior to the 1980s, U.S. bond investors invested exclusively in U.S. domestic bonds. Among the reasons for their lack of participation in the non-U.S. bond markets are: lack of familiarity with the structure of these markets; lack of familiarity with interest rate movements in these markets; concern about the liquidity of these markets; unfamiliarity with and concern about foreign sovereign and private credit risk; and, foreign withholding taxes on U.S. investors.

In recent years, however, U.S. investors have become increasingly aware of non-U.S. interest rate movements and their relationship with U.S. interest rates. In addition, foreign countries have liberalized their bond markets, making them more liquid and more accessible to international investors. In many cases, withholding taxes have been eliminated or reduced. Futures and options markets have been developed on government bonds in several major countries, permitting the more effective implementation of hedging and arbitrage strategies. And, in general, there is an increased awareness of the non-U.S. bond markets as potential sources of return enhancement and/or risk reduction. As a result, U.S. bond managers—mainly money managers who manage pension funds or other institutional monies, and mutual funds or others who manage retail monies—have increasingly adopted a global approach and invested in bonds from several countries.

Many global investors participate only in the foreign government bond markets, rather than the nongovernment bond markets, because of the low credit risk, the liquidity, and the simplicity of the government markets. While nongovernment markets ("semigovernment," local government, corporate, and mortgage bond markets) provide higher yields, they also have greater credit risks, and foreign investors may not be ready to accept alien credit risks, and less liquidity.

The focus of this chapter is on several non-U.S. bond markets, more specifically, the Eurobond market, non-U.S. government bond markets, and the two largest non-U.S. bond markets, Japan and Germany.

CLASSIFICATION OF GLOBAL BOND MARKETS

There is no uniform system for classifying the sectors of the global bond market, although one possible classification is as follows. From the perspective of a given country, the global bond market can be classified into two markets: an *internal bond market* and an *external bond market*. The internal bond market is also called the *national bond market*. It can be decomposed into two parts: the domestic bond market and the foreign bond market. The domestic bond market is where issuers domiciled in the country issue bonds and where those bonds are subsequently traded.

The foreign bond market of a country is where bonds of issuers not domiciled in the country are issued and traded. For example, in the U.S. the foreign bond market is the market where bonds are issued by non-U.S. entities and then subsequently traded. Bonds traded in the U.S. foreign bond market are nicknamed *Yankee bonds*. In Japan, a yen-denominated bond issued by a British corporation and subsequently traded in Japan's bond market is part of the Japanese foreign bond market. Yen-denominated bonds issued by non-Japanese entities are nicknamed *Samurai bonds*. Foreign bonds in the United Kingdom are referred to as *Bulldog bonds*, in the Netherlands *Rembrandt bonds*, and in Spain *Matador bonds*.

Regulatory authorities in the country where the bond is issued impose certain rules governing the issuance of foreign bonds. These may include (1) restrictions on the bond structures that may be issued (e.g., unsecured debt, zero-coupon bonds, convertible bonds, etc.), (2) restrictions on the minimum or maximum size of an issue and/or the frequency with which an issuer may come to market, (3) a waiting period before an issuer can bring the issue to market (imposed to avoid an oversupply of issues), (4) a minimum quality standard (credit rating) for the issue or issuer, (5) disclosure and periodic reporting requirements, and (6) restrictions on the types of financial institutions permitted to underwrite issues. The 1980s have been characterized by general government relaxation or abolition of these restrictions so as to open up their bond markets to issuers.

The *external bond market*, also called the *international bond market*, includes bonds with the following distinguishing features: (1) they are underwritten by an international syndicate, (2) at issuance they are offered simultaneously to investors in a number of countries, (3) they are issued outside the jurisdiction of any single country, and (4) they are in unregistered form. The external bond market is commonly referred to as the *offshore bond market*, or, more popularly, the *Eurobond market*. The classification we use is by no means universally accepted. Some market observers refer to the external bond market as consisting of the foreign bond market and the Eurobond market.

In September 1989 the first true "global bond" was issued. This was a ten-year $1.5 billion offering of the World Bank. What makes this issue a global bond is its simultaneous offering in the U.S. Yankee bond market and in the Eurobond market. It represents the first attempt to surmount the fragmented market for U.S. dollar-denominated bonds. Since then global bonds have accounted for three-quarters of the $3 to $4 billion raised by the World Bank.

A few corporations have since begun to issue global bonds. Since June 1990, Citicorp has had several global bond issues ranging from $1 to $1.5 billion. Each issue was backed by credit–card receivables and denominated in U.S. dollars. Two Canadian utility companies, Ontario–Hydro and Hydro–Quebec, have had several global bond offerings. The first global non–U.S. dollar issue was done by Ontario–Hydro in December 1990, denominated in Canadian dollars. No global bond issues have been denominated in European currencies or Japanese yen.[1]

FOREIGN EXCHANGE RISK AND BOND RETURNS

The return to U.S. investors from investments in non-U.S. bonds that are denominated in a foreign currency consists of two components: (1) the return on the security measured in the currency in which the bond is denominated (called "local currency" return), which results from coupon payments, reinvestment income, and capital gains/losses; and (2) changes in the foreign exchange rate.

An *exchange rate* is the amount of one currency that can be exchanged for another currency, or the price of one currency in terms of another currency. Since the early 1970s, exchange rates between currencies have been free to float, with market forces determining the

---

[1] In general, it is felt that the following three characteristics must be met for a corporation to issue global bonds. First, the issuer must have a consistent demand for funds. Second, the amount of funds needed on a regular basis must be around $1 billion. Finally, the issuer must have a high credit rating. Since there are not many corporations that would satisfy these conditions, the opportunity to raise funds via a global bond offering is limited. These three characteristics were suggested by Dan Roth, treasurer of the World Bank. (Desmond Dodd, "New Currencies Seen as Next Test for Global Issues," *Corporate Financing Week*, Special Supplement (November 25, 1991), p.9.)

relative value of a currency.[2] Thus, each day a currency's value may stay the same, increase, or decrease relative to that of another currency. When a currency declines in value relative to another currency, it is said to have depreciated relative to the other currency. Alternatively, this is the same as saying that the other currency has appreciated.

From the perspective of a U.S. investor, the cash flows of assets denominated in a foreign currency expose the investor to uncertainty as to the cash flow in U.S. dollars. The actual U.S. dollars that the investor gets depend on the exchange rate between the U.S. dollar and the foreign currency at the time the nondollar cash flow is received and exchanged for U.S. dollars. If the foreign currency depreciates (declines in value) relative to the U.S. dollar, the dollar value of the cash flows will be proportionately less. This risk is referred to as *foreign exchange risk.*

Skeptics of global bond investment strategies have asserted that during periods when the U.S. dollar is strengthening, global bond investment strategies will not be popular with U.S. investors. Even in a period of dollar stability or strength, however, nondollar bond investments may continue to be used by U.S. investors for three basic reasons. First, the currency component of the investment may be hedged with foreign exchange spot, forwards, futures, or options instruments (although there is a cost of hedging). The decision not to hedge the currency component can then be regarded as an active currency play. Second, global investment—with the currency hedged —permits investment strategies based on interest rate changes in various countries, thereby providing additional dimensions to the actual investment decision or a broader range of investment choices. Finally, diversifying bond investments across countries—particularly with the currency hedged—may provide diversification resulting in a reduction in risk. Thus, it is likely that global bond investing will continue to increase in any U.S. dollar environment, with the dollar either weakening or strengthening.

EUROBOND MARKET

The Eurobond market is divided into sectors depending on the currency in which the issue is denominated. For example, when Eurobonds are denominated in U.S. dollars, they are referred to as *Eurodollar bonds.* Eurobonds denominated in Japanese yen are referred to as *Euroyen bonds.*

In recent years, it has become increasingly difficult to classify a bond

---

[2] In practice, national monetary authorities can intervene in the foreign exchange market for their currency for a variety of economic reasons, so the current foreign exchange system is sometimes referred to as a "managed" floating–rate system.

issue as a foreign bond or Eurobond based on the distinguishing characteristics that we cited earlier.[3] We noted that, the most important characteristic of a Eurobond offering is the composition of the underwriting syndicate. Yet "bought deals"—when there is only one underwriter—are becoming increasingly common. A bond offering in which there is only one underwriter, and in which the issue is placed primarily outside the national market of both the issuer and underwriter, would not traditionally be classified as a Eurobond offering. Another characteristic of a Eurobond is that it is not regulated by the single country whose currency is used to pay bondholders. In practice, however, only the U.S. and Canada do not place restrictions on U.S. dollar- or Canadian dollar-denominated issues sold outside their two countries. Regulators of other countries whose currencies are used in Eurobond issues have closely supervised such offerings. Their power to regulate Eurobond offerings comes from their ability to impose foreign exchange and/or capital restrictions.

Although Eurobonds are typically registered on a national stock exchange, the most common being the Luxembourg, London, or Zurich exchanges, the bulk of all trading is in the over-the-counter market. Listing is purely to circumvent restrictions imposed on some institutional investors who are prohibited from purchasing securities that are not listed on an exchange. Some of the stronger issuers privately place issues with international institutional investors.

Securities Issued in the Eurobond Market

The Eurobond market has been characterized by new and innovative bond structures to accommodate particular needs of issuers and investors. There are, of course, the "plain vanilla," fixed-rate coupon bonds, referred to as *Euro straights*. Because these are issued on an unsecured basis, they are usually issued by high-quality entities.

Coupon payments are made annually, rather than semiannually, because of the higher cost of distributing interest to geographically dispersed bondholders.[4] There are also zero-coupon bond issues, deferred-coupon issues, and step-up issues, all of which were described in Chapter 6.

Dual Currency Bonds: There are issues that pay coupon interest in one currency but pay the principal in a different currency. Such issues are called *dual currency issues*. For the first type of dual-currency bond, the exchange rate that is used to convert the principal and coupon payments into a specific currency is specified at the time the bond is issued. The

---

[3] Michael Bowe, *Eurobonds* (Kent, U.K.: Square Mile Books, 1988), pp.16–17.

second type differs from the first in that the applicable exchange rate is the rate that prevails at the time a cash flow is made (i.e, at the spot exchange rate at the time a payment is made). The third type is one that offers to either the investor *or* the issuer the choice of currency. These bonds are commonly referred to as option currency bonds. A specific example is the Index Currency Option Note (ICONs) introduced by the Long-Term Credit Bank of Japan in 1985.

Convertible Bonds and Bonds with Warrants: A convertible Eurobond is one that can be converted into another asset. Bonds with attached warrants represent a large part of the Eurobond market. A warrant grants the owner of the warrant the right to enter into another financial transaction with the issuer if the owner will benefit as a result of exercising. Most warrants are detachable from the host bond; that is, the bondholder may detach the warrant from the bond and sell it.

There are a wide array of bonds with warrants: *equity warrants*, *debt warrants*, and *currency warrants*. An equity warrant permits the warrant owner to buy the common stock of the issuer at a specified price. A debt warrant entitles the warrant owner to buy additional bonds from the issuer at the same price and yield as the host bond. The debt warrant owner will benefit if interest rates decline because a bond with a higher coupon can

---

[4] Consequently, an adjustment is required to make a direct comparison between the yield to maturity on a U.S. fixed-rate bond and that on a Eurodollar fixed-rate bond. Given the yield to maturity on a Eurodollar fixed-rate bond, its bond-equivalent yield is computed as follows:

Bond-equivalent yield of a Eurodollar bond =

$$2\left[(1 + \text{ytm on Eurodollar bond})^{1/2} - 1\right]$$

For example, suppose that the yield to maturity on a Eurodollar bond is 10%. Then the bond-equivalent yield is:

$$2\left[(1.10)^{1/2} - 1\right] = .09762 = 9.762\%$$

Notice that the bond-equivalent yield will always be less than the Eurodollar bond's yield to maturity.

To convert the bond-equivalent yield of a U.S. bond issue to an annual-pay basis so that it can be compared to the yield to maturity of a Eurodollar bond, the following formula can be used:

Yield to maturity on an annual-pay basis =

$$\left[\left(1 + \frac{\text{ytm on a bond - equivalent basis}}{2}\right)^2 - 1\right]$$

For example, suppose that the yield to maturity of a U.S. bond issue quoted on a bond–equivalent yield basis is 10%. The yield to maturity on an annual–pay basis would be:

$$\left[(1.05)^2 - 1\right] = .1025 = 10.25\%$$

The yield to maturity on an annual basis is always greater than the yield to maturity on a bond–equivalent basis.

be purchased from the same issuer. A currency warrant permits the warrant owner to exchange one currency for another at a set price (i.e., a fixed exchange rate). This feature protects the bondholder against a depreciation of the foreign currency in which the bond's cash flows are denominated. There are also gold warrants, which allow the warrant holder to purchase gold from the issuer of the bond.

Floating-Rate Notes: There are a wide variety of floating-rate Eurobond notes. In the Eurobond market, almost all floating-rate notes are denominated in U.S. dollars with non-U.S. banks being the major issuers. The coupon rate on a Eurodollar floating-rate note is some stated margin over the London Interbank Offered Rate (LIBOR), the bid on LIBOR (referred to as LIBID), or the arithmetic average of LIBOR and LIBID (referred to as LIMEAN).[5] The size of the spread reflects the perceived credit risk of the issuer, margins available in the syndicated loan market, and the liquidity of the issue. Typical reset periods for the coupon rate are either every six months or every quarter, with the rate tied to six-month or three-month LIBOR, respectively. That is, the length of the reset period and the maturity of the index used to establish the rate for the period are matched.

Many issues have either a minimum coupon rate (or floor) that the coupon rate cannot fall below and a maximum coupon rate (or cap) that the coupon rate cannot rise above. An issue that has both a floor and a cap is said to be *collared.* There are some issues that grant the borrower the right to convert the floating coupon rate into a fixed coupon rate at some time. There are some issues referred to as *drop-lock bonds*, which automatically change the floating coupon rate into a fixed coupon rate under certain circumstances.

A floating-rate note issue will either have a stated maturity date, or it may be a *perpetual*, also called *undated*, issue (i.e., with no stated maturity date). The perpetual issue was introduced into the Eurobond market in 1984. For floating-rate notes that do mature, the term is usually greater than 5 years, with the typical maturity being between 7 and 12 years. There are callable and putable floating-rate notes; some issues are both callable and putable.

NON-U.S. GOVERNMENT BOND MARKETS

Exhibit 8-1 shows the size of the major non-U.S.government bond markets. The institutional settings for these markets vary considerably, and these variations may affect liquidity and the ways in which strategies

---

[5] A less commonly used index is the Singapore Interbank Offered Rate (SIBOR).

are implemented, or, more precisely, affect the tactics of the investment strategies. For example, in the government bond market different primary market issuance practices may affect the liquidity and the price behavior of specific government bonds in a country. The nature of the secondary market affects the ease and cost of trading. The importance of the benchmark effect in various countries may influence which bonds to trade and hold. In addition, yields are calculated according to different methods in various countries, and these differences will affect the interpretation of yield spreads. Withholding and transfer tax practices also affect global investment strategies.

While the cash flows of a government bond issue are typically in the currency of the issuing country, in recent years there have been an increasing number of issues denominated in European Currency Units (ECU). An ECU is a composite currency created by the European Economic Community. The currencies included in the ECU are those that are members of the European Monetary System (EMS). The weight of each country's currency is figured according to the relative importance of a country's economic trade and financial sector within the European Economic Community.[6]

We review below the Japanese, German, United Kingdom, French, Canadian, Dutch, and Australian government bond markets in order to

Exhibit 8-1   Size of the Nine Largest Non–U.S. Government Bond Markets (as of June 1, 1990, in billions of U.S. dollars)

Country	Principal Amount	Market Value
Japan	$ 472.1	$ 460.4
Germany	213.7	201.6
United Kingdom	167.1	155.6
France	153.1	155.2
Canada	101.8	101.6
Netherlands	100.1	97.2
Denmark	33.3	34.0
Australia	21.8	21.1
Switzerland	7.1	6.6
Total (Non-U.S.)	$ 1,270.1	$ 1,233.3

Source: Salomon Brothers Inc

---

[6] The countries whose currencies are included in the ECU are Germany, the United Kingdom, France, Italy, the Netherlands, Belgium, Luxembourg, Denmark, Ireland, Greece, Spain, and Portugal. Exchange rates between the ECU and those countries not part of the EEC float freely. The exchange rate between countries in the EEC, however, may fluctuate only within a narrow range.

provide a flavor of the variety of government bonds available.[7] Short-term government issues, referred to as Treasury bills, are not stressed, although, just as in the U.S., the Treasury bill is often the largest sector of the government debt market.

Japanese Government Bonds

There are four types of Japanese government securities issued publicly: (1) short-term Treasury bills, (2) medium-term bonds, (3) long-term bonds, and (4) super long-term bonds.

There are two types of medium-term bonds: bonds with coupons and zero-coupon bonds. Bonds with coupons have maturities of two, three, and four years. The market for medium-term bonds tends to be illiquid because such bonds are typically purchased by individuals and investment trust funds who tend to be buy-and-hold investors. The other type of medium-term bond is the five-year zero coupon bond. These are sold primarily to individual investors; consequently, the market for these securities likewise tends to be illiquid.

Ten-year bonds are coupon bearing and are referred to as *long-term bonds*. During October 1986, 20-year fixed-rate bonds, referred to as *super long-term bonds*, were issued publicly for the first time. There were three subsequent issues during 1987 and additional issues during 1988. As a rule, 10-year bonds are issued each month; 20-year bonds recently have been issued at a rate of three times per year; and 5-year discount bonds recently have been issued at a rate of once a quarter. Auctions of coupon-bearing medium-term bonds are held nearly every month, although in recent years only two-year bonds have been issued.

Long-term bonds and super long-term bonds are noncallable, but the government can repurchase bonds in the secondary market. Both long-term bonds and super long-term bonds are numbered serially and referred to by number rather than maturity and coupon. For example, the No. 129 10-year is the 6.4% of 03/20/00, and the No. 16 super-long is the 6.8% of 09/20/11. All coupon bonds pay semiannual interest, just as in the U.S. Treasury coupon market.

In recent years, the Japanese government has cut back sharply on the issuance of medium-term and super long-term bonds. Issuance of long-term (ten-year) bonds has been reduced somewhat, while the issuance of Treasury bills has been increased substantially.

Additional information about the primary and secondary markets for Japanese government bonds is provided at the end of this chapter.

---

[7] Brief descriptions of each market come from Frank J. Jones and Frank J. Fabozzi, *International Government Bond Markets* (Chicago: Probus Publishing, 1992).

German Government Bonds

The Federal Republic of Germany issues four types of securities: (1) Treasury discount paper (*Unverzinsliche Schatzanweisungen*, often abbreviated to U-Schatze); (2) Federal government notes *Bundeskassenobligationen*, (also called "Kassens"; (3) *Bundesobligationen* (often called "OBLEs"); and (4) Federal government bonds (*Bundasanleihen*, also referred to as "Bunds"). With the unification of West and East Germany in October 1990, the German Unity Fund began to issue Unity Fund bonds ("Unities"), which are fully guaranteed by the federal government. Government agency bonds are also issued by the Federal Railway (*Bundesbahn*) and the Post Office (*Bundespost*) with the full faith and credit of the federal government.

U-Schatze are discount money market instruments with maturities of up to two years. Kassens are notes issued to satisfy short- and medium-term needs of the German government and its agencies. Maturities range from two to six years. They are bullet issues with no call features. Kassens are issued irregularly several times a year by tender. OBLEs are five-year federal government debt issues.

Bunds have original maturities from 6 to 30 years, although recently no issues have been longer than 10 years. Ten-year bunds are the largest sector of the German government securities market in terms of amount outstanding and secondary market turnover. While 10-year Bunds typically have been issued on a monthly basis, this schedule has not been rigid.

All coupon payments are annual rather than semiannual, as in the U.S. and Japan; this is the convention followed in the European bond market overall.

Additional information about the German government bond market follows at the end of the chapter.

United Kingdom Government Bonds

Gilts (gilt-edged stock) are bonds issued and guaranteed by the British government. Four types of gilts are available: (1) straights (most are bullet bonds, but some are callable); (2) convertibles; (3) index-linked; and (4) irredeemables (perpetuals also called "undateds").

Generally, *convertibles* have short maturities that give the holder the option to convert into a specified amount of a longer–maturity gilt (or more than one gilt) for a number of years. Convertibles have a series of conversion dates with varying (decreasing) conversion values. For example, convertibles may offer conversion dates every half year for two and a half years, with the conversion value decreasing from £102 to £98.

Thus, every convertible bond has a conversion schedule (or more than one) indicating the issues into which it can be converted, with conversion dates and corresponding conversion prices for each bond into which it can be converted. *Index-linked gilts* have coupons and final redemption amounts linked to the General Index of Retail Price (RPI), an index which is released each month by the Central Statistical Office. Index-linked gilts have low coupons, 2% to 2 1/2%, which, in effect, reflect the real rate of return. Maturities of index-linked gilts vary from short-term to 2024. *Irredeemable gilts* are issued without a final maturity, but redeemable after a specified date on three-months' notice from the government. The largest of these is the War Loan 3 1/2% or After. Twenty-five years ago, this was the largest of all gilt issues, with £1.9 billion outstanding. These gilts were issued when yields were low and have coupons in the 2 1/2% to 4% range. There are currently six irredeemable issues outstanding.

There are more types of gilts than there are types of issues in other government bond markets. Over 100 gilt-edged bond issues are outstanding. Each gilt is specified by name, coupon, redemption (maturity) date (if any; irredeemables have no maturity date), and callability (callable gilts are also called "double-dated"). Gilts have nine different names: Exchequer, Treasury, Funding, Redemption, Transport, Gas, Conversion, Consols, and War Loan (redemptions have reduced War Loans to only one outstanding issue). Each name refers specifically to the government department that issued the bond or the reason for the issue. For example, "Conversion" indicates that the gilts are converted gilts resulting from the conversion of previously issued convertible gilts; "Transport" and "Gas" refer to bonds issued upon nationalization of these industries. The names have no practical significance, however, and do not affect value. Recently, all new issues have been either Treasury or Exchequer. There is no distinction between these two types of issues.

Maturities range from 1 to 30 years. Recently, the government has issued less long-term debt. Typical categories for gilts by maturity are: (1) short-dated gilts: 0-7 years; (2) medium-dated gilts: 7-15 years; (3) long-dated gilts: greater than 15 years; and (4) undated gilts: no redemption date (for example, the War Loan).

French Government Bonds

The French Treasury issues instruments with maturities of 3 months to 30 years. Treasury bills, in general, are called BTNs (*Bons du Trésor Negotiables*) and include discount Treasury bills (*Bons Taux Fixe* [BTF]) that have maturities of 13, 26, and 52 weeks, and interest-bearing Treasury bills (Treasury Notes–*Bons Taux Fixe et a Intérêts Annuels*

[BTAN]) that have a fixed-coupon rate and are currently issued with 2- and 5-year maturities.

The market for French government bonds, the *Obligation Assimilables du Trésor* (OAT), has been reformed significantly since May 1985. This reform has increased the liquidity of the market, making it more attractive to foreign investors. OATs are fungible Treasury bonds with both fixed rates and floating rates.[8] OATs are not callable. They were first issued (via auction) during May 1985, and all government bond issues since have been OATs. Beginning in 1987, the French Treasury harmonized its auction cycle by issuing five types of OATs on a monthly basis.

There are two types of floaters: one based on bond yields and the other on bill yields. OAT TME (*Taux Moyen d'Emprunts d'Etat*, or, more explicitly, *Taux Mensuel de Rendement d'Emprunts d'Etat à Long Terme*) are floating-rate bonds based on bond yields. The coupon is fixed annually based on an index of government bond yields on issues with maturities of seven years or more. Coupon is paid annually. OAT TRB (*Taux Révisable des Bons du Trésor*, or, more explicitly, *Taux de Rendement Poscompte des Bons du Tresor à 13 semaines*) are floating-rate bonds based on Treasury bill yields.

Since 1985, OATs have been the only type of bonds issued. Before 1985, however, French government bonds had no standard form, and several types of bonds were issued, some of them still outstanding. For example, exchangeable bonds (*Emprunts exchangeables*) allowed either a fixed-rate bond to be converted to a floating-rate bond or a floating-rate to be converted to a fixed-rate bond during prespecified time periods. Bonds with exchange warrants (*Emprunts bon d'enchange*) were a type of exchangeable bond with a detachable warrant that can be sold separately in the secondary market for TME-type variable-rate bonds (as indicated above). Extendable bonds (*Emprunts prorogeables*) granted the owner the right to extend the maturity to a prespecified date. Renewable bonds (*Obligations renouvelables du Trésor* [ORTs]) have been issued with six-year maturities and the right to renew within a three-year period (interest is capitalized and paid either at maturity or time of renewal). In this case, the owner may exchange the old ORT for a new six-year ORT with a new interest rate determined at time of renewal.

---

[8] The word "*assimilables*" means "assimilations" or "fungible," which, in practice, means that within a year new bonds of a given maturity are issued as new tranches of existing bonds.

Canadian Government Bonds

The Canadian government bond has been closely related to the U.S. government debt market and has a similar structure, including types of issues. The Canadian government bond market has a wide variety of issues. Government bonds with maturities of 2 to 30 years are issued. The long maturity ranges have become increasingly important in recent years. Treasury bills with maturities of 3, 6, and 12 months also are issued weekly.

Coupons on Canadian government bonds range from 3% to 18%, and all bonds have fixed coupons. All new Canadian bonds are in "bullet" form; that is, they are not callable or putable. Some previous issues, however, have had purchase funds that permit the government periodically to buy a small proportion (precisely .5% per quarter) if the issue is trading below the original issue price.

In 1991, the Canadian government issued its first issue of real return bonds ($700 million, due in 2021). The issue was priced to yield a real return equal to 4.25%.

Dutch Government Bonds

There are two basic Dutch government bond instruments outstanding. The first type is sinking fund issues. The second type is 3- to 15-year bullet issues. While until recently the Dutch government market was dominated by sinking fund bonds ("sinkers"), since mid-1988 the market has been dominated by bullets, specifically 10-year bullets. Dutch investors have preferred sinkers, but international investors did not, so reorientation of the Dutch market toward sinkers is consistent with growing internationalization of the market. All sinking fund bonds are now quite illiquid. Ten-year Dutch guilders are issued approximately eight times per year.

Australian Government Bonds

The Australian bond market often experiences substantial foreign participation because it has been regarded as a high–yield market and is a stable country. Commonwealth Government Securities are guaranteed with respect to principal and interest by the Commonwealth Government of Australia. The two major types of Australian government securities are Treasury notes and Treasury bonds. There are also small amounts of index-linked Treasury bonds, and retail-oriented Australian savings bonds. Treasury notes are discount securities up to 26 weeks in maturity. Treasury bonds have fixed maturities (up to about 20 years) and pay coupons semiannually. Indexed-linked Treasury bonds have either interest payments or capital linked to the Australian Consumer Price Index.

Interest-indexed securities pay a fixed coupon every six months plus an arrears adjustment that amounts to the increase in the CPI. Capital-indexed securities also pay a fixed coupon (usually 4%) with the increase in the CPI added to the capital value of the bond and paid on maturity. Interest-indexed bonds rarely trade.

JAPANESE AND GERMAN BOND MARKETS

The Japanese and German bond markets are the second and third largest bond markets in the world, respectively. We describe them in more detail here not only because of their importance in the global bond market but also because they typify the trend toward deregulation of financial markets that began in the 1980s.

Japanese Bond Markets

Regulation of the Japanese financial markets is the responsibility of the Ministry of Finance (MOF). All bond issues must be approved by the MOF, which plays a role similar to the SEC in the U.S. The Bank of Japan plays the same role in Japan as the Federal Reserve System in the U.S. The separation of commercial banking and investment banking that was established in the U.S. in the 1930s by the Glass-Steagall Act has been followed by the architects of the Japanese financial system. Japan's securities and exchange law prohibits nonsecurities companies from dealing in any securities except government or government-related bonds. As the wall between commercial banking and investment banking is being chiseled away in the U.S., similar issues are facing Japan's MOF, and reforms are under consideration there too.

While there are more than 200 securities companies in Japan, four dominate the market: Nomura, Daiwa, Nikko, and Yamaichi. These four firms are referred to as the "Big Four," or *Yondai Shoken*. Second–and third-tier securities houses are referred to as *Sho Shoken*. Banks in Japan are classified as either city banks, local banks, long-term credit banks, trust banks, mutual banks, institutions for agriculture and forestry, and credit associations. The most powerful in terms of financial clout are the 13 city banks, so-named because they are headquartered in major Japanese metropolitan areas. These are the primary lenders to private companies. Following city banks in terms of assets are the 64 local banks.[9]

---

[9] Legally there is no distinction between city banks and local banks. The common distinction has to do with size and business focus, with city banks targeting large industrial companies, and local banks focusing on individuals and locally based, medium–sized companies. The three long–term credit banks (Industrial Bank of Japan, Long–Term Credit Bank of Japan, and Nippon Credit Bank) provide long–term financing for Japanese industry. The seven trust banks in Japan conduct both banking business and trust activities (investment management of accounts and custodial activities).

The internal Japanese bond market includes the following sectors: government bonds, government-related organization bonds, local government bonds, bank debentures, and corporate bonds. By far, the largest sector is the Japanese government bond (JGB) market.

Government Bond Market: As we noted earlier, there are three types of JGBs: medium-term government bonds, 10-year government bonds (long-term government bonds), and 20-year government bonds (super long-term government bonds).

There are two methods of issuance of government bonds: syndicate and auction. The syndicate method is used for 10-year bonds and 5-year discount bonds. A new government bond issue is authorized by the Ministry of Finance, with issuance implemented by the Bank of Japan. A fixed syndicate of 788 financial firms, made up of city banks, long-term-credit banks, securities houses, and other financial institutions, is used. The MOF determines the coupon and the size of the issue in consultation with representatives from the underwriting syndicate. Subscriptions are then allocated via a quota system. The members of the underwriting syndicate must also accept and pay for any issues unsubscribed for at the offering. Except for 10-year issues, JGBs are now issued through public auction. Currently, 60% of 10-year JGBs are issued by public auction, with the rest underwritten by the government syndicate at the average auction price.

Once the borrowing authority has been established through the parliamentary process, the MOF has considerable discretion in deciding the composition of new government bond issues, although there are some restrictions on how maturing debt may be refinanced. The overall composition is determined in consultation with representatives of the government bond underwriting syndicate.

For coupon issues, the MOF sets the coupon ahead of the auction after consulting with representatives of the government bond syndicate. An attempt is made to set the coupon at a level that will result in an average auction price below par. Accordingly, bond market conditions, particularly yields on the most recently issued comparable JGB, are a key focus of attention just prior to the auctions.

JGB auctions are conventional price auctions. Since the spring of 1991, all auctions have been carried out in one day. Under present practice, the MOF announces the terms of the issue at 8:30 a.m., bids are accepted between 11:30 a.m. and 1:30 p.m., and the result is announced at 4:30 p.m. the same day. As the coupon is known, bids are made in terms of bond price, to two decimal places. For example, a bid might be yen 99.75. Bids are filled at the price bid beginning with the highest price, until the entire auction amount is sold. If the entire auction amount is sold before all bids can be filled completely, a bid might be filled only partially. Noncompetitive bids are permitted for some JGBs.

Beginning in October 1987, a hybrid auction was used for 10-year JGBs. Eighty percent of new issues were allocated through the standard syndicate, with 20% available from a hybrid auction. In the hybrid auction, investors could bid for up to 1% of the total auction each; no price, however, was bid. The subscription price, coupon rate, and size of the issue were negotiated by the syndicate as usual. If bids for more than 20% of the auction were received, the amounts bid for were reduced proportionally. If bids for less than 20% were received, the remaining amount was allocated to the syndicate. Bidders, according to this method, accepted the results of the syndicate.

A unique feature of the secondary market for JGBs has to do with the benchmark or bellwether bond issue. It is this issue that is the most actively traded and therefore has the greatest liquidity of all issues of similar maturity. In the U.S. Treasury market, the on-the-run issues, that is, the most recently auctioned issue for a given maturity, are the benchmark issues for each maturity. The on-the-run 30-year Treasury issue is the issue in which there is the most trading activity because investors use it to speculate on interest rates in the long-term end of the bond market.

In Japan, the benchmark issue is basically the issue that the Big Four securities houses designate as such. The process of determining the benchmark from among the ten-year bonds is an informal one, usually taking place over a number of weeks. The most important factor in the selection is acceptance by the key market makers. Benchmark issues tend to have certain characteristics: (1) a coupon that is near the prevailing rate; (2) a large outstanding amount (usually yen 1.5 trillion or greater); (3) a wide distribution or placement after its issue; and (4) a remaining maturity as close to ten years as possible. Many observers maintain that the preeminence of the benchmark in the JGB market will decline, and that we will see an evolution toward more issues trading with approximately equal liquidity, although so far there is little indication that such an evolution is underway.

Government-Related Organization Bond Market: The Japanese government-related organization bond sector includes bonds issued by public corporations and special-purpose companies established under Japanese law. There are two types of issues: those with principal and interest guaranteed by the Japanese government, and those that are not. Each year the amount of guaranteed bonds that may be issued is approved by the Japanese Diet (the legislative body). The Japanese government at one time used government-guaranteed bonds of government-related organizations to finance various projects rather than issuing its own bonds. In fact, the Japanese government did not issue any government bonds until 1966. The first, and largest, issuers of government-guaranteed bonds were the Japanese National Railways and the Nippon Telegraph and Telephone Public Corporation in 1953. Both these organizations are now private corporations. Government-guaranteed bonds may be publicly offered or privately placed. The volume of government-guaranteed bonds has declined as a result of privatization in Japan.

Local Government Bond Market: This sector of the bond market consists of debt instruments issued by various Japanese cities, prefectures, towns, and villages. There are 23 entities that now publicly issue bonds. A few local governments (Tokyo, Osaka, Kobe, and Yokohama) have issued nonyen-denominated bonds outside Japan.

Bank Debenture Market: Japanese law permits certain banks to issue bonds to raise funds. These issues, which are called bank debentures, represent the second largest sector of the Japanese bond market. The banks permitted to issue these debentures are the Industrial Bank of Japan, the Long-Term Credit Bank of Japan, the Nippon Credit Bank, the Norinchukin Bank, the Shoko Chukin Bank, and the Bank of Tokyo.

Corporate Bond Market: The corporate bond sector represents yen-denominated bonds issued by Japanese domestic corporations. An interesting institutional feature of the Japanese bond market is the Bond Flotation Committee (*Kisaikai*). This committee of 43 institutions plays an important role in the Japanese corporate bond market by (1) establishing eligibility standards for the issuance of bonds, (2) monitoring the terms and amount of issues, and (3) controlling the coming of new issues to market to avoid flooding the market with issues. The central administration of committee standards is implemented by a group consisting of seven banks (Industrial Bank of Japan, Dai-ichi Kangyo, Fuji Bank, Sumitomo, Mitsubishi, Mitsui, and Sanwa)[10] and the Big Four securities companies.

There is an inherent conflict between the banks and the securities houses. Corporations that issue bonds are substituting this form of borrowing for bank borrowing. As banks are not permitted to underwrite nongovernment bonds, corporate borrowing in the bond market reduces bank lending opportunities, which cannot be recouped from underwriting

---

[10] This group is referred to as "*Hachikokai*," which translated means a committee of eight banks. The group consists of only seven banks because Dai–ichi Bank and Nippon Kangyo Bank merged in 1971.

fees. Consequently, banks have a vested interest in establishing rigid standards to discourage corporate bond offerings; obviously, securities houses would want the issuing rules liberalized. The rules established by the committee are voluntary rules, and the committee's power is expected to diminish with further liberalization of the Japanese bond market.

In 1987, Japan introduced the equivalent of the U.S. shelf registration rule. This rule permits issuers to come to market faster than would be possible by going through standard issuing procedures. A formal corporate bond rating system was introduced in 1977. Equity-linked bonds (convertible bonds and bonds with warrants) have been the most important type of bonds issued by corporations. Prior to 1983, Japanese corporations found it more attractive to issue convertible bonds overseas. Since 1983, the relaxation of restrictions on convertible bond issuance in Japan, coupled with a decline in domestic interest rates, has made domestic issuance more attractive.

Foreign Bond and Euroyen Bond Markets: Several key financial regulatory changes have liberalized the Japanese bond markets. Many of these changes represent attempts to foster the development of the Japanese foreign bond market (the Samurai bond market) and the Euroyen bond market (that is, yen-denominated Eurobonds).[11] For example, while the Bank Flotation Committee has required that all bonds be secured, in 1979 Sears Overseas Finance N.V. issued an unsecured bond in the Samurai bond market, which helped foster the replacement of collateral requirements in the domestic bond market with a credit rating system for bonds. In fact the motivation behind shelf registration was to allow foreign issuers to issue securities in the Samurai bond market.

The Japanese foreign bond market includes both yen-denominated and nonyen-denominated issues. There are three types of foreign bonds that are yen-denominated: *Samurai* bonds, *Daimyo* bonds, and *Shibosai* bonds. Samurai bonds are publicly offered issues. The primary issuers of Samurai bonds are supranational institutions (e.g., the Asian Development Bank and the World Bank), followed by sovereign governments such as the Commonwealth of Australia, or by foreign municipal governments. *Daimyo* bonds were introduced in 1987 to improve liquidity. These publicly issued bonds are listed on the Luxembourg Exchange; rather than being settled in Japan, they are settled through the Euroclear or Cedel systems (discussed later) as are Euroyen bonds. *Shibosai* bonds are privately placed bonds issued by foreigners that are yen-denominated.

---

[11] For a more detailed description of the development of the Japanese bond market, see Issen Sato and E.M. Kanovsky, "Historical Development of the Japanese Bond Market," Chapter 13 in Frank J. Fabozzi (ed.), *The Japanese Bond Markets* (Chicago: Probus Publishing, 1990).

Shogun bonds and *Geisha* bonds are nonyen–denominated bonds issued by foreigners. The former are publicly offered bonds, while the latter are privately placed.

Yield Quotes: A unique feature of the Japanese bond market is the method of quoting yields. As we explained in Chapter 3, the yield to maturity is the measure used in the U.S. to quote bond yields. As explained in that chapter, this measure is deficient because it assumes that the coupon payments can be reinvested at the calculated yield to maturity. In Japan, bond yields are quoted on a "simple yield" basis. The calculation is as follows:

$$\text{Simple yield} = \frac{\text{Annual coupon interest} + \dfrac{(\text{Par Value} - \text{Price})}{\text{Years to maturity}}}{\text{Price}}$$

While this method for calculating yield may seem naive, it can be argued that it is more suitable, because use of the term "simple yield" forewarns the investor that the yield measure may leave a great deal to be desired as a measure of relative value.

German Bond Markets

The Bundesbank is responsible for maintaining an orderly monetary system and establishing regulations for new bond issues, and the German Civil Code requires that domestic issuers obtain permission to issue new bonds.

There are several noteworthy features of the German bond market. First, more than in any other country with a well-developed capital market, the German capital market is more interdependent with its banking system. This is because most intermediation of funds is via banks. Consequently, in the German capital markets, banks are the largest group of investors. There are two types of banks in Germany: universal banks and "special" banks. The activities of universal banks include the usual commercial banking business and any kind of securities business. The latter activity includes the underwriting, trading, and investing in securities. Thus, there is no separation of the banking and securities businesses in Germany. The secondary market for both stocks and bonds as a result is mainly an interbank market. The three major universal banks are Deutsche Bank, Dresdner Bank, and Commerzbank. Special banks are institutions that provide financing for specific needs such as mortgage financing and consumer financing.

A second distinctive feature of the German capital market is that it is one of the most liberal in the world, with a number of measures adopted since 1985 that have opened up the German bond market to foreign entities. In April 1985, the Bundesbank granted subsidiaries of foreign banks domiciled in Germany permission to be lead managers of deutschemark-denominated Eurobonds, called Euro-deutschemark bonds or simply Euro-DM bonds. Also in April 1985, the Bundesbank authorized the issuance of a wide array of Euro-DM issues not previously permitted, such as floating-rate notes, zero-coupon bonds, and dual currency notes.

There are three sectors in the German national bond market: (1) public authority bonds, (2) bank bonds, and (3) nonbank corporate bonds. Public authority bonds include bonds issued by the Federal Republic of Germany, its special agencies—the federal post office (*Bundespost* issues) and the federal railways (*Bundesbahn* issues)—and German state governments (*Lander*) and local authorities (*Gemeinden*). The various types of issues of the Federal Republic of Germany were described in the previous section. *Bundespost* and *Bundesbahn* issues are all guaranteed by the full faith and credit of the Federal Republic of Germany.

The issuing group for *Bunds* is the Federal Bond Syndicate (*Konsortium*), which is composed of 190 financial institutions (including foreign banks). A new issuance procedure for *Bunds* and *Unities* was initiated in July 1990 to promote a more global distribution of government bonds. It combines the traditional underwriting procedure and a new competitive Dutch tender auction.

Two tranches are auctioned. The first tranche has fixed terms, including issue price, and is allocated along traditional guidelines among syndicate members. In this traditional system of issue, all members are allocated a fixed percentage of total issue size, irrespective of the issue terms. Up to 25% of the initial offering is retained by the Bundesbank for intervention and market-making purposes. The second tranche is auctioned on the next day with bid prices made by eligible members in DM .05 increments for bonds with the same terms as the first tranche (except price). No selling commissions are paid on this tranche. Bids may be placed until the morning (10:00 a.m. to 11:30 a.m.) after the underwriting date, with allocation by the Bundesbank taking place within two hours thereafter. The two tranches plus the Bundesbank quota form one issue with identical terms and one security code. The total issue volume is announced by the Bundesbank after allocation. The proportions of total volume raised via the two tranches are flexible in order to suit market conditions at the same time of issuance. Foreigners may not tender at issue.

Although there is no strict benchmark issue in Germany (as there is in the United States and Japan), a benchmark system has been evolving. For example, in mid-1991 the benchmark was the 8 3/8% of May 2001. The benchmark has typically been the most recently issued ten-year *Bund*.

Previously, no yield distinction existed between government and agency bonds, but in recent years, because international investors prefer *Bund* issues, a small yield spread has emerged between *Bunds* and the two agency issues.

The second largest sector, roughly 40% of the German national bond market, is the market for bank bonds. Within this sector, the two major types of bank bonds are municipal bonds (*Kommunalobligationen*) and mortgage bonds (*Pfandbriefe*). Municipal bonds are debt obligations issued by banks but secured by public authorities. By far the smallest sector of the German national bond market is the nonbank corporate market. German corporations borrow primarily through bank loans rather than through issuance of bonds. The German foreign bond market is also a small part of the national bond market. Most issues are privately placed.

CLEARING SYSTEMS

Global financial markets require an effective system for the settlement of transactions. That is, buyers must receive the securities purchased, and sellers must receive cash payment, which is complicated when buyer and seller may be in two different countries. Moreover, the broker or dealer firms involved in a transaction may also be in different countries from the buyer and seller. Geographical separation of parties increases the potential for fails (that is, the failure of the seller to deliver securities or of the buyer to make cash payment).

In response to such problems, two clearing systems have developed to handle international transactions: Euroclear, started in December 1968 by Morgan Guaranty Trust Company of New York, and Cedel, started in Luxembourg in September 1970. Their original objective was to handle Eurobond transactions, but now they handle a wide variety of securities and settle international primary and secondary equity transactions. They also provide important services for the effective functioning of global market transactions beyond the settlement of transactions. First, they offer financing services for dealers to finance their positions. Second, they provide a securities borrowing service so that dealers who are short securities can borrow them to cover their positions.

SUMMARY

In this chapter, the Eurobond market and the non-U.S. government bond markets are discussed. When a U.S. investor purchases non-U.S. bonds that are denominated in a foreign currency, the return to be realized will consist of two components. The first component is the local currency return, which results from coupon payments, reinvestment income, and capital gains/losses. The second component is any foreign exchange gain or loss resulting from converting the nondollar cash flows to U.S. dollars. Foreign exchange risk is the risk that the foreign currency depreciates (declines in value) relative to the U.S. dollar, resulting in the U.S. dollar value of the cash flows being lower.

The global bond market can be classified into two markets: the internal or national bond market, which consists of a domestic bond market and a foreign bond market, and the external or international bond market (or Eurobond market).

The Eurobond market is divided into sectors based on the currency in which the issue is denominated. Many innovative bond structures have been introduced in the Eurobond market, such as dual–currency issues and various types of convertible bonds and bonds with warrants. The floating-rate sector of the Eurobond market is dominated by U.S. dollar-denominated issues.

Many investors who have made the decision to invest in non-U.S. bonds participate only in the foreign government bond markets, rather than the nongovernment bond markets. This is because of the low credit risk, the liquidity, and the simplicity of the government markets. In this chapter, we reviewed the Japanese, German, United Kingdom, French, Canadian, Dutch, and Australian government bond markets.

The Japanese bond market, the second largest bond market in the world, is regulated by the Ministry of Finance. The internal Japanese bond market includes government bonds (the largest sector), government-related organization bonds, local government bonds, bank debentures, and corporate bonds. The Japanese foreign bond market includes both yen-denominated (*Samurai* bonds, *Daimyo* bonds, and *Shibosai* bonds) and nonyen-denominated issues.

The third largest bond market is the German bond market. The German capital market, which is more interdependent with its banking system than any other developed capital market, has two types of banks: universal banks and special banks. The three sectors in the German national bond market include public authority bonds, bank bonds, and nonbank corporate bonds.

Euroclear and Cedel are two clearing systems that handle Eurobond transactions as well as provide dealer financing and a securities borrowing service.

QUESTIONS FOR CHAPTER 8

1. What risk is faced by a U.S. life insurance company that buys British government bonds?

2. Why do U.S. investors who invest in non-U.S. bonds prefer foreign government bonds?

3. What institutional factors of a foreign government bond market affect implementation of investment strategies?

4. What is the difference between LIBID and LIMEAN?

5. Describe the role of Cedel and Euroclear.

6. Describe each of the following bonds:

   a. A Eurobond

   b. A Euro-straight bond.

   c. A dual-currency bond.

7. What is the European Currency Unit?

8. a. What are the four types of securities issued by the Japanese government?

   b. How is the benchmark government issue determined in the Japanese bond market?

   c. Explain how yields are quoted in the Japanese bond market.

9. What is a "gilt"?

10. The quotation following is from an article entitled "Spanish Bonds to be Tops," that appeared in the March 4, 1991, issue of *Bondweek*:

    The Spanish bond market will be one of the best performing European markets this year due to its relatively high yields, a strong peseta [the Spanish currency] and moves by the Spanish government to liberalize the market, according to analysts. The Spanish government's recent move to lower short-term rates from 14.7% to 14.5%, hold monthly auctions and abolish the 25% withholding tax on bonds (government bonds) for non-residents has also helped increase liquidity in the market, they said.

    Explain why the relatively high yields, a strong peseta, and the government's liberalization policies will contribute to the projected favorable performance of the Spanish bond market cited in this quotation.

11. A withholding tax is a tax imposed by a country on interest or dividends to be paid to foreign (i.e., nonresident) investors who have purchased securities in that country. Foreign investors, of course, want to avoid withholding taxes. The excerpt below discussing withholding taxes is taken from the *International Capital Market in 1989* published by the European Investment Bank:

During 1989 changes in withholding tax regimes—actual and proposed—made for additional gyrations in securities prices. Speculation as to the permanence of the 10% withholding tax on coupon income of all domestically issued bonds in Germany was already alive when it was introduced on 1 January 1989. When the decision was finally taken in May to abolish the tax as from 1 July, yield relations between the euro-Deutsche Mark and the domestic markets had already begun to change. Yields on euro-Deutsche Mark bonds by supranational borrowers, for instance, which had traded below German Government bonds ("Bunds"), started to rise in early April and returned to their traditional level above those of "Bunds." Issuing patterns also fell back to those of the pre-withholding tax period: German entities reduced sharply their issuing activity in the euromarket. The heavy outflow of long-term funds from Germany which had preceded the introduction of the withholding tax was also partly reversed.

a. What is a "euro-Deutsche Mark" bond?

b. Why would proposed withholding taxes cause "gyrations in securities prices"?

c. Explain why imposition of the German 10% withholding tax in January 1989 caused yields on euro-Deutsche Mark bonds issued by supranational borrowers to trade at a lower yield than German government bonds.

d. Why did issuing patterns fall "back to those of the pre-withholding tax period"?

Chapter 9

THE TERM STRUCTURE
OF INTEREST RATES

The yield on Treasury securities is a benchmark for determining the yield on non-Treasury securities. Consequently, all market participants are interested in the relationship between yield and maturity for Treasury securities. In this chapter we will see how information embedded in Treasury yields can be used by market participants to price bonds. At the end of the chapter, we will look at the relationship between the credit spread on corporate bonds and maturity.

ANALYSIS OF THE TREASURY YIELD CURVE

The graphical depiction of the relationship between the yield on Treasury securities for different maturities is known as the *yield curve*. Exhibit 9-1 shows four hypothetical yield curves.

While a yield curve is typically constructed on the basis of observed yields and maturities, the term structure of interest rates is the relationship between the yield on zero-coupon Treasury securities and their maturities. Any noncallable security can be considered a package of zero-coupon securities. That is, each zero-coupon security in the package has a maturity equal to its coupon payment date and, in the case of the principal, the maturity date. The value of the security should equal the value of all the component zero-coupon securities. If this equality does not hold, it will be possible to create arbitrage profits. To determine the value of each zero-coupon security, it is necessary to know the yield on the zero-coupon Treasury corresponding to that maturity. This yield is called the *spot rate*, and the graphical depiction of the relationship between the spot rate and its maturity is called the *spot rate curve.*

The theoretical spot rate plays a key role in the pricing of all financial instruments because all securities can be viewed as a package of zero-coupon securities and options. However, the cash flows on non-Treasury

EXHIBIT 9-1   Four Hypothetical Yield Curves

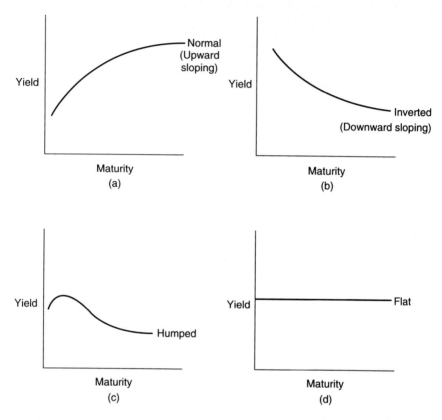

securities are not risk-free. The interest rate used to discount a risky cash flow will be equal to the interest rate on a theoretical zero-coupon Treasury security with a maturity equal to the time of receipt of the risky cash flow plus a spread that reflects credit risk.

In this section we explain how the theoretical spot rate curve is constructed, along with the implications for arbitrage opportunities if the actual yields depart from that specified by the theoretical spot rate curve. More specifically, the process of coupon stripping described in Chapter 5 may be profitable. In turn, this process will drive market yields toward the theoretical spot rates.

Constructing the Theoretical Spot Rate Curve

It is possible to construct a theoretical spot rate curve from the observed yields on Treasury bills and Treasury coupon securities. To see how this is done, we'll use the hypothetical price, yield (yield to maturity), and maturity for the 20 Treasury securities shown in Exhibit 9-2.[1]

EXHIBIT 9-2   Maturity and Yield to Maturity for 20 Hypothetical Treasury Securities

Maturity	Coupon	Yield to Maturity	Price
.50	.0000	.0800	96.15
1.00	.0000	.0830	92.19
1.50	.0850	.0890	99.45
2.00	.0900	.0920	99.64
2.50	.1100	.0940	103.49
3.00	.0950	.0970	99.49
3.50	.1000	.1000	100.00
4.00	.1000	.1040	98.72
4.50	.1150	.1060	103.16
5.00	.0875	.1080	92.24
5.50	.1050	.1090	98.38
6.00	.1100	.1120	99.14
6.50	.0850	.1140	86.94
7.00	.0825	.1160	84.24
7.50	.1100	.1180	96.09
8.00	.0650	.1190	72.62
8.50	.0875	.1200	82.97
9.00	.1300	.1220	104.30
9.50	.1150	.1240	95.06
10.00	.1250	.1250	100.00

The basic principle is that the value of a Treasury coupon security should be equal to the value of a package of zero-coupon Treasury securities. Consider first the six-month Treasury bill in Exhibit 9-2. Because a Treasury bill is a zero-coupon instrument, its yield of 8% is equal to the spot rate. Similarly, for the one-year Treasury, the yield of 8.3% is the one-year spot rate. Given these two spot rates, we can compute the spot rate for a 1.5-year zero-coupon Treasury. The value or price of a 1.5-year zero-coupon Treasury should equal the present value of the three cash flows from the 1.5-year coupon Treasury, where the yield used for discounting is the spot rate corresponding to the cash flow. Using $100 as par, the cash flow for the 1.5-year coupon Treasury is as follows:

0.5 years	.085 × $100 × .5	= $ 4.25		
1.0 year	.085 × $100 × .5	= $ 4.25		
1.5 years	.085 × $100 × .5 + 100	= $104.25		

[1] In practice, when the yield curve is constructed using the methodology described here, only the observed yields of bonds selling at par (current coupon issues) are used. The resulting yield curve is called the *par yield curve*.

The present value of the cash flow is then:

$$\frac{4.25}{\left(1+y_1\right)^1} + \frac{4.25}{\left(1+y_2\right)^2} + \frac{104.25}{\left(1+y_3\right)^3}$$

where y_1 = one-half the six-month theoretical spot rate
y_2 = one-half the one-year theoretical spot rate
y_3 = one-half the 1.5-year theoretical spot rate

Because the six-month spot rate and one-year spot rate are 8.0% and 8.3%, respectively, then

$$y_1 = .04 \quad \text{and} \quad y_2 = .0415$$

Therefore the present value of the 1.5-year coupon Treasury security is:

$$\frac{4.25}{(1.0400)^1} + \frac{4.25}{(1.0415)^2} + \frac{104.25}{\left(1+y_3\right)^3}$$

As the price of the 1.5-year coupon Treasury security is $99.45, the following relationship must hold:

$$99.45 = \frac{4.25}{(1.0400)^1} + \frac{4.25}{(1.0415)^2} + \frac{104.25}{\left(1+y_3\right)^3}$$

We can now solve for the theoretical 1.5-year spot as follows:

$$99.45 = 4.08654 + 3.91805 + \frac{104.25}{\left(1+y_3\right)^3}$$

$$91.4451 = \frac{104.25}{\left(1+y_3\right)^3}$$

$$\left(1+y_3\right)^3 = 1.140024$$

$$y_3 = .04465$$

Doubling this yield, we obtain the bond-equivalent yield of .0893 or 8.93%, which is the theoretical 1.5-year spot rate.

Given the theoretical 1.5-year spot rate, we can obtain the theoretical two-year spot rate. The cash flow for the two-year coupon Treasury in Exhibit 9-2 is given below:

0.5 years	.090 × $100	× .5	=	$	4.50
1.0 year	.090 × $100	× .5	=	$	4.50
1.5 years	.090 × $100	× .5	=	$	4.50
2.0 years	.090 × $100	× .5 + 100	=	$	104.50

The present value of the cash flow is as follows:

$$\frac{4.50}{\left(1+y_1\right)^1} + \frac{4.50}{\left(1+y_2\right)^2} + \frac{4.50}{\left(1+y_3\right)^3} + \frac{104.50}{\left(1+y_4\right)^4}$$

where y_4 = one-half the two-year thoretical spot rate

The six-month spot rate, one-year spot rate, and 1.5-year spot rate are 8.0%, 8.3%, and 8.93%, respectively, so:

$$y_1 = .04 \qquad y_2 = .0415 \qquad \text{and } y_3 = .04465$$

Therefore the present value of the two-year coupon Treasury security is:

$$\frac{4.50}{(1.0400)^1} + \frac{4.50}{(1.0415)^2} + \frac{4.50}{(1.04465)^3} + \frac{104.50}{\left(1+y_4\right)^4}$$

Because the price of the two-year coupon Treasury security is $99.64, the following relationship must hold:

$$99.64 = \frac{4.50}{(1.0400)^1} + \frac{4.50}{(1.0415)^2} + \frac{4.50}{(1.04465)^3} + \frac{104.50}{\left(1+y_4\right)^4}$$

We can now solve for the theoretical two-year spot rate as follows:

$$99.64 = 4.32692 + 4.14853 + 3.94730 + \frac{104.50}{\left(1+y_4\right)^4}$$

$$87.21725 = \frac{104.50}{\left(1+y_4\right)^4}$$

$$\left(1+y_4\right)^4 = 1.198158$$

$$y_4 = .046235$$

Doubling this yield, we obtain the theoretical two-year spot rate bond-equivalent yield of 9.247%.

We can then use the theoretical two-year spot rate and the 2.5-year coupon Treasury in Exhibit 9-2 to compute the 2.5-year theoretical spot rate. In general, to compute the theoretical spot rate for the nth six-month period, the following equation must be solved:

$$P_n = \frac{C^*}{\left(1+y_1\right)^1} + \frac{C^*}{\left(1+y_2\right)^2} + \frac{C^*}{\left(1+y_3\right)^3} + \ldots + \frac{C^*+100}{\left(1+y_n\right)^n}$$

where P_n = price of the coupon Treasury with n periods to maturity (per $100 of par value)

C^* = semiannual coupon interest for the coupon Treasury with n periods to maturity (per $100 of par value)

y_t for t = 1,2,..., $n-1$ are the theoretical spot rates that are known

This expression can be rewritten as follows:

$$P_n = C^* \sum_{t=1}^{n-1} \frac{1}{\left(1+y_t\right)^t} + \frac{C^*+100}{\left(1+y_n\right)^n}$$

Solving for y_n, we get:

$$y_n = \left[\frac{C^*+100}{P_n - C^* \sum_{t=1}^{n-1} \frac{1}{\left(1+y_t\right)^t}} \right]^{1/n} - 1$$

Doubling y_n gives the theoretical spot rate on a bond-equivalent basis.

The equation above is used to determine the theoretical spot rates for each hypothetical Treasury security shown in Exhibit 9-2. The theoretical spot rates are presented in Exhibit 9-3. *It is this yield/maturity structure that would be used to construct the theoretical spot rate curve that is referred to as the term structure of interest rates.* The methodology described above for deriving the spot rate curve is called *bootstrapping*.[2]

In Chapter 5 we discussed stripped Treasury securities that are zero-coupon Treasury securities created by dealer firms. It would seem logical that the observed yield on stripped Treasury securities can be used to construct an actual spot rate curve rather than go through the procedure we just described. There are three problems with using the observed yields on stripped Treasury securities to construct the term structure of interest rates. First, the liquidity of the stripped Treasury market is not as great as that of the Treasury coupon market. Thus, the observed yields on stripped Treasury securities reflect a premium for liquidity (in the sense of marketability). Second, there are maturity sectors of the stripped Treasury securities market that attract specific investors who may be willing to trade off yield in exchange for an attractive feature associated with that particular maturity sector, thereby distorting the term structure relationship. For example, unlike domestic taxable entities, certain foreign governments

---

[2] The same methodology is used in the swap market to derive a zero-coupon swap curve. See Chapter 19.

EXHIBIT 9-3   Theoretical Spot Rates

Maturity	Yield to Maturity	Theoretical Spot Rate
.50	.0800	.08000
1.00	.0830	.08300
1.50	.0890	.08930
2.00	.0920	.09247
2.50	.0940	.09468
3.00	.0970	.09787
3.50	.1000	.10129
4.00	.1040	.10592
4.50	.1060	.10850
5.00	.1080	.11021
5.50	.1090	.11175
6.00	.1120	.11584
6.50	.1140	.11744
7.00	.1160	.11991
7.50	.1180	.12405
8.00	.1190	.12278
8.50	.1200	.12546
9.00	.1220	.13152
9.50	.1240	.13377
10.00	.1250	.13623

may grant investors preferential tax treatment on zero-coupon Treasuries. As a result, these foreign investors invest heavily in long-maturity stripped Treasury securities, driving down yields in that maturity sector. Finally, the tax treatment of stripped Treasury securities is different from that of Treasury coupon securities. Specifically, the accrued interest on stripped Treasury securities is taxed even though no cash is received by the investor. Thus they are negative cash flow securities to taxable entities, and, as a result, their yield reflects this tax disadvantage.

Term Structure Modeling

The bootstrapping methodology for constructing the theoretical spot rate curve, although useful, is in practice more complex for several reasons. First, there may be more than one Treasury issue with the same maturity selling at different yields.[3] This reflects other factors that affect

---

[3] A procedure for computing the theoretical spot rate curve by using Treasuries with different coupons but the same maturity is explained in John Caks, "The Coupon Effect on Yield to Maturity," *Journal of Finance*, March 1977, pp. 103-115. For a mathematically simpler version of this approach, see Alden L. Toevs and Lawrence Dyer, *The Term Structure of Interest Rates and Its Use in Asset and Liability Management* (New York: Morgan Stanley, October 1986), p. 47.

yield: difference in coupon and the presence of a call future. Second, there is not a current Treasury issue for every possible maturity, so that a continuous yield curve cannot be constructed using the procedure we just illustrated.

The objective in empirical estimation of the term structure is to construct a spot rate curve that (1) fits the data sufficiently well and (2) is a sufficiently smooth function.[4] Several methodologies have been suggested to estimate the term structure.[5] Vasicek and Fong propose an approach that has been applied to historical price data on Treasury securities with satisfactory results.[6] The approach produces forward rates (discussed below) that are a smooth, continuous function of maturity. The model has desirable asymptotic properties for long maturities, and exhibits both sufficient flexibility to fit a wide variety of shapes of the term structure and sufficient robustness to produce stable forward rates.

STRIPPED TREASURY SECURITIES AND
THE TERM STRUCTURE OF INTEREST RATES

The potential profit in creating zero-coupon Treasury securities depends on the actual yields on Treasury securities and the theoretical spot rate curve. To see how a government dealer can realize a profit from coupon stripping (creating zero-coupon Treasury securities), consider a ten-year, 12.5% coupon Treasury selling at par (offering a yield to maturity of 12.5 %). Suppose that a government dealer buys the issue at par and strips the issue, expecting to sell the zero-coupon Treasury securities at the yields indicated for the corresponding maturity shown in Exhibit 9-3.

Exhibit 9-4 shows the price that would be received for each zero-coupon Treasury security created. The price of the Treasury coupon

---

[4] For a further discussion of the desirable properties of models for estimating the term structure, see Terence C. Langetieg and Stephen J. Smoot, "An Appraisal of Alternative Spline Methodologies for Estimating the Term Structure of Interest Rates," working paper, University of Southern California, December 1981.

[5] See, for example, Willard R. Carleton and Ian Cooper, "Estimation and Uses of the Term Structure of Interest Rates," *Journal of Finance*, September 1976, pp. 1067-1083; J. Huston McCulloch, "Measuring the Term Structure of Interest Rates,"*Journal of Business*, January 1971, pp. 19-31, and J. Huston McCulloch, "The Tax Adjusted Yield Curve," *Journal of Finance*, June 1975, pp. 811-830.

[6] Earlier approaches have attempted to estimate the term structure of interest rates by fitting polynomial splines of the second or third order. Splines, being piecewise polynomials, are inherently ill-suited to fit an exponential-type curve that would represent the term structure. (See Langetieg and Smoot, "An Appraisal of Alternative Spline Methodologies for Estimating the Term Structure of Interest Rates.") Vasicek and Fong propose an approach that can be termed *exponential spline fitting*, which overwhelms the drawbacks of using piecewise splines. See Oldrich A. Vasicek and H. Gifford Fong, "Term Structure Modeling Using Exponential Splines," *Journal of Finance*, May 1982, pp. 339-348.

security is just the total present value of all the cash flows from the stripped Treasury securities, each discounted at the yield corresponding to its maturity (from Exhibit 9-3). The proceeds received from selling the zero-coupon Treasury securities would be $104.1880 per $100 of par value of the Treasury issue purchased by the dealer. This would result in a profit of $4.1880 per $100 purchased.

EXHIBIT 9-4 Profit Opportunity from Coupon Stripping Using Observed Yield for the Maturity

Maturity	Cash Flow	Present Value at 12.5%	Yield to Maturity	Present Value at Yield to Maturity
.50	6.25	5.8824	.0800	6.0096
1.00	6.25	5.5363	.0830	5.7618
1.50	6.25	5.2017	.0890	5.4847
2.00	6.25	4.9042	.0920	5.2210
2.50	6.25	4.6157	.0940	4.9676
3.00	6.25	4.3442	.0970	4.7040
3.50	6.25	4.0886	.1000	4.4418
4.00	6.25	3.8481	.1040	4.1663
4.50	6.25	3.6218	.1060	3.9267
5.00	6.25	3.4087	.1080	3.6938
5.50	6.25	3.2082	.1090	3.4863
6.00	6.25	3.0195	.1120	3.2502
6.50	6.25	2.8419	.1140	3.0402
7.00	6.25	2.6747	.1160	2.8384
7.50	6.25	2.5174	.1180	2.6451
8.00	6.25	2.3693	.1190	2.4789
8.50	6.25	2.2299	.1200	2.3210
9.00	6.25	2.0987	.1220	2.1528
9.50	6.25	1.9753	.1240	1.9930
10.00	106.25	31.6046	.1250	31.6046
Total		100.0000		104.1880

To understand why the government dealer has the opportunity to realize this profit, look at the third column of Exhibit 9-4. That column shows how much the government dealer paid for each of the cash flows by buying the entire package of cash flows (i.e., by buying the bond). For example, consider the $6.25 coupon payment in four years. By buying the ten-year Treasury bond priced to yield 12.5%, the dealer pays a price based on 12.5% (6.25% semiannual) for that coupon payment, or equivalently,

$3.8481. However, under the assumptions in this illustration, investors were willing to accept a lower yield, 10.4% (5.2% semiannual) to purchase a zero-coupon Treasury security with four years to maturity. Thus, investors were willing to pay $4.1663. On this one coupon payment, the government dealer realizes a profit equal to the difference between $4.1663 and $3.8481 (or $.3182). From all the cash flows, the total profit is $4.1880. Coupon stripping is a good example where "the sum of the parts is greater than the whole."

Suppose that instead of the observed yield to maturity from Exhibit 9-3, the yields that investors want is the same as the theoretical spot rates shown in the exhibit. Exhibit 9-5 demonstrates that, in this case, the total proceeds from the sale of the zero-coupon Treasury securities would be approximately equal to $100, making coupon stripping uneconomic. If the Treasury security is not priced based on the theoretical spot rates, coupon stripping may be profitable.

EXHIBIT 9-5   Profit Opportunity from Coupon Stripping Using Theoretical Spot Rate Curve

Maturity	Cash Flow	Present Value at 12.5%	Theoretical Spot Rate	Present Value at Spot Rate
.50	6.25	5.8824	.08000	6.0096
1.00	6.25	5.5363	.08300	5.7618
1.50	6.25	5.2017	.08930	5.4824
2.00	6.25	4.9042	.09247	5.2163
2.50	6.25	4.6157	.09468	4.9595
3.00	6.25	4.3442	.09787	4.6923
3.50	6.25	4.0886	.10129	4.4227
4.00	6.25	3.8481	.10592	4.1360
4.50	6.25	3.6218	.10850	3.8850
5.00	6.25	3.4087	.11021	3.6553
5.50	6.25	3.2082	.11175	3.4367
6.00	6.25	3.0195	.11584	3.1801
6.50	6.25	2.8419	.11744	2.9766
7.00	6.25	2.6747	.11991	2.7660
7.50	6.25	2.5174	.12405	2.5343
8.00	6.25	2.3693	.12278	2.4092
8.50	6.25	2.2299	.12546	2.2217
9.00	6.25	2.0987	.13152	1.9861
9.50	6.25	1.9753	.13377	1.8266
10.00	106.25	31.6046	.13623	28.4426
Total		100.0000		100.0010

It is the process of coupon stripping that will prevent the price of a Treasury security from selling at a price that is materially different from its theoretical price based on the theoretical spot rate curve. As more stripping is done, forces of demand and supply will cause rates to move toward their theoretical spot rate levels. This is, in fact, what has happened in the Treasury market.

IMPLIED FORWARD RATES

We have just seen how the theoretical spot rate curve can be constructed from the yield curve. But there may be more information contained in the yield curve. Specifically, can we use the yield curve to infer the market's expectations of future interest rates? Let's explore this possibility.

Suppose that an investor has a one-year investment horizon and is faced with the following two alternatives:

Alternative 1: Buy a one-year Treasury bill
Alternative 2: Buy a six-month Treasury bill, and when it matures in six months buy another six-month Treasury bill

The investor will be indifferent between the two alternatives if they produce the same yield or the same number of dollars per dollar invested over the one-year investment horizon. Investors know the spot rate on the six-month Treasury bill and the one-year Treasury bill, but they do not know what yield will be available on a six-month Treasury bill purchased six months from now. The yield on a six-month Treasury bill six months from now is called the *forward rate*. Given the spot rate for the six-month Treasury bill and the one-year Treasury bill rate, the forward rate on a six-month Treasury bill that will make investors indifferent to the two alternatives can be determined as described below.

By investing in the one-year Treasury bill, the investor will receive the maturity value at the end of one year. Suppose that the maturity value of the one-year Treasury bill is $100. The price (cost) of the one-year Treasury bill would be as follows:

$$\frac{100}{\left(1+y_2\right)^2}$$

where y_2 is one-half the bond-equivalent yield of the theoretical one-year spot rate.

Suppose that the investor purchases a six-month Treasury bill for P dollars. At the end of six months, the value of this investment would be

$$P\left(1+y_1\right)$$

where y_1 is one-half the bond-equivalent yield of the theoretical six-month spot rate.

Let f be one-half the forward rate on a six-month Treasury bill available six months from now. Then the future dollars available at the end of one year from the P dollars invested would be given by

$$P(1+y_1)(1+f)$$

Suppose that today we want to know how many P dollars the investor must invest in order to get $100 one year from now. This can be found as follows:

$$P(1+y_1)(1+f) = 100$$

Solving, we get

$$P = \frac{100}{(1+y_1)(1+f)}$$

The investor will be indifferent between the two alternatives confronting him if he makes the same dollar investment and receives $100 from both investments at the end of one year. That is, the investor will be indifferent if

$$\frac{100}{(1+y_2)^2} = \frac{100}{(1+y_1)(1+f)}$$

Solving for f, we get

(9.1) $$f = \frac{(1+y_2)^2}{(1+y_1)} - 1$$

Doubling f gives the bond-equivalent yield for the six-month forward rate.

To illustrate equation (9.1), we will use the theoretical spot rates shown in Exhibit 9-3. We know that:

Six-month bill spot rate $= .080$; therefore $y_1 = .0400$
One-year bill spot rate $= .083$; therefore $y_2 = .0415$

Substituting into the equation, we have

$$f = \frac{(1.0415)^2}{1.0400} - 1$$

$$= .043$$

The forward rate on a six-month security, quoted on a bond-equivalent basis, is 8.60% ($.043 \times 2$).

Let's confirm these results. The price of a one-year Treasury bill with a $100 maturity value is

$$\frac{100}{(1.0415)^2} = 92.19$$

If 92.19 is invested for six months at the six-month spot rate of 8%, the amount at the end of six months would be

$$92.19(1.0400) = 95.8776$$

If 95.8776 is reinvested for another six months in a six-month Treasury offering 4.3% for six months (8.6% annually), the amount at the end of one year is

$$95.8876\,(1.043) = 100$$

Both alternatives will have the same $100 payoff if the six-month Treasury bill yield six months from now is 4.3% (8.6% on a bond-equivalent basis). This means that if investors are guaranteed a 4.3% yield (8.6% bond-equivalent basis) on a six-month Treasury bill six months from now, they will be indifferent between the two alternatives.

Because we use the theoretical spot rates to compute the forward rate, the resulting forward rate is called the *implied forward rate*.

While we have restricted our example to calculation of the implied six-month forward rate six months from now, we can follow the same methodology to determine the implied forward rate six months from now for an investment for a period longer than six months. That is, the yield curve or, more specifically, the spot rate curve generated from the yield curve can be used to construct an implied forward rate six months from now for one-year investments, 1.5-year investments, two-year investments, 2.5-year investments, and so on.

We can even take this one step farther. It is not necessary to limit ourselves to implied forward rates six months from now. The yield curve can be used to calculate the implied forward rate for any time into the future for any investment horizon. As examples, the following can be calculated:

- The two-year implied forward rate five years from now
- The six-year implied forward rate ten years from now
- The seven-year implied forward rate three years from now

How is this done? To demonstrate how, we must introduce some notation. We will continue to let f represent the forward rate. But now we must identify two aspects of the forward rate. First, we want to denote when the forward rate begins. Second, we want to denote the length of time of the forward rate. To identify these two aspects of the forward rate, we use the following notation:

$_nf_t$ = the forward rate n periods from now for t periods

Remember that in our examples each period is equal to six months. The following examples will illustrate this notation. Consider first our earlier example of the six-month forward rate six months from now. In this case, because we are looking at a forward rate six months from now, this is equal to one period from now. Thus n is 1. The length of the forward rate is six months, so t is equal to 1. Consequently, the six-month forward rate six months from now is denoted by $_1f_1$. The six-month forward rates can then be expressed as follows:

$_2f_1$ = six-month forward rate one year (two periods) from now
$_3f_1$ = six-month forward rate 1.5 years (three periods) from now
$_4f_1$ = six-month forward rate two years (four periods) from now, etc.

For forward rates four years (eight periods) from now, we would have the following:

$_8f_1$ = six-month forward rate four years (eight periods) from now
$_8f_2$ = one-year (two period) forward rate four years (eight periods) from now
$_8f_3$ = 1.5-year forward rate four years (eight periods) from now, etc.

Now let's see how the spot rates can be used to calculate the implied forward rate. We shall assume in the illustration that there are zero-coupon Treasury securities available.[7] Suppose that an investor has a five-year investment horizon and is faced with the following two alternatives:

Alternative 1:   Buy a five-year (ten-period) zero-coupon Treasury security
Alternative 2:   Buy a three-year (six-period) zero-coupon Treasury security, and when it matures in three years buy a two-year Treasury security.

Investors will be indifferent between the two alternatives if they produce the same yield or the same number of dollars per dollar invested over the five-year investment horizon. Investors know the spot rate on the five-year Treasury security and the three-year Treasury security, but they do not know what yield will be available on a two-year Treasury security purchased three years from now. That is, the investor does not know the two-year forward rate three years from now. In terms of our notation, the unknown is $_6f_4$.

---

[7] The existence of zero-coupon Treasury securities is not necessary for determination of the implied forward rates. The assumption just simplifies the presentation.

The price of the five-year zero-coupon Treasury security with a maturity value of $100 would be

$$\frac{100}{\left(1+y_{10}\right)^{10}}$$

where y_{10} is one-half the bond-equivalent yield of the theoretical five-year spot rate.

Suppose that the investor purchases a three-year zero-coupon Treasury security for P dollars. At the end of three years, the value of this investment would be

$$P\left(1+y_6\right)^6$$

where y_6 is one-half the bond-equivalent yield of the theoretical three-year spot rate. Let $_6f_4$ be the semiannual two-year forward rate three years from now. Then the future dollars available at the end of five years from the P dollars invested are

$$P\left(1+y_6\right)^6\left(1+{}_6f_4\right)^4$$

Suppose that today we want to know how many P dollars the investor must invest in order to get $100 one year from now. This can be found as follows:

$$P\left(1+y_6\right)^6\left(1+{}_6f_4\right)^4 = 100$$

Solving we get,

$$P = \frac{100}{\left(1+y_6\right)^6\left(1+{}_6f_4\right)^4}$$

Investors will be indifferent between the two alternatives if they make the same dollar investment and receive $100 at the end of five years from both alternatives. That is, the investor will be indifferent if

$$\frac{100}{\left(1+y_{10}\right)^{10}} = \frac{100}{\left(1+y_6\right)^6\left(1+{}_6f_4\right)^4}$$

Solving for $_6f_4$, we get

$$_6f_4 = \left[\frac{\left(1+y_{10}\right)^{10}}{\left(1+y_6\right)^6}\right]^{1/4} - 1$$

Doubling $_6f_4$ gives the bond-equivalent yield for the two-year forward rate three years from now.

To illustrate this, we use the theoretical spot rates shown in Exhibit 9-3. We know that:

Three-year spot rate $=$ .09787; therefore y_6 $=$ .048935
Five-year spot rate $=$ .11021; therefore y_{10} $=$ .055105

Substituting into the equation, we have

$$_6f_4 = \left[\frac{(1.055105)^{10}}{(1.048935)^6}\right]^{1/4} - 1$$

$$= \left[\frac{(1.709845)^{10}}{(1.331961)^6}\right]^{1/4} - 1$$

$$= .0644$$

The forward rate on a two-year Treasury security three years from now, quoted on a bond-equivalent basis, is 12.88% (.0644 × 2). Let's confirm our results. The price of a five-year zero-coupon Treasury security with a $100 maturity value is

$$\frac{100}{(1.055105)^{10}} = 58.48$$

If 58.48 is invested for three years at the three-year spot rate of 9.878%, the amount at the end of six periods would be

$$58.48\,(1.048935)^6 = 77.8931$$

If 77.8931 is reinvested for another two years (four periods) at 6.44% (12.88% annually), the amount at the end of the fifth year is

$$77.8931(1.0644)^4 = 100$$

Both alternatives will have the same $100 payoff if the two-year Treasury rate three years from now is 6.44% (12.88% on a bond-equivalent basis).

In general, the formula for the implied forward rate is:

(9.2) $$_nf_t = \left[\frac{(1+y_{n+t})^{n+t}}{(1+y_n)^n}\right]^{1/t} - 1$$

where y_n is a semiannual spot rate. Doubling $_nf_t$ gives the implied forward rate on a bond-equivalent basis.

To illustrate how to apply equation (9.2), consider the earlier example where we sought the six-month forward rate six months from now. That is, we sought $_1f_1$. Because n is equal to 1 and t is equal to 1, equation (9.2) becomes

$$_1f_1 = \left[\frac{\left(1+y_{1+1}\right)^{1+1}}{\left(1+y_1\right)^1} \right]^{1/1} - 1$$

or

$$= \frac{\left(1+y_2\right)^2}{\left(1+y_1\right)^1} - 1$$

This agrees with equation (9.1)

In our previous example, we sought the two-year forward rate three years from now. If we substitute 6 for n and 4 for t in the general formula, we would obtain the same formula we used to compute the forward rate we derived earlier.

Relationship Between Long Spot Rates and Short-Term Implied Forward Rates

While we have shown that there is a relationship between the implied forward rate and two spot rates, we can also demonstrate that there is a relationship between a spot rate and the implied short-term forward rates. To demonstrate this relationship, suppose our investor purchases a five-year zero-coupon Treasury security for $58.48 with a maturity value of $100. The investor instead could buy a six-month Treasury bill and reinvest the proceeds every six months for five years. The number of dollars that will be realized will depend on the six-month forward rates. Suppose that the investor can actually reinvest the proceeds maturing every six months at the implied six-month forward rates. Let's see how many dollars would accumulate at the end of five years. The implied six-month forward rates were calculated for the yield curve given in Exhibit 9-2. The semiannual implied forward rates from Exhibit 9-3 are:

$$_1f_1 = .043000$$
$$_2f_1 = .050980$$
$$_3f_1 = .051005$$
$$_4f_1 = .051770$$
$$_5f_1 = .056945$$
$$_6f_1 = .060965$$
$$_7f_1 = .069310$$
$$_8f_1 = .064625$$
$$_9f_1 = .062830$$

By investing the $58.48 at the six-month spot rate of 4% (8% on a bond-equivalent basis) and reinvesting at the forward rates above, the number of dollars accumulated at the end of five years would be

$54.48 (1.04) (1.043) (1.05098) (1.051005) (1.05177) (1.056945)
(1.060965) (1.06931) (1.064625) (1.06283) = $100

Therefore, we see that if the implied forward rates are realized, the $54.48 investment will produce the same number of dollars as an investment in a five-year zero-coupon Treasury security at the five-year spot rate. From this illustration, we can see that the five-year spot rate is related to the current six-month spot rate and the implied six-month forward rates.

In general the relationship among a t-period spot rate, the current six-month spot rate, and the implied six-month forward rates is as follows:

$$y_t = \left[\left(1 + y_1\right)\left(1 + {}_1 f_1\right)\left(1 + {}_2 f_1\right)\left(1 + {}_3 f_1\right) \cdots \left(1 + {}_t f_1\right) \right]^{1/t} - 1$$

DETERMINANTS OF THE SHAPE OF THE TERM STRUCTURE

Two major theories have evolved to account for the observed shapes of the yield curve: the expectations theory and the market segmentation theory.

There are several forms of the expectations theory—the pure expectations theory, the liquidity theory, and the preferred habitat theory. All share a hypothesis about the behavior of short-term forward rates, and all also assume that forward rates negotiated in current long-term contracts are closely related to the market's expectations about future short-term rates. They differ, however, on whether other factors also affect forward rates, and how. The pure expectations theory postulates that no other systematic factors affect forward rates; the liquidity theory and the preferred habitat theory assert that there are other factors. Accordingly, the last two forms of the expectations theory are sometimes referred to as *biased expectations* theories. To date, however, with some exceptions, empirical evidence does not provide support for the expectations theory.[8]

The Pure Expectations Theory

According to the pure expectations theory, forward rates exclusively represent expected future rates. Thus, the entire term structure at a given time reflects the market's current expectations of the family of future

---

[8] For a summary of the numerous studies on the expectations theory, see Richard McEnally and James V. Jordan, "The Term Structure of Interest Rates," Chapter 56 in Frank J. Fabozzi (ed.), *The Handbook of Fixed Income Securities* (Homewood, IL: BusinessOne–Irwin, Third Edition, 1991).

short-term rates. Under this view, a rising term structure, as in Panel A of Exhibit 9-1, must indicate that the market expects short-term rates to rise throughout the relevant future. Similarly, a flat term structure reflects an expectation that future short-term rates will remain relatively constant, while a falling term structure must reflect an expectation that future short-term rates will decline steadily.

We can illustrate these assumptions by considering how an expectation of a rising short-term future rate would affect the behavior of various market participants so as to result in a rising yield curve. Assume initially a flat term structure, and suppose that economic news subsequently leads market participants to expect interest rates to rise.

1. Any market participants interested in a long-term investment would not want to buy long-term bonds because they would expect yields to rise sooner or later, resulting in a price decline for the bonds and a capital loss on the long-term bonds they had purchased. They would want to invest instead in short-term debt obligations until the rise in yield had occurred, permitting them then to reinvest their funds at the higher yield.

2. Speculators expecting rising rates would anticipate a decline in the price of long-term bonds and therefore would want to sell or short them. (If interest rates rise as expected, the price of longer-term bonds will fall. As the speculator sold these bonds short and could then purchased them at a lower price to cover the short sale, a profit will be earned.) The proceeds received from the shorting of longer-term bonds will be invested in the meantime in short-term debt obligations.

3. Borrowers wishing to acquire long-term funds would be pulled toward borrowing in the long end of the market now, in the expectation that borrowing at a later time would be more expensive.

All these responses would tend to lower the net demand for long-maturity bonds (partly by increasing the supply), and increase demand for short-term debt obligations. This would raise long-term yields in relation to short-term yields; that is, the response would tilt the term structure upward until it is consistent with expectations of future interest rates. By analogous reasoning, an unexpected event leading to the expectation of lower future rates will result in the yield curve sloping down.

Unfortunately the pure expectations theory suffers from one shortcoming, which is quite serious, at least qualitatively. It says nothing about the risks inherent in investing in bonds and like instruments (or in borrowing). If forward rates were perfect predictors of future interest rates, then the future prices of bonds would be known with certainty. The total return over any investment horizon (or the cost of borrowing for any required period of financing) would be certain, and independent of the maturity of the instrument initially acquired (or sold) and of the time at which the investor needs to liquidate the instrument (or the borrower to refinance the debt). But where there is uncertainty about future interest rates and hence about future prices of bonds, these instruments become risky investments, with the risk depending on the maturity of the instrument and the intended investment horizon.

What are the implications of the pure expectations theory for bond portfolio management? There are five interpretations of the pure expectations theory put forth by economists, which are not exact equivalents nor necessarily consistent with each other (because of the risks associated with future interest rates that were noted above).[9] The broadest interpretation of the pure expectations theory suggests that the expected total return for any investment horizon period will be the same regardless of the maturity strategy selected.[10] For example, if an investor has a five-year investment horizon, it would make no difference whether a 5-year, a 10-year, or a 20-year bond is purchased and held for five years, because the total return from all three bonds will be the same over five years. It can be demonstrated that, because of the risks associated with investing in long-term bonds, this interpretation cannot be generally valid.[11]

The second interpretation, referred to as the *local expectations* form of the pure expectations theory,[12] suggests that the total return will be the same over a short-term investment horizon starting today. For example, if an investor has a 6-month investment horizon, buying a 5-year, a 10-year or a 20-year bond will produce the same 6-month total return. Cox, Ingersoll, and Ross demonstrate that the local expectations formulation is the only one of the five interpretations that can be sustained in equilibrium.

The third interpretation, the *unbiased expectations* form of the pure expectations theory, is the one we assumed at the outset of this section. It suggests that the implied forward rates are an unbiased forecast of the market's expectation of future interest rates.[13]

---

[9] These formulations are summarized by John Cox, Jonathan Ingersoll, Jr., and Stephen Ross, "A Re-examination of Traditional Hypotheses About the Term Structure of Interest Rates," *Journal of Finance*, September 1981, pp. 769-799.

[10] F. Lutz, "The Structure of Interest Rates," *Quarterly Journal of Economics* (1940–41), pp. 36–63.

[11] Cox, Ingersoll, and Ross, pp. 774–775.

[12] The labels for this theory, and the three to follow, are those used by Cox, Ingersoll, and Ross.

[13] Burton Malkiel, *The Term Structure of Interest Rates: Expectations and Behavior Patterns* (Princeton, NJ: Princeton University Press, 1966), p. 23.

The fourth interpretation of the pure expectations theory suggests that the total return that an investor will realize by rolling over short-term bonds to some investment horizon will be the same as holding a zero-coupon bond with a maturity that is the same as that investment horizon. (Recall that the zero-coupon bond has no reinvestment risk so that future interest rates over the investment horizon do not affect the total return.) This variant is called the *return to maturity expectations* interpretation. For example, once again assume that an investor has a five-year investment horizon. By buying a five-year zero-coupon bond and holding it to maturity, the investor's total return is the difference between the maturity value and the price of the bond all divided by the price of the bond. According to return to maturity expectations, by buying a six-month instrument and rolling it over for five years, the investor will realize the same total return.

Closely related to the return to maturity expectations is the *yield to maturity expectations* interpretation. This variant proposes that the total return will be the same for each period within the investment horizon, suggesting more than just the total return at the end of the investment horizon being equal by rolling over short-term instruments. Continuing with the example, an investor with a five-year investment horizon should expect to find that, at the end of six months, the total return from holding a five-year zero-coupon bond will be the same as holding a six-month instrument. At the end of three years, the total return from holding a five-year zero-coupon bond will be the same as rolling over a six-month instrument for three years. Under special conditions, the yield to maturity expectations and the unbiased expectations interpretations are the same.[14]

The Liquidity Theory

The drawback of the pure expectations theory is that it does not consider the risks associated with investing in bonds. Yet it can be shown that there is uncertainty about the one-period return from holding a bond that has a maturity longer than one period, and the uncertainty about the one-period return increases systematically with the maturity of the bond.[15]

Given this observation, and the reasonable consideration that investors typically do not like uncertainty, J.R. Hicks has hypothesized that to induce investors to hold longer-term maturities requires offering them a long-term rate higher than the average of expected future rates by a risk premium that increases, the longer the term to maturity.[16] Put

---

[14] As Cox, Ingersoll, and Ross demonstrate, this occurs when the analysis takes place in a continuous time framework.

[15] See Frank J. Fabozzi and Franco Modigliani, *Capital Markets: Institutions and Instruments* (Englewood Cliffs, NJ: Prentice–Hall, 1992), pp. 382–386.

[16] John R. Hicks, *Value and Capital* (London: Oxford University Press, 1946), 2nd ed., pp. 141–145.

differently, the forward rates should reflect both interest rate expectations and a "liquidity" premium (really a risk premium).

According to this theory, which is called the *liquidity theory* of the term structure, the implied forward rates will not be an unbiased estimate of the market's expectations of future interest rates because they embody a liquidity premium. An upward-sloping yield curve may reflect expectations that future interest rates either (1) will rise, or (2) will be flat or even fall, but with a liquidity premium increasing fast enough with maturity so as to produce an upward-sloping yield curve.

The Preferred Habitat Theory

Another theory originally formulated by Modigliani and Sutch also adopts the view that the term structure reflects the expectation of the future path of interest rates as well as a risk premium, but rejects the assertion that the risk premium must rise uniformly with maturity.[17] The latter conclusion could be accepted if all investors intend to liquidate their investment at the shortest possible date while all borrowers are eager to borrow long, an assumption that is not realistic for a number of reasons. Risk aversion dictates that investors should not buy a short-term instrument but rather an instrument with a maturity matching their investment objective. If investors buy a shorter instrument, they will bear reinvestment risk, i.e., the risk of a fall in the interest rates available for reinvesting proceeds of the shorter instrument. Investors can avoid that risk only by "locking in" the current long rate, through a long-term bond. Similarly, if they buy an instrument with maturity longer than the time they wish to invest for, they will bear the risk of a loss in the price of the asset (price risk) when liquidating it before its maturity, because of a rise in interest rates. Entirely analogous considerations apply to borrowers; prudence and safety call for borrowing for a maturity matching the length of time for which funds are required.

To illustrate this preference for maturity sectors, consider a life insurance company that has issued a five-year guaranteed investment contract. The insurance company will not want to invest in six-month instruments because of the associated reinvestment risk. As another example, assume a thrift has borrowed funds at a fixed rate for one year from the issuance of a one-year certificate of deposit. The thrift is exposed to price (or interest-rate) risk if the borrowed funds are invested in a bond with 20 years to maturity. For either of these institutions there is a risk of shifting out of their preferred maturity sector.

---

[17] Franco Modigliani and Richard Sutch, "Innovations in Interest Rate Policy," *American Economic Review*, May 1966, pp. 178–197.

The preferred habitat theory asserts that, to the extent that the demand and supply of funds in a given maturity range do not match, some lenders and borrowers will be induced to shift to maturities showing the opposite imbalances, but they will need to be compensated by an appropriate risk premium whose size will reflect the extent of risk aversion.[18]

Thus, the shape of the yield curve is determined by both expectations of future interest rates and a risk premium, positive or negative, to induce market participants to shift out of their preferred habitat. Clearly, according to this theory, upward-sloping, downward-sloping, flat, or humped yield curves are all possible.

Market Segmentation Theory

The market segmentation theory also recognizes that investors have preferred habitats and that the major reason for the shape of the yield curve lies in asset/liability management constraints (either regulatory or self-imposed) and/or creditors (borrowers) restricting their lending (financing) to specific maturity sectors.[19] The market segmentation theory differs from the preferred habitat theory, however, in that it assumes that neither investors nor borrowers are willing to shift from one maturity sector to another to take advantage of opportunities arising from differences between expectations and forward rates. Thus, for this theory the shape of the yield curve is determined by supply of and demand for securities within each maturity sector.

This formulation seems untenable because it presupposes the prevalence of absolute risk aversion, while the evidence does not support that proposition. That is, market participants will tend to shift away from their preferred habitat when there are sufficiently large discrepancies between market and expected rates, therefore insuring that the differences between them will not grow too large, which leads back to the preferred habitat model.

THE TERM STRUCTURE OF CREDIT SPREADS

Thus far, our focus in this chapter has been on the term structure of U.S. Treasury securities—default-free securities. The Treasury spot rates can then be used to price any default-free security. As we illustrated earlier, failure of Treasury securities to be priced according to the Treasury spot rates creates the opportunity for arbitrage profits.

---

[18] Cox, Ingersoll, and Ross demonstrate this relationship between the degree of risk aversion and the premium.

[19] This theory is suggested in J.M. Culbertson, "The Term Structure of Interest Rates," *Quarterly Journal of Economics*, November 1957, pp. 489–504.

For a corporate bond, price is not as simple. The price of a corporate bond must reflect not only the spot rate for default-free bonds but also a risk premium to reflect default risk and any options embedded in the issue. For now, we skip options embedded in bonds, a complexity addressed in Chapters 13 through 15.

In practice, the spot rate that has been used to discount the cash flows from a corporate bond is the Treasury spot rate plus a constant credit spread. For example, if the six-month Treasury spot rate is 5%, and the ten-year Treasury spot rate is 6.5%, and a suitable credit spread is deemed to be 100 basis points, then a 6% spot rate is used to discount a six-month cash flow of a corporate bond and a 7.5% discount rate to discount a ten-year cash flow. The drawback of this approach is that there is no reason to expect the credit spread to be the same, whenever the cash flow is expected to be received. Instead, logic indicates that the credit spread increases with the maturity of the corporate bond. That is, there is a term structure of credit spreads.

Until recently, little work has been done to estimate the term structure of credit spreads. The problem for academicians in estimating the term structure of credit spreads has been the lack of data on corporate bonds. Recently, two researchers at Goldman Sachs, Robert Litterman and Thomas Iben, have developed a procedure to estimate the term structure of credit spreads and have applied their model using actual corporate bond trading data.[20] The basic principle is described below.[21]

Consider four hypothetical zero-coupon securities, two Treasury issues and two securities issued by the same corporation:

Type	Maturity	Price per $1 par	Yield
Treasury	1 year	.930	7.39%
Corporate	1 year	.926	7.84%
Treasury	2 years	.848	8.42%
Corporate	2 years	.840	8.91%

Focus first on the two issues with one year to maturity. Investors are willing to pay 93.0 cents to receive $1 by purchasing the one-year Treasury and 92.6 cents to receive $1 by purchasing the one-year corporate security. The 4-cent difference produces a credit spread of 45 basis points (7.84% minus 7.39%). The lower price for the corporate

---

[20] Robert Litterman and Thomas Iben, "Corporate Bond Valuation and the Term Structure of Credit Spreads," *Journal of Portfolio Management*, Spring 1991, pp. 52–64. The original research was published by Goldman Sachs in 1988.

[21] The numerical example is the one used by Litterman and Iben, pp. 53–54

security reflects default risk; that is, it reflects the probability that the issuer will default. For the same expected return to result by holding either bond, the price of the corporate bond must be equal to the price of the Treasury times the probability of solvency (i.e., not defaulting).[22] Thus,

Price of corporate zero = Price of Treasury zero × (Probability of solvency)

or, equivalently, because the probability of solvency is equal to one minus the probability of default:

Price of corporate zero = Price of Treasury zero × (1 − Probability of default)

Solving for the probability of default,

$$\text{Probability of default} = 1 - \frac{\text{Price of Corporate zero}}{\text{Price of Treasury zero}}$$

In our example,

$$\text{Probability of default} = 1 - \frac{.926}{.930} = .0043$$

Now let's focus on the two zero-coupon securities that mature two years from now. The two-year corporate zero will pay off $1 in the second year only if the corporation that has issued both one-year and two-year securities does not default in either the first or the second year. The probability of default in the first year has already been determined (.0043). The next step is to determine the conditional probability of default in the second year, given that the corporation does not default in the first year. Litterman and Iben refer to this probability as the *forward probability of default*.

Given the assumption that the expected return from holding a Treasury zero for two years must equal the return from holding a corporate zero for two years times the probability of solvency, the forward probability of default can be calculated. In this example it is .0052. This procedure can be used to determine a term structure of credit spreads for zero-coupon corporates for a *given* corporate issuer.

In practice, the difficulty of applying this technique is that there are no issuers that offer a sufficiently wide range of corporate coupon securities to construct a zero-coupon spread curve. The procedure Litterman and Iben use is to construct a generic-zero spread curve by credit rating and industry using actual trading data.

Exhibit 9-6 shows a generic zero-coupon spread curve for financial corporations by credit rating as of January 14, 1991. Notice that the credit

---

[22] This simple illustration assumes that if default occurs, the investor realizes nothing. In practice, this is not true, and the formulation can be modified to reflect this.

**EXHIBIT 9-6   Generic-Zero Spread Curves for Financial
Corporations (January 14, 1991)**

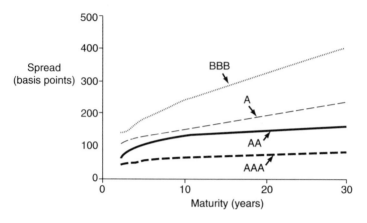

Source: Robert Litterman and Thomas Iben, "Corporate Bond Valuation and the Term Structure of Credit Spreads," *Journal of Portfolio Management,* Spring 1991, p. 55.

spread increases with maturity. Litterman and Iben indicate that this is a typical shape for the credit spread. The lower the credit rating, the steeper the curve.

One implication of an upward-sloping term structure for credit spreads is that it is inappropriate to discount the cash flows from a corporate bond at a constant spread to the Treasury spot rate curve. The shorter-term cash flows will be undervalued, and the long-term cash flows will be overvalued.

SUMMARY

The yield on Treasury securities provides the base rate off which non-Treasury securities are priced. More specifically, we have seen in this chapter that it is the term structure of interest rates, which is represented by the theoretical spot rate curve for zero-coupon Treasuries, that is used for pricing securities. While the yield curve for actual zero-coupon Treasuries can be used to construct the spot rate curve, this approach has limitations in estimating the term structure. A simplified approach for estimating the term structure is presented in this chapter; more sophisticated econometric techniques have been developed. We also demonstrate that the profitability of stripping coupon Treasury securities to create zero-coupon Treasury securities and of creating synthetic coupon

Treasury securities from zero-coupon Treasury securities depends on the shape and level of the actual yield curve.

Several theories have been proposed for what determines the term structure of interest rates: expectations theories and the market segmentation theory. There are three forms of the expectations theory: the pure expectations theory, the liquidity theory, and the preferred habitat theory. With the pure expectations theory the only factor that affects the term structure is expectations about future interest rates.

Because corporate bonds expose an investor to default risk, a credit spread must be added to the Treasury spot rates to obtain the appropriate spot rate to discount cash flows. The common practice of adding a constant spread to each Treasury spot rate is inappropriate, because there is a term structure of credit spreads that reflect the probability of default. Estimation of the term structure of credit spreads is much more difficult than estimation of the term structure of interest rates, and a methodology for its estimation has been suggested.

QUESTIONS FOR CHAPTER 9

1. You are a pension fund consultant. At various times you hear comments on interest rates from some of your clients. How would you respond to each comment?

   a. "The yield curve is upward-sloping today. This suggests that the market consensus is that interest rates are expected to increase in the future."

   b. "I can't make any sense out of today's term structure. For short-term yields (up to three years), the yields increase with maturity; for maturities greater than three years but less than eight years, yields decline with maturity; and for maturities greater than eight years yields are virtually the same for each maturity. There is simply no theory that explains a yield curve with this shape."

   c. "When I want to determine the market's consensus of future interest rates, I calculate the implied forward rates."

2. Determine the value of the following risk-free debt instrument, which promises to make the particular payments when the corresponding spot rates are as shown in the last column:

Year	Cash Payment	Spot Rate
1	$15,000	8.0%
2	17,000	8.5
3	20,000	9.0
4	21,000	9.5

3. You observe the yield curve below for Treasury securities (all yields are shown on a bond-equivalent basis):

Year	Yield to Maturity	Spot Rate
.5	5.25%	5.25%
1.0	5.50	5.50
1.5	5.75	5.76
2.0	6.00	?
2.5	6.25	?
3.0	6.50	?
3.5	6.75	?
4.0	7.00	?
4.5	7.25	?
5.0	7.50	?
5.5	7.75	7.97
6.0	8.00	8.27
6.5	8.25	8.59
7.0	8.50	8.92
7.5	8.75	9.25
8.0	9.00	9.61
8.5	9.25	9.97

9.0	9.50	10.36
9.5	9.75	10.77
10.0	10.00	11.20

All the securities maturing from 1.5 years on are selling at par. The .5-year and one-year securities are zero-coupon instruments.

a. Calculate the missing spot rates.

b. What should the price of a six-year Treasury security be?

c. What is the implied six-month forward rate starting in the sixth year?

4. You observe the following yield curve for Treasury securities (all yields are shown on a bond-equivalent basis):

Year	Yield to Maturity	Spot Rate
.5	10.00%	10.00%
1.0	9.75	9.75
1.5	9.50	9.48
2.0	9.25	9.22
2.5	9.00	8.95
3.0	8.75	8.68
3.5	8.50	8.41
4.0	8.25	8.14
4.5	8.00	7.86
5.0	7.75	7.58
5.5	7.50	7.30
6.0	7.25	7.02
6.5	7.00	6.74
7.0	6.75	6.46
7.5	6.50	6.18
8.0	6.25	5.90
8.5	6.00	5.62
9.0	5.75	5.35
9.5	5.50	?
10.0	5.25	?

All the securities maturing from 1.5 years on are selling at par. The .5-year and one-year securities are zero-coupon instruments.

a. Calculate the missing spot rates.

b. What should the price of a four-year Treasury security be?

5. a. The following is from the February 1991 monthly report published by Blackstone Financial Management:

On February 1, 1991, the Federal Reserve lowered the discount rate from 6.5% to 6.0% and moved the fed funds target rate from 6.75% to 6.25%. The aggressive easing of monetary policy prompted a significant steepening of the yield curve. Two-year Treasury notes fell 41 basis points to 6.82% while Treasury bonds declined only 16 basis points.

Explain how the "aggressive easing of monetary policy" resulted in a "steepening of the yield curve."

b. In the March 1991 monthly report, the following appears:

The further perception that the Federal Reserve had largely concluded its aggressive easing of monetary policy, along with a sell-off of short and intermediate Treasuries by Middle Eastern accounts to raise cash to finance war costs, produced a flatter yield curve. . . .

Explain why the yield curve became flatter as a result of the actions described above.

6. (*This question is from CFA Examination II, June 1, 1991, Morning Section, Question 2*):

a. Calculate the two-year spot rate implied by the U.S. Treasury yield curve data given below. Assume interest is paid annually for purposes of this calculation. Show all calculations.

Years to Maturity	Current Coupon (Yield-to-Maturity)	Spot Rate
1	7.5%	7.5%
2	8.0	?

b. Explain why a spot rate curve can be derived entirely from the current coupon (yield to maturity) yield curve.

c. Given a U.S. Treasury one-year spot rate of 9.0% and U.S. Treasury two-year spot rate of 9.5%, calculate the implied one-year forward rate for the two-year U.S. Treasury security with one year remaining to maturity. Explain why a one-year forward rate of 9.6% would not be expected to prevail in a market given these spot rates.

d. Describe *one* practical application of the spot rate concept and *one* practical application of the forward rate concept.

7. (*This question is from CFA Examination II, June 2, 1990, Morning Section, Question 2*):

The following are average yields on U.S. Treasury bonds at two different times:

Term to Maturity	Yield to Maturity	
	January 15, 19XX	May 15, 19XX
1 year	7.25%	8.05%
2 years	7.50	7.90
5 years	7.90	7.70
10 years	8.30	7.45
15 years	8.45	7.30
20 years	8.55	7.20
25 years	8.60	7.10

a. Assuming a pure expectations hypothesis, define a forward rate. Describe how you would calculate the forward rate for a three-year

U.S. Treasury bond two years from May 15, 19XX, using the actual term structure above.

b. Discuss how *each* of the *three* major term structure hypotheses could explain the January 15, 19XX, term structure shown above.

c. Discuss what happened to the term structure over the time period and the effect of this change on the U.S. Treasury bonds of two years and ten years.

8. a. Why has coupon stripping resulted in pricing of Treasuries based on theoretical spot rates?

b. If the actual price of a Treasury is less than its theoretical price based on spot rates, how can a market participant take advantage of this situation?

9. Give five interpretations of the pure expectations theory and their implications for bond portfolio management.

10. a. What is meant by the term structure of credit spreads?

b. What is a generic zero-coupon spread curve?

c. What is the implication of an upward-sloping term structure for credit spreads?

Chapter 10

Mortgage Loans

While the American dream may be to own a home, the major portion of the funds to purchase one must be borrowed. The market where these funds are borrowed is called the mortgage market. This sector of the debt market is by far the largest in the world, with an estimated size at the beginning of 1990 of roughly $3.5 trillion, far exceeding the $1.9 trillion U.S. government securities market and the $1.4 trillion corporate bond market.

This chapter and the two to follow describe mortgage loans and the various securities created by using mortgage loans as collateral. In this chapter we focus on individual mortgage loans: the characteristics of mortgage loans, the participants (mortgage originators and investors) in this market, the more popular mortgage loan designs, and the market for mortgage loans.

WHAT IS A MORTGAGE?

A mortgage is a loan secured by the collateral of some specified real estate property, which obliges the borrower to make a predetermined series of payments. The mortgage gives the lender (the mortgagee) the right of foreclosure on the loan, if the borrower (the mortgager) defaults. That is, if the borrower fails to make the contracted payments, the lender can seize the property in order to ensure that the debt is paid off.

When the lender makes the loan based on the credit of the borrower and on the collateral for the mortgage, the mortgage is said to be a conventional mortgage. The lender also may take out mortgage insurance to provide a guarantee for the fulfillment of the borrower's obligations. There are two forms of mortgage insurance that are guaranteed by the U.S. government if the borrower can qualify: Federal Housing Administration (FHA) and Veterans Administration (VA) insurance. There are also private mortgage insurers. The cost of mortgage insurance is paid to the guarantor by the mortgage originator but passed along to the borrower in the form of higher mortgage payments.

The types of real estate properties that can be mortgaged are divided into two broad categories: residential and nonresidential properties. The former category includes houses, condominiums, cooperatives, and apartments. Residential real estate can be subdivided into single-family (one-to-four-family) structures and multifamily structures (apartment buildings in which more than four families reside). Nonresidential property includes commercial and farm properties. Our focus in this chapter and the next two is on residential mortgage loans.

PARTICIPANTS IN THE MORTGAGE MARKET

In addition to the ultimate lenders of funds and the government agencies described in the next chapter, there are three groups involved in the market: mortgage originators, mortgage servicers, and mortgage insurers.

Mortgage Originators

The original lender is called the mortgage originator. Mortgage originators include thrifts, commercial banks, mortgage bankers, life insurance companies, and pension funds. The three largest originators for all types of residential mortgages are thrifts, commercial banks, and mortgage bankers. These three groups originated $475 billion (or 98%) of the $485 billion of residential mortgages originated in 1990. Prior to 1990, thrifts were the largest originators, followed by commercial banks. In 1990, thrift origination declined; with an increase in commercial bank origination, the share of thrift origination dropped below that of commercial banks. In 1990 mortgage bankers' share of origination was the largest.

Originators may generate income for themselves in one or more ways. First, they typically charge an origination fee. This fee is expressed in terms of points, where each point represents 1% of the borrowed funds. For example, an origination fee of two points on a $100,000 mortgage represents $2,000. Originators also charge application fees and certain processing fees.

The second source of revenue is the profit that might be generated from selling a mortgage at a higher price than it originally cost. This profit is called *secondary marketing profit*. Of course, if mortgage rates rise, an originator will realize a loss when the mortgages are sold in the secondary market. Finally, the mortgage originator may hold the mortgage in its investment portfolio.

A potential homeowner who wants to borrow funds to purchase a home will apply for a loan from a mortgage originator. Upon completion of the application form, which provides financial information about the applicant, and payment of an application fee, the mortgager originator will perform a credit evaluation of the applicant.

The two primary factors in determining whether the funds will be lent are the payment-to-income (PTI) ratio and the loan-to-value (LTV) ratio. The PTI, the ratio of monthly payments (both mortgage and real estate tax payments) to monthly income, is a measure of the ability of the applicant to make monthly payments. The lower this ratio, the greater the likelihood that the applicant will be able to meet the required payments. The difference between the purchase price of the property and the amount borrowed is the borrower's down payment. The LTV is the ratio of the amount of the loan to the market (or appraised) value of the property. The lower this ratio, the more protection the lender has if the applicant defaults and the property must be repossessed and sold.

Mortgage originators can either (1) hold the mortgage in their portfolio, (2) sell the mortgage to an investor who wishes to hold the mortgage or who will place the mortgage in a pool of mortgages to be used as collateral for the issuance of a security, or (3) use the mortgage themselves as collateral for the issuance of a security. When a mortgage is used as collateral for the issuance of a security, the mortgage is said to be *securitized*. In the next chapter, we discuss the process of securitizing mortgages.

When a mortgage originator intends to sell the mortgage, it will obtain a commitment from the potential investor (buyer). Two federally sponsored credit agencies and several private companies buy mortgages. As these agencies and private companies pool these mortgages and sell them to investors, they are called *conduits*.

The two agencies, the Federal Home Loan Mortgage Corporation and the Federal National Mortgage Association (discussed further below), purchase only *conforming* mortgages. A *conforming mortgage* is one that meets the underwriting standards established by these agencies for being in a pool of mortgages underlying a security that they guarantee. Three underwriting standards established by these agencies in order to qualify as a conforming mortgage are (1) a maximum PTI, (2) a maximum LTV, and (3) a maximum loan amount. If an applicant does not satisfy the underwriting standards, the mortgage is called a *nonconforming mortgage*.[1]

---

[1] Loans that exceed the maximum loan amount and therefore do not qualify as conforming mortgages are called *jumbo* loans.

Mortgages acquired by the agency may be held as investments in their portfolio or securitized. The securities offered are discussed in the next chapter.

Examples of private conduits are Citimae, Inc. (a subsidiary of Citicorp), Bear Stearns Mortgage Capital Corporation, Residential Funding Corporation (a subsidiary of GMAC), FBS Mortgage Corporation (a subsidiary of First Boston), Sears Mortgage Securities Corporation, and Shearson Lehman Hutton Mortgage Corporation. Private conduits typically will securitize the mortgages purchased rather than hold them as an investment. Both conforming and nonconforming mortgages are purchased. Nonconforming mortgages do not necessarily have greater credit risk. For example, an individual with an annual income of $500,000 may apply for a mortgage loan of $200,000 on real estate that she wants to purchase for $1 million. This would be a nonconforming mortgage because the amount of the mortgage exceeds the limit currently established for a conforming mortgage. The individual's income, however, can easily accommodate the monthly mortgage payments. Moreover, the lender's risk exposure is minimal, for it has lent $200,000 backed by collateral of $1 million.

Mortgage Servicers

Every mortgage loan must be serviced. Servicing of a mortgage loan involves collecting monthly payments and forwarding proceeds to owners of the loan; sending payment notices to mortgagors; reminding mortgagors when payments are overdue; maintaining records of principal balances; administering an escrow balance for real estate taxes and insurance purposes; initiating foreclosure proceedings if necessary; and furnishing tax information to mortgagors when applicable.

Servicers include bank-related entities, thrift-related entities, and mortgage bankers. As of 1989, an *American Banker* survey found that bank-related servicers had 43% of the market share and thrift-related servicers 20%. There is a secondary market for servicing rights (i.e., the market for the transfer of the right to service a mortgage loan).

There are five sources of revenue from mortgage servicing. The primary source is the *servicing fee*. This fee is a fixed percentage of the outstanding mortgage balance. Consequently, the revenue from servicing declines over time as the mortgage balance amortizes. The second source of servicing income arises from the interest that can be earned by the servicer from the escrow balance that the borrower often maintains with the servicer. The third source of revenue is the float earned on the monthly mortgage payment. This opportunity arises because of the delay permitted between the time the servicer receives the payment and the time that the payment must be sent to the investor. Fourth, there are several sources of ancillary income. First, a late fee is charged by the servicer if the payment is not made on time. Second, many servicers receive commissions from cross selling their borrowers for credit life and other insurance products. Third, fees can also be generated from selling mailing lists.

Finally, there are other benefits of servicing rights for servicers who are also lenders. Their portfolio of borrowers is a potential source for other loans such as second mortgages, automobile loans, and credit cards.

Mortgage Insurers

There are two types of mortgage-related insurance. The first type, originated by the lender to insure against default by the borrower, is called mortgage insurance or private mortgage insurance. It is usually required by lenders on loans with loan-to-value (LTV) ratios greater than 80%. The amount insured will be some percentage of the loan and may decline as the LTV ratio declines. While the insurance is required by the lender, its cost is borne by the borrower, usually through a higher contract rate. Mortgage insurance can be obtained from a mortgage insurance company such as Mortgage Guaranty Insurance Company (owned by Northwestern Mutual) and PMI Mortgage Insurance Company (owned by Sears, Roebuck), or, if the borrower qualifies, from the Federal Housing Administration or Veterans Administration.

The second type of mortgage-related insurance is acquired by the borrower, usually with a life insurance company, and is typically called credit life. Unlike mortgage insurance, this type of insurance is not required by the lender. The policy provides for a continuation of mortgage payments after the death of the insured person, which allows the survivors to continue living in the house. Because the insurance coverage decreases as the mortgage balance declines, this type of mortgage insurance is simply a term policy.

While both types of insurance have a beneficial effect on the creditworthiness of the borrower, the first type is more important from the lender's perspective. Mortgage insurance is sought by the lender when the borrower is viewed as being capable of meeting the monthly mortgage payments, but does not have enough funds for a large down payment. For example, suppose a borrower seeks financing of $100,000 to purchase a single-family residence for $110,000, thus making a down payment of $10,000. The LTV ratio is 90%, exceeding the uninsured maximum LTV of 80%. Even if the lender's credit analysis indicates that the borrower's payment-to-income ratio is acceptable, the mortgage loan cannot be extended. However, if a private mortgage insurance company insures a portion of the loan, then the lender is afforded protection. Mortgage insurance companies will write policies to insure a maximum of 20% of loans with an LTV ranging from 80% to 90%, and a maximum of 25% of loans with an LTV ranging from 90% to 95%. The lender is still exposed to default by the borrower on the noninsured portion of the mortgage loan, and, in the case of private mortgage insurers, exposed as well to the risk that the insurer will default.

ALTERNATIVE MORTGAGE INSTRUMENTS

There are many types of mortgage loans from which a borrower can select. We review several of the more popular mortgage designs here.

The interest rate on a mortgage loan is greater than the risk-free interest rate, in particular the yield on a Treasury security of comparable maturity. The spread reflects the higher costs of collection, the costs associated with default, which are not eliminated despite the collateral, poorer liquidity, and uncertainty concerning the timing of the cash flow (which we explain later). The frequency of payment is typically monthly, and the prevailing term of the mortgage is 20 to 30 years, although in recent years an increasing number of 15-year mortgages have been originated.

Level-Payment, Fixed-Rate Mortgage

The basic idea behind the design of the level-payment, fixed-rate mortgage, or simply level-payment mortgage, is that the borrower pays interest and repays principal in equal installments over an agreed-upon period of time, called the maturity or term of the mortgage. Thus at the end of the term the loan has been fully amortized.

Each monthly mortgage payment for a level-payment mortgage is due on the first of each month and consists of:

1. Interest of 1/12th of the fixed annual interest rate times the amount of the outstanding mortgage balance at the beginning of the previous month, and
2. A repayment of a portion of the outstanding mortgage balance (principal).

The difference between the monthly mortgage payment and the portion of the payment that represents interest equals the amount that is applied to reduce the outstanding mortgage balance. The monthly mortgage payment is designed so that after the last scheduled monthly payment of the loan is made, the amount of the outstanding mortgage balance is zero (i.e., the mortgage is fully repaid).

To illustrate a level-payment fixed-rate mortgage, consider a 30-year (360-month), $100,000 mortgage with a 9.5% mortgage rate. The monthly mortgage payment would be $840.85. (The formula for calculating the monthly mortgage payment is given later.)

Exhibit 10-1 shows how each monthly mortgage payment is divided between interest and repayment of principal. At the beginning of month 1, the mortgage balance is $100,000, the amount of the original loan. The mortgage payment for month 1 includes interest on the $100,000 borrowed for the month. The interest rate is 9.5%, so the monthly interest rate is 0.0079167 (.095 divided by 12). Interest for month 1 is therefore $791.67 ($100,000 times 0.0079167). The $49.18 difference between the monthly mortgage payment of $840.85 and the interest of $791.67 is the portion of the monthly mortgage payment that represents repayment of principal. This $49.18 in month 1 reduces the mortgage balance.

The mortgage balance at the end of month 1 (beginning of month 2) is then $99,950.81 ($100,000 minus $49.19).2 The interest for the second monthly mortgage payment is $791.28, the monthly interest rate (0.0079167) times the mortgage balance at the beginning of month 2 ($99,950.81). The difference between the $840.85 monthly mortgage payment and the $791.28 interest is $49.57, representing the amount of the mortgage balance paid off with that monthly mortgage payment. Notice in Exhibit 10-1 that the last monthly mortgage payment is sufficient to pay off the remaining mortgage balance. When a loan repayment schedule is structured in this way, so that the payments made by the borrower will completely pay off the interest and principal, the loan is said to be *self-amortizing*. Exhibit 10-1 is then referred to as an *amortization schedule*.

As Exhibit 10-1 clearly shows, the portion of the monthly mortgage payment applied to interest declines each month, and the portion applied to reducing the mortgage balance increases. The reason for this is that as the mortgage balance is reduced with each monthly mortgage payment, the interest on the mortgage balance declines. Because the monthly mortgage payment is fixed, a larger part of the monthly payment is applied to reduce the principal in each subsequent month.

Determining the Monthly Mortgage Payment: To compute the monthly mortgage payment for a level-payment mortgage requires application of the formula for the present value of an annuity presented in Chapter 2. The formula is

---

[2] Because Exhibit 10-1 is computer-generated, rounding results in slightly different values in the table.

EXHIBIT 10-1 Amortization Schedule for a Level-Payment, Fixed-Rate Mortgage

Mortgage loan: $100,000
Mortgage rate: 9.5%
Monthly payment: $840.85
Term of loan: 30 years (360 months)

Month	Beginning Mortgage Balance	Monthly Mortgage Payment	Interest for Month	Principal Repayment	Ending Mortgage Balance
1	$100,000.00	$840.85	$791.67	$ 49.19	$99,950.81
2	99,950.81	840.85	791.28	49.58	99,901.24
3	99,901.24	840.85	790.88	49.97	99,851.27
4	99,851.27	840.85	790.49	50.37	99,800.90
5	99,800.90	840.85	790.09	50.76	99,750.14
6	99,750.14	840.85	789.69	51.17	99,698.97
7	99,698.97	840.85	789.28	51.57	99,647.40
8	99,647.40	840.85	788.88	51.98	99,595.42
9	99,595.42	840.85	788.46	52.39	99,543.03
10	99,543.03	840.85	788.05	52.81	99,490.23
. . .	. . .	. . .	. . .	. . .	. . .
. . .	. . .	. . .	. . .	. . .	. . .
. . .	. . .	. . .	. . .	. . .	. . .
98	$99,862.54	840.85	735.16	105.69	92,756.85
99	92,756.85	840.85	734.33	106.53	92,650.32
100	92,650.32	840.85	733.48	107.37	92,542.95
101	92,542.95	840.85	732.63	108.22	92,434.72
102	92,434.72	840.85	731.77	109.08	92,325.64
103	92,325.64	840.85	730.91	109.94	92,215.70
104	92,215.70	840.85	730.04	110.81	92,104.89
105	92,104.89	840.85	729.16	111.69	91,993.20
106	91,993.20	840.85	728.28	112.57	91,880.62
. . .	. . .	. . .	. . .	. . .	. . .
. . .	. . .	. . .	. . .	. . .	. . .
. . .	. . .	. . .	. . .	. . .	. . .
209	74,177.40	840.85	587.24	253.62	73,923.78
210	73,923.78	840.85	585.23	255.62	73,668.16
211	73,668.16	840.85	583.21	257.65	73,410.51
212	73,410.51	840.85	581.17	259.69	73,150.82
. . .	. . .	. . .	. . .	. . .	. . .
. . .	. . .	. . .	. . .	. . .	. . .
. . .	. . .	. . .	. . .	. . .	. . .
354	5,703.93	840.85	45.16	795.70	4,908.23
355	4,908.23	840.85	38.86	802.00	4,106.24
356	4,106.24	840.85	32.51	808.35	3,297.89
357	3,297.89	840.85	26.11	814.75	2,483.14
358	2,483.14	840.85	19.66	821.20	1,661.95
359	1,661.95	840.85	13.16	827.70	834.25
360	834.25	840.85	6.60	834.25	0.00

$$PV = A \left[\frac{1 - (1+i)^{-n}}{i} \right]$$

where

A = amount of the annuity ($)
n = number of periods
PV = present value of an annuity ($)
i = periodic interest rate

We can redefine these terms for a level-payment mortgage as follows:

$$MB_0 = MP \left[\frac{1 - (1+i)^{-n}}{i} \right]$$

where

MP = monthly mortgage payment ($)
n = number of months
MB_0 = original mortgage balance ($)
i = simple monthly interest rate (annual interest rate/12)

Solving for the monthly mortgage payment (MP) gives

$$MP = \frac{MB_0}{\left[\dfrac{1 - (1+i)^{-n}}{i} \right]}$$

Alternatively, this can be expressed in a simplified form as follows:

$$MP = MB_0 \left[\frac{[i(1+i)^n]}{[(1+i)^n - 1]} \right]$$

The term in brackets is called the *payment factor* or *annuity factor*. It is the monthly payment for a $1 mortgage loan with an interest rate of i and a term of n months.

To illustrate how the formula is applied, we'll use the $100,000, 30-year, 9.5% mortgage that we discussed above.

n = 360;
MB_0 = $100,000;
i = .0079167 (=.095/12).

The monthly mortgage payment is then

$$MP = \$100,000 \left[\frac{\left[.0079167\,(1.0079167)^{360} \right]}{\left[(1.0079167)^{360} - 1 \right]} \right]$$

$$= \$100,000 \left[\frac{\left[.0079167\,(17.095) \right]}{\left[17.095 - 1 \right]} \right]$$

$$= \$100,000 \left[.0084085 \right]$$

$$= \$840.85$$

This agrees with the monthly mortgage payment used in Exhibit 10-1. The payment factor or annuity factor is .0084085.

Graduated Payment Mortgage

With a graduated-payment mortgage (GPM), both the interest rate and the term of the mortgage are fixed, as they are with a level-payment, fixed-rate mortgage. The difference is that the monthly mortgage payment for a GPM is smaller in the initial years than for a level-payment, fixed-rate mortgage with the same mortgage rate, but then becomes larger in the remaining years of the mortgage term. The terms of a GPM plan include: (1) the mortgage rate; (2) the term of the mortgage; (3) the number of years over which the monthly mortgage payment will increase (and when the level payments will begin); and (4) the annual percent increase in the mortgage payments.

Monthly mortgage payments in the earlier years of a GPM are generally not sufficient to pay the entire interest due on the outstanding mortgage balance. The difference between the monthly mortgage payment and the monthly interest due (based on the outstanding mortgage balance) is added to the outstanding mortgage balance, so that in the earlier years of a GPM there is *negative amortization*. The higher-level mortgage payments in the later years of the GPM are designed to fully amortize the outstanding mortgage balance, which is, by then, greater than the original amount borrowed.

The Federal Housing Administration introduced GPMs in late 1979. GPMs became eligible for pooling in certain types of mortgage-backed securities in 1979. Origination of GPMs has faded in popularity in recent years with the growing popularity of the other mortgage instruments discussed in this section.

Growing Equity Mortgages

A growing equity mortgage (GEM) is a fixed-rate mortgage whose monthly mortgage payments increase over time. In contrast with a GPM, there is no negative amortization. The initial monthly mortgage payment is the same as for a level-payment, fixed-rate mortgage. The higher monthly mortgage payments are applied to paying off the principal, which means that the principal of a GEM is repaid faster. For example, a 30-year $100,000 GEM loan with a contract rate of 9.5% might call for an initial monthly payment of $840.85 (the same as a level payment 9.5% 30-year mortgage loan). The GEM payment would gradually increase, however, and the GEM might be fully paid off in only 15 years.

Pools of GEMs have been securitized.

Tiered-Payment Mortgages

Another mortgage design with a fixed rate and a monthly payment that graduates over time is the tiered-payment mortgage (TPM). The initial monthly mortgage payments again are below those of a level payment mortgage as with a GPM. In this case, however, unlike in a GPM, there is no negative amortization because withdrawals are made from a buydown account to supplement the initial monthly payments and cover the shortfall of interest. The buydown account is established at the time the loan is originated by the borrower, the lender, or a third party such as a home builder or developer.

In the second half of 1989, 15-year TPMs were used as collateral for a mortgage-backed security.

Adjustable-Rate Mortgage

An adjustable-rate mortgage (ARM) is a loan whose contract rate is reset periodically in accordance with some appropriately chosen benchmark index (or reference base), typically one based on a short-term interest rate.

Outstanding ARMs call for resetting the interest rate either every month, six months, year, two years, three years, or five years. In recent years ARMs typically have had reset periods of six months, one year, or five years. The interest rate at the reset date is equal to a benchmark index plus a spread. The spread is typically between 100 and 200 basis points, reflecting market conditions, the features of the ARM, and the increased cost of servicing an ARM compared to a fixed-rate mortgage.

Benchmark Indexes: Two categories of benchmark indexes have been used in ARMs: (1) indexes based on market-determined rates, and (2) indexes based on the cost of funds for thrifts. Market-determined rates have been limited to Treasury-based indexes, unlike the more popular benchmark index used in the Eurodollar floating-rate market, the London Interbank Offered Rate (LIBOR). The benchmark index will have an important impact on the pricing and performance of an ARM.

Three Treasury-based indexes have been used as benchmarks: the one-year constant-maturity Treasury (CMT) rate, the five-year CMT, and the six-month Treasury bill rate. CMT rates are based on the CMT yield curve constructed for each trading day by the Federal Reserve Bank of New York and published weekly in the Federal Reserve's *Statistical Release H-15*. The CMT yield curve has yields for the most actively traded Treasuries with maturities of 1, 2, 3, 5, 7, 10, and 30 years based on closing bid yields submitted by five major dealer firms. The one-year CMT and five-year CMT are taken from the CMT yield curve. The six-month Treasury bill index is based on the weekly competitive auction of six-month Treasury bills, where there is a range of rates realized by winning bidders. The six-month Treasury bill index that is reported weekly in the *Statistical Release H-15* is the weighted average of the winning yield bids, where the weight is the amount sold at each bid rate.

There are at least four rates published for each of the Treasury-based indexes each month, so a mortgage agreement will specify which weekly rate should be used. Typically, the weekly index rate used to set the new mortgage rate is the one just before the 15th of the month in which the rate will be reset.

Treasury-based indexed ARMs are preferred by nonthrift investors. Of the three indexes, the most popular is the one-year CMT. Because liabilities are closely tied to the calculated cost of funds index, thrifts prefer ARMs benchmarked to cost of funds indexes.

Cost of funds for thrifts indexes are calculated according to the monthly weighted average interest cost for liabilities of thrifts. The two most popular are the 11th District Federal Home Loan Bank Board Cost of Funds and the National Cost of Funds Index. Another index that has been used is the Federal Home Loan Bank Contract Rate.

The 11th District includes the states of California, Arizona, and Nevada. The cost of funds is calculated by first computing the monthly interest expenses for all thrifts included in the 11th District. Interest expenses are summed and then divided by the average of the beginning and ending monthly balance. The index value is reported with a one-month lag. June's 11th District cost of funds, for example, is reported in July. The contract rate for an 11th District cost of funds-based index is usually reset based on the previous month's reported index rate. That is, if the reset date is August, the index rate reported in July will be used to set the contract rate. Consequently, there is a two-month lag by the time the average cost of funds is reflected in the contract rate. This obviously is an advantage to the borrower when interest rates are rising and a disadvantage to the investor. The opposite is true when interest rates are falling.

The National Cost of Funds Index is calculated based on all federally insured S&Ls. A median cost of funds is calculated rather than an average. This index is reported with about a one and a half-month delay. The contract rate is typically reset based on the most recently reported index value.

The index chosen has considerable impact on the performance of an ARM. A comparison of the movement of the one-year CMT rate and the 11th District Cost of Funds Index for the period January 1983 to December 1989 indicates that the 11th District Cost of Funds exhibits less volatility than the one-year CMT rate and has a tendency to lag behind movements of the one-year Treasury rate.[3] These two characteristics for the 11th District Cost of Funds are a result of the manner in which it is calculated. The index is a composite cost of funds, which includes both historical and current costs. When interest rates are rising, the composite interest cost will include the lower historical cost and the higher current costs. The average will therefore be lower than the current cost. The opposite is true when interest rates are falling. The implication is that when interest rates are falling (rising), an ARM indexed off the 11th District Cost of Funds will pay a higher (lower) rate than an ARM indexed off the one-year Treasury rate.

The frequency with which the contract rate resets varies with the index used. For ARMs indexed to the one-year Treasury rate, the mortgage rate is generally reset once a year. The monthly mortgage payments for the year are then based on the new indexed mortgage rate. For an 11th District Cost of Funds index-based ARM, the mortgage rate typically adjusts monthly, while the monthly mortgage payments are adjusted once a year.

Features of Adjustable-Rate Mortgages: To encourage borrowers to accept ARMs rather than fixed-rate mortgages, mortgage originators generally offer an initial contract rate that is less than the prevailing market mortgage rate. This below-market initial contract rate, set by the mortgage originator under competitive market conditions, is commonly referred to as a teaser rate. At the reset date, the benchmark index plus the spread determines the new contract rate. For example, suppose that one-year ARMs are typically offering a 100 basis point spread over the one-

---

[3] Robert Gerber, "Adjustable Rate Mortgages," in Frank J. Fabozzi, ed., *The Handbook of Mortgage-Backed Securities* (Chicago: Probus Publishing, 1992.)

year CMT rate. Suppose also that the current one-year CMT rate is 6.5%, so that the initial contract rate should be 7.5%. The mortgage originator might set an initial contract rate of 6.75%, a rate 75 basis points below the current index rate plus the spread.

A pure ARM is one that resets periodically and has no other terms that affect the monthly mortgage payment. The monthly mortgage payment, however, and the investor's cash flow are affected by other terms setting (1) periodic rate caps, and (2) lifetime rate caps and floors.

Rate caps limit the amount that the contract rate may increase or decrease at the reset date. The rate cap is expressed in percentage points. The most common rate cap on annual reset loans is 2%.

We can look at a periodic cap on the interest rate in terms of an option. Effectively the lender or investor has given the homeowner the right to borrow money at a below-market interest rate. Thus, the lender or investor has sold an option on an interest rate to the homeowner. In fact, because the cap goes into effect each year, the lender or investor has not sold one option but a package of options to the homeowner. The lender must be compensated for selling these options.

Prior to 1987, most ARMs had an upper limit on the contract rate that could be charged over the life of the loan. The Competitive Equality Banking Act of 1987 requires that all single-family mortgages originated have such a limit on the contract rate. This lifetime loan cap is expressed in terms of the initial rate, the most common lifetime cap being 5% to 6%. For example, if the initial mortgage rate is 7%, and the lifetime cap is 5%, the maximum interest rate that the lender can charge over the life of the loan is 12%. Many ARMs also have a lower limit on the interest rate that can be charged over the life of the loan.

Once again, looking at the lifetime cap from the perspective of an option, the lender or investor has effectively sold an option on an interest rate to the homeowner. What about a lifetime floor? In this case, the homeowner is compensating the lender or investor should the interest rate fall below the floor. Therefore, the homeowner has sold the lender or investor an option. From the lender's or investor's perspective, an ARM with a lifetime cap and floor is equivalent to a "collar" — a maximum and minimum interest rate. This, then, is equivalent to selling an option (the cap) at one interest rate and buying an option (the floor) at a lower interest rate.

Balloon/Reset Mortgages

Another form of adjustable-rate mortgage is the balloon/reset mortgage. In a balloon/reset mortgage loan, the borrower is given long-term financing by the lender, but at specified future dates the contract rate is renegotiated. Thus, the lender provides long-term funds for what is effectively short-term borrowing; how short depends on the frequency of the renegotiation period. Effectively this is a short-term balloon loan where the lender agrees to provide financing for the remainder of the term of the mortgage. The balloon payment is the original amount borrowed less the amount amortized.

This mortgage design, while much discussed in the late 1970s and throughout the 1980s, did not catch on until 1990. Two government-sponsored entities to be discussed in later chapters, the Federal National Mortgage Association (Fannie Mae) and the Federal Home Loan Mortgage Corporation (Freddie Mac) have programs for the purchase of these mortgages. Freddie Mac's 30-year balloon/resets, for example, can have either a renegotiation period of 5 years ("30-due-in-5" FRMs) or 7 years ("30-due-in-7" FRMs). If certain conditions are met, Freddie Mac guarantees the extension of the loan.

MORTGAGE CASH FLOW WITH SERVICING FEE

An investor who acquires a mortgage may service the mortgage or sell the right to service the mortgage. In the former case, the investor's cash flow is the entire cash flow from the mortgage. In the latter case, it is the cash flow net of the servicing fee. The monthly cash flow from a mortgage loan, regardless of the mortgage design, can therefore be decomposed into three parts:

1. The servicing fee
2. The interest payment net of the servicing fee
3. The scheduled principal repayment

For example, consider once again the $100,000 30-year level-payment, fixed-rate mortgage loan with a mortgage rate of 9.5%. Suppose the servicing fee is 0.5% per year. Exhibit 10-2 shows the cash flow for the mortgage with this servicing fee. The monthly mortgage payment is unchanged. The amount of the principal repayment is the same as in Exhibit 10-1. The difference is that the interest is reduced by the amount of the servicing fee. The amount of the servicing fee, just like the amount of interest, declines each month because the mortgage balance declines.

RISKS ASSOCIATED WITH INVESTING IN MORTGAGES

Investors are exposed to four main risks by investing in whole loans: (1) default risk; (2) liquidity risk; (3) interest-rate risk; and (4) prepayment risk.

EXHIBIT 10-2   Cash Flow for a Mortgage with Servicing Fee

Mortgage loan: $100,000
Mortgage rate: 9.5%
Servicing fee: 0.5%
Monthly payment: $840.85
Term of loan: 30 years (360 months)

Month	Beginning mortgage balance	Monthly mortgage payment	Net Interest for month	Servicing fee	Principal repayment	Ending mortgage balance
1	$100,000.00	$840.85	$750.00	$41.67	$49.19	$99,950.81
2	99,950.81	840.85	749.63	41.65	49.58	99,901.24
3	99,901.24	840.85	749.26	41.63	49.97	99,851.27
4	99,851.27	840.85	748.88	41.60	50.37	99,800.90
5	99,800.90	840.85	748.51	41.58	50.76	99,750.14
6	99,750.14	840.85	748.13	41.56	51.17	99,698.97
7	99,698.97	840.85	747.74	41.54	51.57	99,647.40
8	99,647.40	840.85	747.36	41.52	51.98	99,595.42
9	99,595.42	840.85	746.97	41.50	52.39	99,543.03
10	99,543.03	840.85	746.57	41.48	52.81	99,490.23
...	...	...	...	...	...	..
...	...	...	...	...	...	..
...	...	...	...	...	...	..
98	$99,862.54	840.85	696.47	38.69	105.69	92,756.85
99	92,756.85	840.85	695.68	38.65	106.53	92,650.32
100	92,650.32	840.85	694.88	38.60	107.37	92,542.95
101	92,542.95	840.85	694.07	38.56	108.22	92,434.72
102	92,434.72	840.85	693.26	38.51	109.08	92,325.64
103	92,325.64	840.85	692.44	38.47	109.94	92,215.70
104	92,215.70	840.85	691.62	38.42	110.81	92,104.89
105	92,104.89	840.85	690.79	38.38	111.69	91,993.20
106	91,993.20	840.85	689.95	38.33	112.57	91,880.62
...	...	...	...	...	...	..
...	...	...	...	...	...	..
...	...	...	...	...	...	..
209	74,177.40	840.85	556.33	30.91	253.62	73,923.78
210	73,923.78	840.85	554.43	30.80	255.62	73,668.16
211	73,668.16	840.85	552.51	30.70	257.65	73,410.51
212	73,410.51	840.85	550.58	30.59	259.69	73,150.82
...	...	...	...	...	...	..
...	...	...	...	...	...	..
...	...	...	...	...	...	..
354	5,703.93	840.85	42.78	2.38	795.70	4,908.23
355	4,908.23	840.85	36.81	2.05	802.00	4,106.24
356	4,106.24	840.85	30.80	1.71	808.35	3,297.89
357	3,297.89	840.85	24.73	1.37	814.75	2,483.14
358	2,483.14	840.85	18.62	1.03	821.20	1,661.95
359	1,661.95	840.85	12.46	.69	827.70	834.25
360	834.25	840.85	6.25	.35	834.25	0

Default Risk

The default or credit risk is the risk that the homeowner/borrower will default. For FHA- and VA-insured mortgages, this risk is minimal. For privately insured mortgages, the risk can be gauged by the credit rating of the private insurance company that has insured the mortgage. For conventional mortgages the credit risk depends on the borrower.

Liquidity Risk

While there is an active secondary market for whole loans, the fact is that bid-ask spreads are large compared to other debt instruments. That is, mortgage loans tend to be rather illiquid because they are large and indivisible.

The bid-ask spread on whole loans varies. Typical spreads are around 10/32nds, with aggressive bidding reducing spreads to 8/32nds when collateral is needed to create mortgage-backed securities. For whole loans with unusual collateral, spreads are much wider—the odder the collateral, the higher the spread.

Interest-Rate Risk

Because a mortgage is a debt instrument, and a long-term one on average—indeed one of the longest—its price will move in the direction opposite from market interest rates. Moreover, because the borrower can repay the loan at any time, the investor faces the same problem of negative convexity when rates decline as does the holder of any callable bond (as we discuss in Chapter 13).

Prepayment Risk

In our illustration of the cash flow from a level-payment, fixed-rate mortgage, we assume that the homeowner does not pay off any portion of the mortgage balance prior to the scheduled due date. But homeowners do pay off all or part of their mortgage balance prior to the maturity date. Payments made in excess of the scheduled principal repayments are called *prepayments*.

Prepayments occur for one of several reasons. First, homeowners prepay the entire mortgage when they sell their home, either because of (1) a change of employment that necessitates moving, (2) the purchase of a more or less expensive home, or (3) a divorce where settlement requires sale of the marital residence. Second, as we note earlier in the chapter, the borrower has the right to pay off all or part of the mortgage balance at any time. Effectively, someone who invests in a mortgage has granted the borrower an option to prepay the mortgage, and the borrower will have an incentive to do so as market rates fall below the contract rate. Third, in the case of homeowners who cannot meet their mortgage obligations, the property is repossessed and sold. The proceeds from the sale are used to pay off the mortgage in the case of a conventional mortgage. For an insured mortgage, the insurer will pay off the mortgage balance. Finally, if property is destroyed by fire or another insured catastrophe occurs, insurance proceeds are used to pay off the mortgage.

The effect of prepayments is that the cash flow from a mortgage is not known with certainty. This is true for all mortgage loans, not just level-payment, fixed-rate mortgages.

In the next chapter we describe securities backed by a pool of mortgage loans that overcome many of the risks associated with investing directly in mortgage loans.

SUMMARY

A mortgage is a loan secured by the collateral of some specified real estate property, which obliges the borrower to make a predetermined series of payments. There are basically three professional groups involved in the market: mortgage originators, mortgage servicers, and mortgage insurers. The original lender is called the mortgage originator.

The interest rate on a mortgage loan is generally above the risk-free interest rate, in particular the yield on a Treasury security of comparable maturity, with the spread reflecting the higher costs of collection, costs associated with default that are not eliminated despite the collateral, poorer liquidity, and uncertainty concerning the timing of the cash flow. There is a wide range of mortgage designs. These include the level-payment, fixed-rate mortgage, the graduated payment mortgage, the growing equity mortgage, the tiered-payment mortgage, the adjustable-rate mortgage, and the balloon reset mortgage.

The monthly cash flow from a mortgage loan, regardless of the mortgage design, can be decomposed into three parts: (1) the servicing fee, (2) the interest payment, and (3) the scheduled principal repayment. There is uncertainty associated with investing in a mortgage because of prepayments; that is, the cash flow is not known with certainty. This uncertainty is called prepayment risk. Those investing in mortgages also face liquidity risk and price risk, and may be exposed to credit risk.

QUESTIONS FOR CHAPTER 10

1. a. What are the sources of revenue arising from mortgage origination?
   b. What are the two primary factors in determining whether funds will be lent to an applicant for a mortgage loan?
   c. What can mortgage originators do with a loan after originating it?

2. What is meant by a conforming mortgage and a nonconforming mortgage?

3. What are the sources of revenue from mortgage servicing?

4. Why is the interest rate on a mortgage loan not necessarily the same as the interest rate that the investor receives?

5. a. What are the two types of mortgage insurance?
   b. Which is the more important type of insurance from the lender's perspective?

6. a. What are the three components of the cash flow of a mortgage loan?
   b. Why is the cash flow of a mortgage unknown?
   c. In what sense has the investor in a mortgage granted the borrower (homeowner) a call option?

7. a. What are the two categories of benchmark indexes used in adjustable-rate mortgages?
   b. Which category of index would you expect to increase faster when interest rates are rising? Why?
   c. What types of features are included in an adjustable-rate mortgage to restrict how the contract rate may change at the reset date?

8. What is a balloon/reset loan?

9. Consider the following level-payment, fixed-rate mortgage:
   Maturity = 360 months
   Amount borrowed = $150,000
   Annual mortgage rate = 8%
   a. What is the monthly mortgage payment?
   b. Construct an amortization schedule for the first ten months.

Chapter 11

MORTGAGE PASS-THROUGH SECURITIES

A mortgage pass-through security, or simply a pass-through, is created when one or more mortgage holders form a collection (pool) of mortgages and sell shares or participation certificates in the pool. From the pass-through, two further derivative mortgage-backed securities are created: collateralized mortgage obligations and stripped mortgage-backed securities, which we discuss in the next chapter. The pass-through is the subject of this chapter.

CASH FLOW CHARACTERISTICS

The cash flow of a pass-through depends on the cash flow of the underlying mortgages. It consists of monthly mortgage payments representing interest, the scheduled repayment of principal, and any prepayments.

Payments are made to securityholders each month. Neither the amount nor the timing, however, of the cash flow from the pool of mortgages is identical to that of the cash flow passed through to investors. The monthly cash flow for the pass-through is less than the monthly cash flow of the underlying mortgages by an amount equal to servicing and other fees that are charged by the issuer or guarantor of the pass-through for guaranteeing the issue.[1] The coupon rate on a pass-through is less than the contract rate on the underlying pool of mortgage loans by an amount equal to these servicing and guaranteeing fees.

The timing of the cash flow is also different. The monthly mortgage payment is due from each mortgagor on the first day of each month. There is a delay in passing through the corresponding monthly cash flow to the securityholders, which varies by the type of pass-through. Because of

---

[1] Actually, their servicer pays the guarantee fee to the issuer or guarantor.

prepayments, the cash flow of a pass-through is also not known with certainty. The various conventions for estimating the cash flow are discussed later in the chapter.

AGENCY PASS-THROUGHS

There are three major types of pass-throughs, guaranteed by three organizations: Government National Mortgage Association ("Ginnie Mae"), Federal Home Loan Mortgage Corporation ("Freddie Mac"), and Federal National Mortgage Association ("Fannie Mae"). These are called *agency pass-throughs*.

An agency can provide one of two types of guarantees. One type of guarantee is the timely payment of both interest and principal, meaning that interest and principal will be paid when due, even if some of the mortgagors fail to make their monthly mortgage payments. Pass-throughs with this type of guarantee are referred to as *fully modified pass-throughs*. The second type also guarantees both interest and principal payments, but it guarantees only the timely payment of interest. The scheduled principal is passed through as it is collected with a guarantee that the scheduled payment will be made no later than a specified date. Pass-throughs with this type of guarantee are called *modified pass-throughs*.

Government National Mortgage Association MBS

Ginnie Mae pass-throughs are guaranteed by the full faith and credit of the U.S. government. For this reason, Ginnie Mae pass-throughs are viewed as risk-free in terms of default risk, just like Treasury securities. The security guaranteed by Ginnie Mae is called a *mortgage-backed security* (MBS). All Ginnie Mae MBS are fully modified pass-throughs.

Only mortgage loans insured or guaranteed by either the Federal Housing Administration, the Veterans Administration, or the Farmers Home Administration can be included in a mortgage pool guaranteed by Ginnie Mae.

Ginnie Mae MBSs are issued under one of two programs: GNMA I (established in 1970) and GNMA II (established in 1983). The two programs differ in terms of the collateral underlying the pass-throughs. In both programs, pass-throughs are issued backed by single-family (SF) mortgages, graduated-payment mortgages (GPM), growing equity mortgages (GEM), and mobile or manufactured home loans. The large majority of GNMA MBSs are backed by single-family mortgages, where a single-family mortgage is a loan for a one-to-four family primary residence with a level-payment fixed-rate mortgage.

Mortgage-backed securities backed by adjustable-payment mortgages (APM) are issued under the GNMA II program. The monthly mortgage payment for an APM changes periodically, according to some index. An example of an adjustable-payment mortgage is the adjustable-rate mortgage (ARM). Not all ARMs qualify for inclusion in the pools that collateralize Ginnie Mae APM mortgage-backed securities. To qualify, the ARM must (1) adjust annually, and (2) be indexed off the weekly average yield of the one-year constant-maturity Treasury.

Federal Home Loan Mortgage Corporation PC

The second largest type of agency pass-through is the *participation certificate* (PC) issued by Freddie Mac. Although a guarantee of Freddie Mac is not a guarantee by the U.S. government, most market participants view Freddie Mac PCs as similar, although not identical, in credit-worthiness to Ginnie Mae pass-throughs.

Freddie Mac has two programs by which it creates PCs: the *Cash Program* and the *Guarantor/Swap Program*. In the former, the individual mortgages that back the PC are those purchased from mortgage originators, then pooled by Freddie Mac and sold in the market or through its dealer network through daily auctions. The PCs created under this program are called *Cash PCs* or *Regular PCs*. Under the Guarantor/Swap Program, Freddie Mac allows originators to swap pooled mortgages for PCs in those same pools. For example, a thrift may have $50 million of mortgages. It can swap these mortgages for a Freddie Mac PC in which the underlying mortgage pool is the same $50 million in mortgage loans that the thrift swapped for the PC. The PCs created under this program are called *Swap PCs*.

In the fall of 1990, Freddie Mac introduced its *Gold PC*, which, as will be explained below, has stronger guarantees. Gold PCs are issued in both programs, and will be the only type of PC issued in the future.

Freddie Mac offers both modified pass-throughs and fully modified pass-throughs. All non-Gold PCs that have been issued as part of its Cash Program and almost all that have been issued as part of its Guarantor/Swap Program are modified pass-throughs. There are a very small number of non-Gold PCs in the latter program that are fully modified pass-throughs. All Gold PCs issued are fully modified pass-throughs.

For modified PCs issued by Freddie Mac, the scheduled principal is passed through as it is collected, with Freddie Mac guaranteeing only that the scheduled payment will be made no later than one year after it is due.

There are pools with fixed-rate, level-payment mortgage loans, adjustable-rate mortgage loans, and balloon/reset mortgage loans. A wide variety of ARM PCs are issued under both the Cash and Guarantor/Swap Programs. There are Treasury-indexed ARM pools and cost-of-funds-indexed ARM pools. The latter includes the 11th District Cost of Funds, the National Cost of Funds, and the Federal Home Loan Bank Contract Rate.

Federal National Mortgage Association MBS

The pass-throughs issued by Fannie Mae are called *mortgage-backed securities* (MBS). Like a Freddie Mac PC, a Fannie Mae MBS is not an obligation of the federal government. Fannie Mae also has a swap program similar to that of Freddie Mac, through which it issues most of its MBSs. All Fannie Mae MBSs are fully modified pass-throughs.

There are four standard MBS programs established by Fannie Mae. Besides these regular programs, Fannie Mae issues securities known as "boutique" securities, which are securities issued through negotiated transactions and not backed by one of the mortgage loan types in the regular program.

Three of the four standard programs have pools backed by mortgage loans that are level-payment fixed-rate mortgages. The fourth standard program is an MBS collateralized by adjustable-rate mortgage loans. These ARMs are adjusted to the one-year Treasury index, and have a 2% annual adjustment cap and a lifetime cap of 6%. Pass-throughs in the boutique program can be backed by either fixed-rate or adjustable-rate conventional mortgage loans. In the former case, there are boutique securities for which the underlying mortgage loans are GPMs, GEMs, and balloons. The boutique securities backed by adjustable-rate mortgage loans can have, as their underlying mortgages, conventional ARMs indexed to the Federal Home Loan Bank's 11th District Cost of Funds.

CONVENTIONAL PASS-THROUGHS

Conventional pass-throughs, also called *private label pass-through securities* and *A/B pass-throughs*, are issued by thrifts, commercial banks, and private conduits. Private conduits purchase nonconforming mortgages, pool them, and then sell pass-throughs in which the collateral is the underlying pool of nonconforming mortgages. The private conduits that issue pass-throughs are doing what the government created the agency conduits to do, without any guarantees (implicit or explicit) from the U.S. government.

Unlike agency pass-throughs, conventional mortgage pass-throughs must be registered with the Securities and Exchange Commission. Conventional mortgage pass-throughs are rated by commercial rating agencies such as Moody's and Standard & Poor's. The development of private credit enhancement has been the key to the success of this market.

Credit Enhancement

Credit enhancement may take any one of several forms: (1) corporate guarantees; (2) letters of credit; (3) bond insurance; or (4) senior/subordinated interests.

With a corporate guarantee, the issuer of a conventional pass-through uses its own credit rating to back the security. The cost of a letter of credit is relatively high because of the limited number of financial institutions willing to issue such guarantees, and therefore this form of credit enhancement is not common. For the third form of credit enhancement, an insurance bond is obtained to cover timely payment of interest and principal. The rating of the insurance company that writes the policy must be equal to or higher than the rating that the issuer seeks for the pass-through. For example, if an issuer seeks a double-A rating for the pass-through, it cannot obtain insurance from an insurance company with a single-A rating. Financial Guarantee Insurance Corporation (FGIC), Financial Security Assurance (FSA), and Capital Markets Assurance Corporation (CAPMAC) are insurance companies that underwrite policies for conventional pass-throughs.

The fourth form of credit enhancement is the senior/subordinated structure, also known as the *A/B pass-through*. Since 1988, this structure has become the most common. It calls for partitioning a mortgage pool into senior certificates and subordinated certificates. The senior certificate holder has priority on the cash flow from the underlying collateral. It is the senior certificates that are rated and sold to investors as conventional pass-throughs. The subordinated certificates absorb the default risk. They can be either retained or sold to investors willing to accept the greater default risk. The larger the share of subordinated certificates relative to senior certificates that a mortgage pool is divided into will determine its credit rating. The greater the portion of subordinated certificates relative to senior certificates, the higher the credit rating that can be obtained.

PRICE AND YIELD CONVENTIONS

We know that the price of a financial asset is equal to the present value of its expected cash flow. Because of prepayments, however, the cash flow of a pass-through cannot be known with certainty. Conventions for calculating the price and yield of a pass-through have been developed using prepayment benchmarks that have been established in the industry. As we observe earlier in this book, yield measures have well-known deficiencies, so they are not appropriate to use in assessing the value of any fixed-income instrument except a zero-coupon instrument. In Chapter 15 we explain several specific methodologies to evaluate pass-throughs.

Prepayment Benchmark Conventions

Estimating the cash flow from a pass-through requires forecasting prepayments. The Public Securities Association (PSA) prepayment benchmark, which is based on a series of constant prepayment rates, is the current choice.

Constant Prepayment Rate: One way to project prepayments and the cash flow of a pass-through is to assume that some fraction of the remaining principal in the pool is prepaid *each* month for the remaining term of the mortgages. The prepayment rate assumed for a pool, called the *constant prepayment rate (CPR)*, is based on a pool's particular characteristics (including its historical prepayment experience) and the current and expected future economic environment.

The CPR is an annual prepayment rate. To estimate monthly prepayments, the CPR must be converted into a monthly prepayment rate, commonly referred to as the *single monthly mortality rate* (SMM), as follows:

$$(11.1) \quad SMM = 1 - (1 - CPR)^{1/12}$$

For example, suppose that the CPR used to project prepayments is 6%. The corresponding SMM is:

$$SMM = 1 - (1 - .06)^{1/12}$$
$$= 1 - (.94)^{.083333}$$
$$= .005143$$

An SMM of $w\%$ means that approximately $w\%$ of the remaining mortgage balance at the beginning of the month after subtracting the scheduled principal payment will prepay that month. That is,

Prepayment for month = SMM $\times$
(Beginning mortgage balance − Scheduled principal payment for month)

For example, suppose that an investor owns a pass-through in which the remaining mortgage balance at the beginning of some month is $50,525. Assuming that the SMM is .5143% and the scheduled principal payment is $67, then the estimated prepayment for the month is:

$$.005143 \times (\$50,525 - \$67) = \$260$$

PSA Standard Prepayment Benchmark: The Public Securities Association (PSA) standard prepayment benchmark is expressed as a monthly series of annual CPRs.[2] The benchmark PSA model assumes that prepayment rates will be low for newly originated mortgages and then will speed up as the mortgages become seasoned.

More specifically, the PSA standard benchmark assumes the following prepayment rates for 30-year mortgages:

1. A CPR of .2% for the first month, increased by .2% per month for the next 30 months when it reaches 6% per year, and
2. A 6% CPR for the remaining years.

This benchmark is referred to as "100% PSA" and can be expressed as follows:

$$\text{if } t \leq 30 \text{ then } \text{CPR} = \frac{6\% \, t}{30}$$

$$\text{if } t > 30 \text{ then } \text{CPR} = 6\%$$

where t is the number of months since the pass-through was originated.

Slower or faster speeds are then referred to as some percentage of PSA. For example, 50% PSA means one-half the CPR of the PSA prepayment rate; 150% PSA means one-and-a-half the CPR of the PSA prepayment rate.

The CPR is converted to an SMM using equation (11.1). For example, the SMMs for month 5, month 20, and months 31 through 360, assuming 100% PSA are calculated as follows:

$$\text{for month 5: CPR} = \frac{6\%(5)}{30} = 1\% = .01$$

$$\text{SMM} = 1 - (1-.01)^{1/12}$$

$$= 1 - (.99)^{.083333}$$

$$= .000837$$

$$\text{for month 20: CPR} = \frac{6\%(20)}{30} = 4\% = .04$$

$$\text{SMM} = 1 - (1-.04)^{1/12}$$

$$= 1 - (.96)^{.083333}$$

$$= .003396$$

---

[2] This benchmark is commonly referred to as a prepayment model, suggesting that it can be used to estimate prepayments. Strictly speaking, characterization of this benchmark as a prepayment model is inappropriate.

for months $31-360$: CPR $= 6\% = .06$

$$\text{SMM} = 1 - (1 - .06)^{1/12}$$

$$= 1 - (.94)^{.083333}$$

$$= .005143$$

The SMMs for month 5, month 20, and months 31 through 360 assuming 150% PSA are computed as follows:

for month 5: CPR $= \dfrac{6\%(5)}{30} = 1\% = .01$

150% PSA $= 1.5\,(.01) = .015$

SMM $= 1 - (1 - .015)^{1/12}$

$= 1 - (.985)^{.083333}$

$= .001259$

for month 20:   CPR $= \dfrac{6\%(20)}{30} = 4\% = .04$

150% PSA $= 1.5\,(.04) = .06$

SMM $= 1 - (1 - .06)^{1/12}$

$= 1 - (.94)^{.083333}$

$= .005143$

for months $31-360$: CPR $= 6\%\ =.06$

150% PSA $= 1.5\,(.06) = .09$

SMM $= 1 - (1 - .09)^{1/12}$

$= 1 - (.91)^{.083333}$

$= .007828$

Notice that the SMM assuming 150% PSA is not just 1.5 times the SMM assuming 100% PSA. It is the CPR that is a multiple of the CPR assuming 100% PSA.

Constructing the Projected Cash Flow

The cash flow to the investor in a pass-through is the sum of (1) the projected monthly interest net of the servicing fee, (2) the projected monthly scheduled principal payment, and (3) the projected monthly principal prepayment. As we explain earlier, the projected monthly principal prepayment is found by multiplying the SMM by the difference between the outstanding balance at the beginning of the month (the ending balance in the previous month) and the projected scheduled principal payment for the month.

An illustration shows how the monthly cash flow for a pass-through is constructed for several different assumptions about the PSA prepayment rates. Suppose that an investor owns a pass-through with an original mortgage balance of $100,000, mortgage rate of 9.5%, a 0.5% servicing fee, and 360 months to maturity. Suppose that the PSA prepayment model is used to project prepayments for the pass-through. In particular, assume that the investor believes that the mortgages will prepay at 100% PSA. Exhibit 11-1 shows the cash flow for the pass-through for selected months. The SMMs shown in the third column agree with those computed above.

Let's look at the components of the cash flow for the first month. The initial monthly mortgage payment for this pass-through, shown in the fourth column of the exhibit, is $841. The monthly interest is the monthly interest rate of .0079166 (.095 divided by 12) multiplied by the original mortgage balance, $100,000. The regularly scheduled principal is the difference between the monthly mortgage payment for the month, $841 in the first month, and the monthly interest of $792. The difference, $49, is shown in the fifth column. The prepayment for the month is found by multiplying the SMM for the month by the difference between the mortgage balance at the beginning of the month and the regularly scheduled principal repayment. In the first month, since the SMM is 0.000166 and the difference between the beginning mortgage balance of $100,000 and the projected scheduled principal payment of $49 is $99,951, the projected prepayment for the month is $17, shown in the seventh column. The amount of the monthly servicing fee is found by multiplying the mortgage balance at the beginning of the month by the servicing fee. For the first month, in our illustration it is 0.0004166 (0.005 divided by 12) multiplied by $100,000. The product is $42, which is shown in the eighth column. The monthly cash flow is then the projected monthly mortgage payment ($841) plus the projected monthly prepayment ($17) minus the amount of the servicing fee ($42), or $816. Alternatively, the monthly cash flow is the monthly interest net of servicing ($792 minus $42) plus the projected principal repayment which consists of the projected monthly regularly scheduled principal repayment ($49) and the monthly projected prepayment ($17). In any case, the projected monthly cash flow of $816 is shown in the ninth column. Finally, the last column shows the end-of-month mortgage balance, found by subtracting from the

EXHIBIT 11-1   Projected Cash Flow Assuming 100% PSA

Original balance $100,000
Mortgage rate   9.5%   Term   360 months
Servicing fee   .5%   PSA   100%

Month (1)	Beg. MB (2)	SMM (3)	Mort. Pay. (4)	Sch Prin. (5)	Int. (6)	Pre-pay. (7)	Serv-icing (8)	Cash Flow (9)	End. MB (10)
1	100,000	.000166	841	49	792	17	42	816	99,934
2	99,934	.000333	841	50	791	33	42	832	99,851
3	99,851	.000501	840	50	790	50	42	849	99,751
4	99,751	.000669	840	50	790	67	42	865	99,634
5	99,634	.000837	839	51	789	83	42	881	99,500
6	99,500	.001005	839	51	788	100	41	897	99,349
7	99,349	.001174	838	51	787	117	41	913	99,181
8	99,181	.001343	837	52	785	133	41	929	98,996
18	96,584	.003050	819	55	765	294	40	1,074	96,235
19	96,235	.003223	817	55	762	310	40	1,087	95,870
20	95,870	.003396	814	55	759	325	40	1,100	95,489
21	95,489	.003569	812	56	756	341	40	1,113	95,093
31	90,860	.005143	777	58	719	467	38	1,206	90,336
32	90,336	.005143	773	58	715	464	38	1,200	89,814
33	89,814	.005143	769	58	711	462	37	1,193	89,294
34	89,294	.005143	765	58	707	459	37	1,187	88,777
99	60,354	.005143	547	69	478	310	25	832	59,975
100	59,975	.005143	544	70	475	308	25	827	59,597
209	27,372	.005143	310	94	217	140	11	439	27,138
210	27,138	.005143	309	94	215	139	11	436	26,905
211	26,905	.005143	307	94	213	138	11	434	26,673
359	283	.005143	143	141	2	1	0	144	141
360	141	.005143	142	141	1	0	0	142	0

Beg. MB	=	projected mortgage balance at the beginning of month
SMM	=	single monthly mortality rate
Mort. Pay.	=	projected monthly mortgage payment
Sch. Prin.	=	projected monthly scheduled principal payment
Int.	=	projected monthly interest
Prepay.	=	projected prepayment for the month
Servicing	=	projected servicing fee for the month
Cash Flow	=	projected cash flow for month
End. MB	=	projected ending mortgage balance for month

mortgage balance at the beginning of the month the projected principal repayment. In the first month, the ending mortgage balance is $100,000 minus $66 ($49 + $17), or $99,934. This amount is then the beginning mortgage balance for month 2. Using this amount, the cash flow can be calculated for the second month.

Notice that the monthly mortgage payment declines over time. This is because mortgages in the pool are assumed to be prepaying. Equation (11.2) is used to determine what the monthly mortgage payment would be for any month:

$$(11.2) \quad \overline{MP}_t = \overline{MB}_{t-1} \left[\frac{\left[i(1+i)^{n-t+1} \right]}{\left[(1+i)^{n-t+1} - 1 \right]} \right]$$

where

$\overline{MP}_t$ = projected monthly mortgage payment for month t

$\overline{MB}_{t-1}$ = projected mortgage balance at the end of month $t-1$ given prepayments have occurred in the past (which is the projected mortgage balance at the beginning of month t)

n = original number of months of mortgage

i = simple monthly interest rate (annual interest rate/12)

For example, the mortgage payment for month 21 in Exhibit 11-1 of $812 is calculated as follows:

$$i = .0079166 (0.095 / 12)$$

$$n = 360$$

$$\overline{MB}_{20} = \$95,489$$

$$\overline{MB}_{21} = \$95,489 \left[\frac{\left[0.0079166 (1.0079166)^{360-21+1} \right]}{\left[(1.0079166)^{360-21+1} - 1 \right]} \right]$$

$$= 812$$

Exhibit 11-2 shows the projected cash flow assuming 150% PSA.

Cash Flow Yield

Given the projected cash flow and the price of a pass-through, we can calculate the yield. The yield is the interest rate that will make the present value of the expected cash flow equal to the price. A yield computed in this manner is known as a *cash flow yield*.

EXHIBIT 11-2   Projected Cash Flow Assuming 150% PSA

Original balance $100,000
Mortgage rate   9.5%   Term   360 months
Servicing fee   .5%   PSA   150%

Month (1)	Beg. MB (2)	SMM (3)	Mort. Pay. (4)	Sch Prin. (5)	Int. (6)	Pre-pay. (7)	Serv-icing (8)	Cash Flow (9)	End. MB (10)
1	100,000	.000250	841	49	792	25	42	824	99,926
2	99,926	.000501	841	50	791	50	42	849	99,826
3	99,826	.000753	840	50	790	75	42	874	99,701
4	99,701	.001005	840	50	789	100	42	898	99,551
5	99,551	.001258	839	51	788	125	41	923	99,375
6	99,375	.001512	838	51	787	150	41	947	99,174
7	99,174	.001767	836	51	785	175	41	970	98,947
8	98,947	.002022	835	52	783	200	41	994	98,695
18	95,324	.004615	809	54	755	440	40	1,209	94,830
19	94,830	.004878	805	54	751	462	40	1,228	94,313
20	94,313	.005143	801	54	747	485	39	1,247	93,774
21	93,774	.005407	797	55	742	507	39	1,266	93,213
31	87,224	.007828	746	55	691	682	36	1,392	86,487
32	86,487	.007828	740	55	685	677	36	1,381	85,755
33	85,755	.007828	734	55	679	671	36	1,369	85,028
34	85,028	.007828	728	55	673	665	35	1,358	84,308
99	48,211	.007828	437	55	382	377	20	794	47,779
100	47,779	.007828	434	55	378	374	20	787	47,350
209	16,241	.007828	184	56	129	127	7	304	16,059
210	16,059	.007828	183	56	127	125	7	301	15,878
211	15,878	.007828	181	56	126	124	7	299	15,699
359	112	.007828	57	56	1	0	0	57	56
360	56	.007828	56	56	0	0	0	56	0

Beg. MB	=	projected mortgage balance at the beginning of month
SMM	=	single monthly mortality rate
Mort. Pay.	=	projected monthly mortgage payment
Sch. Prin.	=	projected monthly scheduled principal payment
Int.	=	projected monthly interest
Prepay.	=	projected prepayment for the month
Servicing	=	projected servicing fee for the month
Cash Flow	=	projected cash flow for month
End. MB	=	projected ending mortgage balance for month

For a pass-through, the yield that makes the present value of the cash flow equal to the price is a monthly interest rate. The next step is to annualize the monthly yield. According to market convention, to compare the yield for a pass-through to that of a Treasury or corporate bond, the monthly yield should not be annualized simply by multiplying the monthly yield by 12. The reason is that a Treasury bond and a corporate bond pay interest semiannually, while a pass-through has a monthly cash flow. Reinvestment of monthly cash flows gives the pass-through holder the opportunity to generate greater interest than can be earned by a bondholder who has only semiannual coupon payments to reinvest. Therefore, the yield on a pass-through must be calculated so as to make it comparable to the yield to maturity for a bond.

This is accomplished by computing the *bond-equivalent yield*. As we explain in Chapter 3, this is simply a market convention for annualizing the yield of any fixed-income instrument that pays interest more than one time per year. The bond-equivalent yield is found by doubling a semiannual yield. For a pass-through security, the semiannual yield is:

$$\text{Semiannual cash flow yield} = \left(1 + y_M\right)^6 - 1$$

where y_M = monthly interest rate that will equate the present value of the projected monthly cash flow to the price of the pass-through

The bond equivalent yield is found by doubling the semiannual cash flow yield; that is

$$\text{bond-equivalent yield} = 2\left[\left(1 + y_M\right)^6 - 1\right]$$

Illustration

For example, suppose that a pass-through backed by 9.5% mortgages, a servicing fee of .5%, 360 months remaining to maturity (a newly originated pass-through), and original principal of $100,000 can be purchased for $94,521. To compute the cash flow yield, we need to make a prepayment assumption. Assuming that the prepayment rate is 100% PSA, the cash flow would be as shown in Exhibit 11-1. Assuming that the first monthly cash flow is 30 days from now, the interest rate that will make the present value of the cash flow, assuming 100% PSA equal to the price of $94,521 is .8333% (.008333). The bond-equivalent yield is then 10.21%, as shown below:

$$y_M = .0083333$$
$$\text{Bond-equivalent yield} = 2\left[(1.008333)^6 - 1\right] = .1021 = 10.21\%$$

Suppose that the pass-through security in this previous illustration can be purchased instead for $105,985. Assuming a prepayment rate of 200% PSA, the interest rate that will make the present value of the cash flow equal to $105,985 is .6667% (.006667). The bond-equivalent yield is

$$y_M = .006667$$
Bond-equivalent yield $= 2 [(1.006667)^6 - 1] = .0813 = 8.13\%$

Price

Given the required yield for a pass-through, its price is simply the present value of the projected cash flow. Care needs to be paid to determining the monthly interest rate that should be used to compute the present value of each monthly cash flow.

To convert a bond-equivalent yield to a monthly interest rate, the following equation can be used:

$$y_M = [1 + (.5) \text{ bond-equivalent yield}]^{1/6} - 1$$

For example, consider the pass-through used in the previous illustration. Suppose that (1) the investor requires an 8.13% yield on a bond-equivalent basis, and (2) the prepayment rate assumed by the investor is 150% PSA. The corresponding monthly interest rate for a bond-equivalent yield of 8.13% is .6667% (0.006667) as we show below:

$$
\begin{aligned}
y_M &= [1 + (.5) .0813]^{1/6} - 1 \\
&= [1.04065]^{.16667} - 1 \\
&= .006667
\end{aligned}
$$

The projected cash flow based on 150% PSA would be the same as in Exhibit 11-2. Discounting the projected cash flow at 0.6667% gives a price of $106,710.

Suppose that instead 8.13%, the investor wants a yield of 12.30%. Also assume that the investor believes that a 25% PSA rate is appropriate to project the cash flow. The monthly interest rate then is determined as follows:

$$
\begin{aligned}
y_M &= [1 + (.5) .1230]^{1/6} - 1 \\
&= [1.0615]^{.16667} - 1 \\
&= .01
\end{aligned}
$$

Discounting the projected cash flow based on 25% PSA would give a price of $79,976.

Beware of Conventions

The PSA prepayment benchmark is simply a market convention. It is the product of a study by the PSA based on FHA prepayment experience.

Data that the PSA committee examined seemed to suggest that mortgages became seasoned (i.e., prepayment rates tended to level off) after 30 months and the CPR tended to be 6%. How, though, did the PSA come up with the CPRs used for months 1 through 29? In fact, these numbers are not based on empirical evidence, but instead on a linear increase from month 1 to month 30 so that at month 30 the CPR is 6%. Moreover, the same benchmark or seasoning process is used in quoting pass-throughs regardless of the collateral — 30- and 15-year loans, fixed- or adjustable-rate loans, and conventional or VA/FHA-insured loans.

Astute money managers recognize that the CPR is a convenient shorthand enabling market participants to quote yield and/or price, but that as a convention in determining value it has many limitations. Studies have demonstrated that the seasoning process assumed by the PSA benchmark does not fit recent prepayment experience. One study of fixed-rate pass-throughs finds that the seasoning process takes considerably longer than 30 months.[3] How much longer depends on the type of collateral. Freddie Mac and Fannie Mae pass-throughs (which are backed by conventional mortgage loans) were found to take longer to season than Ginnie Mae pass-throughs (which are backed by FHA/VA-insured mortgage loans). In a study of the prepayment behavior of one-year constant maturity Treasury ARMs, it is found that prepayments tended to season in about 26 months at a CPR of 15.6% for about 20 months, then gradually declined for 30 months, finally reaching a second seasoning pattern at a 12.3% CPR.[4] Cost of funds-indexed ARMs investigated exhibited a similar seasoning behavior pattern. This two-plateau seasoning pattern is far different from the PSA's single-plateau seasoning assumption.

These findings indicate that yield measures based on the PSA prepayment benchmark should be regarded with a great deal of caution.

SECONDARY MARKET TRADING

Pass-throughs are quoted in the same manner as U.S. Treasury coupon securities. A quote of 94-05 means 94 and 5/32nds of par value, or 94.15625% of par value. As we explain in our discussion of prepayments, the yield corresponding to a price must be qualified by an assumption concerning prepayments.

---

[3] David Jacob, Clark McGranery, Sean Gallop, and Lynn Tong, "The Seasoning of Prepayment Speeds and its Effect on the Average Lives and Values of MBS," Chapter 31 in Frank J. Fabozzi, ed., *The Handbook of Mortgage-Backed Securities*, 3rd edition (Chicago: Probus Publishing, 1992).

[4] Scott F. Richard and Lynn M. Edens, "Prepayment and Valuation Modeling for Adjustable Rate Mortgage-Backed Securities," Chapter 11 in *The Handbook of Mortgage-Backed Securities,* 3rd edition.

Pass-throughs are identified by a pool prefix and pool number provided by the agency. The prefix indicates the type of pass-through. For example, a pool prefix of 20 for a Freddie Mac PC means that the underlying pool consists of conventional mortgages with an original maturity of 15 years. A pool prefix of *AR* for a Ginnie Mae MBS means that the underlying pool consists of adjustable-rate mortgages. The pool number indicates the specific mortgages underlying the pass-through and the issuer of the pass-through.

Many trades occur while a pool is still unspecified, and therefore no pool information is known at the time of the trade. This kind of trade is known as a "TBA" (to be announced) trade. When an investor purchases, say, $1 million GNMA 8's on a TBA basis, the investor can receive up to three pools, with pool numbers being announced shortly before the settlement date. Three pools can be delivered because the Public Securities Association (PSA) has established guidelines for standards of delivery and settlement of mortgage-backed securities,[5] under which our hypothetical TBA trade permits three possible pools to be delivered. The option of what pools to deliver is left to the seller, as long as selection and delivery satisfy the PSA guidelines. In contrast to TBA trades, a pool number may be specified. In this case the transaction will involve delivery of the pool specifically designated.[6]

There are many seasoned issues of the same agency with the same coupon rate outstanding at a given point in time. Exhibit 11-3, for example, shows the number of pools of 30-year Ginnie Mae MBSs outstanding by coupon as of May 1992. One pass-through may be backed by a pool of mortgage loans in which all the properties are located in California, while another may be backed by a pool of mortgage loans in which all the properties are in Minnesota. Yet another may be backed by a pool of mortgage loans in which the properties are from several regions in the country. So which pool are dealers referring to when they talk about Ginnie Mae 8's? They do not refer to any specific pool but instead to a generic security, although the prepayment characteristics of pass-throughs with underlying pools from different parts of the country are different. Thus, the projected prepayment rates for pass-throughs reported by dealer firms are for generic pass-throughs. A particular pool purchased may have a materially different prepayment speed from the generic. Moreover, when

---

[5] Public Securities Association, *Uniform Practices for the Clearance and Settlement of Mortgage-Backed Securities*. More specifically, the requirement for good delivery permits a maximum of three pools per $1 million traded, or a maximum of four pools per $1 million for coupons of 12% or more.

[6] For further discussion of specified pools, see Chuck Ramsey and J. Michael Henderson, "Specified Pools," Chapter 6 in *The Handbook of Mortgage-Backed Securities*.

EXHIBIT 11-3   30-Year Ginnie Mae MBS Outstanding by Coupon as of May 1992

Coupon	Number of Pools	Remaining Balance ($Million)
7	612	1,282
7 1/2	6,662	16,773
8	18,843	54,280
8 1/2	14,397	44,545
9	34,236	126,376
9 1/2	28,276	100,933
10	21,362	69,209
10 1/2	7,086	16,839
11	11,026	31,273
11 1/2	8,984	29,042

an investor purchases a pass-through without specifying a pool number, the seller can deliver the worst-paying pools as long as the pools delivered satisfy good delivery requirements.

TBA trades give another advantage to the seller. PSA delivery standards permit an under- or overdelivery tolerance of 2.5% per million traded. This means that if $1 million of par value is sold at par, the seller may deliver to the buyer pass-throughs with a par value anywhere between $975,000 and $1,025,000. This delivery option is valuable. To understand why, suppose that interest rates decline between the trade date and the settlement date. The value of pass-throughs will rise, and therefore it will be beneficial for the seller to deliver less than $1 million. The opposite is true if interest rates rise between the trade date and the settlement date: the seller will deliver $1,025,000.

Investors need to recognize the valuable delivery options that are granted to the seller in a TBA trade, and they can deny these options to the seller by engaging in a specified trade. The cost of such a trade, however, as measured by the bid-ask spread, will be larger than for a TBA trade, with the difference depending on the specific pool sought by the buyer.

PREPAYMENT RISK AND ASSET/LIABILITY MANAGEMENT

To explore prepayment risk further, suppose an investor buys a 10% coupon Ginnie Mae MBS at a time when mortgage rates are 10%. Let's consider what will happen to prepayments if mortgage rates decline to, say, 6%. When mortgage rates decline, the adverse consequences for investors in a pass-through are the same as those faced by holders of a callable bond. In both cases, the upside price potential of the instrument is truncated because of the embedded option granted to the borrower; that is, a pass-through will exhibit price compression or negative convexity. This should not be surprising because a mortgage loan effectively grants the borrower the right to call the loan at par value. Moreover, the investor must reinvest the proceeds at a lower interst rate. The adverse consequences we just described when mortgage rates decline is referred to as *contraction risk*.

Now let's look at what happens if mortgage rates rise to, say, 15%. The price of the pass-through, like that of any bond, will decline. But again it will decline more because the higher rates will tend to slow down the rate of prepayment, in effect increasing the amount invested at the pool coupon rate, which is lower than the market rate. Prepayments will slow down because homeowners have no interest in refinancing or partial prepayment when mortgage rates are higher than their contractual rate of 10%. Yet this is just the time when investors want prepayments to speed up so that they can reinvest the prepayments at the higher market interest rate. This adverse consequence of rising mortgage rates is called *extension risk*.

Therefore, prepayment risk encompasses contraction risk and extension risk, both attributable to the option granted to the borrower/homeowner to prepay a mortgage loan—in whole or in part—at any time.

It should be understood that prepayments are not necessarily an adverse event for an investor. The effect on investment performance will depend upon whether the pass-through is purchased at a discount or premium. Prepayments enhance the return from holding a pass-through if it is purchased at a discount for two reasons. First, the investor realizes a capital gain equal to the difference between the par value and the price paid. Second, a pass-through will trade at a discount because the pass-through's coupon rate is lower than the current coupon rate for newly issued pass-throughs. Consequently, prepayments allow the investor to reinvest the proceeds at a higher coupon rate. For a pass-through purchased at a premium to par, prepayments reduce investment returns for two reasons: (1) the investor realizes a capital loss equal to the difference between the price paid and par, and (2) the proceeds must be reinvested at a lower coupon rate.

Motivation for the Development of the CMO Structure

Prepayment risk has a number of implications for the attractiveness of pass-throughs for certain institutional investors. These issues have motivated the development of the collateralized mortgage obligation (CMO), which is the subject of the next chapter.

From an asset/liability perspective, pass-throughs are an unattractive investment for many institutional investors because of prepayment risk. The CMO structure was developed to broaden the appeal of mortgage-backed products to traditional fixed-income investors. Consider, for example, commercial banks and thrifts (S&Ls, savings banks, and credit unions). Their objective is to lock in a spread over their cost of funds, and they raise funds on a short-term basis either through the issuance of short-term money market obligations or the issuance of certificates of deposit. If they invest the proceeds in fixed-rate pass-throughs, assets and liabilities will be mismatched because a pass-through is a long-term security.

Pass-throughs may not be useful for satisfying certain obligations of insurance companies. More specifically, consider a life insurance company that has issued a four-year guaranteed investment contract (GIC). A GIC is an insurance product in which the insurance company agrees to pay a specified interest rate over a predetermined time period in return for a specified sum of money, the premium. If the insurance company purchases a pass-through with the premium received, the security could have a life considerably longer than four years or any other maturity that is anticipated when the pass-through is purchased. That is, the insurance company is exposed to extension risk.

Finally, consider a pension fund or a life insurance company with a predetermined set of liabilities that must be paid over the next 15 years. In the case of a pension fund, this would be the defined-benefit payments it must make to beneficiaries; for the life insurance company, it might be obligations resulting from an annuity policy that it has sold. Buying a pass-through exposes these institutional investors to the risk that prepayments will speed up, and, as a result, the pass-through's maturity will shorten to considerably less than 15 years. Prepayments will speed up if interest rates decline, thereby forcing reinvestment of prepayments at a lower interest rate. In this case, the pension fund and the life insurance company are exposed to contraction risk.

Some institutional investors are concerned with extension risk, others with contraction risk, when they invest in a pass-through. As we explain in the next chapter, redirection of cash flows in collateralized mortgage obligations allows the redistribution of such prepayment risk, giving investors the opportunity to reduce their exposure to prepayment risk.

SUMMARY

A mortgage pass-through security is created when one or more mortgage holders form a collection (pool) of mortgages and sell shares or participation certificates in the pool. The monthly cash flow of a pass-through depends on the cash flow of the underlying mortgages and therefore consists of monthly mortgage payments representing interest, the scheduled repayment of principal, and any prepayments. The cash flow is less than that of the underlying mortgages by an amount equal to servicing and any guarantor fees. As with individual mortgage loans, because of prepayments the cash flow of a pass-through is not known with certainty.

The major types of pass-throughs are agency pass-throughs issued by Ginnie Mae, Freddie Mac, and Fannie Mae. There are two types of guarantees that may be provided by an agency: (1) timely payment of both interest and principal, and (2) timely payment of interest and eventual payment of the scheduled principal when it is collected, but no later than a specified date. Ginnie Mae pass-throughs are guaranteed by the full faith and credit of the U.S. government and consequently are viewed as risk-free in terms of default risk. Freddie Mac and Fannie Mae are government sponsored entities, and therefore their guarantee does not carry the full faith and credit of the U.S. government.

Conventional pass-throughs or private label pass-throughs are issued by entities such as thrifts, commercial banks, and private conduits. Unlike agency pass-throughs, these pass-throughs are rated by commercial rating agencies and require some form of credit enhancement to obtain a high credit rating. Credit enhancement may take any one of several forms: (1) corporate guarantees; (2) letters of credit; (3) bond insurance; or (4) senior/subordinated interests. The senior/subordinated (or A/B pass-through) structure is the most common.

Estimating the cash flow from a pass-through requires forecasting prepayments. The current convention is to use the Public Securities Association (PSA) prepayment benchmark, which is a series of constant prepayment rates, to obtain the cash flow. Given the projected cash flow and the market price of a pass-through, a cash flow yield can be calculated. Investors must recognize that the PSA prepayment benchmark is a convention enabling market participants to quote yield and/or price but that it has many limitations for determining the value of a pass-through.

Pass-throughs are quoted in the same manner as U.S. Treasury coupon securities. They are identified by a pool prefix and pool number. A TBA trade occurs while a pool is still unspecified, and therefore no pool information is known at the time of the trade. The seller has the right in this case to deliver pass-throughs backed by pools that satisfy the PSA requirements for good delivery.

As a result of prepayment risk, when mortgage rates decline, the adverse consequences for investors in a pass-through are the same as those faced by holders of a callable bond. Prepayment risk can be decomposed into two components: contraction risk and extension risk. Prepayment risk means that pass-throughs are an unattractive investment for many institutional investors from an asset/liability perspective. The CMO structure is designed to broaden the appeal of mortgage-backed products to traditional fixed-income investors.

QUESTIONS FOR CHAPTER 11

1. a. What is a mortgage pass-through security?

    b. Describe the investment characteristics of a mortgage pass-through security.

2. a. What are the different types of agency pass-through securities?

    b. Which type of agency pass-through carries the full faith and credit of the U.S. government?

3. a. What is meant by a fully modified pass-through?

    b. What is meant by a modified pass-through?

4. What is an agency swap program?

5. a. What is a conventional pass-through security?

    b. Describe various ways that issuers have enhanced the credit quality of a conventional pass-through security.

6. Why is it necessary to forecast prepayments?

7. Indicate whether you agree or disagree with the following statement: "The PSA prepayment benchmark is a model for forecasting prepayments for a pass-through security."

8. a. What is the CPR for each month given below assuming the PSA shown in each column?

	CPR assuming		
Month	100% PSA	70% PSA	320% PSA
1			
4			
9			
27			
40			
120			
340			

    b. Calculate the SMM for each month given below assuming the PSAs shown in each column.

	SMM assuming		
Month	100% PSA	70% PSA	320% PSA
1			
4			
9			
27			
40			
120			
340			

9. Complete this table

	Original balance	$100,000						
	Mortgage rate	9.5%	Term	360 months				
	Servicing fee	.5%	PSA	170%				

Month	Beg MB	SMM	Mort. pay	Sch prin	Int.	Pre-pay.	Serv-icing	Cash flow	End. MB
(1)	(2)	(3)	(4)	(5)	(6)	(7)	(8)	(9)	(10)
1	100,000		841	49	792		42		
2	99,934		841						

10. a. What is meant by the cash flow yield of a mortgage pass-through security?

   b. What are the limitations of cash flow yield measures for a mortgage pass-through security?

   c. What is the bond-equivalent yield if the monthly cash flow yield is .7%?

11. What is meant by contraction risk and extension risk?

12. a. Distinguish between a TBA and specified pool trade.

   b. What delivery options are granted to the seller in a TBA trade?

Chapter 12

COLLATERALIZED MORTGAGE OBLIGATIONS AND STRIPPED MBS

In this chapter we discuss collateralized mortgage obligations and stripped mortgage-backed securities. Because these securities derive their cash flow from underlying mortgage collateral such as pass-throughs or a pool of whole loans, they are referred to as "derivative" products.

COLLATERALIZED MORTGAGE OBLIGATIONS

At the close of the previous chapter, we discussed the prepayment risks associated with investing in pass-throughs: contraction risk and extension risk. We note there that some institutional investors are concerned with extension risk when they invest in a pass-through, while others are more concerned with contraction risk. Fortunately, redirecting cash flows from a pass-through to different bond classes makes it possible to redistribute prepayment risk for investors who want to reduce their exposure to prepayment risk. Because the total prepayment risk of a pass-through will not be changed by altering the cash flows, other investors must be found who are willing to accept the unwanted prepayment risk.

Collateralized mortgage obligations (CMOs) are bond classes created by redirecting the cash flows of mortgage-related products (pass-throughs and whole loans) so as to mitigate prepayment risk.[1] The mere creation of a CMO cannot eliminate prepayment risk; it can only transfer the various forms of this risk among different classes of bondholders. The technique of redistributing the coupon interest and principal from the underlying mortgage-related products to different classes, so that a CMO class has a different coupon rate from that for the underlying collateral, results in instruments that have varying convexity characteristics that may be more suitable to the needs and expectations of investors, thereby broadening the appeal of mortgage-backed products to various traditional fixed-income investors.

---

[1] As explained later in this chapter, collateralized mortgage obligations can also be created from the cash flow of stripped mortgage-backed securities.

The CMO Structure

A CMO is a security backed by a pool of pass-throughs, whole loans, or stripped mortgage-backed securities (explained later in the chapter). CMOs are structured so that there are several classes of bondholders with varying *stated* maturities. The principal payments from the underlying collateral are used to retire the bonds on a priority basis according to terms specified in the prospectus.

The first generation of CMOs was structured so that each class of bond would be retired sequentially; hence such structures are referred to as *sequential-pay* CMOs. In a "plain vanilla" CMO structure, there may be four classes of bonds, which we shall refer to as class A, class B, class C, and class Z. (The classes are commonly referred to as *tranches*.) The first three classes, with class A representing the shortest-maturity bond, receive periodic interest payments from the underlying collateral; class Z is an accrual bond that receives no periodic interest until the other three classes are retired. When principal payments, both scheduled payments and prepayments, are received by the trustee for the CMO, they are applied to retire the class A bonds. After all the class A bonds are retired, all principal payments received are applied to retire the class B bonds. Once all the class B bonds are retired, class C bonds are paid off in the same fashion. Finally, after the first three classes of bonds are retired, the cash flow payments from the remaining underlying collateral are used to satisfy the obligations on the Z-bonds (original principal plus accrued interest). These bonds are referred to as *accrual or Z-bonds*.

As an example, consider one of the early CMO issues, which had four classes: the M.D.C. Mortgage Funding Corporation, Series J CMO, a $100 million issue priced on July 7, 1986.[2] The underlying collateral is Ginnie Mae pass-throughs with a weighted average coupon of 9.5% and 297 months remaining to maturity. The original maturity for the Ginnie Mae pass-throughs was 360 months. Basic information for each class is summarized in the upper panel of Exhibit 12-1.

Cash Flow of a CMO: The cash flow for each class can be derived only by assuming some prepayment rate for the underlying mortgage collateral. The yield cited for each class of a CMO is the cash flow yield explained in the previous chapter, a measure that depends on a prepayment assumption. The prepayment benchmark that mortgage-backed securities dealers use to quote CMO cash flow yields is the PSA standard prepayment model. The issuer of the CMO illustrated in Exhibit 12-1 priced the issue according to

---

[2] This information is taken from Lakhbir S. Hayre, David Foulds, and Lisa Pendergast, "Introduction to Collateralized Mortgage Obligations," in Frank J. Fabozzi, ed., *The Handbook of Mortgage-Backed Securities*, rev. ed. (Chicago: Probus Publishing, 1988).

EXHIBIT 12-1   Summary Information for M.D.C. Mortgage Funding, Series J

Class	Par (in millions)	Stated Maturity	Coupon	Price
A	$35.5	5/99	8.05%	99.87500
B	15.5	2/02	8.75	99.84575
C	40.5	2/07	9.35	99.71875
Z	9.0	8/16	9.50	93.15625

Class	Expected Maturity	Average Life (years)	Duration	Projected Yield	Benchmark Treasury	Spread over Treasury (in Basis Points)
A	5/91	2.30	2.10	7.87%	2 year	120
B	8/93	5.80	4.61	8.72	5	160
C	11/99	10.10	6.58	9.38	10	210
Z	8/11	18.50	17.05	10.00	20	235

Source: Lakhbir S. Hayre, David Foulds, and Lisa Pendergast, "Introduction to Collateralized Mortgage Obligations," in Frank J. Fabozzi, ed., *The Handbook of Mortgage-Backed Securities*, rev. ed. (Chicago: Probus Publishing, 1988), p. 346.

a prepayment rate of 110% PSA. The expected maturity, average life, duration, projected yield, and spread to Treasuries based on 110% PSA are summarized in the lower panel of Exhibit 12-1.

Considerations in Structuring a CMO: A number of considerations are important in structuring a CMO. First, the CMO must be structured to ensure that the cash flow structure will satisfy the bond obligations even under adverse prepayment conditions. This is necessary in order to get a high quality rating from commercial rating companies. Second, to avoid adverse tax consequences, the issue must be structured so that the trust is not treated as a taxable entity. This enables it to avoid double taxation—a tax at both the trust and security holder levels; that is, it does away with the possibility that the distributions made to securityholders are treated as dividends and therefore would not be tax-deductible by the trust.[3] The third consideration is that the issuer wants the CMO to be considered as a sale of assets so that it will not appear as debt on its balance sheet. Last— but certainly not least—is the arbitrage available to the issuer in the transaction. The issuer must be able to acquire the collateral for the transaction at a price that will permit a profit. The factors that affect the arbitrage profit are the yield curve shape, general prepayment levels, client demand for CMOs, and the demand for the underlying collateral.

Credit Risk: The credit quality for most CMOs is high enough to earn a triple-A rating by the major commercial rating agencies. The credit risk is determined by the quality of the underlying mortgage collateral and the CMO structure, and generally not by the creditworthiness of the issuer of the CMO.

With respect to the collateral, for CMOs backed by agency pass-throughs or FHA/VA-guaranteed mortgage loans, credit risk is minimal. CMOs issued by Freddie Mac and Fannie Mae carry their guarantee and are perceived to have low credit risk. CMOs that do not fall into one of these two categories typically carry pool insurance that guarantees the timely payment of interest and principal.

The second key element in determining the credit quality of the CMO is the manner in which the cash flows are structured. In order to receive a triple-A quality rating, the cash flows must be sufficient to meet all of the obligations under any prepayment scenario. Also, the reinvestment rate assumed to be earned on the cash flow until it is distributed to bondholders must be low.

Because of the safeguards built into a CMO structure, a CMO with a triple-A rating is generally viewed as having less credit risk than a corporate bond with the same rating.

CMO Classes

The numerous innovations in structuring CMOs have resulted in the creation of classes of bonds with one or more of the following characteristics: (1) greater stability of cash flows over a wide range of prepayment speeds; (2) better matching of floating-rate liabilities; (3) substantial upside potential in a declining interest rate environment but less downside risk in a rising interest rate environment;[4] or (4) properties that allow them to be used for hedging mortgage-related products. Below we discuss how CMO classes allow these characteristics to be realized.

---

[3] An entity that issues a pass-through structured as a grantor trust is not treated as a taxable entity, although prior to the Tax Reform Act of 1986, the IRS ruled that multiple-class pass-throughs such as CMOs were taxable entities even if structured as a grantor trust. To circumvent this provision in the tax code so that the issuer of a CMO would not be treated as the issuer of a multiple-class pass-through and therefore as a taxable entity, issuers designed cash flow structures that would be classified as debt payments for tax purposes. This, however, meant that the CMO would be treated as debt on the balance sheet, thereby not satisfying the issuer's objective of avoiding this adverse financial reporting consequence.

The Real Estate Mortgage Investment Conduits (REMIC) provision in the Tax Reform Act of 1986 allows issuers to issue a multiple-class pass-through without being treated as a taxable entity. This means that a CMO can now be structured so that the issuer can treat it as a sale of assets for tax purposes, and the transaction will not be treated as debt for financial reporting purposes. The issuer does this by electing to have the CMO treated as a REMIC. Thus a REMIC CMO is not a new security but a tax election made by an issuer.

[4] In the terminology of the analytical framework discussed in Chapter 13, these classes have substantial positive convexity.

Accrual Bonds: In the CMO structure shown in Exhibit 12-1, the Z-bond class is the accrual bond. In most of the earlier CMO structures, the accrual bond was the last class to be paid off and therefore the class with the longest stated maturity. Such a bond appeals to long-term investors who seek to mitigate the risk associated with the reinvestment of coupon and principal payments. As we explain when we discuss planned amortization class bonds later, accrual bonds with intermediate stated maturities are now available.

The inclusion of an accrual bond in a CMO structure is important because it is this class of bondholders that protects earlier classes from extension risk. Moreover, the higher the principal amount of the accrual class, the more bonds with a short stated maturity that can be included in a CMO. In terms of the economics of the transaction, inclusion of more bonds with a short stated maturity leads to greater arbitrage profits for the issuer in a positive sloping yield curve environment.

Floating-Rate/Inverse Floating-Rate CMOs: A class in a CMO structure that has a coupon rate that varies directly with the London Interbank Offered Rate (LIBOR) or some other reference interest rate, is called a floating-rate class. Such a CMO class appeals to financial institutions (both domestic and foreign) that seek investments whose interest rates vary with the floating rates they must pay on their liabilities.

One feature of the floating-rate CMO necessary to ensure that the collateral will be sufficient to meet all obligations of the CMO issue is a cap placed on the maximum lifetime interest rate that could be paid to the floating-rate class. Such a feature has made floating-rate CMOs a less attractive vehicle for financial institutions and foreign investors seeking instruments for asset/liability management.

To overcome this drawback, an inverse floating-rate class has been introduced into some CMO structures. This is a class whose coupon rate changes in the direction *opposite* from the change in interest rates. Inclusion of an inverse floater in a CMO structure along with a floating-rate class means that the maximum coupon rate that could be paid to the floating-rate class is higher than would be possible without an inverse floater.

To illustrate the inverse floater and how it affects the cap on a floating-rate class, we can use an actual CMO deal, the FHLMC Series 128 CMO issued in January 1990. The coupon rate on the underlying collateral is 9% and the principal amount at the time of issuance was $1 billion. The CMO structure includes a floating-rate class with a principal of $64 million and an inverse floater with a principal of $16 million. Therefore, the floater and inverse floater represented $80 million of the $1 billion structure.

The coupon rate for the floating-rate class is:

LIBOR + .65

For the inverse floater the coupon rate is:

$42.4 - 4 \times \text{LIBOR}$

The weighted-average coupon rate is:

$$\frac{64}{80}\left(\text{Floater coupon rate}\right) + \frac{16}{80}\left(\text{Inverse floater coupon rate}\right)$$

The weighted-average coupon rate is 9% regardless of the level of LIBOR. For example, if LIBOR is 10%, then

Floater coupon rate = 10 + .65 = 10.65
Inverse floater coupon rate = 42.4 − 4 × 10 = 2.4

The weighted-average coupon rate is:

$$\frac{64}{80}(10.65) + \frac{16}{80}(2.4) = 9$$

Consequently, the coupon rate on the underlying collateral, 9%, can support the aggregate interest payments that must be made to these two classes.

Because LIBOR is always positive, the coupon rate paid to the floating-rate class cannot be negative. However, if there are no restrictions placed on the coupon rate for the inverse floater, it is possible for the coupon rate for that class to be negative. To prevent this, a floor is set on the coupon rate for the inverse floater. In this deal, the floor is set at zero. By imposing this floor, a restriction is placed on the maximum coupon rate that can be paid to the floating-rate class. The maximum coupon rate is 11.25%. This is found by substituting zero for the coupon rate of the inverse floater in the formula for the weighted average coupon rate and then setting the formula equal to 9.

Notice also that, in the absence of the inverse floater, the coupon rate that the floating-rate class can be paid cannot go to far above 9%, the coupon rate on the underlying collateral. The reason that it can be slightly above 9% is explained later when we discuss the CMO residual.

The multiple by which the coupon interest rate on the inverse floater will change is called the *coupon leverage*. In our illustration, the multiple is 4. The higher the coupon leverage, the more the inverse floater's coupon interest rate will change for a given change in LIBOR. For example, a coupon leverage of 4 means that a 100-basis point change in LIBOR will change the coupon interest rate on the inverse floater by 400 basis points;

a coupon leverage of .7 means that the coupon interest rate will change by 70 basis points for a 100-basis point change in LIBOR. Inverse floaters with a wide variety of coupon leverages are available in the market.

A special type of inverse floater is the *two-tiered index bond*. With this bond, the coupon is fixed within a specified range for the reference rate. Once the upper range for the reference rate (the strike rate) is reached, the coupon resets according to a specified formula so that, as the reference rate rises, the coupon rate falls. The rate at which the coupon is fixed represents the cap on the bond; a floor is set at a coupon rate of 0%. For example, a two-tiered index bond may be structured as follows: (1) for one-month LIBOR (the reference rate) between 0% and 9%, the coupon rate is fixed at 9.3%, and (2) if one-month LIBOR is greater than 9% (the strike rate), the coupon rate is set by the formula:

$$\text{Coupon rate} = 69 - 6 \times \text{one-month LIBOR}$$

with a floor of 0% which is reached when LIBOR is 11.5% or greater.

A variant of the floating-rate CMO is the *superfloater*. In a conventional floating-rate class, the coupon rate resets at a fixed spread above LIBOR. For example, the coupon rate may be LIBOR plus 60 basis points. A superfloater is a floating-rate class whose initial coupon rate is set below LIBOR but changes by some multiple of the change in LIBOR. For example, the initial coupon rate for a superfloater may be:

$$\text{Initial LIBOR} - 50 \text{ Basis points} + 2 \times (\text{Change in LIBOR})$$

To illustrate, suppose that initial LIBOR is 8%. Then the coupon rate for a conventional floater of, say, LIBOR plus 60 basis points and the superfloater with a coupon rate based on the formula above is as follows if LIBOR changes:

Coupon Rate if LIBOR Changes (in Basis Points) by:

	−300	−200	−100	0	+100	+200	+300
Conventional floater	5.6	6.6	7.6	8.6	9.6	10.6	11.6
Superfloater	1.5	3.5	5.5	7.5	9.5	11.5	13.5

The spread to LIBOR if LIBOR changes is then:

Spread to LIBOR if LIBOR Changes (in Basis Points) by:

	−300	−200	−100	0	+100	+200	+300
Conventional floater	60	60	60	60	60	60	60
Superfloater	−350	−250	−150	−50	50	150	250

Notice in the table that the spread to LIBOR (1) provides a substantially higher yield than a conventional floater when interest rates are rising, and (2) provides a substantially lower yield than a conventional floater when interest rates are falling or stable. The superfloater has been suggested for hedging fixed-rate mortgage loans or pass-throughs.[5]

PAC Bonds: In the 1980s, traditional corporate bond buyers who contemplated investing in CMOs sought a structure with the characteristics of a corporate bond and with high credit quality. While CMOs satisfied the second condition, they did not satisfy the first.

A Planned Amortization Class (PAC) bond is a CMO product that was created so as to have a similar cash flow structure as a sinking fund corporate bond within a specified range of prepayment rates; that is, the cash flow pattern to the bondholder is known. The cash flow for PAC bonds is more predictable because there is a principal repayment schedule that must be satisfied. The PAC bondholders, therefore, have priority over all other classes in the CMO issue in receiving principal payments from the underlying collateral in order to satisfy the repayment schedule. The greater certainty of the cash flow for the PAC bonds comes at the expense, of course, of the non-PAC classes, called the *companion* or *support* classes. Should the actual prepayment speed be faster than the upper limit of the PAC range, then the companion bonds receive the excess. This means that the companion bonds absorb the contraction risk. Should the actual prepayment speed be slower than the lower limit of the range, then in subsequent periods the PAC bondholders have priority on principal payments (both scheduled payments and prepayments). This reduces extension risk, which is absorbed by the companion bondholders. Because there may be more than one class of bonds receiving principal payments at the same time, structures with PAC bonds are called *simultaneous-pay* CMOs.

Exhibit 12-2 illustrates how a PAC bond can be constructed from underlying collateral. Exhibit 12-2a shows the principal payments that will result if the prepayment speed for the life of some hypothetical collateral is 80% PSA. Specifically, if the prepayment speed does in fact turn out to be 80% PSA, the solid curve in Exhibit 12-2a represents a principal

---

[5] For an illustration, see Frank J. Fabozzi and Franco Modigliani, *Mortgage and Mortgage-Backed Securities Markets* (Boston, MA: Harvard Business School Publications, 1992), Chapter 11. The return pattern provided by a superfloater when hedging can be replicated by purchasing (1) a conventional floater, and (2) LIBOR-based caps that are paid for with a combination of cash and premium income received from writing both in- and out-of-the money LIBOR-based options. (Caps are discussed in Chapter 19.) Sounds complicated, doesn't it? The superfloater is much simpler; which is why it was created. For a discussion of the complications associated with using superfloaters for hedging, see Michael Smirlock, "Superfloaters: A CMO Innovation," *MBS Letter*, March 21, 1988, pp. 7, 10.

EXHIBIT 12-2   Creation of a PAC Bond Schedule

(a) Principal Cash Flow at 80% PSA

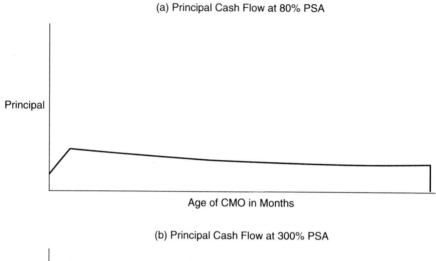

Age of CMO in Months

(b) Principal Cash Flow at 300% PSA

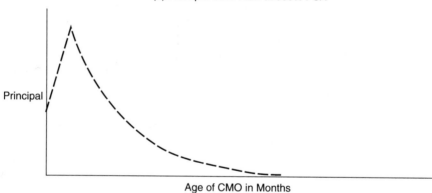

Age of CMO in Months

(c) Principal Cash Flow Common to 80% PSA and 300% PSA

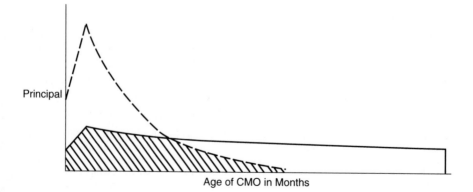

Age of CMO in Months

payment schedule that can be satisfied by the underlying collateral. Next consider Exhibit 12-2b, which shows the principal payments if the prepayment speed is considerably faster, 300% PSA. Here, the broken line in Exhibit 12-2b represents a principal payment schedule that can be satisfied by the underlying collateral if the prepayment speed is in fact 300% PSA. Notice that the principal payments are higher in the earlier years in comparison to Exhibit 12-2a, but that in later years the principal payments are lower because of the faster prepayments.

Exhibit 12-2c combines the solid line in Exhibit 12-2a and the broken line in Exhibit 12-2b. The shaded area in Exhibit 12-2c represents the principal payments that will be available to pay bondholders as long as the prepayment rate is either 80% or 300% PSA. In fact, it tells us even more. The shaded area represents the principal payment schedule that will be available to pay bondholders at every possible PSA rate between 80% and 300% PSA.

The upper and lower PSA levels used to construct the principal payment schedule shown in Exhibit 12-2c are called the *initial PAC collar*. The key is that prepayment protection is ensured as long as the companion bonds are not fully paid off. Consequently, the degree of prepayment protection changes over time as actual prepayments occur. For example, if prepayments over the first few years are at the lower end of the initial PAC collar, there will be more companion bonds remaining, which will result in greater prepayment protection for the PAC bonds. A new collar can be determined that will allow PAC bondholders to realize their original principal payment schedule so long as prepayments are within the collar. This new collar is called the *effective collar*.

The breaking of the initial collar does not mean that the principal payment schedule will not be met. It depends on when the initial collar is broken, the amount of the deviation from the collar, and for how long the collar is broken. For example, if for the PAC bond in Exhibit 12-2 the prepayment rate is within the initial PAC collar for the first three years but then speeds up to, say, 350% PSA for two months, this will not affect the principal payment schedule. The reason is that the prepayments within the initial PAC collar in the first three years result in more companion bonds at the end of three years than originally anticipated. The faster prepayment for two months then will be easily absorbed by the companion bonds. If the prepayment rate for the first ten months had been 400% PSA, however, there would be a good chance that the principal payment schedule will not be satisfied, because the companion bonds will be paid off at a faster rate, thereby offering less prepayment protection.

In practice, there is more than one class of PAC bonds in a CMO structure. For example, instead of the one PAC bond depicted in Exhibit

12-2, several sequential series of PAC bonds can be carved out of the cash flow, each with a different projected starting and terminal point for the principal repayment. Specification of the PACs to be created will depend on investor demand for classes with certain average lives and windows. The *window* for a PAC refers to the time between the first payment of principal and the estimated final principal payment. The tighter the PAC window, the more a PAC resembles a corporate bond with a bullet payment (i.e., a corporate term bond).

CMO PAC structures have been created with a sequential series of accrual PAC (or Z-PAC) bond classes.[6] Z-PAC bonds have had a variety of average lives, from intermediate-term to long-term. Moreover, unlike the traditional accrual bond, Z-PAC bonds have less uncertainty about the cash flow. The Z-PAC bonds broadened the interest of traditional zero-coupon bond buyers in CMOs.

Earlier we discussed floating-rate and inverse floating-rate classes. These bonds have been created from the companion bonds in a CMO deal with PAC bonds. However, they can be created from a PAC. For example, the PAC in Exhibit 12-2 can be split into a floater and inverse floater class.

Companions with Schedules: The creation of floaters and inverse floaters from a companion bond is but one example of how a companion bond's cash flow can be distributed in order to create a bond or bonds that can be used for better asset/liability matching or hedging. The companion bonds absorb prepayment risk, thereby protecting the PAC bonds. However, companion bonds themselves can have cash flows prioritized so as to reduce prepayment risk. Companion bonds with schedules resulting from the prioritization of cash flows still have greater prepayment risk than the PAC bonds they support, but prepayment risk is less than it would be in the absence of a schedule.

Companion bonds with schedules, also referred to as *PAC II level bonds*, are supported by other companion bonds without schedules. (PACs in a structure where there are PAC II level bonds are called PAC I level bonds.) There have been CMO structures with PAC III level bonds, these being bonds where the companion (support) bonds for the level II PAC bonds have schedules.

TAC Bonds: A Targeted Amortization Class, or TAC, bond, just as a PAC bond, has priority over other bonds classes that do not have a schedule for principal repayments. The prepayment protection afforded TAC bonds,

---

[6] Structurers have also included some unusual features for turning the accrual mechanism on and off. Under certain conditions—either relating to a particular date, level of interest rates, or amount of principal available to pay other classes in the CMO structure—a Z-PAC bond could be converted into a coupon-paying bond. Such bonds are referred to as "jump Z-bonds."

however, is less than that of PAC bonds. It is designed to provide protection against contraction risk but exposes the investor to extension risk. This is accomplished by specifying a narrower PSA prepayment range or just a single PSA prepayment rate over which the principal is guaranteed.

Some institutional investors are interested in protection against extension risk but are willing to accept contraction risk. This is opposite from the protection that is sought by TAC bondholders. The structures that have been created to provide such protection are referred to as *reverse TAC bonds.*

The use of TAC bonds in a CMO structure in the earlier deals is quite different from its use today. Today TAC and reverse TAC bonds are created from companion bonds. They accordingly provide support for PAC bondholders.

VADM Bonds: Accrual or Z-bonds have been used in CMO structures as support for bonds called *very accurately determined maturity* (VADM) or *guaranteed final maturity* bonds. Specifically, the interest accruing (i.e., not being paid out) on a Z-bond is used to pay the interest and principal on a VADM bond. What this effectively does is provide protection against extension risk even if prepayments slow down, because the interest accruing on the Z-bond will be sufficient to pay off the scheduled principal and interest on the VADM bond. Thus, the *maximum* final maturity can be determined with a high degree of certainty. However, if prepayments are high, resulting in the supporting Z-bond being paid off faster, a VADM bond can shorten.

A VADM is similar in character to a reverse TAC. For structures with similar collateral, however, a VADM bond offers greater protection against extension risk. Moreover, most VADMs that have been created will not shorten significantly if prepayments speed up. Thus, they offer greater protection against contraction risk compared to a reverse TAC with the same underlying collateral. Compared to PACs, VADM bonds have greater absolute protection against extension risk, and while VADM bonds do not have as much protection against contraction risk, the CMOs that have included these bonds are structured so that contraction risk is generally not significant.

CMO Residuals: The excess of the cash flow generated by the underlying collateral over the amount needed to pay interest, retire the bonds, and pay administrative expenses is called the CMO residual. Investors can purchase an equity position in the residual cash flow. The excess cash flow is not known with certainty. It depends on several factors: (1) current and future interest rates; (2) the coupon rate on the underlying mortgage collateral; (3) the type of collateral; (4) the prepayment rate on the underlying collateral; and (5) the structure of the CMO issue.

The three most common sources of CMO residual cash flow are (1) premium interest, (2) bond coupon differential, and (3) reinvestment income.[7] The first and most important component is the cash flow generated from premium interest. This represents the difference between the coupon rate on the collateral and the coupon rate paid on the highest-coupon rate bond in the CMO structure. For example, if the coupon rate on the collateral is 9.5% and 9.125% is the highest coupon rate paid on a bond class, the premium interest is .375%. The bond coupon differential arises because a CMO structure is designed to support bond payments assuming that each bond class has a coupon rate equal to the highest-coupon rate bond class. For example, if the coupon rate on the highest-coupon rate bond is 9.125%, and there are three other classes with coupon rates of 7.75%, 8.0%, and 8.9%, the bond coupon differential would be generated from 137.5-, 112.5-, and 22.5-basis point differentials, respectively. The third source of residual cash flow is the income generated by the reinvestment of cash flow payments from the collateral between the time it is received and the time payments must be made to bondholders.

The CMO residual is an interesting instrument, because its value should move in the same direction as the change in interest rates and not in the opposite direction. To understand why, consider what happens when interest rates/mortgage rates fall. There are two adverse effects. First, prepayments are expected to speed up. The result is that the classes receiving the lower coupon rate will be paid off faster, thereby reducing the cash flow to the CMO residual that results from the premium income and bond coupon differential. Second, the cash flow that is reinvested until it is paid to each CMO class will be invested at a lower interest rate. Together, these two effects will result in a lower expected cash flow for the CMO residual owners and a lower price for the CMO residual.[8] If interest rates/mortgage rates rise, the expected cash flow for the CMO residual will increase, because prepayments will be expected to slow down, and cash flow before payout to CMO bondholders will be reinvested at a higher interest rate. The result should be an increase in the price of the CMO residual.

---

[7] Mark Stanley, Helene Halperin, Robert Kulason, and William Calan, *CMO Residuals: Structure and Performance* (Merrill Lynch Capital Markets, January 1988).

[8] The cash flow will be discounted at a lower interest rate, but typically the overall effect is a lower price.

Because the price of a CMO residual moves in the same direction as the change in interest rates, it can be used by institutions for hedging portfolios of pass-throughs.

IOettes and PAC IOs: In the earlier CMO structures, the premium interest and the coupon bond differential accrued to the benefit of the residual class. This is no longer the practice in structuring CMOs. Instead, the premium interest is now stripped off and used to pay a class known as the *interest-only* (IO) class, and the coupon bond differential is stripped off to create a class known as a *PAC IO*.

This structure can be illustrated using the FHLMC 1044 CMO. This issue includes five PAC I level bonds and one PAC II level bond. The coupon rate for each of these bonds is:

A	PAC I level	7.75%
B	PAC I level	8.00
C	PAC I level	8.60
D	PAC I level	8.90
E	PAC I level	8.50
F	PAC II level	8.40

The coupon rate for the underlying collateral for this structure was 9.5%. The residual class was given a fixed coupon rate of 9.125%. A bond class called Class L was given the difference between the collateral coupon rate of 9.5% and the maximum coupon rate of the PACs and residual class; that is, Class L received the premium interest. At the maximum coupon rate of 9.125%, the coupon rate of the residual class, Class L received 37.5 basis points. Because this class is entitled to receive only interest, it is called an IO. Prior to 1992, a provision in the tax law did not permit a CMO structure to have a class that receives no principal. Consequently, structurers had to include a nominal principal for an IO class included in a CMO structure, effectively making the class a bond with an extremely high coupon rate. Because of this nominal principal, an IO included in a CMO is referred to as an *IOette*.

Notice also that in the FHLMC 1044 CMO there is still excess coupon interest available, because only 9.125% of the 9.5% is paid out to the IOette and the residual class (which we earlier called earlier bond coupon differential). The difference between the coupon interest rate that had to be paid to the PAC I level and PAC II level bonds, given the level of interest rates at the time this structure was created, allowed for the additional stripping of interest. In this structure, the bond coupon differential between 9.125% and the coupon rate on PAC bonds A, B, and C was used to create an IO bond, Class I. Because this IO class is created out of the stripped interest from PACs, it is called a PAC IO. In fact, in the FHLMC 1044 deal a second PAC IO, Class J, was created by stripping off the interest from the two PAC Classes D and E. By stripping off the interest between 9.125% and the coupon interest of 8.4% on the PAC II level bond (Class F), a PAC II level IO was created (Class K).

Number of Classes in CMO Structures

Given the vast number of CMO classes that can be included in a deal structure, it is not surprising to see structures issued today with as many as 70 classes. Prior to 1988, the average number of classes in a CMO deal was 4. With the introduction of PACs, the average number of classes per deal increased to about 6 by 1988. The deals between 1986 (when PACs were introduced) and 1988 typically included only one or two PAC classes. By 1989, there was an average of 9 classes per deal, and in 1990 and 1991 there were about 11 classes per deal.

STRIPPED MORTGAGE-BACKED SECURITIES

Stripped mortgage-backed securities, introduced by Fannie Mae in 1986, are another example of derivative products. A pass-through divides the cash flow from the underlying pool of mortgages on a pro rata basis across the securityholders. A stripped MBS is created by altering the distribution of principal and interest from a pro rata distribution to an *unequal* distribution. Some of the securities thus created will have a price/yield relationship that is different from the price/yield relationship of the underlying mortgage pool.

Types of Stripped MBS

There are three types of stripped MBS: (1) synthetic-coupon pass-throughs, (2) interest-only/principal-only securities, and (3) CMO strips.

Synthetic-Coupon Pass-Throughs: The first generation of stripped mortgage-backed securities is called synthetic-coupon pass-throughs. This is because the unequal distribution of coupon and principal results in a synthetic coupon rate that is different from that of the underlying collateral.

Interest-Only/Principal-Only Strips: In early 1987, stripped MBS began to be issued where all the interest is allocated to one class (the interest-only or IO class) and all the principal to the other class (the principal-only or PO class). The IO class receives no principal payments.

The PO security is purchased at a substantial discount from par value. The yield an investor will realize depends on the speed at which prepayments are made. The faster the prepayments, the higher the yield the investor will realize. For example, suppose that there is a pass-through backed by 30-year mortgages with $400 million in principal and that investors can purchase POs backed by this pass-through for $175 million. The dollar return on this investment will be $225 million. How quickly that dollar return is recovered by PO investors determines the yield that will be realized. In the extreme case, if all the homeowners in the underlying mortgage pool decide to prepay their mortgage loans immediately, PO investors will realize the $225 million immediately. At the other extreme, if all homeowners decide to keep their houses for 30 years and make no prepayments, the $225 million will be spread out over 30 years, which will result in a lower yield for PO investors.

Let's look at how the price of the PO can be expected to change as mortgage rates in the market change. When mortgage rates decline below the coupon rate, prepayments are expected to speed up, accelerating payments to the PO holder. Thus, the cash flow of a PO improves (in the sense that principal repayments are received earlier). The cash flow will be discounted at a lower interest rate because the mortgage rate in the market has declined. The result is that the price of a PO will increase when mortgage rates decline. When mortgage rates rise above the coupon rate, prepayments are expected to slow down. The cash flow deteriorates (in the sense of its taking longer to recover principal repayments). Coupled with a higher discount rate, the price of a PO will fall when mortgage rates rise.

When an IO is purchased there is no par value. In contrast to the PO investor, the IO investor wants prepayments to be slow. The reason is that the IO investor receives only interest on the amount of the principal outstanding. As prepayments are made, the outstanding principal declines, and less dollar interest is received. In fact, if prepayments are too fast, the IO investor may not recover the amount paid for the IO.

Let's look at the expected price response of an IO to changes in mortgage rates. If mortgage rates decline below the coupon rate, prepayments are expected to accelerate. This results in a deterioration of the expected cash flow for an IO. Although the cash flow will be discounted at a lower rate, the net effect is typically a decline in the price of an IO. If mortgage rates rise above the coupon rate, the expected cash flow improves, but the cash flow is discounted at a higher interest rate. The net effect may be either a rise or fall for the IO. Thus, we see an interesting characteristic of an IO: its price tends to move in the same direction as the change in mortgage rates. This effect occurs (1) when mortgage rates fall below the coupon rate, and (2) for some range of mortgage rates above the coupon rate.

An example of this effect can be seen in Exhibit 12-3, which shows for various mortgage rates the price of (1) a 9% pass-through, (2) a PO created from this pass-through, and (3) an IO created from this pass-through. Notice that as mortgage rates decline below 9%, the price of the pass-through does not respond much. This is the negative convexity (or price compression) property of pass-throughs. For the PO security, the price falls monotonically as mortgage rates rise. For the IO security, at mortgage rates above approximately 10%, the price declines as mortgage rates rise; as mortgage rates fall below about 10%, the price of an IO falls as mortgage rates decline.

Both POs and IOs exhibit substantial price volatility when mortgage rates change. The greater price volatility of the IO and PO compared to the pass-through from which they were created can be seen by the steepness of a tangent line to the curves at any given mortgage rate.

CMOs that are backed by POs, are referred to as *PO-collateralized CMOs*.

EXHIBIT 12-3   Relationship between Price and Mortgage Rates for a Pass-Through, PO and IO

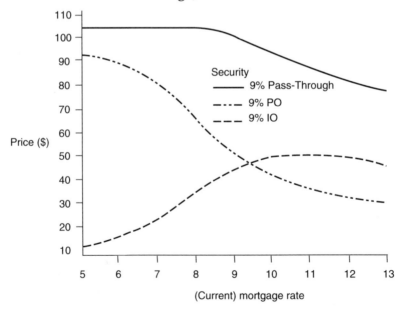

Source: Adapted from Steven J. Carlson and Timothy D. Sears, "Stripped Mortgage Pass-Throughs: New Tools for Investors," in Frank J. Fabozzi, ed., *The Handbook of Mortgage-Backed Securities*, rev. ed. (Chicago: Probus Publishing, 1988), p. 564.

CMO Strips: One of the classes in a CMO structure can be a principal-only or an interest-only class. These are called CMO strips. A CMO strip may be a PAC or TAC. When a CMO strip is a PO class that is neither a PAC nor a TAC, it is called a *Super PO*. The reason for referring to such a class as a Super PO relates to its potential price performance if prepayments increase in speed as interest rates decline. When this occurs, the Super PO bondholders are paid off faster; because these bonds are issued at a substantial discount from par, the result is "super" price performance.

SUMMARY

To address the prepayment risks associated with investing in mortgage pass-through securities—contraction risk and extension risk—CMOs were created. They accomplish this by redirecting cash flows from a pass-through to different bond classes, according to a set of rules for distribution of interest and principal (both regularly scheduled principal payments and prepayments), so as to redistribute prepayment risk to investors who want to reduce their exposure to it. Because the total prepayment risk of a pass-through is not changed by altering the cash flows, other investors must be willing to accept the unwanted prepayment risk. The credit quality for most CMOs is high enough to be rated triple-A by the major commercial rating agencies.

In a sequential-pay CMO, a bond class does not receive principal payments until all classes before it that have priority with respect to receipt of principal payments are fully paid off. Numerous innovations in structuring CMOs have resulted in the creation of classes of bonds with: (1) greater stability of cash flows over a wide range of prepayment speeds; (2) better matching of floating-rate liabilities; (3) substantial upside potential in a declining interest rate environment, but less downside risk in a rising interest rate environment; or (4) usefulness for hedging mortgage-related products. These structures include accrual bonds, floating-rate and inverse floating-rate bonds, PAC bonds (and companion or support bonds), companions with schedules, TAC bonds, VADMs, and residuals. When one or more PAC bonds are included, the structure is referred to as a simultaneous-pay CMO.

A stripped MBS is created by assigning distribution of principal and interest of the underlying pass-through security in unequal portions to two classes of bonds. The result is that the two bonds will have a different price/yield relationship from that of the underlying pass-through. There are three types of stripped MBS: (1) synthetic-coupon pass-throughs, (2) interest-only/principal only-securities, and (3) CMO strips.

QUESTIONS FOR CHAPTER 12

1. How does a collateralized mortgage obligation alter the cash flow from mortgages so as to shift the prepayment risk across various classes of bondholders?

2. "By creating a CMO, an issuer eliminates the prepayment risk associated with the underlying mortgages." Do you agree with this statement?

3. This quotation is taken from a 1991 issue of *Bondweek*:

   First Interstate Bank of Texas will look into buying several different types of collateralized mortgage obligation tranches when it starts up its buy program sometime after the second quarter of 1991, according to Jules Pollard, v.p. Pollard said he will consider replacing maturing adjustable-rate mortgage pass-throughs with short companion tranches and planned and targeted amortization classes because the ARMS have become rich. . . Pollard did not provide a dollar figure on the planned investments, which will be made to match fund the bank's liabilities. When he does invest he said he prefers government-guaranteed securities or those with implied guarantees.

   a. Explain the types of securities that Mr. Pollard is planning to buy.
   b. Given the preference stated in the last sentence of the quotation, what issuers is he likely to prefer? What issuers would he reject?

4. The following questions are to be answered by referring to the selected pages taken from prospectus supplement that appears on pages 281-305. As indicated on S-30 and S-31, the structure and the distribution payments are based on mortgage loans with a 12% mortgage rate and an initial mortgage term of 360 months, and the underlying pass-throughs have a coupon rate of 10.125% and a remaining term to maturity of 356 months.

   a. Is the CMO structure described in the supplement a sequential-pay or simultaneous-pay CMO?
   b. How many classes are there in this CMO structure?
   c (i) Which class is the floating-rate class?
      (ii) What is the benchmark interest rate used for the floating-rate, and what is the spread to the benchmark?
      (iii) What are the cap and the floor on the floating-rate after August 24, 1990? How is the floor determined?
   d. (i) Which class is the inverse floating-rate class?
      (ii) What is the formula used to determine the coupon rate for the inverse floater?
      (iii) What is the coupon leverage?
      (iv) What are the cap and the floor on the inverse floater after August 24, 1990?

    (v) How was the cap on the inverse floater determined?

    (vi) How was the cap on the floating-rate class determined?

e. Assuming the initial principal outstanding of both the floating-rate and inverse floating-rate class and a LIBOR of 9%, then what is

    (i) The dollar coupon interest that will be paid to the floating-rate class?

    (ii) The dollar coupon interest that will be paid to the inverse floater?

    (iii) The total dollar coupon interest to both classes?

    (iv) The total dollar coupon interest on the underlying pass-through, assuming a coupon rate of 10.125%.

f. Based on your answer in the previous question, what is the weighted-average coupon paid to the sum of the floating- and inverse floating-rate classes?

g. Are the floating-rate and inverse floating-rate classes in this structure PAC or support classes?

h. (i) How many PAC bonds are in this CMO structure?

    (ii) What is the initial PAC collar?

i. Based on the planned principal balances shown on pages S-16 to S-24:

    (i) When is Class 89-A scheduled to make its first principal payment?

    (ii) When is Class 89-A scheduled to make its final principal payment?

    (iii) What is the window for Class 89-A?

    (iv) When is Class 89-G scheduled to make its first principal payment?

    (v) When is Class 89-G scheduled to make its final principal payment?

    (vi) What is the window for Class 89-G?

j. Which bond is an accrual PAC bond? How did you determine which PAC bond was an accrual PAC bond?

k. What are the support bonds in this CMO structure?

l. (i) Why is the coupon rate on Class 89-R not indicated in the prospectus supplement?

    (ii)What is the source of the interest payment that will be made to Class R?

m. Based on the percent of original principal balance outstanding reported on pages S-30 to S-34:

    (i) To what extent is Class 89-A subject to extension risk?

    (ii) To what extent is Class 89-B subject to contraction risk?

    (iii) Explain why the support classes are subject to substantial pre-payment risk.

    (iv) For the PAC bonds, why is the weighted-average life constant between 90% PSA and 275% PSA?

5. In a CMO structure with several PAC bonds, explain why once the support bonds are paid off, the structure will be just like a sequential-pay CMO.

6. Suppose that for the first four years of a CMO, prepayments are well within the initial PAC collar. What will happen to the effective upper collar?

7. a. Why in a steep yield curve environment can the creation of a CMO be attractive to an issuer?

   b. Why in a CMO structure do you think an issuer would want to create as many short-term classes as possible?

8. a. What is a principal-only security? An interest-only security?

   b. How is the price of an interest-only security expected to change when interest rates change?

9. Suppose that 8% coupon pass-throughs are stripped into two classes. Class X-1 receives 75% of the principal and 10% of the interest. Class X-2 receives 25% of the principal and 90% of the interest.

   (i) What type of stripped MBS would this be?

   (ii) What is the effective coupon rate on Class X-1?

   (iii) What is the effective coupon rate on Class X-2?

Prospectus Supplement to Prospectus Dated January 4, 1990
$500,000,000
Federal National Mortgage Association

FannieMae

Guaranteed REMIC Pass-Through Certificates
Fannie Mae REMIC Trust 1990-89

The Guaranteed REMIC Pass-Through Certificates offered hereby (the "REMIC Certificates") represent beneficial ownership interests in one of two trust funds. The REMIC Certificates, other than the Class 89-RL REMIC Certificates, represent beneficial ownership interests in Fannie Mae REMIC Trust 1990-89 (the "Trust"). The assets of the Trust consist of the "regular interests" in a separate trust fund (the "Lower Tier REMIC"), consisting of Fannie Mae Guaranteed Mortgage Pass-Through Certificates (the "MBS Certificates"), each of which represents a beneficial interest in a pool (the "Pool") of first lien, single-family, fixed-rate residential mortgage loans (the "Mortgage Loans") having the characteristics described in this Prospectus Supplement. The Class 89-RL REMIC Certificates will be the "residual interest" in the Lower Tier REMIC. The general characteristics of the REMIC Certificates, including the terms of Fannie Mae's guaranty thereof, are described in the attached Prospectus dated January 4, 1990 (the "REMIC Prospectus"). The general characteristics of the MBS Certificates, including the terms of Fannie Mae's guaranty thereof, are described in the attached MBS Prospectus dated April 1,1990 (the "MBS Prospectus").

(Continued on page 283)

THE OBLIGATIONS OF FANNIE MAE UNDER ITS GUARANTY OF THE REMIC CERTIFICATES ARE OBLIGATIONS OF FANNIE MAE ONLY AND ARE NOT BACKED BY THE FULL FAITH AND CREDIT OF THE UNITED STATES. THE REMIC CERTIFICATES ARE EXEMPT FROM THE REGISTRATION REQUIREMENTS OF THE SECURITIES ACT OF 1933 AND ARE "EXEMPTED SECURITIES" WITHIN THE MEANING OF THE SECURITIES EXCHANGE ACT OF 1934.

	Original Principal Amount	Interest Rate	Final Distribution Date
Class 89-A	$37,101,000	9.00%	March 2000
Class 89-B	31,474,000	9.00%	August 2003
Class 89-X	18,984,000	9.50%	July 2011
Class 89-C	40,000,000	9.50%	March 2014
Class 89-D	40,000,000	9.50%	March 2016
Class 89-E	16,168,000	9.50%	December 2016
Class 89-G	22,028,000	8.75%	October 2017
Class 89-H	15,856,000	8.75%	May 2018
Class 89-J	35,884,000	8.50%	July 2019
Class 89-K	36,683,000	6.50%	July 2020
Class 89-L	209,000	1009.00%	July 2020
Class 89-M	88,649,000	9.50%	July 2020
Class 89-F	9,120,000	(1)	November 2017
Class 89-S	11,400,000	(2)	November 2017
Class 89-N	14,528,000	9.50%	August 2017
Class 89-0	5,991,000	9.50%	November 2017
Class 89-P	51,566,000	9.50%	October 2018
Class 89-Y	7,000,000	9.50%	July 2020
Class 89-Z	6,833,000	9.50%	July 2020
Class 89-R	10,516,000	(3)	July 2020
Class 89-RL	10,000	9.50%	July 2020

(1) During their initial Interest Accrual Period of July 25, 1990 through August 24, 1990, the Class 89-F REMIC Certificates will bear interest at a rate of 8.8125% per annum. During each Interest Accrual Period thereafter, the Class 89-F REMIC Certificates will bear interest, subject to a maximum rate of 11.00% per annum and a minimum rate of 0.50% per annum, at a rate per annum equal to 50 basis points in excess of the London interbank offered rate for one-month U.S. dollar deposits ("LIBOR"), as more fully described herein.

(2) During their initial Interest Accrual Period of July 25, 1990 through August 24, 1990, the Class 89-S REMIC Certificates will bear interest at a rate of 10.05% per annum. During each Interest Accrual Period thereafter, the Class 89-S REMIC Certificates will bear interest, subject to a maximum rate of 16.7% per annum and a minimum rate of 8.3% per annum, at a per annum rate equal to 16.7% - (0.8 X LIBOR).

(3) Holders of the Class 89-R REMIC Certificates will be entitled on each Distribution Date to receive all Surplus Cash. See "Description of the REMIC Certificates—Additional Characteristics of the Class 89-R and Class 89-RL REMIC Certificates" herein.

This Prospectus Supplement does not contain complete information regarding this offering and should be read only in conjunction with the REMIC Prospectus and the MBS Prospectus.

The date of this Prospectus Supplement is June 22, 1990.

(Continued from page 283)

Interest on each Class of REMIC Certificates, other than the Class 89-R REMIC Certificates, at the applicable per annum interest rate described on the cover hereof will be distributed on the 25th day of each month (or, if such 25th day is not a business day, on the first business day next succeeding such 25th day), commencing in August 1990 (each, a "Distribution Date"), except for interest distributions on the Class 89-X, Class 89-Y and Class 89-Z REMIC Certificates, which are Accrual Certificates. Interest will accrue on the Accrual Certificates as described under "Description of the REMIC Certificates—Distributions of Interest" herein. Interest to be distributed or added to principal with respect to each REMIC Certificate on a Distribution Date will consist of one month's interest on the outstanding principal amount of such REMIC Certificate immediately prior to such Distribution Date.

The principal distribution on each Distribution Date will be in an amount equal to the sum of the aggregate distributions of principal concurrently made on the MBS Certificates and interest that accrues and is unpaid on the Accrual Certificates. On each Distribution Date, distributions of principal of the REMIC Certificates will be allocated among the Classes of REMIC Certificates in accordance with the priorities described herein.

The Final Distribution Dates of the respective Classes of REMIC Certificates have been determined so that distributions on the underlying MBS Certificates will be sufficient to make timely distributions of interest on the REMIC Certificates and to retire each such Class on or before its Final Distribution Date without the necessity of any call on Fannie Mae under its guaranty of the REMIC Certificates. The rate of distribution of principal of the REMIC Certificates will depend on the rate of payment (including prepayments) of the principal of the Mortgage Loans underlying the MBS Certificates. Both the Trust and the Lower Tier REMIC are subject to early termination only under the limited circumstances described in the REMIC Prospectus under "The Trust Agreement—Termination."

The yields on the REMIC Certificates will be sensitive in varying degrees to the rate of principal payments (including prepayments) of the Mortgage Loans, which generally can be prepaid at any time. An extremely rapid rate of principal payments (including prepayments) may have a negative effect on the yield on the Class 89-L REMIC Certificates, which initially will be offered at a substantial premium to their original principal amount and could result in a failure by investors in the Class 89-L REMIC Certificates to recoup their initial investment. In addition, the Class 89-F and Class 89-S REMIC Certificates will be sensitive to fluctuations in the level of LIBOR. Furthermore, the weighted average life of the Class 89-Y REMIC Certificates may decrease significantly, and the weighted average lives of the Class 89-M, Class 89-F, Class 89-S, Class 89-N, Class 89-0, Class 89-P and Class 89-Z REMIC Certificates may increase in varying degrees, if the prepayment rates of the Mortgage Loans exceed approximately 169% PSA (as defined herein) for any Distribution Date. Such changes in weighted average lives may have a significant effect on the yields on the REMIC Certificates.

The Class 89-R and Class 89-RL REMIC Certificates will be subject to certain transfer restrictions. See "Description of the REMIC Certificates—Additional Characteristics of the Class 89-R and Class 89-RL REMIC Certificates" herein. In addition, any transferee of a Class 89-R or Class 89-RL REMIC Certificate will be required to execute and deliver an affidavit as provided in the REMIC Prospectus. See "Description of the REMIC Certificates—Additional Characteristics of Residual Certificates" and "Certain Federal Income Tax Consequences—Sales of Certificates—*Residual Certificates Transferred to or Held by Disqualified Organizations*" in the REMIC Prospectus.

Elections will be made to treat the Lower Tier REMIC and the Trust as "real estate mortgage investment conduits" ("REMICs") pursuant to their original principal amount and could result in a as amended (the "Code"). The REMIC Certificates, other than the Class 89-R and Class 89-RL REMIC Certificates, will be designated as "regular interests" in the REMIC constituted by the Trust, and the Class 89-R REMIC Certificates will be designated as the "residual interest" in such REMIC. The interests in the Lower Tier REMIC, with the exception of the Class 89-RL REMIC Certificates (the "Lower Tier Interests"), will be designated as the "regular interests," and the Class 89-RL REMIC Certificates will be designated as the "residual interest," in the Lower Tier REMIC. See "Certain Federal Income Tax Consequences" in the REMIC Prospectus.

THE MBS CERTIFICATES

General

The MBS Certificates underlying the REMIC Certificates are Fannie Mae Guaranteed Mortgage Pass-Through Certificates, which will have an aggregate unpaid principal amount of $500,000,000, Pass-Through Rates of 9.50% and the general characteristics described in the attached MBS Prospectus. The Mortgage Loans that underlie the MBS Certificates are conventional Level Payment Mortgage Loans, each secured by a first mortgage or deed of trust on a one- to four-family ("single-family") residential property, and all of which have an original maturity of up to 30 years, as described under "The Mortgage Pools" and "Yield Considerations" in the MBS Prospectus. The weighted average coupon of the Mortgage Loans in each Pool at the Issue Date of the related MBS Certificate ("WAC") was within the range of 9.75% to 12.00% per annum. The weighted average remaining term to maturity, in months, of the Mortgage Loans in each Pool at the Issue Date of the related MBS Certificate ("WAM"), less the number of months elapsed from such Issue Date through the July 1, 1990 REMIC Issue Date ("Adjusted WAM"), or the current WAM, if available, will not be less than 180 or greater than 360. The weighted average of the Adjusted WAMs (or current WAMs, to the extent available) of all the MBS Certificates underlying the REMIC Certificates is expected to be approximately 356 months. Following the issuance of the REMIC Certificates, Fannie Mae will prepare a Final Data Statement setting forth the Pool number, the WAC at the Issue Date (or current WAC, to the extent available) and the Adjusted WAM (or current WAM, to the extent available) of each MBS Certificate underlying the REMIC Certificates, along with the weighted average of all the WACs (or of any available current WACs) and the weighted average of all the Adjusted WAMs (or of any available current WAMs) based on the current unpaid principal balances of the MBS Certificates as of the REMIC Issue Date. The Final Data Statement will also include the MBS Percentage Schedule as further described herein. Final Data Statements will not accompany Prospectus Supplements but will be made available by Fannie Mae. To request Final Data Statements, telephone Fannie Mae at (202) 752-7585. The contents of the Final Data Statement and other data specific to the REMIC Certificates are available in electronic form by calling Fannie Mae at (202) 782-6000.

Prepayment Considerations and Risks

The rate of principal payments of the MBS Certificates, and therefore of distributions on the REMIC Certificates, is related directly to the rate of payments of principal of the underlying Mortgage Loans, which may be in the form of scheduled amortization or prepayments (for this purpose, the term "prepayment" includes prepayments and liquidations resulting from default, casualty, condemnation and payments made pursuant to any guaranty of payment by, or option to repurchase of, Fannie Mae). In general, when the level of prevailing interest rates declines significantly below the interest rates on fixed-rate mortgage loans, the rate of prepayment is likely to increase, although the prepayment rate is influenced by a number of other factors, including general economic conditions and homeowner mobility. See "Maturity and Prepayment Assumptions" in the MBS Prospectus.

Acceleration of mortgage payments as a result of transfers of the mortgaged property is another factor affecting prepayment rates. The Mortgage Loans underlying the MBS Certificates will generally provide by their terms that, in the event of the transfer or prospective transfer of title to the underlying mortgaged property, the full unpaid principal balance of the Mortgage Loan is due and payable at the option of the holder. As set forth under "Description of Certificates—Collection and Other Servicing Procedures" in the MBS Prospectus, Fannie Mae is required to exercise its right to accelerate the maturity of Mortgage Loans containing enforceable "due-on-sale" provisions upon certain transfers of the mortgaged property.

Prepayments of mortgage loans commonly are measured relative to a prepayment standard or model. The model used in this Prospectus Supplement, the Public Securities Association's standard prepayment model ("PSA"), represents an assumed rate of prepayment each month of the then outstanding principal balance of a pool of new mortgage loans. *PSA does not purport to be either a historical description of the prepayment experience of any pool of mortgage loans or a prediction of the anticipated rate of prepayment of any pool of mortgage loans, including the Mortgage Loans underlying the MBS Certificates backing the PEMIC Certificates.* 100% PSA assumes prepayment rates of 0.2% per annum of the then unpaid principal balance of such mortgage loans in the first month of the life of the mortgage loans and an additional 0.2% per annum in each month thereafter (for example, 0.4% per annum in the second month) until the 30th month. Beginning in the 30th month and in each month thereafter during the life of the mortgage loans, 100% PSA assumes a constant prepayment rate of 6% per annum. Multiples will be calculated from this prepayment rate series; for example, 165% PSA assumes prepayment rates will be 0.33% per annum in month one, 0.66% per annum in month two, reaching 9.9% per annum in month 30 and remaining constant at 9.9% per annum thereafter. 0% PSA assumes no prepayments.

DESCRIPTION OF THE REMIC CERTIFICATES

The following summaries describing certain provisions of the REMIC Certificates do not purport to be complete and are subject to, and are qualified in their entirety by reference to, the REMIC Prospectus and the provisions of the Trust Agreement.

General

Two separate trust funds will be created pursuant to the Trust Agreement, and elections will be made to treat each trust fund as a REMIC for federal income tax purposes.

One trust fund (the "Lower Tier REMIC") will consist of the MBS Certificates. The entire beneficial ownership interest in the Lower Tier REMIC will be evidenced by the Lower Tier Interests and the Class 89-RL REMIC Certificates. Each of the Lower Tier Interests will be designated as a "regular interest" in the REMIC constituted by the Lower Tier REMIC and will bear interest at the rate of 9.50% per annum. The initial aggregate principal amount of the Lower Tier Interests, together with the initial principal amount of the Class 89-RL REMIC Certificates, equals the initial aggregate principal amount of the REMIC Certificates. The Lower Tier Interests, together with the Class 89-RL REMIC Certificates, in the aggregate, will evidence the entire beneficial ownership interest in the distributions of principal and interest on the MBS Certificates. The Class 89-RL REMIC Certificates will be designated as the "residual interest" in the REMIC constituted by the Lower Tier REMIC and will have the characteristics described herein.

The second trust fund (the "Trust") will consist of the Lower Tier Interests. The entire beneficial ownership interest in the Trust will be evidenced by the REMIC Certificates, other than the Class 89-RL REMIC Certificates, as described herein.

Distributions of Interest

The REMIC Certificates, other than the Class 89-R REMIC Certificates, will bear interest at the respective per annum interest rates described on the cover hereof. Interest on the REMIC Certificates is calculated on the basis of a 360-day year consisting of twelve 30-day months and is payable monthly on each Distribution Date, commencing (except in the case of the Class 89-X, Class 89-Y and Class 89-Z REMIC Certificates, which are Accrual Certificates) in August 1990. Interest to be distributed or added to principal of each REMIC Certificate on a Distribution Date will consist of one month's interest on the outstanding principal amount of such REMIC Certificate immediately prior to such Distribution Date. Interest to be distributed or added to principal on a Distribution Date will accrue on the REMIC Certificates, other than the Class 89-F, Class 89-S and Class 89-R REMIC Certificates, during the calendar month preceding the month in which such Distribution Date occurs. In the case of the Class 89-F and Class 89-S REMIC Certificates, such interest will accrue during the one-month period beginning on the 25th day of such preceding month and ending on the 24th day of the month of such Distribution Date (each, an "Interest Accrual Period").

Interest will accrue on the Accrual Certificates at the per annum interest rate of 9.50%; however, such interest will not be distributed to Holders of the Accrual Certificates but rather will be added to the principal balances thereof on each Distribution Date (i) until after the principal balance of the Class 89-B REMIC Certificates has been reduced to zero, in the case of the Class 89-X REMIC Certificates, and (ii) in the case of the Class 89-Y and Class 89-Z REMIC Certificates, for so long as the Class 89-Y and Class 89-Z REMIC Certificates, respectively, are outstanding. Interest so accrued and unpaid on theAccrual Certificates will be added to the principal amounts thereof on the applicable Distribution Dates.

Interest will accrue on the Class 89-F REMIC Certificates at the per annum rate of 8.8125% during the initial Interest Accrual Period, and will accrue during each Interest Accrual Period thereafter, subject to a maximum per annum interest rate of 11.00% and a minimum per annum rate of 0.50%, at a variable per annum rate equal to 50 basis points in excess of the London interbank offered rate for one-month U.S. dollar deposits ("LIBOR"). Interest will accrue on the Class 89-S REMIC Certificates at the per annum rate of 10.05% during the initial Interest Accrual Period, and will accrue during each Interest Accrual Period thereafter, subject to a maximum per annum interest rate of 16.7% and a minimum per annum interest rate of 8.3%, at a variable per annum rate equal to 16.7%— (0.8 X LIBOR). In each case, the applicable rate will be determined monthly on the second business day prior to the first day of the related Interest Accrual Period (the "LIBOR Determination Date"). The yields with respect to the Class 89-F and Class 89-S REMIC Certificates will be affected by changes in LIBOR, which may not correlate with changes in mortgage interest rates. It is possible that lower mortgage interest rates could occur concurrently with an increase in the level of LIBOR. Conversely, higher mortgage interest rates could occur concurrently with a decrease in the level of LIBOR.

The effective yield on the REMIC Certificates, other than the Class 89-F, Class 89-S and Class 89-R REMIC Certificates, will be reduced below the yield otherwise produced because interest payable with respect to an Interest Accrual Period will not be distributed until the 25th day following the end of such Interest Accrual Period and will not bear interest during such delay.

Calculation of LIBOR

Commencing on August 23, 1990 and thereafter on each LIBOR Determination Date, until the principal amounts of the Class 89-F and Class 89-S REMIC Certificates have been reduced to zero, Fannie Mae or its agent (initially State Street Bank and Trust Company in Boston, Massachusetts, hereinafter referred to as "State Street") will request each of the designated reference banks meeting the criteria set forth herein (the "Reference Banks") to inform State Street of the quotation offered by its principal London office for making one-month United States dollar deposits in leading banks in the London interbank market, as of 11:00 a.m. (London time) on such LIBOR Determination Date. (For purposes of calculating LIBOR, "business day" means a day on which banks are open for dealing in foreign currency and exchange in London, Boston and New York City.) In lieu of making a request of the Reference Banks, State Street may rely on the quotations for those Reference Banks that appear at such time on the Reuters Screen LIBO Page (as defined in the International Swap Dealers Association, Inc. Code of Standard Wording, Assumptions and Provisions for Swaps, 1986 Edition), to the extent available.

LIBOR will be established by State Street on each LIBOR Determination Date as follows:

(a) If on any LIBOR Determination Date two or more Reference Banks provide such offered quotations, LIBOR for the next Interest Accrual Period shall be the arithmetic mean of such offered quotations (rounded upwards if necessary to the nearest whole multiple of 1/32%).

(b) If on any LIBOR Determination Date only one or none of the Reference Banks provides such offered quotations, LIBOR for the next Interest Accrual Period shall be whichever is the higher of (i) LIBOR as determined on the previous LIBOR Determination Date or (ii) the Reserve Interest Rate. The "Reserve Interest Rate" shall be the rate per annum which State Street determines to be either (i) the arithmetic mean (rounded upwards if necessary to the nearest whole multiple of 1/32%) of the one-month United States dollar lending rates that New York City banks selected by State Street are quoting, on the relevant LIBOR Determination Date, to the principal London offices of at least two of the Reference Banks to which such quotations are, in the opinion of State Street being so made, or (ii) in the event that State Street can determine no such arithmetic mean, the lowest one-month United States dollar lending rate which New York City banks selected by State Street are quoting on such LIBOR Determination Date to leading European banks.

(c) If on the August 23, 1990, LIBOR Determination Date, State Street is required but is unable to determine the Reserve Interest Rate in the manner provided in paragraph (b) above, LIBOR shall be 8.3125%.

Each Reference Bank (i) shall be a leading bank engaged in transactions in Eurodollar deposits in the international Eurocurrency market; (ii) shall not control, be controlled by, or be under common control with Fannie Mae; and (iii) shall have an established place of business in London. If any such Reference Bank should be unwilling or unable to act as such or if Fannie Mae should terminate the appointment of any such Reference Bank, State Street will promptly appoint another leading bank meeting the criteria specified above.

The establishment of LIBOR on each LIBOR Determination Date by State Street and State Street's calculation of the rate of interest applicable to the Class 89-F and Class 89-S REMIC Certificates for the related Interest Accrual Period shall (in the absence of manifest error) be final and binding. Each such rate of interest may be obtained by telephoning State Street at (617) 654-4067 or Fannie Mae at (202) 752-6547.

Distributions of Principal

Principal will be distributed monthly on the Lower Tier Interests and the Class 89-RL REMIC Certificates in an amount equal to the aggregate distributions of principal concurrently made on the MBS Certificates (the "Cash Flow Distribution Amount"). On each Distribution Date, the Class 89-RL REMIC Certificates will receive approximately .002% of the Cash Flow Distribution Amount, which percentage is equal to the proportion that the original principal amount of such Class bears to the aggregate original principal amount of the Lower Tier Interests plus the Class 89-RL REMIC Certificates. The balance of the Cash Flow Distribution Amount (the "Lower Tier Regular Distribution Amount") will be distributed as principal of the Lower Tier Interests held by the Trust.

The principal distribution on the REMIC Certificates, other than the Class 89-RL REMIC Certificates, on each Distribution Date (the "Principal Distribution Amount") will be in an amount equal to the sum of (i) the Lower Tier Regular Distribution Amount and (ii) any interest accrued and added on such Distribution Date to the principal amounts of the Accrual Certificates.

The Class 89-A, Class 89-B, Class 89-X, Class 89-C, Class 89-D, Class 89-E, Class 89-G, Class 89-H, Class 89-J, Class 89-K, Class 89-L and Class 89-R REMIC Certificates are "Planned Principal REMIC Certificates" and the amount necessary to reduce the outstanding principal balances of the Planned Principal REMIC Certificates to their respective Planned Principal Balances on any Distribution Date is referred to herein as the "Planned Principal Amount."

On each Distribution Date, the Principal Distribution Amount will be applied to the distribution of principal of the Classes of REMIC Certificates in the following order of priority:

(i) to the Classes of Planned Principal REMIC Certificates, in the following order and in the proportions set forth below, in an amount up to the amount necessary to reduce their outstanding principal balances to their respective Planned Principal Balances as set forth in the table beginning on page S-16 for such Distribution Date (which amount will be zero, except in the case of the Class 89-L and Class 89-R REMIC Certificates, until the Distribution Date in June 1992):

	Allocated to	
	Class listed in preceding Column	**Class 89-L**
Class 89-R	99.997507370%	0.002492630%
Class 89-A	99.950000000%	0.050000000%
Class 89-B	99.950000000%	0.050000000%
Class 89-X	100%	
Class 89-C	100%	
Class 89-D	100%	
Class 89-E	100%	
Class 89-G	99.925018745%	0.074981255%
Class 89-H	99.925018745%	0.074981255%
Class 89-J	99.900049975%	0.099950025%
Class 89-K	99.700748129%	0.299251871%

(ii) on each and every Distribution Date, beginning on the Distribution Date, if any, for which the Cash Flow Distribution Amount is greater than the related MBS Payment Amount (as defined below), to the Class 89-Y REMIC Certificates (the "Class 89-Y Priority Amount"), until the principal balance thereof has been reduced to zero;

(iii) to the Class 89-M REMIC Certificates, in an amount up to the amount necessary to reduce their outstanding principal balance to their Targeted Principal Balance (the "Targeted Principal Amount") as set forth in the table beginning on Page 289 for such Distribution Date;

(iv) concurrently, to the Class 89-F, Class 89-S and Class 89-N REMIC Certificates, in the proportions of 22.2227637126%, 27.7784546407% and 49.9987816467%, respectively, until the principal balance of the Class 89-N REMIC Certificates has been reduced to zero;

(v) concurrently, to the Class 89-F, Class 89-S and Class 89-0 REMIC Certificates, in the proportions of 22.2227637126%, 27.7784546407% and 49.9987816467%, respectively, until the principal balances thereof have been reduced to zero;

(vi) to the Class 89-P REMIC Certificates, until the principal balance thereof has been reduced to zero;

(vii) if the Class 89-Y REMIC Certificates are then outstanding, concurrently, to the Class 89-Y and Class 89-Z REMIC Certificates, in proportion to their original principal balances (or approximately 50.6% and 49.4%, respectively), until the principal balance of the Class 89-Y REMIC Certificates has been reduced to zero;

(viii) if the Class 89-Z REMIC Certificates are then outstanding, to the Class 89-Z REMIC Certificates, until the principal balance thereof has been reduced to zero;

(ix) to the Class 89-M REMIC Certificates, without regard to their Targeted Principal Balance and until the principal balance thereof has been reduced to zero; and

(x) to the Planned Principal REMIC Certificates, in the order and in the proportions set forth in clause (i) above, without regard to their respective Planned Principal Balances and until their respective principal balances have been reduced to zero.

Because the timing and amount of distributions of principal of the REMIC Certificates will depend on the rate of principal payments (including prepayments) of the Mortgage Loans underlying the MBS Certificates, there can be no assurance as to the timing of distributions of principal of the REMIC Certificates.

The MBS Payment Amount will equal the product of the corresponding MBS percentage on the MBS Percentage Schedule (as described below) for each Distribution Date multiplied by the aggregate unpaid principal amount of the MBS Certificates (the "MBS Balance") immediately preceding such Distribution Date. An MBS Balance Schedule will be calculated by Fannie Mae based upon the actual characteristics of the MBS Certificates delivered to the Trust (which characteristics will vary from the characteristics assumed herein). Such MBS Balance Schedule will reflect the MBS Balance for each Distribution Date assuming that the Mortgage Loans underlying the MBS Certificates prepay at a constant rate of approximately 169% PSA and that all of the Mortgage Loans underlying each Pool have the same interest rate and remaining term as the WAC (or current WAC, if available) and Adjusted WAM (or current WAM, if available) of the respective Pool. The MBS Percentage Schedule will represent the percentage decrease from one Distribution Date to the next in the MBS Balance Schedule. Consequently, at prepayment levels higher than approximately 169% PSA, the Cash Flow Distribution Amount for each Distribution Date will be greater than the related MBS Payment Amount. The determination by Fannie Mae of the MBS Percentage Schedule will be final and binding and will be included in the Final Data Statement referred to herein under "The MBS Certificates—General." The MBS Balance Schedule will not be included in the Final Data Statement.

PLANNED AND TARGETED PRINCIPAL BALANCES

Distribution Date	Class 89-R Planned Principal Balance	Class 89-A Planned Principal Balance	Class 89-B Planned Principal Balance	Class 89-X Planned Principal Balance	Class 89-C Planned Principal Balance
Initial Balance	$10,516,000.00	$37,101,000.00	$31,474,000.00	$18,984,000.00	$40,000,000.00
August 1990	9,656,730.88	37,101,000.00	31,474,000.00	19,134,290.00	40,000,000.00
September 1990	8,718,585.84	37,101,000.00	31,474,000.00	19,285,769.80	40,000,000.00
October 1990	7,701,706.87	37,101,000.00	31,474,000.00	19,438,448.81	40,000,000.00
November 1990	6,606,271.43	37,101,000.00	31,474,000.00	19,592,336.53	40,000,000.00
December 1990	5,432,492.33	37,101,000.00	31,474,000.00	19,747,442.52	40,000,000.00
January 1991	4,180,617.75	37,101,000.00	31,474,000.00	19,903,776.44	40,000,000.00
February 1991	2,850,931.08	37,101,000.00	31,474,000.00	20,061,348.01	40,000,000.00
March 1991	1,443,750.87	37,101,000.00	31,474,000.00	20,220,167.01	40,000,000.00
April 1991	0.00	37,101,000.00	31,474,000.00	20,380,243.33	40,000,000.00
May 1991	0.00	37,101,000.00	31,474,000.00	20,541,586.93	40,000,000.00
June 1991	0.00	37,101,000.00	31,474,000.00	20,704,207.82	40,000,000.00
July 1991	0.00	37,101,000.00	31,474,000.00	20,868,116.14	40,000,000.00
August 1991	0.00	37,101,000.00	31,474,000.00	21,033,322.06	40,000,000.00
September 199	0.00	37,101,000.00	31,474,000.00	21,199,835.86	40,000,000.00
October 1991.	0.00	37,101,000.00	31,474,000.00	21,367,667.89	40,000,000.00
November 1991	0.00	37,101,000.00	31,474,000.00	21,536,828.59	40,000,000.00
December 1991	0.00	37,101,000.00	31,474,000.00	21,707,328.49	40,000,000.00
January 1992	0.00	37,101,000.00	31,474,000.00	21,879,178.17	40,000,000.00
February 1992	0.00	37,101,000.00	31,474,000.00	22,052,388.33	40,000,000.00
March 1992	0.00	37,101,000.00	31,474,000.00	22,226,969.74	40,000,000.00
April 1992	0.00	37,101,000.00	31,474,000.00	22,402,933.26	40,000,000.00
May 1992	0.00	37,101,000.00	31,474,000.00	22,580,289.80	40,000,000.00
June 1992	0.00	34,594,057.88	31,474,000.00	22,759,050.43	40,000,000.00
July 1992.	0.00	32,019,331.02	31,474,000.00	22,939,226.25	40,000,000.00
August 1992	0.00	29,377,691.25	31,474,000.00	23,120,828.45	40,000,000.00
September 1992	0.00	26,670,038.96	31,474,000.00	23,303,868.35	40,000,000.00
October 1992	0.00	23,969,949.25	31,474,000.00	23,488,357.30	40,000,000.00
November 1992	0.00	21,277,352.18	31,474,000.00	23,674,306.80	40,000,000.00
December 1992	0.00	18,592,177.87	31,474,000.00	23,861,728.40	40,000,000.00
January 1993	0.00	15,914,356.46	31,474,000.00	24,050,633.75	40,000,000.00
February 1993	0.00	13,243,818.18	31,474,000.00	24,241,034.60	40,000,000.00
March 1993	0.00	10,580,493.32	31,474,000.00	24,432,942.79	40,000,000.00
April 1993	0.00	7,924,312.18	31,474,000.00	24,626,370.25	40,000,000.00
May 1993	0.00	5,275,205.16	31,474,000.00	24,821,329.01	40,000,000.00
June 1993	0.00	2,633,102.66	31,474,000.00	25,017,831.20	40,000,000.00
July 1993	0.00	0.00	31,471,935.16	25,215,889.03	40,000,000.00
August 1993	0.00	0.00	28,843,633.17	25,415,514.82	40,000,000.00
September 1993	0.00	0.00	26,222,127.22	25,616,720.98	40,000,000.00
October 1993	0.00	0.00	23,607,347.92	25,819,520.02	40,000,000.00
November 1993	0.00	0.00	20,999,225.87	26,023,924.55	40,000,000.00
December 1993	0.00	0.00	18,397,691.74	26,229,947.29	40,000,000.00
January 1994	0.00	0.00	15,802,676.20	26,437,601.04	40,000,000.00
February 1994	0.00	0.00	13,214,109.96	26,646,898.71	40,000,000.00
March 1994	0.00	0.00	10,631,923.77	26,857,853.33	40,000,000.00
April 1994	0.00	0.00	8,056,048.37	27,070,478.00	40,000,000.00
May 1994	.00	0.00	5,486,414.56	27,284,785.95	40,000,000.00
June 1994	0.00	0.00	2,922,953.12	27,500,790.51	40,000,000.00
July 1994	0.00	0.00	365,594.88	27,718,505.10	40,000,000.00
August 1994	0.00	0.00	0.00	25,751,120.52	40,000,000.00
September 1994	0.00	0.00	0.00	23,425,663.23	40,000,000.00
October 1994	0.00	0.00	0.00	21,107,855.58	40,000,000.00
November 1994	0.00	0.00	0.00	18,797,642.23	40,000,000.00
December 1994	0.00	0.00	0.00	16,494,967.99	40,000,000.00

Distribution Date	Class 89-D Planned Principal Balance	Class 89-E Planned Principal Balance	Class 89-G Planned Principal Balance	Class 89-H Planned Principal Balance
Initial Balance	$40,000,000.00	$16,168,000.00	$22,028,000.00	$15,856,000.00
August 1990	40,000,000.00	16,168,000.00	22,028,000.00	15,856,000.00
September 1990	40,000,000.00	16,168,000.00	22,028,000.00	15,856,000.00
October 1990	40,000,000.00	16,168,000.00	22,028,000.00	15,856,000.00
November 1990	40,000,000.00	16,168,000.00	22,028,000.00	15,856,000.00
December 1990	40,000,000.00	16,168,000.00	22,028,000.00	15,856,000.00
January 1991	40,000,000.00	16,168,000.00	22,028,000.00	15,856,000.00
February 1991	40,000,000.00	16,168,000.00	22,028,000.00	15,856,000.00
March 1991	40,000,000.00	16,168,000.00	22,028,000.00	15,856,000.00
April 1991	40,000,000.00	16,168,000.00	22,028,000.00	15,856,000.00
May 1991	40,000,000.00	16,168,000.00	22,028,000.00	15,856,000.00
June 1991	40,000,000.00	16,168,000.00	22,028,000.00	15,856,000.00
July 1991	40,000,000.00	16,168,000.00	22,028,000.00	15,856,000.00
August 1991	40,000,000.00	16,168,000.00	22,028,000.00	15,856,000.00
September 1991	40,000,000.00	16,168,000.00	22,028,000.00	15,856,000.00
October 1991	40,000,000.00	16,168,000.00	22,028,000.00	15,856,000.00
November 1991	40,000,000.00	16,168,000.00	22,028,000.00	15,856,000.00
December 1991	40,000,000.00	16,168,000.00	22,028,000.00	15,856,000.00
January 1992	40,000,000.00	16,168,000.00	22,028,000.00	15,856,000.00
February 1992	40,000,000.00	16,168,000.00	22,028,000.00	15,856,000.00
March 1992	40,000,000.00	16,168,000.00	22,028,000.00	15,856,000.00
April 8 1992	40,000,000.00	16,168,000.00	22,028,000.00	15,856,000.00
May 1992	40,000,000.00	16,168,000.00	22,028,000.00	15,856,000.00
June 1992	40,000,000.00	16,168,000.00	22,028,000.00	15,856,000.00
July 1992	40,000,000.00	16,168,000.00	22,028,000.00	15,856,000.00
August 1992	40,000,000.00	16,168,000.00	22,028,000.00	15,856,000.00
September 1992	40,000,000.00	16,168,000.00	22,028,000.00	15,856,000.00
October 1992	40,000,000.00	16,168,000.00	22,028,000.00	15,856,000.00
November 1992	40,000,000.00	16,168,000.00	22,028,000.00	15,856,000.00
December 1992	40,000,000.00	16,168,000.00	22,028,000.00	15,856,000.00
January 1993	40,000,000.00	16,168,000.00	22,028,000.00	15,856,000.00
February 1993	40,000,000.00	16,168,000.00	22,028,000.00	15,856,000.00
March 1993	40,000,000.00	16,168,000.00	22,028,000.00	15,856,000.00
April 1993	40,000,000.00	16,168,000.00	22,028,000.00	15,856,000.00
May 1993	40,000,000.00	16,168,000.00	22,028,000.00	15,856,000.00
June 1993	40,000,000.00	16,168,000.00	22,028,000.00	15,856,000.00
July 1993	40,000,000.00	16,168,000.00	22,028,000.00	15,856,000.00
August 1993	40,000,000.00	16,168,000.00	22,028,000.00	15,856,000.00
September 1993	40,000,000.00	16,168,000.00	22,028,000.00	15,856,000.00
October 1993	40,000,000.00	16,168,000.00	22,028,000.00	15,856,000.00
November 1993	40,000,000.00	16,168,000.00	22,028,000.00	15,856,000.00
December 1993	40,000,000.00	16,168,000.00	22,028,000.00	15,856,000.00
January 1994	40,000,000.00	16,168,000.00	22,028,000.00	15,856,000.00
February 1994	40,000,000.00	16,168,000.00	22,028,000.00	15,856,000.00
March 1994	40,000,000.00	16,168,000.00	22,028,000.00	15,856,000.00
April 1994	40,000,000.00	16,168,000.00	22,028,000.00	15,856,000.00
May 1994	40,000,000.00	16,168,000.00	22,028,000.00	15,856,000.00
June 1994	40,000,000.00	16,168,000.00	22,028,000.00	15,856,000.00
July 1994	40,000,000.00	16,168,000.00	22,028,000.00	15,856,000.00
August 1994	40,000,000.00	16,168,000.00	22,028,000.00	15,856,000.00
September 1994	40,000,000.00	16,168,000.00	22,028,000.00	15,856,000.00
October 1994	40,000,000.00	16,168,000.00	22,028,000.00	15,856,000.00
November 1994	40,000,000.00	16,168,000.00	22,028,000.00	15,856,000.00
December 1994	40,000,000.00	16,168,000.00	22,028,000.00	15,856,000.00

Distribution Date	Class 89-J Planned Principal Balance	Class 89-K Planned Principal Balance	Class 89-L Planned Principal Balance	Class 89-M Targeted Principal Balance
Initial Balance	$35,884,000.00	$36,683,000.00	$209,000.00	$88,649,000.00
August 1990	35,884,000.00	36,683,000.00	208,978.58	88,433,307.10
September 1990	35,884,000.00	36,683,000.00	208,955.20	88,174,628.99
October 1990	35,884,000.00	36,683,000.00	208,929.85	87,873,135.24
November 1990	35,884,000.00	36,683,000.00	208,902.54	87,529,051.74
December 1990	35,884,000.00	36,683,000.00	208,873.28	87,142,660.69
January 1991	35,884,000.00	36,683,000.00	208,842.08	86,714,300.47
February 1991	35,884,000.00	36,683,000.00	208,808.93	86,244,365.46
March 1991	35,884,000.00	36,683,000.00	208,773.86	85,733,305.69
April 1991	35,884,000.00	36,683,000.00	208,737.87	85,153,938.79
May 1991	35,884,000.00	36,683,000.00	208,737.87	83,496,802.48
June 1991	35,884,000.00	36,683,000.00	208,737.87	81,748,128.50
July 1991	35,884,000.00	36,683,000.00	208,737.87	79,908,896.82
August 1991	35,884,000.00	36,683,000.00	208,737.87	77,980,163.49
September 1991	35,884,000.00	36,683,000.00	208,737.87	75,963,059.54
October 1991	35,884,000.00	36,683,000.00	208,737.87	73,858,789.83
November 1991	35,884,000.00	36,683,000.00	208,737.87	71,668,631.79
December 1991	35,884,000.00	36,683,000.00	208,737.87	69,393,934.01
January 1992	35,884,000.00	36,683,000.00	208,737.87	67,036,114.78
February 1992	35,884,000.00	36,683,000.00	208,737.87	64,596,660.47
March 1992	35,884,000.00	36,683,000.00	208,737.87	62,077,123.88
April 8 1992	35,884,000.00	36,683,000.00	208,737.87	59,479,122.40
May 1992	35,884,000.00	36,683,000.00	208,737.87	56,804,336.19
June 1992	35,884,000.00	36,683,000.00	207,483.77	55,766,253.12
July 1992	35,884,000.00	36,683,000.00	206,195.76	54,701,209.41
August 1992	35,884,000.00	36,683,000.00	204,874.28	53,610,465.91
September 1992	35,884,000.00	36,683,000.00	203,519.78	52,495,318.28
October 1992	35,884,000.00	36,683,000.00	202,169.06	51,397,114.29
November 1992	35,884,000.00	36,683,000.00	200,822.09	50,315,682.15
December 1992	35,884,000.00	36,683,000.00	199,478.83	49,250,851.69
January 1993	35,884,000.00	36,683,000.00	198,139.25	48,202,454.38
February 1993	35,884,000.00	36,683,000.00	196,803.31	47,170,323.27
March 1993	35,884,000.00	36,683,000.00	195,470.98	46,154,293.01
April 1993	35,884,000.00	36,683,000.00	194,142.23	45,154,199.83
May 1993	35,884,000.00	36,683,000.00	192,817.01	44,169,881.52
June 1993	35,884,000.00	36,683,000.00	191,495.30	43,201,177.41
July 1993	35,884,000.00	36,683,000.00	190,177.06	42,247,928.37
August 1993	35,884,000.00	36,683,000.00	188,862.25	41,309,976.79
September 1993	35,884,000.00	36,683,000.00	187,550.84	40,387,166.56
October 1993	35,884,000.00	36,683,000.00	186,242,79	39,479,343.08
November 1993	35,884,000.00	36,683,000.00	184,938.08	38,586,353.19
December 1993	35,884,000.00	36,683,000.00	183,636.66	37,708,045.25
January 1994	35,884,000.00	36,683,000.00	182,338.51	36,844,269.02
February 1994	35,884,000.00	36,683,000.00	181,043.58	35,994,875.74
March 1994	35,884,000.00	36,683,000.00	179,751.84	35,159,718.04
April 1994	35,884,000.00	36,683,000.00	178,463.26	34,338,650.01
May 1994	35,884,000.00	36,683,000.00	177,177.80	33,531,527.09
June 1994	35,884,000.00	36,683,000.00	175,895.42	32,738,206.14
July 1994	35,884,000.00	36,683,000.00	174,616.11	31,958,545.39
August 1994	35,884,000.00	36,683,000.00	174,433.22	31,192,404.42
September 1994	35,884,000.00	36,683,000.00	174,433.22	30,439,644.18
October 1994	35,884,000.00	36,683,000.00	174,433.22	29,700,126.96
November 1994	35,884,000.00	36,683,000.00	174,433.22	28,973,716.35
December 1994	35,884,000.00	36,683,000.00	174,433.22	28,260,277.27

Distribution Date	Class 89-R Planned Principal Balance	Class 89-A Planned Principal Balance	Class 89-B Planned Principal Balance	Class 89-X Planned Principal Balance	Class 89-C Planned Principal Balance
January 1995	$0.00	$0.00	$0.00	$14,199,777.77	$40,000,000.00
February 1995	0.00	0.00	0.00	11,912,016.57	40,000,000.00
March 1995	0.00	0.00	0.00	9,631,629.53	40,000,000.00
April 1995	0.00	0.00	0.00	7,358,561.88	40,000,000.00
May 1995	0.00	0.00	0.00	5,092,758.96	40,000,000.00
June 1995	0.00	0.00	0.00	2,834,166.21	40,000,000.00
July 1995	0.00	0.00	0.00	582,729.17	40,000,000.00
August 1995	0.00	0.00	0.00	0.00	38,338,393.49
September 1995	0.00	0.00	0.00	0.00	36,101,104.92
October 1995	0.00	0.00	0.00	0.00	33,870,809.30
November 1995	0.00	0.00	0.00	0.00	31,647,452.57
December 1995	0.00	0.00	0.00	0.00	29,430,980.75
January 1996	0.00	0.00	0.00	0.00	27,221,339.99
February 1996	0.00	0.00	0.00	0.00	25,018,476.48
March 1996	0.00	0.00	0.00	0.00	22,822,336.55
April 1996	0.00	0.00	0.00	0.00	20,632,866.58
May 1996	0.00	0.00	0.00	0.00	18,450,013.06
June 1996	0.00	0.00	0.00	0.00	16,273,722.55
July 1996	0.00	0.00	0.00	0.00	14,103,941.70
August 1996	0.00	0.00	0.00	0.00	11,940,617.25
September 1996	0.00	0.00	0.00	0.00	9,783,696.00
October 1996	0.00	0.00	0.00	0.00	7,633,124.85
November 1996	0.00	0.00	0.00	0.00	5,488,850.75
December 1996	0.00	0.00	0.00	0.00	3,350,820.76
January 1997	0.00	0.00	0.00	0.00	1,218,981.98
February 1997	0.00	0.00	0.00	0.00	0.00
March 1997	0.00	0.00	0.00	0.00	0.00
April 1997	0.00	0.00	0.00	0.00	0.00
May 1997	0.00	0.00	0.00	0.00	0.00
June 1997	0.00	0.00	0.00	0.00	0.00
July 1997	0.00	0.00	0.00	0.00	0.00
August 1997	0.00	0.00	0.00	0.00	0.00
September 1997	0.00	0.00	0.00	0.00	0.00
October 1997	0.00	0.00	0.00	0.00	0.00
November 1997	0.00	0.00	0.00	0.00	0.00
December 1997	0.00	0.00	0.00	0.00	0.00
January 1998	0.00	0.00	0.00	0.00	0.00
February 1998	0.00	0.00	0.00	0.00	0.00
March 1998	0.00	0.00	0.00	0.00	0.00
April 1998	0.00	0.00	0.00	0.00	0.00
May 1998	0.00	0.00	0.00	0.00	0.00
June 1998	0.00	0.00	0.00	0.00	0.00
July 1998	0.00	0.00	0.00	0.00	0.00
August 1998	0.00	0.00	0.00	0.00	0.00
September 1998	0.00	0.00	0.00	0.00	0.00
October 1998	0.00	0.00	0.00	0.00	0.00
November 1998	0.00	0.00	0.00	0.00	0.00
December 1998	0.00	0.00	0.00	0.00	0.00
January 1999	0.00	0.00	0.00	0.00	0.00
February 1999	0.00	0.00	0.00	0.00	0.00
March 1999	0.00	0.00	0.00	0.00	0.00
April 1999	0.00	0.00	0.00	0.00	0.00
May 1999	0.00	0.00	0.00	0.00	0.00
June 1999 and thereafter	0.00	0.00	0.00	0.00	0.00

Distribution Date	Class 89-D Planned Principal Balance	Class 89-E Planned Principal Balance	Class 89-G Planned Principal Balance	Class 89-H Planned Principal Balance
January 1995	$40,000,000.00	$16,168,000.00	$22,028,000.00	$15,856,000.00
February 1995	40,000,000.00	16,168,000.00	22,028,000.00	15,856,000.00
March 1995	40,000,000.00	16,168,000.00	22,028,000.00	15,856,000.00
April 1995	40,000,000.00	16,168,000.00	22,028,000.00	15,856,000.00
May 1995	40,000,000.00	16,168,000.00	22,028,000.00	15,856,000.00
June 1995	40,000,000.00	16,168,000.00	22,028,000.00	15,856,000.00
July 1995	40,000,000.00	16,168,000.00	22,028,000.00	15,856,000.00
August 1995	40,000,000.00	16,168,000.00	22,028,000.00	15,856,000.00
September 1995	40,000,000.00	16,168,000.00	22,028,000.00	15,856,000.00
October 1995	40,000,000.00	16,168,000.00	22,028,000.00	15,856,000.00
November 1995	40,000,000.00	16,168,000.00	22,028,000.00	15,856,000.00
December 1995	40,000,000.00	16,168,000.00	22,028,000.00	15,856,000.00
January 1996	40,000,000.00	16,168,000.00	22,028,000.00	15,856,000.00
February 1996	40,000,000.00	16,168,000.00	22,028,000.00	15,856,000.00
March 1996	40,000,000.00	16,168,000.00	22,028,000.00	15,856,000.00
April 1996	40,000,000.00	16,168,000.00	22,028,000.00	15,856,000.00
May 1996	40,000,000.00	16,168,000.00	22,028,000.00	15,856,000.00
June 1996	40,000,000.00	16,168,000.00	22,028,000.00	15,856,000.00
July 1996	40,000,000.00	16,168,000.00	22,028,000.00	15,856,000.00
August 1996	40,000,000.00	16,168,000.00	22,028,000.00	15,856,000.00
September 1996	40,000,000.00	16,168,000.00	22,028,000.00	15,856,000.00
October 1996	40,000,000.00	16,168,000.00	22,028,000.00	15,856,000.00
November 1996	40,000,000.00	16,168,000.00	22,028,000.00	15,856,000.00
December 1996	40,000,000.00	16,168,000.00	22,028,000.00	15,856,000.00
January 1997	40,000,000.00	16,168,000.00	22,028,000.00	15,856,000.00
February 1997	39,093,281.60	16,168,000.00	22,028,000.00	15,856,000.00
March 1997	36,973,666.89	16,168,000.00	22,028,000.00	15,856,000.00
April 1997	34,860,085.16	16,168,000.00	22,028,000.00	15,856,000.00
May 1997	32,752,483.80	16,168,000.00	22,028,000.00	15,856,000.00
June 1997	30,650,810.29	16,168,000.00	22,028,000.00	15,856,000.00
July 1997	28,555,012.13	16,168,000.00	22,028,000.00	15,856,000.00
August 1997	26,465,036.91	16,168,000.00	22,028,000.00	15,856,000.00
September 1997	24,380,832.28	16,168,000.00	22,028,000.00	15,856,000.00
October 1997	22,302,345.94	16,168,000.00	22,028,000.00	15,856,000.00
November 1997	20,229,525.65	16,168,000.00	22,028,000.00	15,856,000.00
December 1997	18,162,319.23	16,168,000.00	22,028,000.00	15,856,000.00
January 1998	16,100,674.54	16,168,000.00	22,028,000.00	15,856,000.00
February 1998	14,044,539.51	16,168,000.00	22,028,000.00	15,856,000.00
March 1998	11,993,862.11	16,168,000.00	22,028,000.00	15,856,000.00
April 1998	9,948,590.36	16,168,000.00	22,028,000.00	15,856,000.00
May 1998	7,908,672.33	16,168,000.00	22,028,000.00	15,856,000.00
June 1998	5,874,056.14	16,168,000.00	22,028,000.00	15,856,000.00
July 1998	3,844,689.94	16,168,000.00	22,028,000.00	15,856,000.00
August 1998	1,820,521.94	16,168,000.00	22,028,000.00	15,856,000.00
September 1998	0.00	15,969,S00.37	22,028,000.00	15,856,000.00
October 1998	0.00	13,955,S73.51	22,028,000.00	15,856,000.00
November 1998	0.00	11,962,322.48	22,028,000.00	15,856,000.00
December 1998	0.00	9,999,692.02	22,028,000.00	15,856,000.00
January 1999	0.00	8,067,219.56	22,028,000.00	15,856,000.00
February 1999	0.00	6,164,449.45	22,028,000.00	15,856,000.00
March 1999	0.00	4,290,932.87	22,028,000.00	15,856,000.00
April 1999.	0.00	2,446,227.75	22,028,000.00	15,856,000.00
May 1999	0.00	629,898.63	22,028,000.00	15,856,000.00
June 1999 and thereafter	0.00	0.00	20,870,385.26	15,856,000.00
July 1999			19,110.848.17	15,856,000.00
August 1999			17,378,399.22	15,856,000.00

Distribution Date	Class 89-J Planned Principal Balance	Class 89-K Planned Principal Balance	Class89-L Planned Principal Balance	Class 89-M Targeted Principal Balance
January 1995	$35,884,000.00	$36,683,000.00	$174,433.22	$27,559,675.96
February 1995	35,884,000.00	36,683,000.00	174,433.22	26,871,779.93
March 1995	35,884,000.00	36,683,000.00	174,433.22	26,196,457.96
April 1995	35,884,000.00	36,683,000.00	174,433.22	25,533,580.13
May 1995	35,884,000.00	36,683,000.00	174,433.22	24,883,017.76
June 1995	35,884,000.00	36,683,000.00	174,433.22	24,244,643.40
July 1995	35,884,000.00	36,683,000.00	174,433.22	23,618,330.86
August 1995	35,884,000.00	36,683,000.00	174,433.22	23,003,955.15
September 1995	35,884,000.00	36,683,000.00	174,433.22	22,401,392.51
October 1995	35,884,000.00	36,683,000.00	174,433.22	21,810,520.37
November 1995	35,884,000.00	36,683,000.00	174,433.22	21,231,217.36
December 1995	35,884,000.00	36,683,000.00	174,433.22	20,663,363.26
January 1996	35,884,000.00	36,683,000.00	174,433.22	20,106,839.07
February 1996	35,884,000.00	36,683,000.00	174,433.22	19,561,526.89
March 1996	35,884,000.00	36,683,000.00	174,433.22	19,027,310.02
April 1996	35,884,000.00	36,683,000.00	174,433.22	18,504,072.85
May 1996	35,884,000.00	36,683,000.00	174,433.22	17,991,700.93
June 1996	35,884,000.00	36,683,000.00	174,433.22	17,490,080.92
July 1996	35,884,000.00	36,683,000.00	174,433.22	16,999,100.57
August 1996	35,884,000.00	36,683,000.00	174,433.22	16,518,648.75
September 1996	35,884,000.00	36,683,000.00	174,433.22	16,048,615.40
October 1996	35,884,000.00	36,683,000.00	174,433.22	15,588,891.53
November 1996	35,884,000.00	36,683,000.00	174,433.22	15,139,369.25
December 1996	35,884,000.00	36,683,000.00	174,433.22	14,699,941.68
January 1997	35,884,000.00	36,683,000.00	174,433.22	14,270,503.04
February 1997	35,884,000.00	36,683,000.00	174,433.22	13,850,948.54
March 1997	35,884,000.00	36,683,000.00	174,433.22	13,441,174.45
April 1997	35,884,000.00	36,683,000.00	174,433.22	13,041,078.04
May 1997	35,884,000.00	36,683,000.00	174,433.22	12,650,557.62
June 1997	35,884,000.00	36,683,000.00	174,433.22	12,269,512.46
July 1997	35,884,000.00	36,683,000.00	174,433.22	11,897,842.85
August 1997	35,884,000.00	36,683,000.00	174,433.22	11,535,450.05
September 1997	35,884,000.00	36,683,000.00	174,433.22	11,182,236.31
October 1997	35,884,000.00	36,683,000.00	174,433.22	10,838,104.83
November 1997	35,884,000.00	36,683,000.00	174,433.22	10,502,959.77
December 1997	35,884,000.00	36,683,000.00	174,433.22	10,176,706.24
January 1998	35,884,000.00	36,683,000.00	174,433.22	9,859,250.29
February 1998	35,884,000.00	36,683,000.00	174,433.22	9,550,498.89
March 1998	35,884,000.00	36,683,000.00	174,433.22	9,250,359.95
April 1998	35,884,000.00	36,683,000.00	174,433.22	8,958,742.29
May 1998	35,884,000.00	36,683,000.00	174,433.22	8,675,555.62
June 1998	35,884,000.00	36,683,000.00	174,433.22	8,400,710.56
July 1998	35,884,000.00	36,683,000.00	174,433.22	8,134,118.61
August 1998	35,884,000.00	36,683,000.00	174,433.22	7,875,692.18
September 1998	35,884,000.00	36,683,000.00	174,433.22	7,625,344.51
October 1998	35,884,000.00	36,683,000.00	174,433.22	7,382,989.74
November 1998	35,884,000.00	36,683,000.00	174,433.22	7,137,874.07
December 1998	35,884,000.00	36,683,000.00	174,433.22	6,883,091.18
January 1999	35,884,000.00	36,683,000.00	174,433.22	6,618,838.21
February 1999	35,884,000.00	36,683,000.00	174,433.22	6,345,308.44
March 1999	35,884,000.00	36,683,000.00	174,433.22	6,062,691.30
April 1999	35,884,000.00	36,683,000.00	174,433.22	5,771,172.51
May 1999	35,884,000.00	36,683,000.00	174,433.22	5,470,934.05
June 1999	35,884,000.00	36,683,000.00	173,564.57	5,162,154.28
July 1999	35,884,000.00	36,683,000.00	172,244.26	4,845,008.00
August 1999	35,884,000.00	36,683,000.00	170,944.27	4,519,666.46

Distribution Date	Class 89-G Planned Principal Balance	Class 89-H Planned Principal Balance	Class 89-J Planned Principal Balance
September 1999	$15,672,628.83	$15,856,000.00	$35,884,000.00
October 1999	13,993,133.55	15,856,000.00	35,884,000.00
November 1999	12,339,515.98	15,856,000.00	35,884,000.00
December 1999	10,711,384.71	15,856,000.00	35,884,000.00
January 2000	9,108,354.17	15,856,000.00	35,884,000.00
February 2000	7,530,044.59	15,856,000.00	35,884,000.00
March 2000	5,976,081.92	15,856,000.00	35,884,000.00
April 2000	4,446,097.69	15,856,000.00	35,884,000.00
May 2000	2,939,728.99	15,856,000.00	35,884,000.00
June 2000	1,456,618.33	15,856,000.00	35,884,000.00
July 2000	0.00	15,852,413.61	35,884,000.00
August 2000	0.00	14,414,768.01	35,884,000.00
September 2000	0.00	12,999,339.91	35,884,000.00
October 2000	0.00	11,605,792.83	35,884,000.00
November 2000	0.00	10,233,795.32	35,884,000.00
December 2000	0.00	8,883,020.94	35,884,000.00
January 2001	0.00	7,553,148.12	35,884,000.00
February 2001	0.00	6,243,860.15	35,884,000.00
March 2001	0.00	4,954,845.05	35,884,000.00
April 2001	0.00	3,685,795.54	35,884,000.00
May 2001	0.00	2,436,408.95	35,884,000.00
June 2001	0.00	1,206,387.15	35,884,000.00
July 2001	0.00	0.00	35,879,437.66
August 2001	0.00	0.00	34,687,566.84
September 2001	0.00	0.00	33,514,188.43
October 2001	0.00	0.00	32,359,021.91
November 2001	0.00	0.00	31,221,790.94
December 2001	0.00	0.00	30,102,223.36
January 2002	0.00	0.00	29,000,051.10
February 2002	0.00	0.00	27,915,010.10
March 2002	0.00	0.00	26,846,840.29
April 2002	0.00	0.00	25,795,285.48
May 2002	0.00	0.00	24,760,093.36
June 2002	0.00	0.00	23,741,015.41
July 2002	0.00	0.00	22,737,806.83
August 2002	0.00	0.00	21,750,226.51
September 2002	0.00	0.00	20,778,036.96
October 2002	0.00	0.00	19,821,004.27
November 2002	0.00	0.00	18,878,898.04
December 2002	0.00	0.00	17,951,491.35
January 2003	0.00	0.00	17,038,560.66
February 2003	0.00	0.00	16,139,885.83
March 2003	0.00	0.00	15,255,250.01
April 2003	0.00	0.00	14,384,439.62
May 2003	0.00	0.00	13,527,244.27
June 2003	0.00	0.00	12,683,456.78
July 2003	0.00	0.00	11,852,873.05
August 2003	0.00	0.00	11,035,292.07
September 2003	0.00	0.00	10,230,515.84
October 2003	0.00	0.00	9,438,349.36
November 2003	0.00	0.00	8,658,600.54
December 2003	0.00	0.00	7,891,080.21
January 2004	0.00	0.00	7,135,602.02
February 2004	0.00	0.00	6,391,982.44
March 2004	0.00	0.00	5,660,040.71
April 2004	0.00	0.00	4,939,598.77

Distribution Date	Class 89-K Planned Principal Balance	Class 89-L Planned Principal Balance	Class 89-M Targeted Principal Balance
September 1999	$36,683,000.00	$169,664.30	$4,186,297.47
October 1999	36,683,000.00	168,404.05	3,845,065.40
November 1999	36,683,000.00	167,163.22	3,496,131.30
December 1999	36,683,000.00	165,941.51	3,139,652.90
January 2000	36,683,000.00	164,738.63	2,775,784.67
February 2000	36,683,000.00	163,554.31	2,404,677.90
March 2000	36,683,000.00	162,388.26	2,026,480.75
April 2000	36,683,000.00	161,240.19	1,641,338.24
May 2000	36,683,000.00	160,109.85	1,249,392.39
June 2000	36,683,000.00	158,996.96	850,782.19
July 2000	36,683,000.00	157,901.26	445,643.70
August 2000	36,683,000.00	156,822.49	34,110.07
September 2000	36,683,000.00	155,760.38	0.00
October 2000	36,683,000.00	154,714.70	0.00
November 2000	36,683,000.00	153,685.19	0.00
December 2000	36,683,000.00	152,671.60	0.00
January 2001	36,683,000.00	151,673.70	0.00
February 2001	36,683,000.00	150,691.24	0.00
March 2001	36,683,000.00	149,724.00	0.00
April 2001	36,683,000.00	148,771.73	0.00
May 2001	36,683,000.00	147,834.22	0.00
June 2001	36,683,000.00	146,911.25	0.00
July 2001	36,683,000.00	146,001.44	0.00
August 2001	36,683,000.00	144,808.97	0.00
September 2001	36,683,000.00	143,635.01	0.00
October 2001	36,683,000.00	142,479.26	0.00
November 2001	36,683,000.00	141,341.46	0.00
December 2001	36,683,000.00	140,221.33	0.00
January 2002	36,683,000.00	139,118.61	0.00
February 2002	36,683,000.00	138,033.03	0.00
March 2002	36,683,000.00	136,964.32	0.00
April 2002	36,683,000.00	135,912.24	0.00
May 2002	36,683,000.00	134,876.53	0.00
June 2002	36,683,000.00	133,856.94	0.00
July 2002	36,683,000.00	132,853.23	0.00
August 2002	36,683,000.00	131,865.16	0.00
September 2002	36,683,000.00	130,892.48	0.00
October 2002	36,683,000.00	129,934.97	0.00
November 2002	36,683,000.00	128,992.39	0.00
December 2002	36,683,000.00	128,064.52	0.00
January 2003	36,683,000.00	127,151.14	0.00
February 2003	36,683,000.00	126,252.01	0.00
March 2003	36,683,000.00	125,366.93	0.00
April 2003	36,683,000.00	124,495.69	0.00
May 2003	36,683,000.00	123,638.06	0.00
June 2003	36,683,000.00	122,793.85	0.00
July 2003	36,683,000.00	121,962.85	0.00
August 2003	36,683,000.00	121,144.86	0.00
September 2003	36,683,000.00	120,339.69	0.00
October 2003	36,683,000.00	119,547.12	0.00
November 2003	36,683,000.00	118,766.98	0.00
December 2003	36,683,000.00	117,999.08	0.00
January 2004	36,683,000.00	117,243.22	0.00
February 2004	36,683,000.00	116,499.23	0.00
March 2004	36,683,000.00	115,766.92	0.00
April 2004	36,683,000.00	115,046.12	0.00

Distribution Date	Class 89-G Planned Principal Balance	Class 89-H Planned Principal Balance	Class 89-J Planned Principal Balance	Class 89-K Planned Principal Balance	Class 89-L Planned Principal Balance	Class 89-M Targeted Principal Balance
May 2004	$0.00	$0.00	$4,230,481.27	$36,683,000.00	$114,336.65	$0.00
June 2004	0.00	0.00	3,532,515.47	36,683,000.00	113,638.33	0.00
July 2004	0.00	0.00	2,845,531.26	36,683,000.00	112,951.01	0.00
August 2004	0.00	0.00	2,169,361.07	36,683,000.00	112,274.50	0.00
September 2004	0.00	0.00	1,503,839.87	36,683,000.00	111,608.64	0.00
October 2004	0.00	0.00	848,805.10	36,683,000.00	110,953.28	0.00
November 2004	0.00	0.00	204,096.66	36,683,000.00	110,308.25	0.00
December 2004	0.00	0.00	0.00	36,253,415.61	108,814.65	0.00
January 2005	0.00	0.00	0.00	35,630,135.08	106,943.88	0.00
February 2005	0.00	0.00	0.00	35,016,695.24	105,102.64	0.00
March 2005	0.00	0.00	0.00	34,412,945.72	103,290.48	0.00
April 2005	0.00	0.00	0.00	33,818,738.42	101,506.97	0.00
May 2005	0.00	0.00	0.00	33,233,927.47	99,751.66	0.00
June 2005	0.00	0.00	0.00	32,658,369.21	98,024.12	0.00
July 2005	0.00	0.00	0.00	32,091,922.12	96,323.93	0.00
August 2005	0.00	0.00	0.00	31,534,446.84	94,650.67	0.00
September 2005	0.00	0.00	0.00	30,985,806.11	93,003.92	0.00
October 2005	0.00	0.00	0.00	30,445,864.72	91,383.29	0.00
November 2005	0.00	0.00	0.00	29,914,489.52	89,788.36	0.00
December 2005	0.00	0.00	0.00	29,391,549.35	88,218.76	0.00
January 2006	0.00	0.00	0.00	28,876,915.06	86,674.08	0.00
February 2006	0.00	0.00	0.00	28,370,459.40	85,153.95	0.00
March 2006	0.00	0.00	0.00	27,872,057.08	83,658.00	0.00
April 2006	0.00	0.00	0.00	27,381,584.70	82,185.85	0.00
May 2006	0.00	0.00	0.00	26,898,920.69	80,737.13	0.00
June 2006	0.00	0.00	0.00	26,423,945.34	79,311.49	0.00
July 2006	0.00	0.00	0.00	25,956,540.74	77,908.58	0.00
August 2006	0.00	0.00	0.00	25,496,590.77	76,528.04	0.00
September 2006	0.00	0.00	0.00	25,043,981.06	75,169.53	0.00
October 2006	0.00	0.00	0.00	24,598,598.94	73,832.71	0.00
November 2006	0.00	0.00	0.00	24,160,333.48	72,517.26	0.00
December 2006	0.00	0.00	0.00	23,729,075.40	71,222.84	0.00
January 2007	0.00	0.00	0.00	23,304,717.08	69,949.13	0.00
February 2007	0.00	0.00	0.00	22,887,152.53	68,695.80	0.00
March 2007	0.00	0.00	0.00	22,476,277.36	67,462.56	0.00
April 2007	0.00	0.00	0.00	22,071,988.73	66,249.09	0.00
May 2007	0.00	0.00	0.00	21,674,185.40	65,055.08	0.00
June 2007	0.00	0.00	0.00	21,282,767.63	63,880.24	0.00
July 2007	0.00	0.00	0.00	20,897,637.19	62,724.27	0.00
August 2007	0.00	0.00	0.00	20,518,697.34	61,586.88	0.00
September 2007	0.00	0.00	0.00	20,145,852.80	60,467.79	0.00
October 2007	0.00	0.00	0.00	19,779,009.74	59,366.71	0.00
November 2007	0.00	0.00	0.00	19,418,075.73	58,283.37	0.00
December 2007	0.00	0.00	0.00	19,062,959.76	57,217.49	0.00
January 2008	0.00	0.00	0.00	18,713,572.17	56,168.80	0.00
February 2008	0.00	0.00	0.00	18,369,824.69	55,137.04	0.00
March 2008	0.00	0.00	0.00	18,031,630.35	54,121.95	0.00
April 2008	0.00	0.00	0.00	17,698,903.51	53,123.27	0.00
May 2008	0.00	0.00	0.00	17,371,559.85	52,140.75	0.00
June 2008	0.00	0.00	0.00	17,049,516.29	51,174.14	0.00
July 2008	0.00	0.00	0.00	16,732,691.01	50,223.18	0.00
August 2008	0.00	0.00	0.00	16,421,003.47	49,287.65	0.00
September 2008	0.00	0.00	0.00	16,114,374.29	48,367.31	0.00
October2008	0.00	0.00	0.00	15,812,725.34	47,461.91	0.00
November 2008	0.00	0.00	0.00	15,515,979.64	46,571.22	0.00
December 2008	0.00	0.00	0.00	15,224,061.41	45,695.03	0.00

Distribution Date	Class 89-G Planned Principal Balance	Class 89-H Planned Principal Balance	Class 89-J Planned Principal Balance	Class 89-K Planned Principal Balance	Class 89-L Planned Principal Balance	Class 89-M Targeted Principal Balance
January 2009	$0.00	$0.00	$0.00	$14,936,895.98	$44,833.10	$0.00
February 2009	0.00	0.00	0.00	14,654,409.83	43,985.22	0.00
March 2009	0.00	0.00	0.00	14,376,530.57	43,151.17	0.00
April 2009	0.00	0.00	0.00	14,103,186.88	42,330.73	0.00
May 2009	0.00	0.00	0.00	13,834,308.53	41,523.69	0.00
June 2009	0.00	0.00	0.00	13,569,826.35	40,729.84	0.00
July 2009	0.00	0.00	0.00	13,309,672.24	39,948.99	0.00
August 2009	0.00	0.00	0.00	13,053,779.11	39,180.93	0.00
September 2009	0.00	0.00	0.00	12,802,080.88	38,425.45	0.00
October 2009	0.00	0.00	0.00	12,554,512.51	37,682.38	0.00
November 2009	0.00	0.00	0.00	12,311,009.91	36,961.50	0.00
December 2009	0.00	0.00	0.00	12,071,509.98	36,232.65	0.00
January 2010	0.00	0.00	0.00	11,835,950.56	35,525.61	0.00
February 2010	0.00	0.00	0.00	11,604,270.46	34,830.23	0.00
March 2010	0.00	0.00	0.00	11,376,409.40	34,146.30	0.00
April 2010	0.00	0.00	0.00	11,152,308.02	33,473.66	0.00
May 2010	0.00	0.00	0.00	10,931,907.86	32,812.13	0.00
June 2010	0.00	0.00	0.00	10,715,151.35	32,161.53	0.00
July 2010	0.00	0.00	0.00	10,501,981.78	31,521.71	0.00
August 2010	0.00	0.00	0.00	10,292,343.34	30,892.48	0.00
September 2010	0.00	0.00	0.00	10,086,181.02	30,273.68	0.00
October 2010	0.00	0.00	0.00	9,883,440.67	29,665.15	0.00
November 2010	0.00	0.00	0.00	9,684,068.97	29,066.74	0.00
December 2010	0.00	0.00	0.00	9,488,013.39	28,478.28	0.00
January 2011	0.00	0.00	0.00	9,295,222.22	27,899.62	0.00
February 2011	0.00	0.00	0.00	9,105,644.52	27,330.60	0.00
March 2011	0.00	0.00	0.00	8,919,230.13	26,771.08	0.00
April 2011	0.00	0.00	0.00	8,735,929.65	26,220.90	0.00
May 2011	0.00	0.00	0.00	8,555,694.44	25,679.92	0.00
June 2011	0.00	0.00	0.00	8,378,476.60	25,148.00	0.00
July 2011	0.00	0.00	0.00	8,204,228.94	24,625.00	0.00
August 2011	0.00	0.00	0.00	8,032,905.00	24,110.77	0.00
September 2011	0.00	0.00	0.00	7,864,459.04	23,605.18	0.00
October 2011	0.00	0.00	0.00	7,698,846.00	23,108.09	0.00
November 2011	0.00	0.00	0.00	7,536,021.51	22,619.37	0.00
December 2011	0.00	0.00	0.00	7,375,941.88	22,138.89	0.00
January 2012	0.00	0.00	0.00	7,218,564.08	21,666.52	0.00
February 2012	0.00	0.00	0.00	7,063,845.74	21,202.14	0.00
March 2012	0.00	0.00	0.00	6,911,745.13	20,745.61	0.00
April 2012	0.00	0.00	0.00	6,762,221.17	20,296.81	0.00
May 2012	0.00	0.00	0.00	6,615,233.38	19,855.63	0.00
June 2012	0.00	0.00	0.00	6,470,741.91	19,421.94	0.00
July 2012	0.00	0.00	0.00	6,328,707.55	18,995.62	0.00
August 2012	0.00	0.00	0.00	6,189,091.63	18,576.56	0.00
September 2012	0.00	0.00	0.00	6,051,856.10	18,164.65	0.00
October 2012	0.00	0.00	0.00	5,916,963.51	17,759.77	0.00
November 2012	0.00	0.00	0.00	5,784,376.94	17,361.81	0.00
December 2012	0.00	0.00	0.00	5,654,060.07	16,970.66	0.00
January 2013	0.00	0.00	0.00	5,525,977.10	16,586.22	0.00
February 2013	0.00	0.00	0.00	5,400,092.82	16,208.38	0.00
March 2013	0.00	0.00	0.00	5,276,372.51	15,837.04	0.00
April 2013	0.00	0.00	0.00	5,154,782.01	15,472.08	0.00
May 2013	0.00	0.00	0.00	5,035,287.69	15,113.42	0.00
June 2013	0.00	0.00	0.00	4,917,856.40	14,760.95	0.00
July 2013	0.00	0.00	0.00	4,802,455.53	14,414.57	0.00
August 2013	0.00	0.00	0.00	4,689,052.95	14,074.20	0.00

Distribution Date	Class 89-G Planned Principal Balance	Class 89-H Planned Principal Balance	Class 89-J Planned Principal Balance	Class 89-K Planned Principal Balance	Class 89-L Planned Principal Balance	Class 89-M Targeted Principal Balance
September 2013	$0.00	$0.00	$0.00	$4,577,617.03	$13,739.72	$0.00
October 2013	0.00	0.00	0.00	4,468,116.61	13,411.05	0.00
November 2013	0.00	0.00	0.00	4,360,521.03	13,088.11	0.00
December 2013	0.00	0.00	0.00	4,254,800.08	12,770.78	0.00
January 2014	0.00	0.00	0.00	4,150,924.01	12,459.00	0.00
February 2014	0.00	0.00	0.00	4,048,863.55	12,152.67	0.00
March 2014	0.00	0.00	0.00	3,948,589.85	11,851.69	0.00
April 2014	0.00	0.00	0.00	3,850,074.52	11,556.00	0.00
May 2014	0.00	0.00	0.00	3,753,289.60	11,265.50	0.00
June 2014	0.00	0.00	0.00	3,658,207.56	10,980.11	0.00
July 2014	0.00	0.00	0.00	3,564,801.28	10,699.75	0.00
August 2014	0.00	0.00	0.00	3,473,044.07	10,424.34	0.00
September 2014	0.00	0.00	0.00	3,382,909.65	10,153.81	0.00
October 2014	0.00	0.00	0.00	3,294,372.13	9,888.06	0.00
November 2014	0.00	0.00	0.00	3,207,406.03	9,627.03	0.00
December 2014	0.00	0.00	0.00	3,121,986.26	9,370.64	0.00
January 2015	0.00	0.00	0.00	3,038,088.10	9,118.82	0.00
February 2015	0.00	0.00	0.00	2,955,687.22	8,871.50	0.00
March 2015	0.00	0.00	0.00	2,874,759.68	8,628.59	0.00
April 2015	0.00	0.00	0.00	2,795,281.88	8,390.04	0.00
May 2015	0.00	0.00	0.00	2,717,230.60	8,155.77	0.00
June 2015	0.00	0.00	0.00	2,640,582.97	7,925.71	0.00
July 2015	0.00	0.00	0.00	2,565,316.47	7,699.80	0.00
August 2015	0.00	0.00	0.00	2,491,408.94	7,477.96	0.00
September 2015	0.00	0.00	0.00	2,418,838.54	7,260.14	0.00
October 2015	0.00	0.00	0.00	2,347,583.77	7,046.27	0.00
November 2015	0.00	0.00	0.00	2,277,623.49	6,836.29	0.00
December 2015	0.00	0.00	0.00	2,208,936.85	6,630.12	0.00
January 2016	0.00	0.00	0.00	2,141,503.33	6,427.72	0.00
February 2016	0.00	0.00	0.00	2,075,302.74	6,229.02	0.00
March 2016	0.00	0.00	0.00	2,010,315.18	6,033.96	0.00
April 2016	0.00	0.00	0.00	1,946,521.08	5,842.48	0.00
May 2016	0.00	0.00	0.00	1,883,901.15	5,654.53	0.00
June 2016	0.00	0.00	0.00	1,822,436.41	5,470.04	0.00
July 2016	0.00	0.00	0.00	1,762,108.18	5,288.97	0.00
August 2016	0.00	0.00	0.00	1,702,898.04	5,111.25	0.00
September 2016	0.00	0.00	0.00	1,644,787.88	4,936.83	0.00
October 2016	0.00	0.00	0.00	1,587,759.87	4,765.66	0.00
November 2016	0.00	0.00	0.00	1,531,796.44	4,597.69	0.00
December 2016	0.00	0.00	0.00	1,476,880.30	4,432.86	0.00
January 2017	0.00	0.00	0.00	1,422,994.43	4,271.12	0.00
February 2017	0.00	0.00	0.00	1,370,122.06	4,112.42	0.00
March 2017	0.00	0.00	0.00	1,318,246.70	3,956.72	0.00
April 2017	0.00	0.00	0.00	1,267,352.09	3,803.96	0.00
May 2017	0.00	0.00	0.00	1,217,422.25	3,654.09	0.00
June 2017	0.00	0.00	0.00	1,168,441.42	3,507.08	0.00
July 2017	0.00	0.00	0.00	1,120,394.11	3,362.86	0.00
August 2017	0.00	0.00	0.00	1,073,265.05	3,221.41	0.00
September 2017	0.00	0.00	0.00	1,027,039.21	3,082.66	0.00
October 2017	0.00	0.00	0.00	981,701.79	2,946.58	0.00
November 2017	0.00	0.00	0.00	937,238.24	2,813.12	0.00
December 2017	0.00	0.00	0.00	893,634.22	2,682.24	0.00
January 2018	0.00	0.00	0.00	850,875.61	2,553.90	0.00
February 2018	0.00	0.00	0.00	808,948.51	2,428.06	0.00
March 2018	0.00	0.00	0.00	767,839.24	2,304.67	0.00
April 2018	0.00	0.00	0.00	727,534.33	2,183.69	0.00

Distribution Date	Class 89-G Planned Principal Balance	Class 89-H Planned Principal Balance	Class 89-J Planned Principal Balance	Class 89-K Planned Principal Balance	Class 89-L Planned Principal Balance	Class 89-M Targeted Principal Balance
May 2018	$0.00	$0.00	$0.00	$688,020.53	$2,065.09	$0.00
June 2018	0.00	0.00	0.00	649,284.77	1,948.83	0.00
July 2018	0.00	0.00	0.00	611,314.22	1,834.86	0.00
August 2018	0.00	0.00	0.00	574,096.21	1,723.15	0.00
September 2018	0.00	0.00	0.00	537,618.30	1,613.66	0.00
October 2018	0.00	0.00	0.00	501,868.23	1,506.36	0.00
November 2018	0.00	0.00	0.00	466,833.92	1,401.20	0.00
December 2018	0.00	0.00	0.00	432,503.49	1,298.16	0.00
January 2019	0.00	0.00	0.00	398,865.26	1,197.19	0.00
February 2019	0.00	0.00	0.00	365,907.70	1,098.27	0.00
March 2019	0.00	0.00	0.00	333,619.49	1,001.36	0.00
April 2019	0.00	0.00	0.00	301,989.46	906.42	0.00
May 2019	0.00	0.00	0.00	271,006.63	813.43	0.00
June 2019	0.00	0.00	0.00	240,660.20	722.34	0.00
July 2019	0.00	0.00	0.00	210,939.51	633.13	0.00
August 2019	0.00	0.00	0.00	181,834.10	545.77	0.00
September 2019	0.00	0.00	0.00	153,333.65	460.23	0.00
October 2019	0.00	0.00	0.00	125,428.01	376.47	0.00
November 2019	0.00	0.00	0.00	98,107.19	294.47	0.00
December 2019	0.00	0.00	0.00	71,361.34	214.19	0.00
January 2020	0.00	0.00	0.00	45,180.80	135.61	0.00
February 2020	0.00	0.00	0.00	19,556.03	58.70	0.00
March 2020 and thereafter	0.00	0.00	0.00	0.00	0.00	0.00

Using the assumptions with respect to the Mortgage Loans specified in the final paragraph of this Prospectus Supplement (other than for O% PSA), the principal balances of the Planned Principal REMIC Certificates will be reduced to their respective Planned Principal Balances for each Distribution Date if prepayments on the Mortgage Loans underlying the MBS Certificates occur at a constant level between approximately 90% PSA and 275% PSA, and the principal balance of the Class 89-M REMIC Certificates will be reduced to their Targeted Principal Balance for each Distribution Date if prepayments occur at a constant level of approximately 165% PSA.

There is no assurance that the principal balances of the Planned Principal REMIC Certificates or the Class 89-M REMIC Certificates will conform on any Distribution Date to the applicable level specified for such Distribution Date in the schedule above. Because any excess of the Principal Distribution Amount over the sum of the Planned and Targeted Principal Amounts for any month will be distributed, the ability to pay the Planned or Targeted Principal Amount for any Distribution Date will not be enhanced by the averaging of high and low principal prepayments, as might be the case if any such excess amounts were held for future applications and not distributed monthly. Moreover, with respect to the Planned Principal REMIC Certificates, the amount of principal available on any Distribution Date may be insufficient to reduce such Classes to their respective Planned Principal Balances for such Distribution Date if prepayments on the Mortgage Loans do not occur at a constant rate, even if such prepayments remain within the range of approximately 90% PSA to 275% PSA. This result could occur, for example, if principal payments on the Mortgage Loans initially occur at a relatively fast rate within such range and subsequently occur at a significantly slower rate within such range. The amount of principal available on any Distribution Date may be insufficient to reduce the principal balance of the Class 89-M REMIC Certificates to their Targeted Principal Balance for such Distribution Date if prepayments on the Mortgage Loans do not occur at a constant rate of approximately 165% PSA. Furthermore, there is no assurance that distributions of principal will begin or end on the Distribution Dates specified in the schedule of Planned and Targeted Principal Balances. See "Final Distribution Dates and Weighted Average Lives of the REMIC Certificates" herein for a further discussion of the effect of prepayments on the Mortgage Loans on the rate of payments of principal and on the weighted average lives of the Classes of REMIC Certificates.

The following table indicates the percentages of the initial principal amount of each Class of REMIC Certificates that would be outstanding after each of the dates shown at various *constant* percentages of PSA and the corresponding weighted average life of each Class of REMIC Certificates. The table has been prepared on the basis of assumptions concerning the characteristics of the Mortgage Loans that will underlie the MBS Certificates, including (i) with respect to the information set forth under 0% PSA, that each Mortgage Loan underlying the MBS Certificates bears an interest rate of 12.00% per annum and has an original and remaining term to maturity of 360 months and (ii) with respect to the remaining information, that each Mortgage Loan underlying the MBS

Percent of Original Principal Balance Outstanding

Date	Class 89-A PSA Prepayment Assumption					Class 89-B PSA Prepayment Assumption					Class 89-X PSA Prepayment Assumption					Class 89-C PSA Prepayment Assumption				
	0%	90%	165%	275%	500%	0%	90%	165%	275%	500%	0%	90%	165%	275%	500%	0%	90%	165%	275%	500%
Initial Percent	100	100	100	100	100	100	100	100	100	100	100	100	100	100	100	100	100	100	100	100
July 1991	100	100	100	100	100	100	100	100	100	100	110	110	110	110	110	100	100	100	100	100
July 1992	100	86	86	86	86	100	100	100	100	100	121	121	121	121	121	100	100	100	100	100
July 1993	83	0	0	0	0	100	100	100	100	19	133	133	133	133	133	100	100	100	100	100
July 1994	64	0	0	0	0	100	1	1	1	0	146	146	146	146	0	100	100	100	100	0
July 1995	43	0	0	0	0	100	0	0	0	0	161	3	3	3	0	100	100	100	100	0
July 1996	20	0	0	0	0	100	0	0	0	0	176	0	0	0	0	100	35	35	35	0
July 1997	0	0	0	0	0	94	0	0	0	0	194	0	0	0	0	100	0	0	0	0
July 1998	0	0	0	0	0	61	0	0	0	0	213	0	0	0	0	100	0	0	0	0
July 1999	0	0	0	0	0	24	0	0	0	0	234	0	0	0	0	100	0	0	0	0
July 2000	0	0	0	0	0	0	0	0	0	0	229	0	0	0	0	100	0	0	0	0
July 2001	0	0	0	0	0	0	0	0	0	0	178	0	0	0	0	100	0	0	0	0
July 2002	0	0	0	0	0	0	0	0	0	0	122	0	0	0	0	100	0	0	0	0
July 2003	0	0	0	0	0	0	0	0	0	0	60	0	0	0	0	100	0	0	0	0
July 2004	0	0	0	0	0	0	0	0	0	0	0	0	0	0	0	95	0	0	0	0
July 2005	0	0	0	0	0	0	0	0	0	0	0	0	0	0	0	58	0	0	0	0
July 2006	0	0	0	0	0	0	0	0	0	0	0	0	0	0	0	17	0	0	0	0
July 2007	0	0	0	0	0	0	0	0	0	0	0	0	0	0	0	0	0	0	0	0
July 2008	0	0	0	0	0	0	0	0	0	0	0	0	0	0	0	0	0	0	0	0
July 2009	0	0	0	0	0	0	0	0	0	0	0	0	0	0	0	0	0	0	0	0
July 2010	0	0	0	0	0	0	0	0	0	0	0	0	0	0	0	0	0	0	0	0
July 2011	0	0	0	0	0	0	0	0	0	0	0	0	0	0	0	0	0	0	0	0
July 2012	0	0	0	0	0	0	0	0	0	0	0	0	0	0	0	0	0	0	0	0
July 2013	0	0	0	0	0	0	0	0	0	0	0	0	0	0	0	0	0	0	0	0
July 2014	0	0	0	0	0	0	0	0	0	0	0	0	0	0	0	0	0	0	0	0
July 2015	0	0	0	0	0	0	0	0	0	0	0	0	0	0	0	0	0	0	0	0
July 2016	0	0	0	0	0	0	0	0	0	0	0	0	0	0	0	0	0	0	0	0
July 2017	0	0	0	0	0	0	0	0	0	0	0	0	0	0	0	0	0	0	0	0
July 2018	0	0	0	0	0	0	0	0	0	0	0	0	0	0	0	0	0	0	0	0
July 2019	0	0	0	0	0	0	0	0	0	0	0	0	0	0	0	0	0	0	0	0
July 2020	0	0	0	0	0	0	0	0	0	0	0	0	0	0	0	0	0	0	0	0
Weighted Average Life (years)**	4.6	2.5	2.5	2.5	2.4	8.3	3.5	3.5	3.5	2.9	11.9	4.6	4.6	4.6	3.3	15.2	5.8	5.8	5.8	3.7

* Indicates an amount above zero and less than 0.5% of the original principal balance is outstanding.

** The weighted average life of a REMIC Certificate is determined by (a) multiplying the amount of the reduction, if any, of the principal amount of such REMIC Certificate from one Distribution Date to the next Distribution Date by the number of years from the date of issuance to the second such Distribution Date, (b) summing the results and (c) dividing the sum by the aggregate amount of the reductions in principal amount of such REMIC Certificate referred to in clause (a).

Certificates bears an interest rate of 10.125% per annum, had an original term to maturity of 360 months and has a remaining term to maturity of 356 months. It is not likely that (i) all of the underlying Mortgage Loans will have the interest rate or remaining term to maturity assumed or (ii) the underlying Mortgage Loans will prepay at a *constant* level of PSA. In addition, the diverse remaining terms to maturity of the Mortgage Loans (which will include recently originated Mortgage Loans) could produce slower or faster principal distributions than indicated in the table at the various *constant* percentages of PSA specified (except 0% PSA), even if the weighted average remaining term to maturity of the Mortgage Loans is 356 months.

Class 89-D					Class 89-E					Class 89-G					Class 89-H				
PSA Prepayment Assumption					PSA Prepayment Assumption					PSA Prepayment Assumption					PSA Prepayment Assumption				
0%	90%	165%	275%	500%	0%	90%	165%	275%	500%	0%	90%	165%	275%	500%	0%	90%	165%	275%	500%
100	100	100	100	100	100	100	100	100	100	100	100	100	100	100	100	100	100	100	100
100	100	100	100	100	100	100	100	100	100	100	100	100	100	100	100	100	100	100	100
100	100	100	100	100	100	100	100	100	100	100	100	100	100	100	100	100	100	100	100
100	100	100	100	100	100	100	100	100	100	100	100	100	100	100	100	100	100	100	100
100	100	100	100	96	100	100	100	100	100	100	100	100	100	100	100	100	100	100	100
100	100	100	100	0	100	100	100	100	26	100	100	100	100	100	100	100	100	100	100
100	100	100	100	0	100	100	100	100	0	100	100	100	100	0	100	100	100	100	43
100	71	71	71	0	100	100	100	100	0	100	100	100	100	0	100	100	100	100	0
100	10	10	10	0	100	100	100	100	0	100	100	100	100	0	100	100	100	100	0
100	0	0	0	0	100	0	0	0	0	100	87	87	87	0	100	100	100	100	0
100	0	0	0	0	100	0	0	0	0	100	0	0	0	0	100	100	100	100	0
100	0	0	0	0	100	0	0	0	0	100	0	0	0	0	100	0	0	0	0
100	0	0	0	0	100	0	0	0	0	100	0	0	0	0	100	0	0	0	0
100	0	0	0	0	100	0	0	0	0	100	0	0	0	0	100	0	0	0	0
100	0	0	0	0	100	0	0	0	0	100	0	0	0	0	100	0	0	0	0
100	0	0	0	0	100	0	0	0	0	100	0	0	0	0	100	0	0	0	0
71	0	0	0	0	100	0	0	0	0	100	0	0	0	0	100	0	0	0	0
19	0	0	0	0	100	0	0	0	0	100	0	0	0	0	100	0	0	0	0
0	0	0	0	0	4	0	0	0	0	100	0	0	0	0	100	0	0	0	0
0	0	0	0	0	0	0	0	0	0	0	0	0	0	0	80	0	0	0	0
0	0	0	0	0	0	0	0	0	0	0	0	0	0	0	0	0	0	0	0
0	0	0	0	0	0	0	0	0	0	0	0	0	0	0	0	0	0	0	0
0	0	0	0	0	0	0	0	0	0	0	0	0	0	0	0	0	0	0	0
0	0	0	0	0	0	0	0	0	0	0	0	0	0	0	0	0	0	0	0
0	0	0	0	0	0	0	0	0	0	0	0	0	0	0	0	0	0	0	0
0	0	0	0	0	0	0	0	0	0	0	0	0	0	0	0	0	0	0	0
0	0	0	0	0	0	0	0	0	0	0	0	0	0	0	0	0	0	0	0
0	0	0	0	0	0	0	0	0	0	0	0	0	0	0	0	0	0	0	0
0	0	0	0	0	0	0	0	0	0	0	0	0	0	0	0	0	0	0	0
17.4	7.4	7.4	7.4	4.4	18.7	8.5	8.5	8.5	4.9	19.5	9.4	9.4	9.4	5.4	20.2	10.5	10.5	10.5	6.0

Percent of Original Principal Balance Outstanding—(Continued)

Date	Class 89-J					Class 89-K					Class 89-L					Class 89-M						
	PSA Prepayment Assumption					PSA Prepayment Assumption					PSA Prepayment Assumption					PSA Prepayment Assumption						
	0%	90%	165%	275%	500%	0%	90%	165%	275%	500%	0%	90%	165%	275%	500%	0%	90%	165%	169%	170%	275%	500%
Initial Percent	100	100	100	100	100	100	100	100	100	100	100	100	100	100	100	100	100	100	100	100	100	100
July 1991	100	100	100	100	100	100	100	100	100	100	100	100	100	100	100	100	94	90	90	94	90	90
July 1992	100	100	100	100	100	100	100	100	100	100	100	99	99	99	99	100	71	62	62	62	62	55
July 1993	100	100	100	100	100	100	100	100	100	100	98	91	91	91	85	100	71	48	48	48	48	0
July 1994	100	100	100	100	100	100	100	100	100	100	97	84	84	84	83	100	71	36	36	36	36	0
July 1995	100	100	100	100	100	100	100	100	100	100	95	83	83	83	83	100	71	27	27	27	27	0
July 1996	100	100	100	100	100	100	100	100	100	100	93	83	83	83	72	100	71	19	19	19	12	0
July 1997	100	100	100	100	51	100	100	100	100	100	91	83	83	83	61	100	71	13	13	13	4	0
July 1998	100	100	100	100	4	100	100	100	100	100	88	83	83	83	53	100	71	9	9	9	*	0
July 1999	100	100	100	100	0	100	100	100	100	72	85	82	82	82	38	100	69	5	5	5	*	0
July 2000	100	100	100	100	0	100	100	100	100	49	83	76	76	76	26	100	65	1	1	1	*	0
July 2001	100	100	100	100	0	100	100	100	100	34	83	70	70	70	18	100	57	0	0	0	*	0
July 2002	100	63	63	63	0	100	100	100	100	23	83	64	64	64	12	100	47	0	0	0	*	0
July 2003	100	33	33	33	0	100	100	100	100	16	83	58	58	58	8	100	34	0	0	0	*	0
July 2004	100	8	8	8	0	100	100	100	100	11	83	54	54	54	6	100	20	0	0	0	*	0
July 2005	100	0	0	0	0	100	87	87	87	7	83	46	46	46	4	100	4	0	0	0	*	0
July 2006	100	0	0	0	0	100	71	71	71	5	83	37	37	37	3	100	0	0	0	0	*	0
July 2007	100	0	0	0	0	100	57	57	57	3	83	30	30	30	2	100	0	0	0	0	*	0
July 2008	100	0	0	0	0	100	46	46	46	2	83	24	24	24	1	100	0	0	0	0	*	0
July 2009	100	0	0	0	0	100	36	36	36	2	83	19	19	19	1	100	0	0	0	0	*	0
July 2010	100	0	0	0	0	100	29	29	29	1	74	15	15	15	1	100	0	0	0	0	*	0
July 2011	55	0	0	0	0	100	22	22	22	1	62	12	12	12	*	100	0	0	0	0	*	0
July 2012	0	0	0	0	0	66	17	17	17	*	35	9	9	9	*	100	0	0	0	0	*	0
July 2013	0	0	0	0	0	13	13	13	13	*	7	7	7	7	*	81	0	0	0	0	*	0
July 2014	0	0	0	0	0	10	10	10	10	*	5	5	5	5	*	37	0	0	0	0	*	0
July 2015	0	0	0	0	0	7	7	7	7	*	4	4	4	4	*	0	0	0	0	0	*	0
July 2016	0	0	0	0	0	5	5	5	5	*	3	3	3	3	*	0	0	0	0	0	*	0
July 2017	0	0	0	0	0	3	3	3	3	*	2	2	2	2	*	0	0	0	0	0	*	0
July 2018	0	0	0	0	0	2	2	2	2	*	1	1	1	1	*	0	0	0	0	0	*	0
July 2019	0	0	0	0	0	1	1	1	1	*	*	*	*	*	*	0	0	0	0	0	*	0
July 2020	0	0	0	0	0	0	0	0	0	0	0	0	0	0	0	0	0	0	0	0	0	0
Weighted Average Life (years)**	21.1	12.5	12.5	12.5	7.1	22.6	18.6	18.6	18.6	10.8	19.3	13.8	13.8	13.8	8.1	23.7	9.4	3.6	3.6	3.7	3.3	1.9

* Indicates an amount above zero and less than 0.5% of the original principal balance is outstanding.

** The weighted average life of a REMIC Certificate is determined by (a) multiplying the amount of the reduction, if any, of the principal amount of such REMIC Certificate from one Distribution Date to the next Distribution Date by the number of years from the date of issuance to the second such Distribution Date, (b) summing the results and (c) dividing the sum by the aggregate amount of the reductions in principal amount of such REMIC Certificate referred to in clause (a).

Class 89-F and Class 89-S

PSA Prepayment Assumption						
0%	90%	165%	169%	170%	275%	500%
100	100	100	100	100	100	100
100	100	90	89	100	100	23
100	100	62	58	78	81	0
100	100	47	42	63	0	0
100	100	36	29	52	0	0
100	100	26	18	43	0	0
100	100	19	10	37	0	0
100	100	13	3	34	0	0
100	100	9	0	32	0	0
100	100	5	0	32	0	0
100	100	0	0	31	0	0
100	100	0	0	18	0	0
100	100	0	0	1	0	0
100	100	0	0	0	0	0
100	100	0	0	0	0	0
100	73	0	0	0	0	0
100	34	0	0	0	0	0
100	0	0	0	0	0	0
100	0	0	0	0	0	0
100	0	0	0	0	0	0
100	0	0	0	0	0	0
100	0	0	0	0	0	0
100	0	0	0	0	0	0
72	0	0	0	0	0	0
0	0	0	0	0	0	0
0	0	0	0	0	0	0
0	0	0	0	0	0	0
25.2	16.6	3.6	3.0	5.8	1.4	0.8

Class 89-N

PSA Prepayment Assumption						
0%	90%	165%	169%	170%	275%	500%
100	100	100	100	100	100	100
100	100	86	85	100	100	0
100	100	46	41	69	73	0
100	100	26	18	48	0	0
100	100	9	0	32	0	0
100	100	0	0	20	0	0
100	100	0	0	12	0	0
100	100	0	0	7	0	0
100	100	0	0	5	0	0
100	100	0	0	4	0	0
100	100	0	0	3	0	0
100	100	0	0	0	0	0
100	100	0	0	0	0	0
100	100	0	0	0	0	0
100	100	0	0	0	0	0
100	62	0	0	0	0	0
100	6	0	0	0	0	0
100	0	0	0	0	0	0
100	0	0	0	0	0	0
100	0	0	0	0	0	0
100	0	0	0	0	0	0
100	0	0	0	0	0	0
61	0	0	0	0	0	0
0	0	0	0	0	0	0
0	0	0	0	0	0	0
0	0	0	0	0	0	0
25.1	16.2	2.2	2.0	3.5	1.2	0.7

Class 89-O

PSA Prepayment Assumption						
0%	90%	165%	169%	170%	275%	500%
100	100	100	100	100	100	100
100	100	100	100	100	100	78
100	100	100	100	100	0	0
100	100	100	98	100	0	0
100	100	90	62	100	0	0
100	100	64	33	100	0	0
100	100	44	11	100	0	0
100	100	30	0	100	0	0
100	100	17	0	100	0	0
100	100	0	0	61	0	0
100	100	0	0	5	0	0
100	100	0	0	0	0	0
100	100	0	0	0	0	0
100	100	0	0	0	0	0
100	100	0	0	0	0	0
100	100	0	0	0	0	0
100	100	0	0	0	0	0
100	0	0	0	0	0	0
100	0	0	0	0	0	0
100	0	0	0	0	0	0
100	0	0	0	0	0	0
100	0	0	0	0	0	0
100	0	0	0	0	0	0
0	0	0	0	0	0	0
0	0	0	0	0	0	0
0	0	0	0	0	0	0
25.5	17.5	7.0	5.5	11.2	1.9	1.1

Class 89-P

PSA Prepayment Assumption						
0%	90%	165%	169%	170%	275%	500%
100	100	100	100	100	100	100
100	100	100	100	100	100	100
100	100	100	100	100	100	0
100	100	100	100	100	46	0
100	100	100	100	100	7	0
100	100	100	100	100	0	0
100	100	100	100	100	0	0
100	100	100	99	100	0	0
100	100	96	92	100	0	0
100	100	69	78	100	0	0
100	100	50	61	87	0	0
100	100	30	42	72	0	0
100	100	8	22	56	0	0
100	94	0	2	40	0	0
100	59	0	0	24	0	0
100	22	0	0	7	0	0
100	0	0	0	0	0	0
100	0	0	0	0	0	0
100	0	0	0	0	0	0
100	0	0	0	0	0	0
100	0	0	0	0	0	0
61	0	0	0	0	0	0
0	0	0	0	0	0	0
0	0	0	0	0	0	0
0	0	0	0	0	0	0
26.1	19.3	12.9	12.5	15.4	3.0	1.5

Percent of Original Principal Balance Outstanding—(Continued)

Date	Class 89-Y							Class 89-Z							Class 89-R					Class 89-RL				
	PSA Prepayment Assumption							PSA Prepayment Assumption							PSA Prepayment Assumption					PSA Prepayment Assumption				
	0%	90%	165%	169%	170%	275%	500%	0%	90%	165%	169%	170%	275%	500%	0%	90%	185%	275%	500%	0%	90%	185%	275%	500%
Initial Percent	100	100	100	100	100	100	100	100	100	100	100	100	100	100	100	100	100	100	100	100	100	100	100	100
July 1991	110	110	110	110	110	0	0	110	110	110	110	110	110	110	52	0	0	0	0	100	98	96	94	89
July 1992	121	121	121	121	121	0	0	121	121	121	121	121	121	121	0	0	0	0	0	99	93	88	82	68
July 1993	133	133	133	133	133	0	0	133	133	133	133	133	133	133	0	0	0	0	0	99	87	79	68	48
July 1994	146	146	146	146	146	0	0	146	146	146	146	146	146	146	0	0	0	0	0	98	82	71	56	33
July 1995	161	161	161	161	161	0	0	161	161	161	161	161	161	15	0	0	0	0	0	98	77	63	46	23
July 1996	176	176	176	176	176	0	0	176	176	176	176	176	176	0	0	0	0	0	0	97	72	56	38	16
July 1997	194	194	194	194	194	0	0	194	194	194	194	194	0	0	0	0	0	0	0	96	67	50	32	11
July 1998	213	213	213	213	213	0	0	213	213	213	213	213	0	0	0	0	0	0	0	95	63	45	26	8
July 1999	234	234	234	234	234	0	0	234	234	234	234	234	0	0	0	0	0	0	0	94	59	40	22	5
July 2000	258	258	258	258	258	0	0	258	258	258	258	258	0	0	0	0	0	0	0	93	55	35	18	4
July 2001	283	283	283	283	283	0	0	283	283	283	283	283	0	0	0	0	0	0	0	92	51	31	15	2
July 2002	311	311	311	311	311	0	0	311	311	311	311	311	0	0	0	0	0	0	0	91	47	28	12	2
July 2003	342	342	342	342	342	0	0	342	342	342	342	342	0	0	0	0	0	0	0	89	44	24	10	1
July 2004	376	376	376	376	376	0	0	376	376	376	376	376	0	0	0	0	0	0	0	88	40	21	8	1
July 2005	413	413	413	413	413	0	0	413	413	413	413	413	0	0	0	0	0	0	0	86	37	19	6	*
July 2006	454	454	403	380	0	0	0	454	454	403	380	454	0	0	0	0	0	0	0	84	34	16	5	*
July 2007	500	500	362	340	0	0	0	500	500	362	340	500	0	0	0	0	0	0	0	81	31	14	4	*
July 2008	549	549	322	303	0	0	0	549	549	322	303	549	0	0	0	0	0	0	0	78	28	12	3	*
July 2009	604	604	284	266	0	0	0	604	604	284	266	531	0	0	0	0	0	0	0	75	25	11	3	*
July 2010	664	664	248	232	0	0	0	664	664	248	232	462	0	0	0	0	0	0	0	72	23	9	2	*
July 2011	729	668	214	200	0	0	0	729	668	214	200	397	0	0	0	0	0	0	0	68	20	8	2	*
July 2012	802	590	182	169	0	0	0	802	590	182	169	337	0	0	0	0	0	0	0	63	18	6	1	*
July 2013	881	512	152	141	0	0	0	881	512	152	141	280	0	0	0	0	0	0	0	58	15	5	1	*
July 2014	969	434	124	115	0	0	0	969	434	124	115	228	0	0	0	0	0	0	0	53	13	4	1	*
July 2015	1,065	356	97	90	0	0	0	1,065	356	97	90	179	0	0	0	0	0	0	0	46	10	3	1	*
July 2016	1,171	279	73	68	0	0	0	1,171	279	73	68	135	0	0	0	0	0	0	0	39	8	2	*	*
July 2017	1,111	203	51	47	0	0	0	1,111	203	51	47	93	0	0	0	0	0	0	0	31	6	2	*	*
July 2018	785	126	31	28	0	0	0	785	126	31	28	56	0	0	0	0	0	0	0	22	4	1	*	*
July 2019	417	51	12	11	0	0	0	417	51	12	11	21	0	0	0	0	0	0	0	12	1	*	*	*
July 2020	0	0	0	0	0	0	0	0	0	0	0	0	0	0	0	0	0	0	0	0	0	0	0	0
Weighted Average Life (years)**	28.4	25.1	21.5	21.3	0.6	0.3	0.2	28.4	25.1	21.5	21.3	23.3	4.7	1.9	1.1	0.4	0.4	0.4	0.4	22.5	12.6	8.9	6.1	3.7

* Indicates an amount above zero and less than 0.5% of the original principal balance is outstanding.

** The weighted average life of a REMIC Certificate is determined by (a) multiplying the amount of the reduction, if any, of the principal amount of such REMIC Certificate from one Distribution Date to the next Distribution Date by the number of years from the date of issuance to the second such Distribution Date, (b) summing the results and (c) dividing the sum by the aggregate amount of the reductions in principal amount of such REMIC Certificate referred to in clause (a).

Chapter 13

ANALYSIS OF BONDS WITH EMBEDDED OPTIONS I

In our explanation of bond pricing, return measures, and price volatility in Chapters 2-4, we confined the discussion to bonds in which neither the issuer nor the bondholder has the option to do anything. In this chapter and the next, we look at how to value bonds that have embedded options. Because the most common type of option embedded in a bond is a call option, our primary focus will be on callable bonds. Mortgage-backed securities are also securities with embedded call options, and Chapter 15 focuses on valuing those securities.

This chapter has four objectives. We first explain the disadvantages of the call feature. Second, we discuss the conventional methodology that has been used to evaluate these bonds. Third, the price/yield relationship for a callable bond is illustrated. Finally, we provide a technique that can be used to value bonds with embedded options. In the next chapter, an alternative technique to value bonds with embedded options is explained.

DISADVANTAGES OF CALLABLE BONDS

The holder of a callable bond has given the issuer the right to call the issue prior to the maturity date. This has two disadvantages for the bondholder. First, an issuer will call a bond when the yield on bonds in the market is lower than the issue's coupon rate. For example, if the coupon rate on a callable corporate bond is 13%, and prevailing market yields are 7%, the issuer will find it economical to call the 13% issue and refund it with a 7% issue. From the investor's perspective, the proceeds received then will have to be reinvested at a lower interest rate. Thus, callable bonds expose bondholders to reinvestment risk.

Second, as we explain later in this chapter, the price appreciation potential for a bond in a declining interest rate environment is limited when it is callable. The price of the callable bond will remain near its call price rather than rising to the higher price that would result for an otherwise comparable noncallable bond. This phenomenon for a callable bond is referred to as *price compression.*

Given these disadvantages of a callable bond, why would any investor want to own one? If the investor receives sufficient compensation in the form of higher potential yield, an investor willing to accept call risk will be willing to hold a callable corporate bond.

TRADITIONAL METHODOLOGY

When a bond is callable, the practice has been to calculate a yield to call as well as a yield to maturity. The former yield calculation assumes that the issuer will call the bond at the first call date. As we explain in Chapter 3, the procedure for calculating the yield to call is the same as for any yield calculation: determine the interest rate that will make the present value of the expected cash flows equal to the price. In the case of yield to call, the expected cash flows are the coupon payments to the first call date and the call price.

According to the traditional approach, conservative investors will compute the yield to call and yield to maturity for a callable bond selling at a premium, and use the lower of the two to evaluate the relative value. More recently, the traditional approach has been extended to compute not just the yield to the first call date, but the yield to all possible call dates. As most bonds can be called at any time after the first call date, the approach has been to compute the yield to every coupon anniversary date following the first call date. Then, all yield to calls calculated and the yield to maturity are compared. The lowest of these yields is called the *yield to worst.* It is this yield that the traditional approach would have one believe should be used in relative value analysis.

We explain the limitations of the yield to call as a measure of the potential return of a security in Chapter 3. The yield to call does consider all three sources of potential return from owning a bond, but as in the case of the yield to maturity, it assumes that all cash flows can be reinvested at the computed yield—in this case the yield to call—until the assumed call date. Moreover, the yield to call assumes that (1) the investor will hold the bond to the assumed call date, and (2) the issuer will call the bond on that date.

These assumptions underlying the yield to call are oftentimes unrealistic. They do not take into account how an investor will reinvest the proceeds if the issue is called. For example, consider two bonds, M and N. Suppose that the yield to maturity for bond M, a five-year noncallable bond, is 10%, while the yield to call for bond N is 10.5%, assuming the bond will be called in three years. Which bond is better for an investor with a five-year investment horizon? It's not possible to tell for the yields cited. If the investor intends to hold the bond for five years and the issuer calls the bond after three years, the total dollars that will be available at the end of five years depend on the interest rate that can be earned from investing funds from the call date to the end of the investment horizon.

PRICE/YIELD RELATIONSHIP FOR A CALLABLE BOND

We explain in Chapter 4 that the price/yield relationship for an option-free (i.e., noncallable/nonputable) bond is convex. Exhibit 13-1 shows the price/yield relationship for both a noncallable bond and the same bond if it is callable. The convex curve a-a' is the price/yield relationship for the noncallable (option-free) bond. The unusual shaped curve denoted by a-b is the price/yield relationship for the callable bond.

The reason for the shape of the price/yield relationship for the callable bond is as follows. When the prevailing market yield for comparable bonds is higher than the coupon rate on the bond, it is unlikely that the issuer will call the bond. For example, if the coupon rate on a bond is 8%, and the prevailing yield on comparable bonds is 16%, the issuer will hardly call the 8% bond so that it can issue a 16% bond. As long as the bond is unlikely to be called, the callable bond will have the same price/yield relationship as a noncallable bond. However, even when the coupon rate is just below the market yield, investors may not pay the same price for the bond than had it been a noncallable bond, because there is still the chance the market yield may drop further so that it will become beneficial for the issuer to call the bond.

As yields in the market decline, the likelihood that yields will decline further so that the issuer will benefit from calling the bond increases. The exact yield level at which investors begin to view the issue as likely to be called may not be known, but we do know that there is some level. In Exhibit 13-1, at yield levels below y^*, the price/yield relationship for the callable bond departs from the price/yield relationship for the noncallable bond. If, for example, the market yield is such that a bond would be selling for 109, but because it is callable it would be called at 104, investors would not pay 109. If they do, and the bond is called, investors would receive 104 (the call price) for a bond they purchased for 109. Notice that for a range of yields below y^*, there is price compression — that is, there is limited price appreciation as yields decline. The portion of the callable bond price/yield relationship below y^* is said to be *negatively convex*. This means that a decline in yields by a given number of basis

EXHIBIT 13-1 Price/Yield Relationship for a Noncallable and a Callable Bond

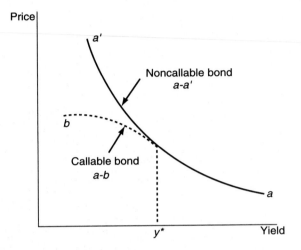

points will result in a greater price decline compared to the price appreciation if yields decline by the same number of basis points.

THE COMPONENTS OF A BOND WITH AN EMBEDDED OPTION

To develop an analytical framework for assessing relative value and evaluating the potential performance of bonds with embedded options over some investment horizon, it is necessary to segment the components of the bond.

Components of a Callable Bond

A callable bond is a bond in which the bondholder has sold the issuer an option (more specifically, a call option) that allows the issuer to repurchase the contractual cash flows of the bond from the time the bond is first callable until the maturity date.

Consider two bonds for example: (1) a callable bond with an 8% coupon, 20 years to maturity, and callable in 5 years at 104, and (2) a 10-year 9% coupon bond callable immediately at par. For the first bond, the bondholder owns a 20-year noncallable bond and has sold a call option granting the issuer the right to call away from the bondholder 15 years of cash flows 5 years from now for a price of 104. The investor who owns the second bond has a 10-year noncallable bond and has sold a call option granting the issuer the right immediately to call away the entire 10-year contractual cash flows, or any cash flows remaining at the time the issue is called, for 100.

Effectively, owners of a callable bond enter into two separate transactions. First, they buy a noncallable bond from the issuer for which they pay some price. Then, they sell the issuer a call option for which they receive the option price from the issuer. Therefore, we can summarize the position of a callable bondholder as follows:

Long a callable bond = Long a noncallable bond + Sold a call option

In terms of price, the price of a callable bond is therefore equal to the price of the two component parts. That is,

(13.1)   Callable bond price = Noncallable bond price − Call option price

The reason the call option price is subtracted from the price of the noncallable bond is that upon sale of a call option, the bondholder receives the option price. Graphically this can be seen in Exhibit 13-1. At a given yield, the difference between the price of the noncallable bond and the callable bond is the price of the embedded call option.

Actually, the position is more complicated than this. The issuer may be entitled to call the bond at the first call date and anytime thereafter, or at the first call date and any subsequent coupon anniversary. Thus the investor has effectively sold a strip (or a package) of call options to the issuer. The call price may vary with the date the issue may be called. The underlying bond for the call option is the remaining coupon payments that would have been made by the issuer had the bond not been called. For expositional purposes, it is easier to understand the principles associated with the investment characteristics of callable bonds if we describe the investor's position as long a noncallable bond and short a call option.

Components of a Putable Bond

The same logic applies to putable bonds. In the case of a putable bond, the bondholder has the right to sell the bond to the issuer at a designated price and time. A putable bond can be seen as representing two separate transactions. First, the investor buys a nonputable bond. Second, the investor buys an option from the issuer that allows the investor to sell the bond to the issuer. This type of option is called a *put* option. Therefore, the position of a putable bondholder can be described as:

Long a putable bond = Long a nonputable bond + Long a put option

The price of a putable bond is then

(13.2)   Putable bond price = Nonputable bond price + Put option price

BASICS OF OPTION PRICING

The *option pricing approach* is a valuation technique that relies on estimating the value of the embedded option. To employ this approach, it is necessary to have a basic understanding of option pricing. More detailed information on options and option pricing models is covered in Chapter 18.

An option is an agreement in which the writer of the option grants the buyer of the option the right to purchase from or sell to the writer a designated instrument at a specified price within a specified period of time. The writer, also referred to as the seller, grants this right to the buyer in exchange for a certain sum of money called the *option price* or *option premium*. The price at which the instrument may be bought or sold is called the *exercise* or *strike price*. The date after which an option is void is called the *expiration date* or *maturity date*.

When an option grants the buyer the right to purchase the designated instrument from the writer, it is called a *call option*. When the option buyer has the right to sell the designated instrument to the writer (seller), the option is called a *put option*. The buyer of an option is said to be *long the option*; the writer (seller) is said to be *short the option*.

Basic Components of the Option Price

The cost to the buyer of an option is primarily a reflection of the option's *intrinsic value* and any additional amount over its intrinsic value. The premium over intrinsic value is often referred to as the *time value of an option*.

The intrinsic value of an option is the economic value of the option if it is exercised immediately. Because the buyer of an option need not exercise the option, and, in fact, will not do so if there is no economic value that will result from exercising, the intrinsic value cannot be less than zero.

The intrinsic value of a call option on a bond is the difference between the current bond price and the strike price. When a call option has intrinsic value, it is said to be "in the money." When the strike price of a call option exceeds the current bond price, the call option is said to be "out of the money" and has no intrinsic value. A call option for which the strike price is equal to the current bond price is said to be "at the money."

These relationships in terms of strike price and current bond price, or alternatively in terms of prevailing market rate and coupon rate, are summarized below for a call option:

- If current bond price > strike price (or if prevailing market rate < coupon rate), then

  1. The intrinsic value is the difference between the current bond price and strike price.
  2. The option is said to be "in the money."

- If current bond price = strike price (or the prevailing market rate = coupon rate), then

  1. The intrinsic value is zero.
  2. The option is said to be "at the money."

- If current bond price < strike price (or the prevailing market rate > coupon rate) then

  1. The intrinsic value is zero.
  2. The option is said to be "out of the money."

For a put option, the intrinsic value is equal to the amount by which the current bond price is below the strike price. When the put option has intrinsic value, the option is said to be in the money.

These relationships are summarized below for a put option:

- If current bond price < strike price (or the prevailing market rate > coupon rate), then

  1. The intrinsic value is the difference between the strike price and current bond price.
  2. The option is said to be "in the money."

- If current bond price = strike price (or prevailing market rate = coupon rate), then

  1. The intrinsic value is zero.
  2. The option is said to be "at the money."

- If current bond price > strike price (or the prevailing market rate < coupon rate), then

  1. The intrinsic value is zero.
  2. The option is said to be "out of the money."

The time value of an option is the amount by which the option price exceeds the intrinsic value. That is,

$$\text{Time value of an option} = \text{Option price} - \text{Intrinsic value}$$

For an at-the-money or out-of-the-money option, the time value of the option is equal to the option price since the intrinsic value is zero. At the expiration date, the time value of the option will be zero. The option price at the expiration date will be equal to its intrinsic value.

Why would an option buyer be willing to pay a premium over the intrinsic value for an option? The reason is that the option buyer believes that at some time prior to expiration changes in the market yield will increase the value of the rights conveyed by the option.

Price Sensitivity of the Option Price

As the price of a bond with an embedded option will be affected by how the price of the embedded option changes, we will look at the sensitivity of the option price to the price of the underlying bond. We focus our attention on call options.

Exhibit 13-2 shows the theoretical price of a call option based on the price of the underlying bond. The horizontal axis is the price of the underlying bond at any given time. The vertical axis is the option price. The shape of the theoretical price of a call option, given the price of the underlying bond, would be the same regardless of the actual option pricing model used. In particular, the relationship between the price of the underlying bond and the theoretical call option price is convex. Thus, option prices also exhibit convexity.

EXHIBIT 13-2   Theoretical Call Price and Price of Underlying Bond

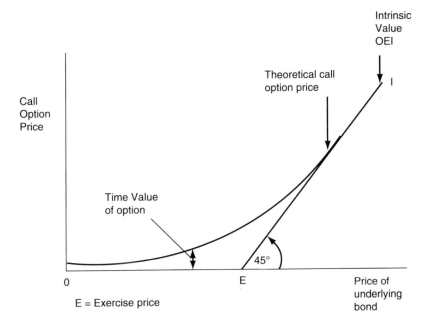

The line from the origin to the strike price on the horizontal axis in Exhibit 13-2 is the intrinsic value of the call option when the price of the underlying bond is less than the strike price because the intrinsic value is zero. The 45 degree line extending from the horizontal axis is the intrinsic value of the call option once the price of the underlying bond exceeds the strike price. The reason is that the intrinsic value of the call option will increase by the same dollar amount as the increase in the price of the underlying bond. For example, if the exercise price is $100 and the price of the underlying bond increases from $100 to $101, the intrinsic value will increase by $1. If the price of the bond increases from $101 to $110, the intrinsic value of the option will increase from $1 to $9. Thus, the slope of the line representing the intrinsic value after the strike price is reached is 1.

Because the theoretical call option price is shown by the convex curve, the difference between the theoretical call option price and the intrinsic value at any given price for the underlying bond is the time value of the option.

Exhibit 13-3 shows the theoretical call option price but with a tangent line drawn at the price of $P*$. The tangent line in Exhibit 13-3 can be used to estimate what the new option price will be (and therefore what the change in the option price will be) if the price of the underlying bond changes. Because of the convexity of the relationship between the option

EXHIBIT 13-3   Estimating The Theoretical Option Price with a Tangent Line

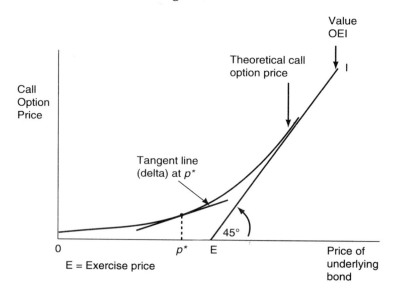

price and the price of the underlying bond, the tangent line does a good job of approximating what the new option price will be for a small change in the price of the underlying bond. For large changes, however, the tangent line does not do as good a job in approximating what the new option price will be.

The slope of the tangent line shows how the theoretical call option price will change for small changes in the price of the underlying bond. The slope of the tangent line is commonly referred to as the *delta* or *hedge ratio* of the option. Specifically,

$$\text{Delta} = \frac{\text{Change in price of call option}}{\text{Change in price of underlying bond}}$$

For example, a delta of .5 means that a $1 change in the price of the underlying bond will change the price of the call option by $.50.

Exhibit 13-4 shows the theoretical call option price with three tangent lines drawn. The steeper the slope of the tangent line, the greater the delta. When an option is deep out of the money (that is, the price of the underlying bond is substantially below the strike price), the slope of the tangent line is relatively flat (see line 1 in Exhibit 13-4). This means a delta close to zero. To understand why, consider a call option with a strike

**EXHIBIT 13-4 Delta of a Call Option at Three Prices
for the Underlying Bond**

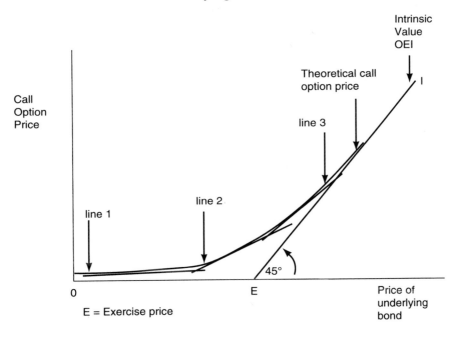

E = Exercise price

price of 100 and 2 months to expiration. If the price of the underlying bond is $20, its price would not increase by much if the price of the underlying bond increases by $1 from $20 to $21.

For a call option that is deep in the money, the delta will be close to 1. That is, the call option price will increase almost dollar for dollar with an increase in the price of the underlying bond. In terms of Exhibit 13-4, the slope of the tangent line approaches the slope of the intrinsic value line after the strike price. As we stated earlier, the slope of that line is 1. Thus, the delta for a call option varies from zero (for deep out of the money call options) to 1 (for deep in the money call options). The delta for an at-the-money call option is approximately .5.

We also can measure the convexity of a call option. Recall from Chapter 4 that the convexity of a bond measures the change in the dollar duration. For call options, convexity measures the change in delta. The measure of convexity for options is commonly referred to as *gamma* and is measured as follows:

$$\text{Gamma} = \frac{\text{Change in delta}}{\text{Change in price of underlying bond}}$$

OPTION PRICING APPROACH

To illustrate the option pricing approach, consider the General Motors Acceptance Corporation (GMAC) 12% coupon bond of June 2005 that is callable in June 1990 at 102. A bondholder who owned this bond on April 1, 1988, effectively owned a noncallable bond with 17 years and 2 months to maturity and sold a call option granting the issuer (GMAC) the right to call away from the bondholder 15 years of cash flows beginning June 1, 1990. The exercise price for this call option is 102.

The price of the noncallable bond and the theoretical price of the embedded call option at each yield level are shown in Exhibit 13-5. The theoretical price of the call option is based on a binomial option pricing model.[1] As we explain in Chapter 17, a key determinant of the value of an option is the expected future interest rate volatility. The volatility assumption used to compute the theoretical call option price in Exhibit 13-5 is 12% per year.

The difference between the price of the noncallable bond and the theoretical price of the call option is the price of the callable bond. A graph of the price/yield relationship in Exhibit 13-5 is shown in Exhibit

---

[1] The theoretical option price for this illustration was provided by Andrew Ho of Kidder Peabody.

13-6. The shape is consistent with the price/yield relationship for callable bonds in Exhibit 13-1.

A property of the price of a call option is that it increases when the expected interest rate volatility increases. Exhibit 13-7 shows the theoretical price of the call option when interest rate volatility is assumed to be 20% per year. The theoretical price of the call option is greater in Exhibit 13-7 than in Exhibit 13-5 because of the higher interest rate volatility assumed. Since the theoretical price of the call option is higher, the price of the callable bond is lower in Exhibit 13-7 than in Exhibit 13-5.

EXHIBIT 13-5   Price/Yield Relationship and Theoretical Option Price for GMAC 12% of June 2005 Callable at 102 in June 1990 (Settlement 6/1/88, 12% Interest Rate Volatility Assumption)

Assumptions to compute theoretical call option price:
Binomial option pricing model
Interest rate volatility: 12%
Short-term interest rate: 6%

Yield	Noncallable Bond Price	Theoretical Option Price	Theoretical Callable Bond Price
20.51	60	.000	60.000
20.18	61	.000	61.000
19.86	62	.000	62.000
19.55	63	.000	63.000
19.24	64	.000	64.000
18.95	65	.000	65.000
18.66	66	.000	66.000
18.39	67	.000	67.000
18.11	68	.000	68.000
17.85	69	.001	68.999
17.59	70	.001	69.999
17.34	71	.001	70.999
17.10	72	.002	71.998
16.86	73	.002	72.998
16.63	74	.003	73.997
16.40	75	.005	74.995
16.18	76	.006	75.994
15.96	77	.008	76.992
15.75	78	.012	77.988
15.54	79	.016	78.984
15.33	80	.020	79.980
15.13	81	.027	80.973
14.94	82	.036	81.964
14.75	83	.046	82.954
14.56	84	.057	83.943
14.38	85	.075	84.925
14.20	86	.095	85.905

Yield	Noncallable Bond Price	Theoretical Option Price	Theoretical Callable Bond Price
14.02	87	.116	86.884
13.85	88	.146	87.854
13.68	89	.183	88.817
13.51	90	.223	89.777
13.35	91	.265	90.735
13.19	92	.330	91.670
13.03	93	.398	92.602
12.87	94	.469	93.531
12.72	95	.557	94.443
12.57	96	.667	95.333
12.42	97	.783	96.217
12.28	98	.904	97.096
12.00	100	1.235	98.765
11.73	102	1.606	100.394
11.46	104	2.112	101.888
11.33	105	2.380	102.620
11.20	106	2.661	103.339
11.07	107	3.012	103.988
10.95	108	3.373	104.627
10.83	109	3.742	105.258
10.71	110	4.134	105.866
10.59	111	4.596	106.404
10.47	112	5.067	106.933
10.35	113	5.548	107.452
10.24	114	6.056	107.944
10.13	115	6.631	108.369
10.02	116	7.215	108.785
9.91	117	7.808	109.192
9.80	118	8.429	109.571
9.69	119	9.111	109.889
9.59	120	9.801	110.199
9.48	121	10.499	110.501
9.38	122	11.220	110.780
9.28	123	11.996	111.004
9.18	124	12.778	111.222
9.08	125	13.567	111.433
8.98	126	14.372	111.628
8.89	127	15.224	111.776
8.79	128	16.080	111.920
8.60	130	17.813	112.187
8.42	132	19.632	112.368
8.24	134	21.466	112.534
8.07	136	23.362	112.638
7.90	138	25.267	112.733
7.73	140	27.210	112.790
7.24	146	33.106	112.894
6.79	152	39.075	112.925
6.36	158	45.066	112.934
5.96	164	51.064	112.936
5.57	170	57.064	112.936

EXHIBIT 13-6   Price / Yield Relationship for GMAC 12%,
June 2005, Callable at 102 in June 1990
(June 1, 1988, Settlement)

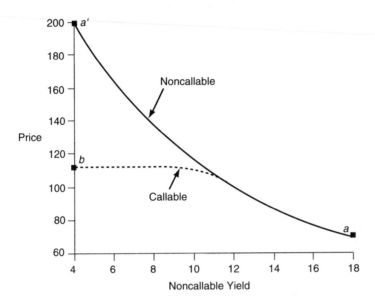

EXHIBIT 13-7   Price/Yield Relationship and Theoretical Option
Price for GMAC 12% of June 2005 Callable at 102 in
June 1990 (Settlement 6/1/88, 20% Interest Rate
Volatility Assumption)

Assumptions to compute theoretical call option price:
Binomial option pricing model
Interest rate volatility: 20%
Short-term interest rate: 6%

Yield	Noncallable Bond Price	Theoretical Option Price	Theoretical Callable Bond Price
20.51	60	.019	59.981
20.18	61	.024	60.976
19.86	62	.029	61.971
19.55	63	.035	62.965
19.24	64	.044	63.956
18.95	65	.055	64.945
18.66	66	.066	65.934
18.39	67	.078	66.922
18.11	68	.092	67.908
17.85	69	.112	68.888
17.59	70	.134	69.866
17.34	71	.158	70.842

Yield	Noncallable Bond Price	Theoretical Option Price	Theoretical Callable Bond Price
17.10	72	.182	71.818
16.86	73	.208	72.792
16.63	74	.248	73.752
16.40	75	.290	74.710
16.18	76	.334	75.666
15.96	77	.379	76.621
15.75	78	.427	77.573
15.54	79	.491	78.509
15.33	80	.564	79.436
15.13	81	.640	80.360
14.94	82	.718	81.282
14.75	83	.800	82.200
14.56	84	.887	83.113
14.38	85	1.006	83.994
14.20	86	1.128	84.872
14.02	87	1.254	85.746
13.85	88	1.384	86.616
13.68	89	1.518	87.482
13.51	90	1.665	88.335
13.35	91	1.851	89.149
13.19	92	2.041	89.959
13.03	93	2.235	90.765
12.87	94	2.434	91.566
12.72	95	2.637	92.363
12.57	96	2.855	93.145
12.42	97	3.125	93.875
12.28	98	3.399	94.601
12.00	100	3.964	96.036
11.73	102	4.550	97.450
11.46	104	5.285	98.715
11.33	105	5.664	99.336
11.20	106	6.049	99.951
11.07	107	6.439	100.561
10.95	108	6.835	101.165
10.83	109	7.272	101.728
10.71	110	7.752	102.248
10.59	111	8.238	102.762
10.47	112	8.730	103.270
10.35	113	9.228	103.772
10.24	114	9.731	104.269
10.13	115	10.240	104.760
10.02	116	10.821	105.179
9.91	117	11.414	105.586
9.80	118	12.013	105.987
9.69	119	12.618	106.382
9.59	120	13.227	106.773
9.48	121	13.842	107.158
9.38	122	14.479	107.521
9.28	123	15.172	107.828
9.18	124	15.871	108.129
9.08	125	16.575	108.425

Yield	Noncallable Bond Price	Theoretical Option Price	Theoretical Callable Bond Price
8.98	126	17.283	108.717
8.89	127	17.996	109.004
8.79	128	18.713	109.287
8.60	130	20.250	109.750
8.42	132	21.832	110.168
8.24	134	23.431	110.569
8.07	136	25.076	110.924
7.90	138	26.797	111.203
7.73	140	28.529	111.471
7.24	146	33.925	112.075
6.79	152	39.541	112.459
6.36	158	45.311	112.689
5.96	164	51.183	112.817
5.57	170	57.117	112.883

This also can be seen in Exhibit 13-8, which shows the price/yield relationship assuming: (1) the issue is not callable, (2) the issue is callable and interest rate volatility is assumed to be 12% per year, and (3) the issue is callable and interest rate volatility is assumed to be 20% per year. Notice that the price/yield relationship for the callable bond assuming 20% interest rate volatility begins to depart from the price/yield relationship for the bond if it is not callable at a higher yield than the price/yield relationship for the callable bond assuming 12% interest rate volatility. When the market yield is deep in the money, the price/yield relationship for the callable bond is the same regardless of the interest rate volatility assumption.

Option-Adjusted Yield

Given these relationships for a callable bond, an investor wants to know if the noncallable bond is correctly priced in the sense that there is adequate reward for the credit risk associated with owning the bond. Although in our previous illustrations we have started with the price of the noncallable bond and computed the theoretical price of the callable bond by subtracting the theoretical price of the call option, in fact the price that the noncallable bond will sell at in the market is not directly observable. It can be estimated by rewriting equation (13.1) as:

(13.3) Noncallable bond price = Callable bond price + Call option price

The price of the noncallable bond can be determined if the price of the callable bond and the call option price are known. Given the estimated call option price based on some option pricing model and the observed

EXHIBIT 13-8   Price/Yield Relationship for GMAC Callable Bond for June 1, 1988, Settlement, Based on Two Interest Rate Volatility Assumptions

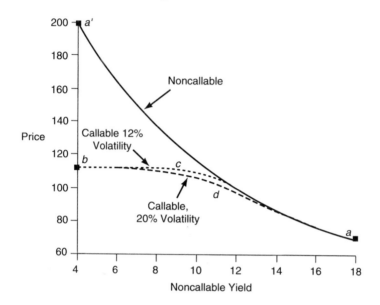

market price of the callable bond, we can add the two prices to get the *implied price of the noncallable bond.*

Given the implied price of the noncallable bond, it is then simple to compute the yield on this bond if it is not called but held to maturity. The yield is the interest rate that will make the present value of the cash flows for the bond, if held to maturity, equal to the implied price of the noncallable bond. The yield computed is referred to as the *option-adjusted yield.*[2]

To illustrate the option-adjusted yield, suppose an investor is considering an 8% coupon callable corporate bond selling at 102 with 20 years to maturity and callable at 104. Suppose also that, using an option pricing model, the call option price is estimated to be 4.21. Then the option-adjusted yield is computed by first calculating the implied price for the noncallable bond as follows:

> Observed callable bond price = 102
> Theoretical call option price = 4.21
> Implied price for noncallable bond = 102 + 4.21 = 106.21

---

[2] When the analysis is applied to callable bonds that have no other embedded options, the term *call-adjusted yield* is commonly used.

The option-adjusted yield is computed by finding the interest rate that will make the present value of 40 coupon payments of $4 every six months plus $100 at the end of 40 6-month periods equal to $104.21. The calculated 6-month interest rate that satisfies this is 3.7%. Doubling this interest rate gives the option-adjusted yield of 7.4% on a bond-equivalent yield basis.

For an actual application, consider once again the GMAC callable bond. Suppose that the *observed* price for the bond assuming June 1, 1988, settlement is 106.933. Also suppose that based on an option pricing model and a volatility assumption of 12% per year, the theoretical option price for the call option is 5.067. The implied noncallable bond price is found as follows:

> Observed callable bond price = 106.933
> Theoretical call option price = 5.067
> Implied noncallable bond price = 106.933 + 5.067 = 112

The option-adjusted yield is found by determining the interest rate that will make the present value of the cash flows equal to the implied price of the noncallable bond (112). The cash flow in this case assumes that the bond is not called and held to maturity. The semiannual interest rate that will make the present value of the cash flows equal to 112 is 5.237%. Doubling this interest rate gives the option-adjusted yield computed on a bond-equivalent basis. The option-adjusted yield is therefore 10.474%.

The option-adjusted yield is the implied yield on the noncallable bond. A noncallable bond is priced fairly if the option-adjusted yield for a callable bond is the proper yield for a noncallable bond with the same features and of the same issuer. A bond is rich, or overvalued, if the option-adjusted yield is less; it is cheap, or undervalued, if the option-adjusted yield is more.

An option-adjusted yield spread can be calculated by computing the difference between the yield on a comparable but otherwise noncallable bond and the option-adjusted yield. Herein lies a problem with the option pricing approach: how do we determine the benchmark to which the callable bond should be compared? In the option-adjusted spread valuation technique that is described in the next chapter, a benchmark bond is not needed.

Option-Adjusted Duration

For a callable bond, it is inappropriate to use modified duration because the expected cash flow changes as the yield changes. To understand the price volatility of a callable bond resulting from a change in interest rates, it is necessary to look at how the two components of the callable bond react. A change in interest rates will affect the price volatility of the noncallable bond component depending on the duration of the noncallable bond. It will also affect the price of the embedded call option.

More specifically, if interest rates rise: (1) the price of the noncallable bond component will fall, and (2) the price of the call option will fall. The latter will fall because the call option becomes less valuable as interest rates rise. As the price of a callable bond is the difference between the price of the noncallable bond and the price of the embedded call option, a rise in interest rates will reduce the price of a callable bond but not by as much as the price of the noncallable bond because the price of the call option falls. The opposite occurs if interest rates fall. That is, the price of the noncallable bond component rises, and the price of the embedded call option rises. The net effect is an increase in the price of the callable bond but by less than the price of the noncallable bond.

As shown in the appendix to this chapter, the duration of a callable bond after adjusting for the call option, commonly referred to as the *option-adjusted duration*, is equal to:

Option-adjusted duration =

$$(13.4) \quad \frac{Price_{NCB}}{Price_{CB}} \times Dur_{NCB} \times (1 - Delta)$$

where

$$
\begin{aligned}
Price_{NCB} &= \text{Price of noncallable bond} \\
Price_{CB} &= \text{Price of callable bond} \\
Dur_{NCB} &= \text{Modified duration of the noncallable bond} \\
Delta &= \text{Delta of the call option}
\end{aligned}
$$

The delta measures the change in the price of the call option when the price of the underlying bond changes. As explained earlier, the delta varies between 0 and 1.

As can be seen from equation (13.4), the option-adjusted duration depends on the following three elements:

1. The ratio of the price of the noncallable bond to the price of the callable bond. Recall that the difference between the price of a noncallable bond and a callable bond is equal to the price of the call option. The higher (lower) the price of the call option, the greater (smaller) the ratio. Thus we see that the option-adjusted duration will depend on the price of the call option.

2. The duration of the corresponding noncallable (option- free) bond.

3. The delta of the call option.

Let's apply the option-adjusted duration to two extreme cases — a deep-discount callable bond and a premium callable bond with a coupon rate considerably above the prevailing market yield. First consider the deep-discount bond.

For a deep-discount bond, the coupon rate is substantially below the current market yield. For example, a 20-year bond with a coupon rate of 5% will trade at a deep discount when the current market yield on comparable bonds is 15%. Since it would not be economical for the issuer to call the 5% coupon bond and replace it with a 15% coupon bond, the call option is deep out of the money. The option price would be low for this bond, and therefore the ratio of the noncallable bond price to the callable bond price would be close to 1. When the option is deep out of the money, the delta is close to 0. Therefore,

$$\frac{\text{Price}_{\text{NCB}}}{\text{Price}_{\text{CB}}} = 1$$

$$\text{Delta} = 0$$

Substituting into equation (13.4) gives:

$$\text{Option - adjusted duration} = 1 \times \text{Dur}_{\text{NCB}} \times (1-0)$$
$$= \text{Dur}_{\text{NCB}}$$

Thus, the option-adjusted duration of a deep discount callable bond will be the same as its duration assuming it is noncallable.

Now let's consider the duration of a premium callable bond with a coupon rate substantially higher than the current market yield. As an example, consider a 20-year bond with a coupon rate of 16% when the current market yield is 6% (the bond would sell at a premium). The call option would be deep in the money because it would be highly beneficial for the issuer to call the issue and issue new bonds with a coupon rate of 6%. Once again, recall that the delta of a deep in-the-money call option is 1. Substituting 1 for delta into equation (13.4) gives:

$$\text{Option - adjusted duration} = \frac{\text{Price}_{\text{NCB}}}{\text{Price}_{\text{CB}}} \times \text{Dur}_{\text{NCB}} \times (1-1)$$

$$= 0$$

Thus, the option-adjusted duration for a premium callable bond in which the coupon rate is substantially higher than the current market yield would be 0.

Anywhere in between a deep-discount bond and a premium bond with a high coupon rate relative to the prevailing market yield, the option-adjusted duration of a callable bond will be less than the duration of a noncallable bond.

Let's see how we can apply these concepts to the GMAC callable bonds. Suppose that the observed price is 106.933 and the theoretical call option price is 5.067. The implied price of the noncallable bond is 112, and the option-adjusted yield is 10.474%. The modified duration of the noncallable bond selling for 112 and with a yield of 10.474% would be 7.67. Based on the same option pricing model that generated the theoretical call option price of 5.067, the delta for the call option would be .486. The option-adjusted duration for the GMAC callable bond based on the information given would be:

P_{NCB}	=	Implied price of noncallable bond	=	112
P_{CB}	=	Observed price of callable bond	=	106.933
Dur_{NCB}	=	Duration of noncallable bond	=	7.67
Delta	=	Delta of call option	=	.486

$$\text{Option - adjusted duration} = \frac{112}{106.933} \times 7.67 \times (1-.486)$$

$$= 4.13$$

Option-Adjusted Convexity

As shown in the appendix to this chapter, the option-adjusted convexity can be found as follows:

Option-adjusted convexity =

$$(13.5) \quad \frac{\text{Price}_{NCB}}{\text{Price}_{CB}} \left[\text{Con}_{NCB} \times (1 - \text{Delta}) - \text{Price}_{NCB} \times \text{Gamma} \times (\text{Dur}_{NCB})^2 \right]$$

where

Con_{NCB}	=	Convexity of the noncallable bond
Gamma	=	Gamma of the call option

The gamma of a call option measures the convexity of the call option.

The option-adjusted duration depends on the price of the call option (i.e., the ratio of the price of the noncallable bond to the price of the callable bond), the duration of the noncallable bond, and the delta. The option-adjusted convexity depends on the same three factors plus the convexity of the noncallable bond and the gamma of the call option.

Because the gamma of a call option is positive and the delta is between 0 and 1, option-adjusted convexity will be less than the convexity of the noncallable bond. Unlike the convexity for an option-free bond, which is always positive, the option-adjusted convexity may be negative. This occurs when the term in brackets in equation (13.5) is negative. That is, when

$$\text{Con}_{NCB} \times (1 - \text{Delta}) < \text{Price}_{NCB} \times \text{Gamma} \times \left(\text{Dur}_{NCB}\right)^2$$

This will occur when the yield falls so that the call option moves deep in the money, and the delta will approach 1. The term on the left-hand side will approach 0, and the term on the right hand side will be positive, resulting in a negative value for the term in the brackets in the option-adjusted convexity formula.

Continuing with the GMAC callable bond, assume the same information earlier. The convexity of the noncallable bond is 91.82. The gamma for the call option (based on the option pricing model used to calculate the theoretical call option price) is .02878. The option-adjusted convexity is then:

P_{NCB}	=	Implied price of noncallable bond	=	112
P_{CB}	=	Observed price of callable bond	=	106.933
Dur_{NCB}	=	Duration of noncallable bond	=	7.67
Con_{NCB}	=	Convexity of noncallable bond	=	91.82
Delta	=	Delta of call option	=	.486

Option-adjusted convexity =

$$\frac{112}{106.933}\left[91.82 \times (1-.486) - 112 \times .02878 \times (7.67)^2\right]$$

$$= -149$$

The option-adjusted convexity is negative in this example because the option-adjusted yield is 10.474%, which is less than the coupon rate of 12%. The call option is therefore in the money.

Exhibits 13-9 and 13-10 show the price/yield relationship for the GMAC callable bond, the duration for the noncallable bond, the duration for the callable bond, the convexity of the noncallable bond, the delta of the call option, the gamma of the call option, and the convexity of the callable bond. Exhibit 13-9 assumes that interest rate volatility will be 12%; Exhibit 13-10 assumes 20%. Notice in both exhibits that the duration of the callable bond approaches the duration of the noncallable bond as the yield rises above the coupon rate of 12%. As yields decline below 12%, the difference between the duration of the callable bond and the noncallable bond increases.

EXHIBIT 13-9 Option Adjusted Duration and Convexity for GMAC 12% of June 2005 Callable at 102 in June 1990 (Settlement 6/1/88, 12% Interest Rate Volatility Assumption)

Assumptions to compute theoretical call option price:
Binomial option pricing model
Interest rate volatility: 12%
Short-term interest rate: 6%

	Noncallable Bond			Call Option			Callable Bond		
Yield	Price	Dur.	Con.	Price	Delta	Gamma	Price	Dur.	Con.
20.51	60	4.96	45.4	.000	.00	.000001	60.000	4.9	45.4
20.18	61	5.03	46.5	.000	.00	.000003	61.000	5.0	46.5
19.86	62	5.10	47.6	.000	.00	.000004	62.000	5.1	47.6
19.55	63	5.17	48.7	.000	.00	.000007	63.000	5.1	48.7
19.24	64	5.24	49.7	.000	.00	.000011	64.000	5.2	49.7
18.95	65	5.30	50.8	.000	.00	.000016	65.000	5.3	50.8
18.66	66	5.37	51.8	.000	.00	.000026	66.000	5.3	51.8
18.39	67	5.43	52.9	.000	.00	.000037	67.000	5.4	52.8
18.11	68	5.49	53.9	.000	.00	.000051	68.000	5.4	53.8
17.85	69	5.56	54.9	.001	.00	.000077	68.999	5.5	54.8
17.59	70	5.62	55.9	.001	.00	.000105	69.999	5.6	55.7
17.34	71	5.68	57.0	.001	.00	.000139	70.999	5.6	56.6
17.10	72	5.74	58.0	.002	.00	.000198	71.998	5.7	57.5
16.86	73	5.80	59.0	.002	.00	.000262	72.998	5.8	58.3
16.63	74	5.86	59.9	.003	.00	.000331	73.997	5.8	59.0
16.40	75	5.92	60.9	.005	.00	.000455	74.995	5.9	59.6
16.18	76	5.98	61.9	.006	.00	.000587	75.994	5.9	60.2
15.96	77	6.04	62.8	.008	.00	.000725	76.992	6.0	60.7
15.75	78	6.09	63.8	.012	.00	.000942	77.988	6.0	60.9
15.54	79	6.15	64.7	.016	.00	.001187	78.984	6.1	60.9
15.33	80	6.20	65.7	.020	.00	.001441	79.980	6.1	60.9
15.13	81	6.26	66.6	.027	.00	.001775	80.973	6.2	60.5
14.94	82	6.31	67.5	.036	.01	.002191	81.964	6.2	59.7
14.75	83	6.36	68.4	.046	.01	.002620	82.954	6.2	58.9
14.56	84	6.42	69.4	.057	.01	.003079	83.943	6.3	57.7
14.38	85	6.47	70.3	.075	.01	.003725	84.925	6.3	55.8
14.20	86	6.52	71.1	.095	.02	.004383	85.905	6.3	53.6
14.02	87	6.57	72.0	.116	.02	.005054	86.884	6.4	51.2
13.85	88	6.62	72.9	.146	.03	.005875	87.854	6.4	48.0
13.68	89	6.67	73.8	.183	.03	.006795	88.817	6.4	44.1
13.51	90	6.72	74.6	.223	.04	.007724	89.777	6.4	39.9
13.35	91	6.77	75.5	.265	.05	.008673	90.735	6.4	35.4

Yield	Noncallable Bond			Call Option			Callable Bond		
	Price	Dur.	Con.	Price	Delta	Gamma	Price	Dur.	Con.
13.19	92	6.82	76.3	.330	.06	.009839	91.670	6.4	29.5
13.03	93	6.86	77.2	.398	.07	.011006	92.602	6.3	23.3
12.87	94	6.91	78.0	.469	.08	.012174	93.531	6.3	16.8
12.72	95	6.96	78.8	.557	.09	.013406	94.443	6.3	9.5
12.57	96	7.00	79.6	.667	.11	.014725	95.333	6.2	1.4
12.42	97	7.05	80.4	.783	.12	.016032	96.217	6.2	−7.0
12.28	98	7.09	81.2	.904	.14	.017327	97.096	6.1	−15.8
12.00	100	7.18	82.8	1.235	.18	.019921	98.765	5.9	−35.2
11.73	102	7.27	84.4	1.606	.22	.022422	100.394	5.8	−55.9
11.46	104	7.35	85.9	2.112	.26	.024551	101.888	5.4	−76.7
11.33	105	7.39	86.7	2.380	.29	.025551	102.620	5.3	−87.4
11.20	106	7.43	87.4	2.661	.31	.026493	103.339	5.2	−98.1
11.07	107	7.47	88.2	3.012	.34	.027128	103.988	5.0	−107.5
10.95	108	7.51	88.9	3.373	.37	.027716	104.627	4.8	−117.0
10.83	109	7.55	89.6	3.742	.40	.028259	105.258	4.6	−126.4
10.71	110	7.59	90.3	4.134	.42	.028689	105.866	4.5	−135.5
10.59	111	7.63	91.1	4.596	.45	.028756	106.404	4.3	−142.5
10.47	112	7.67	91.8	5.067	.48	.028778	106.933	4.1	−149.3
10.35	113	7.71	92.5	5.548	.51	.028757	107.452	3.9	−155.9
10.24	114	7.75	93.2	6.056	.54	.028601	107.944	3.7	−161.7
10.13	115	7.78	93.9	6.631	.57	.028099	108.369	3.5	−165.1
10.02	116	7.82	94.6	7.215	.59	.027564	108.785	3.3	−168.2
9.91	117	7.86	95.2	7.808	.62	.026997	109.192	3.1	−170.9
9.80	118	7.89	95.9	8.429	.65	.026317	109.571	2.9	−172.7
9.69	119	7.93	96.6	9.111	.67	.025370	109.889	2.7	−172.0
9.59	120	7.96	97.2	9.801	.70	.024405	110.199	2.5	−171.0
9.48	121	8.00	97.9	10.499	.72	.023425	110.501	2.3	−169.6
9.38	122	8.03	98.6	11.220	.75	.022384	110.780	2.2	−167.3
9.28	123	8.07	99.2	11.996	.77	.021192	111.004	2.0	−163.1
9.18	124	8.10	99.9	12.778	.79	.020000	111.222	1.8	−158.6
9.08	125	8.14	100.5	13.567	.81	.018809	111.433	1.7	−153.6
8.98	126	8.17	101.1	14.372	.83	.017610	111.628	1.5	−148.1
8.89	127	8.20	101.8	15.224	.84	.016387	111.776	1.4	−141.7
8.79	128	8.24	102.4	16.080	.86	.015178	111.920	1.2	−134.9
8.60	130	8.30	103.6	17.813	.89	.012809	112.187	1.0	−120.3
8.42	132	8.36	104.8	19.632	.91	.010663	112.368	.8	−105.4
8.24	134	8.43	106.0	21.466	.93	.008606	112.534	.6	−89.6
8.07	136	8.49	107.2	23.362	.95	.006928	112.638	.4	−75.7
7.90	138	8.55	108.4	25.267	.96	.005337	112.733	.3	−61.3
7.73	140	8.61	109.5	27.210	.97	.004155	112.790	.2	−50.0
7.24	146	8.78	112.8	33.106	.99	.001608	112.894	.0	−22.1
6.79	152	8.94	116.0	39.075	.99	.000538	112.925	.0	−8.4
6.36	158	9.10	119.1	45.066	.99	.000135	112.934	.0	−2.3
5.96	164	9.25	122.0	51.064	1.00	.000029	112.936	.0	−.5
5.57	170	9.39	124.8	57.064	1.00	.000004	112.936	.0	−.0

EXHIBIT 13-10 Option Adjusted Duration and Convexity for GMAC 12% of June 2005 Callable at 102 in June 1990 (Settlement 6/1/88, 20% Interest Rate Volatility Assumption)

Assumptions to compute theoretical call option price:
Binomial option pricing model
Interest rate volatility: 20%
Short-term interest rate: 6%

Yield	Noncallable Bond			Call Option			Callable Bond		
	Price	Dur.	Con.	Price	Delta	Gamma	Price	Dur.	Con.
20.51	60	4.96	45.4	.019	.00	.000845	59.981	4.9	44.0
20.18	61	5.03	46.5	.024	.00	.000987	60.976	5.0	44.8
19.86	62	5.10	47.6	.029	.00	.001130	61.971	5.0	45.5
19.55	63	5.17	48.7	.035	.00	.001274	62.965	5.1	46.2
19.24	64	5.24	49.7	.044	.00	.001493	63.956	5.1	46.7
18.95	65	5.30	50.8	.055	.01	.001716	64.945	5.2	47.1
18.66	66	5.37	51.8	.066	.01	.001939	65.934	5.3	47.5
18.39	67	5.43	52.9	.078	.01	.002161	66.922	5.3	47.9
18.11	68	5.49	53.9	.092	.01	.002397	67.908	5.4	48.2
17.85	69	5.56	54.9	.112	.01	.002718	68.888	5.4	48.1
17.59	70	5.62	55.9	.134	.02	.003036	69.866	5.5	48.1
17.34	71	5.68	57.0	.158	.02	.003352	70.842	5.5	47.9
17.10	72	5.74	58.0	.182	.02	.003665	71.818	5.5	47.7
16.86	73	5.80	59.0	.208	.03	.003982	72.792	5.6	47.4
16.63	74	5.86	59.9	.248	.03	.004400	73.752	5.6	46.7
16.40	75	5.92	60.9	.290	.04	.004812	74.710	5.7	45.9
16.18	76	5.98	61.9	.334	.04	.005218	75.666	5.7	45.0
15.96	77	6.04	62.8	.379	.05	.005621	76.621	5.7	44.0
15.75	78	6.09	63.8	.427	.05	.006018	77.573	5.7	43.0
15.54	79	6.15	64.7	.491	.06	.006480	78.509	5.7	41.5
15.33	80	6.20	65.7	.564	.07	.006963	79.436	5.8	39.8
15.13	81	6.26	66.6	.640	.07	.007438	80.360	5.8	38.1
14.94	82	6.31	67.5	.718	.08	.007906	81.282	5.8	36.2
14.75	83	6.36	68.4	.800	.09	.008367	82.200	5.8	34.2
14.56	84	6.42	69.4	.887	.10	.008828	83.113	5.8	32.1
14.38	85	6.47	70.3	1.006	.11	.009336	83.994	5.8	29.6
14.20	86	6.52	71.1	1.128	.12	.009835	84.872	5.8	26.9
14.02	87	6.57	72.0	1.254	.13	.010323	85.746	5.7	24.1
13.85	88	6.62	72.9	1.384	.14	.010803	86.616	5.7	21.2
13.68	89	6.67	73.8	1.518	.15	.011274	87.482	5.7	18.2
13.51	90	6.72	74.6	1.665	.16	.011739	88.335	5.7	15.0
13.35	91	6.77	75.5	1.851	.17	.012198	89.149	5.7	11.6
13.19	92	6.82	76.3	2.041	.18	.012646	89.959	5.6	8.0
13.03	93	6.86	77.2	2.235	.20	.013084	90.765	5.6	4.4
12.87	94	6.91	78.0	2.434	.21	.013511	91.566	5.5	.6
12.72	95	6.96	78.8	2.637	.22	.013929	92.363	5.5	−3.2
12.57	96	7.00	79.6	2.855	.24	.014328	93.145	5.4	−7.2
12.42	97	7.05	80.4	3.125	.25	.014669	93.875	5.4	−11.1
12.28	98	7.09	81.2	3.399	.27	.015000	94.601	5.3	−15.2

	Noncallable Bond			Call Option			Callable Bond		
Yield	Price	Dur.	Con.	Price	Delta	Gamma	Price	Dur.	Con.
12.00	100	7.18	82.8	3.964	.30	.015630	96.036	5.2	−23.7
11.72	102	7.27	84.4	4.550	.33	.016222	97.450	5.1	−32.5
11.46	104	7.35	85.9	5.285	.36	.016563	98.715	4.9	−40.6
11.33	105	7.39	86.7	5.664	.38	.016714	99.336	4.8	−44.8
11.20	106	7.43	87.4	6.049	.39	.016857	99.951	4.7	−49.0
11.07	107	7.47	88.2	6.439	.41	.016991	100.561	4.6	−53.2
10.95	108	7.51	88.9	6.835	.43	.017117	101.165	4.5	−57.5
10.83	109	7.55	89.6	7.272	.44	.017167	101.728	4.4	−61.5
10.71	110	7.59	90.3	7.752	.46	.017135	102.248	4.3	−65.1
10.59	111	7.63	91.1	8.238	.48	.017097	102.762	4.2	−68.6
10.47	112	7.67	91.8	8.730	.50	.017051	103.270	4.1	−72.2
10.35	113	7.71	92.5	9.228	.51	.017000	103.772	4.0	−75.7
10.24	114	7.75	93.2	9.731	.53	.016942	104.269	3.9	−79.3
10.13	115	7.78	93.9	10.240	.55	.016879	104.760	3.8	−82.9
10.02	116	7.82	94.6	10.821	.56	.016680	105.179	3.7	−85.5
9.91	117	7.86	95.2	11.414	.58	.016465	105.586	3.6	−87.9
9.80	118	7.89	95.9	12.013	.60	.016246	105.987	3.5	−90.3
9.69	119	7.93	96.6	12.618	.61	.016023	106.382	3.4	−92.7
9.59	120	7.96	97.2	13.227	.63	.015797	106.773	3.2	−95.0
9.48	121	8.00	97.9	13.842	.64	.015568	107.158	3.1	−97.3
9.38	122	8.03	98.6	14.479	.66	.015308	107.521	3.0	−99.3
9.28	123	8.07	99.2	15.172	.67	.014961	107.828	2.9	−100.4
9.18	124	8.10	99.9	15.871	.69	.014613	108.129	2.8	−101.4
9.08	125	8.14	100.5	16.575	.70	.014265	108.425	2.7	−102.3
8.98	126	8.17	101.1	17.283	.72	.013915	108.717	2.6	−103.1
8.89	127	8.20	101.8	17.996	.73	.013564	109.004	2.5	−103.8
8.79	128	8.24	102.4	18.713	.75	.013212	109.287	2.4	−104.4
8.60	130	8.30	103.6	20.250	.77	.012414	109.750	2.2	−104.1
8.42	132	8.36	104.8	21.832	.79	.011589	110.168	2.0	−103.0
8.24	134	8.43	106.0	23.431	.82	.010769	110.569	1.8	−101.3
8.07	136	8.49	107.2	25.076	.84	.009946	110.924	1.6	−98.9
7.90	138	8.55	108.4	26.797	.86	.009118	111.203	1.4	−95.4
7.73	140	8.61	109.5	28.529	.87	.008301	111.471	1.3	−91.5
7.24	146	8.78	112.8	33.925	.92	.006038	112.075	.8	−77.0
6.79	152	8.94	116.0	39.541	.95	.004126	112.459	.5	−60.3
6.36	158	9.10	119.1	45.311	.97	.002635	112.689	.3	−43.8
5.96	164	9.25	122.0	51.183	.98	.001563	112.817	.1	−29.3
5.57	170	9.39	124.8	57.117	.99	.000854	112.883	.1	−17.9

SUMMARY

Most bonds issued in bond markets throughout the world have some type of embedded option, and we have provided here a framework for evaluating such bonds. Our primary focus has been on bonds that are callable. The disadvantages of the call feature from the investor's perspective as interest rates decline is twofold. First, there is reinvestment risk. Second, the upside potential of a callable bond is limited compared to an otherwise noncallable bond, a feature referred to as price compression or negative convexity. The limitations of using the conventional methodology for evaluating callable bonds were explained.

The option pricing approach can be employed to value bonds with embedded options. This approach requires that the value of the embedded options be estimated using an option pricing model. It allows calculation of an option-adjusted yield, duration, and convexity.

APPENDIX

DERIVATION OF OPTION-ADJUSTED DURATION AND CONVEXITY

Call-Adjusted Duration

The price of a callable bond can be expressed as follows:

Price of a callable bond = Price of a noncallable bond − Call option price

or

(A13.1) $P_{CB} = P_{NCB} - P_{CO}$

where

$$
\begin{aligned}
P_{CB} &= \text{Price of a callable bond} \\
P_{NCB} &= \text{Price of a noncallable bond} \\
P_{CO} &= \text{Price of a call option}
\end{aligned}
$$

Taking the first derivative of equation (A13.1) with respect to yield (y), we have

(A13.2) $\dfrac{dP_{CB}}{dy} = \dfrac{dP_{NCB}}{dy} - \dfrac{dP_{CO}}{dy}$

Dividing both sides by the price of the callable bond:

$$
\frac{dP_{CB}}{dy}\frac{1}{P_{CB}} = \frac{dP_{NCB}}{dy}\frac{1}{P_{CB}} - \frac{dP_{CO}}{dy}\frac{1}{P_{CB}}
$$

Multiplying the numerator and denominator of the right-hand side by the price of a noncallable bond:

$$
\frac{dP_{CB}}{dy}\frac{1}{P_{CB}} = \frac{dP_{NCB}}{dy}\frac{1}{P_{NCB}}\frac{P_{NCB}}{P_{CB}} - \frac{dP_{CO}}{dy}\frac{1}{P_{NCB}}\frac{P_{NCB}}{P_{CB}}
$$

Let's look at each of the components.

$$\frac{dP_{CB}}{dy}\frac{1}{P_{CB}} = \text{Modified duration of callable bond} = \text{Dur}_{CB}$$

This relationship can be seen by looking at equation (4.8) in Chapter 4.[3]

$$\frac{dP_{NCB}}{dy}\frac{1}{P_{NCB}} = \text{Duration of a noncallable bond} = \text{Dur}_{NCB}$$

Thus, we have

$$(A13.3) \quad \text{Dur}_{CB} = \text{Dur}_{NCB}\frac{P_{NCB}}{P_{CB}} - \frac{dP_{CO}}{dy}\frac{1}{P_{NCB}}\frac{P_{NCB}}{P_{CB}}$$

The change in the value of the call option for a change in yield is

$$(A13.4) \quad \frac{dP_{CO}}{dy}$$

The change in the value of the call option, however, depends on the change in the price of the noncallable bond for a given change in yield. That is,

$$P_{CO} = f\left(P_{NCB}\right) \text{ and } P_{NCB} = g(y)$$

Using the function-of-a-function rule from calculus, equation (A13.4) can be expressed as

$$(A13.5) \quad \frac{dP_{CO}}{dy} = \frac{dP_{CO}}{dP_{NCB}}\frac{dP_{NCB}}{dy}$$

The first term on the right-hand side of equation (A13.5) is the change in the value of the call option for a change in the price of the noncallable bond. As explained in the chapter, this is the *delta* of an option. Thus,

$$(A13.6) \quad \frac{dP_{CO}}{dy} = \text{Delta} \times \frac{dP_{NCB}}{dy}$$

Substituting equation (A13.6) into equation (A13.3) and rearranging terms,

---

[3] Actually, it is equal to $-\text{Dur}_{CB}$, but because we are omitting the negative sign for the durations on the right-hand side, this does not affect our derivation

$$(A13.7) \quad \text{Dur}_{CB} = \text{Dur}_{NCB} \times \frac{P_{NCB}}{P_{CB}} \times (1 - \text{Delta})$$

The duration for the callable bond given by equation (A13.7) is the same as the call-adjusted duration presented in the chapter.

Call-Adjusted Convexity

Convexity is equal to the second derivative multiplied by the reciprocal of the price. Equation (A13.2) gives the first derivative for the price of a callable bond. Once again, since the price of a call option depends on the price of the underlying noncallable bond and, in turn, the price of the noncallable bond depends on its yield, the function-of-a-function rule allows equation (A13.2) to be expressed as

$$(A13.8) \quad \frac{dP_{CB}}{dy} = \frac{dP_{NCB}}{dy} - \frac{dP_{CO}}{dP_{NCB}} \frac{dP_{NCB}}{dy}$$

The second derivative is:

$$(A13.9) \quad \frac{d^2 P_{CB}}{dy^2} = \frac{d^2 P_{NCB}}{dy^2} - \left[\frac{d^2 P_{CO}}{dP^2_{NCB}} \left(\frac{dP_{NCB}}{dy} \right)^2 + \frac{dP_{CO}}{dP_{NCB}} \frac{d^2 P_{NCB}}{dy^2} \right]$$

Let's look at each of the components on the right-hand side of equation (A13.9). First consider the second derivative of the price of the noncallable bond with respect to yield, i.e.,

$$\frac{d^2 P_{NCB}}{dy^2}$$

Multiplying the numerator and the denominator by the price of the noncallable bond gives

$$\frac{d^2 P_{NCB}}{dy^2} \times \frac{P_{NCB}}{P_{NCB}}$$

which is equivalent to the convexity of the noncallable bond times the price of the noncallable bond:

$$(A13.10) \quad \text{Con}_{NCB} \times P_{NCB}$$

Next let's look at

$$\frac{d^2P_{NCB}}{dP^2_{NCB}} \left(\frac{dP_{NCB}}{dy}\right)^2$$

The first term is the rate of change of the delta of the call option with respect to a change in the price of the noncallable bond. As explained in the chapter, this is the gamma of the call option. Thus, we have

$$\text{Gamma} \times \left(\frac{dP_{NCB}}{dy}\right)^2$$

which can also be expressed as

$$\text{Gamma} \times \left(\frac{dP_{NCB}}{dy}\right)^2 \times \frac{P^2_{NCB}}{P^2_{NCB}}$$

which is equivalent to

(A13.11) $\text{Gamma} \times \left(\text{Dur}_{NCB}\right)^2 \times P^2_{NCB}$

Now look at

$$\frac{dP_{CO}}{dP_{NCB}} \frac{d^2P_{NCB}}{dy^2}$$

The first term is the delta of the call option, so

$$\text{Delta} \times \frac{d^2P_{NCB}}{dy^2}$$

Multiplying the numerator and the denominator by the price of the noncallable bond, we have

$$\text{Delta} \times \frac{d^2P_{NCB}}{dy^2} \times \frac{P_{NCB}}{P_{NCB}}$$

but recall that the second derivative of the price of a noncallable bond times the reciprocal of its price is the convexity of the noncallable bond. Therefore, the term becomes

(A13.12) $\text{Delta} \times \text{Con}_{NCB} \times P_{NCB}$

Substituting equations (A13.10), (A13.11), and (A13.12) into equation (A13.9),

(A13.13) $\dfrac{d^2 P_{CB}}{dy^2} = \text{Con}_{NCB} \times P_{NCB}$

$$- \left[\text{Gamma} \times \left(\text{Dur}_{NCB} \right)^2 \times P^2_{NCB} + \text{Delta} \times \text{Con}_{NCB} \times P_{NCB} \right]$$

Multiplying the left-hand side of equation (A13.12) by the reciprocal of the price of the callable bond gives the convexity of the callable bond. Multiplying the right-hand side of equation (A13.12) by the reciprocal of the price of the callable bond and rearranging terms gives

$$\text{Con}_{CB} = \dfrac{P_{NCB}}{P_{CB}} \left[\text{Con}_{NCB} \times (1 - \text{Delta}) - P_{NCB} \times \text{Gamma} \times \left(\text{Dur}_{NCB} \right)^2 \right]$$

This is the equation presented in the chapter for the call-adjusted convexity of a callable bond.

QUESTIONS FOR CHAPTER 13

1. a. What is meant by negative convexity?

   b. Does a callable bond have negative or positive convexity?

2. a. Describe the position of the owner of a callable bond in terms of a noncallable bond and a call option on a noncallable bond.

   b. How can the price of a callable bond be expressed in terms of the noncallable bond and the call option?

   c. Why is the call option in a callable bond complicated to evaluate?

3. A Merrill Lynch note structure called a Liquid Yield Option Note (LYON) has the following characteristics:

   it is a zero-coupon instrument;

   it is convertible into the common stock of the issuer;

   it is putable;

   it is callable.

   a. Describe all the embedded options granted to the corporation that issues a LYON.

   b. Describe all the embedded options granted to the investor who purchases a LYON.

4. a. What is the intrinsic value of an option?

   b. What is the time value of an option?

   c. What is meant by an in-the-money call option?

5. a. What does a delta of .2 mean for a call option?

   b. What is the range of values for delta that can be realized for a call option?

6. Suppose an investor is considering a 10% coupon callable corporate bond selling at 104 with 10 years to maturity and callable at 103. Suppose also that, using an option pricing model, the call option price is estimated to be 5.27.

   a. Demonstrate that the option-adjusted yield is 8.6%.

   b. Suppose that expected interest rate volatility increases. What would happen to the call option price and the call-adjusted yield?

7. a. What is the range for the call-adjusted duration of a callable bond?

   b. Given the information below, calculate the call-adjusted duration:

   Observed price of callable bond = 105
   Estimated call option price = 4
   Duration of noncallable bond = 5
   Delta = .4

8. This excerpt is taken from an article entitled "Call Provisions Drop Off," that appeared in the January 27, 1992, issue of *BondWeek*, p. 2:

   Issuance of callable long-term bonds dropped off further last year as interest rates fell, removing the incentive for many issuers to pay extra for the provision, said Street capital market officials...The shift toward noncallable issues, which began in the late 1980s, reflects the secular trend of investors' unwilling to bear prepayment risk and possibly the cyclical trend that corporations believe that interest rates have hit all time lows....

Though investors are more aware of the value of call protection, the price of a 10-year call provision has dropped to 13-15 basis points from 25-30 a few years ago, investment bankers said....Junk bond issuers have not given up on calls....

    a. What "incentive" is this article referring to in the first sentence of the excerpt?

    b. Why would issuers not be willing to pay for this incentive if they feel that interest rates will continue to decline?

    c. Why has the value of call protection decreased?

    d. Why do you think issuers of junk (high-yield) bonds have not eliminated call provisions?

9. The following excerpt comes from an article entitled "Eagle Eyes High-Coupon Callable Corporates," that appeared in the January 20, 1992, issue of *BondWeek*, p. 7:

If the bond market rallies further, Eagle Asset Management may take profits, trading $8 million of seven to 10-year Treasuries for high-coupon single-A industrials that are callable in two to four years according to Joseph Blanton, senior v.p. He thinks a further rally is unlikely, however.
The corporates have a 95% chance of being called in two to four years and are treated as two-to-four year paper in calculating the duration of the portfolio, Blanton said....

    a. Why is modified duration an inappropriate measure for a high-coupon callable bond?

    b. What would be a better measure than modified duration?

    c. Why would the replacement of 10-year Treasuries with high-coupon callable bonds reduce the portfolio's duration?

10. This excerpt, which discusses dual currency bonds, is taken from the *International Capital Market*, published in 1989 by the European Investment Bank:

    The generic name of dual-currency bonds hides many different variations which are difficult to characterize in detail. These variations on the same basic concept have given birth to specific names like Index Currency Option notes (ICON), foreign interest payment bonds (FIPS), forex-linked bonds, heaven and hell bonds, to name but a few. Despite this diversity it is, however, possible to attempt a broad-brush classification of the various types of dual-currency bonds.

    The first category covers bond issues denominated in one currency but for which coupon and repayment of the principal are made in another designated currency at an exchange rate fixed at the time of issue. A second category comprises dual-currency bonds in which coupon payments and redemption proceeds are made in a currency different from the currency of denomination at the spot exchange rate that will prevail at the time of payment.

Within this category, one finds the forex-linked bonds, foreign currency bonds and heaven and hell bonds. A final category includes bonds which offer to issuers or the holder the choice of the currency in which payments and/or redemptions are to be made at the future spot exchange rate. ICONs fall into this latter category because there is an implicit option due to the exchange rate revision formula. Usually, these bonds are referred to as option currency bonds.

Irrespective of the above-mentioned categories, all dual-currency bonds expose the issuers and the holders to some form of foreign exchange risk .... Pricing dual-currency bonds is therefore an application of option pricing, as the bonds can be looked at as a combination of a straight bond and a currency option. The value of the straight bond component is obtained according to traditional fixed-rate bond valuation models. The pricing of the option component is, ex post, equal to the difference between the dual currency bond price and its straight bond component ....

There has been some considerable debate whether investors in dual-currency bonds have been properly compensated for the risks taken. This is a difficult question and one unlikely to draw a definitive conclusion.

a. Why do all currency bonds "expose the issuers and the holders to some form of foreign exchange risk" regardless of the category of bond?

b. Do you agree that the pricing of all dual-currency bonds is an application of option pricing?

c. Why should the price of the option component be "equal to the difference between the dual currency bond price and its straight bond component"?

d. Why is the debate over whether investors in dual-currency bonds have been properly compensated "one unlikely to draw a definitive conclusion"?

Chapter 14

ANALYSIS OF BONDS WITH EMBEDDED OPTIONS II:

Option-Adjusted Spread

This chapter presents an alternative to the option pricing approach to valuing bonds with embedded options. Although corporate bonds are used in our examples, the analysis is equally applicable to agency securities, municipal securities, and mortgage-backed securities. In the next chapter, the option-adjusted spread technology is applied to mortgage-backed securities.

DRAWBACK OF TRADITIONAL YIELD SPREAD ANALYSIS

Traditional analysis of the yield premium for a non-Treasury bond involves calculating the difference between the yield to maturity (or yield to call) of the bond in question and the yield to maturity of a comparable maturity coupon Treasury. The latter is obtained from the Treasury yield curve. For example, consider two 8.8% coupon, 25-year bonds:

Issue	Price	Yield to maturity
Treasury	96.6133	9.15%
Corporate	87.0798	10.24%

The yield spread for these two bonds as traditionally computed is 109 basis points (10.24% minus 9.15%). The drawbacks of this convention, however, are (1) the yield for both bonds fails to take into consideration the term structure of interest rates, and (2) in the case of callable and/or putable bonds, expected interest rate volatility may alter the cash flow of a bond. For now, let's focus only on the first problem: failure to incorporate the term structure of interest rates.

STATIC SPREAD

In traditional yield spread analysis, an investor compares the yield to maturity of a bond with the yield to maturity of a similar maturity on-the-run Treasury security. This means that the yield to maturity of both a 25-year zero-coupon corporate bond and an 8.8% coupon 25-year corporate coupon bond would both be compared to a benchmark 25-year Treasury security. Such a comparison makes little sense, because the cash flow characteristics of the two corporate bonds will not be the same as that of the benchmark Treasury.

The proper way to compare non-Treasury bonds of the same maturity but with different coupon rates is to compare them to a portfolio of Treasury securities that have the same cash flow. For example, consider the 8.8%, 25-year corporate bond selling for 87.0798. The cash flow per $100 par value for this corporate bond, assuming that interest rates do not change (that is, assuming static interest rates), is 49 6-month payments of $4.40 and a payment in 25 years (50 6-month periods) of $104.40. A portfolio that will replicate this cash flow would include 50 zero-coupon Treasury securities with maturities coinciding with the amount and timing of the cash flows of the corporate bond.

The corporate bond's value is equal to the present value of all of the cash flows. The corporate bond's value, assuming the cash flows are riskless, will equal the present value of the replicating portfolio of Treasury securities. In turn, these cash flows are valued at the Treasury spot rates. Exhibit 14-1 shows how to calculate the price of a risk-free 8.8%, 25-year bond assuming the Treasury spot rate curve shown in the exhibit. The price would be 96.6133. The corporate bond's price is 87.0798, less than the package of zero-coupon Treasury securities, because investors in fact require a yield premium for the risk associated with holding a corporate bond rather than a riskless package of Treasury securities.

The *static spread* is a measure of the spread that the investor would realize over the entire Treasury spot rate curve if the bond is held to maturity. It is not a spread off one point on the Treasury yield curve, as is the traditional yield spread. The static spread is calculated as the spread that will make the present value of the cash flows from the corporate bond, when discounted at the Treasury spot rate plus the spread, equal to the corporate bond's price. A trial-and-error procedure is required to determine the static spread.

To illustrate how this is done, let's use the corporate bond in the first illustration. Select some spread, say, 100 basis points. To each Treasury spot rate shown in the third column in Exhibit 14-2, 100 basis points is added. So, for example, the 14-year (period 28) spot rate is 10.0% (9% plus 1%). The spot rate plus 100 basis points is then used to calculate the present value of 88.5473. Because the present value is not equal to the corporate bond's price (87.0798), the static spread is not 100 basis points. If a spread of 110 basis points is tried, it can be seen from the next-to-last column of Exhibit 14-2 that the present value is 87.8031; again, because this is not equal to the corporate bond's price, 110 basis points is not the static spread. The last column of Exhibit 14-2 shows the present value when a 120 basis point spread is tried. The present value is equal to the corporate bond price. Therefore 120 basis points is the static spread, compared to the traditional yield spread of 109 basis points.

Exhibit 14-3 shows the static spread and the traditional yield spread for bonds with various maturities and prices, assuming the Treasury spot rates shown in Exhibit 14-1. Notice that the shorter the maturity of the bond, the less the static spread will differ from the traditional yield spread. The magnitude of the difference between the traditional yield spread and the static spread also depends on the shape of the yield curve. The steeper the yield curve, the more the difference for a given coupon and maturity.

Another reason for the small differences in Exhibit 14-3 is that the corporate bond makes a bullet payment at maturity. The difference between the traditional yield spread and the static spread will be considerably greater for sinking fund bonds and mortgage-backed securities in a steep yield curve environment.

EXHIBIT 14-1   Calculation of Price of a 25-Year, 8.8% Coupon Bond Using Treasury Spot Rates

Period	Cash Flow	Treasury Spot Rate	Present Value
1	4.4	7.00000%	4.2512
2	4.4	7.04999	4.1055
3	4.4	7.09998	3.9628
4	4.4	7.12498	3.8251
5	4.4	7.13998	3.6922
6	4.4	7.16665	3.5622
7	4.4	7.19997	3.4351
8	4.4	7.26240	3.3077
9	4.4	7.33315	3.1820
10	4.4	7.38977	3.0611
11	4.4	7.44517	2.9434
12	4.4	7.49135	2.8302
13	4.4	7.53810	2.7200
14	4.4	7.57819	2.6141
15	4.4	7.61959	2.5112
16	4.4	7.66205	2.4111
17	4.4	7.70538	2.3139
18	4.4	7.74391	2.2207
19	4.4	7.78888	2.1291

Period	Cash Flow	Treasury Spot Rate	Present Value
20	4.4	7.83434	2.0404
21	4.4	8.22300	1.8879
22	4.4	8.33333	1.7923
23	4.4	8.40000	1.7080
24	4.4	8.50000	1.6204
25	4.4	8.54230	1.5465
26	4.4	8.72345	1.4500
27	4.4	8.90000	1.3581
28	4.4	9.00000	1.2829
29	4.4	9.01450	1.2252
30	4.4	9.23000	1.1367
31	4.4	9.39000	1.0611
32	4.4	9.44840	1.0045
33	4.4	9.50000	.9514
34	4.4	9.50000	.9083
35	4.4	9.50000	.8671
36	4.4	9.50000	.8278
37	4.4	9.55000	.7833
38	4.4	9.56000	.7462
39	4.4	9.58000	.7095
40	4.4	9.58000	.6771
41	4.4	9.60000	.6436
42	4.4	9.70000	.6020
43	4.4	9.80000	.5625
44	4.4	9.90000	.5251
45	4.4	10.00000	.4897
46	4.4	10.10000	.4563
47	4.4	10.30000	.4154
48	4.4	10.50000	.3774
49	4.4	10.60000	.3503
50	104.4	10.80000	7.5278

Theoretical price			96.6133

EXHIBIT 14-2   Calculation of the Static Spread for a 25-Year, 8.8% Coupon Corporate Bond

Period	Cash Flow	Treasury spot rate	Present value if spread used is		
			100 BP	110 BP	120 BP
1	4.4	7.00000%	4.2308	4.2287	4.2267
2	4.4	7.04999	4.0661	4.0622	4.0583
3	4.4	7.09998	3.9059	3.9003	3.8947
4	4.4	7.12498	3.7521	3.7449	3.7377
5	4.4	7.13998	3.6043	3.5957	3.5871
6	4.4	7.16665	3.4607	3.4508	3.4408
7	4.4	7.19997	3.3212	3.3101	3.2990
8	4.4	7.26240	3.1828	3.1706	3.1584
9	4.4	7.33315	3.0472	3.0340	3.0210
10	4.4	7.38977	2.9174	2.9034	2.8895

Period	Cash Flow	Treasury Spot Rate	Present value if spread used is		
			100 BP	110 BP	120 BP
11	4.4	7.44517	2.7917	2.7770	2.7624
12	4.4	7.49135	2.6715	2.6562	2.6409
13	4.4	7.53810	2.5552	2.5394	2.5236
14	4.4	7.57819	2.4440	2.4277	2.4115
15	4.4	7.61959	2.3366	2.3198	2.3032
16	4.4	7.66205	2.2327	2.2157	2.1988
17	4.4	7.70538	2.1325	2.1152	2.0981
18	4.4	7.74391	2.0368	2.0193	2.0020
19	4.4	7.78888	1.9435	1.9259	1.9085
20	4.4	7.83434	1.8536	1.8359	1.8184
21	4.4	8.22300	1.7072	1.6902	1.6733
22	4.4	8.33333	1.6131	1.5963	1.5796
23	4.4	8.40000	1.5300	1.5132	1.4967
24	4.4	8.50000	1.4446	1.4282	1.4119
25	4.4	8.54230	1.3722	1.3559	1.3398
26	4.4	8.72345	1.2806	1.2648	1.2492
27	4.4	8.90000	1.1938	1.1785	1.1635
28	4.4	9.00000	1.1224	1.1075	1.0929
29	4.4	9.01450	1.0668	1.0522	1.0378
30	4.4	9.23000	.9852	.9712	.9575
31	4.4	9.39000	.9154	.9020	.8888
32	4.4	9.44840	.8625	.8495	.8367
33	4.4	9.50000	.8131	.8004	.7880
34	4.4	9.50000	.7725	.7601	.7480
35	4.4	9.50000	.7340	.7219	.7100
36	4.4	9.50000	.6974	.6855	.6739
37	4.4	9.55000	.6568	.6453	.6341
38	4.4	9.56000	.6227	.6116	.6007
39	4.4	9.58000	.5893	.5785	.5679
40	4.4	9.58000	.5597	.5492	.5389
41	4.4	9.60000	.5295	.5193	.5093
42	4.4	9.70000	.4929	.4832	.4737
43	4.4	9.80000	.4585	.4492	.4401
44	4.4	9.90000	.4260	.4172	.4086
45	4.4	10.00000	.3955	.3871	.3789
46	4.4	10.10000	.3668	.3588	.3511
47	4.4	10.30000	.3323	.3250	.3179
48	4.4	10.50000	.3006	.2939	.2873
49	4.4	10.60000	.2778	.2714	.2652
50	104.4	10.80000	5.9416	5.8030	5.6677
	Total present value		88.5473	87.8031	87.0798

OPTION-ADJUSTED SPREAD

We stated at the outset of the chapter that there are two drawbacks to the traditional yield spread analysis and have showed how to overcome the first problem: failure to incorporate the term structure of interest rates. This led to development of the static spread. Now we look at the second

EXHIBIT 14-3 Comparison of Traditional Yield Spread and Static Spread for Various Bonds(*)

Bond	Price	Yield to maturity	Spread (in basis points) Traditional	Static	Difference
— 25-year, 8.8% coupon bond —-					
Treasury	96.6133	9.15%	—	—	—
A	88.5473	10.06%	91	100	9
B	87.8031	10.15%	100	110	10
C	87.0798	10.24%	109	120	11
— 15-year, 8.8% coupon bond —					
Treasury	101.9603	8.57%	—	—	—
D	94.1928	9.54%	97	100	3
E	93.4639	9.63%	106	110	4
F	92.7433	9.73%	116	120	4
— 10-year, 8.8% coupon bond —					
Treasury	107.4906	7.71%	—	—	—
G	100.6137	8.71%	100	100	0
H	99.9585	8.81%	110	110	0
I	99.3088	8.91%	120	120	0
—5-year, 8.8% coupon bond —					
Treasury	105.9555	7.36%	—	—	—
J	101.7919	8.35%	99	100	1
K	101.3867	8.45%	109	110	1
L	100.9836	8.55%	119	120	1

*Assumes Treasury spot rate curve given in Exhibit 14-1.

drawback: failure to take into account future interest rate volatility that would affect the expected cash flow for a callable bond.

To understand why this is a drawback, consider an 8.8%, 10-year corporate bond that is immediately callable, and assume current interest rates are 8.8%. The likelihood that the issuer will call the bond increases as interest rates decline. If interest rates do fall and the bond is called, the investor's cash flows will change. A small drop in rates, of course, will not be sufficient to justify the issuer's calling the bond. The rate must drop enough so that it will be economic for the issuer to call the bond. For example, a decline of interest rates from 8.8% to 8.5% 6 months from now may not make it attractive to call the issue, given the cost of refunding. In addition to the interest rate, that cost is a function of (1) the remaining maturity on the bond, (2) the call price, and (3) fees associated with registering and underwriting the new issue.

The refinancing opportunities will depend on how interest rates change over the life of the bond. For example, suppose that 6-month interest rates are now 7%. Consider the 10 possible interest rate paths from that level for 6-month forward rates for the subsequent 19 6-month periods shown in Exhibit 14-4, assuming that the 6-month forward interest rates can rise or fall by 10% every 6 months.

The refinancing opportunity for the corporation will be based not on the short-term forward rate but on a longer-term rate that reflects how much the issuer would have to pay to refund a bond issue. Let's make the simple assumption that the refinancing rate for the corporation is 100 basis points higher than the short-term forward rate. Exhibit 14-5 shows the ten possible paths for the refinancing rate, with each rate in the exhibit 100 basis points higher than in Exhibit 14-4.

Suppose that the following rule is established for calling of the bond: If the refinancing rate is below 5.8% with at least three years remaining to maturity, then the bond will be called. Given this rule for calling, the bond would not be called if five of the paths are realized (paths 1, 2, 4, 8, and 10).

EXHIBIT 14-4   Ten Possible Paths for Six-Month Forward Rates Assuming an Initial Forward Rate of 7% and 10% Volatility

———————————— Path of short-term forward rates ————————————

Period	1	2	3	4	5	6	7	8	9	10
1	7.0%	7.0%	7.0%	7.0%	7.0%	7.0%	7.0%	7.0%	7.0%	7.0%
2	7.7	7.7	7.7	6.3	6.3	6.3	7.7	6.3	7.7	7.7
3	8.5	6.9	6.9	6.9	5.7	5.7	8.5	5.7	8.5	8.5
4	7.6	6.2	6.2	7.6	5.1	6.2	9.3	6.2	9.3	9.3
5	6.9	6.9	5.6	8.4	4.6	6.9	8.4	6.9	8.4	8.4
6	7.5	7.5	5.1	9.2	4.1	6.2	7.5	7.5	7.5	7.5
7	8.3	8.3	4.5	10.1	4.5	5.6	6.8	8.3	6.8	6.8
8	9.1	9.1	5.0	11.2	5.0	5.0	6.1	9.1	6.1	6.1
9	10.0	10.0	5.5	12.3	5.5	4.5	5.5	8.2	6.7	6.7
10	9.0	9.0	6.1	13.5	6.1	4.1	5.0	7.4	6.1	7.4
11	9.9	8.1	6.7	12.2	6.7	4.5	4.5	8.1	5.4	6.7
12	8.9	8.9	7.3	10.9	7.3	4.0	4.0	8.9	4.9	6.0
13	8.1	9.8	8.1	9.8	8.1	4.4	3.6	9.8	4.4	5.4
14	8.9	8.9	7.2	8.9	7.2	4.0	3.2	10.8	4.0	4.9
15	9.7	8.0	6.5	8.0	6.5	4.4	2.9	9.7	4.4	5.3
16	8.8	7.2	7.2	8.8	7.2	3.9	3.2	10.7	4.8	4.8
17	7.9	6.5	7.9	9.6	7.9	3.5	3.5	9.6	5.3	4.3
18	7.1	7.1	8.7	10.6	8.7	3.2	3.9	10.6	5.8	4.8
19	7.8	7.8	7.8	11.7	9.6	2.9	4.3	11.7	6.4	5.2
20	8.6	7.0	8.6	10.5	8.6	3.2	4.7	12.8	7.0	4.7

EXHIBIT 14-5   Ten Possible Paths for the Refinancing Rate Assuming It is 100 Basis Points Higher than the Short-term Forward Rate

———————— Path of refinancing rate ————————

Period	1	2	3	4	5	6	7	8	9	10
1	8.0%	8.0%	8.0%	8.0%	8.0%	8.0%	8.0%	8.0%	8.0%	8.0%
2	8.7	8.7	8.7	7.3	7.3	7.3	8.7	7.3	8.7	8.7
3	9.5	7.9	7.9	7.9	6.7	6.7	9.5	6.7	9.5	9.5
4	8.6	7.2	7.2	8.6	6.1	7.2	10.3	7.2	10.3	10.3
5	7.9	7.9	6.6	9.4	5.6	7.9	9.4	7.9	9.4	9.4
6	8.5	8.5	6.1	10.2	5.1	7.2	8.5	8.5	8.5	8.5
7	9.3	9.3	5.5	11.1	5.5	6.6	7.8	9.3	7.8	7.8
8	10.1	10.1	6.0	12.2	6.0	6.0	7.1	10.1	7.1	7.1
9	11.0	11.0	6.5	13.3	6.5	5.5	6.5	9.2	7.7	7.7
10	10.0	10.0	7.1	14.5	7.1	5.1	6.0	8.4	7.1	8.4
11	10.9	9.1	7.7	13.2	7.7	5.5	5.5	9.1	6.4	7.7
12	9.9	9.9	8.3	11.9	8.3	5.0	5.0	9.9	5.9	7.0
13	9.1	10.8	9.1	10.8	9.1	5.4	4.6	10.8	5.4	6.4
14	9.9	9.9	8.2	9.9	8.2	5.0	4.2	11.8	5.0	5.9
15	10.7	9.0	7.5	9.0	7.5	5.4	3.9	10.7	5.4	6.3
16	9.8	8.2	8.2	9.8	8.2	4.9	4.2	11.7	5.8	5.8
17	8.9	7.5	8.9	10.6	8.9	4.5	4.5	10.6	6.3	5.3
18	8.1	8.1	9.7	11.6	9.7	4.2	4.9	11.6	6.8	5.8
19	8.8	8.8	8.8	12.7	10.6	3.9	5.3	12.7	7.4	6.2
20	9.6	8.0	9.6	11.5	9.6	4.2	5.7	13.8	8.0	5.7

Therefore, the cash flow for the bond at each 6-month period is not different from that of a noncallable bond. For the other paths, the bond would be called.

Exhibit 14-6 shows the cash flow for this corporate bond given the call rule and assuming that the bond has a call price of 103 regardless of when it is called. In the period a bond is called, the cash flow is 107.40 (the call price of 103 plus the semiannual coupon interest of 4.40). After the call period, the cash flow is zero.

There are obviously an enormous number of interest rate paths. Let's imagine for the moment that we could analyze each path. For each path, we would then calculate the present value of the cash flow of the bond using as a discount rate the Treasury spot rate at each period plus a spread. Recall from Chapter 9 that the forward rates can be calculated from the spot rates. Similarly, the spot rates can be calculated from the forward rates. Exhibit 14-7 shows the spot rates for each period given the short-term forward rates in Exhibit 14-4.

So, for each path we calculate a present value by using the spot rate plus some assumed spread. Then we compute an average of all the present

EXHIBIT 14-6 Cash Flow for Each Refinancing Path of an 8.8%, 10-Year Corporate Bond Callable at 103

Call Rule: Call if refinancing rate falls to 5.8% or less and bond has at least three years to maturity

	Path									
Period	1	2	3	4	5	6	7	8	9	10
1	4.4	4.4	4.4	4.4	4.4	4.4	4.4	4.4	4.4	4.4
2	4.4	4.4	4.4	4.4	4.4	4.4	4.4	4.4	4.4	4.4
3	4.4	4.4	4.4	4.4	4.4	4.4	4.4	4.4	4.4	4.4
4	4.4	4.4	4.4	4.4	4.4	4.4	4.4	4.4	4.4	4.4
5	4.4	4.4	4.4	4.4	107.4	4.4	4.4	4.4	4.4	4.4
6	4.4	4.4	4.4	4.4	0.0	4.4	4.4	4.4	4.4	4.4
7	4.4	4.4	107.4	4.4	0.0	4.4	4.4	4.4	4.4	4.4
8	4.4	4.4	0.0	4.4	0.0	4.4	4.4	4.4	4.4	4.4
9	4.4	4.4	0.0	4.4	0.0	107.4	4.4	4.4	4.4	4.4
10	4.4	4.4	0.0	4.4	0.0	0.0	4.4	4.4	4.4	4.4
11	4.4	4.4	0.0	4.4	0.0	0.0	107.4	4.4	4.4	4.4
12	4.4	4.4	0.0	4.4	0.0	0.0	0.0	4.4	107.4	4.4
13	4.4	4.4	0.0	4.4	0.0	0.0	0.0	4.4	0.0	4.4
14	4.4	4.4	0.0	4.4	0.0	0.0	0.0	4.4	0.0	4.4
15	4.4	4.4	0.0	4.4	0.0	0.0	0.0	4.4	0.0	4.4
16	4.4	4.4	0.0	4.4	0.0	0.0	0.0	4.4	0.0	4.4
17	4.4	4.4	0.0	4.4	0.0	0.0	0.0	4.4	0.0	4.4
18	4.4	4.4	0.0	4.4	0.0	0.0	0.0	4.4	0.0	4.4
19	4.4	4.4	0.0	4.4	0.0	0.0	0.0	4.4	0.0	4.4
20	104.4	104.4	0.0	104.4	0.0	0.0	0.0	104.4	0.0	104.4

values for all the paths. If the average present value is equal to the market price of the bond, then the spread added to the Treasury spot rates is called the *option-adjusted spread*. If it is not, the present value along each path is calculated again using a different spread. Once again, if the average present value is equal to the market price of the bond, this new spread is the option-adjusted spread. If not, the process continues until a spread is found that satisfies this condition.

This is illustrated in Exhibit 14-8. The first column specifies the spread added to each Treasury spot rate in Exhibit 14-7. The next ten columns show the present value for each path based on that spread. The last column shows the average present value. For example, if the market price of this corporate bond is 105.4, then the option-adjusted spread is 40 basis points.

The option-adjusted spread can be interpreted as follows. It is the average spread over the Treasury spot rate curve based on potential paths that can be realized in the future for interest rates. The reason why the

EXHIBIT 14-7   Treasury Spot Rate on Each Path Constructed from Six-Month Forward Rates

Period	1	2	3	4	5	6	7	8	9	10
1	7.00%	7.00%	7.00%	7.00%	7.00%	7.00%	7.00%	7.00%	7.00%	7.00%
2	7.35	7.35	7.35	6.65	6.65	6.65	7.35	6.65	7.35	7.35
3	7.72	7.21	7.21	6.74	6.32	6.32	7.72	6.32	7.72	7.72
4	7.70	6.97	6.97	6.96	6.02	6.30	8.12	6.30	8.12	8.12
5	7.53	6.95	6.69	7.25	5.73	6.41	8.17	6.41	8.17	8.17
6	7.53	7.05	6.42	7.57	5.46	6.37	8.07	6.60	8.07	8.07
7	7.64	7.22	6.15	7.94	5.33	6.26	7.89	6.84	7.89	7.89
8	7.83	7.46	6.01	8.34	5.29	6.10	7.66	7.13	7.66	7.66
9	8.07	7.75	5.95	8.77	5.31	5.92	7.42	7.25	7.56	7.56
10	8.17	7.88	5.96	9.24	5.39	5.73	7.17	7.26	7.41	7.54
11	8.33	7.90	6.02	9.51	5.50	5.62	6.93	7.34	7.23	7.46
12	8.38	7.99	6.13	9.62	5.65	5.48	6.68	7.48	7.03	7.34
13	8.36	8.13	6.28	9.64	5.84	5.40	6.44	7.66	6.83	7.19
14	8.39	8.18	6.35	9.59	5.94	5.30	6.21	7.88	6.63	7.02
15	8.48	8.17	6.36	9.48	5.98	5.24	5.99	8.01	6.47	6.91
16	8.50	8.11	6.41	9.43	6.05	5.15	5.82	8.17	6.37	6.78
17	8.46	8.01	6.50	9.45	6.16	5.06	5.68	8.26	6.31	6.63
18	8.39	7.96	6.62	9.51	6.30	4.95	5.58	8.39	6.28	6.53
19	8.36	7.95	6.68	9.62	6.47	4.84	5.51	8.56	6.28	6.46
20	8.37	7.90	6.78	9.67	6.58	4.76	5.47	8.77	6.32	6.37

EXHIBIT 14-8   Present Value of Each Path and Average Present Value Using Various Spreads

	Present Value of Path										
Spread	1	2	3	4	5	6	7	8	9	10	Average PV
40 bp	100.6	103.5	107.5	93.73	108.5	111.5	107.9	100.4	107.7	112.4	105.4
50 bp	100.0	102.9	107.3	93.14	108.3	111.1	107.4	99.77	107.2	111.6	104.9
60 bp	99.35	102.2	107.0	92.55	108.0	110.7	106.9	99.13	106.7	110.8	104.3
70 bp	98.70	101.5	106.7	91.97	107.8	110.3	106.5	98.49	106.2	110.1	103.8
80 bp	98.06	100.8	106.4	91.40	107.5	109.9	106.0	97.86	105.7	109.3	103.3
90 bp	97.43	100.2	106.1	90.83	107.3	109.5	105.5	97.24	105.3	108.6	102.8
100 bp	96.80	99.58	105.9	90.26	107.1	109.1	105.1	96.62	104.8	107.9	102.3
110 bp	96.18	98.93	105.6	89.70	106.8	108.7	104.6	96.00	104.3	107.1	101.8
120 bp	95.56	98.29	105.3	89.14	106.6	108.3	104.2	95.39	103.8	106.4	101.3

spread is "option-adjusted" is because on the potential paths the cash flows are adjusted to reflect the options embedded in the bond.

Taking Into Consideration Credit Risk

What has been ignored in demonstration of the option-adjusted spread framework thus far is that the spread over the Treasury spot rate curve also reflects credit risk. We can incorporate credit risk, however, by adding a generic zero coupon spread to the Treasury spot rate curve so that the cash flows on a path will then be discounted using this combined rate.

The amount of the generic zero coupon spread will depend on the quality rating of the issue. Moreover, as explained in Chapter 9, there is no reason to expect that the zero coupon spread should be the same for each period. The evidence in Chapter 9 suggests that the zero coupon spread rises with maturity. While it is theoretically correct to incorporate a term structure of credit risk into an option-adjusted spread model, there are models in current use that assume a constant credit risk spread (i.e., a flat term structure for credit risk).

Some Technical Issues

There are several additional technical issues that must be addressed in developing an option-adjusted spread model. First, in the simplified illustration, we use only ten possible paths. This is too small a sample to provide any confidence about the potential cash flows that could be realized by an investor. In practice, paths can be generated using Monte Carlo simulation. To do this, it is necessary to specify how the term structure will shift each period. This is accomplished by specifying a probability distribution for the short-term Treasury rate. A change in the short-term Treasury rate will determine how the entire term structure will shift.

A second technical consideration is to assure that the assumed probability distribution is consistent with the existing term structure of interest rates. This means that when the on-the-run Treasury securities are evaluated, their option-adjusted spread should be zero. This is accomplished by adding a drift term to the short-term return generating process.[1]

A third technical issue is determination of the relationship between short-term rates and refinancing rates. In our simplified illustration, we conveniently assume that the spread between the two is 100 basis points. Empirical evidence is necessary to determine the relationship.

The call rule, that is, the conditions that must exist for the corporation to call the bond, must be specified. In our simplified illustration, it is assumed that the refinancing rate must be 5.8% or less and there must be at least three years remaining to maturity. In practice, the

---

[1] For an explanation of how this is done, see Lakhbir S. Hayre and Kenneth Lauterbach, "Stochastic Valuation of Debt Securities," in Frank J. Fabozzi (ed.), *Managing Institutional Assets* (New York: Harper & Row, 1990), pp. 321-364.

call rule will be more complex. It will take into consideration the after-tax interest cost savings, the call premium (which declines over time), the legal and or underwriting fees, and the time remaining to maturity.[2]

The last technical issue involves the need for an estimate of interest rate volatility, which will have an impact on the option-adjusted spread. The volatility assumption is introduced when a probability distribution for the short-term Treasury securities is selected. One parameter that must be specified in selecting a probability distribution is the variance (or standard deviation). The larger the variance assumed, the greater the volatility assumed for interest rates.

Our illustration assumes a constant volatility of 10% per period for the short-term forward rate. Instead of assuming a constant volatility, we can develop a model that takes the short-term forward rate as a random variable or that assumes volatility is different for different periods. The importance of the volatility assumption for the option-adjusted spread is illustrated later in this section.

Because of these technical issues, the option-adjusted spread reported by dealers for the same corporate bond can differ by 20 basis points.[3] For mortgage-backed securities, the differences in the option-adjusted spreads reported by dealers can be considerably greater.

Summary of Option-Adjusted Spread Calculation

We can summarize the procedure to calculate the option-adjusted spread as follows:

1. From the Treasury yield curve estimate the term structure of interest rates (spot rates) and the implied forward rates.
2. Select a probability distribution for short-term Treasury spot rates. The probability distribution should be selected so that it is consistent with (a) the current term structure of interest rates, and (b) the historical behavior of interest rates. This will prevent the possibility of arbitrage along the yield curve.
3. Use the probability distribution and Monte Carlo simulation to determine randomly a large number of interest rate paths (say, 1,000).
4. For bonds with embedded options (such as callable or putable bonds), develop rules for determining the exercise of an option.

---

[2] For a more detailed discussion of the factors to be considered in refunding a bond issue, see John D. Finnerty, Andrew J. Kalotay, and Francis X. Farrell, Jr., *The Financial Manager's Guide to Evaluating Bond Refunding Opportunities* (Cambridge, MA: Ballinger Publishing, 1988).

[3] John D. Finnerty and Michael Rose, "Arbitrage-Free Spread: A Consistent Measure of Relative Value," *Journal of Portfolio Management* (Spring 1991), p.77.

5. For each path found in (3), determine the cash flows, given (a) information about the bond issue (e.g., call provisions), and (b) the rules established in (4).

6. For an assumed spread and the term structure along a path, calculate a present value for each path.

7. Calculate the average present value for all paths.

8. Compare the average present value to the market price of the bond. If they are equal, the assumed spread used in (6) is the option-adjusted spread. If they are not, try another spread and repeat (7) and (8).

Application

While it is too complicated to work through the calculation of an actual application of option-adjusted spread analysis here, let's look at the result of one such analysis. Exhibit 14-9 summarizes the results of an option-adjusted spread analysis by Hayre and Lauterbach for three callable bond issues.[4] The analysis is based on closing prices as of September 20, 1988.

The traditional yield spread analysis would suggest that the ITT bond is particularly attractive because it is trading at 168 basis points over the Treasury yield curve. In fact, in terms of just spread off Treasuries, it would seem that this issue is the most attractive of the three issues. The option-adjusted spread analysis in the last three columns, however, suggests just the opposite. Regardless of the assumed volatility of interest rates, the ITT issue is the least attractive on an option-adjusted spread basis.

Notice also the impact of the volatility assumption on the option-adjusted spread. The higher the assumed volatility of interest rates, the lower the option-adjusted spread. In the case of the ITT issue, if assumed volatility is 20% annually, the option-adjusted spread is negative — quite a different story from what traditional yield spread analysis would tell us.

Valuing the Embedded Option

In the previous chapter, we demonstrated that the price of a callable bond is equal to the price of a noncallable bond minus the value of the embedded call option. A by-product of the option-adjusted spread analysis provides the implied value of the embedded call option.

The procedure for obtaining this value after estimating an option-adjusted spread is as follows. First, use the option-adjusted spread to

---

[4] See Hayre and Lauterbach, "Stochastic Valuation of Debt Securities."

Exhibit 14-9   Option-Adjusted Spread for Three Callable Corporate Bonds

OAS at Volatility of

Issuer	S&P Rating	Maturity	Next Call Date	Next Call Price	Curr. Price	Coupon (%)	YTM	Trsy. Yield Spread	10%	15%	20%
ITT Fin.	A	07/01/92	07/01/89	100.00	101.58	10.800	10.27	168	57	30	−4
Marriot	A−	02/01/96	02/01/93	100.00	99.59	9.625	9.70	85	65	50	37
GMAC	AA−	07/15/07	now	104.00	84.19	8.000	9.86	82	71	54	41

Note: Based on closing prices and Treasury rates on September 20, 1988.

Source: Lakhbir Hayre and Kenneth Lauterbach, "Stochastic Valuation of Debt Securities," in Frank J. Fabozzi (ed.), *Managing Institutional Assets* (New York, NY: Harper & Row, 1990.)

determine what a noncallable bond would sell for. This price, which is called the implied noncallable bond price, is determined by adding the option-adjusted spread to the Treasury spot rates and calculating the present value of the cash flows to maturity. Next, subtract the callable bond's market price from the implied noncallable bond price. The difference is the value of the embedded call option.

For the ITT issue, the value of the embedded call option, as calculated by Hayre and Lauterbach, is as follows:

	Volatility Assumed 10%	15%	20%
Option-adjusted spread (bp)	57.00	30.00	−4.00
Implied noncallable price	105.06	105.94	107.07
Market price	101.58	101.58	101.58
Value of embedded call option	3.48	4.36	5.49

Notice that the value of the embedded call option is a by-product of the option-adjusted spread analysis, and that the option is not valued explicitly by using an option pricing model as in the previous chapter.

In basis points, the option cost is found by subtracting the OAS from the static spread. That is

Option cost = Static spread − OAS

Applications to Other Bond Structures with Embedded Options

While our focus has been on callable corporate bonds, the option-adjusted spread analysis can be extended to any corporate bond structure such as putable bonds, floating-rate notes, and sinking fund bonds. It can easily accommodate more than one embedded option simultaneously. For example, if a corporate bond is both callable and putable, the value of the cash flow along a path will take into account that the bond may be called before it is put if interest rates fall sufficiently (based on the call rule), or be put before it is called if interest rates rise (based on a put rule that must be developed). In the case of floating-rate notes, the presence of any interest rate cap or floor can be easily accommodated.

High-yield ("junk") bond structures typically have multiple embedded options. Consider, for example, the payment-in-kind (PIK) bond. If rates decline sufficiently, the bond may be called; if interest rates rise, however, the issuer has the option of putting to the bondholder another bond with the same coupon as the issue. The option-adjusted spread approach can handle this structure.

APPROXIMATING DURATION AND CONVEXITY

In the previous chapter, we describe the price performance characteristics of callable bonds. Modified duration and convexity measures for option-free bonds are inappropriate both for callable bonds and, as explained in the next chapter, mortgage-backed securities. Here we present formulas for approximating duration and convexity that can be used for any bond.

Effective Duration and Effective Convexity

Duration is a measure of the percentage change in price for small changes in interest rates, so an *effective duration* formula which allows for changes in the cash flow if interest rates change can be used to approximate duration:

$$\text{Effective duration} = \frac{P_- - P_+}{(P_0)(y_+ - y_-)}$$

where

$$\begin{aligned}
P_0 &= \text{Initial price (per \$100 of par value)} \\
P_- &= \text{Price if yield is decreased by } x \text{ basis points} \\
P_+ &= \text{Price if yield is increased by } x \text{ basis points} \\
y_- &= \text{Initial yield minus } x \text{ basis points} \\
y_+ &= \text{Initial yield plus } x \text{ basis points}
\end{aligned}$$

To illustrate the calculation of effective duration, we shall apply it to an option-free bond. (In the next chapter, effective duration will be calculated for a mortgage pass-through security.) Consider a 20-year 7%

coupon bond selling at 74.26 to yield 10%. Suppose we evaluate the price changes for a 20-basis point change up and down. Then,

$$
\begin{aligned}
P_0 &= 74.26 \\
P_- &= 75.64 \\
P_+ &= 72.92 \\
y_- &= .098 \\
y_+ &= .102
\end{aligned}
$$

$$
\text{Effective duration} = \frac{75.64 - 72.92}{(74.26)(.102 - .098)} = 9.16
$$

The modified duration for this bond is 9.18. The effective duration is 9.16, indicating a good approximation.

To approximate convexity, an *effective convexity* formula can be used:

$$
\text{Effective convexity} = \frac{P_+ + P_- - 2\left(P_0\right)}{\left(P_0\right)\left[.5\left(y_+ - y_-\right)\right]^2}
$$

Consider the 20-year 7% coupon bond selling at 74.26 to yield 10%. Effective convexity is:

$$
\frac{75.64 + 72.92 - 2\,(74.26)}{(74.26)\left[.5(.102 - .98)\right]^2} = 134.66
$$

The convexity is equal to 132.08. The effective convexity (134.66) proves itself to be a good approximation of convexity (132.08).

Application to Option-Adjusted Spread Framework

Within the option-adjusted spread framework, effective duration and convexity can be computed by increasing and decreasing short-term Treasury rates by a small amount, while the option-adjusted spread is kept constant. This will produce two average prices: one when short-term interest rates are increased, and one when short-term interest rates are decreased. The average prices are then substituted into the formula for effective duration and convexity given in the previous section.

For the three issues in Exhibit 14-9, the effective duration and convexity are shown in Exhibit 14-10. Also shown is the effective duration and convexity for the bonds if they are not callable, which are essentially the modified durations. Look at the ITT bond, which was callable in less than one year from the date that the analysis was performed. Notice that effective duration for the ITT callable bond is much lower than if it had been a noncallable bond. The convexity for this bond is negative. The lower effective duration and the negative convexity are attributable to the fact that the ITT bond has a coupon rate that is higher than the prevailing market yield (10.8% coupon versus 10.27% using the yield to maturity as the prevailing market yield — see Exhibit 14-9). In contrast, the effective duration for the callable GMAC bond is almost identical to its noncallable duration despite the fact that the bond is immediately callable. The reason is that the coupon rate on the issue is 8% while the prevailing yield (as measured by the bond's yield to maturity) is 9.86%. Therefore, this bond is trading as if it were a noncallable bond.

EXHIBIT 14-10   Effective Duration and Convexity for Three Callable Corporate Bonds

Issuer	Maturity	Next Call Date	Current Price	Effective Duration Callable	Effective Duration Non-Callable	Effective Convexity Callable	Effective Convexity Non-Callable
ITT Fin	07/01/92	07/01/89	101.58	1.1	3.0	−0.3258	0.1872
Marriot	02/01/96	02/01/93	99.59	4.6	5.1	0.2135	0.5683
GMAC	07/15/07	now	84.19	8.1	8.4	0.5328	1.6818

Note: Volatility assumption is 15% per annum.

Source: Lakhbir Hayre and Kenneth Lauterbach, "Stochastic Valuation of Debt Securities," in Frank J. Fabozzi (ed.), *Managing Institutional Assets* (New York, NY: Harper & Row, 1990.)

PRICE PERFORMANCE

In the previous chapter, we explain that the price/yield relationship for a noncallable bond will exhibit negative convexity as yields drop. The option-adjusted spread analysis can be used to construct the price/yield relationship for changes in interest rates. This is done by changing the short-term Treasury rate, holding the option-adjusted spread constant, and calculating the average present value along all the paths. The average present value is then the projected price. This procedure will trace out the price/yield relationship.

When this is done for the ITT bond, the result is the price/yield relationship shown in Exhibit 14-11, which also shows the relationship for the bond if it were noncallable. Compare this exhibit with Exhibit 13-1 in the previous chapter. The shapes are identical. For the ITT bond, once the short-term Treasury rate falls below about 12%, the bond will exhibit negative convexity. That is what the calculated values for effective duration and convexity for the ITT bond tell us in Exhibit 14-10.

EXHIBIT 14-11   Projected Price Paths for the ITT Bond

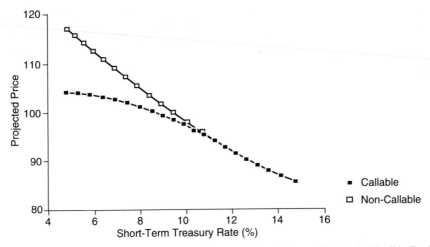

Source: Lakhbir Hayre and Kenneth Lauterbach, "Stochastic Valuation of Debt Securities," in Frank J. Fabozzi (ed.), *Managing Institutional Assets* (New York, NY: Harper & Row, 1990.)

THE LIMITATIONS OF OPTION-ADJUSTED SPREAD ANALYSIS

While the option-adjusted spread analysis technique is clearly superior to traditional yield spread analysis, it does have its limitations. Option-adjusted spread analysis helps us identify securities that promise to pay a spread after adjusting for the embedded option specifically assuming (1) the bond is held to the effective maturity date, and (2) the cash flows from the bond can be reinvested in investment vehicles with a yield equal to the yield on the noncallable bond plus the option-adjusted spread.

Key ingredients in the model are (1) a probability distribution for the short-term forward rates, (2) expected interest rate volatility, and (3) a rule for determining when an embedded option will be exercised. If these components are incorrectly specified, the results of the analysis will be misleading.[5]

A more appropriate way to evaluate the investment merits of a bond with an embedded option to accomplish an investment objective over some horizon is to use the total return framework discussed in Chapter 3. The option-adjusted spread analysis is used in the total return framework to compute the price at the end of the investment horizon.

---

[5] For a more detailed criticism of the option-adjusted spread methodology and, an alternative valuation technique, see Finnerty and Rose, "Arbitrage-Free Spread: A Consistent Measure of Relative Value." See also the response by Labhbir S. Hayre in the same issue.

SUMMARY

This chapter has explained the option-adjusted spread approach to valuing a bond with an embedded option(s). This approach takes into into account (1) the term structure of interest rates, (2) the options embedded in the bond, and (3) the expected volatility of interest rates. The traditional yield spread approach fails to take these factors into account.

The static spread measures the spread over the Treasury spot rate curve, assuming that interest rates will not change in the future. The option-adjusted spread is the spread over the Treasury spot rate curve taking into account that the embedded option(s) will cause the cash flow of the bond to change as interest rates change. It is an average spread because it is based on a large number of potential paths for interest rates. The cost of the embedded option is a by-product of the model. It is not estimated using an option pricing model directly.

Because there are many technical issues in developing an option-adjusted spread model, there can be considerable differences in the values reported by dealer firms. A portfolio manager using an option-adjusted spread reported by a dealer or one from a model developed by a vendor firm must recognize why these differences may occur. Moreover, a portfolio manager must understand the limitations of using option-adjusted spread analysis in selecting bonds to satisfy asset/liability objectives.

QUESTIONS FOR CHAPTER 14

1. What are the two drawbacks of the traditional approach to valuation of bonds with embedded options?

2. In Robert Litterman, José Scheinkman, and Laurence Weiss, "Volatility and the Yield Curve," *The Journal of Fixed Income*, Premier Issue, 1991, p. 49, the following statement is made:

    Many fixed-income securities — e.g., callable bonds — contain embedded options whose prices are sensitive to the level of volatility. Modeling the additional impact of volatility on the value of the coupons allows for a better understanding of the price behavior of these securities.

    Explain why.

3. Is the static spread for a 3-year, 9% coupon corporate bond selling at 105.58, given the theoretical Treasury spot rate curve below, 50, 100, or 120 basis points?

Six-Month Period	Annual Spot Rate
1	4.0%
2	4.2
3	4.9
4	5.4
5	5.7
6	6.0

4. Under what conditions would the traditional yield spread be close to the static spread?

5. What is the option cost for a callable bond if it is determined that the option-adjusted spread is 80 basis points and the static spread is 130 basis points?

6. What is the option-adjusted spread for an on-the-run Treasury security?

7. How does the option-adjusted spread approach take into consideration credit risk?

8. a. Calculate the effective duration of a 10% coupon Treasury bond with 5 years to maturity selling at par. (In your calculation of effective duration change the yield up and down by 40 basis points.)

    b. Calculate the modified duration of the bond in 8(a).

    c. How well does effective duration approximate modified duration?

9. a. Explain how the option-adjusted spread approach can be incorporated into the total return framework.

    b. In the option-adjusted spread approach, how is effective duration calculated?

Chapter 15

ANALYSIS OF MORTGAGE-BACKED SECURITIES

There are two approaches to value mortgage-backed securities (including pass-throughs, collateralized mortgage obligations, and stripped mortgage-backed securities): (1) the static cash flow yield methodology, and (2) the option-adjusted spread methodology described in the previous chapter.

STATIC CASH FLOW YIELD METHODOLOGY

The static cash flow yield methodology is the simplest to use, although we shall see that it offers little insight into the relative value of an MBS.

Cash Flow Yield

The static cash flow yield methodology is based on the cash flow yield measure that we described for pass-throughs in Chapter 11. And a cash flow yield is based on some prepayment assumption.

As we have noted several times already, the yield to maturity has two shortcomings as a measure of a bond's potential return: (1) it is assumed that the coupon payments can be reinvested at a rate equal to the yield to maturity, and (2) it is assumed that the bond is held to maturity. These shortcomings are equally present in application of the cash flow yield measure: (1) the projected cash flows are assumed to be reinvested at the cash flow yield, and (2) the mortgage-backed security is assumed to be held until the final payout based on some prepayment assumption.

The importance of reinvestment risk, the risk that the cash flow will be reinvested at a rate less than the cash flow yield, is particularly important for many mortgage-backed securities because payments come as frequently as every month. The cash flow yield, moreover, is dependent on realization of the projected cash flow according to some prepayment rate. If actual prepayments vary from the prepayment rate assumed, the cash flow yield will not be realized.

Spread to Treasuries

It should be clear that at the time of purchase it is not possible to determine an exact yield for a mortgage-backed security; the yield will depend on the actual prepayment experience of the mortgages in the pool. Nevertheless, the convention in all fixed-income markets is to measure the yield on a non-Treasury security to that of a "comparable" Treasury security.

The repayment of principal over time makes it inappropriate to compare the yield of a mortgage-backed security to a Treasury of a stated maturity. Instead, market participants have used two measures: Macaulay duration (as explained in Chapter 4), and average life. The average life is the average time to receipt of principal payments (projected scheduled principal payments and projected principal prepayments), weighted by the amount of principal expected divided by the total principal to be repaid. Symbolically, the average life is calculated as:

$$\text{Average life} = \frac{1}{12} \sum_{t=1}^{n} \frac{t\,(\text{Principal expected at time } t)}{\text{Total principal}}$$

where n is the number of months remaining.

Effective Duration and Convexity

Modified duration is a measure of the sensitivity of a bond's price to interest rate changes, assuming that the expected cash flow does not change with interest rates. Modified duration is consequently not an appropriate measure for mortgage-backed securities, because prepayments do cause the projected cash flow to change as interest rates change. When interest rates fall (rise), prepayments are expected to rise (fall). As a result, when interest rates fall (rise), duration may decrease (increase) rather than increase (decrease). This property, as we explained in Chapter 13, is referred to as negative convexity.

Negative convexity has the same impact on the price performance of a mortgage-backed security as it does on the performance of a callable bond (discussed in Chapter 13). When interest rates decline, a bond with an embedded call option, which is what a mortgage-backed security is, will not perform as well as an option-free bond.

While modified duration is an inappropriate measure of interest rate sensitivity, there is a way to allow for changing prepayment rates on cash flow as interest rates change. This is achieved by using the formula for approximating duration and convexity that we presented in Chapter 14.

When allowing for changing cash flow, the resulting duration and convexity are called *effective duration* and *effective convexity*. As indicated in the previous chapter:

$$\text{Effective duration} = \frac{P_- - P_+}{\left(P_0\right)\left(y_+ - y_-\right)}$$

Where

$$
\begin{aligned}
P_0 &= \text{Initial price (per \$100 of par value)} \\
P_- &= \text{Price if yield is decreased by } x \text{ basis points} \\
P_+ &= \text{Price if yield is increased by } x \text{ basis points} \\
y_- &= \text{Initial yield minus } x \text{ basis points} \\
y_+ &= \text{Initial yield plus } x \text{ basis points}
\end{aligned}
$$

The price of the security at the higher and lower interest rates will depend on the prepayment rate assumed. The prepayment rate typically is assumed to be greater at a lower interest rate than at a higher interest rate. Thus, calculation of effective duration requires a prepayment model to determine how prepayments are expected to change as interest rates change.

To illustrate how to calculate effective duration, consider the pass-through described in Exhibit 11-1 of Chapter 11. The price assuming 100% PSA and a yield of 10.21% is \$94,521, or 94.521 per \$100 of par value. Let's look at what would happen to the price if the yield were to change by 50 basis points. Suppose that if the yield decreases by 50 basis points to 9.71%, the prepayment rate is assumed to be unchanged at 100% PSA. However, if the yield instead increases by 50 basis points to 10.71%, the prepayment rate is assumed to decrease to 75% PSA. The price at 9.71% would be \$97,520 (97.520 per \$100 of par value), and the price at 10.71% would be \$90,992 (90.992 per \$100 of par value). Therefore,

$$
\begin{aligned}
P_0 &= 94.521 \\
P_- &= 97.520 \\
P_+ &= 90.992 \\
y_- &= .0971\ (.1021 - .50) \\
y_+ &= .1071\ (.1021 + .50)
\end{aligned}
$$

$$\text{Effective duration} = \frac{97.520 - 90.992}{94.521(.1071 - .0971)} = 6.91$$

An effective duration of 6.91 means that the price will change by approximately 6.91% per 100-basis point change in interest rates after allowing for changes in prepayments.

The formula for effective convexity is:

$$\text{Effective convexity} = \frac{P_+ + P_- - 2\left(P_0\right)}{\left(P_0\right)\left[.5\left(y_+ - y_-\right)\right]^2}$$

Using values for the pass-through in the previous illustration:

$$\text{Effective convexity} = \frac{90.992 + 97.520 - 2(94.521)}{(94.521)\left[.5(.1071 - .0971)\right]^2}$$

$$= \frac{-.530}{94.521\,(.005)^2} = -224.29$$

Notice that the convexity of this pass-through is negative.

OPTION-ADJUSTED SPREAD METHODOLOGY

We have noted that for the static cash flow yield methodology, the yield spread for a mortgage-backed security is the difference between the cash flow yield and the yield to maturity of a comparable Treasury. The latter is obtained from the yield curve. The drawback of this procedure is that the cash flow yield for neither the mortgage-backed security nor the Treasury security is calculated properly because the calculation fails to take into consideration (1) the term structure of interest rates for Treasuries (i.e., the theoretical spot rate curve), and (2) expected interest rate volatility which will alter the expected cash flow for the pass-through because of changes in prepayments. The option-adjusted spread methodology, based on some assumed interest rate volatility, takes these into consideration.

Static Spread

We explain in Chapter 14 that the proper way to evaluate mortgage-backed securities of the same duration but with different coupon rates is to compare them with a portfolio of zero-coupon Treasury securities that have the same cash flow as projected for the mortgage-backed security. Assuming the mortgage-backed security's cash flow is riskless, its value is equal to the portfolio value of all of the zero-coupon Treasuries. In turn, these cash flows are valued at the spot rates. A mortgage-backed security's value will be less than the portfolio of zero-coupon Treasury securities because investors demand a spread for the risk associated with holding a mortgage-backed security rather than a riskless package of Treasury securities (riskless in the sense of default risk and certainty of the cash flow).

The static spread to Treasuries is the spread that will make the present value of the projected cash flow from the mortgage-backed security, when discounted at the spot rate plus a spread, equal to its market price. A trial-and-error procedure is required to determine the spread.

Option Cost

Using the decomposition principle for a callable bond discussed in Chapter 13, we can obtain the implied cost of the option of a mortgage-backed security by calculating the difference between the option-adjusted spread at the assumed volatility of interest rates and the static spread. That is,

Option cost = Static spread − Option-adjusted spread

The option cost measures the prepayment (or option) risk embedded in the security.

Illustrations

In this section we will show how the option-adjusted spread (OAS) is applicable to analysis of several types of mortgage-backed securities.

Application to Pass-Throughs: The OAS concepts we describe will be made clearer with some illustrations from the option-adjusted spreads reported by Hayre and Lauterbach for six GNMAs, which we reproduce as Exhibit 15-1.[1] The analysis is based on closing prices as of May 5, 1988. The cash flow yield in the fourth column is based on a projected PSA prepayment rate shown in the third column (reached using the Prudential-Bache prepayment model). The spreads shown in the next-to-last column of the exhibit are the difference between the GNMA (cash flow) yield and the yield to maturity of a Treasury with a maturity equal to the same average life as the GNMA. (The average life is shown in the fifth column.) The last column shows the option-adjusted spread.

According to the static cash flow yield methodology, the respective spreads for the GNMA 8 and GNMA 11 of 106 and 108 basis points suggest that both have similar returns over a comparable Treasury security. The OAS methodology, however, indicates that the GNMA 8 is more attractive than the GNMA 11 because of its higher option-adjusted spread (88 basis points versus 48 basis points). This result reflects the negative convexity of the higher-coupon GNMA and its higher prepayment volatility as interest rates change.

---

[1] See Lakhbir S. Hayre and Kenneth Lauterbach, "Stochastic Valuation of Debt Securities," in Frank J. Fabozzi, ed., *Managing Institutional Assets* (New York: Harper & Row, 1990), pp. 321-364.

EXHIBIT 15-1   Yield Spreads and OASs for GNMAs.

Coupon	(1) Price[a]	(2) Rem. Term	(3) Proj. PSA[b]	(4) Yield	(5) Avg. Life	(6) Spread[c]	(7) OAS[d]
GNMA 8	91-18	18-09	100	9.84	8.0	106	88
GNMA 9	96-08	20-08	108	9.87	8.5	105	80
GNMA 10	99-31	28-02	130	10.14	9.6	123	80
GNMA 11	105-21	26-00	199	9.77	6.9	108	48
GNMA 12	109-00	26-03	331	9.19	4.4	88	33
GNMA 13	111-12	25-00	396	8.89	3.6	70	50

a. Prices and prepayment projection as of May 5, 1988.
b. Projected prepayment rate is expressed as a percentage of the benchmark Public Securities Association (PSA) curve.
c. Spread is the difference between the yield of the GNMA and the Treasury curve yield at the average life.
d. OAS is calculated using a volatility of 15%.

Source: Lakhbir S. Hayre and Kenneth Lauterbach, "Stochastic Valuation of Debt Securities," in Frank J. Fabozzi, ed., *Managing Institutional Assets* (New York: Harper & Row, 1990), Table 3, p. 339.

The sensitivity of the OAS to the interest rate volatility assumption for each of the GNMA pass-throughs in Exhibit 15-1 is shown in Exhibit 15-2, which looks at four annual interest rate volatilities. As expected, the higher the expected interest rate volatility, the lower the OAS. The difference between the OAS at a nonzero interest rate volatility and the OAS at a zero interest rate volatility (that is, the static spread as calculated by these researchers) is the assumed cost of the option. As can be seen from Exhibit 15-2, the lower the coupon rate, the lower the option cost.

EXHIBIT 15-2   Sensitivity of GNMA OASs to Volatility Changes

	OAS at Volatility of:			
	0%	10%	15%	20%
GNMA 8	105	96	88	79
GNMA 9	106	94	80	64
GNMA 10	130	106	80	55
GNMA 11	119	82	48	17
GNMA 12	116	68	33	3
GNMA 13	115	77	50	26

Source: Lakhbir S. Hayre and Kenneth Lauterbach, "Stochastic Valuation of Debt Securities," in Frank J. Fabozzi (ed.), *Managing Institutional Assets* (new York: harper & Row, 1990), Table 4, p. 340.

CMO Application: An illustration will show how CMOs can be analyzed using the OAS methodology (analysis was provided by Scott Richard of Goldman, Sachs).[2] Exhibit 15-3 shows the OAS for a plain vanilla sequential-pay structure, FNMA 89-97. The structure includes five bond classes, A, B, C, D and Z, and a residual class. The Z class is an accrual bond, and the D class is an IOette. Analysis focuses on the A, B, C, and Z classes. The top panel of Exhibit 15-3 shows the OAS and the option cost for the collateral and four classes in the CMO structure. The option-adjusted spread for the collateral is 70 basis points. As the option cost is 45 basis points, the static spread is 115 basis points (70 basis points plus 45 basis points). Note that the classes do not share the option-adjusted spread equally. The A class does not receive a significant portion of the OAS, but only 23 basis points. The longer maturity structures, particularly the Z class, receive much of the option-adjusted spread. The option cost is also distributed unequally among the four classes. The Z class, which is exposed to the greatest prepayment risk, has the highest option cost, a cost that is greater than even for the collateral.

The next panel in the exhibit shows for the collateral and the four classes (1) how the option-adjusted spread changes if prepayments are at 80% and 120% of the prepayment speed assumed in estimat'ng the option-adjusted spread in the base case (the top panel), and (2) the change in the dollar price at these prepayment rates, assuming that the option-adjusted spread is constant. Let's look first at the collateral. If the prepayment speed is 80% of the assumed prepayment speed in the base case, the option-adjusted spread does not change, and there would be no change in the collateral price. Note in contrast the dramatic changes for the four classes.

To see how an investor might use this information, consider the A class. At 80% of the prepayment speed, the option-adjusted spread for this class declines from 23 basis points to 8 basis points. For a buyer of the A class, if the option-adjusted spread is held constant, the panel also indicates that the investor would lose $0.43 per $100 par value. The reason for the adverse effect of a slowdown in prepayment speed on the A class is obvious. If prepayments slow down, class A (the class with the shortest stated maturity) extends. The option-adjusted spreads for the two longer classes (C and Z) do not change materially.

Should the prepayment speed be 120% greater than in the base case assumption, the second panel in Exhibit 15-3 indicates that the collateral's option-adjusted spread will increase only slightly (one basis point), but

---

[2] This illustration was presented by Scott Richard at the Collateralized Mortgage Obligations tutorial sponsored by Frank J. Fabozzi Associates on September 27, 1991.

that the option-adjusted spread for the other classes does not change equally. If prepayments are faster, the option-adjusted spread of the Z class rises dramatically, and its price increases substantially ($2.70 per $100 par) assuming the option-adjusted spread is held constant at the base case of 74 basis points.

EXHIBIT 15-3   Option-Adjusted Spread Analysis of FNMA 89-97 Classes A, B, C, and Z (as of 4/27/90)

Base case (assumes 12% interest rate volatility)

	Option-adjusted Spread (in Basis Points)	Option Cost (in Basis Points)
Collateral	70	45
Class		
A	23	29
B	46	41
C	59	36
Z	74	50

Prepayments at 80% and 120% of Prepayment Model (assumes 12% interest rate volatility)

	New Option-Adjusted Spread (in Basis Points)		Change in Price per $100 Par (Holding OAS Constant)	
	80%	120%	80%	120%
Collateral	70	71	$ .00	$ .04
Class				
A	8	40	−.43	.48
B	31	65	−.86	1.10
C	53	73	−.41	.95
Z	72	93	−.28	2.70

Interest rate volatility of 8% and 16%

	New Option-Adjusted Spread (in Basis Points)		Change in Price per $100 Par (Holding OAS Constant)	
	8%	16%	8%	16%
Collateral	92	46	$1.03	−$1.01
Class				
A	38	5	.42	−.51
B	67	21	1.22	−1.45
C	77	39	1.22	−1.36
Z	99	50	3.55	−3.41

Source: Data provided by Scott Richard of Goldman, Sachs, Inc.

The second panel basically indicates that while the option-adjusted spread and change in collateral price are not sensitive to the prepayment assumption (for plus and minus 20%), the same cannot be said for the classes in the structure.

The third panel shows what happens if interest rate volatility is less or more than the 12% assumed in the base case. Lower interest rate volatility (8%) results in an increase in the option-adjusted spread for the collateral to 92 basis points and an increase in the collateral price (assuming a constant option-adjusted spread of 70 basis points) by $1.03 per $100 par value. Thus, if actual volatility is less than that used to model this deal (the base case of 12%), the collateral and the classes would be priced cheap. The greatest increase in value resulting from underestimation of future market volatility comes in the Z class.

If volatility is higher instead of lower (16% instead of 12%), there will be more instances when the homeowner is likely to prepay. Consequently, the option-adjusted spread and the change in price (holding the option-adjusted spread constant) will decline for the collateral and the four classes.

Effective Duration and Convexity

The option-adjusted spread methodology allows effective duration and convexity to be computed by increasing and decreasing short-term Treasury rates by a small amount. At the same time, the option-adjusted spread is kept constant. This produces two average total present values: one when short-term interest rates are increased and one when short-term interest rates are decreased. These average total present values can be viewed as the theoretical prices, given small interest rate changes. These are the prices that can be substituted into the formulas for effective duration and convexity.

SUMMARY

There are two methodologies commonly used to value mortgage-backed securities: static cash flow yield and option-adjusted spread. The cash flow yield is the yield that will make the present value of the cash flow, according to a particular prepayment assumption, equal to the market price of the mortgage-backed security. An effective duration and convexity can also be computed. The drawback of this framework is the difficulty of selecting an appropriate benchmark Treasury security.

The option-adjusted spread methodology was outlined in the previous chapter, and explained further here. Its application to mortgage-backed securities assumes cash flow along predicted paths according to a prepayment model. The methodology can be used to determine the option-adjusted spread and the option cost of mortgage-backed securities.

QUESTIONS FOR CHAPTER 15

1. Suppose you are told that the cash flow yield of a pass-through security is 9% and that you are seeking to invest in a security with a yield greater than 8.8%.

   a. What additional information would you need to know before you might acquire this pass-through security?

   b. What are the limitations of the cash flow yield for assessing the potential return from investing in a mortgage-backed security?

2. The cash flow yield methodology requires calculation of a spread over a comparable Treasury security. How is a comparable Treasury determined?

3. In the calculation of effective duration and effective convexity, why is a prepayment model needed?

4. The following excerpt is taken from an article entitled "Fidelity Eyes $250 Million Move Into Premium PACs and I-Os," which appeared in the January 27, 1992, issue of *BondWeek*, pp. 1 and 21:

   Three Fidelity investment mortgage funds are considering investing this quarter a total of $250 million in premium planned amortization classes of collateralized mortgage obligations and some interest-only strips, said Jim Wolfson, portfolio manager.... Wolfson...will look mainly at PACs backed by 9-10% Federal Home Loan Mortgage Corp. and Federal National Mortgage Association pass-throughs. These have higher option-adjusted spreads than regular agency pass-throughs, or similar premium Government National Mortgage-backed PACs, he said. He expects I-Os will start to perform better as prepayments start to slow later in this quarter.

   The higher yields on I-Os and premium PACs compensate for their higher prepayment risk, said Wolfson. "You get paid in yield to take on negative convexity," he said. He does not feel prepayments will accelerate ....

   a. Why would premium PACs and interest-only strips offer higher yields if the market expects prepayments will accelerate or are highly uncertain?

   b. What does Wolfson mean when he says "You get paid in yield to take on negative convexity"?

   c. What measure is Wolfson using to assess the risks associated with prepayments?

5. In an article entitled "CUNA Mutual Looks for Noncallable Corporates," which appeared in the November 4, 1991, issue of *BondWeek*, p. 6, Joe Goglia, a portfolio manager for CUNA Mutual Insurance Group, stated that he invests in "planned amortization class tranches, which have less exposure to prepayment risk and are more positively convex than other mortgage-backeds." Is this true?

6. What is the effect of greater expected interest rate volatility on the option-adjusted spread of a pass-through security?

7. Why would the option-adjusted spread reported by dealer firms for the same mortgage-backed security differ?

8. What do you think that a negative option cost means for a class of a collateralized mortgage obligation?

Chapter 16

ANALYSIS OF CONVERTIBLE BONDS

In Chapter 6, we described convertible bonds. This chapter explains methodologies for analyzing them, beginning with a review of the basic provisions of convertible bonds.

CONVERTIBLE BOND PROVISIONS

The conversion provision in a corporate bond issue grants the bondholder the right to convert the bond into a predetermined number of shares of common stock of the issuer. A convertible bond is therefore a corporate bond with a call option to buy the common stock of the issuer.

Exchangeable bonds grant the bondholder the right to exchange the bonds for the common stock of a firm *other* than the issuer of the bond. For example, Dart & Kraft has an outstanding bond issue that is exchangeable for the common stock of Minnesota Mining and Manufacturing. (Dart & Kraft obtained the 3M common stock in exchange for the sale of Riker Laboratories.) Some Ford Motor Credit bonds are exchangeable for the common stock of the parent company, Ford Motor Company. A few issues are exchangeable into more than one security. General Cinema, for example, has an outstanding issue that is convertible into the common stock of R.J. Reynolds and Sea-Land Corporation.

The number of shares of common stock that the bondholder will receive from exercising the call option of a convertible bond or an exchangeable bond is called the *conversion ratio*. The conversion privilege may extend for all or only some portion of the bond's life, and the stated conversion ratio may fall over time. It is always adjusted proportionately for stock splits and stock dividends.

At the time of issuance of a convertible bond, the issuer has effectively granted the bondholder the right to purchase the common stock at a price equal to:

$$\frac{\text{Par value of convertible bond}}{\text{Conversion ratio}}$$

This price is referred to as the *par conversion price* and often in the indenture simply as the *conversion price*.

Along with the conversion privilege granted to the bondholder, most convertible bonds are callable at the option of the issuer, and some are putable. In our initial analysis, we ignore these embedded options.

Illustration

To illustrate how to analyze a convertible bond, we use the same hypothetical bond throughout the chapter:

XYZ bond

Maturity = 10 years

Coupon rate = 10%

Conversion ratio = 50

Par value = $1,000

Current market price of XYZ bond = $950

Current market price of XYZ common stock = $17

Dividends per share = $1

The conversion price for XYZ bond is:

$$\text{Conversion price} \; = \; \frac{\$1,000}{50} \; = \; \$20$$

MINIMUM VALUE OF A CONVERTIBLE BOND

The *conversion value* of a convertible bond is the value of the bond if it is converted immediately.[1] That is,

Conversion value = Market price of common stock x Conversion ratio

The minimum price of a convertible bond is the greater of

1. Its conversion value, or
2. Its value as a corporate bond without the conversion option — that is, based on the convertible bond's cash flows if not converted (i.e., a plain vanilla bond). This value is called its *straight value*.

---

[1] Technically, the standard textbook definition of conversion value given here is theoretically incorrect because as bondholders convert, the price of the stock will decline. The theoretically correct definition for the conversion value is that it is the product of the conversion ratio and the stock price *after* conversion.

To estimate the straight value, we must determine the required yield on a nonconvertible bond with the same quality rating and similar investment characteristics. Given this estimated required yield, the straight value is then the present value of the bond's cash flows using this yield to discount the cash flows.

If the convertible bond does not sell for the greater of these two values, arbitrage profits could be realized. For example, suppose the conversion value is greater than the straight value, and the bond trades at its straight value. An investor can buy the convertible bond at the straight value and convert it. By doing so, the investor realizes a gain equal to the difference between the conversion value and the straight value. Suppose, instead, the straight value is greater than the conversion value, and the bond trades at its conversion value. By buying the convertible at the conversion value, the investor will realize a higher yield than a comparable straight bond.

Illustration

For the XYZ convertible bond, the conversion value is equal to:

Conversion value = $\$17 \times 50 = \$850$

To determine the straight value, it is necessary to determine what comparable bonds are trading for in the market. Suppose that comparable bonds are trading to yield 14%. The straight value is then the price of a 10%, 10-year bond selling to yield 14%. The price for such a bond would be $788.[2]

Given a conversion value of $850 and a straight value of $788, the minimum price for the XYZ bond is $850. To see this, note that if the bond is selling at its straight value rather than its conversion value, an investor could buy the bond for $788 and simultaneously sell 50 shares of XYZ stock at $17 per share. When the short sale of the stock is covered when the bond is converted, the transaction would produce an arbitrage profit of $62 per XYZ bond purchased. The only way to eliminate this arbitrage profit is for the XYZ bond to sell for $850, its conversion value.

Suppose instead that comparable nonconvertible bonds are trading to yield 11.8%. Then the straight value of XYZ bond would be $896. The minimum price for the XYZ bond must be its straight value in this case, because that is a value higher than the conversion value of $850. To see this, suppose that the market price of the XYZ bond is $850. At this price, the yield would be about 12.7%, 90 basis points greater than comparable

---

[2] Actually, it is $788.10, but $788 will be used in our illustrations.

nonconvertible bonds. Investors would find the bond attractive. As investors buy the bond, they will bid up its price to where the new yield is 11.8%.

MARKET CONVERSION PRICE

The price that an investor effectively pays for the common stock if the convertible bond is purchased and then converted into the common stock is called the *market conversion price*.[3] It is found as follows:

$$\text{Market conversion price} = \frac{\text{Market price of convertible bond}}{\text{Conversion ratio}}$$

The market conversion price is a useful benchmark because once the actual market price of the stock rises above the market conversion price, any further stock price increase is certain to increase the value of the convertible bond by at least the same percentage. Therefore, the market conversion price can be viewed as a break-even point.

An investor who purchases a convertible bond rather than the underlying stock typically pays a premium over the current market price of the stock. This premium per share is equal to the difference between the market conversion price and the current market price of the common stock. That is,

Market conversion premium per share =
Market conversion price – Current market price

The market conversion premium per share is usually expressed as a percentage of the current market price as follows:

$$\text{Market conversion premium ratio} = \frac{\text{Market conversion premium per share}}{\text{Market price of common stock}}$$

Why would someone be willing to pay a premium to buy this stock? Recall that the minimum price of a convertible bond is the greater of its conversion value or its straight value. Thus, as the stock price declines, the price of the convertible bond will not fall below its straight value. The straight value therefore acts as a floor for the convertible bond price.

Viewed in this context, the market conversion premium per share can be seen as the price of a call option. As explained in Chapter 13, the buyer of a call option limits the downside risk to the option price. In the case of a convertible bond, for a premium, the bondholder limits the downside risk to the straight value of the bond. The difference between the buyer of a call

---

[3] The market conversion price is also called the conversion parity price.

option and the buyer of a convertible bond is that the former knows precisely the dollar amount of the downside risk, while the latter knows only that the most that can be lost is the difference between the convertible bond price and the straight value. The straight value at some future date, however, is not known; the value will change as the interest rate changes.

Illustration

At a market price of $950, a stock price of $17, and a conversion ratio of 50, the market conversion price, market conversion premium per share, and market conversion premium ratio of the XYZ convertible bond are calculated as follows:

$$\text{Market conversion price} = \frac{\$950}{50} = \$19$$

$$\text{Market conversion premium per share} = \$19 - \$17 = \$2$$

$$\text{Market conversion premium ratio} = \frac{\$2}{\$17} = .118 \text{ or } 11.8\%$$

CURRENT INCOME OF CONVERTIBLE BOND VERSUS STOCK

As an offset to the market conversion premium per share, investing in the convertible bond rather than buying the stock directly generally means that the investor realizes higher current income from the coupon interest paid on the convertible bond than would be received as dividends paid on the number of shares equal to the conversion ratio. Analysts evaluating a convertible bond typically compute the time it takes to recover the premium per share by computing the *premium payback period* (which is also known as the *break-even time*). This is computed as follows:

$$\frac{\text{Market conversion premium per share}}{\text{Favorable income differential per share}}$$

where the favorable income differential per share is equal to:[4]

$$\frac{\text{Coupon interest from bond} - \left(\text{Conversion ratio} \times \text{Dividend per share}\right)}{\text{Conversion ratio}}$$

---

[4] A more precise methodology for calculating the favorable income from holding the convertible is recommended in Luke Knecht and Mike McCowin, "Valuing Convertible Securities," in Frank J. Fabozzi (ed.), *Advances and Innovations in Bond and Mortgage Markets* (Chicago: Probus Publishing, 1989). In most cases the conventional formula presented in the text is sufficient.

Notice that the premium payback period does *not* take into account the time value of money.

Illustration

For the XYZ convertible bond, the market conversion premium per share is $2. The favorable income differential per share is found as follows:

Coupon interest from bond = .10   x $1,000 = $100
Conversion ratio   x   Dividend per share = 50   x $1 = $50

Therefore,

$$\text{Favorable income differential per share} = \frac{\$100 - \$50}{50} = \$1$$

and

$$\text{Premium payback period} = \frac{\$2}{\$1} = 2 \text{ years}$$

Without considering the time value of money, the investor would recover the market conversion premium per share in two years.

DOWNSIDE RISK WITH A CONVERTIBLE BOND

Investors usually use the straight value of the bond as a measure of the downside risk of a convertible bond, because the price of the convertible bond cannot fall below this value. Thus, the straight value acts as the *current* floor for the price of the convertible bond. The downside risk is measured as a percentage of the straight value and computed as follows:

$$\text{Premium over straight value} = \frac{\text{Market price of the convertible bond}}{\text{Straight value}} - 1$$

The higher the premium over straight value, all other factors constant, the less attractive the convertible bond.

Despite its use in practice, this measure of downside risk is flawed because the straight value (the floor) changes as interest rates change. If interest rates rise (fall), the straight value falls (rises) making the floor fall (rise). Therefore, the downside risk changes as interest rates change.

Illustration

Earlier we said that if comparable nonconvertible bonds are trading to yield 14%, the straight value of the XYZ bond would be $788. The premium over straight value is then

$$\text{Premium over straight value} = \frac{\$950}{\$788} - 1 = .21 \text{ or } 21\%.$$

If the yield on a comparable nonconvertible bond is 11.8% instead of 14%, the straight value would be $896 and the premium over straight value would be

$$\text{Premium over straight value} = \frac{\$896}{\$788} - 1 = .14 \text{ or } 14\%.$$

INVESTMENT CHARACTERISTICS OF A CONVERTIBLE BOND

The investment characteristics of a convertible bond depend on the stock price. If the price of the stock is low, so that the straight value is considerably higher than the conversion value, the bond will trade much like a straight bond. The convertible bond in such instances is referred to as a *bond equivalent* or a *busted convertible*.

When the price of the stock is such that the conversion value is considerably higher than the straight value, then the convertible bond will trade as if it were an equity instrument; in this case it is said to be an *equity equivalent*. In such cases, the market conversion premium per share will be small.

Between these two cases, bond equivalent and equity equivalent, the convertible bond trades as a *hybrid security*, having the characteristics of both a bond and an equity instrument.

THE PROS AND CONS OF INVESTING IN A CONVERTIBLE BOND

So far we have presented several measures that can be used to analyze convertible bonds. Let's use the XYZ convertible bond to drive home the pros and cons of investing in a convertible bond.

Suppose that an investor is considering purchase of a stock or a convertible bond. The stock can be purchased in the market for $17. By buying the convertible bond, the investor is effectively purchasing the stock for $19 (the market conversion price per share).

Look at the outcome one month from now, assuming that XYZ stock rises to $34. An investor buying the stock would realize a gain of $17 ($34 − $17) on a $17 investment, or a 100% return. In contrast, the conversion value for the bond would be $1,700 ($34 x 50). Because the price of XYZ bond is $950, the investor would realize a return of about 79%. The return in fact would probably be slightly higher because the convertible bond would trade at a slight premium to its conversion value. The reason for the lower return by buying the convertible bond rather than the stock directly is that the investor has effectively paid $2 per share more for the stock. Thus, the investor realizes a gain based on a stock price of $19 rather than $17.

So far, we've illustrated the advantage of owning the stock rather than the bond when the price of the stock rises. Let's look at the situation where the stock declines in value to $7. The investor who buys the stock now realizes a loss of $10 per share for a return of −59%. The conversion value of the XYZ bond likewise drops, to $350 ($7 x 50). Its price, however, will not fall to that level. Recall from our earlier discussion that the minimum price of a convertible bond will be the greater of its conversion value or its straight value. Assuming that the straight value is $788, and it does not change over the one-month period, the value of XYZ bond will fall to only $788. This means that the investor realizes a loss of only 21% (the downside risk or the premium over straight value calculated earlier). The loss would be even less in fact because the convertible bond would trade at a premium to its conversion value.

The critical assumption in this analysis is that the straight value does not change, although it can change for any of the reasons cited in Chapter 2. More specifically, if interest rates rise in the economy, the straight value will decline. Even if interest rates do not rise, the perceived creditworthiness of the issuer may deteriorate, causing investors to demand a higher yield. In fact, the stock price and the yield required by investors are not independent. When the price of the stock drops precipitously, as in our $17 to $7 illustration, the perceived creditworthiness of the issuer may decline, causing a decline in the straight value. In any event, although the straight value may decline, it still is a floor (albeit a moving floor) for the convertible bond price. In our illustration, the straight value would have to fall about $390 (59% loss on $950), to equal the loss on the stock purchase.

The illustration clearly demonstrates that there are benefits and drawbacks of investing in convertible bonds. The disadvantage is the upside potential give up because a premium per share must be paid. An advantage is the reduction in downside risk (as determined by the straight value), with the opportunity to recoup the premium per share through the higher current income from owning the convertible bond.

Call Risk

Convertible issues are callable by the issuer. This is a valuable feature for issuers, who deem the current market price of their stock undervalued enough so that selling stock directly would dilute the equity of current stockholders. The firm would prefer to raise equity funds over incurring debt, so it issues a convertible setting the conversion ratio on the basis of a stock price it regards as acceptable. Once the market price reaches the conversion point, the firm will want to see the conversion happen in view of the risk that the price may drop in the future. This gives the firm an interest in forcing conversion, even though this is not in the interest of the owners of the security whose price is likely to be adversely affected by the call.

Takeover Risk

Corporate takeovers represent another risk to investing in convertible bonds. If an issuer is acquired by another company or by its own management (as in the case of a management-led leveraged buyout), the stock price may not appreciate sufficiently for the holders of the convertible bond to benefit from the conversion feature. As the stock of the acquired company may no longer trade after a takeover, the investor can be left with a bond that pays a lower coupon rate than comparable-risk corporate bonds.

AN OPTIONS APPROACH

In our discussion of convertible bonds, we did not address the following questions:

1. What is a fair value for the conversion premium per share?
2. How do we handle convertible bonds with call and/or put options?
3. How does a change in interest rates affect the stock price?

The option pricing approach to valuation described in Chapter 13 can help us answer these questions.

Consider first a noncallable/nonputable convertible bond. The investor who purchases this bond would be entering into two separate transactions: (1) buying a noncallable/nonputable straight bond, and (2) buying a call option (or warrant) on the stock, where the number of shares that can be purchased with the call option is equal to the conversion ratio.

The question is: What is the fair value for the call option? The fair value depends on the factors (discussed in Chapter 13) that affect the price of a call option. One key factor is the expected price volatility of the stock: the more the expected price volatility, the greater the value of the call option. The theoretical value of a call option can be valued using the Black-Scholes option pricing model[5] or the binomial option pricing model.[6] As a first approximation to the value of a convertible bond, the formula would be:

Convertible bond value = Straight value + Price of the call option on the stock

The price of the call option is added to the straight value because the investor has purchased a call option on the stock.

Now let's add in a common feature of a convertible bond: the issuer's right to call the bond. The issuer can force conversion by calling the bond. For example, suppose that the call price is $1,030 per $1,000 par and the conversion value is $1,700. If the issuer calls the bonds, the optimal strategy for the investor is to convert the bond and receive shares worth $1,700.[7] The investor, however, loses any premium over the conversion value that is reflected in the market price. Therefore, the analysis of convertible bonds must take into account the value of the issuer's right to call the bond. This depends, in turn, on (1) future interest rate volatility, and (2) economic factors that determine whether it is optimal for the issuer to call the bond.

The Black-Scholes option pricing model cannot handle this situation. Instead, the binomial option pricing model can be used simultaneously to value the bondholder's call option on the stock and the issuer's right to call the bonds. The bondholder's put option can also be accommodated. To link interest rates and stock prices together (the third question we raised above), statistical analysis of historical movements of these two variables must be estimated and incorporated into the model.

While the option pricing approach offers a great deal of promise and

---

[5] Fischer Black and Myron Scholes, "The Pricing of Corporate Liabilities," *Journal of Political Economy* (May-June 1973), pp. 637-659.

[6] John C. Cox, Stephen A. Ross, and Mark Rubinstein, "Option Pricing: A Simplified Approach," *Journal of Financial Economics* (September 1979), pp. 229-263; Richard J. Rendleman and Brit J. Bartter, "Two-State Option Pricing," *Journal of Finance* (December 1979), pp. 1093-1110; and William F. Sharpe, *Investments* (Englewood Cliffs, N.J.: Prentice-Hall, 1981), Chapter 16.

[7] Actually, the conversion value would be less than $1,700, because the per share value after conversion would decline.

models have been proposed as far back as 1977, we have not seen widespread use of this approach.[8]

SUMMARY

In this chapter we have discussed the basic provisions of convertible bonds and explored a framework for evaluating these bonds. Analysis of a convertible bond requires calculation of the conversion value, straight value, market conversion price, market conversion premium ratio, and premium payback period.

The downside risk of a convertible bond usually is estimated by calculating the premium over straight value. The limitation of this measure is that the straight value (the floor) changes as interest rates change. Convertible bond investors are also subject to call risk and takeover risk.

The option pricing approach can be used to determine the fair value of the embedded call option. The value of the call option following this approach is estimated using some equity option pricing model such as the Black-Scholes model. While this represents a superior approach to the valuation of convertible bonds, the method has not been widely used.

---

[8] See, for example: Michael Brennan and Eduardo Schwartz, "Convertible Bonds: Valuation and Optimal Strategies for Call and Conversion," *Journal of Finance* (December 1977), pp. 1699-1715; Jonathan Ingersoll, "A Contingent-Claims Valuation of Convertible Securities," *Journal of Financial Economics* (May 1977), pp. 289-322; Michael Brennan and Eduardo Schwartz, "Analyzing Convertible Bonds," *Journal of Financial and Quantitative Analysis* (November 1980), pp. 907-929; and George Constantinides, "Warrant Exercise and Bond Conversion in Competitive Markets," *Journal of Financial Economics* (September 1984), pp. 371-398.

QUESTIONS FOR CHAPTER 16

1. This excerpt is taken from an article entitled "Caywood Looks for Convertibles," which appeared in the January 13, 1992, issue of *BondWeek*, p. 7:

   Caywood Christian Capital Management will invest new money in its $400 million high-yield portfolio in "busted convertibles," double-and triple-B rated convertible bonds of companies ...., said James Caywood, ceo. Caywood likes these convertibles as they trade at discounts and are unlikely to be called, he said.

   a. What is a "busted convertible"?
   b. What is the premium over straight value at which these bonds would trade?
   c. Why does Mr. Caywood seek convertibles with higher investment-grade ratings?
   d. Why is Mr. Caywood interested in call protection?

2. Explain the limitation of using premium over straight value as a measure of the downside risk of a convertible bond.

3. This excerpt comes from an article entitled "Bartlett Likes Convertibles," in the October 7, 1991, issue of *BondWeek*, p. 7:

   Bartlett & Co. is selectively looking for opportunities in convertible bonds that are trading cheaply because the equity of the issuer has dropped in value, according to Dale Rabiner, director of fixed income at the $800 million Cincinnati-based fund. Rabiner said he looks for five-year convertibles trading at yields comparable to straight bonds of companies he believes will rebound.

   Discuss this strategy for investing in convertible bonds.

4. Consider a convertible bond as follows:
   par value = $1,000
   coupon rate = 9.5%
   market price of convertible bond = $1,000
   conversion ratio = 37.383
   estimated straight value of bond = $510
   yield to maturity of straight bond = 18.7%

   Assume that the price of the common stock is $23 and that the dividend per share is $.75 per year.

   a. Calculate each of the following:
      (i)   Conversion value
      (ii)   Market conversion price
      (iii) Conversion premium per share
      (iv)   Conversion premium ratio
      (v)   Premium over straight value
      (vi)   Yield advantage of bond
      (vii) Premium payback period

   b. Suppose that the price of the common stock increases from \$23 to \$46.

      (i) What will be the approximate return realized from investing in the convertible bond?

      (ii) What would be the return realized if \$23 had been invested in the common stock?

      (iii) Why would the return on investing in the common stock directly be higher than investing in the convertible bond?

   c. Suppose that the price of the common stock declines from \$23 to \$8.

      (i) What will be the approximate return realized from investing in the convertible bond?

      (ii) What would be the return realized if \$23 had been invested in the common stock?

      (iii) Why would the return on investing in the convertible bond be higher than investing in the common stock directly?

5. A Merrill Lynch note structure called a Liquid Yield Option Note (LYON) is a zero-coupon instrument that is convertible into the common stock of the issuer. The conversion ratio is fixed for the entire life of the note. If investors wish to convert to the shares of the issuer, they must exchange the LYON for the stock. As a result, the conversion price increases over time. Why?

6. [This question is from CFA Examination III, June 1, 1991, Afternoon Session, Question 13]

     Simon Evans, CFA, is researching SOC Corporation, a company which has issued both convertible and straight bonds. A major broker/dealer makes an over-the-counter market in options on SOC's common stock. Evans is considering two possible portfolios:

Portfolio X - five SOC convertible bonds (total par value \$5,000) with a conversion ratio of 20

Portfolio Y- five SOC straight bonds (total par value \$5,000) and a call option for 100 SOC shares

     Evans believes that Portfolios X and Y are similar in some ways, because each portfolio holds SOC bonds and rights to own SOC stock.

     In preparing to make a portfolio decision, Evans obtained the current information presented in the following table:

SOC bonds data	Convertible	Straight
Coupon	5.5%	10.5%
Maturity	5 years	5 years
Conversion ratio	20.0	—
Market price	93.75	100.00
Yield-to-maturity	7.0%	10.5%

SOC call/option data (American style)

Strike price	$50.00
Expiration date	5 years
Call premium	$7.50

a. Certain steps are required to change each portfolio from SOC bonds to SOC common stock. Using *only* the information provided above, compare Portfolios X and Y with respect to *each* of the following:

  - transactions required to change holdings from bonds to stocks,
  - parties involved in the transactions, and
  - potential risks or costs associated with the changes.

b. Complete the following table. (Use 8.5302 as the present value of an ordinary annuity of $1 paid semi-annually for five years discounted at a 6% risk-free annual discount rate.)

	Straight SOC Bonds	Convertible SOC Bonds	Difference
Cost of five bonds	_____	_____	_____
Dollar amount of semi-annual coupon for five bonds	_____	_____	_____
Present value of cash flow differences		_____	

c. Recommend and justify the purchase of either Portfolio X or Portfolio Y, using your analysis in parts (a) and (b) above.

Chapter 17

INTEREST RATE FUTURES
CONTRACTS

A futures contract is an agreement that requires a party to the agreement either to buy or sell something at a designated future date at a predetermined price. In this chapter we describe interest rate futures contracts. Interest rate options and options on futures are covered in the next chapter. Interest rate swaps and interest rate agreements are the subject of Chapter 19.

With the advent of interest rate futures, options, swaps, caps, and floors, proactive portfolio risk management, in its broadest sense, assumes a new dimension. Money managers can achieve new degrees of freedom. It is now possible to alter the interest-rate sensitivity of a bond portfolio or an asset/liability position economically and quickly. These derivative contracts, so called because they derive their value from an underlying asset, offer money managers risk and return patterns that previously were either unavailable or too costly.

MECHANICS OF FUTURES TRADING

A futures contract is a firm legal agreement between a buyer (seller) and an established exchange or its clearinghouse in which the buyer (seller) agrees to take (make) delivery of something at a specified price at the end of a designated period of time. The price at which the parties agree to transact in the future is called the *futures price*. The designated date at which the parties must transact is called the *settlement* or *delivery date*.

To illustrate, suppose there is a futures contract traded on an exchange where the something to be bought or sold is bond XYZ, and the settlement is three months from now. Assume further that Bob buys this futures contract, and Sally sells this futures contract, and the price at which they agree to transact in the future is $100. Then $100 is the futures price. At the settlement date, Sally will deliver bond XYZ to Bob. Bob will give Sally $100, the futures price.

Most financial futures contracts have settlement dates in the months of March, June, September, or December. This means that at a predetermined time in the contract settlement month the contract stops trading, and a price is determined by the exchange for settlement of the contract. The contract with the soonest settlement date is called the *nearby futures contract*. The next futures contract is the one that settles just after the nearby contract. The contract farthest away in time from settlement is called the *most distant futures contract*.

Opening Position

When an investor takes a position in the market by buying a futures contract, the investor is said to be in a *long position* or to be *long futures*. If, instead, the investor's opening position is the sale of a futures contract, the investor is said to be in a *short position* or *short futures*.

Liquidating a Position

A party to a futures contract has two choices on liquidation of the position. First, the position can be liquidated prior to the settlement date. For this purpose, the party must take an offsetting position in the same contract. For the buyer of a futures contract, this means selling the same number of identical futures contracts; for the seller of a futures contract, this means buying the same number of identical futures contracts.

The alternative is to wait until the settlement date. At that time the party purchasing a futures contract accepts delivery of the underlying asset at the agreed-upon price; the party that sells a futures contract liquidates the position by delivering the underlying asset at the agreed-upon price. For some futures contracts that we shall describe in this chapter, settlement is made in cash only. Such contracts are referred to as *cash-settlement contracts*.

The Role of the Clearinghouse

Associated with every futures exchange is a clearinghouse, which performs several functions. One of these functions is guaranteeing that the two parties to the transaction will perform. To see the importance of this function, consider potential problems in the futures transaction described earlier from the perspective of the two parties—Bob the buyer, and Sally the seller. Each must be concerned with the other's ability to fulfill the obligation at the settlement date. Suppose that at the settlement date the price of bond XYZ in the cash market is $70. Sally can buy bond XYZ for $70 and deliver it to Bob who, in turn, must pay her $100. If Bob does not have the capacity to pay $100 or refuses to pay, however, Sally has lost the opportunity to realize a profit of $30. Suppose, instead, that the price of bond XYZ in the cash market is $150 at the settlement date. In this case, Bob is ready and willing to accept delivery of bond XYZ and pay the agreed-upon price of $100. If Sally does not have the ability or refuses to deliver bond XYZ, Bob has lost the opportunity to realize a profit of $50.

The clearinghouse exists to meet this problem. When an investor takes a position in the futures market, the clearinghouse takes the opposite position and agrees to satisfy the terms set forth in the contract. Because the clearinghouse exists, the investor need not worry about the financial strength and integrity of the party taking the opposite side of the contract. After initial execution of an order, the relationship between the two parties ends. The clearinghouse interposes itself as the buyer for every sale and the seller for every purchase. Thus investors are free to liquidate their positions without involving the other party in the original contract, and without worry that the other party may default. This is the reason why we define a futures contract as an agreement between a party and a clearinghouse associated with an exchange.

Besides its guarantee function, the clearinghouse makes it simple for parties to a futures contract to unwind their positions prior to the settlement date. Suppose that Bob wants to get out of his futures position. He will not have to seek out Sally and work out an agreement with her to terminate the original agreement. Instead, Bob can unwind his position by selling an identical futures contract. As far as the clearinghouse is concerned, its records will show that Bob has bought and sold an identical futures contract. At the settlement date, Sally will not deliver bond XYZ to Bob but will be instructed by the clearinghouse to deliver to someone who bought and still has an open futures position. In the same way, if Sally wants to unwind her position prior to the settlement date, she can buy an identical futures contract.

Margin Requirements

When a position is first taken in a futures contract, the investor must deposit a minimum dollar amount per contract as specified by the exchange. This amount, which is called *initial margin*, is required as deposit for the contract.[1] The initial margin may be in the form of an interest-bearing security such as a Treasury bill. As the price of the futures contract fluctuates, the value of the investor's equity in the position changes. At the end of each trading day, the exchange determines the

---

[1] Individual brokerage firms are free to set margin requirements above the minimum established by the exchange.

settlement price for the futures contract. This price is used to mark-to-market the investor's position, so that any gain or loss from the position is reflected in the investor's equity account.

Maintenance margin is the minimum level (specified by the exchange) by which an investor's equity position may fall as a result of an unfavorable price movement before the investor is required to deposit additional margin. The additional margin deposited is called *variation margin*, and it is an amount necessary to bring the equity in the account back to its initial margin level. Unlike initial margin, variation margin must be in cash, not interest-bearing instruments. Any excess margin in the account may be withdrawn by the investor. If a party to a futures contract who is required to deposit variation margin fails to do so within 24 hours, the futures position is closed out.

Although there are initial and maintenance margin requirements for buying securities on margin, the concept of margin differs for securities and futures. When securities are acquired on margin, the difference between the price of the security and the initial margin is borrowed from the broker. The security purchased serves as collateral for the loan, and the investor pays interest. For futures contracts, the initial margin, in effect, serves as "good faith" money, an indication that the investor will satisfy the obligation of the contract. Normally no money is borrowed by the investor.

Commissions

Commissions on futures contracts are fully negotiable. They are usually quoted on the basis of a "round-turn," meaning a price that includes the opening and closing out of the futures contract. In most cases, the commission is the same regardless of the maturity date or type of the underlying instrument. Commissions for institutional accounts vary enormously, ranging from a low of about $11 to a high of about $30 per contract.

FUTURES VERSUS FORWARD CONTRACTS

A *forward contract*, just like a futures contract, is an agreement for the future delivery of something at a specified price at the end of a designated period of time. Futures contracts are standardized agreements as to the delivery date (or month) and quality of the deliverable, and are traded on organized exchanges. A forward contract differs in that it is usually nonstandardized (that is, the terms of each contract are negotiated individually between buyer and seller), there is no clearinghouse, and secondary markets are often nonexistent or extremely thin. Unlike a futures contract, which is an exchange-traded product, a forward contract is an over-the-counter instrument.

Although both futures and forward contracts set forth terms of delivery, futures contracts are not intended to be settled by delivery. In fact, generally fewer than 2% of outstanding contracts are settled by delivery. Forward contracts, in contrast, are intended for delivery.

Futures contracts are marked-to-market at the end of each trading day, while forward contracts usually are not. Consequently, futures contracts are subject to interim cash flows as additional margin may be required in the case of adverse price movements, or as cash is withdrawn in the case of favorable price movements. There are no interim cash flow effects with forward contracts because no variation margin is required.

Finally, the parties in a forward contract are exposed to credit risk because either party may default on the obligation. Credit risk is minimal in the case of futures contracts because the clearinghouse associated with the exchange guarantees the other side of the transaction.

Other than these differences, most of what we say about futures contracts applies equally to forward contracts.

RISK AND RETURN CHARACTERISTICS OF FUTURES CONTRACTS

The buyer of a futures contract will realize a profit if the futures price increases; the seller of a futures contract will realize a profit if the futures price decreases. For example, suppose that one month after Bob and Sally take their positions in the futures contract, the futures price of bond XYZ increases to $120. Bob, the buyer of the futures contract, could then sell the futures contract and realize a profit of $20. Effectively, at the settlement date he has agreed to buy bond XYZ for $100 and agreed to sell bond XYZ for $120. Sally, the seller of the futures contract, will realize a loss of $20.

If the futures price falls to $40 and Sally buys the contract, she realizes a profit of $60 because she agreed to sell bond XYZ for $100 and now can buy it for $40. Bob would realize a loss of $60. Thus, if the futures price decreases, the buyer of the futures contract realizes a loss while the seller of a futures contract realizes a profit.

Leveraging Aspect of Futures

When a position is taken in a futures contract, the party need not put up the entire amount of the investment. Instead, only initial margin must be put up. If Bob has $100 and wants to invest in bond XYZ because he believes its price will appreciate as a result of a decline in interest rates, he can buy one bond if bond XYZ is selling for $100. If the exchange where the futures contract for bond XYZ is traded requires initial margin of $5, however, Bob can purchase 20 contracts with his $100 investment. (This example ignores the fact that Bob may need funds for variation margin.) His payoff will then depend on the price action of 20 XYZ bonds, not the one he could buy with $100. Thus he can leverage the use of his funds. While the degree of leverage available in the futures market varies from contract to contract, the leverage attainable is considerably greater than in the cash market.

At first, the leverage available in the futures market may suggest that the market benefits only those who want to speculate on price movements. This is not true. Futures markets can be used to reduce price risk. Without the leverage possible in futures transactions, the cost of reducing price risk using futures would be too high for many market participants.

CURRENTLY TRADED INTEREST RATE FUTURES CONTRACTS

In October 1975, the Chicago Board of Trade (CBT) pioneered trading in a futures contract based on a fixed-income instrument—Government National Mortgage Association certificates. Three months later, the International Monetary Market (IMM) of the Chicago Mercantile Exchange began trading futures contracts based on 13-week Treasury bills. Other exchanges soon followed with their own interest rate futures contracts. The more actively traded interest rate futures contracts in the United States are described below. Most major financial markets outside of the United States have similar futures contracts in which the underlying is a fixed-income security issued by the central government.

Treasury Bill Futures

Treasury bill futures, as well as the Eurodollar futures contracts described next, are futures contracts whose underlying instrument is a short-term debt obligation. The Treasury bill futures contract, which is traded on the IMM, is based on a 13-week (3-month) Treasury bill with a face value of $1 million. More specifically, the seller of a Treasury bill futures contract agrees to deliver to the buyer at the settlement date a Treasury bill with 13 weeks remaining to maturity and a face value of $1 million. The Treasury bill delivered can be newly issued or seasoned. The futures price is the price at which the Treasury bill will be sold by the short and purchased by the buyer. For example, a Treasury bill futures contract that settles in 9 months requires that 9 months from now the short deliver to the long $1 million face value of a Treasury bill with 13 weeks remaining to maturity. The Treasury bill could be a newly issued 13-week Treasury bill or a Treasury bill that was issued one year prior to the settlement date and therefore at the settlement has only 13 weeks remaining to maturity.

As explained in Chapter 5, Treasury bills are quoted in the cash market in terms of the annualized yield on a bank discount basis, where

$$Y_d = \frac{D}{F} \times \frac{360}{t}$$

where Y_d = annualized yield on a bank discount basis (expressed as a decimal)

$\quad D$ = dollar discount, which is equal to the difference between the face value and the price of a bill maturing in t days

$\quad F$ = face value; and

$\quad t$ = number of days remaining to maturity.

The dollar discount (D) is found by

$$D = Y_d \times F \times \frac{t}{360}$$

In contrast, the Treasury bill futures contract is quoted not directly in terms of yield but instead on an index basis which is related to the yield on a bank discount basis as follows:

Index price = $100 - (Y_d \times 100)$

For example, if Y_d is 8%, the index price is

$100 - (.08 \times 100) = 92$

Given the price of the futures contract, the yield on a bank discount basis for the futures contract is determined as follows:

$$Y_d = \frac{100 - \text{Index price}}{100}$$

To see how this works, suppose that the index price for a Treasury bill futures contract is 92.52. The yield on a bank discount basis for this Treasury bill futures contract is:

$$Y_d = \frac{100 - 95.52}{100} = .0748 \text{ or } 7.48\%$$

The invoice price that the buyer of $1 million face value of 13-week Treasury bills must pay at settlement is found by first computing the dollar discount, as follows:

$$D = Y_d \times \$1,000,000 \times \frac{t}{360}$$

where t is either 90 or 91 days.

Typically, the number of days to maturity of a 13-week Treasury bill is 91 days. The invoice price is then:

Invoice price = $\$1,000,000 - D$

For example, for the Treasury bill futures contract with an index price of 92.52 (and a yield on a bank discount basis of 7.48%), the dollar discount for the 13-week Treasury bill to be delivered with 91 days to maturity is:

$$D = .0748 \times \$1,000,000 \times \frac{91}{360}$$

$$= \$18,907.78$$

The invoice price is:

Invoice price = $\$1,000,000 - \$18,907.78 = \$981,092.22$

The minimum index price fluctuation or "tick" for this futures contract is .01. A change of .01 for the minimum index price translates into a change in the yield on a bank discount basis of one basis point (.0001). The change in the value of one basis point will change the dollar discount, and therefore the invoice price, by:

$$.0001 \times \$1,000,000 \times \frac{t}{360}$$

For a 13-week Treasury bill with 91 days to maturity, the change in the dollar discount is:

$$.0001 \times \$1,000,000 \times \frac{91}{360} = \$25.28$$

For a 13-week Treasury bill with 90 days to maturity, the change in the dollar discount would be $25. Despite the fact that a 13-week Treasury bill typically has 91 days to maturity, market participants commonly refer to the value of a basis point for this futures contract as $25.

Eurodollar CD Futures

Eurodollar certificates of deposit (CDs) are denominated in dollars but represent the liabilities of banks outside the United States. The contracts are traded on both the International Monetary Market of the Chicago Mercantile Exchange and the London International Financial Futures Exchange.

The rate paid on Eurodollar CDs is the London Interbank Offered Rate (LIBOR).[2] The three-month Eurodollar CD is the underlying instrument for the Eurodollar CD futures contract. As with the Treasury bill futures contract, this contract is for $1 million of face value and is traded on an index price basis with a minimum price fluctuation (tick) of .01 (or .0001 in terms of LIBOR).

The Eurodollar CD futures contract is a cash settlement contract. That is, the parties settle in cash for the value of a Eurodollar CD based on LIBOR at the settlement date.

The Eurodollar CD futures contract is one of the most heavily traded futures contract in the world. It is frequently used to trade the short end of the yield curve, and many hedgers have found this contract to be the best hedging vehicle for a wide range of hedging situations.

Treasury Bond Futures

The underlying instrument for a Treasury bond futures contract is $100,000 par value of a hypothetical 20-year, 8% coupon bond. While prices and yields of the Treasury bond futures contract are quoted in terms of this hypothetical Treasury bond, the seller of the futures contract has the choice of several actual Treasury bonds that are acceptable to deliver. The Chicago Board of Trade allows the seller to deliver any Treasury bond that has at least 15 years to maturity from the date of delivery if not callable; in the case of callable bonds, the issue must not be callable for at least 15 years from the first day of the delivery month. To settle the contract an acceptable bond must be delivered. That is, the contract is not a cash-settlement contract.

The minimum price fluctuation for the Treasury bond futures contract is a 32nd of 1%. The dollar value of a 32nd for a $100,000 par value (the par value for the underlying Treasury bond) is $31.25. Thus, the minimum price fluctuation is $31.25 for this contract.

The delivery process for the Treasury bond futures contract makes the contract interesting. At the settlement date, the seller of a futures contract (the short) is required to deliver the buyer (the long) $100,000 par value of an 8%, 20-year Treasury bond. Because no such bond exists, however, the seller must choose from other acceptable deliverable bonds that the exchange has specified. Suppose the seller is entitled to deliver $100,000 of a 6%, 20-year Treasury bond to settle the futures contract.

---

[2] The yield on the Eurodollar CD futures contract is quoted in terms of an add-on, or simple, interest rate. Rates on Eurodollar CD futures contract are thus directly comparable to the rates on domestic CDs or interbank deposits. However, to compare the Eurodollar CD rate to the Treasury bill rate, one of the rates must be converted so that both rates will be in the same terms.

The value of this bond of course is less than the value of an 8%, 20-year bond. If the seller delivers the 6%, 20-year, this would be unfair to the buyer of the futures contract who contracted to receive $100,000 of an 8%, 20-year Treasury bond. Alternatively, suppose the seller delivers $100,000 of a 10%, 20-year Treasury bond. The value of a 10%, 20-year Treasury bond is greater than that of an 8%, 20-year bond, so this would be a disadvantage to the seller.

How can this problem be resolved? To make delivery equitable to both parties, and to tie cash to futures prices, the CBT has introduced *conversion factors* for determining the invoice price of each acceptable deliverable Treasury issue against the Treasury bond futures contract. The conversion factor is determined by the CBT before a contract with a specific settlement date begins trading. The conversion factor is based on the price that a deliverable bond would sell for at the beginning of the delivery month if it were to yield 8%. The conversion factor is constant throughout the trading period of the futures contract. The short must notify the long of the actual bond that will be delivered one day before the delivery date.

The invoice price paid by the buyer of the Treasury bonds delivered by the seller is determined using the formula:

Invoice price = Contract size × Futures contract settlement price
  × Conversion factor

Suppose the Treasury bond futures contract settles at 96 (.96 in decimal form) and that the short elects to deliver a Treasury bond issue with a conversion factor of 1.15. As the contract size is $100,000, the invoice price is:

$100,000 × .96 × 1.15 = $110,400

The invoice price in the formula is just for the principal. The buyer of the futures contract must also pay the seller accrued interest on the bond delivered.

In selecting the issue to be delivered, the short will select from all the deliverable issues the one that is cheapest to deliver. This issue is referred to as the *cheapest-to-deliver* or the *most deliverable issue*; it plays a key role in the pricing of this futures contract. The cost to deliver is the difference between the cost of purchasing the Treasury issue and the invoice price for the principal. That is,

Cost to deliver = Cost of purchasing issue − Invoice price

This is equivalent to selecting the issue that would generate the greatest profit as measured by the invoice price for the principal minus the cost of purchasing the issue. Notice that computation of the cost of delivery does not consider the accrued interest that the seller (short position) must pay to acquire the issue. The reason is that the cost of accrued interest would be offset by the long when the issue is purchased from the short.

In addition to the option of which acceptable Treasury issue to deliver—sometimes referred to as the *quality* or *swap option*—the short position has two more options granted under CBT delivery guidelines. The short position is permitted to decide when in the delivery month delivery actually will take place. This is called the *timing option*. The other option is the right of the short position to give notice of intent to deliver up to 8:00 p.m. Chicago time after the closing of the exchange (3:15 p.m. Chicago time) on the date when the futures settlement price has been fixed. This option is referred to as the *wild card option*. The quality option, the timing option, and the wild card option (in sum referred to as the *delivery options*) mean that the long position can never be sure of which Treasury bond will be delivered or when it will be delivered.

Treasury Note Futures

Modeled after the Treasury bond futures contract, the underlying instrument for the Treasury note futures contract is $100,000 par value of a hypothetical 10-year, 8% Treasury note. There are several acceptable Treasury issues that may be delivered by the short. An issue is acceptable if the maturity is not less than 6.5 years and not more than 10 years from the first day of the delivery month. The delivery options granted to the short position and the minimum price fluctuation are the same as for the Treasury bond futures contract.

Bond Buyer's Municipal Bond Index Futures

Traded on the CBT, the underlying product for this contract is a basket, or index, of 40 municipal bonds. The Bond Buyer, publisher of *The Bond Buyer* (a trade publication of the municipal bond industry), serves as the index manager for the contract and prices each bond in the index based on prices received between 1:30 and 2:00 p.m. (Central Standard Time) from five municipal bond brokers. It is necessary to obtain several independent prices from brokers because municipal bonds trade in the over-the-counter market.

Once the prices are received from the five pricing brokers for a given issue, the lowest and the highest prices are dropped. The remaining three prices then are averaged, and the resulting value is referred to as the appraisal value. The appraisal value for each issue then is divided by a conversion factor that equates the bond to an 8% issue. This gives a converted price for each issue. The converted prices then are summed and divided by 40, for an average converted price on the index. The index is revised bimonthly, when newer issues are added, and older issues or issues that no longer meet the criteria for inclusion in the index are dropped.[3] A smoothing coefficient is calculated on the index revision date so that the index will not change merely because of changes in the composition of the index. The average converted dollar price for the index is multiplied by this coefficient to get the index value for a particular date.

As delivery on all 40 bonds in the index is not possible, the contract is a cash settlement contract, with settlement price based on the value of the index on the delivery date.

The contract is quoted in points and 32nds of a point. For example, suppose the settlement price for the contract is 93-21. This translates into a price of 93 and 21/32, or 93.65635. The dollar value of a contract is equal to $1,000 times the Bond Buyer Municipal Bond Index. For example, the dollar value based on the settlement price is:

$$\$1,000 \times 93.65635 = \$93,656.35$$

PRICING AND ARBITRAGE IN THE INTEREST RATE MARKET

One of the primary concerns that most traders and investors have when taking a position in futures contracts is whether the futures price at which they transact will be a "fair" price. Buyers are concerned that the price may be too high, and that they will be picked off by more experienced futures traders waiting to profit from the mistakes of the uninitiated. Sellers worry that the price is artificially low, and that savvy traders may have manipulated the markets so that they can buy at bargain basement prices. Furthermore, prospective participants frequently find no rational explanation for the sometimes violent ups and downs that occur in the futures markets. Theories about efficient markets give little comfort to anyone who knows of or has experienced the sudden losses that can occur in the highly leveraged futures markets.

Fortunately, the futures markets are not as irrational as they may at first seem; if they were, they would not have become so successful. The interest rate futures markets are not perfectly efficient markets, but they probably come about as close as any market. Furthermore, there are both very clear reasons why futures prices are what they are and methods by

---

[3] The inclusion criteria, as well as the revision process and pricing of the index, are spelled out in a publication entitled "The Chicago Board of Trade's Municipal Bond Futures Contract," 1987.

which traders, investors, and borrowers can and will quickly eliminate any discrepancy between futures prices and their fair levels.

There are several different ways to price futures contracts. Fortunately, all lead to the same fair price for a given contract. Each approach relies on the "Law of One Price." This law states that a given financial asset (or liability) must have the same price regardless of the means by which it is created. We explain here one way in which futures contracts can be combined with cash market instruments to create cash flows that are identical to other cash securities.[4] The Law of One Price implies that the synthetically created cash securities must have the same price as the actual cash securities. Similarly, cash instruments can be combined to create cash flows that are identical to futures contracts. By the Law of One Price the futures contract must have the same price as the synthetic futures created from cash instruments.

Pricing of Futures Contracts

To understand how futures contracts should be priced, consider the following example. Suppose that a 20-year, 100 par value bond with a coupon rate of 12% is selling at par. Also suppose that this bond is the deliverable for a futures contract that settles in 3 months. If the current 3-month interest rate at which funds can be loaned or borrowed is 8% per year, what should be the price of this futures contract?

Suppose the price of the futures contract is 107. Consider the following strategy:

Sell the futures contract at 107.
Purchase the bond for 100.
Borrow 100 for 3 months at 8% per year.

The borrowed funds are used to purchase the bond, resulting in no initial cash outlay for this strategy. Three months from now, the bond must be delivered to settle the futures contract and the loan must be repaid. These trades will produce the following cash flows:

From settlement of the futures contract:

Flat price of bond	=	107
Accrued interest (12% for 3 months)	=	3
Total proceeds	=	110

---

[4]For the other ways to price futures contracts, see Chapter 5 in Mark Pitts and Frank J. Fabozzi, *Interest Rate Futures and Options* (Chicago: Probus Publishing, 1990).

From the loan:

Repayment of principal of loan	=	100
Interest on loan (8% for 3 months)	=	2
Total outlay	=	102
Profit	=	8

This strategy will guarantee a profit of 8. Moreover, the profit is generated with no initial outlay because the funds used to purchase the bond are borrowed. The profit will be realized *regardless of the futures price at the settlement date*. Obviously, in a well-functioning market, arbitrageurs would buy the bond and sell the futures, forcing the futures price down and bidding up the bond price so as to eliminate this profit.

In contrast, suppose that the futures price is 92 instead of 107. Consider the following strategy:

Buy the futures contract at 92.
Sell (short) the bond for 100.
Invest (lend) 100 for 3 months at 8% per year.

Once again, there is no initial cash outlay. Three months from now a bond will be purchased to settle the long position in the futures contract. That bond will then be used to cover the short position (i.e. to cover the short sale in the cash market). The outcome in 3 months would be as follows:

From settlement of the futures contract:

Flat price of bond	=	92
Accrued interest (12% for 3 months)	=	3
Total outlay	=	95

From the loan:

Principal received from maturing investment	=	100
Interest earned from the 3-month investment (8% for 3 months)	=	2
Total outlay	=	102
Profit	=	7

The 7 profit is a pure arbitrage profit. It requires no initial cash outlay and will be realized regardless of the futures price at the settlement date.

There is a futures price that will eliminate the arbitrage profit, however. There will be no arbitrage if the futures price is 99. Let's look at what would happen if the two previous strategies are followed and the futures price is 99. First, consider the following strategy:

Sell the futures contract at 99.
Purchase the bond for 100.
Borrow 100 for 3 months at 8% per year.

In 3 months, the outcome would be as follows:

From settlement of the futures contract:

Flat price of bond	=	99
Accrued interest (12% for 3 months)	=	3
Total proceeds	=	102

From the loan:

Repayment of principal of loan	=	100
Interest on loan (8% for 3 months)	=	2
Total outlay	=	102
Profit	=	0

There is no arbitrage profit in this case.
Next consider the following strategy:

Buy the futures contract at 99.
Sell (short) the bond for 100.
Invest (lend) 100 for 3 months at 8% per year.

The outcome in 3 months would be as follows:

From settlement of the futures contract:

Flat price of bond	=	99
Accrued interest (12% for 3 months)	=	3
Total outlay	=	102

From the loan:

Principal received from maturing investment	=	100
Interest earned from the 3-month investment (8% for 3 months)	=	2
Total proceeds	=	102
Profit	=	0

Thus neither strategy results in a profit. Hence the futures price of 99 is the equilibrium price, because any higher or lower futures price will permit arbitrage profits.

Theoretical Futures Price Based on Arbitrage Model

Considering the arbitrage arguments just presented, the equilibrium futures price can be determined on the basis of the following information:

1. The price of the bond in the cash market.
2. The coupon rate on the bond. In our example, the coupon rate is 12% per year.
3. The interest rate for borrowing and lending until the settlement date. The borrowing and lending rate is referred to as the *financing rate*. In our example, the financing rate is 8% per year.

We will let

r = financing rate (%)
c = current yield, or coupon rate divided by the cash market price
P = cash market price
F = futures price
t = time, in years, to the futures delivery date

and then consider the following strategy that is initiated on a coupon date:

Sell the futures contract at F.
Purchase the bond for P.
Borrow P until the settlement date at r.

The outcome at the settlement date is

From settlement of the futures contract:

Flat price of bond	$= F$
Accrued interest	$= ctP$
Total proceeds	$= F + ctP$

From the loan:

Repayment of principal of loan	$= P$
Interest on loan	$= rtP$
Total outlay	$= P + rtP$

The profit will equal:

Profit = Total proceeds – Total outlay
Profit = $F + ctP - (P + rtP)$

In equilibrium the theoretical futures price occurs where the profit from this trade is zero. Thus to have equilibrium, the following must hold:

$$0 = F + ctP - (P + rtP)$$

Solving for the theoretical futures price, we have

$$(17.1) \quad F = P + Pt(r - c) = P(1 + t[r - c])$$

Alternatively, consider the following strategy:

Buy the futures contract at F.
Sell (short) the bond for P.
Invest (lend) P at r until the settlement date.

The outcome at the settlement date would be

From settlement of the futures contract:

Flat price of bond	=	F
Accrued interest	=	ctP
Total outlay	=	$F + ctP$

From the loan:

Proceeds received from maturing of investment	=	P
Interest earned	=	rtP
Total proceeds	=	$P + rtP$

The profit will equal:

Profit = Total proceeds − Total outlay

Profit = $P + rtP - (F + ctP)$

Setting the profit equal to zero so that there will be no arbitrage profit and solving for the futures price, we obtain the same equation for the futures price as equation (17.1).

Let's apply equation (17.1) to our previous example in which

r	=	.08
c	=	.12
P	=	100
t	=	.25

Then the theoretical futures price is

$$F = 100 + 100 \times .25 (.08 - .12)$$
$$= 100 - 1 = 99$$

This agrees with the equilibrium futures price we derived earlier.

The theoretical futures price may be at a premium to the cash market price (higher than the cash market price) or at a discount from the cash market price (lower than the cash market price), depending on $(r - c)$. The term $r - c$ is called the *net financing cost* because it adjusts the financing rate for the coupon interest earned. The net financing cost is more commonly called the *cost of carry*, or simply *carry*. *Positive carry* means that the current yield earned is greater than the financing cost; *negative carry* means that the financing cost exceeds the current yield. The relationships can be expressed as follows:

Carry	Futures Price
Positive $(c > r)$	Will sell at a discount to the cash price $(F < P)$
Negative $(c < r)$	Will sell at a premium to the cash price $(F > P)$
Zero $(r = c)$	Will be equal to the cash price $(F = P)$

In the case of interest rate futures, carry (the relationship between the short-term financing rate and the current yield on the bond) depends on the shape of the yield curve. When the yield curve is upward-sloping, the short-term financing rate will generally be less than the current yield on the bond, resulting in positive carry. The futures price will then sell at a discount to the cash price for the bond. The opposite will hold true when the yield curve is inverted.

A Closer Look at the Theoretical Futures Price

To derive the theoretical futures price using the arbitrage argument, we made several assumptions, which have certain implications.

Interim Cash Flows: No interim cash flows due to variation margin or coupon interest payments were assumed in the model. However, we know that interim cash flows can occur for both of these reasons. Because we assumed no variation margin, the price derived is technically the theoretical price for a forward contract (which is not marked-to-market at the end of each trading day). If interest rates rise, the short position in futures will receive margin as the futures price decreases; the margin can then be reinvested at a higher interest rate. In contrast, if interest rates fall, there will be variation margin that must be financed by the short position; however, because interest rates have declined, financing will be possible at a lower cost. Thus, whichever way rates move, those who are short futures gain relative to those who are short forwards. Conversely, those who are long futures lose relative to those who are long forwards. These facts account for the difference between futures and forward prices.

Incorporating interim coupon payments into the pricing model is not difficult. However, the value of the coupon payments at the settlement date will depend on the interest rate at which they can be reinvested. The shorter the maturity of the futures contract and the lower the coupon rate, the less important the reinvestment income is in determining the futures price.

The Short-Term Interest Rate (Financing Rate): In deriving the theoretical futures price it is assumed that the borrowing and lending rates are equal. Typically, however, the borrowing rate is higher than the lending rate.

We will let
$$r_B = \text{borrowing rate}$$
$$r_L = \text{lending rate}$$

Consider the following strategy:

Sell the futures contract at F.
Purchase the bond for P.

Borrow P until the settlement date at r_B. The futures price that would produce no arbitrage profit is

(17.2) $F = P + P(r_B - c)$

Now consider the following strategy:

Buy the futures contract at F.
Sell (short) the bond for P.
Invest (lend) P at r_L until the settlement date.

The futures price that would produce no profit is

(17.3) $F = P + P(r_L - c)$

Equations (17.2) and (17.3) together provide boundaries for the futures price equilibrium. Equation (17.2) provides the upper boundary and equation (17.3) the lower boundary. For example, assume that the borrowing rate is 8% per year, or 2% for three months, while the lending rate is 6% per year, or 1.5% for three months. Then using equation (17.2) and the previous example, the upper boundary is

$$F \text{ (upper boundary)} = \$100 + \$100(.02 - .03)$$
$$= \$99$$

The lower boundary using equation (17.3) is

$$F \text{ (lower boundary)} = \$100 + \$100(.015 - .03)$$
$$= \$98.50$$

In calculating these boundaries, we assume no transaction costs are invoved in taking the position. In actuality, the transaction costs of entering into and closing the cash position as well as the round-trip transaction costs for the futures contract must be considered and do affect the boundaries for the futures contract.

Deliverable Bond is Known: In the pricing model based on arbitrage arguments, it is assumed that only one instrument is deliverable. But the futures contracts on Treasury bonds and Treasury notes are designed to allow the short the choice of delivering one of a number of deliverable issues (the quality or swap option).

Because there may be more than one deliverable, market participants track the price of each deliverable bond and determine which bond is the cheapest to deliver. The futures price will then trade in relation to the cheapest-to-deliver bond. As explained earlier, the cheapest-to-deliver is the bond or note that will result in the smallest loss or the greatest gain on delivering by the short.[5]

There is the risk that while an issue may be the cheapest to deliver at the time a position in the futures contract is taken, it may not be the cheapest to deliver after that time. A change in the cheapest-to-deliver can dramatically alter the futures price.

What are the implications of the quality (swap) option for the futures price? Because the swap option is an option granted by the long to the short, the long will want to pay less for the futures contract. Therefore, the theoretical futures price after adjusting for the quality option granted to the short should be less than the theoretical futures price given above.[6]

Delivery Date is Known: In the pricing model based on arbitrage arguments, a known delivery date is assumed. For Treasury bond and note futures contracts, the short has a timing and wild card option, so the long does not know when the securities will be delivered. The effect of the timing and wild card options on the theoretical futures price is the same as with the quality option. These delivery options should result in a theoretical futures price that is lower than the one suggested above.

Deliverable is not a Basket of Securities: The municipal index futures contract is a cash settlement contract based on a basket of securities. The difficulty in arbitraging this futures contract is that it is too expensive to buy or sell every bond included in the index. Instead, a portfolio including a smaller number of bonds may be constructed to "track" the index. The arbitrage, however, is no longer risk-free because there is tracking error risk.

APPLICATIONS TO PORTFOLIO MANAGEMENT

There are various ways a money manager can use interest rate futures contracts.

Speculating on the Movement of Interest Rates

The price of a futures contract moves in the opposite direction from interest rates: when rates rise, the futures price will fall; when rates fall, the futures price will rise. A portfolio manager who wants to speculate that interest rates will rise (fall) can sell (buy) interest rate futures. Before

---

[5] An alternative procedure is to compute the implied (break-even) repo rate. This rate is the yield that would produce no profit or loss if the bond is purchased and a futures contract is sold against the bond. The cheapest-to-deliver bond is the one with the lowest implied repo rate.

[6] Several studies have investigated the magnitude of the mispricing caused by the delivery option. See, for example: Gerald D. Gay and Steven Manaster, "The Quality Option Implicit in Futures Contracts," *Journal of Financial Economics* (September 1984), pp. 353-370; Gerald D. Gay and Steven Manaster, "Implicit Delivery Options and Optimal Delivery Strategies for Financial Futures Contracts," *Journal of Financial Economics* (May 1986), pp. 41-72; Alex Kane and Alan Marcus, "The Quality Option in the Treasury Bond Futures Market: An Empirical Assessment," *Journal of Futures Markets* (Summer 1986), pp. 231-248; Alex Kane and Alan Marcus, "Valuation and Optimal Exercise of the Wild Card Option in the Treasury Bond Futures Market," *Journal of Finance* (March 1986), pp. 195-207; and Michael J. Hemler, "The Quality Delivery Option in Treasury Bond Futures Contracts,"doctoral dissertation, Graduate School of Business, University of Chicago, March 1988.

interest rate futures were available, investors who wanted to speculate on interest rates did so with the long-term Treasury bond; they shorted the bond if they expected interest rates to rise, and they bought it if they expected interest rates to fall. Using interest rate futures instead of the cash markets (instead of trading long-term Treasuries themselves) has three advantages. First, transactions costs for trading futures are lower than trading in the cash market. Second, margin requirements are lower for futures than for Treasury securities; using futures thus permits greater leverage. Finally, it is easier to sell short in the futures market than in the Treasury market. The leverage advantages in trading futures may encourage speculation on interest rate movements; making speculation easier for investors is not the function of interest rate futures contracts.

Controlling the Interest Rate Risk of a Portfolio

Money managers can use interest rate futures to alter the interest rate sensitivity of a portfolio. Those with strong expectations about the direction of the future course of interest rates will adjust the durations of their portfolios so as to capitalize on their expectations. Specifically, a money manager who expects rates to increase will shorten duration; a money manager who expects interest rates to decrease will lengthen duration. While money managers can use cash market instruments to alter the durations of their portfolios, using futures contracts provides a quicker and less expensive means for doing so (on either a temporary or permanent basis).

Besides adjusting a portfolio for anticipated interest rate movements, money managers can use futures in strategies such as immunization (to be described in Chapter 22) to construct a portfolio with a longer duration than would be available with cash market securities. Suppose that in a given interest rate environment a pension fund manager must structure a portfolio to have a duration of 10 years to accomplish a particular investment objective. Bonds with such a long duration may not be available, but buying the appropriate number and kind of interest rate futures contracts can allow a pension fund manager to increase the portfolio's duration to the target level of 10.

A formula to approximate the number of futures contracts necessary to adjust the portfolio duration to a new level is:[7]

---

[7] This is derived in Frank J. Jones and Beth Krumholz, "Duration Adjustment and Asset Allocation with Treasury Bond and Note Futures Contracts," in Frank J. Fabozzi and T. Dessa Garlicki (eds.), *Advances in Bond Analysis and Portfolio Strategies* (Chicago: Probus Publishing, 1987).

$$\text{Approximate number of contracts} = \frac{\left(D_T - D_I\right) P_I}{D_F \, P_F}$$

where

D_T = Target modified duration for the portfolio
D_I = Initial modified duration for the portfolio
P_I = Initial market value of the portfolio
D_F = Modified duration for the futures contract
P_F = Market value of the futures contract

Notice that if the money manager wishes to increase the duration, then D_T will be greater than D_I, and the equation will have a positive sign. This means that futures contracts will be purchased. The opposite is true if the objective is to shorten the portfolio duration.

Creating Synthetic Securities for Yield Enhancement

A cash market security can be created synthetically by using a position in the futures contract together with the deliverable instrument. The yield on the synthetic security should be the same as the yield on the cash market security. Any difference between the two yields can be exploited so as to enhance the yield on the portfolio.

To see how, consider an investor who owns a 20-year Treasury bond and sells Treasury futures that call for the delivery of that particular bond 3 months from now. While the maturity of the Treasury bond is 20 years, the investor has effectively shortened the maturity of the bond to 3 months.

Consequently, the long position in the 20-year bond and the short futures position are equivalent to a long position in a 3-month riskless security. The position is riskless because the investor is locking in the price to be received 3 months from now–the futures price. By being long the bond and short the futures, the investor has synthetically created a 3-month Treasury bill. The return the investor should expect to earn from this synthetic position should be the yield on a 3-month Treasury bill. If the yield on the synthetic 3-month Treasury bill is greater than the yield on the cash market Treasury bill, the investor can realize an enhanced yield by creating the synthetic short-term security. The fundamental relationship for creating synthetic securities is:

(17.4) $RSP = CBP - FBP$

where

RSP = Riskless short-term security position
CBP = Cash bond position
FBP = Bond futures position

A negative sign before a position means a short position. In terms of our previous example, *CBP* is the long cash bond position, the negative sign before *FBP* refers to the short futures position, and *RSP* is the riskless synthetic 3-month security or Treasury bill.

Equation (17.4) states that an investor who is long the cash market security and short the futures contract should expect to earn the rate of return on a risk-free security with the same maturity as the futures delivery date. Solving equation (17.4) for the long bond position, we have

(17.5) $CBP = RSP + FBP$

Equation (17.5) states that a cash bond position equals a short-term riskless security position plus a long bond futures position, Thus, a cash market bond can be created synthetically by buying a futures contract and investing in a Treasury bill.

Solving equation (17.5) for the bond futures position, we have

(17.6) $FBP = CBP - RSP$

Equation (17.6) tells us that a long position in the futures contract can be created synthetically by taking a long position in the cash market bond and shorting the short-term riskless security. But shorting the short-term riskless security is equivalent to borrowing money. Notice that it was equation (17.6) that we used in deriving the theoretical futures price when the futures contract was underpriced. Recall that when the futures price was 107, the strategy to obtain an arbitrage profit was to sell the futures contract and create a synthetic long futures position by buying the bond with borrowed funds. This is precisely what equation (17.6) states. In this case, instead of creating a synthetic cash market instrument as we did with equations (17.4) and (17.5), we have created a synthetic futures contract. The fact that the synthetic long futures position is cheaper than the actual long futures position provides an arbitrage opportunity.

If we reverse the sign of both sides of equations (17.4), (17.5), and (17.6), we can see how a short futures position can be created synthetically.

In an efficient market the opportunities for yield enhancement should not exist very long. But even in the absence of yield enhancement, money managers can use synthetic securities to hedge a portfolio position that they find difficult to hedge in the cash market either because of lack of liquidity or because of other constraints.[8]

---

[8] For a more detailed discussion of synthetic securities, see Robert W. Kopprasch, Cal Johnson, and Armand H. Tatevossian, "Strategies for the Asset Manager: Hedging and the Creation of Synthetic Assets," in *Advances in Bond Analysis and Portfolio Strategies* and Robert P. Lecky, "Synthetic Asset Strategies," in Frank J. Fabozzi (ed.), *Fixed Income Portfolio Strategies* (Chicago: Probus Publishing, 1989).

Allocating Funds Between Stocks and Bonds

A pension sponsor may wish to alter the composition of the pension's funds between stocks and bonds, that is, change its asset allocation. Suppose that a pension sponsor wants to shift a $1 billion fund from its current allocation of $500 million in stocks and $500 million in bonds to $300 million in stocks and $700 million in bonds. This can be done directly by selling $200 million of stocks and buying a like amount of bonds. The costs associated with shifting funds in this manner are: (1) the transactions costs with respect to commissions and bid-ask spreads, (2) the market impact costs, and (3) the disruption of the activities of the money managers employed by the pension sponsor.

An alternative course of action is to use interest rate futures and stock index futures. Assume the pension sponsor wants to shift $200 million from stocks to bonds. Buying an appropriate number of interest rate futures and selling an appropriate number of stock index futures can achieve the desired exposure to stocks and bonds. Futures positions can be maintained or liquidated slowly as funds invested in the cash markets are actually shifted. The advantages of using financial futures contracts are: (1) transactions costs are lower, (2) market impact costs are avoided or reduced as the sponsor has more time to buy and sell securities in the cash market, and (3) activities of the money managers employed by the pension sponsor are not disrupted.[9]

To determine the approximate number of interest rate futures contracts needed to change the market value of the portfolio allocated to bonds, assuming that the duration of the portfolio is to remain constant, we can use the formula:[10]

$$\text{Approximate number of contracts} = \frac{\left(P_T - P_I\right) D_I}{D_F \, P_F}$$

where P_T = Target market value allocated to bonds and the other terms are the same as in the formula given earlier to approximate the number of contracts to adjust a portfolio's duration.

Notice that if the market value of the portfolio allocated to bonds is to be increased, the numerator of the equation will be positive. This means that

[9]See Roger Clarke, "Asset Allocation Using Futures," Chapter 16 in Robert Arnott and Frank J. Fabozzi (eds.), *Asset Allocation* (Chicago: Probus Publishing, 1988), and Mark Zurak and Ravi Dattatreya, "Asset Allocation Using Futures Contracts," Chapter 20 in Frank J. Fabozzi and Gregory Kipnis (eds.), *The Handbook of Stock Index Futures and Options* (Homewood, IL: Dow Jones-Irwin, 1988).

[10]See Jones and Krumholz, "Duration Adjustment and Asset Allocation with Treasury Bond and Note Futures Contracts."

futures contracts will be purchased. If funds are to be reallocated to stocks and withdrawn from bonds, then the numerator of the equation will be negative, which means that interest rate futures contracts will be sold.

Hedging

Hedging with futures calls for taking a futures position as a temporary substitute for transactions to be made in the cash market at a later date. If cash and futures prices move together, any loss realized by the hedger from one position (whether cash or futures) will be offset by a profit on the other position. When the net profit or loss from the positions are exactly as anticipated, the hedge is referred to as a *perfect* hedge.

In practice, hedging is not that simple. The amount of net profit will not necessarily be as anticipated. The outcome of a hedge will depend on the relationship between the cash price and the futures price both when a hedge is placed and when it is lifted. The difference between the cash price and the futures price is called the *basis*. The risk that the basis will change in an unpredictable way is called *basis risk*.

In most hedging applications, the bond to be hedged is not identical to the bond underlying the futures contract. This kind of hedging is referred to as *cross hedging*. There may be substantial basis risk in cross hedging. An unhedged position is exposed to price risk, the risk that the cash market price will move adversely. A hedged position substitutes basis risk for price risk.

A *short* (or sell) hedge is used to protect against a decline in the cash price of a bond. To execute a short hedge, futures contracts are sold. By establishing a short hedge, the hedger has fixed the future cash price and transferred the price risk of ownership to the buyer of the futures contract. To understand why a short hedge might be executed, suppose that a pension fund manager knows that bonds must be liquidated in 40 days to make a $5 million payment to the beneficiaries of the pension fund. If interest rates rise during the 40-day period, more bonds will have to be liquidated to realize $5 million. To guard against this possibility, the manager can sell bonds in the futures market to lock in a selling price.

A *long* (or buy) hedge is undertaken to protect against an increase in the cash price of a bond. In a long hedge, the hedger buys a futures contract to lock in a purchase price. A pension fund manager might use a long hedge when substantial cash contributions are expected, and the manager is concerned that interest rates will fall. Also, a money manager who knows that bonds are maturing in the near future and expects that interest rates will fall can employ a long hedge to lock in a rate for the proceeds to be reinvested.

Conceptually, cross hedging is somewhat more complicated than hedging deliverable securities, because it involves two relationships. First, there is the relationship between the cheapest-to-deliver security and the futures contract. Second, there is the relationship between the security to be hedged and the cheapest-to-deliver security.

The Hedge Ratio: The key to minimizing risk in a cross hedge is to choose the right hedge ratio. The hedge ratio depends on *volatility weighting*, or weighting by relative changes in value. The purpose of a hedge is to use gains or losses from a futures position to offset any difference between the target sale price and the actual sale price of the asset. Accordingly, the hedge ratio is chosen with the intention of matching the volatility (that is, the dollar change) of the futures contract to the volatility of the asset. Consequently, the hedge ratio is given by:

$$\text{Hedge ratio} = \frac{\text{Volatility of bond to be hedged}}{\text{Volatility of hedging instrument}}$$

As the formula shows, if the bond to be hedged is more volatile than the hedging instrument, more of the hedging instrument will be needed.

While it might be fairly clear why volatility is the key variable in determining the hedge ratio, "volatility" has many definitions. For hedging purposes, however, we are concerned with volatility in absolute dollar terms.[11] To calculate the dollar volatility of a bond, one must know the precise point in time that volatility is to be calculated (because volatility generally declines as a bond ages) as well as the price or yield at which to calculate volatility (because higher yields generally reduce dollar volatility for a given yield change). The relevant point in the life of the bond for calculating volatility is the point at which the hedge will be lifted. Volatility at any other point is essentially irrelevant because the goal is to lock in a price or rate only on that particular day. Similarly, the relevant yield at which to calculate volatility initially is the target yield. Consequently, the "volatility of the bond to be hedged" referred to in the formula is the price value of a basis point for the bond on the hedge lift date, calculated at its current implied forward rate.

An example shows why volatility weighting leads to the correct hedge ratio.[12] Suppose that on April 19. 1985, an investor owned the Southern Bell 11 3/4% bonds of 2023 and sold June 1985 Treasury bond

---

[11] Duration and volatility in terms of percentage change in value may be helpful in deriving the hedge ratio, but offsetting actual dollars is always the bottom line.

[12] This example is adapted from Pitts and Fabozzi, *Interest Rate Futures and Options*.

futures to hedge a future sale of the bonds. This is an example of a cross hedge. Suppose that (1) the Treasury 7 5/8s of 2007 were the cheapest-to-deliver bond on the contract and that they were trading at 11.50%, (2) the Southern Bell bonds were at 12.40%, and (3) the Treasury bond futures were at a price of 70. To simplify, assume also that the yield spread between the two bonds remains at .90% and that the anticipated sale date was the last business day in June 1985.

Because the conversion factor for the deliverable 7 5/8s for the June 1985 contract was .9660, the target price for hedging the 7 5/8s would be 67.62 (from 70 × .9660), and the target yield would be 11.789% (the yield at a price of 67.62). The yield on the telephone bonds is assumed to stay at .90% above the yield on the 7 5/8s, so the target yield for the Southern Bell bonds would be 12.689%, with a corresponding price of 92.628. At these target levels, the price values of a basis point (PVBP) for the 7 5/8s and telephone bonds are, respectively, .056332 and .072564. As indicated earlier, all these calculations are made using a settlement date equal to the anticipated sale date, in this case the end of June 1985. Thus, the relative price volatilities of the bonds to be hedged and the deliverable security are easily obtained from the assumed sale date and target prices.

However, in the formula for the hedge ratio we need the volatility not of the cheapest-to-deliver bond, but of the hedging instrument, that is, of the futures contract. Fortunately, knowing the volatility of the bond to be hedged relative to the cheapest-to-deliver bond and the volatility of the cheapest-to-deliver bond relative to the futures contract, the relative volatilities that define the hedge ratio can be easily obtained as follows:

$$\text{Hedge ratio} = \frac{\text{Volatility of bond to be hedged}}{\text{Volatility of futures contract}}$$

$$= \frac{\text{Volatility of bond to be hedged}}{\text{Volatility of CTD bond}} \times \frac{\text{Volatility of CTD bond}}{\text{Volatility of futures contract}}$$

where CTD = cheapest-to-deliver.
Or, more concisely, assuming a fixed yield spread between the bond to be hedged and the cheapest-to-deliver bond:

$$\text{Hedge ratio} = \frac{\text{PVBP of bond to be hedged}}{\text{PVBP of CTD bond}} \times \text{Conversion factor for CTD bond}$$

The hedge ratio in the example at hand is therefore approximately 1.24 (from .072564/.056332) × .9660). Exhibit 17-1 shows that, if the simplifying assumptions hold, a futures hedge using the recommended hedge ratio very nearly locks in the target price for $10 million face value of the telephone bonds. (Furthermore, most of the remaining error could be eliminated by frequent adjustments to the hedge ratio to account for the fact that the price values of a basis point change as rates move up or down.)

Changing Yield Spreads: Another refinement in the hedging strategy is usually necessary for hedging nondeliverable securities. This refinement concerns the assumption about the relative yield spread between the cheapest-to-deliver bond and the bond to be hedged. In the prior discussion, we assumed that the yield spread was constant over time. Yield spreads, however, are not constant over time. They vary with the maturity of the instruments in question and the level of rates, as well as with many unpredictable and nonsystematic factors.

Regression analysis is a simple technique that allows the hedger to capture the relationship between yield levels and yield spreads and use it to advantage.[13] The regression is a statistical technique that uses historical data to model the imperfect relationship between the two variables. For hedging purposes, the variables are the yield on the bond to be hedged and the yield on the cheapest-to-deliver bond. The regression equation takes the form:

$$\text{Yield on bond to be hedged} = a + b \times \text{Yield on CTD security} + \text{error}$$

The regression procedure provides an estimate of b (the *yield beta*), which is the expected relative change in the two bonds. The "error" term accounts for the fact that the relationship between the yields is not perfect and contains a certain amount of "noise." The regression will, however, give an estimate of a and b so that over the sample period the error is on average zero. Our example that used constant spreads implicitly assumes that the yield beta in the regression equals 1.0 and a equals .90 (because .90 is the assumed spread).

For the two issues in question, that is, the Southern Bell 11 3/4s and the Treasury 7 5/8s, the estimated yield beta was 1.05. Thus, yields on the corporate issue are expected to move 5% more than yields on the Treasury issue. To calculate the relative volatility of the two issues correctly, this fact must be taken into account; thus, the hedge ratio derived in our earlier example is multiplied by the factor 1.05. Consequently, instead of shorting 124 Treasury bond futures contracts to hedge $10 million of telephone bonds, the investor would short 130 contracts.

---

[13]The regression is very useful for noncallable bonds and bonds that are very unlikely to be called, but it will not capture the effects of a call on yield spreads. Strategies for hedging callable instruments can be found in Pitts and Fabozzi, *Interest Rate Futures and Options*, Chapters 11 and 12.

EXHIBIT 17-1   Hedging a Nondeliverable Bond to a Delivery Date with Futures

Instrument to be hedged: Southern Bell 11 3/4% of 4/19/23
Hedge ratio = 1.24
Price of futures contract when sold = 70
Target price for Southern Bell bonds = 92.628

Actual Sale Price of Telephone Bonds	Yield at Sale	Yield on Treas. 7 5/8*	Price of Treas. 7 5/8	Futures Price†	Gain (Loss) on 124 Contracts ($10/.01/ Contract)	Effective Sale Price‡
$7,600,000	15.468%	14.568%	54.590	56.511	$1,672,636	$9,272,636
7,800,000	15.072	14.172	56.167	58.144	1,470,144	9,270,144
8,000,000	14.696	13.796	57.741	59.773	1,268,148	9,268,148
8,200,000	14.338	13.438	59.313	61.401	1,066,276	9,266,276
8,400,000	13.996	13.096	60.887	63.030	864,280	9,264,280
8,600,000	13.671	12.771	62.451	64.649	663,524	9,263,524
8,800,000	13.359	12.459	64.018	66.271	462,396	9,262,396
9,000,000	13.061	12.161	65.580	67.888	261,888	9,261,888
9,200,000	12.776	11.876	67.134	69.497	62,372	9,262,372
9,400,000	12.503	11.603	68.683	71.100	(136,400)	9,263,600
9,600,000	12.240	11.340	70.233	72.705	(335,420)	9,264,580
9,800,000	11.988	11.088	71.773	74.299	(533,076)	9,266,924
10,000,000	11.745	10.845	73.312	75.892	(730,608)	9,269,392
10,200,000	11.512	10.612	74.839	77.473	(926,652)	9,273,348
10,400,000	11.287	10.387	76.364	79.052	(1,122,448)	9,277,552
10,600,000	11.070	10.170	77.884	80.625	(1,317,500)	9,282,500
10,800,000	10.861	9.961	79.394	82.188	(1,511,312)	9,288,688
11,000,000	10.659	9.759	80.899	83.746	(1,704,504)	9,295,496
11,200,000	10.463	9.563	82.403	85.303	(1,897,572)	9,302,428

*By assumption, the yield on the 7 5/8s is 90 basis points lower than the yield on the Southern Bell bond.

†By convergence, the futures price equals the price of the 7 5/8s divided by .9660 (the conversion factor).

‡Transaction costs and the financing of margin flows are ignored.

The formula for the hedge ratio is revised as follows to incorporate the impact of the yield beta:

$$\text{Hedge ratio} = \text{Yield beta} \times \frac{\text{PVBP of the bond to be hedged}}{\text{PVBP of the CTD bond}}$$

$$\times \text{ Conversion factor for CTD bond}$$

where the yield beta is derived from the yield of the bond to be hedged regressed on the yield of the cheapest-to-deliver bond. As before, PVBP stands for the change in price for a one basis point change in yield, calculated at the forward prices, for settlement on the day the hedge is to be lifted.

SUMMARY

A futures contract is a firm legal agreement between a buyer (seller) and an established exchange or its clearinghouse in which the buyer (seller) agrees to take (make) delivery of something at a specified price (called the futures price) at the end of a designated period of time (called the settlement or delivery date). Associated with every futures exchange is a clearinghouse, which guarantees that the two parties to the transaction will perform, and allows parties to unwind their positions without the need to deal with the counterparty to the initial transaction. A party to a futures contract must comply with margin requirements (initial, maintenance, and variation margin). A forward contract differs from a futures contract in that it is usually nonstandardized (that is, the terms of each contract are negotiated individually between buyer and seller), there is no clearinghouse, and secondary markets are often nonexistent or extremely thin.

Currently traded interest rate futures contracts include: Treasury bill futures, Eurodollar CD futures, Treasury bond and note futures, and the Bond Buyer municipal index futures. Interest rate futures are also traded on foreign exchanges where the underlying fixed-income security is foreign debt.

The theoretical price of a futures contract is equal to the cash or spot price plus the cost of carry. The cost of carry is equal to the cost of financing the position less the cash yield on the underlying security. The shape of the yield curve will affect the cost of carry. There are several reasons why the actual futures price will depart from the theoretical futures price. In the case of the Treasury bond futures contracts, the delivery options granted to the seller reduce the actual futures price below the theoretical futures price suggested by the standard arbitrage model.

Money managers can use interest rate futures contracts to speculate on the movement of interest rates, to control the interest rate risk of a portfolio, to allocate funds between stocks and bonds, and to enhance returns when futures are mispriced.

QUESTIONS FOR CHAPTER 17

1. Explain the differences between a futures contract and a forward contract.

2. Suppose that bond ABC is the underlying asset for a futures contract with settlement six months from now. You know the following about bond ABC and the futures contract:

    1. In the cash market ABC is selling for $80 (par value is $100).

    2. ABC pays $8 in coupon interest per year in two semiannual payments of $4, and the next semiannual payment is due exactly six months from now.

    3. The current six-month interest rate at which funds can be loaned or borrowed is 6%.

    a. What is the theoretical (or equilibrium) futures price?

    b. What action would you take if the futures price is $83?

    c. What action would you take if the futures price is $76?

    d. Suppose that bond ABC pays interest quarterly instead of semiannually. If you know that you can reinvest any funds you receive three months from now at 1% for three months, what would the theoretical futures price for six-month settlement be?

    e. Suppose that the borrowing rate and lending rate are not equal. Instead, suppose that the current six-month borrowing rate is 8%, and the six-month lending rate is 6%. What is the boundary for the theoretical futures price?

3. Why would the actual futures price diverge from the theoretical futures market?

4. a. Explain how the shape of the yield curve influences the theoretical price of a Treasury bond futures contract.

    b. How does the shape of the yield curve affect the decision of a person short a bond futures contract as to when to deliver the underlying bond?

5. Consider a hypothetical scenario:

    Treasury Bond Futures Price: 95

    Bond A: Coupon = 12%, conversion factor = .85

    Bond B: Coupon = 10%, conversion factor = .75

    Bond C: Coupon = 6.5%, conversion factor = 1.25

    Bond A is selling at 105, Bond B at 102, and Bond C at 95.

    The current month is the delivery month, and a short has agreed to make delivery tomorrow.

    a. Ignoring accrued interest, calculate the invoice price for each of the three bonds.

    b. Which bond is the cheapest-to-deliver?

6. If a money manager wants to reduce a portfolio's duration by using Treasury bond futures contract, should futures contracts be sold or purchased?

7. You work for a conservative investment management firm. You recently asked one of the senior partners for permission to open up a futures account so that you could trade interest rate futures as well as cash instruments. He replied, "Are you crazy? I might as well write you a check, wish you good luck, and put you on a bus to Las Vegas. The futures markets are nothing more than a respectable game of craps. Don't you think you're taking enough risk trading bonds?" How would you try to persuade the senior partner to allow you to use futures?

8. a. What are the risks associated with hedging?

   b. How could a money manager use a Treasury bond futures contract to hedge against higher interest rates over the next quarter?

   c. Suppose an institutional investor wants to hedge a portfolio of mortgage pass-through securities using Treasury bond futures contracts. What are the risks associated with such a hedge?

Chapter 18

INTEREST RATE OPTIONS

This chapter explains the various types of interest rate options, their applications to money management, and how they are priced.

OPTIONS DEFINED

An option is a contract in which the writer of the option grants the buyer of the option the right to purchase from or sell to the writer a designated instrument at a specified price within a specified period of time. The writer, also referred to as the seller, grants this right to the buyer in exchange for a certain sum of money called the *option price* or *option premium*. The price at which the instrument may be bought or sold is called the *exercise* or *strike price*. The date after which an option is void is called the *expiration date*. An *American option* may be exercised at any time up to and including the expiration date. A *European option* may be exercised only on the expiration date.

When an option grants the buyer the right to purchase the designated instrument from the writer, it is called a *call option*. When the option buyer has the right to sell the designated instrument to the writer (seller), the option is called a *put option*. The buyer of any option is said to be *long the option*; the writer (seller) is said to be *short the option*.

The maximum amount that an option buyer can lose in such a transaction is the option price. The maximum profit that the option writer (seller) can realize likewise is the option price. The option buyer has substantial upside return potential, while the option writer has substantial downside risk. We will investigate the risk/reward relationship for option positions later in this chapter.

Differences Between an Option and a Futures Contract

Notice that options differ from futures contracts, in that the buyer of an option has the *right* but not the obligation to perform, while the option seller (writer) has the obligation to perform. In the case of a futures contract, both the buyer and the seller are obligated to perform. Also notice that in a futures contract, the buyer does not pay the seller to accept the obligation; in the case of an option, the buyer pays the seller the option price.

Consequently, the risk/reward characteristics of the two contracts are also different. In a futures contract the long position realizes a dollar-for-dollar gain when the price of the futures increases and suffers a dollar-for-dollar loss when the price of the futures decreases. The opposite occurs for the short position. Options do not provide such a symmetric risk/reward relationship. The most that a long may lose is the option price; yet the long retains all the upside potential, although the gain is always reduced by the option price. The maximum profit that the short may realize is the option price, but this position has substantial downside risk.

TYPES OF INTEREST RATE OPTIONS

Interest rate options can be written on cash instruments or futures. At one time, there were several exchange-traded option contracts whose underlying instrument was a debt instrument. These contracts are referred to as *options on physicals*. The most liquid exchange-traded option on a fixed-income security at the time of this writing is an option on Treasury bonds traded on the Chicago Board Options Exchange. For reasons to be explained later, options on futures have been far more popular than options on physicals. In recent years, market participants have made increasingly greater use of over-the-counter options on Treasury and mortgage-backed securities.

Certain institutional investors who want to purchase an option on a specific Treasury security or a Ginnie Mae pass-through can do so on an over-the-counter basis.[1] There are government and mortgage-backed securities dealers who make a market in options on specific securities. Over-the-counter (or dealer) options typically are purchased by institutional investors who want to hedge the risk associated with a specific security. For example, a thrift may be interested in hedging its position in a specific mortgage pass-through security.[2] Typically, the maturity of the option coincides with the time period over which the buyer of the option wants to hedge, so the buyer is usually not concerned with the option's liquidity.

---

[1] For a more detailed discussion of over-the-counter options, see Mark Pitts and Frank J. Fabozzi, *Interest Rate Futures and Options* (Chicago: Probus Publishing, 1989), Chapter 2.

[2] For a detailed discussion of over-the-counter options or mortgage-backed securities, see William A. Barr, "Options on Mortgage-Backed Securities," in Frank J. Fabozzi (ed.), *The Handbook of Mortgage-Backed Securities*, Third Edition (Chicago: Probus Publishing, 1992).

Besides options on fixed-income securities, there are OTC options on the shape of the yield curve[3] or the yield spread between two securities (such as the spread between mortgage pass-through securities and Treasuries, or between double-A corporates and Treasuries).

EXCHANGE -TRADED FUTURES OPTIONS

An option on a futures contract, commonly referred to as a *futures option*, gives the buyer the right to buy from or sell to the writer a designated futures contract at a designated price at any time during the life of the option. If the futures option is a call option, the buyer has the right to purchase one designated futures contract at the exercise price. That is, the buyer has the right to acquire a long futures position in the designated futures contract. If the buyer exercises the call option, the writer (seller) acquires a corresponding short position in the futures contract.

A put option on a futures contract grants the buyer the right to sell one designated futures contract to the writer at the exercise price. That is, the option buyer has the right to acquire a short position in the designated futures contract. If the put option is exercised, the writer acquires a corresponding long position in the designated futures contract.

There are futures options on all the interest rate futures contracts reviewed in the previous chapter.

Mechanics of Trading Futures Options

Exercising a Futures Option: As the parties to the futures option will realize a position in a futures contract when the option is exercised, the question is: what will the futures price be? That is, at what price will the long be required to pay for the instrument underlying the futures contract, and at what price will the short be required to sell the instrument underlying the futures contract?

Upon exercise, the futures price for the futures contract will be set equal to the exercise price. The position of the two parties is then immediately marked-to-market in terms of the then-current futures price. Thus, the futures position of the two parties will be at the prevailing futures price. At the same time, the option buyer will receive from the option seller the economic benefit from exercising. In the case of a call futures option, the option writer must pay the difference between the

---

[3] For example, Goldman Sachs offers an option on the slope of the yield curve that it calls SYCURVE. The option represents the right to buy (in the case of a call option) or sell (in the case of a put option) specific segments of the yield curve.

current futures price and the exercise price to the buyer of the option. In the case of a put futures option, the option writer must pay the option buyer the difference between the exercise price and the current futures price.

For example, suppose an investor buys a call option on some futures contract in which the exercise price is 85. Assume also that the futures price is 95 and that the buyer exercises the call option. Upon exercise, the call buyer is given a long position in the futures contract at 85 and the call writer is assigned the corresponding short position in the futures contract at 85. The futures positions of the buyer and the writer are immediately marked-to-market by the exchange. Because the prevailing futures price is 95 and the exercise price is 85, the long futures position (the position of the call buyer) realizes a gain of 10, while the short futures position (the position of the call writer) realizes a loss of 10. The call writer pays the exchange 10 and the call buyer receives from the exchange 10. The call buyer, who now has a long futures position at 95, can either liquidate the futures position at 95 or maintain a long futures position. If the former course of action is taken, the call buyer sells a futures contract at the prevailing futures price of 95. There is no gain or loss from liquidating the position. Overall, the call buyer realizes a gain of 10. The call buyer who elects to hold the long futures position will face the same risk and reward of holding such a position, but still has realized a gain of 10 from the exercise of the call option.

Suppose instead that the futures option is a put rather than a call, and the current futures price is 60 rather than 95. Then if the buyer of this put option exercises it, the buyer would have a short position in the futures contract at 85; the option writer would have a long position in the futures contract at 85. The exchange then marks the position to market at the then-current futures price of 60, resulting in a gain to the put buyer of 25 and a loss to the put writer of the same amount. The put buyer who now has a short futures position at 60 can either liquidate the short futures position by buying a futures contract at the prevailing futures price of 60 or maintain the short futures position. In either case the put buyer realizes a gain of 25 from exercising the put option.

Margin Requirements: There are no margin requirements for the buyer of a futures option once the option price has been paid in full. Because the option price is the maximum amount that the buyer can lose, regardless of how adverse the price movement of the underlying instrument, there is no need for margin.

Because the writer (seller) of an option has agreed to accept all of the risk (and none of the reward) of the position in the underlying instrument, the writer (seller) is required to deposit not only the margin required on the interest rate futures contract position if that is the underlying instrument, but also (with certain exceptions) the option price that is received for writing the option. In addition, as prices adversely affect the writer's position, the writer would be required to deposit variation margin as it is marked-to-market.

Reasons for the Popularity of Futures Options

There are three reasons why futures options on fixed-income securities have largely supplanted options on physicals as the options vehicle of choice for institutional investors.[4] First, unlike options on fixed-income securities, options on Treasury coupon futures do not require payments for accrued interest to be made. Consequently, when a futures option is exercised, the call buyer and the put writer need not compensate the other party for accrued interest.

Second, futures options are believed to be "cleaner" instruments because of the reduced likelihood of delivery squeezes. Market participants who must deliver an instrument are concerned that at the time of delivery the instrument to be delivered will be in short supply, resulting in a higher price to acquire the instrument. As the deliverable supply of futures contracts is more than adequate for futures options currently traded, there is no concern about a delivery squeeze.

Finally, in order to price any option, it is imperative to know at all times the price of the underlying instrument. In the bond market, current prices are not as easily available as price information on the futures contract.

THE INTRINSIC VALUE AND TIME VALUE OF AN OPTION

The cost to the buyer of an option is primarily a reflection of the option's *intrinsic value* and any additional amount over that value. The premium over intrinsic value is often referred to as *time value*.

Intrinsic Value of an Option

The intrinsic value of an option is the economic value of the option if it is exercised immediately. Because the buyer of an option need not exercise the option, and, in fact, will not do so if no economic gain will result from exercising it, the intrinsic value cannot be less than zero.

---

[4] Laurie Goodman, "Introduction to Debt Options," Chapter 1 in Frank J. Fabozzi (ed.), *Winning the Interest Rate Game: A Guide to Debt Options* (Chicago: Probus Publishing, 1985), pp. 13-14.

Call Options: The intrinsic value of a call option on an interest rate futures contract is the difference between the current futures price and the strike price. For example, if the *strike price* for a call option is $100 and the *current futures price* is $105, the intrinsic value is $5. That is, if the option buyer exercises the option and simultaneously sells the futures, the option buyer would realize $105 from the sale of the futures, which would be covered by acquiring the futures from the option writer for $100, thereby netting a $5 gain.

When a call option has intrinsic value, it is said to be "in-the-money." Our call option with a strike price of $100 is in the money when the price of the underlying futures contract is greater than $100. When the strike price of a call option exceeds the current futures price, the call option is said to be "out-of-the-money" and has no intrinsic value. An option for which the strike price is equal to the current futures price is said to be "at-the-money." Both at-the-money and out-of-the-money options have an intrinsic value of zero because it is not profitable to exercise the option.

Put Options: For a put option, the intrinsic value is equal to the amount by which the current futures price is below the strike price. For example, if the strike price of a put option is $100 and the current futures price is $92, the intrinsic value is $8. That is, the buyer of the put option who exercises the put option and simultaneously buys the futures contract will net $8 because the futures contract will be sold to the writer for $100 and purchased in the market for $92.

When the put option has intrinsic value, the option is said to be in-the-money. For our put option with a strike price of $100, the option will be in-the-money when the futures price is less than $100. A put option is out-of-the-money when the current futures price exceeds the strike price. A put option is at-the-money when the strike price is equal to the futures price.

Time Value of an Option

The time value of an option is the amount by which the option price exceeds the intrinsic value. The option buyer hopes that, at some time prior to expiration, changes in the market yield will increase the value of the rights conveyed by the option. For this prospect, the option buyer is willing to pay a premium above the intrinsic value. For example, if the price of a call option with a strike price of $100 is $9 when the current futures price is $105, the time value of this option is $4 ($9 minus the intrinsic value of $5). If the current futures price is $90 instead of $105, then the time value of this option is $9 because the option has no intrinsic value.

There are two ways in which an option buyer may realize the value of a position taken in the option. First, the investor may exercise the option using futures options as an example, by exercising the buyer will be assigned a position in the underlying futures contract at the current futures price and be paid by the writer any difference between the current futures price and the strike price. The investor can sell the futures contract at the current price. For example, for our hypothetical call option with a strike price of $100 and an option price of $9, in which the current futures price is $105, the option buyer can exercise the option. This will produce a long position in the futures contract currently at $105. The call writer will pay the buyer $5 (the difference between the current futures price of $105 and the strike price of $100). By simultaneously selling the underlying futures for $105, the option buyer will realize $5.

The second way of realizing the value of an option position is by selling the call option for $9. Obviously, this is the preferable alternative because the exercise of an option will cause the immediate loss of any time value (in this case, $4).

Whether any option will be exercised prior to the expiration date depends on whether the total proceeds at the expiration date would be greater by holding the option or by exercising and reinvesting any cash proceeds received until the expiration date.

PROFIT AND LOSS PROFILES FOR SIMPLE NAKED OPTION STRATEGIES

To appreciate the opportunities available with interest rate options, the profit and loss profiles for various option strategies must be understood. We begin with simple strategies in only one option on a bond, which are referred to as *naked option strategies*. That is, no other position is taken in another option or bond. *The profit and loss profiles that we present assume that each option position is held to the expiration date and not exercised earlier.* Also, to simplify the illustrations, we assume that there are no transactions costs to implement the strategies.

The four naked option strategies that we illustrate are: (1) long call strategy (buying call options); (2) short call strategy (selling or writing call options); (3) long put strategy (buying put options); and (4) short put strategy (selling or writing put options).

Long Call Strategy (Buying Call Options)

The most straightforward option strategy for participating in an anticipated decrease in interest rates (increase in the price of bonds) is to buy a call option on a debt instrument. This is called a *long call strategy*.

To illustrate this strategy, assume that there is a call option on a particular 8% coupon bond with a par value of $100 and 20 years and 1 month to maturity. The call option expires in 1 month and the strike price is $100. The option price is $3. While this option is an option on a cash market security, the principles apply equally to futures options.

Suppose that the current price of the bond is $100 (i.e., the bond is selling at par), which means that the yield on this bond is currently 8%. As the strike price is equal to the current price of the bond, this option is at-the-money. What would the profit or loss be for the investor who purchases this call option and holds it to the expiration date?

The profit and loss from the strategy will depend on the price of the bond at the expiration date. The price, in turn, will depend on the yield on 20-year bonds with an 8% coupon, because in 1 month the bond will have only 20 years to maturity. Exhibit 18-1 shows the price of a 20-year, 8% coupon bond for interest rates ranging from 4% to 12%. Five outcomes are possible:

1. If the price of the bond at the expiration date is less than $100 (which means that the market yield is greater than 8%), then the investor would not exercise the option. (Why bother exercising the option and paying the option writer $100 when the same bond can be purchased in the market at a lower price?) In this case, the option buyer will lose the entire option price of $3. Notice, however, that this is the maximum loss that the option buyer will realize, no matter how far the price of the bond declines.

2. If the price of the bond is equal to $100 (which means that the market yield is unchanged at 8%), no economic value will result from exercising the option. As in the outcome when the price of the bond is less than $100, the buyer of this call option will lose the entire option price, $3.

3. If the price of the bond is greater than $100 but less than $103 (which means that the market yield is less than 8% but greater than 7.70%—see Exhibit 18-1), the option buyer will exercise the option. By exercising, the option buyer purchases the bond for $100 (the strike price) and can sell it in the market for a higher price. Suppose, for example, the market yield is 7.8%, so that the price of the bond is about $102 at the expiration date. The buyer of this call option will realize a $2 gain by exercising the option, offset by the $3 cost of purchasing the call option. Hence $1 is the total loss on this strategy. If the investor fails to exercise the option, the $3 is lost.

4. If the price of the bond at the expiration date is equal to $103 (a market yield of about 7.70%), the investor will exercise the option. In this case, the investor breaks even, realizing a gain of $3 on the bond, which offsets the cost of the option, $3. Although there is no net gain, the price of the option is recouped.

5. If the price of the bond at the expiration date is greater than $103 (a market yield of less than 7.70%), the investor will exercise the option and realize a profit. For example, if the price of the bond is $113 because the market yield has declined from 8% to 6.8%, exercising the option will generate a profit on the bond of $13. Reducing this gain by the cost of the option ($3) means that the investor realizes a net profit of $10 on this strategy .

EXHIBIT 18-1   Price/Yield Relationship for a 20-Year, 8% Coupon Bond

Yield	Price	Yield	Price
4.0	154.71	8.1	99.02
4.2	151.08	8.2	98.05
4.4	147.56	8.3	97.10
4.6	144.15	8.4	96.16
4.8	140.85	8.5	95.23
5.0	137.65	8.6	94.32
5.2	134.56	8.7	93.42
5.4	131.56	8.8	92.53
5.6	128.66	8.9	91.66
5.8	125.84	9.0	90.80
6.0	123.11	9.1	89.95
6.1	121.78	9.2	89.11
6.2	120.47	9.3	88.29
6.3	119.18	9.4	87.48
6.4	117.91	9.5	86.68
6.5	116.66	9.6	85.89
6.6	115.42	9.7	85.11
6.7	114.21	9.8	84.34
6.8	113.01	9.9	83.59
6.9	111.84	10.0	82.84
7.0	110.68	10.2	81.38
7.1	109.54	10.4	79.96
7.2	108.41	10.6	78.58
7.3	107.30	10.8	77.24
7.4	106.21	11.0	75.93
7.5	105.14	11.2	74.66
7.6	104.08	11.4	73.42
7.7	103.04	11.6	72.22
7.8	102.01	11.8	71.05
7.9	101.00	12.0	69.91
8.0	100.00		

Exhibit 18-2 shows the profit/loss in tabular form for the buyer of the hypothetical call option, while Exhibit 18-3 portrays it graphically. While the break-even point and the loss will depend on the option price and the strike price, the shape shown in Exhibit 18-3 will hold for all buyers of call options. That shape indicates that the maximum loss is the option price, and yet there is substantial upside potential.

EXHIBIT 18-2   Profit/Loss Profile for a Long Call Strategy

Assumptions:

Call option price	= 3
Strike price	= 100
Time to expiration	= 1 month

At expiration date:			At expiration date:		
Market Yield	Price of Bond	Net Profit	Market Yield	Price of Bond	Net Profit
4.0	154.71	51.71	8.1	99.02	−3.00
4.2	151.08	48.08	8.2	98.05	−3.00
4.4	147.56	44.56	8.3	97.10	−3.00
4.6	144.15	41.15	8.4	96.16	−3.00
4.8	140.85	37.85	8.5	95.23	−3.00
5.0	137.65	34.65	8.6	94.32	−3.00
5.2	134.56	31.56	8.7	93.42	−3.00
5.4	131.56	28.56	8.8	92.53	−3.00
5.6	128.66	25.66	8.9	91.66	−3.00
5.8	125.84	22.84	9.0	90.80	−3.00
6.0	123.11	20.11	9.1	89.95	−3.00
6.1	121.78	18.78	9.2	89.11	−3.00
6.2	120.47	17.47	9.3	88.29	−3.00
6.3	119.18	16.18	9.4	87.48	−3.00
6.4	117.91	14.91	9.5	86.68	−3.00
6.5	116.66	13.66	9.6	85.89	−3.00
6.6	115.42	12.42	9.7	85.11	−3.00
6.7	114.21	11.21	9.8	84.34	−3.00
6.8	113.01	10.01	9.9	83.59	−3.00
6.9	111.84	8.84	10.0	82.84	−3.00
7.0	110.68	7.68	10.2	81.38	−3.00
7.1	109.54	6.54	10.4	79.96	−3.00
7.2	108.41	5.41	10.6	78.58	−3.00
7.3	107.30	4.30	10.8	77.24	−3.00
7.4	106.21	3.21	11.0	75.93	−3.00
7.5	105.14	2.14	11.2	74.66	−3.00
7.6	104.08	1.08	11.4	73.42	−3.00
7.7	103.04	0.04	11.6	72.22	−3.00
7.8	102.01	−0.99	11.8	71.05	−3.00
7.9	101.00	−2.00	12.0	69.91	−3.00
8.0	100.00	−3.00			

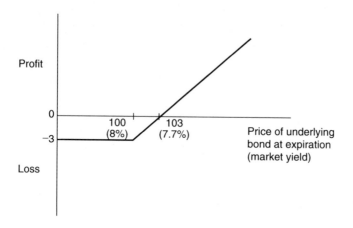

EXHIBIT 18-3   Profit /Loss Diagram for a Long Call Strategy

It is worthwhile to compare the profit and loss profile of a call option buyer to a long bond strategy in the same bond. The payoff from the strategy depends on the price of the bond at the expiration date, which, in turn, depends on the market yield at the expiration date. Consider again the five price outcomes given above:

1. If the price of the bond at the expiration date is less than $100 (market yield rises above 8%), then the investor would lose the entire option price of $3. In contrast, a long bond position will have one of three possible outcomes:

   a. If the price of the bond is lower than $100 (market yield greater than 8%), but higher than $97 (market yield less than about 8.3%), the loss on the long bond position will be less than $3.

   b. If the price of the bond is $97 (market yield of about 8.3%), the loss on the long bond position will be $3.

   c. If the price of the bond is lower than $97, the loss on the long bond position will be more than $3. For example, if the price at the expiration date is $80 because the market yield has risen to 10.4%, the long bond position will result in a loss of $20.

2. If the price of the bond is equal to $100 because the market yield is unchanged, the buyer of the call option will realize a loss of $3 (the cost of the option). There will be no gain or loss on the long bond position.

3. If the price of the bond is higher than $100 because the market yield has fallen below 8% but lower than $103 (market yield above

7.70%), the option buyer will realize a loss of less than $3, while the long bond position will realize a profit.

4. If the market yield falls to about 7.70% so that the price of the bond at the expiration date is equal to $103, there will be no loss or gain from buying the call option. The long bond position will produce a gain of $3.

5. If the price of the bond at the expiration date is higher than $103 because the market yield has fallen below 7.7%, both the call option purchase and the long bond position will result in a profit. However, the profit for the buyer of the call option will be $3 less than that on the long bond position. For example, if the market yield falls to 6.8% so that the price of the bond is $113, the profit from the long call position is $10 while the profit from the long bond position is $13.

Exhibit 18-4 compares the long call strategy and the long bond strategy. This comparison clearly demonstrates the way in which an option can change the risk/return profile available to investors. An investor who takes a long position in the bond realizes a profit of $1 for every $1 increase in the price of the bond as the market yield falls. However, as the market yield rises, this investor loses dollar for dollar. So if the price decreases by more than $3, this strategy will result in a loss of more than $3. The long call strategy, in contrast, limits the loss to only the option price of $3, but retains the upside potential, which will be $3 less than for the long bond position.

We can use this hypothetical call option to demonstrate the speculative appeal of options. Suppose an investor has strong expectations that market yields will fall in three months. With an option price of $3, the speculator can purchase 33.33 call options for each $100 invested. Thus, if the market yield declines, the investor realizes the price appreciation associated with 33.33 bonds of $100 par each (or $3,333 par). With the same $100, the investor could buy only one $100 par value bond and realize the appreciation associated with that one bond if the market yield declines. Now, suppose that in one month the market yield declines to 6% so that the price of the bond increases to $123.11. The long call strategy will result in a profit of $670.26 ($23.11 × 33.33 − $100), or a return of 670% on the $100 investment in the call options. The long bond strategy results merely in a profit of $23.11, or a 23% return on $100.

It is this greater leverage that an option buyer can achieve that attracts investors to options when they wish to speculate on interest rate movements. It does not come without drawbacks, however. Suppose that the market yield is unchanged at the expiration date so that the price of the bond is $100. The long call strategy will result in the loss of the entire investment of $100, while the long bond strategy will produce neither a gain nor a loss.

EXHIBIT 18-4   Comparison of a Long Call Strategy and Long Bond Strategy

Assumptions:
Current price of bond = 100
Call option price   = 3
Strike price   = 100
Time to expiration   = 1 month

| At expiration date: | | Profit: | |
Market Yield	Price of Bond	Long Call	Long Bond
4.0	154.71	51.71	54.71
4.2	151.08	48.08	51.08
4.4	147.56	44.56	47.56
4.6	144.15	41.15	44.15
4.8	140.85	37.85	40.85
5.0	137.65	34.65	37.65
5.2	134.56	31.56	34.56
5.4	131.56	28.56	31.56
5.6	128.66	25.66	28.66
5.8	125.84	22.84	25.84
6.0	123.11	20.11	23.11
6.1	121.78	18.78	21.78
6.2	120.47	17.47	20.47
6.3	119.18	16.18	19.18
6.4	117.91	14.91	17.91
6.5	116.66	13.66	16.66
6.6	115.42	12.42	15.42
6.7	114.21	11.21	14.21
6.8	113.01	10.01	13.01
6.9	111.84	8.84	11.84
7.0	110.68	7.68	10.68
7.1	109.54	6.54	9.54
7.2	108.41	5.41	8.41
7.3	107.30	4.30	7.30
7.4	106.21	3.21	6.21
7.5	105.14	2.14	5.14
7.6	104.08	1.08	4.08
7.7	103.04	0.04	3.04
7.8	102.01	−0.99	2.01
7.9	101.00	−2.00	1.00
8.0	100.00	−3.00	0.00
8.1	99.02	−3.00	−0.98
8.2	98.05	−3.00	−1.95
8.3	97.10	−3.00	−2.90

At expiration date:		Profit:	
Market Yield	Price of Bond	Long Call	Long Bond
8.4	96.16	−3.00	−3.84
8.5	95.23	−3.00	−4.77
8.6	94.32	−3.00	−5.68
8.7	93.42	−3.00	−6.58
8.8	92.53	−3.00	−7.47
8.9	91.66	−3.00	−8.34
9.0	90.80	−3.00	−9.20
9.1	89.95	−3.00	−10.05
9.2	89.11	−3.00	−10.89
9.3	88.29	−3.00	−11.71
9.4	87.48	−3.00	−12.52
9.5	86.68	−3.00	−13.32
9.6	85.89	−3.00	−14.11
9.7	85.11	−3.00	−14.89
9.8	84.34	−3.00	−15.66
9.9	83.59	−3.00	−16.41
10.0	82.84	−3.00	−17.16
10.2	81.38	−3.00	−18.62
10.4	79.96	−3.00	−20.04
10.6	78.58	−3.00	−21.42
10.8	77.24	−3.00	−22.76
11.0	75.93	−3.00	−24.07
11.2	74.66	−3.00	−25.34
11.4	73.42	−3.00	−26.58
11.6	72.22	−3.00	−27.78
11.8	71.05	−3.00	−28.95
12.0	69.91	−3.00	−30.09

Short Call Strategy (Selling or Writing Call Options)

An investor who believes that interest rates will rise or change very little can, if those expectations prove correct, realize income by writing (selling) a call option. This strategy is called a *short call strategy*.

To illustrate this option strategy we shall use the same call option we used to demonstrate the long call strategy. The profit and loss profile of the short call strategy (the position of the call option writer) is the mirror image of the profit and loss profile of the long call strategy (the position of the call option buyer). That is, the profit (loss) of the short call position for any given price of the bond at the expiration date is the same as the loss (profit) of the long call position. Consequently, the maximum profit that the short call strategy can produce is the option price. But the maximum loss is limited only by how high the price of the bond can increase (i.e., how low the market yield can fall) by the expiration date, less the option price. Exhibit 18-5 diagrams the profit/loss profile for a short call strategy.

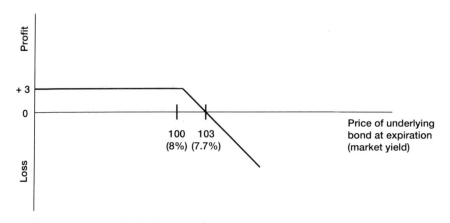

EXHIBIT 18-5   Profit/Loss Profile Diagram for a Short Call Strategy

Long Put Strategy (Buying Put Options)

The most straightforward option strategy for benefitting from an expected increase in interest rates is to buy a put option. This strategy is called a *long put strategy*.

To illustrate this strategy, we'll assume a hypothetical put option for an 8% coupon bond with a par value of $100, 20 years and 1 month to maturity, and a strike price of $100 that is selling for $2. The current price of the bond is $100 (yield of 8%); hence the put option is at-the-money. The profit or loss for this strategy at the expiration date depends on the market yield at the time. The following outcomes are possible:

1. If the price of the bond is higher than $100 because the market yield has fallen below 8%, the buyer of the put option will not exercise it because exercising would mean selling the bond to the writer for a price that is lower than the current market price. Consequently, a loss of $2 (the option price) will result from the long put strategy. Once again, the option price represents the maximum loss to which the buyer of the put option is exposed.

2. If the price of the bond at expiration is equal to $100 because the market yield has remained at 8%, the put will not be exercised, leaving the long put position with a loss equal to the option price of $2.

3. Any price for the bond that is lower than $100 because the market yield has risen above 8% but higher than $98 (market yield of approximately 8.2%) will result in a loss; exercising

the put option, however, limits the loss to less than the option price of $2. For example, suppose that the market yield rises to 8.6%, resulting in a price of $99.03, for the bond at the expiration date. By exercising the option, the option buyer will realize a loss of $1.03. This is because the buyer of the put option can sell the bond, purchased in the market for $99.03, to the writer for $100, realizing a gain of $0.97. Deducting the $2 cost of the option results in a loss of $1.03.

4. At a $98 price for the bond (a market yield of roughly 8.2%) at the expiration date, the long put strategy will break even: the investor will realize a gain of $2 by selling the bond to the writer of the option for $100, offsetting the cost of the option ($2).

5. If the market yield rises above 8.2% so that the price of the bond is below $98 at the expiration date, the long put position will realize a profit. For example, if the market yield rises 260 basis points (from 8% to 10.6%), the price of the bond at expiration will be $78.58. The long put strategy will produce a profit of $19.42: a gain of $21.42, on the bond less the $2 option price.

The profit and loss profile for the long put strategy is shown in tabular form in Exhibit 18-6 and in graphic form in Exhibit 18-7. As with all long option positions, the loss is limited to the option price. However, the profit potential is substantial. The theoretical maximum profit being generated if the bond price falls to zero.

Once again, we can see how an option alters the risk/return profile for an investor by comparing it to a position in the bond. In the case of a long put position, it would be compared to a short bond position, because both strategies realize profits if market yields rise (the price falls). Suppose that an investor sells the bond short for $100. The short bond position would produce the following profit or loss as compared to the long put position:

1. If the price of the bond increases above $100 because the market yield declines, the long put option will result in a loss of $2, but the short bond position will realize one of the following:

   a. If the price of the bond is lower than $102 because the market yield has fallen to below 7.80%, there will be a loss of less than $2.

   b. If the price of the bond is equal to $102, the loss will be $2, the same as for the long put strategy.

   c. If the price of the bond is higher than $102, the loss will be more than $2. For example, if the price is $125.84, because

EXHIBIT 18-6   Profit/Loss Profile for a Long Put Strategy

Assumptions:
Put option price   = 2
Strike price   = 100
Time to expiration   = 1 month

At expiration date:			At expiration date:		
Market Yield	Price of Bond	Net Profit	Market Yield	Price of Bond	Net Profit
4.0	154.71	−2.00	8.1	99.02	−1.02
4.2	151.08`	−2.00	8.2	98.05	−0.05
4.4	147.56	−2.00	8.3	97.10	0.90
4.6	144.15	−2.00	8.4	96.16	1.84
4.8	140.85	−2.00	8.5	95.23	2.77
5.0	137.65	−2.00	8.6	94.32	3.68
5.2	134.56	−2.00	8.7	93.42	4.58
5.4	131.56	−2.00	8.8	92.53	5.47
5.6	128.66	−2.00	8.9	91.66	6.34
5.8	125.84	−2.00	9.0	90.80	7.20
6.0	123.11	−2.00	9.1	89.95	8.05
6.1	121.78	−2.00	9.2	89.11	8.89
6.2	120.47	−2.00	9.3	88.29	9.71
6.3	119.18	−2.00	9.4	87.48	10.52
6.4	117.91	−2.00	9.5	86.68	11.32
6.5	116.66	−2.00	9.6	85.89	12.11
6.6	115.42	−2.00	9.7	85.11	12.89
6.7	114.21	−2.00	9.8	84.34	13.66
6.8	113.01	−2.00	9.9	83.59	14.41
6.9	111.84	−2.00	10.0	82.84	15.16
7.0	110.68	−2.00	10.2	81.38	16.62
7.1	109.54	−2.00	10.4	79.96	18.04
7.2	108.41	−2.00	10.6	78.58	19.42
7.3	107.30	−2.00	10.8	77.24	20.76
7.4	106.21	−2.00	11.0	75.93	22.07
7.5	105.14	−2.00	11.2	74.66	23.34
7.6	104.08	−2.00	11.4	73.42	24.58
7.7	103.04	−2.00	11.6	72.22	25.78
7.8	102.01	−2.00	11.8	71.05	26.95
7.9	101.00	−2.00	12.0	69.91	28.09
8.0	100.00	−2.00			

market yields declined to 5.8%, the short bond position will realize a loss of $25.84, because the short seller must now pay $125.84, for a bond sold short at $100.

2. If the price of the bond at expiration is equal to $100 because the market yield is unchanged, the long put strategy will realize a $2 loss, while there will be no profit or loss on the short bond strategy.

3. Any price for the bond that is lower than $100 but higher than $98 (market yield of about 8.2%) will result in a loss of less than $2 for

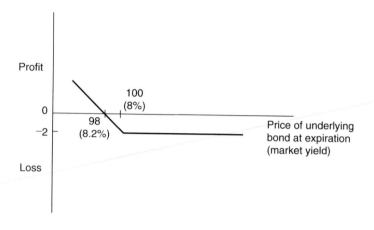

EXHIBIT 18-7 Profit/Loss Profile Diagram for a Long Put Strategy

the long put strategy but a profit for the short bond strategy. For example, a price of $99.02 (market yield of 8.1%) at the expiration date will result in a loss of $1.02 for the long put strategy but a profit of $.98 for the short bond strategy.

4. At a $98 price for the bond at the expiration date, the long put strategy will break even, but the short bond strategy will generate a $2 profit.

5. At a price below $98 (market yield greater than 8.2%) both strategies will generate a profit. However, the profit will always be $2 less for the long put strategy.

Exhibit 18-8 is a tabular comparison of the profit and loss profile for the long put and short bond strategies. While the investor who pursues a short bond strategy participates in all the upside potential and faces all the downside risk, the long put strategy allows the investor to limit the downside risk to the option price while still maintaining upside potential. However, the upside potential is less than that for a short put position by an amount equal to the option price.

Short Put Strategy (Selling or Writing Put Options)

The last naked option position that we shall consider is the short put strategy. The *short put strategy* involves the selling (writing) of put options. This strategy is employed if the investor expects interest rates to fall or stay flat so that the price of the bond will increase or stay the same. The profit and loss profile for a short put option is the mirror image of that

EXHIBIT 18-8 Comparison of a Long Put Strategy and a Short Bond Strategy

Assumptions:
Current price of bond = 100
Put option price   = 2
Strike price   = 100
Time to expiration   = 1 month

	At expiration date:		Profit:	
Market Yield	Price of Bond	Long Put	Short Bond	
4.0	154.71	−2.00	−54.71	
4.2	151.08	−2.00	−51.08	
4.4	147.56	−2.00	−47.56	
4.6	144.15	−2.00	−44.15	
4.8	140.85	−2.00	−40.85	
5.0	137.65	−2.00	−37.65	
5.2	134.56	−2.00	−34.56	
5.4	131.56	−2.00	−31.56	
5.6	128.66	−2.00	−28.66	
5.8	125.84	−2.00	−25.84	
6.0	123.11	−2.00	−23.11	
6.1	121.78	−2.00	−21.78	
6.2	120.47	−2.00	−20.47	
6.3	119.18	−2.00	−19.18	
6.4	117.91	−2.00	−17.91	
6.5	116.66	−2.00	−16.66	
6.6	115.42	−2.00	−15.42	
6.7	114.21	−2.00	−14.21	
6.8	113.01	−2.00	−13.01	
6.9	111.84	−2.00	−11.84	
7.0	110.68	−2.00	−10.68	
7.1	109.54	−2.00	−9.54	
7.2	108.41	−2.00	−8.41	
7.3	107.30	−2.00	−7.30	
7.4	106.21	−2.00	−6.21	
7.5	105.14	−2.00	−5.14	
7.6	104.08	−2.00	−4.08	
7.7	103.04	−2.00	−3.04	
7.8	102.01	−2.00	−2.01	
7.9	101.00	−2.00	−1.00	
8.0	100.00	−2.00	0.00	
8.1	99.02	−1.02	0.98	
8.2	98.05	−0.05	1.95	
8.3	97.10	0.90	2.90	
8.4	96.16	1.84	3.84	
8.5	95.23	2.77	4.77	
8.6	94.32	3.68	5.68	
8.7	93.42	4.58	6.58	
8.8	92.53	5.47	7.47	
8.9	91.66	6.34	8.34	

At expiration date:		Profit:	
Market Yield	Price of Bond	Long Put	Short Bond
9.0	90.80	7.20	9.20
9.1	89.95	8.05	10.05
9.2	89.11	8.89	10.89
9.3	88.29	9.71	11.71
9.4	87.48	10.52	12.52
9.5	86.68	11.32	13.32
9.6	85.89	12.11	14.11
9.7	85.11	12.89	14.89
9.8	84.34	13.66	15.66
9.9	83.59	14.41	16.41
10.0	82.84	15.16	17.16
10.2	81.38	16.62	18.62
10.4	79.96	18.04	20.04
10.6	78.58	19.42	21.42
10.8	77.24	20.76	22.76
11.0	75.93	22.07	24.07
11.2	74.66	23.34	25.34
11.4	73.42	24.58	26.58
11.6	72.22	25.78	27.78
11.8	71.05	26.95	28.95
12.0	69.91	28.09	30.09

for the long put option. The maximum loss is limited only by how low the price of the bond can fall by the expiration date less the option price received for writing the option. Exhibit 18-9 graphically depicts this profit and loss profile.

Summary

To summarize, long calls and short puts allow the investor to gain if bond prices rise (interest rates fall). Short calls and long puts allow the investor to gain if bond prices fall (interest rates rise). An investor would want to use each strategy under the following circumstances:

Circumstance:	Strategy:
Very bullish	Buy call
Slightly bullish	Write put
Slightly bearish	Write call
Very bearish	Buy put

Considering the Time Value of Money

Our illustrations of the four naked option positions do not reflect the time value of money. Specifically, the buyer of an option must pay the seller the option price at the time the option is purchased. Thus the buyer must either finance the purchase price of the option or, if the proceeds do not have to be borrowed, lose the interest that could be earned by investing the option price until the expiration of the option. The seller, in contrast, assuming that the option price does not have to be used as margin for the short position, has the opportunity to invest this option price.

The profit profiles of the naked option positions change when the time value of money is taken into consideration. The break-even price for the buyer and the seller of an option will not be the same as in our illustrations. The break-even price for the underlying instrument at the expiration date is higher for the buyer of the option; for the seller, it is lower.

We also ignored the time value of money in comparing the option strategies with positions in the underlying instrument. In this case, we did not consider the fact that when the underlying instrument is a cash market coupon security, coupon payments may be made between the time the option is purchased and the option's expiration date. When these coupon payments are received, they can be reinvested. Thus reinvestment income must be factored into the analysis of an option position. Also, the effects of financing costs and opportunity costs on the long or short bond positions, respectively, must be factored into the analysis. For the sake of simplicity, however, we shall ignore the time value of money throughout the remainder of this chapter.

HEDGE STRATEGIES

Hedge strategies involve taking a position in an option and a position in the underlying bond in such a way that changes in the value of one

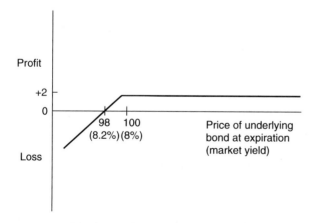

EXHIBIT 18-9   Profit/Loss Profile Diagram for a Short Put Strategy

position will offset any unfavorable price (interest rate) movement in the other position. We discuss two popular hedge strategies here: (1) the covered call writing strategy; and (2) the protective put buying strategy.

Covered Call Writing Strategy

A covered call writing strategy involves writing a call option on bonds held in the portfolio. That is, the investor is in a short position in a call option and a long position in the underlying bond. If the price of the bond declines because interest rates rise, there will be a loss on the long bond position. However, the income generated from the sale of the call option will either (1) fully offset the loss in the long bond position, (2) partially offset the loss in the long bond position, or (3) more than offset the loss in the long bond position so that a profit is generated.

To illustrate this strategy, suppose that an investor owns $100 par of an 8%, 20-year and 1-month bond selling at par. Also suppose that a call option on this bond with a $100 strike price that matures in 1 month can be sold for $3. If the investor has decided to hold the bond and write a call option on the same bond, the profit or loss for this strategy will depend on the market yield on the bond at the expiration date. One of the following outcomes will occur:

1. If the price of the bond is higher than $100 as a result of a decline in the market yield, the call option buyer will exercise the option and pay the option writer $100. The value of the portfolio at the expiration date is then $103 ($100 received from the bond plus $3 received from writing the call option). Thus the profit from this strategy if the price of the bond is higher than $100 is $3 (the option price). The chance for upside potential on the long bond position has been forfeited for the guaranteed $3 option price.

2. If the market yield is unchanged at 8%, the price of the bond is equal to $100 at the expiration date; the call option buyer will not exercise the option. The value of the portfolio will still be $103, resulting in a $3 profit.

3. If the market yield rises such that the price of the bond is lower than $100 but higher than $97, there will be a profit, but it will be less than $3. For example, suppose that the price of the bond is $98 (market yield of about 8.3%). The long bond position will have a value of $98, while the short call position generates $3. The portfolio value is therefore $101, resulting in a profit of $1. The $3 option price received has cushioned the decline in the value of the long position.

4. At a price of $97 (market yield of roughly 8.3%), the long bond position will have a value of $97, and the short call position generates $3. There is no profit or loss for the portfolio because the portfolio value is unchanged at $100.

5. Should market yields rise more than 70 basis points, the price of the bond will be lower than $97 at expiration, and the portfolio will realize a loss. For example, suppose that the price of the bond at expiration is $71 because the market yield increased to 11.8%. The portfolio value will be $74. Hence there is a loss of $26.

The profit and loss profile for this covered call writing strategy is graphically portrayed in Exhibit 18-10. There are two important points to recognize in this illustration. First, this strategy has allowed the investor to reduce the downside risk for the portfolio. In this example, by selling the at-the-money option, the risk is reduced by an amount equal to the option price. In exchange for this reduction of downside risk, the investor has agreed to cap the potential profit. In our illustration, the maximum profit is the option price.

The second point can be seen by comparing Exhibit 18-9 and Exhibit 18-10. Notice that the shape of the two profit and loss profiles is the same. That is, the covered call writing strategy has the same profit and loss profile as a short put strategy. This is not an accident. There is a relationship between put and call options that we shall discuss later in this chapter.

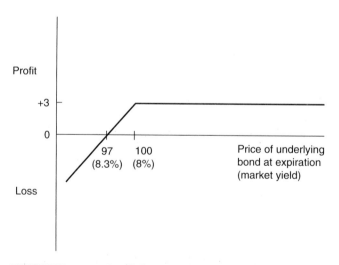

EXHIBIT 18-10 Profit/Loss Profile Diagram for a Covered Call Writing Strategy

Protective Put Buying Strategy

An investor may want to protect the value of bonds held in the portfolio already. A way of doing this with options is to buy a put option. By doing so, the investor is guaranteed to receive the strike price of the put option for the bonds held less the cost of the option. Should the market yield fall, thereby increasing the price of the bonds, the investor will be able to participate in the price increase, with the profit reduced by the cost of the option. This strategy is called a *protective put buying strategy*. It consists of taking a long position in a bond held in the portfolio and a long put position (buying a put option) in which the bond held in the portfolio is the underlying bond for the put option.

For example, suppose than an investor has a $100 par value, 8%, 20-year and 1-month bond whose current market value is $100. Assume further that a 1-month put option selling for $2 can be purchased with a strike price of $100. One month from now at the expiration date the profit or loss can be summarized as follows:

1. If the price of the bond is higher than $102 (a decline in the market yield to less than 7.80%), the investor will realize a profit from this strategy. For example, suppose the market yield declines to 6% so that the bond price is $123.11. Because the cost of purchasing the put option was $2, the net profit for this position will be $21.11. The investor has given up the $2 profit for downside protection on the bond held in the portfolio.
2. If the price of the bond is equal to $102, no profit or loss will be realized from this strategy.
3. There will be a loss of less than $2 if the price of the bond is lower than $102 but more than $100. For example, a price of $101 (market yield of 7.9%) will result in a loss for this strategy of $1: a $1 gain in the long bond position but a cost of $2 to acquire the long put position.
4. In none of the previous outcomes will the investor exercise the put option. However, if the price of the bond is below $100 because the market yield has increased, the option will be exercised. At any price below $100, the investor will be assured of receiving $100 for the bond. Thus the value of the portfolio will be $100 minus the cost of the option ($2), resulting in a maximum loss of $2.

Exhibit 18-11 is a graphic presentation of the profit and loss profile for this protective put buying strategy. By implementing this strategy, the investor has effectively assured a price of $100 (the strike price of the put option) at a cost of $2. The investor has maintained all the upside potential, although this upside potential is reduced by $2, the cost of the put option.

Suppose that, in addition to the put option with a strike price of $100, there is a put option with a strike price of $96. As we shall see shortly, the price for this put option with the same expiration date but a lower strike price would be less than the put option with a strike price of $100. Suppose that the option price is $1.25. The investor who pursues a protective put option strategy using this put option with a strike price of $96 will have guaranteed a minimum price of $96 at a cost of $1.25. The upside potential will be reduced by $1.25. However, the downside risk will be $4 more than that with the put whose strike price is $100.

As can be seen, the strike price determines the minimum price that will be guaranteed by the put option and thus the downside risk of the option. However, the higher the strike price, the greater the cost of guaranteeing the minimum price. This is because the higher the strike price, the more attractive the put option is to an option buyer, resulting in a higher price. Therefore, when implementing a protective put strategy, an investor must evaluate the trade-off between a higher minimum price for the underlying instrument and the associated higher cost of purchasing the put option.

Once again, notice the shape of the payoff pattern for the protective put option in Exhibit 18-11. Note that the profit/loss pattern is the same as that for the long call option strategy shown in Exhibit 18-8.

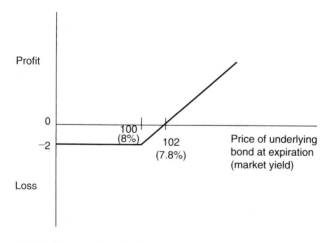

Exhibit 18-11 Profit/Loss Profile Diagram for a Protective Put Buying Strategy

PUT-CALL PARITY RELATIONSHIP
AND EQUIVALENT POSITIONS

Is there a relationship between the price of a call option and the price of a put option on the same underlying instrument, with the same strike price and the same expiration date? There is. To see this relationship, which is commonly referred to as the *put-call parity relationship*, let's use an example.

Previous illustrations have used a put and a call option on the same underlying instrument (a bond currently with 20 years and 1 month to maturity), both options having a strike price of $100 and 1 month to expiration. The price of the underlying bond is assumed to be $100. The call price and put price are assumed to be $3 and $2, respectively. Consider the following strategy.

> Buy the bond at a price of $100
> Sell a call option at a price of $3
> Buy a put option at a price of $2

This strategy therefore involves:

> Long the bond
> Short the call option
> Long the put option

Exhibit 18-12 shows the profit and loss profile at the expiration date for this strategy. Notice that no matter what the price of the underlying bond at expiration date, the strategy produces a profit of $1. Ignoring the cost of financing the long position and the long put position, this situation cannot exist in an efficient market. The actions of market participants in implementing this strategy to capture the $1 profit will result in one or more of the following consequences, which will tend to eliminate the $1 profit: (1) an increase in the price of the bond; (2) a decrease in the call option price; and/or (3) an increase in the put option price.

In our example, assuming the bond price doesn't change, this means that the call price and the put price must be equal. But this is true only when we ignore the time value of money (financing cost, opportunity cost, coupon income, and reinvestment income). Also, in the illustration we did not consider the possibility of early exercise of the options. Thus we have been considering a put-call parity relationship for only European options.

Ignoring the time value of money and considering European options, the outcome from the following position must be one of no arbitrage profits:

(18.1)   Long the bond + Short call option + Long put option = 0

EXHIBIT 18-12 Profit/Loss Profile for a Strategy Involving a Long Bond Position, Short Call Option Position, and Long Put Option Position

Assumptions:

Current price of bond	= 100
Price of call option	= 3
Call strike price	= 100
Price of put option	= 2
Put strike price	= 100
Time to expiration	= 1 month

At expiration date:

Market Yield	Price of Bond	Profit from Long Bond	Price Received for Call	Price Paid for Put	Overall Profit
4.0	154.71	0*	3	−2	1
4.2	151.08	0*	3	−2	1
4.4	147.56	0*	3	−2	1
4.6	144.15	0*	3	−2	1
4.8	140.85	0*	3	−2	1
5.0	137.65	0*	3	−2	1
5.2	134.56	0*	3	−2	1
5.4	131.56	0*	3	−2	1
5.6	128.66	0*	3	−2	1
5.8	125.84	0*	3	−2	1
6.0	123.11	0*	3	−2	1
6.1	121.78	0*	3	−2	1
6.2	120.47	0*	3	−2	1
6.3	119.18	0*	3	−2	1
6.4	117.91	0*	3	−2	1
6.5	116.66	0*	3	−2	1
6.6	115.42	0*	3	−2	1
6.7	114.21	0*	3	−2	1
6.8	113.01	0*	3	−2	1
6.9	111.84	0*	3	−2	1
7.0	110.68	0*	3	−2	1
7.1	109.54	0*	3	−2	1
7.2	108.41	0*	3	−2	1
7.3	107.30	0*	3	−2	1
7.4	106.21	0*	3	−2	1
7.5	105.14	0*	3	−2	1
7.6	104.08	0*	3	−2	1
7.7	103.04	0*	3	−2	1
7.8	102.01	0*	3	−2	1
7.9	101.00	0*	3	−2	1
8.0	100.00	0	3	−2	1
8.1	99.02	0‡	3	−2	1
8.2	98.05	0‡	3	−2	1
8.3	97.10	0‡	3	−2	1
8.4	96.16	0‡	3	−2	1
8.5	95.23	0‡	3	−2	1
8.6	94.32	0	3	−2	1

At expiration date:

Market Yield	Price of Bond	Profit from Long Bond	Price Received for Call	Price Paid for Put	Overall Profit
8.7	93.42	0‡	3	−2	1
8.8	92.53	0‡	3	−2	1
8.9	91.66	0‡	3	−2	1
9.0	90.80	0‡	3	−2	1
9.1	89.95	0‡	3	−2	1
9.2	89.11	0‡	3	−2	1
9.3	88.29	0‡	3	−2	1
9.4	87.48	0‡	3	−2	1
9.5	86.68	0‡	3	−2	1
9.6	85.89	0‡	3	−2	1
9.7	85.11	0‡	3	−2	1
9.8	84.34	0‡	3	−2	1
9.9	83.59	0‡	3	−2	1
10.0	82.84	0‡	3	−2	1
10.2	81.38	0‡	3	−2	1
10.4	79.96	0‡	3	−2	1
10.6	78.58	0‡	3	−2	1
10.8	77.24	0‡	3	−2	1
11.0	75.93	0‡	3	−2	1
11.2	74.66	0‡	3	−2	1
11.4	73.42	0‡	3	−2	1
11.6	72.22	0‡	3	−2	1
11.8	71.05	0‡	3	−2	1
12.0	69.91	0‡	3	−2	1

*If the price of the bond is more than the strike price, the buyer of the call option will exercise the option.

‡If the price of the bond is lower than the strike price, the investor will exercise the put option.

In terms of price, it can be shown that there will be no arbitrage profits at *any* time (not just expiration) if:

(18.2) $P_{po} = P_{co} + S - P_b$

Where P_{po} = Price of put option
P_{co} = Price of call option
S = Strike (exercise) price of option
P_b = Current price of the underlying bond

and the strike price and expiration date are the same for both options. This relationship is one form of the put-call parity relationship for European options when the time value of money is ignored. It is approximately true for American options. Considering the time value of money, the put-call parity relationship for coupon bonds is:

(18.3) $P_{po} = P_{co} + PV(S) + PV(\text{coupon}) - P_b$

where PV (S) = Present value of the strike price
PV (coupon) = Present value of the coupon payments

Equivalent Positions

Working with equation (18.1), we can identify equivalent positions, that is, positions that will provide the same profit profile. For example, subtracting the long put position from both sides of equation (18.1), we have:

(18.4)   Long the bond + Short call option = −Long put option

But the position on the right-hand side of equation (18.4) is the same as a short put position. Therefore:

(18.5)   Long the bond + Short call option = Short put option

We've seen equation (18.5) several places throughout this book. Earlier in this chapter we show that a covered call position, which is a long bond position plus a short call option position on the same bond, has the same profit profile as a short put option position. This is what equation (18.5) states. In our discussion of callable bonds and mortgage-backed securities, we stated that owning such securities is equivalent to a long bond position plus a short call position. Thus, these securities will have a payoff similar to a short put position. But remember, the equivalent position holds only for European options, and a more precise relationship requires that the time value of money be considered.

Manipulating equation (18.1) gives us the following equivalent positions:

Short the bond	+ Short put	=	Short call
Long the bond	+ Long put	=	Long call
Short the bond	+ Long call	=	Long put
Long call	+ Short put	=	Long the bond
Long put	+ Short call	=	Short the bond

Thus an investor can synthetically create any of the positions on the right-hand side of these equations by taking the two positions indicated on the left-hand side.

THE OPTION PRICE

Factors That Influence the Option Price

Six factors will influence the option price:
1. Current price of the underlying instrument
2. Strike price
3. Time to expiration
4. Short-term risk-free interest rate over the life of the option

5. Coupon rate on the bond

6. Expected volatility of yields (or prices) over the life of the option

The impact of each of these factors may depend on whether (1) the option is a call or a put, (2) the option is an American option or a European option, and (3) the underlying instrument is a bond or a futures contract on a bond.[5]

Current Price of the Underlying Instrument: For a call option, as the current price of the underlying instrument increases (decreases), the option price increases (decreases). For a put option, as the current price of the underlying instrument decreases (increases), the option price increases (decreases).

Strike Price: All other factors being constant, the higher the strike price, the lower the price of a call option. For a put option, the opposite is true: the higher the strike price, the higher the price of a put option.

Time to Expiration: For American options (both puts and calls), all other factors held constant, the longer the time to expiration, the higher the option price. No general statement can be made for European options. The impact of the time to expiration on European options will depend on whether the option is a put or a call.

Short-Term Risk-Free Interest Rate Over the Life of the Option: Holding all other factors constant, the price of a call option on a bond will increase as the short-term risk-free interest rate rises. For a put option, the opposite is true: an increase in the short-term risk-free interest rate will decrease the price of a put option. In contrast, for a futures option, the price of both a call and a put option will decrease if the short-term risk-free interest rate rises.[6]

Coupon Rate: For options on bonds, coupons tend to reduce the price of a call option because the coupons make it more attractive to hold the bond than the option. Thus call options on coupon-bearing bonds will tend to be priced lower than similar call options on noncoupon-bearing bonds. Conversely, coupons tend to increase the price of put options.

Expected Volatility of Yields Over the Life of the Option: As the expected volatility of yields over the life of the option increases, the price of the option will also increase. The reason is that the greater the expected volatility, as measured by the standard deviation or variance of yields, the

---

[5] For a more detailed discussion of the impact of these factors on the price of an option, see Pitts and Fabozzi, *Interest Rate Futures and Options*.

[6] Ibid.

greater the probability that the price of the underlying bond or futures contract will move in the direction that will benefit the option buyer.

Theoretical Call Option Price

Exhibit 18-13 shows the shape of the theoretical price of a call option based on the price of the underlying instrument. The line from the origin to the strike price along the horizontal axis is the intrinsic value of the call option when the price of the underlying instrument is lower than the strike price, because the intrinsic value is zero. The 45-degree line extending from the horizontal axis is the intrinsic value of the call option once the price of the underlying instrument exceeds the strike price. The reason for this is that the intrinsic value of the call option will increase by $1 each time the price of the underlying instrument increases by $1. Thus the slope of the line representing the intrinsic value after the strike price is reached is 1.

The theoretical call option price is shown by the convex line. The difference between the theoretical call option price and the intrinsic value at any given price for the underlying instrument is the time value of the option.

Exhibit 18-14 also shows the theoretical call option price, but with three tangent lines drawn. The slope of the tangent line shows how the theoretical price will change for small changes in the price of the underlying instrument. That is, if we let:

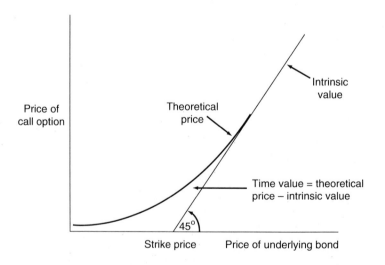

EXHIBIT 18-13   Theoretical Price of a Call Option

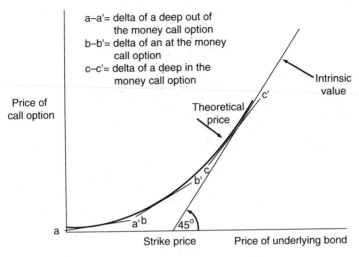

a–a'= delta of a deep out of
the money call option
b–b'= delta of an at the money
call option
c–c'= delta of a deep in the
money call option

Intrinsic value

Price of call option

Theoretical price

c'

c

b'

a'b

45°

a

Strike price   Price of underlying bond

EXHIBIT 18-14   Delta of a Call Option

P_{co} = Theoretical price of the call option
P_b = Price of the underlying bond

then:

$$P_{co} = f(P_b)$$

The slope of the convex curve representing the theoretical call option price at any point is then:

$$\frac{dP_{co}}{dP_b}$$

When we discussed the duration of callable bonds in Chapter 13, we referred to this measure as the *delta* of the option. Delta, also commonly referred to as the *hedge ratio*, plays an important role in (1) portfolio and trading strategies; (2) option pricing models; and (3) assessing the price volatility of a callable bond, as explained in Chapter 13 in determining the call-adjusted duration.

The steeper the slope of the line, the greater the delta. When an option is deep out-of-the-money (that is, the price of the underlying instrument is substantially below the strike price), the slope of the line is relatively flat (see line a-a' in Exhibit 18-14). This means a delta close to zero. To understand why, consider a call option with a strike price of $100 and three months to maturity. If the price of the underlying instrument is $15, how much would you expect the price of the option to increase if the price of the underlying instrument increases by $1, from $15 to $16? Not much, because the price of the underlying instrument is still considerably below the strike price.

For a call option that is deep in-the-money, the delta will be close to 1. That is, the call option price will increase almost dollar-for-dollar with an increase in the price of the underlying instrument. In terms of Exhibit 18-14, the slope of the tangent line approaches the slope of the intrinsic value line after the strike price is reached. The slope of that line is 1. Thus the delta for a call option ranges from zero (for deep out-of-the-money options) to 1 (for deep-in-the-money call options). The delta for an at-the-money option is approximately .5.

Notice that these properties for delta agree with our statements in Chapter 13 when we analyzed the call-adjusted duration.

When analyzing a trading or investment strategy, traders and money managers look at other properties of an option besides its delta. One consideration is the convexity of the option, which is commonly referred to as its *gamma*.[7]

Option Pricing Models

To implement portfolio and trading strategies it is necessary to estimate the theoretical price of an option. Several models have been developed to do this. Like the models we used in discussing the pricing of futures contracts in the previous chapter, options pricing models are based on an arbitrage or riskless hedge argument. The expected price of the underlying instrument is not an input. Option pricing models differ from futures pricing models in that a key factor in the valuation of an option is the expected price or yield volatility over the life of the option.

The most popular option-pricing model for American call options on common stock is the Black-Scholes option pricing model.[8] The key insight of this model is that a synthetic option can be created by taking an appropriate position in the underlying common stock and borrowing or lending funds at the riskless interest rate.

To create a synthetic option, the delta of an option must be computed. As we just explained, the delta indicates how the price of the option will change when the price of the underlying common stock changes. For example, suppose that on the basis of the current price of the

---

[7] The gamma of an option is the change in its delta for a change in the price of the underlying instrument. There are other measures of the price sensitivity of an option to changes in the factors that impact the option price. For example, *kappa* is a measure of the change in the price of an option with a change in the volatility of the underlying instrument. *Theta* is the change in the price of an option with a change in the time to expiration. For a discussion of the role of these measures in options strategies, see Richard M. Bookstaber, *Option Pricing and Investment Strategies* (Chicago: Probus Publishing, 1987), Chapter 4; and James F. Meisner and John A Richards, "Option Premium Dynamics: With Applications to Fixed Income Portfolio Analysis," in Frank J. Fabozzi and T. Dessa Garlicki (eds.), *Advances in Bond Analysis and Portfolio Strategies* (Chicago: Probus Publishing, 1987).

underlying common stock, a call option has a delta of .5. This means that two call options will have the same price movement as one share of the common stock. The profit/loss profile of an option can be created by taking a position in the underlying common stock based on the delta of the option and by borrowing at the riskless interest rate. Because the synthetic option and the option have the same payoff under all possible prices for the underlying common stock at the expiration date, the synthetic option and the option must sell at the same price. From this relationship, the price of the option can be determined.

There are some problems in using the Black-Scholes option pricing model for pricing of interest rate options. Consider a three-month European call option on a three-year zero-coupon bond.[9] The maturity value of the underlying bond is $100, and the strike price is $120. Suppose further that the current price of the bond is $75.13, the three-year risk-free rate is 10% annually, and expected price volatility is 4%. What would be the fair value for this option? Do you really need an option pricing model to determine the value of this option?

Think about it. This zero-coupon bond will never have a price above $100 because that is the maturity value. As the strike price is $120, the option will never be exercised; its value is therefore zero. If you can get anyone to buy such an option, any price you obtain will be free money. Yet an option buyer armed with the Black-Scholes option pricing model will input the variables we assume above and come up with a value for this option of $5.60! Why is the Black-Scholes model off by so much? The answer lies in its underlying assumptions.

There are three assumptions underlying the Black-Scholes model that limit its use in pricing options on interest rate instruments. First, the probability distribution for the prices assumed by the Black-Scholes option pricing model is a lognormal distribution, which permits some probability—no matter how small—that the price can take on any positive value. But in the case of a zero-coupon bond, the price cannot take on a value above $100. In the case of a coupon bond, we know that the price cannot exceed the sum of the coupon payments plus the maturity value. For example, for a five-year 10% coupon bond with a maturity value of $100, the price cannot be greater than $150 (five coupon payments of $10 plus the maturity value of $100). Thus, unlike stock prices, bond prices

---

[8] Fischer Black and Myron Scholes, "The Pricing of Corporate Liabilities," *Journal of Political Economy* (May-June 1973), pp. 637-659.

[9] This example is given in Lawrence J. Dyer and David P. Jacob, "Guide to Fixed Income Option Pricing Models," in Frank J. Fabozzi (ed.), *The Handbook of Fixed Income Options*, (Chicago: Probus Publishing, 1989), pp. 81-82.

have a maximum value. The only way that a bond's price can exceed the maximum value is if negative interest rates are permitted. This is not likely to occur, so any probability distribution for prices assumed by an option pricing model that permits bond prices to be higher than the maximum bond value could generate nonsensical option prices. The Black-Scholes model does allow bond prices to exceed the maximum bond value (or, equivalently, allows negative interest rates). That is one of the reasons why we can get a senseless option price for the three-month European call option on the three-year zero-coupon bond.

The second assumption of the Black-Scholes option pricing model is that the short-term interest rate is constant over the life of the option. Yet the price of an interest rate option will change as interest rates change. A change in the short-term interest rate changes the rates along the yield curve. Therefore, to assume that the short-term rate will be constant is inappropriate for interest rate options. The third assumption is that the variance of prices is constant over the life of the option. Recall from Chapter 4 that as a bond moves closer to maturity, its price volatility declines. Therefore, the assumption that price variance is constant over the life of the option is inappropriate.

While we have illustrated the problem of using the Black-Scholes model to price interest rate options, we can also show that the *binomial option pricing model* based on the price distribution of the underlying bond suffers from the same problems.[10] A way around the problem of negative interest rates is to use a binomial option pricing model based on the distribution of interest rates rather than prices to construct the binomial tree.[11] Once a binomial interest rate tree is constructed, it can be converted into a binomial price tree by using the interest rates on the tree to determine the price of the bond. Then we follow the standard procedure for calculating the option price by working backward from the value of the call option at the expiration date.

---

[10] The binomial option pricing model is commonly used to price equity options. See John Cox, Stephen Ross, and Mark Rubinstein, "Option Pricing: A Simplified Approach," *Journal of Financial Economics* (September 1979), pp. 229-263; Richard Rendleman and Brit Bartter, "Two-State Option Pricing," *Journal of Finance* (December 1979), pp. 1093-1110; and William F. Sharpe, *Investments* (Englewood Cliffs, NJ: Prentice Hall, 1981), Chapter 16.

[11] For example, in constructing the binomial tree based on interest rates, the following formula can be used:

If yield increases: If yield decreases:

$Y_{[t + 1]} = Y_t e^{-s}$ $Y_{[t + 1]} = Y_t e^{-s}$

where $Y_{[t + 1]}$ = Yield to maturity in time period $t + 1$

Y_t = Yield to maturity in time period t

s = Expected interest rate volatility

e = 2.7182818

While the binomial option pricing model based on yields is superior to models based on prices, it still has a theoretical drawback. All option pricing models to be theoretically valid must satisfy the put-call parity relationship explained earlier. The problem with the binomial model based on yields is that it does not satisfy this relationship. It violates the relationship in that it fails to take into consideration the yield curve, thereby allowing arbitrage opportunities.

The most elaborate models that take the yield curve into consideration and as a result do not permit arbitrage opportunities are called *yield curve option pricing models* or *arbitrage-free option pricing models*. These models can incorporate different volatility assumptions along the yield curve. While they are theoretically superior to the other models we have described, they required extensive computer time to solve.[12]

Implied Volatility

Option pricing models provide a theoretical option price depending on the six factors that we discussed at the beginning of this section. The only one of these factors that is not known and must be estimated is the expected volatility of yield or price over the life of the option. A popular methodology to assess whether an option is fairly priced is to assume that the option is priced correctly and then, using an option pricing model, estimate the volatility that is implied by that model, given the observed option price, and the other five factors that determine the price of an option. The estimated volatility computed in this manner is called the *implied volatility*.

For example, suppose that a money manager using some option pricing model, the current price of the option, and the five other factors that determine the price of an option computes an implied yield volatility of 12%. If the money manager expects that the volatility of yields over the life of the option will be greater than the implied volatility of 12%, the option is considered to be undervalued. In contrast, if the money manager's expected volatility of yields over the life of the option is less than the implied volatility, the option is considered to be overvalued.

While we have focused on the option price, the key to understanding the options market is knowing that trading and investment strategies in this market involve buying and selling volatility. Estimating the implied

---

[12]For a discussion of yield curve or arbitrage-free option-pricing models see Chapter 7 of Pitts and Fabozzi, *Interest Rate Futures and Options*; Dyer and Jacob, "Guide to Fixed Income Option Pricing Models," *The Handbook of Fixed Income Options*; and Ravi E. Dattatreya and Frank J. Fabozzi, "A Simplified Model for the Valuation of Debt Options," Chapter 4 in *The Handbook of Fixed Income Options*.

volatility and comparing it to the trader's or money manager's expectations of future volatility is just another way of evaluating options. If an investor uses expected volatility to compute the fair value of the option, the option will appear cheap or expensive in exactly the same cases.

SUMMARY

An option grants the buyer of the option the right either to buy (in the case of a call option) or to sell (in the case of a put option) the underlying asset to the seller (writer) of the option at a stated price called the strike price (exercise price) by a stated date called the expiration date. The price that the option buyer pays to the writer of the option is called the option price or option premium. An American option allows the option buyer to exercise the option at any time up to and including the expiration date; a European option may be exercised only at the expiration date.

Interest rate options include options on fixed-income securities and options on interest rate futures contracts. The latter, more commonly called futures options, are the preferred vehicle for implementing investment strategies. Because of the difficulties of hedging particular bond issues or pass-through securities, many institutions find over-the-counter options more useful; these contracts can be customized to meet specific investment goals.

The buyer of an option cannot realize a loss greater than the option price, and has all the upside potential. By contrast, the maximum gain that the writer (seller) of an option can realize is the option price; the writer is exposed to all the downside risk. Strategies using interest rate options include speculating on interest rate movements and hedging.

The option price consists of two components: the intrinsic value and the time premium. The intrinsic value is the economic value of the option if it is exercised immediately (except that if there is no positive economic value that will result from exercising immediately, then the intrinsic value is zero). The time premium is the amount by which the option price exceeds the intrinsic value. Six factors influence the option price: (1) the current price of the underlying bond; (2) the strike price of the option; (3) the time remaining to the expiration of the option; (4) the expected price volatility of the underlying bond (i.e., expected interest rate volatility); (5) the short-term risk-free interest rate over the life of the option; and (6) coupon payments.

The assumptions underlying the Black-Scholes pricing model and the binomial model based on prices limit their application to options on fixed-income instruments. The binomial option model based on yields is a better model, but it still suffers from the problem that it does not satisfy the put-call parity relationship. More sophisticated models called yield curve or arbitrage-free pricing models overcome this drawback by incorporating the yield curve into the pricing model.

QUESTIONS FOR CHAPTER 18

1. An investor owns a call option on bond X with a strike price of 100. The bond has 10 years to maturity and the coupon rate is 9%. The call option expires today at a time when bond X is selling to yield 8%. Should the investor exercise the call option?

2. An investor wants to protect against a rise in the market yield on a Treasury bond. Should the investor purchase a put option or a call option to obtain protection?

3. What is the intrinsic value and the time value of a call option on bond W given the following information?

   strike price of call option = 97

   current price of bond W = 102

   call option price = 9

4. "There's no real difference between options and futures. Both are hedging tools, and both are derivative products. It's just that with options you have to pay an option premium, while futures require no upfront payment except for a 'good faith' margin. I can't understand why anyone would use options." Do you agree with this statement?

5. What arguments would be given by those who feel that the Black- Scholes model does not apply in pricing interest rate options?

6. Here are some excerpts from an article entitled "It's Boom Time for Bond Options As Interest-Rate Hedges Bloom," published in the November 8, 1990, issue of *The Wall Street Journal.*

   a. The threat of a large interest-rate swing in either direction is driving people to options to hedge their portfolios of long-term Treasury bonds and medium-term Treasury notes, said Steven Northern, who manages fixed-income mutual funds for Massachusetts Financial Services Co. in Boston.

   Why would a large interest rate swing in either direction encourage people to hedge?

   b. If the market moves against an option purchaser, the option expires worthless, and all the investor has lost is the relatively low purchase price, or "premium," of the option.

   Comment on the accuracy of this statement.

   c. Futures contracts also can be used to hedge portfolios, but they cost more, and there isn't any limit on the amount of losses they could produce before an investor bails out.

   Comment on the accuracy of this statement.

   d. Mr. Northern said Massachusetts Financial has been trading actively in bond and note put options. "The concept is simple," he said. "If you're concerned about interest rates but don't want to alter the nature of what you own in a fixed-income portfolio, you can just buy puts."

Why might put options be a preferable means of altering the nature of a fixed-income portfolio?

7. What is the difference between an option on a bond and an option on a bond futures contract?

8. a. What is the motivation for the purchase of an over-the-counter option?

   b. Does it make sense for an investor who wants to speculate on interest rate movements to purchase an over-the-counter option?

Chapter 19

INTEREST RATE SWAPS
AND AGREEMENTS

In the previous two chapters we discuss how interest rate futures and options can be used to control interest rate risk. There are other contracts useful for controlling such risk that commercial banks and investment banks can customize for their clients. These include (1) interest rate swaps and options on swaps, and (2) interest rate agreements (caps and floors) and options on these agreements. These contracts are relatively new. In this chapter we will review each of them and explain how they can be used by institutional investors.

INTEREST RATE SWAPS

In an interest rate swap, two parties (called *counterparties*) agree to exchange periodic interest payments. The dollar amount of the interest payments exchanged is based on some predetermined dollar principal, which is called the *notional principal amount*. The dollar amount each counterparty pays to the other is the agreed-upon periodic interest rate times the notional principal amount. The only dollars that are exchanged between the parties are the interest payments, not the notional principal amount. In the most common type of swap, one party agrees to pay the other party fixed interest payments at designated dates for the life of the contract. This party is referred to as the *fixed-rate payer*. The other party, who agrees to make interest rate payments that float with some index, is referred to as the *floating-rate payer*.

For example, suppose that for the next five years party X agrees to pay party Y 10% per year, while party Y agrees to pay party X six-month LIBOR. Party X is a fixed-rate payer/floating-rate receiver, while party Y is a floating-rate payer/fixed-rate receiver. Assume that the notional principal amount is $50 million, and that payments are exchanged every six months for the next five years. This means that every six months, party X (the fixed-rate payer/floating-rate receiver) will pay party Y $2.5 million (10% times $50 million divided by 2). The amount that party Y (the floating-rate payer/fixed-rate receiver) will pay party X will be six-month LIBOR times $50 million divided by 2. If six-month LIBOR is 7%, party Y will pay party X $1.75 million (7% times $50 million divided by 2). Note that we divide by two because one-half year's interest is being paid.

The interest rate benchmarks that are commonly used for the floating rate in an interest rate swap are those on various money market instruments: Treasury bills, the London Interbank Offered Rate (LIBOR), commercial paper, bankers acceptances, certificates of deposit, the federal funds rate, and the prime rate.

As we illustrate later, market participants can use an interest rate swap to alter the cash flow character of assets or liabilities from a fixed-rate basis to a floating-rate basis, or vice versa.

Risk/Return Characteristics of a Swap

As we explain later in this chapter, there is a secondary market for swaps. The value of an interest rate swap will fluctuate with market interest rates. To see how, let's consider our hypothetical swap. Suppose that interest rates change immediately after parties X and Y enter into the swap. First, consider what would happen if the market demanded that in any five-year swap the fixed-rate payer must pay 11% in order to receive six-month LIBOR. If party X (the fixed-rate payer) wants to sell its position to party A, then party A will benefit by having to pay only 10% (the original swap rate agreed upon) rather than 11% (the current swap rate) to receive six-month LIBOR. Party X will want compensation for this benefit. Consequently, the value of party X's position has increased. Thus, if interest rates increase, the fixed-rate payer will realize a profit and the floating-rate payer will realize a loss.

Next, consider what would happen if interest rates decline to, say, 6%. Now a five-year swap would require the fixed-rate payer to pay 6% rather than 10% to receive six-month LIBOR. If party X wants to sell its position to party B, the latter would demand compensation to take over the position. In other words, if interest rates decline, the fixed-rate payer will realize a loss, while the floating-rate payer will realize a profit.

The risk/return profile of the two positions when interest rates change is summarized in Exhibit 19-1.

Interpreting a Swap Position

There are two ways that a swap position can be interpreted: (1) a

EXHIBIT 19-1   Risk/Return Profile of Counterparties to an Interest Rate Swap

	Interest Rates Decrease	Interest Rates Increase
Floating-rate payer	Gain	Loss
Fixed-rate payer	Loss	Gain

package of forward/futures contracts, and (2) a package of cash flows from buying and selling cash market instruments.

Package of Forward Contracts: Contrast the position of the counterparties in an interest rate swap summarized in Exhibit 19-1 to the position of the long and short futures (forward) contract discussed in Chapter 17. The long futures position gains if interest rates decline and loses if interest rates rise—this is similar to the risk/return profile for a floating-rate payer. The risk/return profile for a fixed-rate payer is similar to that of the short futures position: a gain if interest rates increase and a loss if interest rates decrease. By taking a closer look at the interest rate swap we can understand why the risk/return relationships are similar.

Consider party X's position. Party X has agreed to pay 10% and receive six-month LIBOR. More specifically, assuming a $50 million notional principal amount, X has agreed to buy a commodity called "six-month LIBOR" for $2.5 million. This is effectively a six-month forward contract where X agrees to pay $2.5 million in exchange for delivery of six-month LIBOR. If interest rates increase to 11%, the price of that commodity (six-month LIBOR) is higher, resulting in a gain for the fixed-rate payer, who is effectively long a six-month forward contract on six-month LIBOR. The floating-rate payer is effectively short a six-month forward contract on six-month LIBOR. There is therefore an implicit forward contract corresponding to each exchange date.

Now we can see why there is a similarity between the risk/return relationship for an interest rate swap and a forward contract. If interest rates increase to, say, 11%, the price of that commodity (six-month LIBOR) increases to $2.75 million (11% times $50 million divided by 2). The long forward position (the fixed-rate payer) gains, and the short forward position (the floating-rate payer) loses. If interest rates decline to, say, 9%, the price of our commodity decreases to $2.25 million (9% times $50 million divided by 2). The short forward position (the floating-rate payer) gains, and the long forward position (the fixed-rate payer) loses.

Consequently, interest rate swaps can be viewed as a package of more basic interest rate control tools, such as forwards. The pricing of an interest rate swap will then depend on the price of a package of forward contracts with the same settlement dates in which the underlying for the forward contract is the same index.

While an interest rate swap may be nothing more than a package of forward contracts, it is not a redundant contract for several reasons. First, maturities for forward or futures contracts do not extend out as far as those of an interest rate swap; an interest rate swap with a term of 15 years or longer can be obtained. Second, an interest rate swap is a more transactionally efficient instrument. By this we mean that in one transaction an entity can effectively establish a payoff equivalent to a package of forward contracts. The forward contracts would each have to be negotiated separately. Third, the interest rate swap market has grown in liquidity since its establishment in 1981; interest rate swaps now provide more liquidity than forward contracts, particularly long-dated (i.e., long-term) forward contracts.

Package of Cash Market Instruments: To understand why a swap can also be interpreted as package of cash market instruments, consider an investor who enters into the transaction below:

- buy a $50 million par of a five-year floating-rate bond that pays six-month LIBOR every six months
- finance the purchase of the five-year floating-rate bond by borrowing $50 million for five years on terms requiring 10% annual interest rate paid every six months.

The cash flows for this transaction are described in Exhibit 19-2. The second column of the exhibit sets out the cash flow from purchasing the five-year floating-rate bond. There is a $50 million cash outlay and then ten cash inflows. The amount of the cash inflows is uncertain because they depend on future LIBOR. The next column shows the cash flow from borrowing $50 million on a fixed-rate basis. The last column shows the net cash flow from the entire transaction. As the last column indicates, there is no initial cash flow (no cash inflow or cash outlay). In all ten six-month periods, the net position results in a cash inflow of LIBOR and a cash outlay of $2.5 million. This net position, however, is identical to the position of a fixed-rate payer/floating-rate receiver.

It can be seen from the net cash flow in Exhibit 19-2 that a fixed-rate payer has a cash market position that is equivalent to a long position in a floating-rate bond and borrowing the funds to purchase the floating-rate bond on a fixed-rate basis. But the borrowing can be viewed as issuing a fixed-rate bond, or equivalently, being short a fixed-rate bond. Consequently, the position of a fixed-rate payer can be viewed as being long a floating-rate bond and short a fixed-rate bond.

EXHIBIT 19-2   Cash Flow For the Purchase of a Five-Year Floating-Rate Bond Financed by Borrowing on a Fixed-Rate Basis

Transaction: Purchase for $50 million a five-year floating-rate bond:
floating rate = LIBOR, semiannual pay
Borrow $50 million for five years: fixed rate = 10%,
semiannual payments

Six month period	Cash flow (in millions of dollars) from:		
	Floating-rate bond	Borrowing cost	Net
0	−$ 50	+$ 50.0	$ 0
1	+(LIBOR$_1$/2) x 50	− 2.5	+(LIBOR$_1$/2) x 50 − 2.5
2	+(LIBOR$_2$/2) x 50	− 2.5	+(LIBOR$_2$/2) x 50 − 2.5
3	+(LIBOR$_3$/2) x 50	− 2.5	+(LIBOR$_3$/2) x 50 − 2.5
4	+(LIBOR$_4$/2) x 50	− 2.5	+(LIBOR$_4$/2) x 50 − 2.5
5	+(LIBOR$_5$/2) x 50	− 2.5	+(LIBOR$_5$/2) x 50 − 2.5
6	+(LIBOR$_6$/2) x 50	− 2.5	+(LIBOR$_6$/2) x 50 − 2.5
7	+(LIBOR$_7$/2) x 50	− 2.5	+(LIBOR$_7$/2) x 50 − 2.5
8	+(LIBOR$_8$/2) x 50	− 2.5	+(LIBOR$_8$/2) x 50 − 2.5
9	+(LIBOR$_9$/2) x 50	− 2.5	+(LIBOR$_9$/2) x 50 − 2.5
10	+(LIBOR$_{10}$/2) x 50 + 50	− 52.5	+(LIBOR$_{10}$/2) x 50 − 2.5

Note: The subscript for LIBOR indicates the six-month LIBOR as per the terms of the floating-rate bond at time t.

What about the position of a floating-rate payer? It can be easily demonstrated that the position of a floating-rate payer is equivalent to purchasing a fixed-rate bond and financing that purchase at a floating-rate, where the floating rate is the reference interest rate for the swap. That is, the position of a floating-rate payer is equivalent to a long position in a fixed-rate bond and a short position in a floating-rate bond.

Pricing a Swap

The price of any financial asset is equal to the present value of the expected cash flow. Also, as we explain in Chapter 9, the proper methodology for discounting the cash flow is to use spot or zero-coupon rates. The bootstrapping procedure for extrapolating the theoretical zero-coupon rates is explained in Chapter 9.

In the case of a swap, each cash flow should be discounted at the zero-coupon rate applicable to the time period when the cash flow will be realized (paid or received). Although there is no an active market for zero-coupon swaps from which to determine the appropriate rates, a theoretical zero-coupon swap curve can be extrapolated from the existing coupon swap curve using the bootstrapping procedure illustrated in Chapter 9.

These zero-coupon rates can then be used to price any swap, whether generic or one of the more complex swaps described later.

Duration of a Swap

As with any fixed-income contract, the value of a swap will change as interest rates change, and duration is a measure of the interest rate sensitivity of a fixed-income contract (see Chapter 4). From the perspective of the party who pays floating and receives fixed, the interest rate swap position can be viewed as follows:

Long a fixed-rate bond + Short a floating-rate bond

This means that the duration of an interest rate swap from the perspective of a floating-rate payer is just the difference between the duration of the two bond positions that make up the swap. That is,

Duration of a swap =
Duration of a fixed-rate bond − Duration of a floating-rate bond

Most of the interest rate sensitivity of a swap will result from the duration of the fixed-rate bond because the duration of the floating-rate bond will be small. It will always be less than the length of time to the next reset date. Therefore, the duration of a floating-rate bond for which the coupon rate resets every six months will be less than six months. The duration of a floating-rate bond is smaller, the closer the swap is to its reset date.

Terminology, Conventions, and Market Quotes

Here we review some of the terminology used in the swaps market and explain how swaps are quoted.

The date that the counterparties commit to the swap is called the *trade date*. The date that the swap begins accruing interest is called the *effective date*, while the date that the swap stops accruing interest is called the *maturity date*.

While our illustrations assume that the timing of the cash flows for both the fixed-rate payer and floating-rate payer will be the same, this is rarely the case in a swap. In fact, an agreement may call for the fixed-rate payer to make payments annually but the floating-rate payer to make payments more frequently (semiannually or quarterly). Also, the way interest accrues on each leg of the transaction differs, because there are several day count conventions in the fixed-income markets.

The terminology used to describe the position of a party in the swap markets combines cash market jargon and futures jargon, given that a swap position can be interpreted as a position in a package of cash market instruments or a package of futures/forward positions. The counterparty to an interest rate swap is either a fixed-rate payer or floating-rate payer. There are a number of ways to describe these positions:[1]

Fixed-rate payer
- pays fixed rate in the swap
- receives floating in the swap
- is short the bond market
- has bought a swap
- is long a swap
- has established the price sensitivities of a longer-term liability and a floating-rate asset

Floating-rate payer
- pays floating rate in the swap
- receives fixed in the swap
- is long the bond market
- has sold a swap
- is short a swap
- has established the price sensitivities of a longer-term asset and a floating-rate liability

The first two expressions to describe the position of a fixed-rate payer and floating-rate payer are self-explanatory. To understand why the fixed-rate payer is viewed as short the bond market, and the floating-rate payer is viewed as long the bond market, consider what happens when interest rates change. Those who borrow on a fixed-rate basis will benefit if interest rates rise because they have locked in a lower interest rate. But those who have a short bond position will also benefit if interest rates rise. Thus, a fixed-rate payer can be said to be short the bond market. A floating-rate payer benefits if interest rates fall. A long position in a bond also benefits if interest rates fall, so terminology describing a floating-rate payer as long the bond market is not surprising. From our discussion of interpretation of a swap as a package of cash market instruments and the duration of a swap, description of a swap in terms of the sensitivities of long and short cash positions follows naturally.

The convention that has evolved for quoting swaps levels is that a swap dealer sets the floating rate equal to the index and then quotes the

---

[1] See Robert F. Kopprasch, John Macfarlane, Daniel R. Ross, and Janet Showers, "The Interest Rate Swap Market: Yield Mathematics, Terminology, and Conventions," Chapter 58 in Frank J. Fabozzi and Irving M. Pollack (eds.), *The Handbook of Fixed Income Securities* (Homewood, IL: Dow Jones-Irwin, 1987).

fixed rate that will apply. To illustrate this convention, consider a 10-year swap offered by a dealer to market participants:

Floating-rate payer:

> Pay floating rate of six-month LIBOR
> Receive fixed rate of 8.75%

Fixed-rate payer:

> Pay fixed rate of 8.85%
> Receive floating rate of six-month LIBOR

The offer price that the dealer would quote the fixed-rate payer would be to pay 8.85% and receive LIBOR "flat" ("flat" meaning with no spread to LIBOR). The bid price that the dealer would quote the floating-rate payer would be to pay LIBOR flat and receive 8.75%. The bid-offer spread is ten basis points.

The fixed rate is some spread above the Treasury yield curve with the same term to maturity as the swap. In our illustration, suppose that the 10-year Treasury yield is 8.35%. Then the offer price that the dealer would quote to the fixed-rate payer is the 10-year Treasury rate plus 50 basis points versus receiving LIBOR flat. For the floating-rate payer, the bid price quoted would be LIBOR flat versus the 10-year Treasury rate plus 40 basis points. The dealer would quote such a swap as 40-50, meaning that the dealer is willing to enter into a swap to receive LIBOR and pay a fixed rate equal to the 10-year Treasury rate plus 40 basis points; and it would be willing to enter into a swap to pay LIBOR and receive a fixed rate equal to the 10-year Treasury rate plus 50 basis points. The difference between the Treasury rate paid and received is the bid-offer spread.

Application of a Swap to Asset/Liability Management

So far we have merely described an interest rate swap and looked at its characteristics. We illustrate now how they can be used in asset/liability management. Other types of interest rate swaps have been developed as well beyond the basic or "plain vanilla" swaps described.

An interest rate swap can be used to alter the cash flow characteristics of an institution's assets so as to provide a better match between assets and liabilities. The two institutions we use for illustration are a commercial bank and a life insurance company.

Suppose a bank has a portfolio consisting of five-year term commercial loans with a fixed interest rate. The principal value of the portfolio is $50 million, and the interest rate on all the loans in the portfolio is 10%. The loans are interest-only loans; interest is paid semiannually, and the principal is paid at the end of five years. That is, assuming no default on the loans, the cash flow from the loan portfolio is $2.5 million every six months for the next five years and $50 million at the end of five years. To fund its loan portfolio, assume that the bank is relying on the issuance of six-month certificates of deposit. The interest rate that the bank plans to pay on its six-month CDs is six-month LIBOR plus 40 basis points.

The risk that the bank faces is that six-month LIBOR will be 9.6% or greater. To understand why, remember that the bank is earning 10% annually on its commercial loan portfolio. If six-month LIBOR is 9.6%, it will have to pay 9.6% plus 40 basis points to depositors for six-month funds, or 10%, and there will be no spread income. Worse, if six-month LIBOR rises above 9.6%, there will be a loss; that is, the cost of funds will exceed the interest rate earned on the loan portfolio. The bank's objective is to lock in a spread over the cost of its funds.

The other party in the interest rate swap illustration is a life insurance company that has committed itself to pay a 9% rate for the next five years on a guaranteed investment contract (GIC) it has issued. The amount of the GIC is $50 million. Suppose that the life insurance company has the opportunity to invest $50 million in what it considers an attractive five-year floating-rate instrument in a private placement transaction. The interest rate on this instrument is six-month LIBOR plus 160 basis points. The coupon rate is set every six months.

The risk that the life insurance company faces in this instance is that six-month LIBOR will fall so that the company will not earn enough to realize a spread over the 9% rate that it has guaranteed to the GIC holders. If six-month LIBOR falls to 7.4% or less, no spread income will be generated. To understand why, suppose that six-month LIBOR at the date the floating-rate instrument resets its coupon is 7.4%. Then the coupon rate for the next six months will be 9% (7.4% plus 160 basis points). Because the life insurance company has agreed to pay 9% on the GIC policy, there will be no spread income. Should six-month LIBOR fall below 7.4%, there will be a loss.

We can summarize the asset/liability problems of the bank and the life insurance company as follows:

Bank:

   1. Has lent long term and borrowed short term

   2. If six-month LIBOR rises, spread income declines

Life insurance company:

   1. Has effectively lent short term and borrowed long term

   2. If six-month LIBOR falls, spread income declines

Now let's suppose the market has available a five-year interest rate swap with a notional principal amount of $50 million. The swap terms available to the bank are as follows:

1. Every six months the bank will pay 8.45% (annual rate)
2. Every six months the bank will receive LIBOR

The swap terms available to the insurance company are as follows:

1. Every six months the life insurance company will pay LIBOR
2. Every six months the the life insurance company will receive 8.40%

What has this interest rate contract done for the bank and the life insurance company? Consider first the bank. For every six-month period for the life of the swap agreement, the interest rate spread will be as follows:

Annual interest rate received:

From commercial loan portfolio	= 10.00%
From interest rate swap	= Six-month LIBOR
Total	= 10.00% + Six-month LIBOR

Annual interest rate paid:

To CD depositors	= Six-month LIBOR
From interest rate swap	= 8.45%
Total	= 8.45% + Six-month LIBOR

Outcome:

To be received	= 10.00% + Six-month LIBOR
To be paid	= 8.45% + Six-month LIBOR
Spread income	= 1.15% or 115 basis points

Thus, whatever happens to six-month LIBOR, the bank locks in a spread of 115 basis points.

Now let's look at the effect of the interest rate swap on the life insurance company:

Annual interest rate received:

From floating-rate instrument	= 1.6% + Six-month LIBOR
From interest rate swap	= 8.40%
Total	= 10.00% + Six-month LIBOR

Annual interest rate paid:

To GIC policyholders	= 9.00%
On interest rate swap	= Six-month LIBOR
Total	= 9.00% + Six-month LIBOR

Outcome:

To be received	= 10.00% + Six-month LIBOR
To be paid	= 9.00% + Six-month LIBOR
Spread income	= 1.0% or 100 basis points

Regardless of what happens to six-month LIBOR, the life insurance company locks in a spread of 100 basis points.

The interest rate swap has allowed each party to accomplish its asset/liability objective of locking in a spread.[2] It permits the two financial institutions to alter the cash flow characteristics of its assets: from fixed to floating in the case of the bank, and from floating to fixed in the case of the life insurance company. This type of transaction is referred to as an *asset swap*. Another way the bank and the life insurance company could use the swap market would be to change the cash flow nature of their liabilities. Such a swap is called a *liability swap*.

Of course there are other ways two such institutions can accomplish the same objectives. The bank might refuse to make fixed-rate commercial loans. If borrowers can find someplace else willing to lend on a fixed-rate basis, though, the bank has lost these customers. The life insurance company might refuse to purchase a floating-rate instrument. But suppose that the terms on a private placement instrument offered to the life insurance company were more attractive than those available on a comparable credit risk floating-rate instrument, and that by using the swap market the life insurance company can earn more than it could investing directly in a five-year fixed-rate bond. For example, suppose the life insurance company can invest in a comparable credit risk five-year fixed-rate bond with a yield of 9.8%. Assuming that it commits itself to a GIC with a 9% rate, this would result in spread income of 80 basis points—less than the 100-basis point spread income it achieves by purchasing the floating-rate instrument and entering into the swap.

Consequently, not only can an interest rate swap be used to change the risk of a transaction by changing the cash flow characteristics of assets or liabilities, but under certain circumstances, it also can be used to enhance returns. Obviously, this depends on the existence of market imperfections.

Primary Determinants of Swap Spreads

Earlier we provided two interpretations of a swap: (1) a package of futures/forward contracts, and (2) a package of cash market instruments.

---

[2] Whether the size of the spread is adequate is not an issue to us in this illustration.

The swap spread is determined by the same factors that influence the spread over Treasuries on financial instruments (futures/forward contracts or cash) that produce a similar return or funding profile. As we explain below, the key determinant of the swap spread for swaps with maturities of five years or less is the cost of hedging in the Eurodollar CD futures market. For longer maturity swaps, the key determinant of the swap spread is the credit spreads in the corporate bond market.

Given that a swap is a package of futures/forward contracts, the swap spread can be determined by looking for futures/forward contracts with the same risk/return profile. As we explain in Chapter 17, a Eurodollar CD futures contract is a swap where a fixed dollar payment (i.e., the futures price) is exchanged for three-month LIBOR. There are available Eurodollar CD futures contracts that have maturities every three months for five years. A market participant can put together a (synthetic) fixed-rate security or a fixed-rate funding vehicle of up to five years by taking a position in a strip of Eurodollar CD futures contracts (i.e., a position in every three-month Eurodollar CD up to the desired maturity date).

For example, consider a financial institution that has fixed-rate assets and floating-rate liabilities. Both the assets and liabilities have a maturity of three years. The interest rate on the liabilities resets every three months based on three-month LIBOR. This financial institution can hedge this mismatched asset/liability position by buying a three-year strip of Eurodollar CD futures contracts. By doing so, the financial institution is receiving LIBOR over the three-year period and paying a fixed dollar amount (i.e., the futures price). The financial institution is now hedged because the assets are fixed-rate, and the strip of long Eurodollar CDs futures synthetically creates a fixed-rate funding arrangement. From the fixed dollar amount over the three years, an effective fixed interest rate that the financial institution pays can be calculated. Alternatively, the financial institution can synthetically create a fixed-rate funding arrangement by entering into a three-year swap in which it pays fixed and receives three-month LIBOR. The financial institution will use the vehicle that gives the lowest cost of hedging the mismatched position. This will drive the synthetic fixed rate in the swap market to that available by hedging in the Eurodollar CD futures market.

For swaps with maturities longer than five years, the spread is determined primarily by the credit spreads in the corporate bond market. Since a swap can be interpreted as a package of long and short positions in a fixed-rate bond and a floating-rate bond, it is the credit spreads in those two market sectors that will be the key determinant of the swap spread. Boundary conditions for swap spreads based on prices for fixed-rate and floating-rate corporate bonds can be determined.[3] Several technical factors, such as the relative supply of fixed-rate and floating-rate corporate bonds and the cost to dealers of hedging their inventory position of swaps, influence where between the boundaries the actual swap spread will be.[4]

Development of the Interest Rate Swap Market

The interest rate swap was first developed in late 1981. By 1987, the market had grown to more than $500 billion (in terms of notional principal amount). What is behind this rapid growth? As our asset/liability application should show, an interest rate swap is a quick way for institutional investors to change the nature of assets and liabilities or to exploit any perceived capital market imperfection. The same applies to borrowers such as corporations, sovereigns, and supranationals.

In fact, the initial motivation for the interest rate swap market was borrower exploitation of what were perceived to be "credit arbitrage" opportunities because of differences in quality spreads between lower- and higher-rated credits in the U.S. and Eurodollar bond fixed-rate market and the same spread in these two floating-rate markets. Basically, the value of swaps depends on the well-known economic principle of comparative advantage in international economics. The argument in the case of swaps is that even though a high credit-rated issuer can borrow at a lower cost in both the fixed-rate and floating-rate markets (that is, have an absolute advantage in both), it will have a comparative advantage relative to a lower credit-rated issuer in one of the markets (and a comparative disadvantage in the other). Under these conditions, each borrower can benefit from issuing securities in the market in which it has a comparative advantage and then swapping obligations for the desired type of financing. The swap market became the vehicle for swapping obligations.

Despite arguments that credit arbitrage opportunities are rare in reasonably efficient international capital markets, and that, even if they did exist, they would be eliminated quickly by arbitrage, the number of interest rate swap transactions has grown substantially.[5] One explanation is suggested in a May 1984 contribution sponsored by Citicorp that appeared in *Euromoney*:

> The nature of swaps is that they arbitrage market imperfections. As with any arbitrage opportunity, the more it is exploited, the smaller it becomes....

---

[3] These boundary conditions are derived in the appendix to Ellen Evans and Gioia Parente Bales, "What Drives Interest Rate Swap Spreads?" Chapter 13 in Carl R. Beidleman (ed.), *Interest Rate Swaps* (Homewood, IL: Richard D. Irwin, 1991).

[4] For a discussion of these other factors, see Evans and Bales, "What Drives Interest Rate Swap Spreads," pp. 293-301.

But some of the causes of market imperfections are unlikely to disappear quickly. For example, insurance companies in many countries are constrained to invest mainly in instruments that are domestic in that country. That requirement will tend to favor domestic issuers artificially, and is unlikely to be changed overnight. And even in the world's most liquid markets there are arbitrage opportunities. They are small and exist only briefly. But they exist nevertheless.[6]

As this opinion demonstrates, as early as 1984 it was argued that the difference in quality spreads in the two markets may be attributable to differences in regulations in two countries. Similarly, differences in tax treatment across countries also create market imperfections that can be exploited using swaps.[7] Thus, swaps can be used for regulatory or tax arbitrage.

Rather than relying exclusively on an arbitrage argument, one study suggests that the swaps market has grown because it allows borrowers to raise a type of financing that was not possible prior to the introduction of interest rate swaps.[8]

Finally, another argument suggested for the growth of the interest rate swap market is the increased volatility of interest rates, which has led both borrowers and lenders to hedge or manage their exposure. Even though risk/return characteristics can be replicated by a package of forward contracts, interest rate forward contracts are not as liquid as interest rate swaps. And entering into or liquidating swap transactions has been facilitated by the standardization of documentation published by the

---

[5] Several observers have challenged the notion that "credit arbitrage" exists. It should be evident that the comparative advantage argument, while based on arbitrage, is based not on the assumption of irrational mispricing, but rather on assumptions of equilibrium in segmented markets. If two completely separate markets are each perfectly competitive unto themselves, but set different prices for risk, a transactor in both markets simultaneously sees an imperfectly competitive market and can make money. Those who challenge the "credit arbitrage" notion argue that the differences in quality spreads in the fixed-rate and floating-rate markets represent differences in the risks that lenders face in these two markets. For example, the interest rate for a floating-rate note effectively represents a short-term interest rate. The quality spread on floating-rate notes therefore represents a spread in the short-term market. In contrast, the quality spread on fixed-rate medium- and long-term notes represents the spread in that maturity sector. There is no reason why the quality spreads have to be the same. Two researchers have demonstrated that differences in quality spreads between the fixe-rate and floating-rate markets are consistent with option pricing theory. See Ian Cooper and Antonio Mello, "Default Spreads in the Fixed and in the Floating Rate Markets: A Contingent Claims Approach," *Advances in Futures and Options Research*, Vol. 3 (1988), pp. 269-290.

[6] "Swap Financing Techniques: A Citicorp Guide," Special Sponsored Section, *Euromoney* (May 1984), pp. S1-S7.

[7] Several examples of the use of swaps to exploit differences in taxes are given in Clifford W. Smith, Charles W. Smithson, and Lee MacDonald Wakeman, "The Evolving Market for Swaps," *Midland Corporate Finance Journal* (Winter 1986), pp. 20-32.

[8] Marcelle Arak, Arturo Estrella, Laurie Goodman, and Andrew Silver, "Interest Rate Swaps: An Alternative Explanation," *Financial Management* (Summer 1988), pp. 12-18.

International Swap Dealers Association in early 1987. Moreover, a swap to hedge or manage a position costs less than a package of interest rate forward contracts.

Role of the Intermediary: The role of the intermediary in an interest rate swap sheds some further light on evolution of the market. Intermediaries in these transactions have been commercial banks and investment banks, who in the early stages of the market sought out end users of swaps. That is, they found in their client bases particular entities that needed a swap to accomplish a funding or investing objective, and they matched the two entities. In essence, the intermediary in this type of transaction performed the function of a broker.

The only time that the intermediary intended to take the opposite side of a swap (that is, act as a principal) was to balance out the transaction. For example, an intermediary might have two clients that were willing to do a swap, but one wanted the notional principal amount to be $100 million, while the other wanted it to be $85 million; in this case the intermediary might become the counterparty to the extent of $15 million. That is, the intermediary would warehouse or take a position as a principal to the transaction to make up the $15 million difference between client objectives. To protect itself against an adverse interest rate movement, the intermediary would hedge its position.

As the frequency and the size of the transactions increased, many intermediaries became comfortable with the transactions and became principals at the outset instead of acting as brokers. As long as an intermediary had one entity willing to do a swap, the intermediary was willing to be the counterparty. Consequently, interest rate swaps became part of an intermediary's inventory of product positions. Advances in quantitative techniques and futures products for hedging complex positions such as swaps made the protection of large inventory positions feasible.

Yet another motivation has encouraged intermediaries to become principals rather than brokers in swaps. As more intermediaries entered the swap market, bid-ask spreads on swaps declined sharply. To make money in the swaps market, intermediaries had to do a sufficient volume of business, which could be done only if an intermediary had (1) an extensive client base willing to use swaps, and (2) a large inventory of swaps. This necessitated that intermediaries act as principals.[9]

---

[9] For example, a survey by *Euromoney* asked 150 multinationals and supranationals to identify the characteristics that make a swap house efficient (Special Supplement on Swaps, *Euromoney* (July 1987), p. 14). The results indicate that the speed at which a swap could be arranged for a client is the most important criterion. That speed depends on client base and inventory. The same survey also revealed clients to be less interested in brokered deals than in transactions in which the intermediary is a principal .

At the same time, the parties to swaps have been concerned that the other party might default on its obligation. While a default would not mean any principal was lost, because the notional principal amount had not been exchanged, it would mean that the objective for which the swap was entered into would be impaired. As early transactions tended to involve a higher and a lower credit-rated entity, the former would be concerned with the potential for default of the latter. To reduce the risk of default, many early swap transactions required that the lower credit-rated entity obtain a guarantee from a highly rated commercial bank.

The swap market can be characterized as a market that originated to exploit real or perceived imperfections in the capital market, but that evolved into a transactionally efficient market for accomplishing asset/liability objectives.

Secondary Market for Swaps

There are three general types of transactions in the secondary market for swaps. These include (1) a swap reversal, (2) a swap sale (or assignment), and (3) a swap buy-back (or close-out or cancellation).

In a *swap reversal*, the party that wants out of the transaction will arrange for a swap in which (1) the maturity on the new swap is equal to the time remaining for the original swap, (2) the index is the same, and (3) the notional principal amount is the same. For example, suppose party X enters into a five-year swap with a notional principal amount of $50 million in which it pays 10% and receives LIBOR, but that two years later, X wants out of the swap. In a swap reversal, X would enter into a three-year interest rate swap, with a counterparty different from the original counterparty, let's say Z, in which the notional principal amount is $50 million, and X pays LIBOR and receives a fixed rate. The fixed rate that X receives from Z will depend on prevailing swap terms for floating-rate receivers at the initiation of the three-year swap.

While party X has effectively terminated the original swap in economic terms, there is a major drawback to this approach: party X is still liable to the original counterparty Y, as well as to the new counterparty, Z. That is, party X now has two offsetting interest rate swaps on its books instead of one, and as a result it has increased its default risk exposure.

The *swap sale or swap assignment* overcomes this drawback. In this secondary market transaction, the party that wishes to close out the original swap finds another party that is willing to accept its obligations under the swap. In our illustration, this means that X finds another party, say, A, that will agree to pay 10% to Y and receive LIBOR from Y for the next three years. A might have to be compensated to accept the position of X, or A might have to be willing to compensate X. Who will receive compensation depends on the swap terms at the time. For example, if interest rates have risen so that, to receive LIBOR for three years, a fixed-rate payer would have to pay 12%, then A would have to compensate X because A has to pay only 10% to receive LIBOR. The compensation would be equal to the present value of a three-year annuity of 2% times the notional principal amount.[10] If, instead, interest rates have fallen so that, to receive LIBOR for three years, a fixed-rate payer would have to pay 6%, then X would have to compensate A. The compensation would be equal to the present value of a three-year annuity of 4% times the notional principal amount.

Once the transaction is completed, it is then A not X that is obligated to perform under the swap terms. (Of course an intermediary could act as principal and become party A to help its client X.)

In order to accomplish a swap sale, the original counterparty, Y in our example, must agree to the sale. A key factor in whether Y will agree is whether it is willing to accept the credit of A. For example, if A's credit rating is double-B while X's is double-A, Y would be unlikely to accept A as a counterparty.

A *buy-back or close-out sale* (or *cancellation*) involves the sale of the swap to the original counterparty. As in the case of a swap sale, one party might have to compensate the other, depending on how interest rates and credit spreads have changed since the inception of the swap.

These methods for getting out of or into a swap leave much to be desired for market participants. It is this illiquidity in the secondary market that will hamper swap market growth. There have been proposals to create a swap clearing corporation, similar to the clearing corporations for futures and options, in which case swaps could be marked-to-market and credit exposure to a swap reduced.

Beyond the "Plain Vanilla" Swap

Thus far we have described the "plain vanilla" or generic interest rate swap. A variety of nongeneric or individualized swaps have evolved as a result of the asset/liability needs of borrowers and lenders.

Amortizing, Accreting, and Roller Coaster Swaps: In a generic swap, the notional principal amount does not vary over the life of the swap. Thus, it is sometimes referred to as a *bullet swap.* In contrast, for amortizing,

---

[10] It is three years because this is the time remaining for the swap. The 2% represents the difference between the prevailing rate of 12% and the fixed rate of 10% on the swap.

accreting, and roller coaster swaps, the notional principal amount varies over the life of the swap.

To explain an amortizing swap, we can use the illustration of the interest rate swap between the commercial bank and the life insurance company. Recall that it was the fixed-rate commercial loans that were generating the cash flow that the bank was using to make the fixed-rate payment on the interest rate swap. We assumed then that the loans were interest-only loans and that the principal would be repaid at the end of five years.

Suppose, instead, that the loan is a level-payment, fully amortized one, meaning that the principal outstanding would decline over the five years, and so would the interest payments. In such an instance, the amount received every six months from the commercial loans would be less than the fixed-rate payments to be made on the interest rate swap, if interest rates decline. This is because the principal repaid every six months would have to be reinvested at an interest rate lower than 10% (the interest on the original loan balance). An amortizing swap is the solution in this case. In an amortizing swap, the notional principal amount decreases in a predetermined way over the life of the swap.

In situations where a liability to be funded increases over time, an accreting swap can be used. In an accreting swap, the notional principal amount increases in a predetermined way over time. An accreting swap can be used by a lending institution that has committed to lend increasing amounts to a customer for a long-term project.

In a roller coaster swap, the notional principal amount can rise or fall from period to period according to an institution's liability structure.

Zero-Coupon Swaps: In a zero-coupon swap, the fixed-rate payer does not make any payments until the maturity date of the swap but receives floating-rate payments at regular payment dates. Such a swap exposes the floating-rate payer to significant credit risk because this party makes regular payments but does not receive any payments until the maturity date of the swap.

Basis Rate Swap: The terms of a typical interest rate swap call for the exchange of fixed- and floating-rate payments. In a basis rate swap, both parties exchange floating-rate payments based on a different money market index. As an example, assume a commercial bank has a portfolio of loans at a lending rate based on the prime rate, but the bank's cost of funds is based on LIBOR. The risk the bank faces is that the spread between the prime rate and LIBOR will change. This is referred to as basis risk. The bank can use a basis rate swap to make floating-rate payments based on the prime rate and receive floating-rate payments based on LIBOR.

Forward Rate Swaps: A forward swap is simply a forward contract on an interest rate swap. The terms of the swap are set today, but the parties agree that the swap will begin at a specified date in the future.

Options on Swaps

The second generation of products in the interest rate swap market is options on interest rate swaps, which are referred to as *swaptions*. The buyer of a swaption has the right to enter into an interest rate swap agreement by some specified date in the future. The swaption agreement will specify whether the buyer of the swaption will be a fixed-rate receiver or a fixed-rate payer. The writer of the swaption becomes the counterparty to the swap if the buyer exercises.

If the buyer of the swaption has the right to enter into a swap as a fixed-rate payer, it is called a *call swaption*. The writer therefore becomes the fixed-rate receiver/floating-rate payer. If the buyer of the swaption has the right to enter into a swap as a floating-rate payer, it is called a *put swaption*. The writer of the swaption therefore becomes the floating-rate receiver/fixed-rate payer.

The strike rate of the swaption indicates the fixed rate that will be swapped versus the floating rate. The swaption will also specify the maturity date of the swap. A swaption may be European or American. Of course, as in all options, the buyer of a swaption pays the writer a premium, although the premium can be structured into the swap terms so that no upfront fee has to be paid.

A swaption can be used to hedge a portfolio strategy that uses an interest rate swap but where the cash flow of the underlying asset or liability is uncertain. The cash flow of the asset would be uncertain if it (1) is callable, as in the case of a callable corporate bond, a mortgage loan, or pass-through security, or a loan that can be prepaid, and/or (2) exposes the investor/lender to default risk.[11]

To illustrate the use of a swaption, suppose a savings and loan association enters into a four-year swap in which it agrees to pay 9% fixed and receive LIBOR. The fixed-rate payments will come from a portfolio of mortgage pass-through securities with a coupon rate of 9%. Suppose that one year after the swap begins, mortgage rates decline to 6%, resulting in large prepayments. The prepayments received will have to be reinvested at a rate lower than 9%, but the S&L must still pay 9% under

---

[11] For an explanation of how swaptions can be used to manage a portfolio of callable bonds, see Robert M. Stavis and Victor J. Haghani, "Putable Swaps: Tools for Managing Callable Assets," Chapter 20 in Frank J. Fabozzi (ed.), *The Handbook of Fixed Income Options* (Chicago: Probus Publishing, 1989).

the terms of the swap. As the S&L is paying fixed and receiving floating, it would seek to use a swaption that allows it to unwind the original swap by receiving fixed and paying floating. More specifically, the S&L will enter into a swaption that will allow it to receive 9% and pay LIBOR. The purchase of a call swaption with a strike rate of 9% (and a LIBOR floating-rate) would be the appropriate swaption to terminate the original swap.

INTEREST RATE AGREEMENTS

An *interest rate agreement* is an agreement between two parties whereby one party, for an upfront premium, agrees to compensate the other if a designated interest rate, called the *reference rate*, is different from a predetermined level. When one party agrees to pay the other when the reference rate exceeds a predetermined level, the agreement is referred to as an *interest rate cap* or *ceiling*. The agreement is referred to as an *interest rate floor* when one party agrees to pay the other when the reference rate falls below a predetermined level. The predetermined interest rate level is called the *strike rate*.

The terms of an interest rate agreement include:

1. The reference rate
2. The strike rate that sets the ceiling or floor
3. The length of the agreement
4. The frequency of settlement
5. The notional principal amount

Suppose that C buys an interest rate cap from D with terms as follows:

1. The reference rate is six-month LIBOR
2. The strike rate is 8%
3. The agreement is for seven years
4. Settlement is every six months
5. The notional principal amount is $20 million

Under this agreement, every six months for the next seven years, D will pay C whenever six-month LIBOR exceeds 8%. The payment will equal the dollar value of the difference between six-month LIBOR and 8% times the notional principal amount divided by two. For example, if six months from now six-month LIBOR is 11%, then D will pay C 3% (11% minus 8%) times $20 million divided by 2, or $300,000. If six-month LIBOR is 8% or less, D does not have to pay anything to C.

In the case of an interest rate floor, assume the same terms as the interest rate cap we just illustrated. In this case, if six-month LIBOR is 11%, C receives nothing from D, but if six-month LIBOR is less than 8%,

D compensates C for the difference. For example, if six-month LIBOR is 7%, D will pay C $100,000 (8% minus 7% times $20 million divided by 2).

Interest rate caps and floors can be combined to create an *interest rate collar*. This is done by buying an interest rate cap and selling an interest rate floor. Some commercial banks and investment banking firms now write options on interest rate agreements for customers. Options on caps are called *captions*; options on floors are called *flotions*.

Risk/Return Characteristics

In an interest rate agreement, the buyer pays an upfront fee, which represents the maximum amount that the buyer can lose and the maximum amount that the writer of the agreement can gain. The only party that is required to perform is the writer of the interest rate agreement. The buyer of an interest rate cap benefits if the underlying interest rate rises above the strike rate because the seller (writer) must compensate the buyer. The buyer of an interest rate floor benefits if the interest rate falls below the strike rate, because the seller (writer) must compensate the buyer.

To better understand interest rate caps and interest rate floors, we can look at them in essence as equivalent to a package of interest rate options. As the buyer benefits if the interest rate rises above the strike rate, an interest rate cap is similar to purchasing a package of put options; the seller of an interest rate cap has effectively sold a package of put options. The buyer of an interest rate floor benefits from a decline in the interest rate below the strike rate. Therefore, the buyer of an interest rate floor has effectively bought a package of call options from the writer of the option. An interest rate collar is equivalent to buying a package of put options and selling a package of call options.

Once again, a complex contract can be seen to be a package of basic contracts, or options in the case of interest rate agreements. Captions and flotions can then be viewed as options on a package of options, or *compound options*.

Applications

To see how interest rate agreements can be used for asset/liability management, consider the problems faced by the commercial bank and the life insurance company we discussed in demonstrating use of an interest rate swap.[12]

---

[12] For additional applications in the insurance industry, see David F. Babbel, Peter Bouyoucos, and Robert Stricker, "Capping the Interest Rate Risk in Insurance Products," Chapter 21 in Frank J. Fabozzi (ed.), *Fixed Income Portfolio Strategies* (Chicago: Probus Publishing, 1989). For other applications of interest rate agreements, see Victor J. Haghani and Robert M. Stavis, "Interest Rate Caps and Floors: Tools for Asset/Liability Management," in Frank J. Fabozzi (ed.), *Advances and Innovations in the Bond and Mortgage Markets* (Chicago: Probus Publishing, 1989).

Recall that the bank's objective is to lock in an interest rate spread over its cost of funds. Yet because it borrows short term, its cost of funds is uncertain. The bank may be able to purchase a cap, however, so that the cap rate plus the cost of purchasing the cap is less than the rate it is earning on its fixed-rate commercial loans. If short-term rates decline, the bank does not benefit from the cap, but its cost of funds declines. The cap therefore allows the bank to impose a ceiling on its cost of funds while retaining the opportunity to benefit from a decline in rates. This is consistent with the view of an interest rate cap as simply a package of call options.

The bank can reduce the cost of purchasing the cap by selling a floor. In this case, the bank agrees to pay the buyer of the floor if the underlying rate falls below the strike rate. The bank receives a fee for selling the floor, but it has sold off its opportunity to benefit from a decline in rates below the strike rate. By buying a cap and selling a floor, the bank has created a predetermined range for its cost of funds (i.e., a collar).

Recall the problem of the life insurance company that guarantees a 9% rate on a GIC for the next five years and is considering the purchase of an attractive floating-rate instrument in a private placement transaction. The risk that the company faces is that interest rates will fall so that it will not earn enough to realize the 9% guaranteed rate plus a spread. The life insurance company may be able to purchase a floor to set a lower bound on its investment return, yet retain the opportunity to benefit should rates increase. To reduce the cost of purchasing the floor, the life insurance company can sell an interest rate cap. By doing so, however, it gives up the opportunity of benefiting from an increase in the six-month LIBOR above the strike rate of the interest rate cap.

SUMMARY

An interest rate swap is an agreement specifying that the parties exchange interest payments at designated times. In a typical swap, one party will make fixed-rate payments, and the other will make floating-rate payments, with payments based on the notional principal amount. Participants in financial markets use interest rate swaps to alter the cash flow characteristics of their assets or liabilities, or to capitalize on perceived capital market inefficiencies.

A swap position can be interpreted as either a package of forward/futures contracts or a package of cash flows from buying and selling cash market instruments. The price of an interest rate swap can be determined by first computing a zero-coupon swap rate curve and then using these rates to discount the cash flows from the swap. The interest rate sensitivity or duration of a swap from the perspective of a floating-rate payer is just the difference between the durations of the fixed-rate bond and the floating-rate bond that comprise the swap. Most of the interest rate sensitivity of a swap will result from the duration of the fixed-rate bond because the duration of the floating-rate bond will be small.

There are three general types of transactions in the secondary market for swaps. These include (1) a swap reversal, (2) a swap sale (or assignment), and (3) a swap buy-back (or close-out or cancellation).

A number of types of swaps have been developed to satisfy various needs of market participants. These include swaps in which the notional principal amount varies over the life of the swap (amortizing, accreting, and roller coaster swaps), zero-coupon swaps, and basis rate swaps. The second generation of swaps is options on swaps (swaptions).

An interest rate agreement allows one party for an upfront premium the right to receive compensation from the writer of the agreement if a designated interest rate is different from a predetermined level. An interest rate cap calls for one party to receive a payment if a designated interest rate is above the predetermined level. An interest rate floor lets one party receive a payment if a designated interest rate is below the pre-determined level.

An interest rate cap can be used to establish a ceiling on the cost of funding; an interest rate floor can be used to establish a floor return. Buying a cap and selling a floor creates a collar. There are also options on interest rate caps (called captions) and on floors (called flotions).

QUESTIONS FOR CHAPTER 19

1. Why can a fixed-rate payer in an interest rate swap be viewed as short the bond market, and the floating-rate payer be viewed as long the bond market?

2. Here is a quotation from the March 25, 1991, issue of *Bank Letter*:

   Intense negotiations are underway involving regulatory officials, interested bank and brokerage industry representatives and Senate Staff to try to fashion a compromise floor amendment for a bill that would potentially put interest rate and currency swaps and forward foreign exchange agreements under the regulatory authority of the Commodity Futures Trading Commission, sources said.... Industry forces involved in the $2 trillion market are fighting to block Commodity Futures Trading Commission jurisdiction, arguing that the pending bill, if enacted, would scare the business overseas....

   a. Why is an interest rate swap similar to a futures (or forward) contract?

   b. Why do you think opponents of regulation feel that the bill "would scare the business overseas"?

3. How can the duration of an interest rate swap be calculated?

4. How should an interest rate swap be priced?

5. Describe the role of an intermediary in a swap.

6. What types of transactions occur in the secondary market for an interest rate swap?

7. Suppose that a life insurance company has issued a three-year GIC with a fixed rate of 10%. Under what circumstances might it be feasible for the life insurance company to invest the funds in a floating-rate security and enter into a three-year interest rate swap in which it pays a floating rate and receives a fixed rate?

8. The excerpt following is taken from an article entitled "IRS Rule to Open Swaps to Pension Funds," that appeared in the November 18, 1991, issue of *BondWeek*, pp. 1 and 2:

   A proposed Internal Revenue Service rule that gives tax-free status to income earned on swaps by pension funds and other tax-exempt institutions is expected to spur pension fund use of these products, say swap and pension fund professionals....

   ....UBS Asset Management has received permission from most of its pension fund clients to use interest rate and currency swaps in its fixed-income portfolios and is awaiting the IRS regulation before stepping into the market, says Kenneth Choie, v.p. and head of research and product development.... "The IRS' proposed rule is great news for pension fund managers," as the use of swaps can enhance returns and lower transaction costs, Choie says....

While some pension funds are exploring the swap market, pension fund consultants underscore that the funds' entrance into the market is likely to be slow. Counterparty risk has been a more formidable obstacle than the ambiguity of the tax status of income from interest rate and currency swaps, says Paul Burik, director of research at Ennis, Knupp & Associates, a pension fund consulting firm.

   a. In the article, Choie indicates that one "possible application that UBS is considering is to switch between fixed- and floating-rate income streams without incurring the transaction costs of trading chunks of securities." Explain how an interest rate swap can be used for this application.

   b. What is meant by counterparty risk?

   c. How can counterparty risk be reduced?

9. What is a swaption?

10. What is the relationship between an interest rate agreement and an interest rate option?

11. How can an interest rate collar be created?

Chapter 20

ACTIVE BOND PORTFOLIO
MANAGEMENT STRATEGIES

This chapter and the two that follow discuss bond portfolio management strategies. We begin with an overview of the investment management process and the factors to consider in the selection of a portfolio strategy, distinguishing between active portfolio strategies and structured portfolio strategies. Active strategies are discussed in this chapter, while structured portfolio strategies are the subject of the next two chapters.

OVERVIEW OF THE INVESTMENT MANAGEMENT PROCESS

Regardless of the type of financial institution, the investment management process involves the following five steps:

1. Setting investment objectives
2. Establishing investment policy
3. Selecting the portfolio strategy
4. Selecting the assets
5. Measuring and evaluating performance

Setting Investment Objectives

The first step in the investment management process is setting investment objectives. The investment objective will vary by type of financial institution.

For institutions such as pension funds, the investment objective is to generate sufficient cash flow from investments to satisfy pension obligations. For life insurance companies, the basic objective is to satisfy obligations stipulated in insurance policies and generate a profit. Most insurance products guarantee a dollar payment or a stream of dollar payments at some time in the future. The premium that the life insurance company charges a policyholder for one of its products will depend on the interest rate that the company can earn on its investments. To realize a profit, the life insurance company must earn a higher return on the premium it invests than the implicit (or explicit) interest rate it has guaranteed policyholders.

For institutions such as banks and thrifts, funds are obtained from the issuance of certificates of deposit, short-term money market instruments, or floating-rate notes. These funds are then invested in loans and marketable securities. The objective in this case is to earn a return on invested funds that is higher than the cost of acquiring those funds.

For these sorts of institutions, investment objectives are dictated essentially by the nature of their liabilities — obligations to pension recipients, policyholders, and depositors. For investment companies (mutual funds), the investment objectives will be as set forth in a prospectus. While there are no specific liabilities that must be met, typically the fund establishes a target dividend payout.

Because of the importance of the nature of the liabilities in determining investment objectives, the next chapter examines this topic more closely.

Establishing Investment Policy

The second step in investment management is establishing policy guidelines for meeting the investment objectives. Setting policy begins with the asset allocation decision; that is, there must be a decision as to how the funds of the institution should be distributed among the major classes of investments (cash equivalents, equities, fixed-income securities, real estate, and foreign securities).

Client and regulatory constraints are considerations in establishing an investment policy. Examples of constraints that the sponsor of a pension fund might impose are: No funds may be invested in a bond of an issuer whose credit rating is below some specified level; no more than a predetermined percentage of the fund's assets may be invested in a particular industry; and options and futures may be used only to protect asset values not for speculative purposes. Regulators of state-regulated institutions such as insurance companies (both life and property and casualty companies) may restrict the amount of funds allocated to certain major asset classes. Even the amount allocated within a major asset class may be restricted, depending on the characteristics of the particular asset. In the case of investment companies, restrictions on asset allocation are set forth in the prospectus when the fund is launched and may be changed only with approval of the fund's board.

Tax and financial reporting implications must also be considered in adopting investment policies. For example, life insurance companies enjoy certain tax advantages that make investing in tax-exempt municipal securities generally unappealing. Because pension funds too are exempt from taxes, they also are not particularly interested in tax-exempt municipal securities.

Financial reporting requirements, in particular Financial Accounting Standards Board Statements Nos. 87 and 88 and the Omnibus Budget Reconciliation Act of 1987, affect the ways in which pension funds establish investment policies. It is unfortunate but true that financial reporting considerations can cause institutions to establish investment policies that may not be in the best interest of the institution in the long run.

Selecting a Portfolio Strategy

Selecting a portfolio strategy that is consistent with the objectives and policy guidelines of the client or institution is the third step in the investment management process. Portfolio strategies can be classified as either *active strategies* or *passive strategies*. Essential to all active strategies is specification of expectations about the factors that influence the performance of an asset class. In the case of active equity strategies, this may include forecasts of future earnings, dividends, or price-earnings ratios. In the case of active bond management, this may involve forecasts of future interest rates, future interest rate volatility, or future yield spreads. Active portfolio strategies involving foreign securities will require forecasts of future exchange rates.

Passive strategies involve minimal expectational input. One popular type of passive strategy is *indexing*, whose objective is to replicate the performance of a predetermined index. While indexing has been employed extensively in the management of equity portfolios, the use of indexing for managing bond portfolios is a relatively new practice.

Between the extremes of active and passive strategies have sprung up strategies that have elements of both. For example, the core of a portfolio may be indexed, with the balance managed actively. Or, a portfolio may be primarily indexed but employ low risk strategies to enhance the indexed portfolio's return. This strategy is commonly referred to as "enhanced indexing" or "indexing plus."

In the bond area, several strategies classified as *structured portfolio strategies* have been commonly used. A structured portfolio strategy calls for design of a portfolio to achieve the performance of some predetermined benchmark. Such strategies are frequently followed when funding liabilities. When the predetermined benchmark is the raising of sufficient funds to satisfy a single liability, regardless of the course of future interest rates, a strategy known as *immunization* is often used. When the predetermined benchmark requires funding multiple future liabilities regardless of how interest rates change, strategies such as immunization, *cash flow matching* (or *dedication*), or *horizon matching* can be employed.

As part of the immunization and cash flow matching strategies, low-risk active management strategies can be employed. For example, contingent immunization strategy allows the portfolio manager to manage a portfolio actively until certain parameters are violated. If and when those parameters are violated, the portfolio is then immunized.

Indexing can also be considered a structured portfolio strategy, since the benchmark is to achieve the performance of some predetermined index.[1] The next two chapters describe structured portfolio strategies: Chapter 21 focuses on indexing, and Chapter 22 on immunization and cash flow matching/dedication.

Given the choice between active, structured, or passive management, which should be selected? The answer depends on (1) the client or money manager's view of the pricing efficiency of the market, and (2) the nature of the liabilities to be satisfied. First let's consider the pricing efficiency of a market.

Pricing efficiency is taken to describe a market where prices at all times fully reflect all available information that is relevant to the valuation of securities. When a market is price-efficient, active strategies will not *consistently* produce superior returns after adjusting for (1) risk, and (2) transactions costs.

What strategy should be pursued by an investor who believes that the market is sufficiently efficient so that superior risk-adjusted returns cannot be consistently realized after accounting for transactions costs? Capital market theory argues that indexing is the strategy of choice.

But pricing efficiency is not the sole determinant of the type of investment strategy that should be employed. The nature of the liabilities is also of paramount importance. While indexing may be a reasonable strategy for an institution that does not have a future liability stream to be satisfied, consider the circumstances in which pension funds operate. If a

---

[1] Portfolio insurance strategies—strategies commonly used in the equity area to reproduce the payoff of a put option—where the objective is to insure that the value of the portfolio does not fall below a predetermined level are also viewed as structured portfolio strategies. Portfolio insurance strategies, however, are rarely used in the bond area. For an illustration of the application of portfolio insurance strategies to bonds, see Colin Negrych and Dexter Senft, "Portfolio Insurance Using Synthetic Puts—The Reasons, Rewards and Risks," in Frank J. Fabozzi (ed.), *Handbook of Fixed-Income Options* (Chicago: Probus Publishing, 1989).

pension fund indexes its portfolio, then the fund's return will be roughly the same as the index return. Yet, the index may not provide a return that is sufficient to satisfy the fund's obligations. Consequently, for some institutions such as pension funds and life insurance companies, structured portfolio strategies such as immunization or dedication may be more appropriate to achieve investment objectives. Within the context of these strategies, an active or enhanced return strategy may be followed.

Selecting Assets

Once a portfolio strategy is specified, the next step is to select the specific assets to be included in the portfolio, which requires an evaluation of individual securities. In an active strategy, this means identifying mispriced securities. In the case of bonds, the characteristics of a bond (that is, coupon, maturity, credit quality, and options granted to either the issuer or bondholder) must be carefully examined to determine how these characteristics will influence the performance of the bond over some investment horizon.

It is in this phase that the investment manager attempts to construct an *optimal* or *efficient* portfolio. An optimal or efficient portfolio is one that provides the greatest *expected* return for a given level of risk, or, equivalently, the lowest risk for a given *expected* return.

Measuring and Evaluating Performance

The measurement and evaluation of investment performance is the last step in the investment management process. (Actually, it is technically not the "last" step because investment management is an ongoing process.) This step involves measuring the performance of the portfolio, then evaluating that performance relative to some benchmark. The benchmark selected for evaluating performance is called a *benchmark* or *normal portfolio*.

The benchmark portfolio may be a popular index such as the S&P 500 for equity portfolios or one of the bond indexes discussed in the next chapter. Recently, pension sponsors have worked with money managers and pension consultants to establish customized benchmark portfolios.

Evaluating the performance of a money manager is not simple. Clients typically rely on the services of a firm that specializes in evaluating money managers.

While the performance of a money manager according to some benchmark portfolio may seem superior, this does not necessarily mean that the portfolio satisfies its investment objective. For example, suppose that a life insurance company establishes as its objective the maximization of portfolio return and allocates 75% of the fund to stocks and the balance to bonds. Suppose further that the money manager responsible for the equity portfolio of this pension fund earns a return over a one-year horizon that is 200 basis points higher than the benchmark portfolio which had a return of 2%. Assuming that the risk of the portfolio is similar to that of the benchmark portfolio, it would appear that the money manager outperformed the benchmark portfolio. In spite of this performance, however, suppose that the life insurance company cannot meet its liabilities because the rate it must pay to policyholders is 7%. Then the failure is in establishing the investment objectives and setting policy, not in the money manager's performance.

ACTIVE PORTFOLIO STRATEGIES

The starting point in our discussion of active strategies is an investigation of the various sources of return from holding a fixed-income portfolio. As we explain in Chapter 3, the three sources of return are coupon income, any capital gain (or loss), and reinvestment income. Here we explore the factors that affect one or more of these sources.

In general, the following factors affect a portfolio's return:

1. Changes in the level of interest rates
2. Changes in the shape of the yield curve
3. Changes in yield spreads among bond sectors
4. Changes in the yield spread for a particular bond

A money manager who pursues an active strategy will position a portfolio, subject to client and/or regulatory constraints, to capitalize on expectations about future interest rates, changes in the shape of the yield curve, changes in intersector spreads, and any change in the yield spread of a particular bond. Other active strategies are based not on the traditional yield spread approach but on the option-adjusted spread discussed in Chapter 14.

The total return framework should be employed to analyze the effect of an expected outcome or outcomes on a portfolio's return. Recall from earlier discussions that yield measures are inadequate for assessing the potential performance of an individual bond. For a bond portfolio, the meaning of a "portfolio yield" is questionable and certainly provides no insight into the return for a portfolio over some investment horizon.

INTEREST RATE EXPECTATIONS STRATEGIES

A money manager who believes that he or she can accurately forecast the future level of interest rates will alter the portfolio's sensitivity to interest rate changes. As duration is a measure of interest rate sensitivity, this involves increasing a portfolio's duration if interest rates are expected to fall and reducing it if interest rates are expected to rise. For those money managers whose benchmark is a bond index, this means increasing the portfolio duration relative to the benchmark index if interest rates are expected to fall and reducing it if interest rates are expected to rise. The degree to which the duration of the managed portfolio is permitted to diverge from that of the benchmark index may be limited by the client.

A portfolio's duration may be altered by swapping bonds in the portfolio for new bonds that will achieve the target portfolio duration. Such swaps are commonly referred to as *rate anticipation swaps*. Alternatively, a more efficient means for altering the duration of a bond portfolio is to use interest rate futures contracts. As we explain in Chapter 17, buying futures increases a portfolio's duration, while selling futures decreases it.

The key to this active strategy is, of course, an ability to forecast the direction of future interest rates. The academic literature, however, does not support the view that interest rates can be forecasted so that risk-adjusted excess returns can be consistently realized. It is doubtful whether betting on future interest rates will provide a consistently superior return.

While a money manager may not pursue an active strategy based strictly on future interest rate movements, there can be a tendency to make an interest rate bet to cover inferior performance relative to a benchmark index. For example, suppose a money manager holds himself or herself out to a client as pursuing one of the active strategies discussed later in this chapter. Suppose further that the money manager is evaluated over a one-year investment horizon, and that three months before the end of the investment horizon, the money manager is performing below the client-specified benchmark index. If the money manager believes the account will be lost because of underperformance, there is an incentive to bet on interest rate movements. If the manager is correct, the account will be saved, although an incorrect bet will result in underperforming the benchmark index by a greater amount. In this case, the account will be lost regardless of the level of underperformance. A client can prevent this type of gaming by a money manager by imposing constraints on the degree that the portfolio's duration can vary from that of the benchmark index. Also, in the performance evaluation stage of the investment management process, decomposing the portfolio's return into the factors that generated the return will highlight the extent to which a portfolio's return is attributable to changes in the level of interest rates.

There are other active strategies that rely on forecasts of future interest rate levels. Future interest rates, for instance, will affect the value of options embedded in callable bonds and the value of prepayment options embedded in mortgage-backed securities. Callable corporate and municipal bonds with coupon rates above the expected future interest rate will underperform relative to noncallable bonds or low-coupon bonds. This is because of the negative convexity feature of callable bonds described in Chapter 13. For the wide range of mortgage-backed securities described in Chapters 11 and 12, the effect of interest rates on prepayments will cause some to benefit from higher future interest rates and others to benefit from lower future interest rates.

YIELD CURVE STRATEGIES

As we explain in Chapter 9, the yield curve is the relationship between maturity and yield on U.S. Treasury securities. The shape of the yield curve changes over time. Because a portfolio consists of bonds with varying maturities, changes in the shape of the yield curve will have varying price effects on each bond.

Two portfolios with the same duration will perform differently if the yield curve does not shift in a parallel fashion. To see this point, consider the three bonds and two portfolios shown in Exhibit 20-1.[2] Portfolio I consists of only bond C, the ten-year bond, and is referred to as the "bullet portfolio." Portfolio II consists of 50.2% of bond A and 49.8% of bond B, and we call this portfolio the "barbell portfolio." The dollar duration of the bullet portfolio per 100 basis point change in yield is 6.43409. Recall from Chapter 4 that dollar duration is a measure of the dollar price sensitivity of a bond or a portfolio. Note in Exhibit 20-1 that the dollar duration of the barbell — which is just the weighted average of the dollar duration of the two bonds — is the same as that of the bullet portfolio. In fact, the barbell portfolio was designed to produce this result. As we explained in Chapter 4, duration is just a first approximation of the change in price resulting from a change in interest rates. Convexity provides a second approximation. The dollar convexity

---

[2] This illustration is adapted from Ravi E. Dattatreya and Frank J. Fabozzi, *Active Total Return Management of Fixed Income Portfolios* (Chicago: Probus Publishing, 1989).

EXHIBIT 20-1   Bullet-Barbell Analysis

Three bonds used in analysis

Bond	Coupon	Maturity (Years)	Price Plus Accrued	Yield	Dollar Duration	Dollar Convexity
A	8.50	5	100	8.50%	4.00544	19.8164
B	9.50	20	100	9.50	8.88151	124.1702
C	9.25	10	100	9.25	6.43409	55.4506

Bullet: Bond C
Barbell: Bonds A and B
> Composition of barbell: 50.2% of bond A; 49.8% of bond B
> Dollar duration of barbell =

$$.502 \times 4.00544 + .498 \times 8.88151 = 6.434$$

Average yield of barbell =

$$.502 \times 8.50 + .498 \times 9.5 = 8.998$$

Strategy: Sell the barbell and buy the bullet
Analysis based on average yield
> Yield pickup = Yield on bullet − Average yield of barbell
> = 9.25 − 8.998 = .252, or 25.2 basis points

Analysis based on duration, convexity, and average yield
Dollar convexity of barbell =

$$.502 \times 19.81864 + .498 \times 124.1702 = 71.7846$$

> Yield pickup = Yield on bullet − Average yield of barbell
> = 9.25 − 8.998 = .252, or 25.2 basis points
> Convexity giveup = Convexity of barbell − Convexity of bullet
> = 71.7846 − 55.4506 = 16.334

Analysis based on duration, convexity, and cash flow yield
> Cash flow yield of barbell* =

$$\frac{(8.5 \times .502 \times 4.00544) + (9.5 \times .498 \times 8.88151)}{6.434} = 9.187$$

> Yield pickup = Yield on bullet − Cash flow yield
> = 9.25 − 9.187 = .063, or 6.3 basis points
> Convexity giveup = Convexity of barbell − Convexity of bullet
> = 71.7846 − 55.4506 = 16.334

* The calculation shown is actually a dollar-duration-weighted yield, a very close approximation to cash flow yield.

of the two portfolios, shown in Exhibit 20-1, is not equal. The dollar convexity of the bullet portfolio is less than that of the barbell portfolio.

The "yield" for the two portfolios likewise is not the same. The yield (yield to maturity) for the bullet is simply the yield to maturity of bond C, 9.25%. The traditional yield calculation for the barbell portfolio, which is found by taking a weighted average of the yield to maturity of the two bonds included in the portfolio, is 8.998%. This approach suggests that the "yield" of the bullet portfolio is 25.2 basis points greater than the barbell portfolio. Alternatively, a cash flow yield can be approximated for the barbell portfolio by calculating the dollar duration market-weighted yield of the portfolio. In this case, the cash flow yield of the barbell portfolio is 9.187%, suggesting that the "yield" of the bullet portfolio is 6.3 basis points greater than the barbell portfolio. Although both portfolios have the same dollar duration, the yield of the bullet portfolio, using either yield measure, is greater than the yield of the barbell portfolio. However, the dollar convexity of the barbell portfolio is greater than that of the bullet portfolio. The difference in the two yields is sometimes referred to as the "cost of convexity."

The column labeled "Parallel Shift — Total Return" in Exhibit 20-2 shows the difference in the total return over a six-month investment horizon for the two portfolios assuming that the yield curve shifts in a "parallel" fashion.[3] By parallel it is meant that the yields for the short-term bond (A), the intermediate-term bond (C), and the long-term bond (B) change by the same number of basis points, shown in the "Yield Change" column of the exhibit. The total return reported is:

Bullet portfolio's total return − Barbell portfolio's total return

Thus a positive sign in the total return column means that the bullet portfolio outperformed the barbell portfolio, while a negative sign means that the barbell portfolio outperformed the bullet portfolio.

Which portfolio is the better investment alternative if the yield curve shifts in a parallel fashion and the investment horizon is six months? The answer depends on the amount by which yields change. Notice that when yields change by less than 100 basis points, the bullet portfolio outperforms the barbell portfolio. The reverse is true if yields change by more than 100 basis points.

Now let's look at what happens if the yield curve does not shift in a parallel fashion. The last two columns of Exhibit 20-2 show the relative performance of the two portfolios for a nonparallel shift of the yield curve.

---

[3] Note that no assumption is needed for the reinvestment rate because the three bonds shown in Exhibit 20-1 are assumed to be trading right after a coupon payment has been made and therefore there is no accrued interest.

Specifically, the first nonparallel shift column assumes that if the yield on bond C (the intermediate-term bond) changes by the amount shown in the first column, bond A (the short-term bond) will change by the same amount plus 25 basis points, whereas bond B (the long-term bond) will change by the same amount shown in the first column less 25 basis points. That is, the nonparallel shift assumed is a flattening of the yield curve. For this yield curve shift, the barbell always outperforms the bullet. In the last column, the nonparallel shift assumes that for a change in bond C's yield, the yield on bond A will change by the same amount less 25 basis points, whereas that on bond B will change by the same amount plus 25 points. That is, it assumes that the yield curve will steepen. In this case, the bullet portfolio outperforms the barbell portfolio so long as the yield on bond C does not rise by more than 250 basis points or fall by more than 325 basis points.

The key point here is that looking at measures such as yield (yield to maturity or some type of portfolio yield measure), duration or convexity tells us little about performance over some investment horizon, because performance depends on the magnitude of the change in yields and how the yield curve shifts.

EXHIBIT 20-2 Relative Performance of Bullet Portfolio and Barbell Portfolio Over a Six-Month Investment Horizon*

Yield Change	Parallel Shift*	Nonparallel Shift**	Nonparallel Shift***
−5.000	−7.19%	−10.69%	−3.89%
−4.750	−6.28	−9.61	−3.12
−4.500	−5.44	−8.62	−2.44
−4.250	−4.68	−7.71	−1.82
−4.000	−4.00	−6.88	−1.27
−3.750	−3.38	−6.13	−0.78
−3.500	−2.82	−5.44	−0.35
−3.250	−2.32	−4.82	0.03
−3.000	−1.88	−4.26	0.36
−2.750	−1.49	−3.75	0.65
−2.500	−1.15	−3.30	0.89
−2.250	−0.85	−2.90	1.09
−2.000	−0.59	−2.55	1.25
−1.750	−0.38	−2.24	1.37
−1.500	−0.20	−1.97	1.47
−1.250	−0.05	−1.74	1.53
−1.000	0.06	−1.54	1.57
−0.750	0.15	−1.38	1.58
−0.500	0.21	−1.24	1.57
−0.250	0.24	−1.14	1.53
0.000	0.25	−1.06	1.48
0.250	0.24	−1.01	1.41
0.500	0.21	−0.98	1.32

EXHIBIT 20-2 (Continued)

Yield Change	Parallel Shift*	Nonparallel Shift**	Nonparallel Shift***
0.750	0.16	−0.97	1.21
1.000	0.09	−0.98	1.09
1.250	0.01	−1.00	0.96
1.500	−0.08	−1.05	0.81
1.750	−0.19	−1.10	0.66
2.000	−0.31	−1.18	0.49
2.250	−0.44	−1.26	0.32
2.500	−0.58	−1.36	0.14
2.750	−0.73	−1.46	−0.05
3.000	−0.88	−1.58	−0.24
3.250	−1.05	−1.70	−0.44
3.500	−1.21	−1.84	−0.64
3.750	−1.39	−1.98	−0.85
4.000	−1.57	−2.12	−1.06
4.250	−1.75	−2.27	−1.27
4.500	−1.93	−2.43	−1.48
4.750	−2.12	−2.58	−1.70
5.000	−2.31	−2.75	−1.92

* Performance is based on the difference in total return over a six-month investment horizon. Specifically:

> Bullet portfolio's total return − Barbell portfolio's total return

Therefore a negative value means that the barbell portfolio outperformed the bullet portfolio.

** Change in yield for bond C. Nonparallel shift as follows (flattening of yield curve):

> Yield change bond A = Yield change bond C + 25 basis points
> Yield change bond B = Yield change bond C − 25 basis points

*** Change in yield for bond C. Nonparallel shift as follows (steepening of yield curve):

> Yield change bond A = Yield change bond C − 25 basis points
> Yield change bond B = Yield change bond C + 25 basis points

Types of Changes in the Yield Curve

Frank Jones provides empirical evidence of the importance of changes in the yield curve in determining returns of Treasury securities for various maturity sectors from 1979 to 1990.[4] Historically, three yield curve shifts have been observed, all shown in Exhibit 20-3:

- a parallel shift
- a twist in the slope of the yield curve (i.e., a flattening or steepening of the yield curve)
- a change in the humpedness of the yield curve (such a change is referred to as a *butterfly shift*)

---

[4] Frank J. Jones, "Yield Curve Strategies," *Journal of Fixed Income* (September 1991), pp. 43-51.

Jones finds that parallel shifts and twists in the yield curve are responsible for 91.6% of Treasury returns, while 3.4% of the return is attributable to butterfly shifts and the balance, 5%, to unexplained factor shifts.[5] Moreover, the three types of yield curve shifts are not independent but are correlated. For example, Jones finds that an upward parallel shift in the yield curve and a flattening of the yield curve have a correlation of .41. His statistical analysis, for example, suggests that an upward shift of the yield curve by 10 basis points is consistent with a 2.5 basis point flattening of the yield curve. Moreover, he finds that an upward shift and flattening of the yield curve is correlated with a positive butterfly (less humpedness), while a downward shift and steepening of the yield curve is correlated with a negative butterfly (more humpedness). These two types of shifts in the yield curve are depicted in Exhibit 20-4.

Optimal Strategies

This discussion indicates that yield curve strategies require a forecast of the direction of the shift and a forecast of the type of twist. The two most common types are a downward shift in the yield curve combined with a steepening of the yield curve and an upward shift in the yield curve combined with a flattening of the yield curve.

Jones has examined what would happen to relative returns for shifting of the yield curve in various ways. The framework he employs, the total return framework that we illustrate earlier in this section in the analysis of the bullet and barbell strategies, is one that money managers should use to assess the effect of shifts in the yield curve. Exhibit 20-5 shows Jones's total returns resulting from simulating various types of yield curve shifts for the yield curve existing on November 1, 1990, on 2-year, 10-year, and 30-year Treasuries. The exhibit indicates the optimal (best-performing) sector given the type and magnitude of shifts assumed. In terms of a bullet/barbell strategy, Exhibit 20-6 shows the optimal portfolio position based on shifts and twists shown in Exhibit 20-5.

YIELD SPREAD STRATEGIES

Yield spread strategies involve positioning a portfolio to capitalize on expected changes in yield spreads between sectors of the bond market. Swaps undertaken when the money manager believes that the prevailing yield spread between two bonds in the market is out of line with the historical yield spread, and that the yield spread will realign by the end of the investment horizon, are called *intermarket spread swaps*.

---

5 These findings are consistent with those reported in Robert Litterman and José Scheinkman, "Common Factors Affecting Bond Returns," *Journal of Fixed Income* (June 1991), pp. 54-61.

EXHIBIT 20-3   Types of Yield Curve Shifts

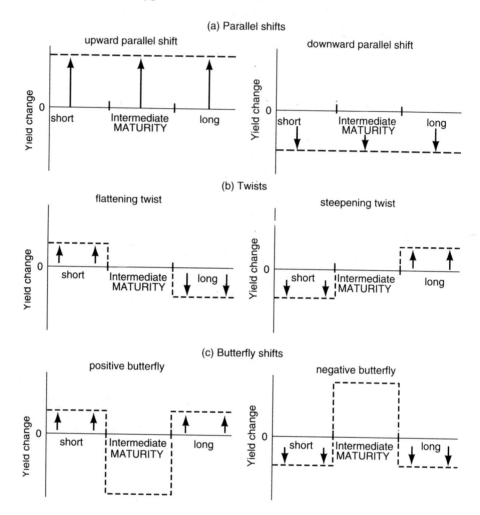

(a) Parallel shifts

upward parallel shift

downward parallel shift

(b) Twists

flattening twist

steepening twist

(c) Butterfly shifts

positive butterfly

negative butterfly

The bond market is classified into sectors in several ways: by type of issuer (Treasury, agencies, corporates, and mortgage-backeds), quality or credit (risk-free Treasuries, triple-A, double-A, etc.), coupon (high-coupon/premium bonds, current-coupon/par bonds, and low-coupon/discount bonds), and maturity (short-, intermediate- or long-term). Yield spreads between maturity sectors involve changes in the yield curve as we have discussed in the previous section.

Credit or quality spreads change because of expected changes in economic prospects. Credit spreads between Treasury and non-Treasury issues widen in a declining or contracting economy and narrow during

EXHIBIT 20-4   Combinations of Yield Curve Shifts

Upward Shift/Flattening/Positive Butterfly

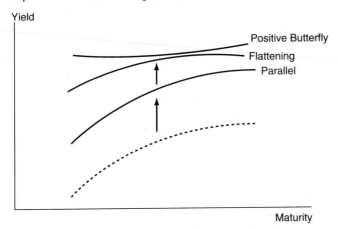

Downward Shift/Steepening/Negative Butterfly

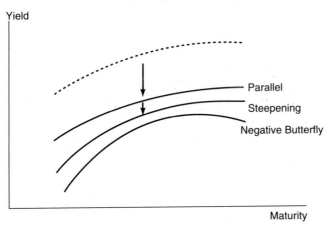

economic expansion. The economic rationale is that in a declining or contracting economy, corporations experience a decline in revenue and reduced cash flow, making it difficult for corporate issuers to service their contractual debt obligations. To induce investors to hold non-Treasury securities of lower quality issuers, the yield spread relative to Treasury securities must widen. The converse is that during economic expansion and brisk economic activity, revenue and cash flow pick up, increasing the likelihood that corporate issuers will have the capacity to service their contractual debt obligations.

Yield spreads between Treasury and federal agency securities will vary depending on investor expectations about the prospects that an implicit government guarantee will be honored. Two examples of changes in yield spreads between Treasury and federal agency securities appear in Chapter 5.

Yield spreads are also related to the level of interest rates. For example, in 1957, when the yield on Treasuries was 3%, the yield spread

EXHIBIT 20-5 Relative Yield Curve Effects on Total Return[+]

Parallel Shift in the Yield Curve (b.p)

		−150	−100	−50	0	+50	+100	+200
		Quadrant (B)				Quadrant (A)		
+200	2	5.02	4.11	3.22	2.33*	1.46*	0.59*	−0.26*
	10–	11.21*	7.54*	4.02*	0.65	−2.57	−5.66	−8.62
	30–	6.24	0.67	−4.41	−9.06	−13.31	−17.21	−20.80
	BB–	5.68	2.23	−0.95	−3.89	−6.61	−9.13	−11.48
Steeper+100	2–	4.11	3.22	2.33	1.46*	0.59*	−0.26*	−1.11*
	10–	11.21	7.54*	4.02*	0.65	−2.57	−5.66	−8.62
	30–	12.35*	6.24	0.67	−4.41	−9.06	−13.31	−17.21
	BB–	8.61	4.87	1.42	−1.75	−4.68	−7.39	9.91
+50	2–	3.66	2.77	1.89	1.03*	0.17*	−0.68*	−1.53*
	10–	11.21	7.54	4.02*	0.65	−2.57	−5.66	−8.62
	30–	15.64*	9.22*	3.39	−1.93	−6.79	−11.23	−15.30
	BB–	10.21	6.30	2.71	−0.59	−3.63	−6.45	−9.05
Slope +0 Change (b.p.)	2–	3.22	2.33	1.46	0.59	−0.26*	−1.11*	−1.94*
	10–	11.21	7.54	4.02	0.65	−2.57	−5.66	−8.62
	30–	19.09*	12.35*	6.24*	0.67*	−4.41	−9.06	−13.31
	BB–	11.89#	7.81#	4.07#	0.63	−2.53#	−5.45#	−8.15
−50	2–	2.77	1.89	1.03	0.17	−0.68*	−1.53*	−2.36*
	10–	11.21	7.54	4.02	0.65	−2.57	−5.66	−8.62
	30–	22.71*	15.64*	9.22*	3.39*	−1.93	−6.79	−11.23
	BB–	13.66#	9.40#	5.50#	1.93#	−1.37#	−4.40#	−7.20#
Flatter −100	2–	2.33	1.46	0.59	−0.26	−1.11	−1.94*	−2.77*
	10–	11.21	7.54	4.02	0.65	−2.57	−5.66	−8.62
	30–	26.51*	19.09*	12.35*	6.24*	0.67*	−4.41	−9.06
	BB–	15.54#	11.09#	7.02#	3.29#	−0.14#	−3.29#	−6.20#
−200	2–	1.46	0.59	−0.26	−1.11	−1.94	−2.77	−3.59
	10–	11.21	7.54	4.02	0.65	−2.57	−5.66	−8.62
	30–	34.72*	26.51*	19.09*	12.35*	6.24*	0.67*	−4.41*
	BB–	19.63#	14.75#	10.31#	6.25#	2.35#	−0.89#	−4.04#
		Quadrant (C)				Quadrant (D)		

+ The yield curve is the one that prevailed on November 1, 1990.
* denotes the optimal of the 2-year, 10-year, and 30-year Treasury.
# indicates that the barbell has a better return than the 10-year.
BB = barbell portfolio
* Adapted from Table 3 of Frank J. Jones, "Yield Curve Strategies," *Journal of Fixed Income* (September 1991), p.46.

EXHIBIT 20-6   Optimal Yield Curve Strategies

	Yield Decreases	Yield Increases
Steeper Yield Curve	*Quadrant B* Intermediate Maturity Bullet	*Quadrant A* Short Maturity Bullet
Flatter Yield Curve	*Quadrant C* Long Maturity Barbell (around long maturity)	*Quadrant D* Short or Long Maturity (greater flattening relative to upward yield shift favors the long maturity)

* Adapted from Table 4 of Frank J. Jones, "Yield Curve Strategies," *Journal of Fixed Income* (September 1991), p.47.

between a triple-B rated utility bond and Treasuries was 40 basis points. This represented a relative yield spread of 13% (.4% divided by 3%). When the yield on Treasuries exceeded 10% in 1985, however, a yield spread of 40 basis points would have meant only a relative yield spread of 4%.[6] Consequently, the yield spread measured in basis points must be greater than 40 basis points. Exhibit 20-7 suggests that the relative yield spread—as measured by the ratio of the yield spread to the level of Treasury yields—and the yield ratio—the ratio of non-Treasury and Treasury yields—tends to be relatively stable over time.

Spreads attributable to differences in callable and noncallable bonds and differences in coupons of callable bonds will change as a result of expected changes in (1) the direction of the change in interest rates, and (2) interest rate volatility. An expected drop in the level of interest rates will widen the yield spread between callable bonds and noncallable bonds as the prospects that the issuer will exercise the call option increase. The reverse is true — the yield spread narrows — if interest rates are expected to rise. As we explain in Chapter 13, an increase in interest rate volatility increases the value of the embedded call option, and thereby increases the yield spread between callable bonds and noncallable bonds. Expectations about the direction of the change in interest rates and interest rate volatility will affect the yield spread between Treasury and pass-through securities and the yield spread between low-coupon and high-coupon pass-throughs in the same way as it affects the yield spreads for corporates.

---

[6] Chris P. Dialynas and David H. Edington, "Bond Yield Spreads—A Postmodern View," *Journal of Portfolio Management* (Fall 1992).

EXHIBIT 20-7 Relative Yield

Period	Average 10-year Treasury Yield	Average BBB Utility Yield	Average Spread (%)	Relative Yield (%)	Yield Ratio
1955-1959	3.46	4.21	75	22	1.217
1960-1964	4.03	4.79	76	19	1.189
1965-1969	5.32	6.22	95	17	1.169
1970-1974	6.82	8.75	197	28	1.283
1975-1979	8.17	10.04	191	23	1.229
1980-1984	12.30	15.18	276	23	1.234
1985-1989	8.81	10.92	209	24	1.240

Source: Chris P. Dialynas and David H. Edington, "Bond Yield Spreads — A Postmodern View," *Journal of Portfolio Management* (Fall 1992).

INDIVIDUAL SECURITY SELECTION STRATEGIES

There are several active strategies that money managers pursue to identify mispriced securities. The most common strategy identifies an issue as undervalued because either (1) its yield is higher than that of comparably rated issues, or (2) its yield is expected to decline (and price therefore rise) because credit analysis indicates that its rating will improve.

A swap in which a money manager exchanges one bond for another bond that is similar in terms of coupon, maturity, and credit quality, but offers a higher yield, is called a *substitution swap*. This swap depends on a capital market imperfection. Such situations sometimes exist in the bond market owing to temporary market imbalances and the fragmented nature of the non-Treasury bond market. The risk the money manager faces in making a substitution swap is that the bond purchased may not be truly identical to the bond for which it is exchanged. Moreover, typically bonds will have similar but not identical maturities and coupon. This could lead to differences in the convexity of the two bonds, and any yield spread may reflect the cost of convexity.

An active strategy used in the mortgage-backed securities market is to identify individual issues of pass-throughs, CMO classes, or stripped MBS that are mispriced, given the assumed prepayment speed to price the security. Recall from the discussion of pass-throughs in Chapter 11 that pass-throughs generally are purchased on a generic basis. That is, the buyer does not know which specific pool (or pools) will be delivered unless the buyer requests the delivery of a specific pool, resulting in a higher cost. Yet, prepayment speeds are not identical for each issuer type and coupon. An investor may be able to identify a pass-through that is mispriced, given the geographical composition of the underlying pool of mortgage loans, and therefore purchase that specific pool.

Another active strategy commonly used in the mortgage-backed securities market is to create a package of securities that will have a better return profile for a wide range of interest rate and yield curve scenarios than similar duration securities available in the market. Because of the fragmented nature of the mortgage-backed securities market and the complexity of the structures, such opportunities are not unusual.

OPTION-ADJUSTED SPREAD BASED STRATEGIES

As Chapter 14 indicates, the practice today is to measure the yield spread on bonds with embedded options in terms of their option-adjusted spread. Money managers can position a portfolio to take advantage of expectations as to how the option-adjusted spread will change over an investment horizon.

There have been several empirical tests of the performance of option-adjusted spread-based trading strategies for mortgage-backed securities. One is an examination by Lakhbir Hayre and Kenneth Lauterbach of the six-month performance of GNMA pass-throughs and similar duration Treasuries using an option-adjusted spread-based trading strategy for the period from mid-1985 to 1988.[7] They find the relative performance of GNMA pass-throughs to be closely related to the option-adjusted spread at the beginning of the six-month investment horizon. These results are reported in Exhibit 20-8. As can be seen, for the period investigated, when the option-adjusted spread at the beginning of the period was less than 100 basis points, the GNMA pass-throughs were outperformed by similar-duration Treasuries more than 68% of the time. When the option-adjusted spread exceeded 100 basis points, however, GNMA pass-throughs were the better performing security class more than 75% of the time.

Hayre and Lauterbach also find an option-adjusted spread-based trading strategy to be superior to a strategy based on the traditional cash flow yield spread described in Chapter 15.[8] Specifically, they report that the correlation between the option-adjusted spread at the beginning of the six-month investment horizon and the subsequent six-month total return was 68%, while the corresponding correlation between the traditional cash flow yield spread and the subsequent six-month total return was only 53%.

---

[7] Lakhbir S. Hayre and Kenneth Lauterbach, "Stochastic Valuation of Debt Securities," in Frank J. Fabozzi (ed.), *Managing Institutional Assets* (New York: Harper & Row, 1990).

[8] Hayre and Lauterbach refer to the cash flow yield spread in their study as the "regular yield spread."

EXHIBIT 20-8   Option-Adjusted Spreads and GNMA Returns over Treasuries

OAS[a]	Frequency of MBS Outperforming Similar-Duration Treasury over Next Six-Months (%)	Average Difference between GNMA and Similar-Duration Treasury Returns[b]
Less than 50	13%	−5.98%
50 to 100	32	−0.82
100 to 150	76	2.86
Greater than 150	100	6.24

Note: Period covered is from mid-1985 to 1988.
a. OASs are calculated assuming a volatility of 15%.
b. Constant reinvestment rate of 6.5% is assumed.

Source: Lakhbir S. Hayre and Kenneth Lauterbach, "Stochastic Valuation of Debt Securities," in Frank J. Fabozzi (ed.), *Managing Institutional Assets* (New York: Harper & Row, 1990), p. 359.

One other test performed by Hayre and Lauterbach is noteworthy. They calculate the six-month total return for the following two strategies:

Strategy A: Purchase at the beginning of each month a GNMA with the highest cash flow yield spread, and finance the acquisition by shorting a comparable duration Treasury.

Strategy B: Purchase at the beginning of each month a GNMA with the highest option-adjusted spread, and finance the acquisition by shorting a comparable duration Treasury.

They find that Strategy A produced positive returns in 62% of the cases, while Strategy B produced positive returns in 81% of the cases. The average return for Strategy A was only 84 basis points, smaller than that for Strategy B, which was 258 basis points. Moreover, in only 8% of the cases did Strategy A outperform Strategy B. These results support the view that an option-adjusted spread-based trading strategy may not only lead to enhanced returns but also be superior to a trading strategy based on traditional yield spreads. These results are similar to those reported by researchers at Morgan Stanley in 1988.[9]

An editorial in the *Financial Analysts Journal* by Alden Toevs documents a growing parity since 1986 in market pricing based on option-adjusted spreads.[10] Exhibit 20-9 summarizes one of his tests for all three agency pass-throughs. The top panel shows information for the two years

---

[9] See David P. Jacob, Gary D. Latainer, and Alden Toevs, "Value and Performance of Mortgage-Backed Securities," Chapter 27 in Frank J. Fabozzi (ed.), *The Handbook of Mortgage-Backed Securities: Revised Edition* (Chicago: Probus Publishing, 1988).

[10] Alden Toevs, "Laser Brains Rejoice: Analytical Methods Can Help Shape Market Equilibrium Prices," *Financial Analysts Journal* (November-December 1990), pp. 8-10.

EXHIBIT 20-9 Mortgage-Backed Securities Segmented by OAS Quartiles: Three-Month Total Return Characteristics Relative to Duration-Matched Treasuries

1986 Through 1987

Quartile	Average Outperformance (basis points)	Average Change in OAS (basis points)
	GNMAs	
1	135	−25
2	94	−11
3	−18	15
4	−152	43
	FNMAs	
1	150	−33
2	68	−8
3	7	6
4	−83	42
	FHLMCs	
1	158	−37
2	55	−5
3	−11	12
4	−70	38

1988 Through 1989

Quartile	Average Outperformance (basis points)	Average Change in OAS (basis points)
	GNMAs	
1	40	0
2	46	−2
3	26	4
4	29	8
	FNMAs	
1	65	−9
2	38	−1
3	33	4
4	40	9
	FHLMCs	
1	69	−7
2	32	1
3	27	4
4	40	8

Source: Alden Toevs, "Laser Brains Rejoice: Analytical Methods Can Help Shape Market Equilibrium Prices," *Financial Analysts Journal* (November-December 1990), Table 1, p. 9.

1986 and 1987, a period when the option-adjusted spread methodology was not widely used by market participants in the mortgage-backed securities market; the lower panel shows the same information for the two years 1988 and 1989, when Toevs argues there was greater acceptance of the option-adjusted spread methodology.

The Toevs study divides all the issues of an agency for each time period into four quartiles according to their option-adjusted spread at the time of purchase. Three-month total returns are calculated for the agency issues in a quartile and for a duration-matched Treasury. The average performance differential is then calculated for a quartile. Consider, for example, the FNMAs in the second quartile in the 1986-1987 period. On average, the three-month total return for the issues in this quartile was better than duration-based Treasuries by 68 basis points.

The relative performance is affected by how the option-adjusted spread changed over the three-month investment horizons. The last column in each panel shows the average change in the option-adjusted spread over a three-month period for each quartile. For example, look at the first and last quartile for the FHLMC issues in the first period. For the first quartile, the average change in the option-adjusted spread was a decline of 37 basis points. That is, on average, the option-adjusted spread became richer by 37 basis points. For the last quartile, the option-adjusted spread became cheaper by 38 basis points on average.

Toevs argues that results for the two time periods provide some indication of how the option-adjusted spread methodology has influenced the pricing of pass-throughs. The comparison shows several trends. First, compared to the first time period, investing based on the option-adjusted spread methodology in the second time period results in average performance for each quartile that is greater than that of a comparable duration-based Treasury security. Second, the range of the average performance differential is narrower in the second time period than in the first time period. Finally, the average change in the option-adjusted spread is insignificant in the second time period. Taken as a whole the results in Exhibit 20-9 seem to support the view that "misvaluations of mortgage prepayment options have been increasingly priced away."[11]

SUMMARY

There are five basic steps involved in investment management. The first main step in the investment management process is setting investment objectives. The second step in the investment management process is

---

[11] Ibid., p.8.

establishing policy guidelines to satisfy the investment objectives; it begins with the asset allocation decision. The third step is selecting a portfolio strategy that is consistent with the objectives and policy guidelines of the client or institution. The fourth step is selecting the specific assets to be included in the portfolio. The measurement and evaluation of investment performance is the "last" step in the ongoing investment management process.

Active strategies seek to capitalize on expectations about changes in factors that will affect the price and therefore the performance of an issue over some investment horizon. The factors that affect a portfolio's return are (1) changes in the level of interest rates; (2) changes in the shape of the yield curve; (3) changes in yield spreads among bond sectors; and (4) changes in the yield spread for a particular bond. The total return framework should be used to assess how changes in these factors will affect the performance of a strategy over some investment horizon.

QUESTIONS FOR CHAPTER 20

1. Why might the investment objective of a portfolio manager of a life insurance company be different from that of a mutual fund manager?

2. What is the essential ingredient in all active portfolio strategies?

3. What are the limitations of using duration and convexity measures in active portfolio strategies?

4. The excerpt following is taken from an article entitled "Smith Plans to Shorten," which appeared in the January 27, 1992, issue of *BondWeek*, p. 6:

   When the economy begins to rebound and interest rates start to move up, Smith Affiliated Capital will swap 30-year Treasuries for 10-year Treasuries and those with average remaining lives of nine years, according to Bob Smith, executive v.p. The New York firm doesn't expect this to occur until the end of this year or early next, however, and sees the yield on the 30-year Treasury first falling below 7%. Any new cash that comes in now will be put into 30-year Treasuries, Smith added.

   What type of portfolio strategy is Smith Affiliated Capital pursuing?

5. The excerpt following is taken from an article entitled "MERUS to Boost Corporates," that appeared in the January 27, 1992, issue of *BondWeek*, p. 6:

   MERUS Capital Management will increase the allocation to corporates in its $790 million long investment-grade fixed-income portfolio by $39.5 million over the next six months to a year, according to George Wood, managing director. MERUS will add corporates rated single A or higher in the expectation that spreads will tighten as the economy recovers and that some credits may be upgraded.

   What types of active portfolio strategies are MERUS Capital Management pursuing?

6. This excerpt comes from an article entitled "Eagle Eyes High-Coupon Callable Corporates," in the January 20, 1992, issue of *BondWeek*, p. 7:

   If the bond market rallies further, Eagle Asset Management may take profits, trading $8 million of seven to 10-year Treasuries for high-coupon single-A industrials that are callable in two to four years according to Joseph Blanton, senior v.p. He thinks a further rally is unlikely, however.

   Eagle has already sold seven- to 10-year Treasuries to buy $25 million of high-coupon, single-A nonbank financial credits. It made the move to cut the duration of its $160 million fixed income portfolio from 3.7 to 2.5 years, substantially lower than the 3.3-year duration of its bogey ... because it thinks the bond rally has run its course.

   ... Blanton said he likes single-A industrials and financials with 9 1/2-10% coupons because these are selling at wide spreads of about 100-150 basis points off Treasuries.

   What types of active portfolio strategies are being pursued by Eagle Asset Management?

7. The excerpt below is taken from an article entitled "W.R. Lazard Buys Triple Bs," which appeared in the November 18, 1991, issue of *BondWeek*, p. 7:

   W.R. Lazard & Co. is buying some corporate bonds rated triple B that it believes will be upgraded and some single As that the market perceives as risky but Lazard does not, according to William Schultz, v.p. The firm, which generally buys corporates rated single A or higher, is making the move to pick up yield, Schultz said.

   What types of active portfolio strategies are being followed by W.R. Lazard & Co.?

8. The excerpt following comes from an article entitled "Investors Move from Taxables to Munis," which appeared in the December 2, 1991, issue of *BondWeek*, p. 1:

   Tax-exempt investors, such as pension funds, mutual funds and large trusts, and taxable investors, such as property and casualty companies, have been switching out of Treasuries and corporates and into municipals for the past couple of weeks, according to market participants. Tax-exempt investors, which typically stick to taxable bonds, expect municipals to outperform governments in the long run because supply in the municipal market is decreasing, while supply in the Treasury market is expected to continue to rise ...

   What type of active portfolio strategy is being pursued here?

9. In an article entitled "Signet to Add Pass-Throughs," which appeared in the October 14, 1991, issue of *BondWeek*, p. 5, it was reported that Christian Goetz, assistant v.p. of Signet Asset Management, "expects current coupons to outperform premium pass-throughs as the Fed lowers rates because mortgage holders will refinance premium mortgages." If Goetz pursues a strategy based on this, what type of active strategy is it?

10. The next excerpt is taken from an article entitled "Fifth Third to Swap into PACs," in the February 17, 1992, issue of *BondWeek*, p. 5:

    Fifth Third Bank is set to invest about $75 million in planned amortization class tranches of collateralized mortgage obligations that it finds undervalued, according to Thomas Atteberry, chief fixed-income strategist and senior portfolio manager.... Atteberry likes PACs because he believes the market has overestimated the speed of prepayments. "The refinancing mania will be short-lived," he predicted.

    ... Atteberry will look for CMOs issued one or two years ago, backed by mortgages issued on the East and West coasts because home values have declined there. As a result, these homeowners are less likely to refinance, he argued. He will sell single-A rated bank, finance and industrial credits because their spreads have tightened a great deal.

    Comment on this portfolio strategy.

11. This excerpt comes from an article entitled "Securities Counselors Eyes Cutting Duration," in the February 17, 1992, issue of *BondWeek*, p. 5:

    Securities Counselors of Iowa will shorten the 5.3 year duration on its $250 million fixed-income portfolio once it is convinced interest rates are moving up and the economy is improving.... It will shorten by holding in cash equivalents the proceeds from the sale of an undetermined amount of 10-year Treasuries and adding a small amount of high-grade electric utility bonds that have short maturities if their spreads widen out at least 100 basis points.

    ...The portfolio is currently allocated 85% to Treasuries and 15% to agencies. It has not held corporate bonds since 1985, when it perceived as risky the barrage of hostile corporate takeovers...

    a. Why would Securities Counselors want to shorten duration if it believes interest rates will rise?

    b. How does the purchase of cash-equivalents and short-maturity high-grade utilities accomplish the goal of shortening the duration?

    c. If the economy does improve, do you think that the spread on short-maturity high-grade corporate bonds will widen out?

    d. In the last sentence of the excerpt, what risk does Securities Counselors indicate that it is seeking to avoid by not buying corporate bonds?

12. The next excerpt is taken from an article entitled "Wood Struthers to Add High-Grade Corporates," which appeared in the February 17, 1992, issue of *BondWeek*, p. 5:

    Wood Struthers & Winthrop is poised to add a wide range of high-grade corporates to its $600 million fixed-income portfolio ... It will increase its 25% corporate allocation to about 30% after the economy shows signs of improving... .It will sell Treasuries and agencies of undetermined maturities to make the purchase.

    ...Its duration is 4 1/2-5 years and is not expected to change significantly ...

    Comment on this portfolio strategy.

13. The excerpt following comes from an article entitled "Wilmington Buys Intermediates," in the February 17, 1992, issue of *BondWeek*, p. 5:

    Wilmington Trust's $100 million Strategic Fixed Income Fund and $150 million Benchmark U.S. Treasury Program will continue to invest new money in three- to five-year securities, including Treasuries, corporates and asset-backs, as it is unclear what interest rates will follow, said Cam Albright, portfolio manager....But conflicting data on the economy will keep yields volatile, and it will be hard to pinpoint when their direction reverses, he contended.

    The Strategic fund holds 60% in Treasuries, with the balance split between investment-grade corporates and mortgage backeds. The latter are mainly in...classes of collateralized mortgage obligations, which Albright likes for their lower prepayment risk.

The Benchmark Program is invested half in Treasuries and half in cash or cash equivalents, which Albright said he holds because of his uncertainty on when rates will move up. Albright plans to keep the portfolios close to market durations ....

a. In the second paragraph above, the class of collateralized mortgage obligation that is held in the Strategic fund is intentionally not indicated. Which class is it, and how do you know?

b. Is this portfolio manager structuring portfolios to capitalize on the direction of interest rate movements?

14. An article entitled "Guinness Fund Likes European Bond Markets," which appeared in the February 3, 1992, issue of *BondWeek*, p. 7, says:

The $350 million Guinness Flight Global Bond Fund plans to halve its 30% U.S. Treasury allocation in the next few months and increase its European holdings as it predicts the latter will outperform this year, according to Philip Saunders, portfolio manager. Saunders expects 10-year Treasury yields to hit bottom ... in the near future. When this occurs, he will sell them before yields start to rise...as the economic recovery grows stronger.

Saunders expects higher returns on markets such as France, the Netherlands and Denmark, where he sees the spreads on 10-year government bonds tightening about 25 basis points to bunds by year end ....

Comment on this portfolio strategy.

15. This quotation appears in an article entitled "Capel Eyes Aussie Swap," which appeared in the February 3, 1992, issue of *BondWeek*, p. 7:

James Capel Fund Managers may trade out of $70 million of seven- to 10-year U.S. Treasuries, or 5% of its $1.4 billion bond portfolio, if 10-year Treasury bond yields rally from 7.21% to 6.75%, which it expects in three to six months, said Theodora Zemek, senior executive. Zemek expects U.S. bond yields will start backing up by year end. Capel may replace some of the U.S. bonds with long Australian government bonds if the Australian bond market still looks attractive, she added.

Comment on this strategy.

16. The excerpt following is taken from an article entitled "Benchmark to Buy Adjustable-Rate Mortgage-Backeds," in the January 13, 1992, issue of *BondWeek*, p. 7:

Following the adoption of a tax package that will likely be perceived by market participants as inflationary, Benchmark Asset Management will swap an undisclosed amount of fixed-rate mortgage-backed securities for variable-rate ones, according to Jack Creden, executive v.p. ....

As a result, the $100 million fixed-income portfolio will likely shorten, but Creden declines to say by how much or what maturities will be swapped.

Comment on this strategy.

17. Describe the different types of yield curve shifts.

Chapter 21

STRUCTURED PORTFOLIO STRATEGIES I: INDEXING

In this chapter and the next, we describe several structured portfolio strategies. Structured strategies generally do not rely on expectations of interest rate movements or changes in yield spread relationships. Their objective instead is to design a portfolio that will achieve the performance of some predetermined benchmark. The target to achieve may be: (1) the return on a specific benchmark index; (2) sufficient dollars to satisfy a future single liability; or (3) sufficient dollars to satisfy each liability of a future liability stream. The structured bond portfolio strategy used when the target to be achieved is replication of a predetermined benchmark index is called an indexing strategy. When the target objective instead is to generate sufficient funds to pay off predetermined future liabilities, the strategy is called a liability funding strategy. Indexing is discussed in this chapter; liability funding is discussed in the chapter to follow.

OVERVIEW OF ASSET/LIABILITY MANAGEMENT

The nature of the liabilities of a financial institution dictates the investment strategy that its money manager will pursue. Depository institutions, for example, seek to generate income from the spread between the return that they earn on assets and the cost of their funds. That is, they are spread businesses. Life insurance companies and, to a certain extent, property and casualty insurance companies also are in the spread business. Pension funds are not in the spread business, in that they do not raise funds themselves in the market. They seek to cover the cost of pension obligations and to do so at a minimum cost that is borne by the sponsor of the pension plan. Investment companies, on the other hand, face no explicit costs for the funds they acquire and must satisfy no specific liability obligations, except in the case of a particular type of investment company that agrees to repurchase shares at any time.

Nature of Liabilities

By the liabilities of a financial institution we mean the amount and timing of the cash outlays that must be made to satisfy the contractual terms of the obligations issued. The liabilities of any financial institution can be categorized according to four types as shown in Exhibit 21-1. Categorizations in the exhibit assume that the entity that must be paid the obligation will not cancel the financial institution's obligation prior to any actual or projected payout date.

EXHIBIT 21-1   Nature of Liabilities of Financial Institutions

Liability Type	Amount of Cash Outlay	Timing of Cash Outlay
Type I	Known	Known
Type II	Known	Uncertain
Type III	Uncertain	Known
Type IV	Uncertain	Uncertain

The descriptions of cash outlays as either known or uncertain are undoubtedly broad. When we refer to a cash outlay as being uncertain, we do not mean that it cannot be predicted. There are some liabilities where the "law of large numbers" makes it easier to predict the timing and/or amount of cash outlays. This is the work typically done by actuaries, but even actuaries cannot predict natural catastrophes such as floods and earthquakes.

Type-I Liabilities: Both the amount and timing of the liabilities are known with certainty. A liability where a financial institution knows that it must pay $50,000 six months from now is one example. Banks and thrifts know the amount that they are committed to pay (principal plus interest) on the maturity date of a fixed-rate deposit, assuming that the depositor does not withdraw funds prior to the maturity date.

Type-I liabilities, however, are not limited to depository institutions. A major product sold by life insurance companies is a *guaranteed investment contract*, popularly referred to as a GIC. The obligation of the life insurance company under this contract is that, for a sum of money (called a premium), it will guarantee an interest rate up to some specified maturity date. For example, suppose a life insurance company for a premium of $10 million issues a five-year GIC agreeing to pay 10% compounded annually. The life insurance company knows that it must pay $16.11 million to the GIC policyholder in five years.[1]

---

[1] This amount is determined as follows: $\$10,000,000 \, (1.10)^5$.

Type-II Liabilities: The amount of the cash outlay is known, but its timing is uncertain. The most obvious example of a Type-II liability is a life insurance policy. There are many types of life insurance policies, but the most basic type is that, for an annual premium, a life insurance company agrees to make a specified dollar payment to policy beneficiaries upon the death of the insured.

Type-III Liabilities: With a Type–III liability, the timing of the cash outlay is known, but the amount is uncertain. A two-year floating-rate CD where the interest rate resets quarterly based on three-month LIBOR is an example. Not surprisingly, there are also floating-rate GICs; these also fall into the Type-III liabilities category.

Type-IV Liabilities: There are numerous insurance products and pension obligations where there is uncertainty as to both the amount and the timing of the cash outlay. Probably the most obvious examples are automobile and home insurance policies issued by property and casualty insurance companies. When, and if, a payment will have to be made to the policyholder is uncertain. Whenever damage is done to an insured asset, the amount of the payment that must be made is uncertain.

Sponsors of pension plans can agree to various types of pension obligations to the beneficiaries of the plan. In defined-benefit plans, retirement benefits depend on the participant's income for a specified number of years before retirement and the total number of years the participant worked. This will affect the amount of the cash outlay. The timing of the cash outlay depends on when the employee elects to retire, and whether the employee remains with the sponsoring plan until retirement. Moreover, both the amount and the timing will depend on how the employee elects to have payments made—over only the employee's life or over the lives of the employee and spouse.

Liquidity Concerns

Because of uncertainty about the timing and/or the amount of the cash outlays, a financial institution must be prepared with sufficient cash to satisfy its obligations. Also keep in mind that our discussion of liabilities did not assume that the entity that holds the obligation against the financial institution has the right to change the nature of the obligation, perhaps incurring some penalty. For example, in the case of a certificate of deposit, the depositor may request the withdrawal of funds prior to the maturity date. Typically, the deposit-accepting institution will grant this request, but assess an early withdrawal penalty. In the case of certain types of investment companies, shareholders have the right to redeem their shares at any time.

Some life insurance products have a cash-surrender value. This means that, at specified dates, the policyholder can exchange the policy for a lump sum payment. Typically, the lump sum payment will penalize the policyholder for turning in the policy. Some life insurance products also have a loan value, which means that the policyholder has the right to borrow against the cash value of the policy.

Besides uncertainty about the timing and amount of the cash outlays, and the potential for the depositor or policyholder to withdraw cash early or borrow against a policy, a financial institution has to be concerned with possible reduction in cash inflows. In the case of a depository institution, this means that deposits will slow down. For insurance companies, it means reduced premiums because of policies that may be cancelled. For certain types of investment companies, it means not being able to find new buyers for redeemed shares.

OBJECTIVE OF AND MOTIVATION FOR BOND INDEXING

Indexing a portfolio means designing a portfolio so that its performance will match the performance of some predetermined index. Performance is measured in terms of total rate of return achieved (or simply, total return) over some investment horizon. Total return over some investment horizon incorporates all three sources of return from holding a portfolio of bonds, that is,

$$\text{Total return} = \frac{\begin{matrix}\text{Coupon interest} \\ \text{received}\end{matrix} + \begin{matrix}\text{Change in} \\ \text{portfolio value}\end{matrix} + \begin{matrix}\text{Reinvestment} \\ \text{income}\end{matrix}}{\text{Portfolio value at beginning of period}}$$

Indexing an equity portfolio is commonplace. On the bond side, indexing is a relatively recent phenomenon. In 1980, for example, only $40 million of assets was managed under bond indexing strategies.[2] Currently, more than $75 billion of funds under fixed-income management is indexed. Since 1980, the number of investment advisors who manage funds on an indexed basis has increased from a few to about 50.[3]

Sharmin Mossavar-Rahmani, a leading expert in index fund management, cites several factors to explain the recent popularity and phenomenal rate of growth of bond indexing.[4] First, the empirical evidence

---

[2] Sharmin Mossavar-Rahmani, "Understanding and Evaluating Index Fund Management," in Frank J. Fabozzi and T. Dessa Garlicki (eds.), *Advances in Bond Analysis and Portfolio Strategies* (Chicago: Probus Publishing, 1987), p. 433.

[3] Sharmin Mossavar-Rahmani, *Bond Index Funds* (Chicago: Probus Publishing, 1991), p. vii.

[4] Ibid., pp. 2-12.

suggests that historically the overall performance of active bond investment advisors has been poor. SEI Funds Evaluation Corporation ranked the performance of active bond investment advisors by total return and compared the relative performance to the Salomon Brothers Investment Grade Index. For various time periods ending in 1989, the median return of the active bond investment advisors was lower than the index return. In fact, in most periods investigated, more than 75% of the advisors underperformed the index.

The second factor explaining the popularity of bond indexing is reduced advisory management fees charged for an indexed portfolio compared to active management advisory fees. Advisory fees charged by active managers typically range from 15 to 50 basis points. The range for indexed portfolios, in contrast, is 1 to 20 basis points, with the upper range representing the fees for enhanced and customized benchmark funds discussed later in this chapter.[5] Some pension funds have decided to do away with advisory fees and to manage some or all of their funds in-house following an indexing strategy.

Lower nonadvisory fees, such as custodian and master fees, is the third explanation for the popularity of indexing. Finally, sponsors have greater control over investment advisors when an indexing strategy is selected. For example, in an actively managed portfolio, a sponsor who specifies a restriction on the portfolio's duration still gives the investment advisor ample leeway to pursue strategies that may significantly underperform the index selected as a benchmark. In contrast, requiring an investment advisor to match an index gives little leeway to the investment advisor, and, as a result, should result in performance that does not significantly diverge from a benchmark.

Critics are quick to point out that while an indexing strategy matches the performance of some index, the performance of that index does not necessarily represent optimal performance. For the five-year period ending September 1981, for example, 50% of active managers outperformed a popular index.[6] Moreover, matching an index does not mean that the money manager will satisfy a client's return requirement objective. For example, if the objective of a life insurance or a pension fund is to have sufficient funds to satisfy a predetermined liability, indexing only reduces the likelihood that performance will not be materially worse than the index. Indexing does not ensure that there will be sufficient funds to

---

[5] Sharmin Mossavar-Rahmani, "Understanding and Evaluating Index Fund Management," p. 434.

[6] As reported in Mossavar-Rahmani, "Understanding and Evaluating Index Fund Management," pp. 436-437.

satisfy a predetermined liability. Finally, matching an index means that a money manager is restricted to the sectors of the bond market that are in the index, even though there may be attractive opportunities in market sectors excluded from the index. While the broad-based bond market indexes typically include agency pass-through securities, other mortgage-backed securities that we discuss in Chapters 11 and 12 such as private label pass-throughs, stripped mortgage-backed securities, and collateralized mortgage obligations are generally not included. Yet it is in these fairly new markets that attractive returns to enhance performance may be available.

At the theoretical level, the index fund approach is supported by the work of Markowitz[7] on the construction of efficient portfolios and by capital market theory as developed by Sharpe,[8] Lintner,[9] and Mossin.[10] Markowitz demonstrates how portfolios can be constructed so as to maximize return for a given level of risk. Such portfolios are referred to as *efficient portfolios*.

The Sharpe-Lintner-Mossin analysis demonstrates that a "market" portfolio offers the highest level of return per unit of risk in an *efficient* market. An efficient market is one in which market participants cannot consistently earn abnormal risk-adjusted returns after considering transactions costs. A combination of securities in a portfolio with characteristics similar to the market is able to capture the efficiency of the market. The theoretical market portfolio consists of all risky assets. The weight of each risky asset in the market portfolio is equal to the ratio of its market value to the aggregate market value of all risky assets. That is, the market portfolio is a capitalization-weighted (value-weighted) portfolio of all risky assets.[11]

FACTORS TO CONSIDER IN SELECTING AN INDEX

A money manager who wishes to pursue an indexing strategy must determine which bond index to replicate. There are a number of bond

---

[7] Harry M. Markowitz,"Portfolio Selection," *Journal of Finance* (March 1952), pp. 71-91, and *Portfolio Selection: Efficient Diversification of Investment* (New York: John Wiley & Sons, 1959).

[8] William F. Sharpe, "Capital Asset Prices: A Theory of Market Equilibrium under Conditions of Risk," *Journal of Finance* (September 1964), pp. 425-442.

[9] John Lintner, "Security Prices, Risk, and Maximal Gains from Diversification," *Journal of Finance* (December 1965), pp. 587-616.

[10] Jan Mossin, "Equilibrium in a Capital Asset Market," *Econometrica* (October 1966), pp. 76-83.

[11] Granito argues that while the theoretical arguments are appropriate for indexing a common stock portfolio, they are inappropriate for justifying indexing of a bond portfolio. See Michael R. Granito, "The Problem with Bond Index Funds," *Journal of Portfolio Management* (Summer 1987), pp. 41-48.

indexes from which to select, and several factors influence the decision. The first is the investor's risk tolerance. Selection of an index that includes corporate bonds will expose the investor to credit risk. If this risk is unacceptable, an investor should avoid an index that includes this sector.

The second factor influencing the selection of an index is the investor's objective. For example, while the total return of the various indexes tends to be highly positively correlated, the variability of total returns has been quite different. Therefore, an investor whose objective may be to minimize the variability of total returns will be biased toward one that has had, and expects to continue to have, low variability (i.e., a shorter duration relative to other indexes). Moreover, variability of total return may not be symmetric in rising and falling markets. Investors who have expectations about the future direction of interest rates will favor the index that is expected to perform better given their expectations. Finally, because the cash flow of different indexes can be quite different, if the objective of an investor is to meet projected liabilities, the index that best matches that liability stream may be the better choice.

A final consideration in selecting an index is constraints on acceptable investments imposed by regulators. An index could include sectors of the bond market in which a regulated entity may not invest. For example, a regulated financial institution that is not permitted to invest in the high-yield sector of the corporate market should not select an index that includes that sector. Even if there is no restriction that prohibits a regulated entity from investing in a given sector of the bond market, there may be restrictions imposed on the proportion of the portfolio that can be allocated to a specific sector. The investor is then limited to indexes whose allocations comply with the regulations imposed.

BOND INDEXES

The wide range of bond market indexes available can be classified as broad-based market indexes and specialized market indexes.

The three broad-based market indexes most commonly used by institutional investors are the Lehman Brothers Aggregate Index, the Salomon Brothers Broad Investment-Grade Bond Index, and the Merrill Lynch Domestic Market Index. The bond market sectors covered by these three indexes are the Treasury, agency, investment-grade corporate, mortgage-backed, and Yankee markets.

The specialized market indexes focus on only one sector of the bond market or a subsector of the bond market. Indexes on sectors of the market are published by the three investment banking firms that produce the broad-based market indexes. For example, Salomon Brothers publishes both a corporate bond index (a sector index) and a high-grade corporate bond index that includes AAA- and AA-rated corporate bonds (a subindex of the corporate bond index). Firms that do not produce one of the three broad-based market indexes may provide specialized indexes. Some examples are the Morgan Stanley Actively Traded MBS Index, the Donaldson Lufkin & Jenrette High Yield Index, the First Boston High Yield Index, the Goldman Sachs Convertible 100, and the Ryan Labs Treasury Index.

In recent years, money managers in consultation with their clients have been moving in the direction of "customized benchmarks." A customized benchmark is a benchmark that is designed to meet a client's requirements and long-term objectives.[12] For example, in December 1986, Salomon Brothers Inc introduced its Large Pension Fund Baseline Bond Index as a standardized customized benchmark tailor-made for large pension funds "seeking to establish long-term core portfolios that more closely match the longer durations of their nominal dollar liabilities."[13]

Why have broker/dealer firms developed and aggressively marketed their bond indexes? Enhancing the firm's image is only a minor reason. The key motivation lies in the potential profit that the firm will make by executing trades to set up an indexed portfolio and rebalance it. Typically, a broker/dealer charges a money manager who wants to set up or rebalance an index a nominal amount for providing the necessary data, but expects that the bulk of the trades will be executed through its trading desks. Also, by keeping the makeup of the index proprietary, those firms attempt to lock in customers to using their index.

INDEXING METHODOLOGIES

Once a money manager has decided to pursue an indexing strategy and has selected an index (broad-based bond market index, specialized market index, or customized benchmark), the next step is to construct a portfolio that will track the index. Any discrepancy between the performance of the indexed portfolio and the index (whether positive or negative) is referred to as *tracking error*. Tracking error has three sources: (1) transactions costs in constructing the indexed portfolio; (2) differences in the

---

12 For a discussion of customized benchmarks and the reasons for the growing interest in them, see Sharmin Mossavar-Rahmani, "Customized Benchmarks in Structured Management," *Journal of Portfolio Management* (Summer 1987), pp. 65-68.

13 Martin L. Leibowitz, Thomas Klaffky, and Steven Mandel, "Introducing the Salomon Brothers Large Pension Fund Baseline Bond Index" (New York, NY: Salomon Brothers Inc, December 1986), p. 1.

composition of the indexed portfolio and the index itself; and (3) discrepancies between prices used by the organization constructing the index and transaction prices paid by the indexer.

One approach in constructing the indexed portfolio is for the money manager to purchase all the issues in the index according to their weight in the benchmark index. However, substantial tracking error will result from the transactions costs (and other fees) associated with purchasing all the issues and reinvesting cash flow (maturing principal and coupon interest). A broad-based market index could include over 5,000 issues, so large transactions costs may make this approach impractical. In addition, some issues in the index may not be available at the prices used in constructing the index.

Instead of purchasing all issues in the index, the money manager may purchase just a sample of issues. While this approach reduces tracking error resulting from high transactions costs, it increases tracking error resulting from the mismatch of the indexed portfolio and the index.

Generally speaking, the fewer the number of issues used to replicate the index, the smaller the tracking error due to transactions costs but the greater the tracking error risk due to the mismatch of the characteristics of the indexed portfolio and the index. In contrast, the more issues purchased to replicate the index, the greater the tracking error due to transactions costs, and the smaller the tracking error risk due to the mismatch of the index portfolio and the index. Obviously, then, there is a trade-off between tracking error and the number of issues used to construct the indexed portfolio.

There are three popular methodologies for designing a portfolio to replicate an index: (1) the stratified sampling or cell approach; (2) the optimization approach; and (3) the variance minimization approach. For each of these approaches, the initial question that the indexer must ask is: What are the factors that affect a bond index's performance? Each approach assumes that the performance of an individual bond depends on a number of systematic factors that affect the performance of all bonds and on a factor unique to the individual issue. The objective of the three approaches is to construct an indexed portfolio that eliminates the performance attributable to the factors unique to all the issues in the indexed portfolio.

Stratified Sampling or Cell Approach

Under this approach, the index is divided into cells, each cell representing a different characteristic of the index. The most common characteristics used to break down an index are: (1) duration; (2) coupon;

(3) maturity; (4) market sectors (Treasury, corporate, mortgage-backed); (5) credit rating; (6) call factors; and (7) sinking fund features. The last two factors are particularly important because the call and sinking fund features of an issue will impact its performance.[14]

For example, suppose that a manager selects the characteristics following to partition a Treasury/agency/corporate bond index:

Characteristic 1—call-adjusted duration range:
　　1. Less than or equal to 5
　　2. Greater than 5

Characteristic 2—maturity range:
　　1. Less than 5 years
　　2. Between 5 and 15 years
　　3. Greater than 15 years

Characteristic 3—market sectors:
　　1. Treasury
　　2. Agencies
　　3. Corporates

Characteristic 4—credit rating:
　　1. Triple A
　　2. Double A
　　3. Single A
　　4. Triple B

The total number of cells would be equal to:

$$2 \times 3 \times 3 \times 4 = 72$$

The objective is then to select from all of the issues in the index one or more issues in each cell that can be used to represent that entire cell. The total dollar amount purchased of the issues from each cell will be based on the percentage of the index's total market value that the cell represents. For example, if 40% of the market value of all the issues in the index is made up of corporate bonds, then 40% of the market value of the indexed portfolio should be composed of corporate bond issues.

The number of cells that the indexer uses will depend on the dollar amount of the portfolio to be indexed. In indexing a portfolio of less than $50 million, for example, using a large number of cells would require purchasing odd lots of issues. This increases the cost of buying the issues to represent a cell, and thus would increase the tracking error. Reducing

---

[14] For a discussion of the importance of call and sinking fund features on performance, see Chris P. Dialynas, "The Active Decisions in the Selection of Passive Management and Performance Bogeys," in *Advances in Bond Analysis and Portfolio Strategies*.

the number of cells to overcome this problem increases tracking error risk of index mismatch because the characteristics of the indexed portfolio may differ materially from those of the index.

Optimization Approach[15]

In this approach the money manager seeks to design an indexed portfolio that will match the cell breakdown just as described, and satisfy other constraints, but also optimize some objective. An objective might be to maximize the yield to maturity or some other yield measure, to maximize convexity, or to maximize expected total returns.[16] Constraints other than matching the cell breakdown might include not purchasing more than a specified amount of one issuer or group of issuers, or overweighing certain sectors for enhanced indexing (discussed later in this chapter).

The computational technique used to derive the optimal solution to the indexing problem in this approach is mathematical programming. When the objective function that the indexer seeks to optimize is a linear function, linear programming (a specific form of mathematical programming) is used. If the objective function is quadratic, then the particular mathematical programming technique used is quadratic programming.

Variance Minimization Approach

The variance minimization approach to designing an index portfolio is by far the most complex. This approach requires using historical data to estimate the variance of the tracking error. This is done by estimating a price function for every issue in the index. The price function is estimated on the basis of two sets of factors: (1) the cash flows from the issue discounted at the theoretical spot rates, and (2) other factors such as the duration or sector characteristics discussed earlier. Using a large universe of issues and elaborate econometric techniques, the price function is estimated from historical data. Once the price function for each issue is obtained, a variance equation for the tracking error can be constructed. The objective then is to minimize the variance of the tracking error in constructing the indexed portfolio. As the variance is a quadratic function (the difference between the benchmark return and the indexed portfolio's

---

[15]For an illustration of this technique, see Philip Galdi, "Indexing Fixed Income Portfolios," *Advances in Bond Analysis and Portfolio Strategies.*

[16]For a mathematical presentation of this approach as well as the variance minimization approach, see Christina Seix and Ravi Akoury, "Bond Indexation: The Optimal Quantitative Approach," *Journal of Portfolio Management* (Spring 1986), pp. 50-53.

return, squared), quadratic programming is used to find the optimal indexed portfolio in terms of minimized tracking error. The biggest problem with this approach is that estimating the price function from historical data is very difficult in the Treasury market, let alone the corporate market or the new issue market. Also, the price function may not be stable.

Although the stratified sampling (or cell) approach seems to be the easiest to use, it is extremely difficult to implement when large, diversified portfolios are taken as the benchmark. In this case, many cells are required, and the problem becomes complex. Also, because the handpicking of issues to match each cell is subjective, tracking error may result. Mathematical programming reduces the complexity of the problem when well-defined constraints are employed, allowing the indexer to analyze large quantities of data optimally.

TRACKING ERROR

How well do indexed portfolios constructed using an optimization approach track benchmark indexes? Exhibit 21-1 presents the results of a study by Salomon Brothers on the tracking error for the Salomon Brothers Broad Based Investment-Grade Bond Index and three subindexes using an optimal indexed portfolio methodology devised by Salomon Brothers. The tracking error is computed each month between January 1985 and November 1986 as the difference between the monthly return on the indexed portfolio and the monthly return on the benchmark index. A positive (negative) tracking error indicates that the monthly return on the indexed portfolio outperformed (underperformed) the monthly return on the index. Summary statistics (standard deviation, mean, high, and low) for the monthly tracking error and the cumulative tracking error over the entire 2-year period are shown in Exhibit 21-1.

The exhibit indicates that tracking error varies according to the benchmark. The smallest tracking error results when the index benchmark comprises only government securities. This is expected, because most government securities have similar features, no credit risk, and minimal call risk if any. By far the more difficult sector to track is the corporate bond market. This is probably because of the difference between the call and sinking fund characteristics of the indexed portfolio and those of the index, as well as the smaller diversification (higher unique risk) for the indexed portfolio relative to the index. For the broad market index, the tracking performance was similar to that of the government index. This is understandable, because the government index made up 60% of the broad market index at the time of the study.

EXHIBIT 21-2   Tracking Error of Monthly Returns in Basis Points*

Sector	Standard Deviation	Mean	High	Low	Total Return Cumulative	Total Return Annualized
Broad market	54	2	13	−6	69	34
Governments	2	2	5	−1	63	31
Corporates	17	9	40	−26	301	156
Mortgages	3	0	6	−7	6	3
Broad market (Including transaction costs)	5	0	11	−8	−12	−6

*Analysis between January 1985 and November 1986.

Source: Sharmin Mossavar-Rahmani, "Understanding and Evaluating Index Fund Management," in Frank J. Fabozzi and T. Dessa Garlicki, eds., *Advances in Bond Analysis and Portfolio Strategies* (Chicago: Probus Publishing, 1987). Based on Salomon Brothers Broad Investment-Grade Bond Index and its components.

LOGISTICAL PROBLEMS IN IMPLEMENTING AN INDEXING STRATEGY[17]

An indexer faces several logistical problems in constructing an indexed portfolio. First of all, the prices for each issue used by the organization that publishes the index may not be execution prices available to the indexer. In fact, they may be materially different from the prices offered by some dealers.

In addition, the prices used by organizations reporting the value of indexes are based on bid prices. Dealer ask prices, however, are the ones that the money manager would have to transact at when constructing or rebalancing the indexed portfolio. Thus there will be a bias between the performance of the index and the indexed portfolio that is equal to the bid-ask spread.

Furthermore, there are logistical problems unique to certain sectors in the bond market. Consider first the corporate bond market. There are typically about 3,500 issues in the corporate bond sector of a broad-based index. Because of the illiquidity of this sector of the bond market, not only may the prices used by the organization that publishes the index be unreliable, but also many of the issues may not even be available. Next, consider the mortgage-backed securities market. There are over 300,000 agency pass-through issues. The organizations that publish indexes lump all these issues into a few hundred generic issues. The indexer is then

---

[17]For a more detailed discussion, see Mossavar-Rahmani, "Understanding and Evaluating Index Fund Management," pp. 438-440.

faced with the difficult task of finding pass-through securities with the same risk/return profiles of these hypothetical issues.[18]

Finally, recall that the total return depends on the reinvestment rate available on coupon interest. If the organization publishing the index regularly overestimates the reinvestment rate, then the indexed portfolio could underperform the index by 10 to 15 basis points a year.[19]

ENHANCED INDEXING

So far we have discussed straight or "plain vanilla" indexing. The objective of this strategy is to replicate the total return performance of some predetermined index. In *enhanced indexing* (also called *"indexing plus"*), the objective is consistently to exceed the total return performance of the index by an amount sufficient to justify a higher management advisory fee and a higher level of risk of underperforming the index. The total return on the index becomes the minimum total return objective rather than the target total return. Thus enhanced indexing brings active strategies back into the portfolio management process, although they are assumed to employ only low-risk strategies.

What are some of the strategies employed in enhanced indexing? We have discussed most of them in the previous chapter. Any of the strategies employed would involve only those issues in the index. Another strategy for enhancing total return is to use securities not included in the index. For example, the broad-based indexes do not include derivative mortgage-backed securities (collateralized mortgage obligations and stripped mortgage-backed securities). If money managers pursuing enhanced index strategies believe that derivative mortgage-backed securities will outperform the agency pass-through securities in the index, they can substitute the former securities for the latter. Or the money manager may be able to create synthetic agency pass-through securities by using stripped mortgage-backed securities (interest-only and principal-only securities) that would exhibit better performance in certain interest rate environments.[20]

---

[18]For an explanation of how to deal with the unique problems associated with tracking a mortgage-backed securities index, see Llewellyn Miller, Edward P. Krawitt, and Michael P. Wands, "Mortgage Index Portfolios," Chapter 39 in Frank J. Fabozzi, ed., *The Handbook of Mortgage-Backed Securities*, 2nd ed. (Chicago: Probus Publishing, 1988).

[19]Fran Hawthorne, "The Battle of the Bond Indexes," *Institutional Investor* (April 1986), p. 122.

[20]For a further discussion of strategies to outperform an index, see Mark L. Dunetz and James M. Mahoney, "Indexation and Optimal Strategies in Portfolio Management," in Frank J. Fabozzi, ed., *Fixed Income Portfolio Strategies* (Chicago: Probus Publishing, 1989).

SUMMARY

Structured portfolio strategies generally do not rely on expectations of interest rate movements or changes in yield spread relationships. The objective instead is to design a portfolio that will achieve the performance of some predetermined benchmark. There are two types of structured portfolio strategies: indexing and liability funding.

The nature of the liabilities dictates the investment strategy a financial institution will pursue. By the nature of liabilities we mean the amount and timing of the cash outlays that are required to satisfy the contractual terms of particular obligations issued.

Indexing a portfolio means designing a portfolio so that its total return will match the performance of some predetermined index. Indexing requires selecting a bond index to be replicated and constructing a portfolio so as to minimize tracking error. The methodologies used to construct an indexed portfolio include the stratified sampling or cell approach, the optimization approach, and the variance minimization approach. In an enhanced indexing strategy the performance of the index becomes the minimum return objective that the portfolio manager attempts to achieve.

QUESTIONS FOR CHAPTER 21

1. What factors led to the use of bond indexing?
2. What are the drawbacks of indexing?
3. Is there any problem with a commercial bank using an indexing strategy to invest one-year funds on which the bank has agreed to pay a fixed rate?
4. What are the three most commonly used broad-based bond market indexes used by institutional investors?
5. a. What is tracking error?
   b. Why does tracking error occur in an indexing strategy?
6. What is the stratified sampling or cell approach to indexing?
7. What are the various types of enhanced indexing strategies?

Chapter 22

STRUCTURED PORTFOLIO STRATEGIES II: LIABILITY FUNDING

In the previous chapter we explain that the objective of a structured portfolio strategy is to design a portfolio that will achieve the performance of some predetermined benchmark. When the predetermined benchmark is either a single liability or multiple liabilities, the strategy is referred to as liability funding. Specifically, when the liability is a single liability, an immunization strategy is employed. When there are multiple liabilities, there are two strategies to choose from: multiperiod immunization and cash flow matching. We begin with the immunization of a single liability.

IMMUNIZATION OF A PORTFOLIO TO SATISFY A SINGLE LIABILITY[1]

To comprehend the basic principles underlying the immunization of a portfolio against interest rate changes so as to satisfy a single liability, consider the situation faced by a life insurance company that sells a guaranteed investment contract (GIC). Under this policy, for a lump sum payment a life insurance company guarantees that specified dollars will be paid to the policyholder at a specified future date. Or, equivalently, the life insurance company guarantees a specified rate of return on the payment. For example, suppose that a life insurance company sells a GIC that guarantees an interest rate of 6.25% every 6 months (12.5% on a bond-equivalent yield basis) for 5.5 years (11 6-month periods). Also suppose that the payment made by the policyholder is $8,820,262. Then the value that the life insurance company has guaranteed the policyholder 5.5 years from now is:[2]

---

[1] The theory of immunization was first set forth in F. M. Redington, "Review of the Principle of Life Office Valuation," *Journal of the Institute of Actuaries* (1952), pp. 286-340.

[2] Actually, the life insurance company will not guarantee the interest rate that it expects to earn, but a lower rate. The spread between the interest rate that the life insurance company can earn and the interest rate it guarantees is the return for the risk of not achieving the target rate.

$$\$8,820,262\,(1.0625)^{11} = \$17,183,033$$

When investing the $8,820,262, the target accumulated value for the portfolio manager of the life insurance company is $17,183,033 after 5.5 years, which is the same as a target yield of 12.5% on a bond-equivalent basis.

Suppose the portfolio manager buys $8,820,262 par value of a bond selling at par with a 12.5% yield to maturity that matures in 5.5 years. Will the portfolio manager be assured of realizing the target yield of 12.5% or, equivalently, a target accumulated value of $17,183,033? As we explain in Chapter 3, the portfolio manager will realize a 12.5% yield only if the coupon interest payments can be reinvested at 6.25% every 6 months. That is, the accumulated value will depend on the reinvestment rate.

To demonstrate this, we will suppose that immediately after investing the $8,820,262 in the 12.5% coupon, 5.5-year maturity bond, yields in the market change and stay at the new level for the remainder of the 5.5 years. Exhibit 22-1 illustrates what happens at the end of 5.5 years. The first column shows the new yield level. The second column shows the total coupon interest payments. The third column gives the interest-on-interest over the entire 5.5 years if the coupon interest payments are reinvested at the new yield level shown in the first column.[3] The price of the bond at the end of 5.5 years shown in the fourth column is the par value. The fifth column is the accumulated value from all three sources: coupon interest, interest-on-interest, and bond price. The total return is

EXHIBIT 22-1 Accumulated Value and Total Return After 5.5 Years: 5.5-Year, 12.5% Bond Selling to Yield 12.5%

Investment horizon (years)	= 5.5
Coupon rate	= 0.125
Maturity (years	= 5.5
Yield to maturity	= 0.125
Price	= 100
Par value purchased	= $8,820,262
Purchase price	= $8,820,262
Target accumulated value	= $17,183,033

			After 5.5 Years		
New Yield*	Coupon Interest	Interest-on-Interest	Price of Bond+	Accumulated Value	Total Return
.160	$6,063,930	$3,112,167	$8,820,262	$17,996,360	.1340
.155	6,063,930	2,990,716	8,820,262	17,874,908	.1326

[3]The formula for computing the interest-on-interest is given in Chapter 3.

			After 5.5 Years		
New Yield*	Coupon Interest	Interest-on-Interest	Price of Bond+	Accumulated Value	Total Return
.145	$6,063,930	2,753,177	8,820,262	17,637,369	.1300
.140	6,063,930	2,637,037	8,820,262	17,521,230	.1288
.135	6,063,930	2,522,618	8,820,262	17,406,810	.1275
.130	6,063,930	2,409,984	8,820,262	17,294,086	.1262
.125	6,063,930	2,298,840	8,820,262	17,183,033	.1250
.120	6,063,930	2,189,433	8,820,262	17,073,625	.1238
.115	6,063,930	2,081,648	8,820,262	16,965,840	.1225
.110	6,063,930	1,975,462	8,820,262	16,859,654	.1213
.105	6,063,930	1,870,852	8,820,262	16,755,044	.1201
.100	6,063,930	1,767,794	8,820,262	16,651,986	.1189
.095	6,063,930	1,666,266	8,820,262	16,550,458	.1178
.090	6,063,930	1,566,246	8,820,262	16,450,438	.1166
.085	6,063,930	1,467,712	8,820,262	16,351,904	.1154
.080	6,063,930	1,370,642	8,820,262	16,254,834	.1143
.075	6,063,930	1,275,014	8,820,262	16,159,206	.1132
.070	6,063,930	1,180,808	8,820,262	16,065,000	.1120
.065	6,063,930	1,088,003	8,820,262	15,972,195	.1109
.060	6,063,930	996,577	8,820,262	15,880,769	.1098
.055	6,063,930	906,511	8,820,262	15,790,703	.1087
.050	6,063,930	817,785	8,820,262	15,701,977	.1077

*Immediate change in yield.
+Maturity value

shown in the last column, according to the formula:[4]

$$2\left[\left(\frac{\text{Accumulated value}}{\$8,820,262}\right)^{1/11} - 1\right]$$

If yields do not change, so that the coupon payments can be reinvested at 12.5% (6.25% every 6 months), the portfolio manager will achieve the target accumulated value. If market yields rise, an accumulated value (total return) higher than the target accumulated value (target yield) will be achieved. This is because the coupon interest payments can be reinvested at a higher rate than the initial yield to maturity. Contrast this with what happens when the yield declines. The accumulated value (total return) will be less than the target accumulated value (target yield). *Therefore investing in a coupon bond with a yield to maturity equal to the target yield and a maturity equal to the investment horizon does not assure that the target accumulated value will be achieved.*

Suppose that instead of investing in a bond maturing in 5.5 years the portfolio manager invests in a 15-year bond with a coupon rate of 12.5% that is selling at par to yield 12.5%. Exhibit 22-2 presents the accumulated

---

[4] The procedure for calculating total return is given in Chapter 3.

EXHIBIT 22-2   Accumulated Value and Total Return After 5.5 Years: 15-Year, 12.5% Bond Selling to Yield 12.5%

Investment horizon (years)	= 5.5
Coupon rate	= .1250
Maturity (years)	= 15
Yield to maturity	= .1250
Price	= 100
Par value purchased	= $8,820,262
Purchase price	= $8,820,262
Target accumulated value	= $17,183,033

			After 5.5 Years		
New Yield*	Coupon Interest	Interest-on-Interest	Price of Bond	Accumulated Value	Total Return
.160	$6,063,930	$3,112,167	$7,337,902	$16,514,000	.1173
.155	6,063,930	2,990,716	7,526,488	16,581,134	.1181
.145	6,063,930	2,753,177	7,925,481	16,742,587	.1200
.140	6,063,930	2,637,037	8,136,542	16,837,510	.1211
.135	6,063,930	2,522,618	8,355,777	16,942,325	.1223
.130	6,063,930	2,409,984	8,583,555	17,057,379	.1236
.125	6,063,930	2,298,840	8,820,262	17,183,033	.1250
.120	6,063,930	2,189,433	9,066,306	17,319,669	.1265
.115	6,063,930	2,081,648	9,322,113	17,467,691	.1282
.110	6,063,930	1,975,462	9,588,131	17,627,523	.1299
.105	6,063,930	1,870,852	9,864,831	17,799,613	.1318
.100	6,063,930	1,767,794	10,152,708	17,984,432	.1338
.095	6,063,930	1,666,266	10,452,281	18,182,477	.1359
.090	6,063,930	1,566,246	10,764,095	18,394,271	.1382
.085	6,063,930	1,467,712	11,088,723	18,620,366	.1406
.080	6,063,930	1,370,642	11,462,770	18,861,342	.1431
.075	6,063,930	1,275,014	11,778,867	19,117,812	.1457
.070	6,063,930	1,180,808	12,145,682	19,390,420	.1485
.065	6,063,930	1,088,003	12,527,914	19,679,847	.1514
.060	6,063,930	996,577	12,926,301	19,986,808	.1544
.055	6,063,930	906,511	13,341,617	20,312,058	.1576
.050	6,063,930	817,785	13,774,677	20,656,393	.1609

*Immediate change in yield.

value and total return if the market yield changes immediately after the bond is purchased and remains at the new yield level. The fourth column of the exhibit is the market price of a 12.5% coupon, 9.5-year bond (since 5.5 years have passed), assuming the market yields shown in the first column. If the market yield increases, the portfolio will fail to achieve the target accumulated value; the opposite will be true if the market yield decreases—the accumulated value (total return) will exceed the target accumulated value (target yield).

The reason for this result can be seen in Exhibit 22-3, which summarizes the change in interest-on-interest and the change in price

EXHIBIT 22-3   Change in Interest–on–Interest and Price Due to Interest Rate Change After 5.5 Years: 15-Year, 12.5% Bond Selling to Yield 12.5%

New Yield	Change in Interest-on-Interest	Change in Price	Total Change in Accumulated Value
.160	$813,327	−$1,482,360	−$669,033
.155	692,875	−1,293,774	−601,898
.145	454,336	−894,781	−440,445
.140	338,197	−683,720	−345,523
.135	223,778	−464,485	−240,707
.130	111,054	−236,707	−125,654
.125	0	0	0
.120	−109,407	246,044	136,636
.115	−217,192	501,851	284,659
.110	−323,378	767,869	444,491
.105	−427,989	1,044,569	616,581
.100	−531,046	1,332,446	801,400
.095	−632,574	1,632,019	999,445
.090	−732,594	1,943,833	1,211,239
.085	−831,128	2,268,461	1,437,333
.080	−928,198	2,606,508	1,678,309
.075	−1,023,826	2,958,605	1,934,779
.070	−1,118,032	3,325,420	2,207,388
.065	−1,210,838	3,707,652	2,496,814
.060	−1,302,263	4,106,039	2,803,776
.055	−1,392,329	4,521,355	3,129,026
.050	−1,481,055	4,954,415	3,473,360

resulting from a change in the market yield. For example, if the market yield rises instantaneously by 200 basis points, from 12.5% to 14.5%, interest-on-interest will be $454,336 greater; however, the market price of the bond will decrease by $894,781. The net effect is that the accumulated value will be $440,445 less than the target accumulated value. The reverse will be true if the market yield decreases. The change in the price of the bond will more than offset the decline in the interest-on-interest, resulting in an accumulated value that exceeds the target accumulated value.

Now we can see what is happening to the accumulated value. There is a trade-off between interest rate (or price) risk and reinvestment risk. For this 15-year bond, the target accumulated value will be realized only if the market yield does not increase.

Because neither a coupon bond with the same maturity nor a bond with a longer maturity ensures realization of the target accumulated value, maybe a bond with a maturity shorter than 5.5 years will. Consider a 12.5% bond with 6 months remaining to maturity selling at par. Exhibit 22-4 shows the accumulated value and total return over the 5.5-year

EXHIBIT 22-4 Accumulated Value and Total Return: 6-Month, 12.5% Bond Selling to Yield 12.5%

Investment horizon (years)	= 5.5
Coupon Rate	= .125
Maturity (years)	= .5
Yield to maturity	= .125
Price	= 100
Par value purchased	= $8,820,262
Purchase price	= $8,820,262
Target accumulated value	= $17,183,033

New Yield *	After 6 Months	After 5.5 Years Accumulated Value	Total Return
.160	$9,371,528	$20,232,427	.1568
.155	9,371,528	19,768,932	.1523
.145	9,371,528	18,870,501	.1432
.140	9,371,528	18,435,215	.1386
.135	9,371,528	18,008,986	.1341
.130	9,371,528	17,591,647	.1295
.125	9,371,528	17,183,033	.1250
.120	9,371,528	16,782,980	.1205
.115	9,371,528	16,391,330	.1159
.110	9,371,528	16,007,924	.1114
.105	9,371,528	15,632,609	.1068
.100	9,371,528	15,265,232	.1023
.095	9,371,528	14,905,644	.0977
.090	9,371,528	14,553,697	.0932
.085	9,371,528	14,209,247	.0886
.080	9,371,528	13,872,151	.0841
.075	9,371,528	13,542,270	.0795
.070	9,371,528	13,219,466	.0749
.065	9,371,528	12,903,604	.0704
.060	9,371,528	12,594,550	.0658
.055	9,371,528	12,292,175	.0613
.050	9,371,528	11,996,349	.0567

*Immediate change in yield

investment horizon. The second column shows the accumulated value after 6 months. The third column shows the value that is accumulated after 5.5 years by reinvesting the value accumulated after 6 months at the yield shown in the first column. That is:

$$\$9,371,528 \left(1 + \frac{\text{New Yield}}{2}\right)^{10}$$

By investing in this 6-month bond, the portfolio manager incurs no interest rate risk, although there is reinvestment risk. The target accumulated value

EXHIBIT 22-5   Accumulated Value and Total Return: 8-Year, 10.125% Bond Selling to Yield 12.5%

Investment horizon (years)	=	5.5
Coupon rate	=	.10125
Maturity (years)	=	8
Yield to maturity	=	.125
Price	=	88.20262
Par value purchased	=	$10,000,000
Purchase price	=	$8,820,262
Target accumulated value	=	$17,183,033

			After 5.5 Years		
New Yield*	Coupon Interest	Interest-on Interest	Price of Bond	Accumulated Value	Total Return
.160	$5,568,750	$2,858,028	$8,827,141	$17,253,919	.1258
.155	5,568,750	2,746,494	8,919,852	17,235,096	.1256
.145	5,568,750	2,528,352	9,109,054	17,206,156	.1253
.140	5,568,750	2,421,697	9,205,587	17,196,034	.1251
.135	5,568,750	2,316,621	9,303,435	17,188,807	.1251
.130	5,568,750	2,213,102	9,402,621	17,184,473	.1250
.125	5,568,750	2,111,117	9,503,166	17,183,033	.1250
.120	5,568,750	2,010,644	9,605,091	17,184,485	.1250
.115	5,568,750	1,911,661	9,708,420	17,188,831	.1251
.110	5,568,750	1,814,146	9,813,175	17,196,071	.1251
.105	5,568,750	1,718,078	9,919,380	17,206,208	.1253
.100	5,568,750	1,623,436	10,027,059	17,219,245	.1254
.095	5,568,750	1,530,199	10,136,236	17,235,185	.1256
.090	5,568,750	1,438,347	10,246,936	17,254,033	.1258
.085	5,568,750	1,347,859	10,359,184	17,275,793	.1260
.080	5,568,750	1,258,715	10,473,006	17,300,472	.1263
.075	5,568,750	1,170,897	10,588,428	17,328,075	.1266
.070	5,568,750	1,084,383	10,705,477	17,358,610	.1270
.065	5,568,750	999,156	10,824,180	17,392,086	.1273
.060	5,568,750	915,197	10,944,565	17,428,511	.1277
.055	5,568,750	832,486	11,066,660	17,467,895	.1282
.050	5,568,750	751,005	11,190,494	17,510,248	.1286

*Immediate change in yield.

will be achieved only if the market yield remains at 12.5% or rises. Once again, the portfolio manager is not assured of achieving the target accumulated value.

If we assume there is a one-time instantaneous change in the market yield, is there a coupon bond that the portfolio manager can purchase to assure the target accumulated value whether the market yield rises or falls? The portfolio manager should look for a coupon bond so that how ever the market yield changes, the change in the interest-on-interest will be offset by the change in the price.

Consider, for example, an 8-year, 10.125% coupon bond selling at

EXHIBIT 22-6   Change in Interest-on-Interest and Price Due to Interest Rate Change After 5.5 Years: 8-Year, 10.125% Bond Selling to Yield 12.5%

New Yield	Change in Interest-on-Interest	Change in Price	Total Change in Accumulated Value
.160	$746,911	−$676,024	$70,887
.155	635,377	−583,314	52,063
.145	417,235	−394,112	23,123
.140	310,580	−297,579	13,001
.135	205,504	−199,730	5,774
.130	101,985	−100,544	1,441
.125	0	0	0
.120	−100,473	101,925	1,452
.115	−199,456	205,254	5,798
.110	−296,971	310,010	13,038
.105	−393,039	416,215	23,176
.100	−487,681	523,894	36,212
.095	−580,918	633,071	52,153
.090	−672,770	743,771	71,000
.085	−763,258	856,019	92,760
.080	−852,402	969,841	117,439
.075	−940,221	1,085,263	145,042
.070	−1,026,734	1,202,311	175,578
.065	−1,111,961	1,321,014	209,053
.060	−1,195,921	1,441,399	245,478
.055	−1,278,632	1,563,494	284,862
.050	−1,360,112	1,687,328	327,216

88.20262 to yield 12.5%. Suppose $10,000,000 of par value of this bond is purchased for $8,820,262. Exhibit 22-5 provides the same information for this bond as Exhibits 22-1 and 22-2 did for the previous bonds. Looking at the last two columns, we see that the accumulated value and the total return are never less than the target accumulated value and the target yield. Thus the target accumulated value is assured regardless of what happens to the market yield. Exhibit 22-6 shows why. When the market yield rises, the change in the interest-on-interest more than offsets the decline in price. When the market yield declines, the increase in price exceeds the decline in interest-on-interest.

What characteristic of this bond assures that the target accumulated value will be realized regardless of how the market yield changes? The Macaulay duration for each of the four bonds we have considered is:

Bond	Macaulay Duration
5.5-year, 12.5% coupon, selling at par	4.14 years
15-year, 12.5% coupon, selling at par	7.12 years
6-month, 12.5% coupon, selling at par	0.50 years
8-year, 10.125% coupon, selling for 88.20262	5.50 years

Notice that the last bond, which assures that the target accumulated value will be achieved regardless of what happens to the market yield, has a Macaulay duration equal to the length of the investment horizon. This is the key. *To immunize a portfolio's target accumulated value (target yield) against a change in the market yield, a portfolio manager must invest in a bond (or a bond portfolio) such that (1) the Macaulay duration is equal to the investment horizon, and (2) the initial present value of the cash flow from the bond (or bond portfolio) equals the present value of the future liability.*

Rebalancing an Immunized Portfolio

Our illustrations of the principles underlying immunization assume a one-time instantaneous change in the market yield. In practice, the market yield will fluctuate over the investment horizon. As a result, the Macaulay duration of the portfolio will change as the market yield changes. In addition, the Macaulay duration will change simply because of the passage of time.

Even in the face of changing market yields, a portfolio can be immunized if it is rebalanced so that its Macaulay duration is equal to the remaining time of the investment horizon. For example, if the investment horizon is initially 5.5 years, the initial portfolio should have a Macaulay duration of 5.5 years. After 6 months the investment horizon will be 5 years, but the Macaulay duration of the portfolio will probably be different from 5 years. Thus the portfolio must be rebalanced so that its Macaulay duration is equal to 5. Six months later the portfolio must be rebalanced again so that its Macaulay duration will equal 4.5 years. And so on.

How often should the portfolio be rebalanced to adjust its Macaulay duration? On the one hand, the more frequent rebalancing increases transactions costs, thereby reducing the likelihood of achieving the target yield. On the other hand, less frequent rebalancing will result in the Macaulay duration wandering from the target Macaulay duration, which will also reduce the likelihood of achieving the target yield. Thus the portfolio manager faces a trade-off: some transactions costs must be accepted to prevent the Macaulay duration from wandering too far from its target; but some maladjustment in the Macaulay duration must be lived with, or transactions costs will become prohibitively high.

Immunization Risk

The sufficient condition for the immunization of a single liability is that the Macaulay duration of the portfolio be equal to the length of the investment horizon. However, a portfolio will be immunized against interest rate changes only if the yield curve is flat and any changes in the yield curve are parallel changes (that is, interest rates move either up or down by the same number of basis points for all maturities). Recall from Chapter 4 that Macaulay duration is a measure of price volatility for parallel shifts in the yield curve. If there is a change in interest rates that does not correspond to this shape-preserving shift, matching the Macaulay duration to the investment horizon will not assure immunization. That is, the target yield will no longer be the minimum total return for the portfolio.

Empirical studies of the effectiveness of immunization strategies based on Macaulay duration clearly demonstrate that immunization does not work perfectly in the real world. In the first study of immunization, Fisher and Weil found that the duration-based immunization strategy would have come closer to the target yield or exceeded it more often than a strategy based on matching the maturity of the portfolio to the investment horizon (for the period 1925 through 1968), even after considering transactions costs.[5] When Ingersoll critically evaluated the Fisher-Weil study, using actual prices rather than the indexes they used, he did not find support for the claim that a duration-matching strategy outperforms a maturity strategy.[6] However, studies by Bierwag, Kaufman, Schweitzer, and Toevs,[7] Hackett,[8] Lau,[9] and Leibowitz and Weinberger[10] all support the theory that a duration-matched portfolio will outperform a maturity-matched portfolio. Yet, contrary to what immunization theory would lead us to expect, a common finding has been that when a duration-matched strategy is employed, the total return is frequently below the target yield. As for the magnitude of the divergence, Leibowitz and Weinberger found that for 5-year investment horizons from January 1958 to January 1975, the total return did not fall below the target yield by more than 25 basis points.

---

[5]Lawrence Fisher and Roman L. Weil, "Coping with the Risk of Interest Rate Fluctuations: Returns to Bondholders from Naive and Optimal Strategies," *Journal of Business* (October 1971), pp. 408-431.

[6]Jonathan E. Ingersoll, "Is Immunization Feasible? Evidence from the CRSP Data," in George K. Kaufman, G. O. Bierwag, and Alden Toevs, eds., *Innovations in Bond Portfolio Management: Duration Analysis and Immunization* (Greenwich, CT: JAI Press, 1983).

[7]G. O. Bierwag, George C. Kaufman, Robert Schweitzer, and Alden Toevs, "The Art of Risk Management in Bond Portfolios," *Journal of Portfolio Management*, (Spring 1981), pp. 27-36.

[8]T. Hackett, "A Simulation Analysis of Immunization Strategies Applied to Bond Portfolios," unpublished doctoral dissertation, University of Oregon, 1981.

[9]Patrick W. Lau, "An Empirical Examination of Alternative Interest Rate Immunization Strategies," unpublished doctoral dissertation, University of Wisconsin at Madison, 1983.

[10]Martin L. Leibowitz and Alfred Weinberger, "Contingent Immunization—Part II: Problem Areas," *Financial Analysts Journal* (January-February 1983), pp. 35-50.

The divergence of the total return from the target yield arises out of the assumption that the yield curve is flat and changes only in a parallel fashion. Several researchers have relaxed this assumption and developed measures of duration based on a yield curve that is not flat and does not shift in a parallel fashion.

Bierwag, Kaufman, Schweitzer, and Toevs, for example, empirically examine how duration strategies based on more complex duration measures assuming different yield curve shifts would perform compared to Macaulay duration. They conclude that Macaulay duration "immunized almost as well as the more complex [duration] strategies and appear to be the most cost effective."[11] Lau reaches the same conclusion—Macaulay duration is just about as effective as the more complex duration measures.

As there are many Macaulay duration-matched portfolios that can be constructed to immunize a liability, is it possible to construct one that has the lowest risk of not realizing the target yield? That is, in light of the uncertain way in which the yield curve may shift, is it possible to develop a criterion for minimizing the risk that a Macaulay duration-matched portfolio will not be immunized? Fong and Vasicek[12] and Bierwag, Kaufman, and Toevs[13] explore this question. Exhibit 22-7 graphically illustrates how to minimize immunization risk.

The spikes in the two panels of Exhibit 22-7 represent actual portfolio cash flows. The taller spikes depict the actual cash flows generated by securities that have matured, and the smaller spikes represent coupon payments. Both Portfolio A and Portfolio B are composed of two bonds with a duration equal to the investment horizon. Portfolio A is, in effect, a barbell portfolio—one composed of short and long maturities and interim coupon payments. For Portfolio B, the two bonds mature very close to the investment horizon, and the coupon payments are nominal over the investment horizon. Portfolio B is, in effect, a bullet portfolio.

We can now see why the barbell portfolio should be riskier than the bullet portfolio. Assume that both portfolios have Macaulay durations equal to the horizon length, so that each is immune to parallel changes in the yield curve. Suppose that the yield curve changes in a nonparallel way so that short-term interest rates decline while long-term interest rates increase. Both portfolios would then produce an accumulated value at the end of the investment horizon that is below the target accumulated value,

[11]Bierwag, Kaufman, Schweitzer, and Toevs, "The Art of Risk Management in Bond Portfolios," p. 33.

[12]H. Gifford Fong and Oldrich Vasicek, "A Risk Minimizing Strategy for Multiple Liability Immunization," *Journal of Finance* (December 1984), pp. 1541-1546.

[13]G. O. Bierwag, George K. Kaufman, and Alden Toevs, "Bond Immunization and Stochastic Process Risk," working paper, Center for Capital Market Research, University of Oregon, July 1981.

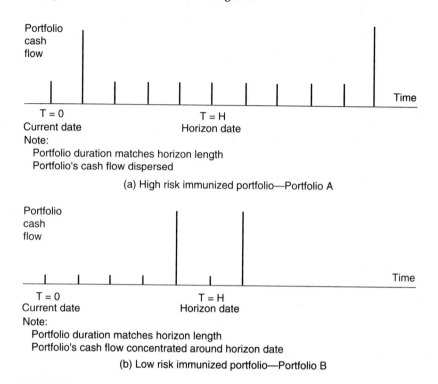

(a) High risk immunized portfolio—Portfolio A

(b) Low risk immunized portfolio—Portfolio B

EXHIBIT 22-7   Illustration of Immunization Risk Measure

because they would experience a capital loss owing to the higher long-term interest rate and less interest-on-interest resulting from the lower reinvestment rate when the short-term interest rate declines. The accumulated value for the barbell portfolio at the end of the investment horizon, however, would miss the target accumulated value by more than the bullet portfolio.

There are two reasons for this. First, the lower reinvestment rates are experienced on the barbell portfolio for larger interim cash flows over a longer time period than on the bullet portfolio. Second, the portion of the barbell portfolio still outstanding at the end of the investment horizon is much longer than the maturity of the bullet portfolio, resulting in a greater capital loss for the barbell compared to the bullet. Thus the bullet portfolio has less risk exposure than the barbell portfolio to any changes in the interest rate structure that might occur.

What should be evident from this analysis is that immunization risk is the risk of reinvestment. The portfolio that has the least reinvestment risk will have the least immunization risk. When there is a high dispersion of cash flows around the investment horizon date, the portfolio is exposed to high reinvestment risk. When the cash flows are concentrated around the investment horizon date, as in the case of the bullet portfolio, the portfolio is subject to low reinvestment risk.

Fong and Vasicek have developed a measure of immunization risk. They have demonstrated that if the yield curve shifts in any arbitrary way, the relative change in the portfolio value will depend on the product of two terms. The first term depends solely on the characteristics of the investment portfolio. The second term is a function of interest rate movement only. The second term characterizes the nature of the change in the shape of the yield curve. Because that change will be impossible to predict *a priori*, it is not possible to control for it. The first term, however, can be controlled for when constructing the immunized portfolio, because it depends solely on the composition of the portfolio. This first term, then, is a measure of risk for immunized portfolios and is equal to:

$$\frac{\dfrac{CF_1(1-H)^2}{(1+y)^1} + \dfrac{CF_2(2-H)^2}{(1+y)^2} + \dots + \dfrac{CF_n(n-H)^n}{(1+y)^n}}{\text{Initial investment value of the portfolio}}$$

where

CF_t = Cash flow of the portfolio at time period t
H = Length of the investment horizon
y = Yield for the portfolio
n = Time to receipt of the last cash flow

The immunization risk measure agrees with our earlier graphic analysis of the relative risk associated with a barbell and a bullet portfolio. For the barbell portfolio (Portfolio A in Exhibit 22-7), the portfolio's cash flow payments are widely dispersed in time, and the immunization risk measure would be high. The portfolio cash flow payments for the bullet portfolio (Portfolio B in Exhibit 22-7) are close to the investment horizon so the immunization risk measure is low. Notice that if all the cash flows are received at the investment horizon, the immunization risk measure is zero. In such a case, the portfolio is equivalent to a pure discount security (zero-coupon security) that matures on the investment horizon date. If a portfolio can be constructed that replicates a pure discount security maturing on the investment horizon date, that portfolio will be the one with the lowest immunization risk. Typically, however, it is not possible to construct such an ideal portfolio.

The objective in constructing an immunized portfolio, then, is to match the Macaulay duration of the portfolio to the investment horizon and select the portfolio that minimizes the immunization risk. The immunization risk measure can be used to construct approximate confidence intervals for the target yield and the target accumulated value.

Zero-Coupon Bonds and Immunization

So far we have dealt with coupon bonds. An alternative approach to immunizing a portfolio against changes in the market yield is to invest in zero-coupon bonds with a maturity equal to the investment horizon. This is consistent with the basic principle of immunization, because the Macaulay duration of a zero-coupon bond is its maturity. However, in practice, the yield on zero-coupon bonds is typically lower than the yield on coupon bonds. Thus using zero-coupon bonds to fund a bullet liability requires more funds, because a lower target yield (equal to the yield on the zero-coupon bond) is being locked in.

Suppose, for example, that a portfolio manager must invest funds to satisfy a known liability of $20 million 5 years from now. If a target yield of 10% on a bond-equivalent basis (5% every 6 months) can be locked in using zero-coupon Treasury bonds, the funds necessary to satisfy the $20 million liability will be the present value of $20 million using a discount rate of 10%:

$$\frac{\$20,000,000}{(1.05)^{10}} = \$12,278,260$$

Suppose, instead, that by using coupon Treasury securities, a target yield of 10.3% on a bond-equivalent basis (5.15% every 6 months) is possible. Then the funds needed to satisfy the $20 million liability will be:

$$\frac{\$20,000,000}{(1.0515)^{10}} = \$12,104,240$$

Thus a target yield higher by 30 basis points would reduce the cost of funding the $20 million by $174,020 ($12,278,260 − $12,104,240). But the reduced cost comes at a price—the risk that the target yield will not be achieved.

Credit Risk and the Target Yield

The target yield may not be achieved if any of the bonds in the portfolio default, or decrease in value because of credit quality deterioration. Restricting the universe of bonds that may be used in constructing an immunized portfolio to Treasury securities eliminates default risk. The target yield that can be achieved, however, will be lower than that for bonds with credit risk, so that the cost of funding a liability would be increased.

In most immunization applications, the client specifies an acceptable level of credit risk. Issues selected for the immunized portfolio are then restricted to those with that quality rating or higher. The more credit risk the client is willing to accept, the higher the achievable target yield, but the greater the risk that the immunized portfolio will fail to meet that target yield because of defaulted or downgraded issues.

Once the minimum credit risk is specified and the immunized portfolio is constructed, the portfolio manager must then monitor the individual issues for possible decreases in credit quality. Should an issue be downgraded below the minimum quality rating, that issue must be sold or the acceptable level of risk changed.

Call Risk

When the universe of acceptable issues includes corporate bonds, the target yield may be jeopardized if a callable issue is included that is subsequently called. Call risk can be avoided by restricting the universe of acceptable bonds to noncallable bonds and deep-discount callable bonds. This strategy does not come without a cost. Because noncallable and deep-discount bonds offer lower yields in a low interest rate environment, restricting the universe to these securities reduces the achievable target yield and therefore increases the cost of funding a liability. Also, it may be difficult to find acceptable noncallable bonds.

An immunized portfolio that includes callable bond issues must be carefully monitored so that issues likely to be called are sold and replaced with bond issues that have a lower probability of being called.

Constructing the Immunized Portfolio

Once the universe of acceptable issues is established and any constraints are imposed, the portfolio manager has a large number of possible portfolios from which to construct an initial immunized portfolio and from which to select to rebalance an immunized portfolio. An objective function can be specified, and a portfolio that optimizes the objective function using mathematical programming tools can be determined. A common objective function, given the risk of immunization discussed earlier, is to minimize the immunization risk measure.[14]

---

[14]For a discussion of alternative objective functions, see H. Gifford Fong and Frank J. Fabozzi, *Fixed Income Portfolio Management* (Homewood: Dow Jones-Irwin, 1985), Chapter 6; Peter C. Christensen and Frank J. Fabozzi, "Bond Immunization: An Asset Liability Optimization Strategy," Chapter 31 in Frank J. Fabozzi and Irving M. Pollack, eds., *The Handbook of Fixed Income Securities* (Homewood: Dow Jones-Irwin, 1987); and Peter C. Christensen and Frank J. Fabozzi, "Dedicated Bond Portfolios," Chapter 32 in *The Handbook of Fixed Income Securities*.

Contingent Immunization

Contingent immunization is a strategy that consists of identifying both the available immunization target rate and a lower safety net level return with which the investor would be minimally satisfied. The money manager pursues an active portfolio strategy until an adverse investment experience drives the then-available potential return—the combined active return from actual past experience and immunized return from expected future experience—down to the safety net level. When that point is reached, the money manager is obligated to immunize the portfolio completely and lock in the safety net level return.

To illustrate this strategy, suppose that a client investing $50 million is willing to accept a 10% rate of return over a 4-year planning horizon at a time when a possible immunized rate of return is 12%. The 10% return is called the *safety net return*. The difference between the immunized return and the safety net return is called the *safety cushion*. In our example, the safety cushion is 200 basis points (12% minus 10%).

Because the initial portfolio value is $50 million, the *minimum* target value at the end of 4 years, based on semiannual compounding, is:

$$\$50,000,000(1.05)^8 = \$73,872,772$$

The rate of return at the time is 12%, so the assets required at this time to achieve the minimum target value of $73,872,772 represent the present value of $73,872,772 discounted at 12% on a semiannual basis:

$$\frac{\$73,872,772}{(1.06)^8} = \$43,348,691$$

Therefore the safety cushion of 200 basis points translates into an initial *dollar safety margin* of $6,651,309 ($50,000,000 − $43,348,691). Had the safety net of return been 11% instead of 10%, the safety cushion would have been 100 basis points and the initial dollar safety margin $1,855,935. In other words, the smaller the safety cushion, the smaller the dollar safety margin.

The money manager initially pursues an active portfolio strategy within the contingent immunization strategy. Suppose that the money manager puts all the funds into a 20-year, 12% coupon bond selling at par to yield 12%. Let's look at what happens if the market yield falls to 9% at the end of 6 months. The value of the portfolio at the end of 6 months would consist of:

Price of the 19.5-year, 12% coupon bond at 9% market yield
6 months' coupon interest

The price of the bond would increase from 100 to 127.34, so that the price of $50 million of these bonds would rise to $63.67 million. Coupon interest is $3 million (.50 × .12 × $50 million). Thus the portfolio value at the end of 6 months is $66.67 million. How much would be necessary to achieve the minimum target return of $73,872,772 if a portfolio can be immunized at the current interest rate of 9%? The required dollar value is found by computing the present value of the minimum target return at 9% for 3.5 years. The required dollar amount is:

$$\frac{\$73,872,772}{(1.045)^7} = \$54,283,888$$

The portfolio value of $66.67 million is greater than the required portfolio value of $54,283,888. The money manager can therefore continue to manage the portfolio actively. The dollar safety margin is now $12,386,112 ($66,670,000 − $54,283,888). As long as the dollar safety margin is positive (that is, the portfolio value is greater than the required portfolio value to achieve the minimum target value at the prevailing interest rate), the portfolio is actively managed.

Suppose that instead of declining to 9% in 6 months, interest rates rose to 14.26%. The market value of the bond would decline to $42,615,776. The portfolio value would then equal $45,615,776 (the market value of the bonds plus $3 million of coupon interest). The required dollar amount to achieve the minimum target value of $73,872,772 at the current interest rate (14.26%) would be:

$$\frac{\$73,872,772}{(1.0713)^7} = \$45,614,893$$

The required dollar amount is approximately equal to the portfolio value (that is, the dollar safety margin is almost zero). Thus the money manager would be required to immunize the portfolio in order to achieve the minimum target value (safety net return) over the investment horizon. The three key factors in implementing a contingent immunization strategy are (1) establishing accurate immunized initial and ongoing available target returns; (2) identifying a suitable and immunizable safety net return; and (3) designing an effective monitoring procedure to ensure that the safety net return is not violated.

STRUCTURING A PORTFOLIO TO SATISFY MULTIPLE LIABILITIES

Thus far we have discussed immunizing a single liability. For pension funds, there are multiple liabilities that must be satisfied—payments to the beneficiaries of the pension fund. A stream of liabilities must also be satisfied for a life insurance company that sells an insurance policy requiring multiple payments to policyholders, such as an annuity policy. There are two strategies that can be used to satisfy a liability stream: (1) multiperiod immunization, and (2) cash flow matching.

Multiperiod Immunization

A portfolio is immunized if there is sufficient cash flow to satisfy all liabilities even if interest rates change. Even if there is a parallel shift in the yield curve, Bierwag, Kaufman, and Toevs demonstrate that matching the duration of the portfolio to the duration of the liabilities is not a sufficient condition to immunize a portfolio seeking to satisfy a liability stream.[15] Instead, it is necessary to decompose the portfolio payment stream in such a way that each liability is immunized by one of the component streams. The key to understanding this approach is recognizing that the payment stream on the portfolio, not the portfolio itself, must be decomposed in this manner. There may be no actual bonds that would give the component payment stream.

In the special case of a parallel shift of the yield curve, Fong and Vasicek demonstrate the conditions that must be satisfied to assure the immunization of multiple liabilities.[16] The necessary and sufficient conditions are: (1) the portfolio's duration must equal the duration of the liabilities; (2) the distribution of durations of individual portfolio assets must have a wider range than the distribution of the liabilities;[17] and (3) the present value of the cash flow from the bond portfolio must equal the present value of the liability stream.

However, these conditions will immunize only in the case of a parallel shift in the yield curve. To cope with the problem of failure to immunize because of nonparallel shifts in the yield curve, Fong and Vasicek generalize the immunization risk measure for a single liability discussed earlier in this chapter to the multiple liability case. An optimal immunization strategy is to minimize this immunization risk measure

---

[15] G. O. Bierwag, George K. Kaufman, and Alden Toevs, "Immunization Strategies for Funding Multiple Liabilities," *Journal of Financial and Quantitative Analysis* (March 1983), pp. 113-124.

[16] Fong and Vasicek, "A Risk Minimizing Strategy for Multiple Liability Immunization."

[17] The reason for the second condition can be illustrated using an example. Suppose that a liability stream with 10 payments of $5 million each year is funded with a zero-coupon bond with a maturity (duration) equal to the duration of the liability stream. Suppose also that when the first $5 million payment is due, interest rates rise so that the value of the zero-coupon bond falls. Even though interest rates have increased, there is no offset to reinvestment income because the bond is a zero-coupon bond. Thus there is no assurance that the portfolio will generate sufficient cash flow to satisfy the remaining liabilities. In the case of a single liability, the second condition is automatically satisfied.

subject to the three constraints above (duration, dispersion of assets and liabilities, and equality of present value of asset cash flow and liability stream), as well as any other constraints that a client may impose.

In a series of articles, Reitano has explored the limitations of the parallel shift assumption.[18] He has also developed models that generalize the immunization of multiple liabilities to arbitrary yield curve shifts. His research makes it clear that classical multiple-period immunization can disguise the risks associated with nonparallel yield curve shifts and that a model that protects against one type of yield curve shift may allow a great deal of exposure and vulnerability to other types of shifts.

Cash Flow Matching

An alternative to multiperiod immunization is cash flow matching. This approach, also referred to as *dedicating a portfolio*, can be summarized as follows. A bond is selected with a maturity that matches the last liability stream. An amount of principal equal to the amount of the last liability stream is then invested in this bond. The remaining elements of the liability stream are then reduced by the coupon payments on this bond, and another bond is chosen for the new, reduced amount of the next-to-last liability. Going backward in time, this cash flow matching process is continued until all liabilities have been matched by the payment of the securities in the portfolio.

Exhibit 22-8 provides a simple illustration of this process for a five-year liability stream. Linear programming techniques can be employed to construct a least-cost cash flow matching portfolio from an acceptable universe of bonds.

The differences between the cash flow matching and multiperiod immunization strategies should be understood. First, unlike the immunization approach, the cash flow matching approach has no duration requirements. Second, with immunization, rebalancing is required even if interest rates do not change. In contrast, no rebalancing is necessary for cash flow matching except to delete and replace any issue whose quality rating has declined below an acceptable level. Third, there is no risk that the liabilities will not be satisfied (barring any defaults) with a cash flow-matched portfolio. For a portfolio constructed using multiperiod immunization, there is immunization risk due to reinvestment risk.

---

[18]Robert R. Reitano, "A Multivariate Approach to Immunization Theory," *Actuarial Research Clearing House*, Vol. 2, 1990; and, "Multivariate Immunization Theory," *Transactions of the Society of Actuaries*, Vol. XLIII, 1991. For a detailed illustration of the relationship between the underlying yield curve shift and immunization, see Robert R. Reitano, "Non-Parallel Yield Curve Shifts and Immunization," *Journal of Portfolio Management* (Spring 1992), pp. 36-43.

EXHIBIT 22-8 Illustration of Cash Flow Matching Process

Assume: 5-year liability stream.
Cash flow from bonds are annual.

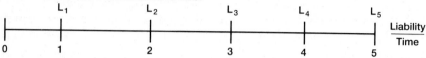

Step 1:
Cash flow from Bond A selected to satisfy L_5
    Coupons = A_c; Principle = A_p and $A_c + A_p = L_5$
Unfunded liabilities remaining:

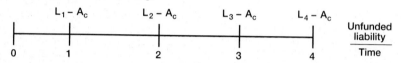

Step 2:
Cash flow from Bond B selected to satisfy L_4
    Unfunded liability = $L_4 - A_c$
    Coupons = B_c; Principle = B_p and $B_c + B_p = L_4 - A_c$
Unfunded liabilities remaining:

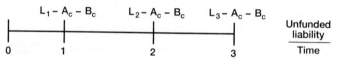

Step 3:
Cash flow from Bond C selected to satisfy L_3
    Unfunded liability = $L_3 - A_c - B_c$
    Coupons = C_c; Principle = C_p and $C_c + C_p = L_3 - A_c - B_c$
Unfunded liabilities remaining:

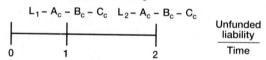

Step 4:
Cash flow from Bond D selected to satisfy L_2
    Unfunded liability = $L_2 - A_c - B_c - C_c$
    Coupons = D_c; Principle = D_p and $D_c + D_p = L_2 - A_c - B_c - C_c$
Unfunded liabilities remaining:

$L_1 - A_c - B_c - C_c - D_c$

|———————|
0   1

Unfunded
liability

Time

Step 5:
Select Bond E with a cash flow of $L_1 - A_c - B_c - C_c - D_c$

The differences just cited may seem to favor the use of cash flow matching. However, what we have ignored is the relative cost of the two strategies. Using the cost of the initial portfolio as an evaluation measure, Gifford Fong Associates has found that cash flow-matched portfolios, using a universe of corporate bonds rated at least double-A, cost from 3% to 7% more in dollar terms than multiperiod immunized portfolios. The reason cash flow matching is more expensive is that, typically, the matching of cash flows to liabilities is not perfect. This means that more funds than necessary must be set aside to match the liabilities. Optimization techniques used to design cash flow-matched portfolios assume that excess funds are reinvested at a conservative reinvestment rate. With multiperiod immunization, all reinvestment returns are assumed to be locked in at a higher target rate of return. Therefore money managers face a trade-off in deciding between the two strategies: avoidance of the risk of not satisfying the liability stream under cash flow matching versus the lower cost attainable with multiperiod immunization.

In the basic cash flow matching technique, only asset cash flows occurring prior to a liability date can be used to satisfy the liability. The technique has been extended to handle situations in which cash flows occurring both before and after the liability date can be used to meet a liability.[19] This technique, called *symmetric cash matching*, allows for the short-term borrowing of funds to satisfy a liability prior to the liability due date. The opportunity to borrow short-term so that symmetric cash matching can be employed results in a reduction in the cost of funding a liability.

A popular variation of multiperiod immunization and cash flow matching to fund liabilities is one that combines the two strategies. This strategy, referred to as *combination matching* or *horizon matching*, creates a portfolio that is duration-matched with the added constraint that it be cash-matched in the first few years, usually five years. The advantage of combination matching over multiperiod immunization is that liquidity needs are provided for in the initial cash flow-matched period. Also, most of the positive slope or inversion of a yield curve tends to take place in the first few years. Cash flow matching the initial portion of the liability stream reduces the risk associated with nonparallel shifts of the yield curve. The disadvantage of combination matching over multiperiod immunization is that the cost is slightly greater.

---

[19]T. Dessa Fabozzi, Tom Tong, and Yu Zhu, "Extensions of Dedicated Bond Portfolio Techniques," Chapter 44 in Frank J. Fabozzi (ed.), *The Handbook of Fixed Income Securities: Third Edition* (Homewood: BusinessOne-Irwin, 1991).

Within the immunization and dedicated cash flow strategies, some portfolio managers are permitted to manage the portfolio actively by entering into bond swaps to enhance portfolio performance. Obviously, only small bets can be made in order to minimize the likelihood that the liability payments will not be satisfied.

EXTENSIONS OF LIABILITY FUNDING STRATEGIES

We note in the previous chapter that liabilities may be uncertain with respect to both timing and amount of the payment. We referred to these liabilities as Type II, III, and IV in Exhibit 21-1. In the techniques we have discussed in this chapter, we have assumed that the timing and the amount of the cash payment are known with certainty. That is, we assume that the liabilities are deterministic.

We assume, moreover, in the models presented in the chapter that the cash flow from the assets is known with certainty, although you have learned that most non-Treasury securities have embedded options that permit the borrower or the investor to alter the cash flow. Thus, the models presented in this chapter are referred to as *deterministic models*, because they assume that the liability payments and the asset cash flows are known with certainty.

Since the mid-1980s, a good number of models have been developed to handle real-world situations in which liability payments and/or asset cash flows are uncertain. Such models are called *stochastic models*.[20] Such models require that the portfolio manager incorporate an interest rate model, that is, a model that describes the probability distribution for interest rates. Optimal portfolios then are solved for using a mathematical programming technique known as *stochastic programming*.

The complexity of stochastic models, however, has limited their application in practice. Nevertheless, they are gaining in popularity as more portfolio managers become comfortable with their sophistication. There is increasing awareness that stochastic models reduce the likelihood that the liability objective will not be satisfied, and that transactions costs can be reduced through less frequent rebalancing of a portfolio derived from these models.

---

[20]For a review of such models, see Randall S. Hiller and Christian Schaack, "A Classification of Structured Bond Portfolio Modeling Techniques," *Journal of Portfolio Management* (Fall 1990), pp. 37-48.

SUMMARY

This chapter has demonstrated liability funding strategies that involve designing a portfolio to produce sufficient funds to satisfy liabilities whether or not interest rates change. When there is only one future liability to be funded, an immunization strategy can be used. An immunization strategy is designed so that, as interest rates change, interest rate risk and reinvestment risk will offset each other in such a way that the minimum cumulative value (or minimum rate of return) becomes the target cumulative value (or target yield). An immunization strategy requires that a money manager create a bond portfolio with a duration equal to the investment horizon. Because immunization theory is based on parallel shifts in the yield curve, the risk is that a portfolio will not be immunized even if the duration-matching condition is satisfied. Immunization risk can be quantified so that a portfolio that minimizes this risk can be constructed.

When there are multiple liabilities to be satisfied, either multiperiod immunization or cash flow matching can be used. Multiperiod immunization is a duration-matching strategy that exposes the portfolio to immunization risk. The cash flow matching strategy does not impose any duration requirement. While the only risk that the liabilities will not be satisfied is that issues will be called or will default, the dollar cost of a cash flow-matched portfolio may be higher than that of a portfolio constructed using a multiperiod immunization strategy.

Liability funding strategies where the liability payments and the asset cash flows are known with certainty are deterministic models. In a stochastic model, either the liability payments or the asset cash flows, or both, are uncertain. Stochastic models require specification of a probability distribution for the process that generates interest rates.

QUESTIONS FOR CHAPTER 22

1. What is meant by immunization of a bond portfolio?
2. a. What is the basic underlying principle in an immunization strategy?

   b. Why may the matching of the maturity of a coupon bond to the maturity of a liability fail to immunize a portfolio?
3. Why must an immunized portfolio be rebalanced periodically?
4. What are the risks associated with a bond immunization strategy?
5. "I can immunize a portfolio by simply investing in zero-coupon bonds." Comment on this statement.
6. Why is there greater risk in a multiperiod immunization strategy than in a cash flow matching strategy?
7. a. What is a contingent immunization strategy?

   b. What is meant by the safety net return and safety cushion in a contingent immunization strategy?
8. What is a combination matching strategy?
9. In a stochastic liability funding strategy, why is an interest rate model needed?
10. *[The question following is from CFA Examination III, June 1, 1991, Morning Session, Question 5]*

    Global Foundation has recently hired Strategic Allocation Associates (SAA) to review and make recommendations concerning allocation of its $5 billion endowment portfolio. Global has indicated an interest in introducing a structured approach (where structured management is broadly defined as indexing, immunization, dedication, etc.) to at least a portion of the fund's fixed-income component.

    After analysis of Global's current asset mix, investment objectives, international exposure, and cash flow data, SAA has recommended that the overall asset mix be: 50% equity, 5% real estate, and 45% fixed-income securities. Within the fixed-income component, SAA further recommended the following allocation:

    –   50% Structured Management;

    –   40% Specialty Active Management (20% Market Timing, 10% High-Yield, 10% Arbitrage); and

    –   10% Nondollar/International Active Management.

    Global's investment committee has asked you, as a senior partner in SAA, to address several issues.

a. Compare structured management to active management with specific focus on *each* of the following aspects:

- predictability of returns,
- level of return, and
- cash flow characteristics.

b. Explain the potential impact on the active managers' strategies and freedoms of action resulting from the introduction of a structured portfolio component.

INDEX